McGraw-Hill Education

Preparation

— for the —

GED® Test

Your Best Study Program for
THE NEW EXAM

McGraw-Hill Education Editors

CONTRIBUTORS

Marion Dausses	Alyssa Grieco
Janet Fitzsimmons	Diane Milne
Madison Gardner	Christel Snelson
Maria Goudiss	Jerimi Walker

New York   Chicago   San Francisco   Athens   London   Madrid
Mexico City   Milan   New Delhi   Singapore   Sydney   Toronto

1 2 3 4 5 6 7 8 9 10   QVS/QVS   1 0 9 8 7 6 5 4

ISBN   978-0-07-184661-5   (book and disk set)
MHID   0-07-184661-1   (book and disk set)

ISBN   978-0-07-185053-7   (book for set)
MHID   0-07-185053-8   (book for set)

e-ISBN   978-0-07-184658-5
e-MHID   0-07-184658-1

Library of Congress Control Number   2014943063

GED® is a registered trademark of the American Council on Education (ACE) and administered exclusively by GED Testing Service LLC under license. This content is not endorsed or approved by ACE or GED Testing Service.

Interior design by THINK Book Works
Interior illustrations by Cenveo® Publisher Services

McGraw-Hill Education products are available at special quantity discounts to use as premiums and sales promotions or for use in corporate training programs. To contact a representative, please visit the Contact Us pages at www.mhprofessional.com.

Contents

PART 2   Physical Science

CHAPTER 3 World History   757

CHAPTER 4 Economics   791

How to Use This Book

Welcome to *McGraw-Hill Education: Preparation for the GED® Test*! This book contains practical test-taking information and review sections for each of the test's four sections. It also contains a pretest and a posttest for every test section. It will give you the information and practice you need to do your best on test day. For best results, follow this five-step plan:

1. **Learn about the GED® test.** Read "Introducing the GED® Test" beginning on page 1. In this section you will learn all about what subjects the test covers, how the test is structured, and how it is scored. You will also see examples of the different question types, including the interactive question formats that appear on the computerized test. This section will also give you valuable test-taking strategies that can raise your score, as well as useful study suggestions and tips for test day.

2. **Start with the pretests.** The pretests in this book are modeled closely on the real GED® test. They have the same number and types of questions and the same degree of difficulty. Take each pretest as your first step in preparing for each part of the real exam. Use the Answers and Explanations section to score yourself, and complete the Evaluation Chart at the end of the test. The chart will help you pinpoint your areas of strength and weakness in your knowledge base and your skill set.

3. **Develop a study plan.** Use your results on the pretest to develop a study plan. Prepare to focus particularly on the topics that were difficult for you on the pretest. Set up a study schedule based on the amount of time you have available. The review sections of this book are broken into short, manageable chunks of information, so you can study one topic at a time at your own pace.

4. **Prepare for each test section.** The four main sections of this book provide a complete review of the subjects you need to master in order to succeed on the GED® test. The Reasoning Through Language Arts (RLA) and Mathematical Reasoning sections include numerous examples to illustrate key concepts. The Science and Social Studies sections contain helpful charts and other graphics to clarify ideas and make learning easier. The RLA and Social Studies sections also include vital information on how to answer extended-response (essay) questions. Work through these sections at your own pace, paying special attention to topics or question types that were particularly difficult for you on the pretests. Check your understanding by completing the exercises and taking the practice quizzes you'll find in each section.

5. **Take the posttests.** When you have completed your review for each test section, take the corresponding posttest you'll find at the end of the book. Like the pretests, the posttests are closely modeled on the real exam in terms of question types, number of questions, and degree of difficulty. Use the posttests to check your progress, to gain experience with the GED® test format, and to learn to pace yourself to get your highest score.

Introducing the GED® Test

Welcome to *McGraw-Hill Education: Preparation for the GED® Test*! Congratulations on choosing the preparation guide from America's leading educational publisher. You probably know us from many of the textbooks you used in school. Now we're ready to help you take the next step—and get the high school equivalency credential you want.

Before you start your study program, this chapter will give you a brief introduction to the exam. In the following pages, you'll learn:

- The history of the GED® test and how it took its current shape
- The structure of each part of the GED® test
- How the test is scored
- Some basic test-taking strategies
- Some dos and don'ts for test day

About the GED® Test

"GED®" stands for General Educational Development. The GED® test is commonly referred to as a "high school equivalency" test because passing scores on all the test sections are usually accepted as equal to a high school diploma.

The GED® program started in 1942 during World War II. Many young people had joined the armed services before completing high school. As a way to help returning veterans reenter civilian life with the equivalent of a high school diploma, which would help them get better jobs or go on to college, the U.S. military asked the American Council on Education (ACE) to develop the GED® test.

The GED® test was revised several times over the years, but many things remained constant. There were five separate test sections: Language Arts–Reading, Language Arts–Writing, Social Studies, Science, and Mathematics. These were standard "paper-and-pencil" tests that featured mostly multiple-choice questions. In 2002 a computerized version of the test was introduced. It did not differ much from the paper-and-pencil version.

ACE, a nonprofit organization, administered the GED® program until 2011. In that year, ACE formed a new partnership with Pearson, a major educational publisher, to create the GED® Testing Service. The first major goal of the new joint venture was to overhaul the old GED® test series and create a new series of tests that use modern computer technology to measure career and college readiness.

The current version of the GED® test is a major departure from the 2002 and earlier versions. Some key differences are:

- There is no paper-and-pencil version of the test. Only a computer version is available.

- There are four, not five, test sections: Reasoning Through Language Arts (RLA), Mathematical Reasoning, Science, and Social Studies.

- The test uses new question formats that may be unfamiliar to test-takers. (But don't worry—we will get you up to speed!)

- Multiple-choice questions have four, not five, answer options.

There are some other major differences that are more important to test designers and teachers than to test-takers like you, but in case you are interested, here they are:

- Instead of using Benjamin Bloom's Taxonomy for measuring the difficulty of questions, the tests now use Norman Webb's Depth of Knowledge measurements.

- Questions are aligned to the Common Core Standards rather than to standards generated by various boards or groups of educators, as they were in the past.

Again, these are not changes you need to be concerned about. These changes tell the test designers what to test and how difficult to make each item.

How Do I Register?

In 2011, more than 700,000 people took at least one of the five GED® test sections. More than 600,000 completed all five (but remember, there are now only four test sections). That makes it one of the most widely administered tests in the world. Luckily, that means you will probably have a lot of options about where to take the test.

The quickest way to register is to do so online at:

ged.com

Visit this website and follow the step-by-step instructions for registering and scheduling your test. You can also locate an official GED® testing location by signing in on the site and clicking "Locate a testing center" at the bottom of the page and register in person. You can find an international or Canadian testing center by visiting this site:

http://www.gedtestingservice.com/testers/locate-a-testing-center

You must register and schedule your test times in advance, and the times tests are offered vary from center to center. Each of the GED® tests is scheduled separately.

Test-taking accommodations are available for those who need them, but test-takers must get approval in advance for these accommodations. Accommodations include:

- An audio version of the test
- A private testing area
- Extended testing periods
- Additional break times
- Font-size options

You must get the appropriate approval form filled out and approved. You can find the forms here:

http://www.gedtestingservice.com/testers/accommodations -for-disability#Accommodations4

In general, you will need documentation from your doctor or your school that proves testing accommodations are recommended and necessary.

What Are the Current Question Formats?

Do not worry too much about the question formats. The bulk of the current version of the GED® test is made up of multiple-choice questions, which almost everyone has experienced at one point or another. But some new question types do take some getting used to. Here is what to expect:

- **Drag and drop:** Drag-and-drop questions can look a variety of different ways, but what they ask you to do is use the computer mouse to select an object (it could be a word, a shape, a set of numbers, or another object) and "drag" it into a correct position in some kind of diagram. If you use a computer, you are probably familiar with the concept of "dragging" and "dropping." It is exactly what you do when you move the icon for a document from one folder to another. Look at the simple question that follows:

Drag and drop the words below into the correct location on the chart.

Words That Describe the Sun	Words That Do Not Describe the Sun

hot

yellow

green

large

extinct

freezing

In this case, it is clear you should drag *hot*, *yellow*, and *large* into the "Words That Describe the Sun" column and *green*, *extinct*, and *freezing* into the "Words That Do Not Describe the Sun" column. Your correct answer would look like this:

Words That Describe the Sun	Words That Do Not Describe the Sun
hot	green
yellow	extinct
large	freezing

This is the basic idea of a drag-and-drop question. You will find many more examples in the practice tests and instructional chapters of this book.

- **Hot spot:** Hot spot items appear mostly in the Mathematical Reasoning test. They require you to plot points on a graph, alter a chart, or complete a similar task. Here is an example:

    Click on the grid below to plot the point indicated by the ordered pair (1, −3).

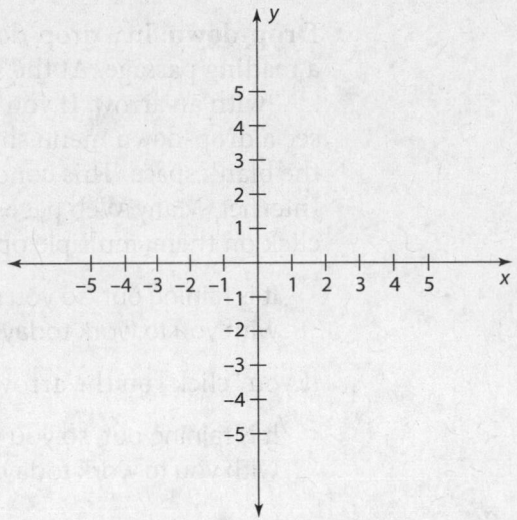

    To answer this question, you have to "click" with your mouse on the correct point on the graph. In this case, you would move one place over along the *x*-axis to 1, and then move down the *y*-axis to −3. Your correct answer would look like this:

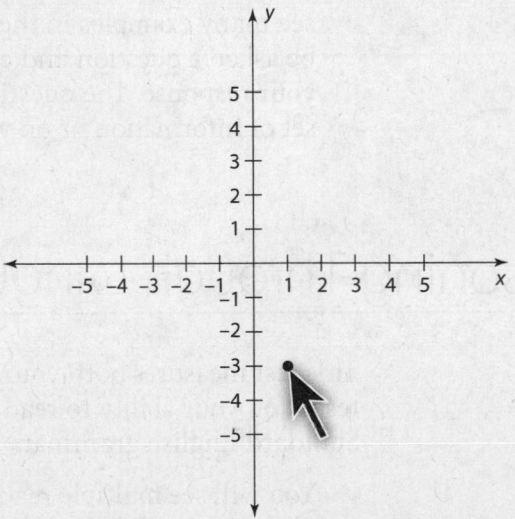

- **Fill in the blank:** This is a question type that is familiar to most people. On the GED® tests, you will simply type in the correct answer. For example, look at this item:

    Do not forget to take (you) _____ umbrella.

This question is testing whether you know when to use apostrophes. So your correct answer would look like this:

Do not forget to take _____ **your** _____ umbrella.

In this case no apostrophe is required because *your* is an adjective describing *umbrella*.

- **Drop-down:** In a drop-down item, you will see a blank space, usually in a reading passage. At the start of the space, you will see the word "Select . . ." with an arrow. If you "click" on the arrow with your mouse, you will see a drop-down menu showing several answer options that could fill the blank space. This concept will be familiar to you if you often use the Internet. Many Web pages have "menus," and if you use your mouse to click on them, multiple options appear. Here is a simple example:

It is raining out, so you should probably take your [Select... ▼] with you to work today.

If you "click" on the arrow, here is what you will see:

It is raining out, so you should probably take your with you to work today.

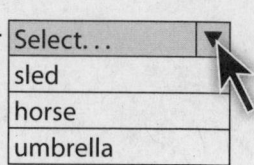

In this case, you should select *umbrella* as the best answer option.

- **Short answer and extended response:** These are two versions of the same thing: an essay question. The only difference is the length. You will see many examples in the practice tests and chapters to come. You will be asked a question and expected to answer in your own words, typing your response. The question will be based either on a passage or another set of information or on your personal experience and opinions.

The Reasoning Through Language Arts (RLA) Test

This test measures both your reading and your writing skills. You will be tested on your ability to read carefully, write clearly, and understand and use Standard English grammar.

You will see multiple reading passages on this test. About 75 percent of these passages will be nonfiction. The rest will be literature. There will be no poetry selections. These items test your reading comprehension.

Your writing abilities will be assessed through short-answer and extended-response questions. Various question formats will test your understanding of Standard English grammar.

You will have 150 minutes to complete the test, which will include 64 questions (mostly multiple choice).

The Mathematical Reasoning Test

The Mathematical Reasoning test is 90 minutes long and features 50 items in a variety of formats. There is a short section on which a calculator is not allowed, but for the bulk of the test, a calculator is allowed. The calculator is available on the computer screen.

About half of the test focuses on quantitative problem solving, and about half focuses on basic algebraic problem solving. There are some geometry questions as well. The test measures skills both with straightforward math problems and with hypothetical real-world situations that require you to decide how to use your problem-solving skills to arrive at the correct answer.

The Science Test

You will have 90 minutes to complete the Science test, which is 40 questions long. About 40 percent of the test focuses on life science, about 40 percent focuses on physical science, and the remaining 20 percent focuses on Earth and space science.

The Science test features a full range of question formats.

The Social Studies Test

The Social Studies test is 90 minutes long, with one break. There is an extended-response question on the test, for which you are allowed 25 minutes. There are a total of 45 questions.

Fully half of the test focuses on civics and government, so get ready to brush up on your knowledge of state and federal government and the duties of citizens. The rest of the test focuses on U.S. history, geography, and economics, with some attention to world history.

More About the Test Interface

Taking a test on a computer understandably makes many people nervous. Test-taking features you may be familiar with, such as the ability to mark skipped questions with a pencil so that you can return to them later, are not available. Scratch paper is not allowed. However, the new test has many features and functions that can improve the test-taking experience.

- **Built-in clock:** Keeping track of the time used to present a challenge, but the test now has a built-in clock that appears in the upper-right-hand corner of the screen.

- **Erasable note boards:** You cannot use scratch paper, but the test offers erasable note boards that work just as well as regular scratch paper. You can request one at the time of your test, and ask for another one or more if you use up all your space. You will be given an erasable marker to use, and you will deliver the note board to the test administrator after completing your test.

- **Marking skipped items:** In the past, when the GED® test was a paper-and-pencil exam, test-takers often marked skipped items on their answer sheets and returned to them as time allowed. The computerized GED® test allows you to either click "Flag for Review" at the upper right of the question screen or just skip questions without marking them, and it provides a Question Review Screen at the end of the test that lists all of the question numbers and indicates whether each one is answered or unanswered and shows a filled-in flag icon next to the questions you flagged for review. You can then click any question number to return to that question to review or answer it if desired. You can also click "Review All," "Review Unanswered," or "Review Flagged" at the bottom of the Question Review Screen to select which questions you wish to review.

- **Zooming and color palette:** You have the option to zoom in on text to make it easier to view, or to change the color palette of the test to improve visibility.

- **No more separate answer sheets:** One of the problems with conventional bubble-in answer sheets is that accidentally skipping one row on the answer sheet can throw off a test-taker's entire score. On the computerized GED® test, you are presented with one question on the screen at a time, and you answer directly on that screen before moving on, so there is no chance of "bubbling in" on the wrong line of an answer sheet.

How the Tests Are Scored

As computerized tests have evolved, there have been two main types of tests: adaptive and linear. Adaptive tests are designed to zero in quickly on the test-taker's ability. Test-takers get a "medium" level question first. If they answer correctly, they get a harder question. If they answer incorrectly, they get an easier question, and so on. Critics of this procedure point out that this format does not necessarily give a full picture of a test-taker's abilities because the test-taker is not able to attempt all of the questions.

A linear test is just a test with a set number of questions, all of which are available to the test-taker. The computerized GED® tests are linear, so scores are determined based on the number of correctly answered questions. All questions, however, are not weighted equally. Because of the new question types, some questions are worth more than others.

The tests are scored in their entirety by an automated scoring engine—even short-response and extended-response items will be scored by computer. Scores are reported within three hours of completion of the test.

Test-Taking Strategies

Clearly, the best preparation for the GED® tests is a solid course of study using a book like the one you have in your hands. The best path to a good score is simply knowing the material. However, no matter how hard you study, there will probably be some questions on the GED® tests that throw you for a loop. In those cases, you need to have some test-taking strategies ready.

A number of tried-and-true test-taking strategies have been proven to help test-takers, particularly in solving multiple-choice questions. The GED® test still relies mainly on multiple-choice questions, so it is a good idea to keep the following strategies in mind:

- **The correct answer is staring you in the face.** Remember, the great thing about multiple-choice questions is that the correct answer is right in front of you. You just have to identify it. You do not have to retrieve it from your memory or come up with it on your own. Use this fact to your advantage.

- **Use the process of elimination.** On the GED® test, there is no penalty for wrong answers, so if you don't know the answer to a question, you have nothing to lose by guessing. And if you must guess, you can improve your chances of guessing correctly by using the "process of elimination," or POE.

  Think about it this way: on the GED® test, multiple-choice items have four answer choices. If you just guess randomly, you still have a one-in-four chance of being correct. But what if you know that one of the answer choices is definitely wrong? Go ahead and eliminate that option. Now you have a one-in-three chance of guessing correctly. Your odds have just improved considerably. If you can eliminate two options, you are up to a 50 percent chance of selecting the correct answer. That's even better. Here is an example of how this works:

  Who was the first person to fly an airplane solo across the Atlantic Ocean?

  A. George Washington
  B. Orville Wright
  C. Charles Lindbergh
  D. Amelia Earhart

Let's say you are not sure of the answer. It seems clear, though, that you can eliminate George Washington as a choice. He was the first at something, of course—the first president of the United States—but airplanes were not even invented when he was alive, so he is not an option. OK, now you are down to three choices. Orville Wright might seem connected to airplanes somehow. You might remember that it was the Wright brothers who built the first airplane to successfully make a controlled, sustained flight. But neither brother flew across the Atlantic. So eliminate Orville. Now you are down to two choices. Both Charles Lindbergh and Amelia Earhart were famous pilots in the early years of aviation. But who was the first to cross the Atlantic? You have no idea? No matter. You are down to two options. Go ahead and guess. You have a 50 percent chance of being correct. (By the way, it was Charles Lindbergh who made the first trans-Atlantic solo flight in 1927. Amelia Earhart became the first woman to complete a solo trans-Atlantic flight five years later.)

- **Keep an eye on the clock, and do not get hung up.** It may be tempting to keep wrestling with a difficult question until you have it mastered, but remember that you do not have all day. You have a set amount of time, and your goal should be to at least attempt every single question on the test. If you do some quick math based on the time limits and question totals given in the previous section, you will see that the longest you should spend on any given question is about two minutes. If you have been struggling and coming up empty for five minutes, skip the question or guess the answer and click "Flag for Review" and move on. You probably have many questions ahead of you that you can answer correctly, so go get those points!

- **Save the last five minutes for guessing . . . and always guess!** Suppose that you have gone through every item on the test. You have returned to skipped items and applied the process of elimination and come up with an acceptable answer. If there are still a few questions that leave you completely stumped, don't sweat it. Just guess. You still have a one-in-four chance of being right on multiple-choice items. The GED® test does not penalize you for wrong answers. They simply count as zeroes. So why miss out on possible points? Pick something, even on one of the new question types. Put down some kind of answer. Never leave a question unanswered.

- **Use short, simple sentences.** On short-answer and extended-response questions, do not try to get too fancy. You can always make sure you are being grammatically correct if you keep your sentences simple and clear.

- **Use your erasable note board to outline your extended responses.** Before just starting to write an answer to an extended-response question, think for a minute or two about what you want to say, in what order, and how you intend to support your opinions or assertions. Make a quick outline. It does not have to follow a formal format. Just know where you are going with a response before you start typing.

- **Proofread your work.** Once you finish your short-answer or extended responses, read through them carefully to make sure there are no obvious mistakes.

Test-Day Tips

This will all sound like very commonsense advice, but you would be surprised at how often people do not prepare properly for test day. So here is your pretest and test-day checklist:

1. Congratulate yourself for having used *McGraw-Hill Education: Preparation for the GED® Test* to prepare yourself thoroughly for your test. You are ready.

2. At least a day or two before the test, make a dry run at getting yourself to the test-taking facility. Are you sure you know *exactly* where to show up—not just which building, but which room on which floor? If you are driving, is there parking available? Where, and how far from the facility? How much does it cost? What is traffic like at the time your test is scheduled? Is there gas in the car? If you are taking public transportation, do you know the quickest, best route to your test-taking facility?

3. Plan to arrive 30 minutes early. Yes, that seems like it is very early. But the unexpected always happens, so be prepared. If you are early, so what? Sit down, relax, and visualize yourself acing the test. But if there is unexpected road construction or if the subway or bus is delayed, you will be glad you had a little time cushion. You do not want to arrive barely in the nick of time, and you definitely do not want to be late. At some facilities, you will not even be admitted if you are late.

4. Don't stay up all night studying the night before the test. Go ahead and review a little, but a good night's sleep is more beneficial than last-minute cramming.

5. Eat breakfast. Or lunch. Or whatever meal comes right before your test time. Just do not let yourself go into the test hungry and thirsty.

6. Dress in layers. Some testing facilities are as cold as freezers. Others are as hot as ovens. Be ready for anything so you can stay comfortable.

How to Use This Book to Set Up a Study Plan

This book features pretests and posttests in all four subject areas. Before you begin your course of study, take the pretest in the subject you plan to tackle first. Use the answer explanations and scoring rubric to see how well you performed. Your performance on the pretest will give you a good idea of which areas you need to work on and which areas you have already mastered.

How much time you decide to devote to each subject area depends completely on your own schedule and your level of mastery of each subject area. There is no set prescription. This book is broken into short, manageable chunks of information, so you can take it one step at a time at your own pace.

If you have a packed daily schedule with very little time to devote to studying and you find that you need a lot of review in a given area, you will probably need to give yourself plenty of time. For example, if you are a parent with a full-time job, you may find that by the time you get the children to bed, you only have enough energy for 30 minutes of studying. That's fine. Just try to do one topic a night, and give yourself at least six weeks to finish your study for each test.

On the other hand, if you want to get through your series of GED® tests as quickly as possible in order to achieve some further goal (get a certain job or promotion, apply to college, or the like) and you have several hours or more of free time every day, you could conceivably prepare yourself for one test in two weeks.

Whatever you decide, write down your plan on a calendar (how many pages per night, for example) and stick to it. It may take a lot of determination, but you can do it.

Finally, turn to family and friends for support and encouragement. What you are doing is important, hard work. You deserve plenty of praise and pats on the back.

We wish you the best of luck—on the test and beyond!

Pretests

How to Use the Pretests

The pretests in this section are designed to help you determine what parts of this book you will want to focus on in order to get your best test score. There are four pretests, one in each GED® test subject area: Reasoning Through Language Arts (RLA), Mathematical Reasoning, Science, and Social Studies. Each one is designed to match the real exam as closely as possible in format and degree of difficulty. When you take these pretests, your results will give you a good idea of how well you would score if you took the GED® test today.

Use the pretests to plan your study by following these five steps:

1. **Take the pretests one at a time.** Do not try to work through all four pretests in one session.

2. **Take each pretest under test conditions.** Find a quiet place where you will not be disturbed. Take the pretest as if it were the actual GED® test. Work though the pretest from beginning to end in one sitting. Mark your answers directly on the test pages. Observe the time limit given at the start of the test. If you have not finished the pretest when time runs out, mark the last question you answered, and then note how much longer it takes you to complete the test. This information will tell you if you need to speed up your pace, and, if so, by how much.

3. **Answer every question.** On the real GED® test, there is no penalty for wrong answers, so it makes sense to answer every question, even if you have to guess. If you don't know an answer, see if you can eliminate one or more of the answer choices. The more choices you can eliminate, the better your chance of guessing correctly!

4. **Check your answers in the Answers and Explanations section at the end of each pretest.** Pay particular attention to the explanations for questions you missed.

5. **Fill out the Evaluation Charts.** These charts are located at the end of each Answers and Explanations section. Mark the numbers of the questions you missed, and the chart will show you the sections of this book where you need to spend the most study time.

The number of questions and time limit for each pretest are shown in the following chart.

Pretest	Number of Questions	Time Limit
Reasoning Through Language Arts		
Part 1: Multiple choice	64	95 minutes
(break)		(10-minute break)
Part 2: Essay	1 essay question	45 minutes
Mathematical Reasoning	50	90 minutes
Science	40	90 minutes
Social Studies	45	90 minutes

Reasoning Through Language Arts (RLA)

This Reasoning Through Language Arts (RLA) Pretest is designed to introduce you to this section of the GED® test and to give you a good idea of your current skill level in this subject area.

This test has the same number of questions as the real GED RLA test: 64 items in multiple-choice or other formats and one essay question. The question formats are the same as the ones on the real exam and are designed to measure the same skills. Most of the questions are based on reading passages that are selections from either fiction or nonfiction sources. Most of the questions are in multiple-choice format, but you will also see questions in other formats, such as fill-in-the-blank items and simulated click-and-drag and drop-down items. On the real GED® test, you will indicate your answers by clicking on the computer screen. For this paper-and-pencil practice test, mark your answers directly on the page. Write your essay on a separate sheet of paper.

To get a good idea of how you will do on the real exam, take this test under actual exam conditions. Complete the test in one session and follow the given time limit. If you do not complete the test in the time allowed, you will know that you need to work on improving your pacing.

Try to answer as many questions as you can. There is no penalty for wrong answers, so guess if you have to. In multiple-choice questions, if you can eliminate one or more answer choices, you can increase your chances of guessing correctly.

After you have finished the test, check your answers in the Answers and Explanations section that follows the pretest. Then use the Evaluation Chart at the end of the Answers and Explanations section to determine the skills and content areas in which you need more practice.

Now turn the page and begin the Reasoning Through Language Arts (RLA) Pretest.

Reasoning Through Language Arts (RLA)

Part 1: Multiple Choice

64 questions | **95 minutes**

Use the excerpt for Items 1 through 5:

Excerpt Adapted from "The Finished Story"

by Lucy Maude Montgomery

1   She always sat in a corner of the west veranda at the hotel, knitting something white and fluffy, or pink and fluffy, or pale blue and fluffy—always fluffy, at least, and always dainty. Shawls and scarfs and hoods the things were, I believe. When she finished one she gave it to some girl and began another.

2   She was old, with that beautiful, serene old age which is as beautiful in its way as youth. Her girlhood and womanhood must have been very lovely to have ripened into such a beauty of sixty years.

3   For the first two days after the arrival at the hotel she sat in her corner alone. There was always a circle of young people around her; old folks and middle-aged people would have liked to join it, but Miss Sylvia, while she was gracious to all, let it be distinctly understood that her sympathies were with youth.

4   Miss Sylvia liked us all, but I was her favorite. She told us so frankly and let it be understood that when I was talking to her and her shawl was allowed to slip under one arm it was a sign that we were not to be interrupted.

5   We were sitting together on the veranda at sunset. Most of the hotel people had gone for a harbor sail.

6   I was reading one of my stories to Miss Sylvia. In my own excuse I must allege that she tempted me to do it. Miss Sylvia had discovered that I was a magazine scribbler, and moreover, that I had shut myself up in my room that very morning and perpetrated a short story. Nothing would do but that I read it to her.

7   It was a rather sad little story. The hero loved the heroine, and she loved him. There was no reason why he should not love her, but there was a reason

why he could not marry her. When he found that he loved her he knew that he must go away. But might he not, at least, tell her his love? Might he not, at least, find out for his consolation if she cared for him? There was a struggle; he won, and went away without a word, believing it to be the more manly course.

8   When I turned the last page of the manuscript and looked up, Miss Sylvia's soft brown eyes were full of tears. She lifted her hands, clasped them together and said in an agitated voice:

9   "Oh, no, no; don't let him go away without telling her—just telling her. Don't let him do it!"

10   "But, you see, Miss Sylvia," I explained, flattered beyond measure that my characters had seemed so real to her, "that would spoil the story. It would have no reason for existence then. Its *motif* is simply his mastery over self. He believes it to be the nobler course."

11   "No, no, it wasn't—if he loved her he should have told her. Think of her shame and humiliation—she loved him, and he went without a word and she could never know he cared for her. Oh, you must change it—you must, indeed! I cannot bear to think of her suffering what I have suffered."

12   Miss Sylvia broke down and sobbed. To appease her, I promised that I would remodel the story, although I knew that the doing so would leave it absolutely pointless.

13   "Oh, I'm so glad," said Miss Sylvia, her eyes shining through her tears. "You see, I know it would make her happier—I know it. I'm going to tell you my poor little story to convince you. But you—you must not tell it to any of the others."

14   "I know I can trust you. But it's such a poor little story. You mustn't laugh at it—it is all the romance I had. Years ago—forty years ago—when I was a young girl of twenty, I—learned to care very much for somebody. I met him at a summer resort like this. I was there with my aunt and he was there with his mother, who was delicate. We saw a great deal of each other for a little while. He was—oh, he was like no other man I had ever seen. You remind me of him somehow. That is partly why I like you so much. I noticed the resemblance the first time I saw you. He was not strong—he coughed a good deal. Then one day he went away—suddenly. I had thought he cared for me, but he never said so—just went away. Oh, the shame of it! After a time I heard that he had been ordered to California for his health. And he died out there the next spring. My heart broke then, I never cared for anybody again—I couldn't. I have always loved him. But it would have been so much easier to bear if I had only known that he loved me—oh, it would have made all the difference in the world. And the sting of it has been there all these years. I can't even permit myself the joy of dwelling on his memory because of the thought that perhaps he did not care."

1. What can be inferred about the narrator?

   A. He has little imagination.
   B. He is worried about Miss Sylvia.
   C. He studies people very carefully.
   D. He already knew Miss Sylvia's story.

2. Which quotation from the passage supports the theme of the passage?

   A. "For the first two days after the arrival at the hotel she sat in her corner alone."
   B. "Miss Sylvia liked us all, but I was her favorite."
   C. "In my own excuse I must allege that she tempted me to do it."
   D. "Oh, no, no; don't let him go away without telling her—just telling her."

3. What effect does the narrator's story have on Miss Sylvia?

   A. It upsets her.
   B. It comforts her.
   C. It irritates her.
   D. It angers her.

4. Indicate each word that DESCRIBES Miss Sylvia and belongs in the character web. (**Note:** On the real GED® test, you will click on the words you choose and "drag" each one into position in the character web.)

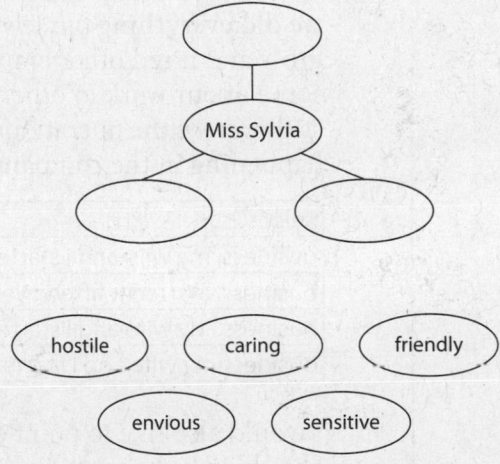

5. Why is it so important to Miss Sylvia to have the ending of the story changed?

   A. It is so close to her own experience.
   B. She thinks it would improve the story.
   C. She feels the ending is overly complicated.
   D. She wants the narrator to make the story shorter.

6. The following letter contains several numbered blanks, each marked "Select. . . ." Beneath each one is a set of choices. Indicate the choice from each set that is correct and belongs in the blank. (**Note:** On the real GED® test, the choices will appear as a "drop-down" menu. When you click on a choice, it will appear in the blank.)

Dear Mr. and Mrs. Taylor:

I want to welcome you to Heart Insurance. We operate our company as a family and think of our clients as extended family as well. Select 1... ▼ We hope that you will be pleased with every aspect of our performance. And I personally promise to act at once if you have any questions or desire any changes made to your policy.

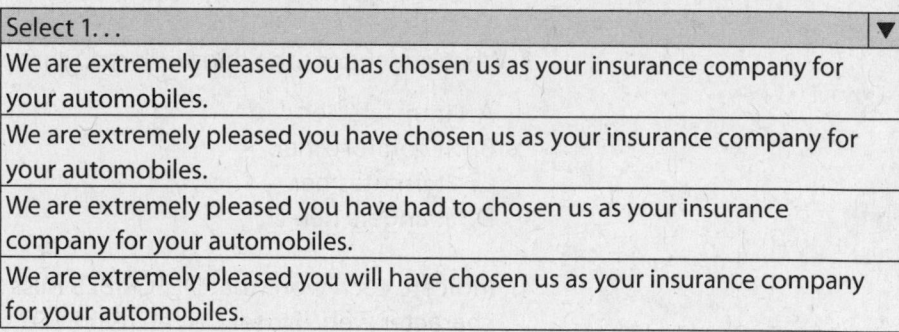

Select 1... ▼
We are extremely pleased you has chosen us as your insurance company for your automobiles.
We are extremely pleased you have chosen us as your insurance company for your automobiles.
We are extremely pleased you have had to chosen us as your insurance company for your automobiles.
We are extremely pleased you will have chosen us as your insurance company for your automobiles.

Heart Insurance is really a mom and pop Select 2... ▼ At first we did everything ourselves to make it successful. After we began to grow and hired other employees, we realized that we needed to delegate some of our work to others, but that does not mean that we do not still oversee the operations very closely. We definitely know what is happening in the company.

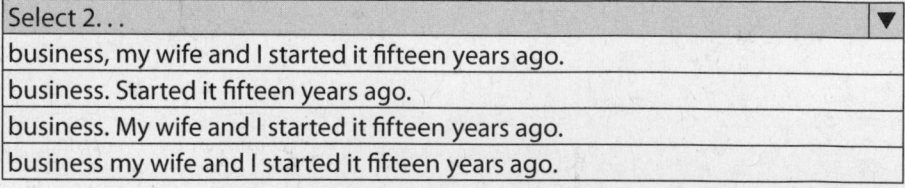

Select 2... ▼
business, my wife and I started it fifteen years ago.
business. Started it fifteen years ago.
business. My wife and I started it fifteen years ago.
business my wife and I started it fifteen years ago.

I would also like to point out that Heart may be able to save you money. Should you choose to insure your home with us as well, you would receive a five percent discount on your insurance rates for both cars and home. We try to work with all our customers so that they can find the best deals for ⌗Select 3...⌗▼⌗ We are extremely competitive pricewise, so you might want to consider making that change. It's just a thought, but it might be a wise decision on your part.

Select 3...	▼
himself.	
theirselves.	
yourselves.	
themselves.	

I am enclosing other information for you about our services. ⌗Select 4...⌗▼⌗ We have many types of umbrella policies that can ensure you will rest easy and have no liability issues.

Select 4...	▼
Operating in all 50 of the United States, we are.	
We, operating in all 50 of the United States, are.	
We operate in all 50 of the United States.	
Operating in all 50 of the United States are we.	

Again, if you have any questions do not hesitate to ⌗Select 5...⌗▼⌗ You can always reach us at our toll-free number, and when you call, you will speak to a person, not a machine. If you choose to write us, make sure to send your correspondence to our main headquarters in Chicago. The address is printed on the pamphlet I am sending you.

Select 5...	▼
call and asking us.	
calling and asking us.	
call and ask us.	
calling and ask us.	

Again, welcome to Heart. We aim to please.

Sincerely,

Donald D. Heart
CEO Heart Insurance

Use the following excerpts for Items 7 through 16:

Excerpt Adapted from "The Dangers of the Proposal of the U.S. Fish and Wildlife Service to Introduce Grizzly Bears into Idaho," a Speech to the U.S. House of Representatives (July 1997)

by Congresswoman Helen Chenoweth

1   The U.S. Fish and Wildlife Service has prepared a plan to introduce grizzly bears into a huge part of my district. Let me explain to the Members that this would affect a significant portion of the State of Idaho. The area we're talking about is over one-third of the state. Just to give Members an idea about how big this area is, let me give a comparison. In this area we could fit the states of Connecticut, Delaware, Maryland, Massachusetts, New Hampshire, Vermont, and Rhode Island, and still have over a million unfilled acres. You should be aware that the area they are talking about contains many populated regions, including the area around the University of Idaho. Moreover, the border of the grizzly bear recovery area runs very close to Boise.

2   The grizzly bear is a huge and dangerous animal, which makes for us a huge and dangerous problem. The grizzly bear is a large predatory mammal. And, provoked or unprovoked, it can move very quickly to viciously attack a human or an animal. In addition, the grizzly has special dietary needs. Just one of them requires between 10 and 168 square miles of land to live on, depending upon the amount of food there is in the area.

3   Bringing back the unpredictable grizzly bear means that people will not be able to behave or work in the way they used to in this part of Idaho. Roads normally open will have to be shut down. Hiking trails will be restricted. Camping areas will be closed. Hunting will be restricted. Livestock and logging practices will be dramatically altered. Bringing back the grizzly bear is really like allowing wildlife to take over.

4   It is a well-known fact that grizzly bears are often violent toward humans and animals. While settlers may have recognized the beauty of these animals, they also understood the horrible threat they pose. At the time, there was no federal act to keep them from killing these animals. Thank goodness. Lewis and Clark described in their journals the absolute terror that they and the Indians had for these animals and how difficult it was to kill a grizzly, even with several shots fired from their 18th-century guns.

5   When I presented to the Fish and Wildlife Service these types of concerns about human risk, they, too, recognized the danger of grizzly bears. In the past few years, because more people are vacationing in our

forests and lands, attacks have increased. Even with this plan, the Fish and Wildlife Service estimates that there could be about one human injury or death each year.

6   Let me say for the record, Mr. Speaker, not one human death or injury resulting from a grizzly bear attack is acceptable to this Congresswoman. In fact, it should not be acceptable to anyone who values human life.

Excerpt from "Final Environmental Impact Statement (EIS) Released on Reintroduction of Grizzly Bears in the Bitterroot Ecosystem in Western Montana and Central Idaho" (2000)

by the U.S. Fish and Wildlife Service

1   The purpose of reintroducing grizzlies would be to enhance the species' potential for recovery in the lower 48 states.

2   An estimated 50,000 grizzly bears lived in the contiguous United States prior to European settlement. Grizzly bears have been eliminated from approximately 98 percent of their historic range in the lower 48 states. Today, approximately 1,000–1,100 grizzly bears remain in five scattered populations in Montana, Idaho, Wyoming, and Washington. Only two areas in the country (the Yellowstone ecosystem and the Northern Continental Divide ecosystem which includes Glacier National Park and the Bob Marshall Wilderness) have populations of several hundred grizzlies. The other three populations have approximately 5 to 50 grizzly bears each.

3   The grizzly bear is a native species of the Bitterroot ecosystem and was once common there. Grizzlies were eliminated from the Bitterroots by the 1940s after a century of intensive persecution. Of all remaining unoccupied grizzly bear habitat in the lower 48 states, the Bitterroot Mountains wilderness area has the best potential for grizzly bear recovery. This area has the components of quality grizzly bear habitat. As such, the Bitterroot ecosystem offers excellent potential to recover a healthy population of grizzly bears and to boost long-term survival and recovery prospects for this species in the contiguous United States. Recovery of endangered species, and their removal from the list of endangered species, is the ultimate goal of the Endangered Species Act.

4   Under the plan outlined in the EIS, the Service would reintroduce a minimum of 25 grizzly bears into 25,140 square miles of the Selway-Bitterroot Wilderness over a period of five years. The bears would be taken from areas in Canada and the United States that have healthy populations of grizzly bears living in habitats similar to those found in the Bitterroot ecosystem.

5   All reintroduced bears would be radio-collared and monitored to determine their movements and how they use their habitat, and to keep the public informed through media outreach of general bear locations and recovery efforts. Under the plan, the Service would only consider bears with no known history of conflicts with people for reintroduction.

6   Suitable bears would be released at remote wilderness sites within the Bitterroot Mountains of east-central Idaho that have high-quality bear habitat and low likelihood of human encounters. By designating the reintroduced grizzly population as nonessential experimental, bears that frequent areas of high human use, act aggressively toward humans, or attack livestock would be relocated or destroyed, based on actions in the Interagency Grizzly Bear Guidelines.

7. What is Congresswoman Chenoweth's viewpoint?

    A. Grizzly bears should be reintroduced into states other than Idaho in a slow and orderly manner.
    B. Grizzly bears should be introduced into Idaho at the discretion of the U.S. Fish and Wildlife Service.
    C. Grizzly bears should not be reintroduced into Idaho or any other part of the country because they are ferocious.
    D. Grizzly bears should not be reintroduced into Idaho in the way that the U.S. Fish and Wildlife Service has planned.

8. Why does Congresswoman Chenoweth compare the area that is to be used for the reintroduction of the grizzly bear to the states of Connecticut, Delaware, Maryland, Massachusetts, New Hampshire, Vermont, and Rhode Island?

    A. She is stressing how large an area it is in contrast to these states.
    B. She is suggesting these states are all smaller in size than Idaho.
    C. She wants everyone to know that there are no grizzlies in these states.
    D. She wants to stress that states in the East coast don't have much wildlife.

9. What is the reason that Congresswoman Chenoweth mentions the Lewis and Clark journals?

   A. to show that even Lewis and Clark were frightened of the grizzlies
   B. to suggest that Lewis and Clark knew very little about grizzlies
   C. to show that she is knowledgeable about the Lewis and Clark expedition
   D. to suggest that the U.S. Fish and Wildlife Service should read the journals

10. According to the Environmental Impact Statement (EIS), what is the purpose of reintroducing grizzlies into the environment?

    A. to study the bears
    B. to make the bears tamer
    C. to increase the number of bears
    D. to improve the bears' environment

11. Which quotation from the Environmental Impact Statement (EIS) supports the underlying premise that grizzlies might pose a hazard to humans when reintroduced?

    A. "Grizzly bears have been eliminated from approximately 98 percent of their historic range in the lower 48 states."
    B. "Grizzlies were eliminated from the Bitterroots by the 1940s after a century of intensive persecution."
    C. "All reintroduced bears would be radio-collared and monitored to determine their movements and how they use their habitat, and to keep the public informed through media outreach of general bear locations and recovery efforts."
    D. "By designating the reintroduced grizzly population as nonessential experimental, bears that frequent areas of high human use, act aggressively toward humans, or attack livestock would be relocated or destroyed, based on actions in the Interagency Grizzly Bear Guidelines."

12. Indicate where each sentence belongs in the chart. (**Note:** On the real GED® test, you will click on each sentence and "drag" it into position in the chart.)

Congresswoman Chenoweth's Speech	The Final Environmental Impact Statement

It is important to reintroduce grizzlies, since they are endangered.

People's lives will be turned upside-down because of the reintroduction of grizzlies in this part of Idaho.

The grizzlies will be carefully monitored and people would be alerted to their presence.

One person killed by a grizzly is too many.

13. In the conclusion of her speech, how does Congresswoman Chenoweth try to make an effective appeal to her listeners?

   A. She provides an objective overview of the project.
   B. She helps her listeners understand the complexity of the project.
   C. She summarizes logical arguments made earlier in her speech.
   D. She stresses emotional issues regarding the reintroduction of grizzlies.

14. How does the tone of the Environmental Impact Statement (EIS) differ from the tone of the speech?

   A. It uses stronger language than the speech does.
   B. It has a more urgent tone than the speech has.
   C. It includes an emotional appeal that the speech is lacking.
   D. It has a more factual tone than the speech has.

15. The Environmental Impact Statement (EIS) includes data on the decline of grizzly populations because the EIS needs to

    A. show why grizzlies were considered dangerous by people.
    B. explain the need for reintroducing grizzlies into the environment.
    C. reassure the audience that grizzlies will become numerous again.
    D. emphasize the amount of time that has passed since grizzlies were numerous.

16. How do the different genres of a speech and of a government document like an Environmental Impact Statement (EIS) affect each text?

    A. A speech is typically better organized than an EIS.
    B. Arguments in a speech are more likely to be based on fact than those in an EIS.
    C. A speech allows for dramatic arguments, while an EIS is more factual and objective.
    D. A speech may contain current ideas, while an EIS is more likely to contain older ideas.

17. The following memo contains several numbered blanks, each marked "Select. . . ." Beneath each one is a set of choices. Indicate the choice from each set that is correct and belongs in the blank. (**Note:** On the real GED® test, the choices will appear as a "drop-down" menu. When you click on a choice, it will appear in the blank.)

To: All Employees

From: HR

Re: Child Care

Great news! In response to all your requests, the company is planning to open a child care facility on the 3rd floor. The location will be in the former Big Kane Division space.

The target opening is set for the 15th of May. All those who want to register a child must stop by HR and pick up the necessary forms. Have your doctor's office fill out the medical data form. [Select 1... ▼] You will also need to fill out the information form so there will be a record of any emergency numbers that may be needed.

Select 1... ▼
The forms which you have completed, and must be returned before a child can attend.
You must return the completed forms to HR before your child can attend.
The forms, and you need to complete them, must be returned before a child can attend.
The completed forms must be returned to HR before a child can even be allowed to attend.

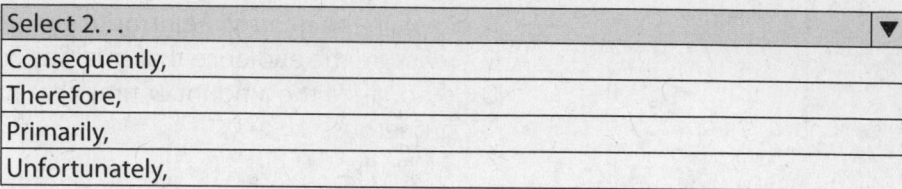 there is a limit on the number of children who can be cared for in the facility, so it would be wise to get your application in sooner rather than later.

Select 2... ▼
Consequently,
Therefore,
Primarily,
Unfortunately,

Certainly, we do realize that some parents already have a good system of care for their children, and most of them will not make a switch. At least that is what we are hoping. But we will be creating a wait list, should more parents apply than we can handle.

Lunch will be provided by the new facility, and 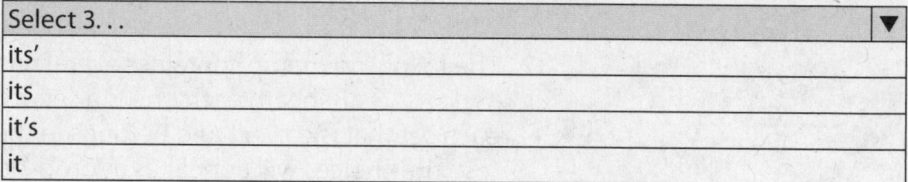 going to be a hot lunch, made possible because of the large kitchen area on the third floor.

Select 3... ▼
its'
its
it's
it

If your child has special dietary needs, you will have to make that clear on the application and provide a list of foods that are acceptable. Snacks will also be provided, but if a parent prefers, a child may bring his or her own food.

The facility will be open Monday through Friday, 7:30 a.m. to 5:30 p.m., and will be under the supervision of Celia Riverton, who has 22 years of child care experience. She will have five assistants. We are seeking an adult to child ratio of one to ten. Select 4... ▼

Select 4... ▼
The cost will vary depending on your current salary, however, we want to make the facility affordable for you.
The cost will vary depending on your current salary. However, we want to make the facility affordable for you.
The cost will vary depending on your current salary however, we want to make the facility affordable for you.
The company sees no need to make a profit off the day care; all that is needed is to cover costs of personnel and food as well other expenses.

If you have any questions, contact Barry Minor. We are all very excited by this new development, which we feel will only result in fewer missed days from work.

Use the following excerpt for Items 18 through 21:

Excerpt Adapted from "The Pendulum"

by O. Henry

1   John walked slowly toward his flat. Slowly, because in the lexicon of his daily life there was no such word as "perhaps." There are no surprises awaiting a man who has been married two years and lives in a flat. As he walked John Perkins prophesied to himself with gloomy and downtrodden cynicism the foregone conclusions of the monotonous day.

2   Katy would meet him at the door. He would remove his coat, sit upon a lounge and read the evening paper. For dinner there would be pot roast, a salad flavored with a dressing warranted not to crack or injure the leather, stewed rhubarb and the bottle of strawberry marmalade blushing at the certificate of chemical purity on its label. After dinner Katy would show him the new patch in her crazy quilt that the iceman had cut for her off the end of his four-in-hand. At half-past seven they would spread newspapers over the furniture to catch the pieces of plastering that fell when the fat man in the flat overhead began to take his physical exercises.

3   John Perkins knew these things would happen. And he knew that at a quarter past eight he would summon his nerve and reach for his hat, and that his wife would deliver this speech in a querulous tone:

4   "Now, where are you going, I'd like to know, John Perkins?"

5   "Thought I'd drop up to McCloskey's," he would answer, "and play a game or two of pool with the fellows."

6   Of late such had been John Perkins's habit. At ten or eleven he would return. Sometimes Katy would be asleep; sometimes waiting up.

7   Tonight John Perkins encountered a tremendous upheaval of the commonplace when he reached his door. No Katy was there with her affectionate, confectionate kiss. The three rooms seemed in portentous disorder. All about lay her things in confusion. Shoes in the middle of the floor, curling tongs, hair bows, kimonos, powder box, jumbled together on dresser and chairs—this was not Katy's way. With a sinking heart John saw the comb with a curling cloud of her brown hair among its teeth. Some unusual hurry and perturbation must have possessed her, for she always carefully placed these combings in the little blue vase on the mantel to be some day formed into the coveted feminine "rat."

8   Hanging conspicuously to the gas jet by a string was a folded paper. John seized it. It was a note from his wife running thus:

9   "Dear John: I just had a telegram saying mother is very sick. I am going to take the 4.30 train. Brother Sam is going to meet me at the depot there. There is cold mutton in the ice box. I will write tomorrow. Hastily, KATY."

10   Never during their two years of being married had he and Katy been separated for a night. John read the note over and over in a dazed way. Here was a change in their routine that had never before varied, and it left him feeling strange.

11   There on the back of a chair hung, pathetically empty and formless, the red apron with black dots that she always wore while getting the meals. Her weekday clothes had been tossed here and there in her haste. A little paper bag of her favorite butterscotch candy lay on the table untouched. A daily newspaper was on the floor, a large rectangular hole gaping where the railroad timetable had been clipped from it. Everything in the room spoke of a loss, of an essence gone, of its soul and life departed. John Perkins stood among the dead remains with a queer feeling of desolation in his heart.

12   He began to tidy up the room as best he could. When he picked up her apron, he had the strangest feeling of terror. He had never thought of life without Katy before. She had become so thoroughly a part of his life that she was like the air he breathed—necessary but scarcely noticed. Now, without warning she was gone, vanished, as though she had never existed. Of course it would only be for a few days, or at most a week or two, but it seemed as though the hand of death had pointed a finger at his secure and uneventful home.

13   John Perkins was not used to thinking about his emotions. But he knew now that Katy was necessary to his happiness. "It is terrible the way I've been treating her. Off every night with the guys to play pool instead of staying here with her. John Perkins, you are the worst of the bunch. I'm going to make it up to her."

14   Suddenly the door opened. Katy walked in carrying her bag. "I'm glad to get back," said Katy. "Mom wasn't that sick. She just had a bit of stomach upset. So I took the next train back."

15   John Perkins felt something shift. It was almost like a machine clicking into position, swinging back to where it should be. He looked at his clock. It was 8:15, the time he left each night to hang out with the guys.

16   He reached for his hat automatically. "Where are you going?" asked Katy. "Thought I'd drop up to McCloskey's and play a game or two of pool with the fellows," he told her.

18. A pendulum is something that swings back and forth. Why do you think O. Henry named this story "The Pendulum"? John Perkins

   A. liked to play pool with his friends in the evening.
   B. changed his feelings from one minute to the next minute.
   C. started to help clean up the house, but then decided it was too much work.
   D. could not go with Katy on the train as he was late getting back from work.

19. Which quotation from the passage supports the idea that John was strongly affected by the absence of Katy?

   A. "As he walked John Perkins prophesied to himself with gloomy and downtrodden cynicism the foregone conclusions of the monotonous day."
   B. "After dinner Katy would show him the new patch in her crazy quilt that the iceman had cut for her off the end of his four-in-hand."
   C. "Everything in the room spoke of a loss, of an essence gone, of its soul and life departed."
   D. "It was 8:15, the time he left each night to hang out with the guys."

20. In the following flow chart, indicate the order in which the events listed occur in the excerpt. (**Note:** On the real GED® test, you will click on the sentences in the boxes and "drag" each one into position in the flow chart.)

Order of Events

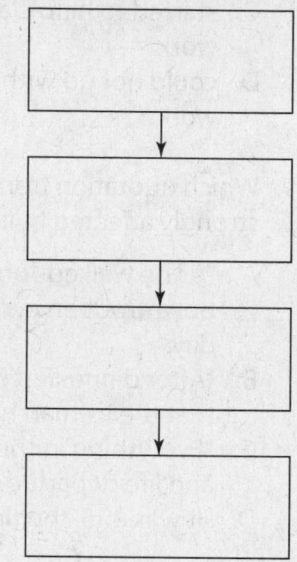

| John starts to tidy up. | John sees the newspaper with a hole in it. |
| John tells Katy he is going out. | John reads Katy's note. |

21. Why was John walking so slowly to his home?

    A. He was not feeling well.
    B. He was tired after working hard.
    C. He knew his wife was not at home.
    D. He knew what the evening would be like.

Use the excerpt for Items 22 through 28:

Excerpt from "Camping with President Roosevelt"

by John Burroughs

1   At the time I made the trip to Yellowstone Park with President Roosevelt in the spring of 1903, I promised some friends to write up my impressions of the President and of the Park, but I have been slow in getting around to it. The President himself, having the absolute leisure and peace of the White House, wrote his account of the trip nearly two years ago! But with the stress and strain of my life at "Slabsides,"—administering the affairs of so many of the wild creatures of the woods about me,—I have not till this blessed season found the time to put on record an account of the most interesting thing I saw in that wonderful land, which, of course, was the President himself.

2   When I accepted his invitation I was well aware that during the journey I should be in a storm center most of the time, which is not always a pleasant prospect to a man of my habits and disposition. The President himself is a good deal of a storm,—a man of such abounding energy and ceaseless activity that he sets everything in motion around him wherever he goes. But I knew he would be pretty well occupied on his way to the Park in speaking to eager throngs and in receiving personal and political homage in the towns and cities we were to pass through. But when all this was over, and I found myself with him in the wilderness of the Park, with only the superintendent and a few attendants to help take up his tremendous personal impact, how was it likely to fare with a non-strenuous person like myself, I asked? I had visions of snow six and seven feet deep where traveling could be done only upon snowshoes, and I had never had the things on my feet in my life. If the infernal fires beneath, that keep the pot boiling so out there, should melt the snows, I could see the party tearing along on horseback at a wolf-bunt pace over a rough country; and as I had not been on a horse's back since the President was born, how would it be likely to fare with me there?

3   I had known the President several years before he became famous, and we had had some correspondence on subjects of natural history. His interest in such themes is always very fresh and keen, and the main motive of his visit to the Park at this time was to see and study in its semi-domesticated condition the great game which he had so often hunted during his ranch days; and he was kind enough to think it would be an additional pleasure to see it with a nature-lover like myself. For my own part, I knew nothing about big game, but I knew there was no man in the country with whom I should so like to see it as Roosevelt.

4   Some of our newspapers reported that the President intended to hunt in the Park. A woman in Vermont wrote me, to protest against the hunting, and hoped I would teach the President to love the animals as much as I

did—as if he did not love them much more, because his love is founded upon knowledge, and because they had been a part of his life. She did not know that I was then cherishing the secret hope that I might be allowed to shoot a cougar or bobcat; but this fun did not come to me. The President said, "I will not fire a gun in the Park; then I shall have no explanations to make." Yet once I did hear him say in the wilderness, "I feel as if I ought to keep the camp in meat. I always have." I regretted that he could not do so on this occasion.

5   I have never been disturbed by the President's hunting trips. It is to such men as he that the big game legitimately belongs—men who regard it from the point of view of the naturalist as well as from that of the sportsman, who are interested in its preservation, and who share with the world the delight they experience in the chase. Such a hunter as Roosevelt is as far removed from the game-butcher as day is from night; and as for his killing of the "varmints,"—bears, cougars, and bobcats,—the fewer of these there are, the better for the useful and beautiful game.

6   The cougars, or mountain lions, in the Park certainly needed killing. The superintendent reported that he had seen where they had slain nineteen elk, and we saw where they had killed a deer, and dragged its body across the trail. Of course, the President would not now on his hunting trips shoot an elk or a deer except to "keep the camp in meat," and for this purpose it is as legitimate as to slay a sheep or a steer for the table at home.

22. In what way does the information about President Roosevelt having a great deal of energy support the main idea?

    A. It explains why Roosevelt was well read.
    B. It suggests that Roosevelt was an excellent hunter.
    C. It suggests that Roosevelt was extremely sensitive.
    D. It explains why Roosevelt was able to accomplish a good deal.

23. Which quotation from the passage supports the idea that Burroughs was worried about his camping trip with President Roosevelt?

    A. "When I accepted his invitation I was well aware that during the journey I should be in a storm center most of the time, which is not always a pleasant prospect to a man of my habits and disposition."
    B. "I had known the President several years before he became famous, and we had had some correspondence on subjects of natural history."
    C. "She did not know that I was then cherishing the secret hope that I might be allowed to shoot a cougar or bobcat; but this fun did not come to me."
    D. "Of course, the President would not now on his hunting trips shoot an elk or a deer except to 'keep the camp in meat,' and for this purpose it is as legitimate as to slay a sheep or a steer for the table at home."

24. Why did it take so long for Burroughs to write about his experience with President Roosevelt?

    A. He did not enjoy writing.
    B. He was not sure what to say.
    C. He was busy doing other things.
    D. He was waiting for President Roosevelt to leave office.

25. Why does Burroughs include details about President Roosevelt's hunting? He wants his readers to

    A. learn how to be hunters themselves.
    B. recognize which animals are best to hunt.
    C. realize that Roosevelt is physically strong.
    D. understand that he approved of Roosevelt's hunting.

26. Indicate each word that DESCRIBES President Roosevelt and belongs in the character web. (**Note:** On the real GED® test, you will click on the words you choose and "drag" each one into position in the character web.)

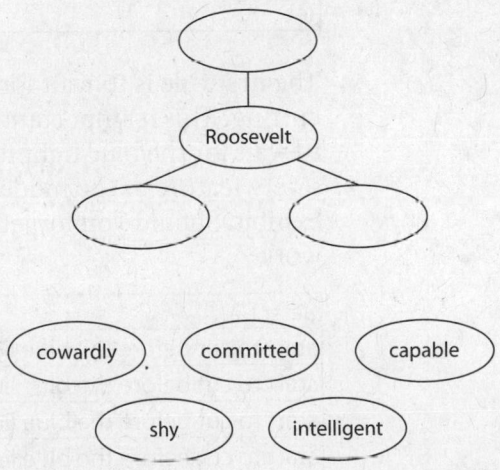

27. Why did President Roosevelt choose not to hunt in the park?

    A. to keep people from criticizing him
    B. to create an image of himself as a nature lover
    C. to show that he was no longer interested in hunting
    D. to stress that hunting should not be done on public lands

28. Why does Burroughs think that cougars should be hunted?

    A. They are wild.
    B. They carry diseases.
    C. They are good to eat.
    D. They kill other animals.

29. The following memo contains several numbered blanks, each marked "Select. . . ." Beneath each one is a set of choices. Indicate the choice from each set that is correct and belongs in the blank. (**Note:** On the real GED® test, the choices will appear as a "drop-down" menu. When you click on a choice, it will appear in the blank.)

Memo

Re: Use of A2 Cutter

To: All Students in Workshop Class 102

This is the first class that we have allowed to use this powerful piece of equipment, so Select 1... ▼ pay a lot of attention to how to do it safely.

Select 1... ▼
lets'
lets
let's
let

The first rule is to wait for the blue light to come on before you begin cutting. This is important, so I'll repeat it. It is of the utmost importance to wait for the blue light to appear before you begin cutting. This is a safety feature of the model A2 cutter, which most other models do not exhibit. Should you forget and Select 2... ▼ and the cutter will not work.

Select 2... ▼
start to cut before the blue light goes on; you will disengage the safety system
start to cut before the blue light goes on, you will disengage the safety system
start to cut before the blue light goes on: you will disengage the safety system
start to cut before the blue light goes on you will disengage the safety system

Another safety rule is to check the material closely for any loose edges. This should be done even before you turn on the cutter. As a general rule, this is the first step in getting started. Select 3... ▼

Select 3... ▼
If you have any questions about what constituted a loose edge, refer to the manual for further explanations and photographs.
If you have any questions about what constitute a loose edge, refer to the manual for further explanations and photographs.
If you have any questions about what constitutes a loose edge, refer to the manual for further explanations and photographs.
If you have any questions about what had constituted a loose edge, refer to the manual for further explanations and photographs.

PRETEST

If you're still not sure, ask me to check it for you. I'd rather check it out with you in the lab than visit you in the hospital.

Once you have determined that there are no loose edges, you may begin by pressing the Start switch. The blue light will come on immediately thereafter. Then you can begin cutting. If the blue light fails, call the head operator. He will have to check whether the cutter is malfunctioning or whether it is simply a problem of a deficient bulb.

When you have finished cutting, press the Stop button and wait for the machine to turn itself off. [Select 4... ▼]

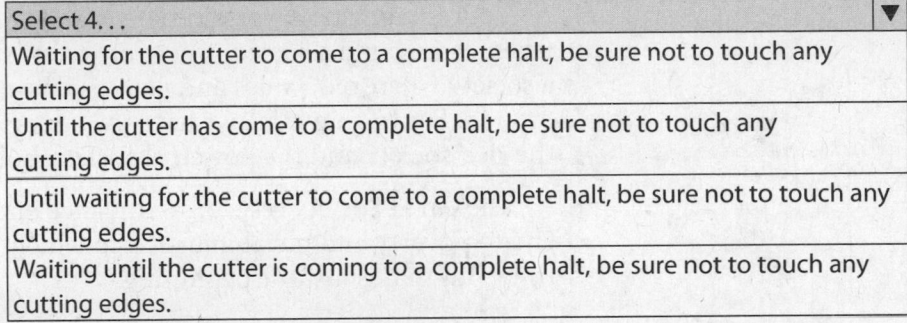

Select 4... ▼
Waiting for the cutter to come to a complete halt, be sure not to touch any cutting edges.
Until the cutter has come to a complete halt, be sure not to touch any cutting edges.
Until waiting for the cutter to come to a complete halt, be sure not to touch any cutting edges.
Waiting until the cutter is coming to a complete halt, be sure not to touch any cutting edges.

The A2 cutter is the first model we've ever employed using laser technology. Those of you who've done the background reading will see important differences between the operation of this machine and the diamond-tipped cutter you've worked with earlier. Later this year we hope to be able to yoke this model to computer-controlled stations and aim for a much higher level of efficiency than we've obtained in prior years. [Select 5... ▼]

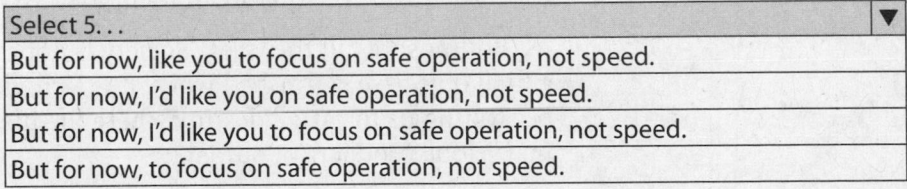

Select 5... ▼
But for now, like you to focus on safe operation, not speed.
But for now, I'd like you on safe operation, not speed.
But for now, I'd like you to focus on safe operation, not speed.
But for now, to focus on safe operation, not speed.

We'll aim for speed later.

Use the two excerpts for Items 30 through 39:

Excerpt from "The Great Society" Speech

by President Lyndon Baines Johnson (given May 22, 1964)

1   The challenge of the next half century is whether we have the wisdom to use that wealth to enrich and elevate our national life, and to advance the quality of our American civilization.

2   Your imagination, your initiative, and your indignation will determine whether we build a society where progress is the servant of our needs, or a society where old values and new visions are buried under unbridled growth. For in your time we have the opportunity to move not only toward the rich society and the powerful society, but upward to the Great Society.

3   The Great Society rests on abundance and liberty for all. It demands an end to poverty and racial injustice, to which we are totally committed in our time. But that is just the beginning.

4   The Great Society is a place where every child can find knowledge to enrich his mind and to enlarge his talents. It is a place where leisure is a welcome chance to build and reflect, not a feared cause of boredom and restlessness. It is a place where the city of man serves not only the needs of the body and the demands of commerce but the desire for beauty and the hunger for community. It is a place where man can renew contact with nature. It is a place which honors creation for its own sake and for what it adds to the understanding of the race. It is a place where men are more concerned with the quality of their goals than the quantity of their goods.

5   But most of all, the Great Society is not a safe harbor, a resting place, a final objective, a finished work. It is a challenge constantly renewed, beckoning us toward a destiny where the meaning of our lives matches the marvelous products of our labor.

6   So I want to talk to you today about three places where we begin to build the Great Society—in our cities, in our countryside, and in our classrooms.

7   Our society will never be great until our cities are great. Today the frontier of imagination and innovation is inside those cities and not beyond their borders.

8   New experiments are already going on. It will be the task of your generation to make the American city a place where future generations will come, not only to live but to live the good life. . . .

9   A second place where we begin to build the Great Society is in our countryside. We have always prided ourselves on being not only America the strong and America the free, but America the beautiful. Today that beauty is

in danger. The water we drink, the food we eat, the very air that we breathe, are threatened with pollution. Our parks are overcrowded, our seashores overburdened. Green fields and dense forests are disappearing.

10   A third place to build the Great Society is in the classrooms of America. There your children's lives will be shaped. Our society will not be great until every young mind is set free to scan the farthest reaches of thought and imagination.

11   These are three of the central issues of the Great Society. While our Government has many programs directed at those issues, I do not pretend that we have the full answer to those problems. But I do promise this: We are going to assemble the best thought and the broadest knowledge from all over the world to find those answers for America.

Excerpt from Fireside Chat 12: On the Recession

by President Franklin Delano Roosevelt (given April 14, 1938)

1   Five years ago we faced a very serious problem of economic and social recovery. For four and a half years that recovery proceeded apace. It is only in the past seven months that it has received a visible setback.

2   And it is only within the past two months, as we have waited patiently to see whether the forces of business itself would counteract it, that it has become apparent that government itself can no longer safely fail to take aggressive government steps to meet it.

3   This recession has not returned to us (to) the disasters and suffering of the beginning of 1933. Your money in the bank is safe; farmers are no longer in deep distress and have greater purchasing power; dangers of security speculation have been minimized; national income is almost 50% higher than it was in 1932; and government has an established and accepted responsibility for relief.

4   But I know that many of you have lost your jobs or have seen your friends or members of your families lose their jobs, and I do not propose that the Government shall pretend not to see these things. I know that the effect of our present difficulties has been uneven; that they have affected some groups and some localities seriously but that they have been scarcely felt in others. But I conceive the first duty of government is to protect the economic welfare of all the people in all sections and in all groups. I said in my Message opening the last session of the Congress that if private enterprise did not provide jobs this spring, government would take up the slack—that I would not let the people down. We have all learned the lesson that government cannot afford to wait until it has lost the power to act. . . .

5   I came to the conclusion that the present-day problem calls for action both by the Government and by the people, that we suffer primarily from a failure of consumer demand because of lack of buying power. Therefore it is up to us to create an economic upturn. "How and where can and should the Government help to start an (upward spiral) economic upturn?" . . .

6   First, I asked for certain appropriations which are intended to keep the Government expenditures for work relief and similar purposes during the coming fiscal year that begins on the first of July, keep that going at the same rate of expenditure as at present. . . .

7   Second, I told the Congress that the Administration proposes to make additional bank reserves available for the credit needs of the country. . . .

8   This third proposal is to make definite additions to the purchasing power of the Nation by providing new work over and above the continuing of the old work. . . .

9   I believe that we have been right in the course we have charted. To abandon our purpose of building a greater, a more stable and a more tolerant America would be to miss the tide and perhaps to miss the port. I propose to sail ahead. I feel sure that your hopes and I feel sure that your help are with me. For to reach a port, we must sail—sail, not lie at anchor, sail, not drift.

30. Which quotation from President Johnson's speech supports the idea that the Great Society will keep changing?

   A. "The challenge of the next half century is whether we have the wisdom to use that wealth to enrich and elevate our national life, and to advance the quality of our American civilization."
   B. "For in your time we have the opportunity to move not only toward the rich society and the powerful society, but upward to the Great Society."
   C. "But most of all, the Great Society is not a safe harbor, a resting place, a final objective, a finished work."
   D. "While our Government has many programs directed at those issues, I do not pretend that we have the full answer to those problems."

31. What can be inferred about President Johnson? He is

   A. artistic.
   B. cautious.
   C. reserved.
   D. idealistic.

32. What is the meaning of the word *unbridled* as it is used in paragraph 2?

    A. uniform
    B. unknown
    C. unaware
    D. uncontrolled

33. What are the three places where President Johnson wants to begin building the Great Society?

    A. oceans, cities, and harbors
    B. schools, frontiers, and parks
    C. countryside, forests, and cities
    D. cities, countryside, and schools

34. Why does President Roosevelt use the metaphor *we must sail—sail, not lie at anchor, sail, not drift* in paragraph 9 of his Fireside Chat?

    A. to criticize people who have little ambition
    B. to explain why he is giving this Fireside Chat
    C. to suggest that he thought of life as a sailing trip
    D. to reinforce the idea that the government must actively do something

35. What did President Roosevelt say would happen if the private sector did not provide jobs?

    A. Government would provide jobs for people.
    B. Congress would take measures to increase consumer demand.
    C. Congress would make bank reserves available.
    D. Government would subsidize the private sector.

36. Which quotation from President Roosevelt's speech supports the idea that he believes in a strong government?

    A. "Five years ago we faced a very serious problem of economic and social recovery."
    B. "It is only in the past seven months that it has received a visible setback."
    C. "And it is only within the past two months, as we have waited patiently to see whether the forces of business itself would counteract it, that it has become apparent that government itself can no longer safely fail to take aggressive government steps to meet it."
    D. "I know that the effect of our present difficulties has been uneven; that they have affected some groups and some localities seriously but that they have been scarcely felt in others."

37. What viewpoint do President Johnson and President Roosevelt have in common? Government should

    A. be smaller and keep taxes low.
    B. assist privately owned businesses.
    C. provide jobs for the nation's people.
    D. take care of the needs of the citizenry.

38. How is the tone of President Johnson's speech different from the tone of President Roosevelt's speech? President Johnson's speech is more

    A. serious than President Roosevelt's speech.
    B. hopeful than President Roosevelt's speech.
    C. complex than President Roosevelt's speech.
    D. objective than President Roosevelt's speech.

39. In what way is President Johnson's speech similar in style to President's Roosevelt's speech? They both

    A. use a comparison to get their point across.
    B. use technical details about what they want to do.
    C. are critical of the way in which the private sector operates.
    D. list important issues that they seek to address.

40. The following e-mail message contains several numbered blanks, each marked "Select. . . ." Beneath each one is a set of choices. Indicate the choice from each set that is correct and belongs in the blank. (**Note:** On the real GED® test, the choices will appear as a "drop-down" menu. When you click on a choice, it will appear in the blank.)

    From: fdaniels@Media.com

    To: All Board Members

    Re: Retreat

    Hello Everyone:

    As president of the board, I am certain that our upcoming retreat will be a great time for us to assess our goals and to get to know each other better. I have heard on great authority that the ⌄Select 1... ▼ is a perfect spot for our retreat since the atmosphere is so unlike what we are used to.

Select 1... ▼
Big 5 Circle Dude Ranch
Big 5 circle dude Ranch
Big 5 Circle Dude ranch
Big 5 circle dude ranch

The ranch consists of a main building and several small cabins near a lovely stream. We will all be staying in the cabins. All of them have two bedrooms and two bathrooms so everyone will be comfortable. You will need to see the assignment sheet that is posted on the HR information board. Most meals will be taken in the main building, although there will be a few lunches that will be cooked in a chuck wagon.

I want to tell all of you about the many voluntary activities that are available at the ranch, such as riding horses and learning to herd cattle. Not all of us will want to partake of these [Select 2... ▼] to pack clothes that are suitable.

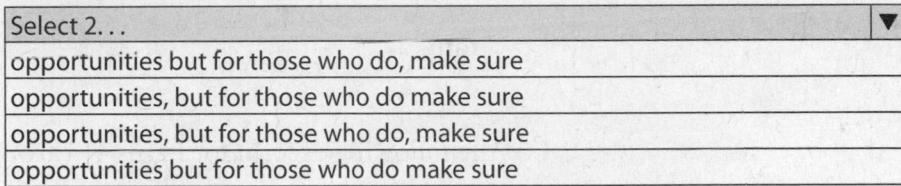

Select 2... ▼
opportunities but for those who do, make sure
opportunities, but for those who do make sure
opportunities, but for those who do, make sure
opportunities but for those who do make sure

Dress for the entire weekend will be casual. No need for suits, heels, or whatever. There will also be opportunities for sleeping under the sky, if you would like. Sleeping bags will be provided in that case.
[Select 3... ▼]

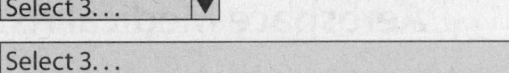

Select 3... ▼
Those people who do not choose to ride or sleeping In bags will still have many somewhat less challenging activities.
Those people who do not choose to be riding or sleeping in bags will still have many somewhat less challenging activities.
Those people who do not choose to ride or sleep in bags will still have many somewhat less challenging activities.
Those people who do not choose to riding or sleeping in bags will still have many somewhat less challenging activities.

Of course there will be ample time for us to get together and talk about our vision for the coming year during the evenings. Also, there is no television on the property and you will need to check your cell phones at the door.

I have been told that the experience is a very grounding one. Since we are for the most part living in our heads, this will indeed be a change. I am sure it will allow us to focus more on our ultimate goals rather than our individual concerns.

We are leaving promptly at 8 a.m. Thursday by vans and will return Sunday evening. I'm attaching the [Select 4... ▼] ad and website address.

Select 4... ▼
ranches'
ranch's
ranches
ranchs'

By the way, I'm bringing my cowboy hat.

Frank

Use the following excerpt for Items 41 through 49:

Excerpt from Remarks Given at the Annual Scientific Meeting of the Aerospace Medical Association (2013)

by NASA Administrator Charles Bolden

1   This conference's theme, "Today's Challenges, Tomorrow's Opportunities," pretty much covers what we at NASA try to address every day. We're in a brand-new era of exploration—one where we're advancing aeronautics and space technology development, transforming the ways we get to low Earth orbit, and setting our sights on farther destinations.

2   Today we celebrate the 40th anniversary of Skylab's launch, and NASA, probably more than any other agency, not only celebrates its history, we learn from it. We build on it, and we make ourselves better. And of course a lot of things we develop along the way don't just go up into space; they also come back down to Earth in the form of very real and practical everyday benefits.

3   Space technologies that have returned to our everyday lives include biomedical technologies such as advanced imaging and infant formula; potential new cancer treatments in the form of microencapsulation; and the protective gear that keeps our military, firefighters, and police safe.

4   That trend is only going to escalate as we reach for even farther horizons. A human mission to Mars is today the ultimate destination in our solar system for humanity. NASA's entire exploration program is aligned to support this goal.

5   You may know that three years ago President Obama paid a visit to Kennedy Space Center, where he set goals of sending humans to an asteroid for the first time in history by 2025 and making a crewed journey to Mars by the 2030s.

6   A few months later, the President signed NASA's 2010 Authorization Act into law, extending the life of the International Space Station and committing the nation to fostering a growing commercial space industry. These measures freed NASA to start work on building the next generation heavy lift rocket and multi-purpose crew vehicle needed to take our astronauts beyond low-Earth orbit into deep space, including that planned mission to Mars.

7   If anyone thinks that interest in human spaceflight has diminished since the end of the shuttle program, let me point out that last year we received the second highest number of astronaut applications in our history—more than 6,300. Less than 20 of them will make the final cut that will be announced in the coming weeks. These astronauts will be among the first to be trained specifically for long duration space flights.

8   Last year we also announced that NASA's Scott Kelly will undertake a one-year mission to the International Space Station in 2015. That mission will add to our knowledge of microgravity's effects on bone density, muscle mass, strength, vision, and other aspects of human health. This research is essential as we plan for a long-duration flight to Mars.

9   Meanwhile, our commercial partners' continued successes in developing space transportation systems to low Earth orbit have demonstrated that our confidence in their approaches was well founded.

10   We now have one partner, SpaceX, regularly resupplying the International Space Station with cargo, while Orbital Science just test launched its *Antares* rocket and is set to become the second.

11   Concurrently, SpaceX, Boeing, and Sierra Nevada are working hard to make commercial crew a reality by 2017, and I know they will. This has allowed NASA to focus on the next destinations, including the asteroid mission that President Obama laid out for us in the FY2014 budget last month.

12   The new asteroid initiative is actually a broad asteroid strategy to identify and find out more about near-Earth asteroids, engage citizen scientists and new partners while we're doing it, and then ultimately send a mission to an asteroid that will relocate it to an orbit closer to Earth where astronauts can visit it using our Space Launch System and *Orion* multipurpose crew vehicle currently under development.

13   Our Space Technology Mission Directorate is hard at work on the technologies that are the underpinning of everything we do. This includes the solar electric propulsion that will power the robotic mission to bring

our target asteroid nearer to Earth so astronauts can explore it and bring samples home.

14   The new budget also has a strong science component, from increasing our fleet of Earth observation satellites, to sending new robots to orbit and land on Mars, to the James Webb Space Telescope targeted for a 2018 launch as the successor to the Hubble Space Telescope.

15   All of this reflects a human imperative to explore and learn. It can be dangerous, but we must not be too risk averse. That's why NASA is doing the necessary planning and development to make space exploration as safe as it can be, and to make sure the things we learn in space have benefits on Earth as well.

16   As we plan those long-duration missions to asteroids and other destinations, there are many extreme dangers we at NASA are trying to mitigate to decrease the risk to our crewmembers.

17   Among these risks are: radiation from solar particle events and cosmic radiation; microgravity-induced harmful changes in human physiology; and the consequences of isolation—be it the psychological effects of being away from family and friends or the problems with communication delays with Earth.

18   NASA is committed to human exploration of the solar system, and the health of our astronauts in preparation for their missions, during launch, and while they are in space, is our top priority. It is also important that space missions do not cause significant harm to crewmembers that might be seen only years after their space missions.

41. Which quotation supports the idea that NASA will attempt to minimize the dangers facing astronauts?

A. "Today we celebrate the 40th anniversary of Skylab's launch, and NASA, probably more than any other agency, not only celebrates its history, we learn from it."

B. "Last year we also announced that NASA's Scott Kelly will undertake a one-year mission to the International Space Station in 2015."

C. "Our Space Technology Mission Directorate is hard at work on the technologies that are the underpinning of everything we do."

D. "It is also important that space missions do not cause significant harm to crewmembers that might be seen only years after their space missions."

42. What is the speech celebrating?

    A. a landing on the moon
    B. a new initiative to explore the asteroids
    C. the anniversary of the launch of Skylab
    D. the launch of the Hubble Space Telescope

43. Which definition best matches the use of the word *engage* in paragraph 12?

    A. to arrange for the use
    B. to contract for the service
    C. to interlock or cause to interlock
    D. to attract and hold the attention

44. Which company has been resupplying the International Space Station with cargo?

    A. Boeing
    B. SpaceX
    C. Sierra Nevada
    D. Orbital Science

45. What is the purpose of Charles Bolden's speech?

    A. to express his thanks to the many astronauts who have served on NASA missions
    B. to detail the many everyday benefits that have resulted from space exploration projects
    C. to show that space exploration projects in the future will be safer than those in the past
    D. to stress that NASA is still a vital organization with significant space exploration missions even though the shuttle program is over

46. In what way does the information about the many breakthroughs for everyday living support the main idea? It supports the idea that

    A. a priority of NASA is a mission to Mars.
    B. outer space is scientists' last frontier.
    C. astronauts face many different challenges.
    D. space exploration produces benefits for ordinary people.

47. Based on the speech, what generalization could be made about long space exploration?

    A. Most of the applicants to NASA want to go on long space explorations.
    B. The long space explorations will need to be funded by private companies.
    C. Most of the planned long space explorations will have to be abandoned due to safety concerns.
    D. It is likely that astronauts on long space explorations will suffer some ill effects.

48. Which definition best matches the use of the word *imperative* in paragraph 15? It means something that is

    A. an option.
    B. a problem.
    C. an outcome.
    D. a necessity.

49. Why does Bolden include the information about the number of people who applied to become an astronaut in paragraph 7? He wants to

    A. show how popular the NASA space program is.
    B. show how difficult it is to become an astronaut.
    C. explain the process of becoming an astronaut.
    D. tell how to apply to become an astronaut.

Use the following excerpt for Items 50 through 55:

Excerpt Adapted from "A Defensive Diamond"

by Saki (H. H. Munro)

1   Treddleford sat in an easy arm-chair in front of a roaring fire, with a book in his hand and the comfortable consciousness that outside the club windows the rain was dripping and pattering with persistent purpose. A chill, wet October afternoon was merging into a bleak, wet October evening, and the club smoking-room seemed warmer and cozier by contrast. It was an afternoon on which to be wafted away from one's climatic surroundings, and "The Golden Journey to Samarkand" promised to bear Treddleford well and bravely into other lands and under other skies. He had just migrated from London the Rain-Swept to Baghdad the Beautiful when an icy breath of imminent annoyance crept between the book and himself. Amblecope, the man with the prominent eyes and the mouth ready mobilized for conversational openings, had planted himself in a neighboring arm-chair.

2   For a many months Treddleford had skillfully avoided making the acquaintance of his talkative fellow-clubman; he had marvelously escaped from the infliction of his relentless record of tedious personal achievements, or alleged achievements, on golf links, turf, and gaming table, by flood and field. Now his season of immunity was coming to an end. There was no escape.

3   The intruder was armed with a copy of "Country Life," not for purposes of reading, but as an aid to conversational ice-breaking.

4   "Rather a good portrait of Throstlewing," he remarked explosively, turning his large challenging eyes on Treddleford; "somehow it reminds me very much of Yellowstep, who was supposed to be such a good thing for the Grand Prix in 1903. Curious race that was; I suppose I've seen every race for the Grand Prix for the last—"

5   "Be kind enough never to mention the Grand Prix to me," said Treddleford desperately; "it brings back acutely distressing memories. I can't explain why without going into a long and complicated story."

6   "Oh, certainly, certainly," said Amblecope hastily; long and complicated stories that were not told by himself were abominable in his eyes. He turned the pages of his magazine and became suddenly interested in the picture of a Mongolian pheasant.

7   "Not a bad representation of the Mongolian variety," he exclaimed, holding it up for his neighbor's inspection. "They do very well in some environments. Take some stopping too, once they're fairly on the wing. I suppose the most pheasants I ever shot in two successive days—"

8   "My aunt," broke in Treddleford, with dramatic abruptness, "possesses perhaps the most remarkable record in the way of taking a pheasant that has ever been achieved. She is seventy-five and can't hit a thing, but she always goes out with the others to hunt. When I say she can't hit a thing, I don't mean to say that she doesn't occasionally endanger the lives of her fellow-gunners, because that wouldn't be true. Well, the other day she winged a pheasant, and brought it to earth with a feather or two knocked out of it; it was a runner, and my aunt saw herself in danger of losing about the only bird she'd hit. Of course she wasn't going to stand that; she followed it through brushwood, and when it took to the open country and started across a plowed field she jumped on a pony and went after it. The chase was a long one, and when the bird at last tired, my aunt was nearer home than she was to the shooting party; she had left that some five miles behind her."

9   "Rather a long run for a wounded pheasant," snapped Amblecope.

10   "The story rests on my aunt's authority," said Treddleford coldly, "and she is local vice-president of the Young Women's Christian Association. Anyway she got her bird."

11   "Some birds, of course, take a lot of killing," said Amblecope; "so do some fish. I remember once I was fishing in the Exe, lovely trout stream, lots of fish, though they don't run to any great size—"

12   "One of them did," announced Treddleford, with emphasis. "My uncle came across a giant trout in a pool just off the main stream of the Exe; he tried to catch it with every kind of fly and worm every day for three weeks without success, and then Fate intervened on his behalf. There was a low stone bridge just over this pool, and on the last day of his fishing holiday a motor van ran violently into it and turned over with its load landing in the stream; no one was hurt. In a couple of minutes the giant trout was twisting on bare mud at the bottom of a waterless pool, and my uncle was able to walk down to him and pick him up. The van-load consisted of blotting-paper, and every drop of water in that pool had been sucked up into the spilt cargo."

13   With that, Amblecope got up from his chair and moved to another part of the room. Treddleford reopened his book.

14   For a half-hour he read of a mysterious world. Then the world of to-day called him back; he was summoned to speak with a friend on the telephone.

15   As Treddleford was about to leave the room he encountered Amblecope, also leaving. Amblecope was about to go through the door, but a new-born pride was surging in Treddleford's breast and he waved him back.

16   "I believe I take precedence," he said coldly; "you are merely the club Bore; I am the club Liar."

50. What can be inferred about Treddleford?

   A. He knows what he wants and how to get it.
   B. He wants to be respected and works hard at it.
   C. He likes to have company, but only when he wants to.
   D. He enjoys reading about other places, but never travels.

51. Which quotation supports the story's main idea?

    A. "Treddleford sat in an easy arm-chair in front of a roaring fire, with a book in his hand and the comfortable consciousness that outside the club windows the rain was dripping and pattering with persistent purpose."
    B. "Now his season of immunity was coming to an end."
    C. "Curious race that was; I suppose I've seen every race for the Grand Prix for the last—"
    D. "My uncle came across a giant trout in a pool just off the main stream of the Exe; he tried to catch it with every kind of fly and worm every day for three weeks without success, and then Fate intervened on his behalf."

52. What does Treddleford think about the book he is reading?

    A. It bores him.
    B. It pleases him.
    C. It is confusing to him.
    D. It is disturbing to him.

53. Why does Treddleford think he should go out the door before Amblecope?

    A. He wants to avoid Amblecope.
    B. He wants to upset Amblecope.
    C. He feels that Amblecope is copying him.
    D. He thinks he is cleverer than Amblecope.

54. What does the expression *wafted away* mean in paragraph 1?

    A. sailed on
    B. carried off
    C. watched over
    D. wanted mostly

55. Why does Amblecope want to tell people stories?

    A. He wants to please people.
    B. He knows it annoys people.
    C. He loves to hear himself talk.
    D. He is a professional storyteller.

56. The following memo contains several numbered blanks, each marked "Select. . . ." Beneath each one is a set of choices. Indicate the choice from each set that is correct and belongs in the blank. (**Note:** On the real GED® test, the choices will appear as a "drop-down" menu. When you click on a choice, it will appear in the blank.)

Memo

All Employees

Re: Computer Problems

We have noticed that a lot of time has been lost due to unresolved computer problems. [Select 1... ▼] In an attempt to improve the situation, we are instituting a new system for dealing with technical issues.

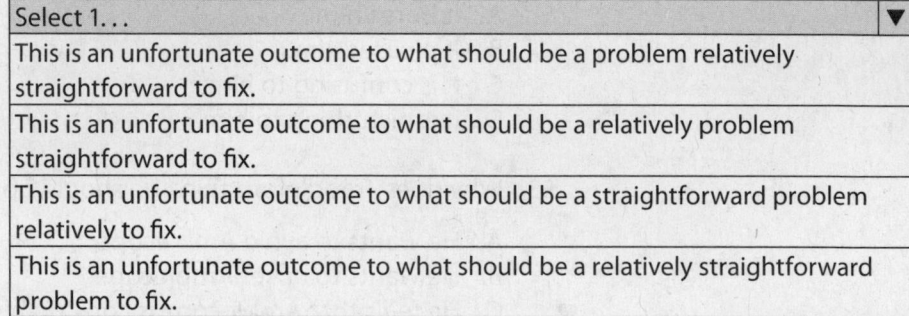

Select 1... ▼
This is an unfortunate outcome to what should be a problem relatively straightforward to fix.
This is an unfortunate outcome to what should be a relatively problem straightforward to fix.
This is an unfortunate outcome to what should be a straightforward problem relatively to fix.
This is an unfortunate outcome to what should be a relatively straightforward problem to fix.

As of this notice, any employee who is experiencing a computer technical difficulty needs to contact IT directly by calling extension 265 rather than giving written notice. You may or may not have an IT person pick up the phone, so if you hear the message that IT is occupied, leave a very specific message and include [Select 2... ▼]

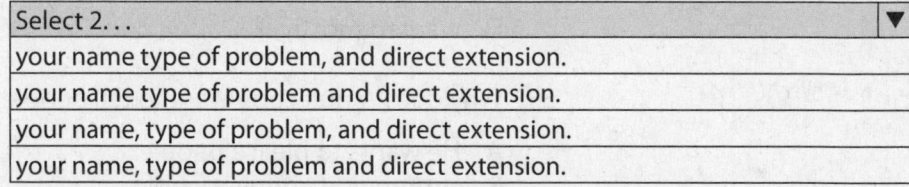

Select 2... ▼
your name type of problem, and direct extension.
your name type of problem and direct extension.
your name, type of problem, and direct extension.
your name, type of problem and direct extension.

You will be contacted within three hours of your call. If that does not happen, call extension 256 and you will be connected with troubleshooting. That will ensure that an IT person returns your call.

All problems will be dealt with in the order that they are reported. When the IT person calls you to discuss the problem, he/she will attempt to resolve the issue or issues that you are facing via the phone. If that effort fails to be effective, [Select 3... ▼]

Select 3... ▼
an IT person will make an appointment will come to your work site and will deal with the matter directly.
an IT person will make an appointment will be coming to your work site and deal with the matter directly.
an IT person will make an appointment to come to your work site and will deal with the matter directly.
an IT person will make an appointment will have come to your work site and dealing with the matter directly.

Be aware that because there usually are many diverse technical issues and there [Select 4... ▼] a limited number of IT staff, it may take up to two days for IT to respond to your report. In the meantime, employees are asked to keep a log of any work that could not be completed because of a computer issue.

Select 4... ▼
is
are
was
were

Should the IT person be unavailable for a longer period of time than two days, please call Ms. Aniela at extension 65 to report that fact and you will be given a temporary work site with a different computer until the issue is successfully resolved. Hopefully this will not happen very often. Should a computer not be repairable, the employee will receive a new one within a week's time.

We hope this new manner of dealing with computer problems will be efficient and thorough and that no work will suffer as a result.

Use the following excerpt for Items 57 through 64:

Excerpt from *Up from Slavery: An Autobiography* (1901)

by Booker T. Washington, Pioneering African-American Educator

1   One day, while at work in the coal-mine, I happened to overhear two miners talking about a great school for coloured people somewhere in Virginia. This was the first time that I had ever heard anything about any kind of school or college that was more pretentious than the little coloured school in our town.

2   In the darkness of the mine I noiselessly crept as close as I could to the two men who were talking. I heard one tell the other that not only was the school established for the members of my race, but that opportunities were provided by which poor but worthy students could work out all or a part of the cost of board, and at the same time be taught some trade or industry.

3   As they went on describing the school, it seemed to me that it must be the greatest place on earth, and not even Heaven presented more attractions for me at that time than did the Hampton Normal and Agricultural Institute in Virginia, about which these men were talking. I resolved at once to go to that school, although I had no idea where it was, or how many miles away, or how I was going to reach it; I remembered only that I was on fire constantly with one ambition, and that was to go to Hampton. This thought was with me day and night.

4   After hearing of the Hampton Institute, I continued to work for a few months longer in the coal-mine. While at work there, I heard of a vacant position in the household of General Lewis Ruffner, the owner of the salt-furnace and coal-mine. Mrs. Viola Ruffner, the wife of General Ruffner, was a "Yankee" woman from Vermont. Mrs. Ruffner had a reputation all through the vicinity for being very strict with her servants, and especially with the boys who tried to serve her. Few of them had remained with her more than two or three weeks. They all left with the same excuse: she was too strict. I decided, however, that I would rather try Mrs. Ruffner's house than remain in the coal-mine, and so my mother applied to her for the vacant position. I was hired at a salary of $5 per month.

5   I had heard so much about Mrs. Ruffner's severity that I was almost afraid to see her, and trembled when I went into her presence. I had not lived with her many weeks, however, before I began to understand her. I soon began to learn that, first of all, she wanted everything kept clean about her, that she wanted things done promptly and systematically, and that at the bottom of everything she wanted absolute honesty and frankness. Nothing must be sloven or slipshod; every door, every fence, must be kept in repair.

6   I cannot now recall how long I lived with Mrs. Ruffner before going to Hampton, but I think it must have been a year and a half. At any rate, I here repeat what I have said more than once before, that the lessons that I learned in the home of Mrs. Ruffner were as valuable to me as any education I have ever gotten anywhere since. Even to this day I never see bits of paper scattered around a house or in the street that I do not want to pick them up at once. I never see a filthy yard that I do not want to clean it, a paling off of a fence that I do not want to put it on, an unpainted or unwhitewashed house that I do not want to paint or whitewash it, or a button off one's clothes, or a grease-spot on them or on a floor, that I do not want to call attention to it.

7   From fearing Mrs. Ruffner I soon learned to look upon her as one of my best friends. When she found that she could trust me she did so implicitly. During the one or two winters that I was with her she gave me an opportunity to go to school for an hour in the day during a portion of the winter months, but most of my studying was done at night, sometimes alone, sometimes under someone whom I could hire to teach me. Mrs. Ruffner always encouraged and sympathized with me in all my efforts to get an education. It was while living with her that I began to get together my first library. I secured a dry-goods box, knocked out one side of it, put some shelves in it, and began putting into it every kind of book that I could get my hands upon, and called it my "library."

8   Notwithstanding my success at Mrs. Ruffner's, I did not give up the idea of going to the Hampton Institute. In the fall of 1872 I determined to make an effort to get there, although, as I have stated, I had no definite idea of the direction in which Hampton was, or of what it would cost to go there. I do not think that anyone thoroughly sympathized with me in my ambition to go to Hampton unless it was my mother, and she was troubled with a grave fear that I was starting out on a "wild-goose chase."

57. Which quotation supports the idea that the author was anxious to get an education?

   A. "This was the first time that I had ever heard anything about any kind of school or college that was more pretentious than the little coloured school in our town."
   B. "I resolved at once to go to that school, although I had no idea where it was, or how many miles away, or how I was going to reach it; I remembered only that I was on fire constantly with one ambition, and that was to go to Hampton."
   C. "I soon began to learn that, first of all, she wanted everything kept clean about her, that she wanted things done promptly and systematically, and that at the bottom of everything she wanted absolute honesty and frankness."
   D. "I cannot now recall how long I lived with Mrs. Ruffner before going to Hampton, but I think it must have been a year and a half."

58. Why does the author refer to Mrs. Ruffner as a "Yankee" in paragraph 4? He wants to suggest that she was

   A. not like the local people.
   B. educated in good schools.
   C. unhappy at being far from her home.
   D. kind to those who worked for her.

59. Fill in the blank.

   Another way to say "wild-goose chase" is _____.

60. Why does the author include information about working for Mrs. Ruffner? The author wants to show that

   A. she enjoyed his company.
   B. he was strong and able to work.
   C. he was adaptable to any situation.
   D. she taught him important life skills.

61. Why was working in a coal mine important to the author's story?

   A. It helped him become strong.
   B. He learned about Hampton there.
   C. He learned to be a good worker there.
   D. It helped him save money to go to Hampton.

62. How does the information that the author did not know where Hampton College was located support the idea that he was committed to obtaining an education? It shows that he

   A. had little awareness of where places were located.
   B. needed to learn basic geography before applying to the institute.
   C. had no real idea of the difficulties involved in entering an institute.
   D. had made up his mind without even knowing much about the institute.

63. Fill in the blank.

   Hampton Institute is located in the state of _____.

64. What main idea can be inferred from the passage?

   A. Washington impressed many people with his wide-ranging knowledge.
   B. Washington took chances that did not always pay off.
   C. Washington was not as organized as he thought he was.
   D. Washington was a person who was committed to bettering himself.

Part 2: Essay

1 question | **45 minutes**

Use the following two excerpts for Item 65:

Excerpt from Remarks Made During a Visit to the Heil Farm in Haverhill, Iowa

by President Barack Obama

1   Well, I want to thank Jeff Heil and his father, Richard, for showing me around the farm. And I think it's remarkable to think that the Heil family has been farming this land since 1902, but they've got a relatively new addition in the wind turbines that you see in the background. They're part of the Laurel wind farm—52 turbines that harvest enough wind power to power an estimated 30,000 Iowa homes in a way that's clean and renewable.

2   And at a moment when we want to pursue every avenue for job creation, it's homegrown energy like wind that's creating good, new jobs in states like Iowa. Let me give you an example. Back when I was first running for this office and spending a lot of time in this state, I visited the town of Newton, about a half an hour down the road. The local Maytag plant was closing its doors and nearly 2,000 jobs were on the line. So you had a once-thriving factory that was going dark and going quiet and, understandably, folks were worried about what would happen to the community.

3   Then wind energy offered a new opportunity. When I returned to Newton to visit that plant as President several months ago, some of the same folks who had lost their jobs at Maytag were back on the line building wind towers to support some of the most advanced wind turbines in the world.

4   Earlier this year, at a different plant about five minutes from there, I met workers building enormous blades for these wind turbines. And I'm proud of the fact that, while we used to have to import parts like those, today they're made in Newton, made in Iowa, made in America by American workers.

5   Unfortunately, what we thought was a bipartisan consensus in supporting wind power has been fraying a little bit during election season. My opponent in this election says he wants to end tax credits for wind energy, wind energy producers that make all this possible. He's called these sources of energy "imaginary"; his new running mate has called them a "fad."

6   I think a lot of folks in Iowa would disagree, because wind farms like this and the good jobs that are down in Newton, they're not a "fad" and they're not "imaginary." Seventy-five thousand jobs across this country depend on wind energy; 7,000 jobs in Iowa alone. That's more than in any other state. These are good, American jobs. And thanks to the hard work of the folks who have these jobs, Iowa generates about 20 percent of its electricity from wind—energy that powers homes and businesses and factories all across the state.

7   Over the past four years, we've doubled the amount of electricity America can generate from wind—from 25 gigawatts to 50 gigawatts. And to put that in perspective, that's like building 12 new Hoover Dams that are powering homes all across the country. We doubled the amount of electricity we generate from solar energy, too. And combined, these energy sources are enough power to make sure that 13 million homes have reliable power and support the paychecks that help more than 100,000 Americans provide for their families.

Excerpt from a Speech on Renewable Energy

by Australian House of Representatives Member Craig Scott

1   Back in 2005, the United Nations Environment Program, with one of those "the science is settled" predictions, asserted that global warming would create millions of climate change refugees. By 2010, it was said, these people would be forced to flee their homes because of rising sea levels from melting ice caps. Well, 2010 has come and gone and there has not been a single person made a climate refugee because of rising sea levels. However, here in Australia we now have some of the world's first climate refugees, forced to flee their homes not by rising sea levels but by government policies subsidizing industrial wind turbines. Dr. Sarah Laurie has documented over 20 Australian families who have been forced to flee their homes in Victoria alone because of wind turbine noise and infrasound. Dr. Laurie states:

2   ". . . current noise guidelines are completely inadequate to protect people's health because they do not involve measurement of infrasound and low-frequency noise."

3   Today I received a letter from Mrs. Pamela Connelly, an Australian climate change refugee forced to flee her home because of inadequate planning regulations which have allowed wind farms to be built too close to her home. I would like to read her letter:

4   "I am writing to share with you our personal experience of living for three years alongside a Pacific Hydro wind turbine and more importantly the contrast after having lived away from them for 18 months.

5   "The first time the turbines started to turn . . . imagine our shock of hearing a constant sort of jet engine/sonic boom whooshing sound and more annoyingly feeling a vibration sometimes in our chest bone every second or so.

6   "When the turbines were at their worst, this noise continued day and night even through closed double-glazed windows. I recall sitting on the couch on one of those earlier nights and being amazed that not only could I clearly hear the turbines, but also feel the wave of vibrations every second or so through my whole body.

7   "Another thing that increased very gradually was headaches, and in the last year or so I was taking Nurofen migraine tablets regularly. . . . The headaches were sometimes so bad that unarmed with Nurofen, the migraines were completely debilitating. . . . These headaches stopped straight away after moving away and in the past 18 months I have only taken two Nurofen tablets."

8   Mrs. Connelly continues:

9   "We asked at a meeting with Pacific Hydro for written proof that it was safe for the health of us and more importantly our children but this could not be supplied.

10   "On further questioning of Pacific Hydro at a meeting at our house we were told no further testing was needed—and nothing could be done." She continues:

11   "It is not until you move away from the turbines that you realize the profound effect that they had on you. You don't particularly connect the symptoms to the wind turbines because they very gradually build up over time and you put it down to coincidence or anything as you really don't want to believe that staying where you love is making you unwell. It really only becomes clear in a short time after you leave the vicinity of the turbines how much of an effect they were having on you when the symptoms disappear."

12   So to the member who bought this motion I say, "Shame," for your motion seeks to inflict the type of pain and suffering experienced by Mrs. Connelly on hundreds if not thousands of rural Australians and strip away their property rights and force them out of their homes.

65. **Extended response**

While President Barack Obama's comments tell about the economic benefits of wind power, Australian House of Representatives Member Craig Scott speaks about some of the drawbacks of wind turbines. Analyze both speeches to determine which position is best supported. Use relevant and specific evidence from both sources to support your response.

Write your response in the box. This task may require approximately 45 minutes to complete.

THIS IS THE END OF THE REASONING THROUGH LANGUAGE ARTS (RLA) PRETEST.

Answers and Explanations

1. **Correct answer: C.** He studies people very carefully. The narrator is a writer; he observes people and what they do and say and look like very carefully, including Miss Sylvia.

2. **Correct answer: D.** "Oh, no, no; don't let him go away without telling her—just telling her." This quotation is directly related to the theme of the passage: that Miss Sylvia had loved someone and never became involved with anyone else, but was upset because he never told her that he cared about her.

3. **Correct answer: A.** It upsets her. Miss Sylvia is clearly upset by the story: her eyes are teary; she begs the narrator to change the story so that the hero in the story tells the young woman of his feelings for her. It reminds her of her own sad story.

4. Words that describe Miss Sylvia:

   Correct answer: caring. From the way Miss Sylvia talks about her great love, and her regard for the narrator, the reader can figure out that Miss Sylvia is a caring person.

   Correct answer: friendly. Miss Sylvia is always surrounded by a circle of young people, and she "liked us all."

   Correct answer: sensitive. Miss Sylvia breaks down when the narrator reads his story to her. She takes in everything around her. She is sensitive to people and to her experiences.

5. **Correct answer: A.** It is so close to her own experience. Miss Sylvia becomes emotional and wants the ending of the story changed because it is so close to her own sad story.

6. Drop-down Select . . . 1–5.

   Select 1 correct answer: We are extremely pleased you have chosen us as your insurance company for your automobiles. The verb *have chosen* agrees with the subject, *you.*

Select 2 correct answer: business. My wife and I started it fifteen years ago. The placement of a period between the two complete thoughts, creating two complete sentences, is the edit that is needed to resolve the issue of the run-on sentence.

Select 3 correct answer: themselves. This is a reflexive pronoun that does agree with the antecedent, *they.* It is a third person plural form, which is required to correctly edit the sentence.

Select 4 correct answer: We operate in all 50 of the United States. The ordering of the sentence is clear and effective as well as logical.

Select 5 correct answer: call and ask us. Both verbs are parallel and are in an infinitive form. The word *to* is understood before *ask.*

7. **Correct answer: C.** Grizzly bears should not be reintroduced into Idaho or any other part of the country because they are ferocious. Chenoweth is highly critical of the plan to reintroduce grizzly bears because they present such a threat to humans and would force many changes in the way people live in the area.

8. **Correct answer: A.** She is stressing how large an area it is in contrast to these states. The reason that Congresswoman Chenoweth includes this information is to contrast the size of these states with the size of the area in Idaho where the grizzlies were to be reintroduced.

9. **Correct answer: A.** To show that even Lewis and Clark were frightened of the grizzlies. The reason that Congresswoman Chenoweth includes this information is to impress on her audience how fierce these animals are.

10. **Correct answer: C.** To increase the numbers of bears. This is the reason that the U.S. Fish

and Wildlife Service wants to reintroduce the bears. This information is found directly in the EIS.

11. **Correct answer: D.** "By designating the reintroduced grizzly population as nonessential experimental, bears that frequent areas of high human use, act aggressively toward humans, or attack livestock would be relocated or destroyed, based on actions in the Interagency Grizzly Bear Guidelines." The information in this quotation does support the underlying premise that the grizzlies might pose a hazard to humans by suggesting that the grizzlies could be aggressive toward humans.

12. **Congresswoman Chenoweth's Speech:**

"People's lives will be turned upside down because of the reintroduction of grizzlies in this part of Idaho."

"One person killed by a grizzly is too many."

The Final Environmental Impact Statement:

"It is important to reintroduce grizzlies since they are endangered."

"The grizzlies will be carefully monitored and people would be alerted to their presence."

13. **Correct answer: D.** She stresses emotional issues regarding the reintroduction of grizzlies. Her conclusion appeals to the emotions of her audience by providing vivid ideas of the harm that may occur when grizzlies are reintroduced in Idaho.

14. **Correct answer: D.** It has a more factual tone than the speech has. A government document like an EIS is factual by nature; a speech, by contrast, is often more personal.

15. **Correct answer: B.** The EIS needs to explain the need for reintroducing grizzlies into the environment. This is the reason this data is found in the EIS and not in the speech. It is there to show the need for reintroducing grizzlies into the environment.

16. **Correct answer: C.** A speech allows for dramatic arguments while a government document like an EIS must be more factual and objective.

17. Drop-down Select . . . 1–4.

Select 1 correct answer: You must return the completed forms to HR before your child can attend. This is the simplest and most straightforward way of communicating the information in this sentence.

Select 2 correct answer: Unfortunately. This is the correct transition word; it is an unfortunate happening, so this word fits with the context of the sentence.

Select 3 correct answer: it's. This is the correct contraction for the words *it is*, which make sense in the sentence.

Select 4 correct answer: The cost will vary depending on your current salary. However, we want to make the facility affordable for you. The placement of a period between the two complete thoughts, creating two complete sentences, is the edit that is needed to resolve the issue of the run-on sentence.

18. **Correct answer: B.** John Perkins' feelings changed from one minute to the next minute. This is the way John Perkins is like a pendulum, swinging back and forth.

19. **Correct answer: C.** "Everything in the room spoke of a loss, of an essence gone, of its soul and life departed." This quotation expresses how much John Perkins was affected by the absence of Katy; the words *loss* and *essence gone* and *life departed* help to illustrate the extent that he was affected.

20. Correct order:

John reads Katy's note.

John sees the newspaper with a hole in it.

John starts to tidy up.

John tells Katy he is going out.

21. **Correct answer: D.** He knew what the evening would be like. In the story, John Perkins knows what his evening will be like, so he does not hurry home; he is bored by the idea of it.

22. **Correct answer: D.** It suggests why Roosevelt was able to accomplish a good deal. This description supports the idea that Roosevelt accomplished many things, including writing about their camping trip two years earlier than Burroughs.

23. **Correct answer: A.** "When I accepted his invitation I was well aware that during the journey I should be in a storm center most of the time, which is not always a pleasant prospect to a man of my habits and disposition." This quotation suggests that Burroughs was somewhat concerned about the camping trip; it supports that main idea.

24. **Correct answer: C.** He was busy doing other things. This information is found in the passage. Burroughs said he was busy at Slabsides and did not have the time to write.

25. **Correct answer: D.** He wants his readers to understand that he approved of Roosevelt's hunting. Burroughs goes out of his way to say that he would like to hunt with Roosevelt; he approves of the manner in which Roosevelt hunts.

26. Words that describe President Roosevelt:

    Correct answer: committed. From the way Burroughs describes him, Roosevelt seems very committed as a president and to all the things he does.

    Correct answer: capable. Roosevelt seems extremely capable of many things according to Burroughs.

    Correct answer: intelligent. The way in which Burroughs talks about Roosevelt reveals that Roosevelt has great intelligence, about nature and about everything he does.

27. **Correct answer: A.** To keep people from criticizing him. The passage talks about how a woman from Vermont did not approve of Roosevelt's hunting. He knew newspapers would report it, so he decided not to make an issue of it.

28. **Correct answer: D.** They kill other animals. This is the reason that Burroughs thinks they should be hunted. The answer is found right in the text.

29. Drop-down Select . . . 1–5.

    Select 1 correct answer: let's. This is the correct contraction for the words *let us*, which make sense in the sentence.

    Select 2 correct answer: start to cut before the blue light goes on, you will disengage the safety system. The correct punctuation to place at the end of an introductory clause is a comma.

    Select 3 correct answer: If you have any questions about what constitutes a loose edge, refer to the manual for further explanations and photographs. The verb *constitutes* agrees in number with the subject and is in the present tense because the action takes place in the present.

    Select 4 correct answer: Until the cutter has come to a complete halt, be sure not to touch any cutting edges. This is the simplest and most straightforward way of communicating the information in this sentence. The others are illogical and/or ungrammatical.

    Select 5 correct answer: But for now, I'd like you to focus on safe operation, not speed. This is the only option that is a complete sentence and not a fragment.

30. **Correct answer: C.** "But most of all, the Great Society is not a safe harbor, a resting place, a final objective, a finished work." This quotation refers to the fact that the Great Society is not a finished work and supports the idea that the Great Society will keep changing.

31. **Correct answer: D.** He is idealistic. Judging from the nature and scope of the speech, President Johnson was extremely idealistic about providing for all people.

32. **Correct answer: D.** Uncontrolled. Something that is unbridled is not under control. This definition fits into the context of the sentence.

33. **Correct answer: D.** Cities, countryside, and schools. These are the three places mentioned by President Johnson where he wants to begin building the Great Society.

34. **Correct answer: D.** to reinforce the idea that the government must actively do something. This is the reason President Roosevelt used this metaphor.

35. **Correct answer: A.** Government would provide jobs for people. President Roosevelt says this in his speech. It is in the text; a close reading will yield the answer.

36. **Correct answer: C.** "And it is only within the past two months, as we have waited patiently to see whether the forces of business itself would counteract it, that it has become apparent that government itself can no longer safely fail to take aggressive government steps to meet it." This quotation supports the idea that President Roosevelt believed in a strong government. The other quotations do not.

37. **Correct answer: D.** Both presidents make it clear that the government has a responsibility to take care of its citizens; this is a priority for both leaders.

38. **Correct answer: B.** President Johnson's tone is more hopeful than President Roosevelt's mostly because during Roosevelt's presidency the country was suffering through a depression; the times were difficult, and consequently Roosevelt's tone was less hopeful.

39. **Correct answer: D.** They both list a set of important national issues that they either plan to address or are already addressing.

40. Drop-down Select . . . 1–4.

    Select 1 correct answer: Big 5 Circle Dude Ranch. All of the first letters of a proper name should be capitalized.

    Select 2 correct answer: opportunities, but for those who do, make sure. The first comma separates clauses, and the second comma follows a prepositional phrase.

    Select 3 correct answer: Those people who do not choose to ride or sleep in bags will still have many somewhat less challenging activities. The verbs *ride* and *sleep* are both in the infinitive form and consequently they are parallel. The other choices are not.

    Select 4 correct answer: ranch's. This is how the possessive form of the word *ranch* is formed, with an apostrophe and the letter *s*.

41. **Correct answer: D.** "It is also important that space missions do not cause significant harm to crewmembers that might be seen only years after their space missions." This information directly supports the idea that NASA is trying to minimize dangers to its astronauts.

42. **Correct answer: C.** The anniversary of the launch of Skylab. This information is found right in the text; a close reading of the speech will yield the answer.

43. **Correct answer: D.** To attract and hold the attention. From the context of the sentence and the text, this is the meaning that is intended.

44. **Correct answer: B.** SpaceX. This information is found right in the text; a close reading of the speech will yield the answer.

45. **Correct answer: D.** To stress that NASA is still a vital organization with significant space exploration projects even though the shuttle program is over. Bolden wants his audience to know that space exploration will still be going on in spite of the loss of the shuttle program;

that is why he cites all of the new projects and all of the advances that have come about because of space exploration.

46. **Correct answer: D.** It supports the idea that space exploration is a benefit to ordinary people in many ways. Bolden mentions the numerous technological and other breakthroughs produced by the space program to show that space exploration has produced many benefits to humanity.

47. **Correct answer: D.** It is likely that astronauts on long space explorations will suffer some ill effects. This is why NASA is studying the challenges of long space travel and trying to make it as safe as possible for astronauts.

48. **Correct answer: D.** An imperative means something that is a necessity. From the context of the sentence and the rest of the text, it can be determined that Bolton thinks that space exploration is a necessity for humans.

49. **Correct answer: A.** He wants to show how popular the NASA space program is. The large number of applicants helps Bolden show how popular the NASA space programs are, even after the end of the shuttle program.

50. **Correct answer: A.** He knows what he wants and how to get it. Treddleford clearly knows what he wants: to be left alone. He also cleverly devises a way to get it.

51. **Correct answer: B.** "Now his season of immunity was coming to an end." This quotation supports the idea that Treddleford was going to be bored by someone telling tedious stories and found a way to avoid that from happening.

52. **Correct answer: B.** It pleases him. Treddleford clearly enjoys reading the book that transports him to Baghdad on a rainy day in London.

53. **Correct answer: D.** He thinks he is cleverer than Amblecope. The text says, "a new-born pride was surging in Treddleford's breast." He thought he was quite clever.

54. **Correct answer: B.** Carried off. From the context of the sentence and the rest of the text, it can be determined that in his mind, Treddleford is carried off to another land by the book that he is reading.

55. **Correct answer: C.** He loves to hear himself talk. Amblecope is concerned only with himself and his desire to show off by telling stories.

56. Drop-down Select . . . 1–4.

Select 1 correct answer: This is an unfortunate outcome to what should be a relatively straightforward problem to fix. The modifiers of the word *problem* should both be before it.

Select 2 correct answer: your name, type of problem, and direct extension. The correct punctuation is to place commas after every item in a series, including the item before the word *and*.

Select 3 correct answer: an IT person will make an appointment to come to your work site and will deal with the matter directly. Both verbs are parallel and are in a correct future form.

Select 4 correct answer: is. The verb *is* agrees with the subject, *number*, which requires a singular verb form. It is also in the present tense, which is called for in this sentence.

57. **Correct answer: B.** "I resolved at once to go to that school, although I had no idea where it was, or how many miles away, or how I was going to reach it; I remembered only that I was on fire constantly with one ambition, and that was to go to Hampton." This quotation directly supports the idea that Washington was anxious to get an education.

58. **Correct answer: A.** He wants to suggest she was not like the local people. The term "Yankee" indicates that Mrs. Ruffner was different from the local Southern people.

59. Blank should be filled in with: **something that leads nowhere**, or a similar expression.

60. **Correct answer: D.** to show that she taught him important life skills. Washington includes the information about Mrs. Ruffner because he learned so much from her about keeping things in order and being honest.

61. **Correct answer: B.** He learned about Hampton there. Had Washington not been working in the coal mine, it is possible he would never have heard about Hampton, which was so important to him.

62. **Correct answer: D.** It shows that Washington had made up his mind without even knowing much about the institute. This description supports the idea that Washington was extremely committed to becoming educated. He didn't even wait to find out where the school was located before deciding to go there.

63. **Correct answer: Virginia.**

64. **Correct answer: D.** Washington was a person who was committed to bettering himself. Washington knew at once what he wanted when he heard about Hampton Institute. He was committed to becoming educated and making a better life.

65. **Extended response.** Decide which of the two arguments you think is stronger. Then support your choice with evidence from the excerpts. In essay questions like this, there is no "right" or "wrong" side.

    Both arguments are effective because both include a strong emotional component. President Obama uses personal stories to strengthen his contention that wind energy is good for the economy. He cites his first visit to Newton when the Maytag plant was closing and people were losing their jobs; and his return there to see the once-empty plant now being used for making wind turbines.

    Australian legislator Scott's arguments are equally emotional when he talks about Mrs. Connelly and what she experienced by living so close to a wind turbine farm. She endured many physical problems as well as the noise and developed health issues, such as migraine headaches. All of her symptoms went away when she abandoned her home.

    If possible, ask an instructor to evaluate your essay. Your instructor's opinions and comments will help you determine what skills you need to practice in order to improve your essay writing.

    You may also want to evaluate your essay yourself using the checklist that follows. Be fair in your evaluation. The more items you can check, the more confident you can be about your writing skills. Items that are not checked will show you the essay-writing skills that you need to work on.

    My essay:

    ☐ Creates a sound, logical argument based on the passage(s).

    ☐ Cites evidence from the passage(s) to support the argument.

    ☐ Analyzes the issue and/or evaluates the validity of the arguments in the passage(s).

    ☐ Organizes ideas in a sensible sequence.

    ☐ Shows clear connections between main points and details.

    ☐ Uses largely correct sentence structure.

    ☐ Follows standard English conventions in regard to grammar, spelling, and punctuation.

Evaluation Chart

Check the Answers and Explanations section of the RLA Pretest to see which answers you got correct and which ones you missed. For each multiple-choice question that you missed, find the item number in the chart below. Check the column on the left to see the test content area for that item. If you missed questions in a particular content area, you need to pay particular attention to that area as you study for the GED® test. The pages of this book that cover that content area are listed in the column on the right.

Content Area	Item Number	Pages to Review
1. Testing Basic English Usage Editing mechanics	6, 17, 29, 40, 56	164–186
2. Testing Reading Comprehension Basic critical reading skills	1, 2, 7, 10, 18, 22, 24, 26, 27, 31, 33, 42, 44, 46, 47, 50, 58, 61, 62, 63, 64	193–203
3. Structure and Author's Choices Sequence of events Structural relationships Author's language	14, 19, 20, 23, 32, 34, 38, 39, 43, 48, 54, 59	209–218
4. Literary Texts (Fiction) Using textual evidence to analyze elements of fiction	1, 2, 3, 4, 5, 18, 19, 21, 50, 51, 52, 53, 55	225–243
5. Informational Texts (Nonfiction) Inferring relationships between ideas Author's viewpoint and purpose Analyzing arguments Rhetorical techniques Author's response to conflicting viewpoints and bias Comparing texts	7, 8, 9, 10, 11, 12, 13, 15, 16, 22, 25, 27, 28, 30, 35, 36, 37, 39, 39, 41, 45, 46, 47, 49, 57, 61, 62	251–270

Mathematical Reasoning

This Mathematical Reasoning Pretest is designed to introduce you to this section of the GED® test and to give you a good idea of your current skill level in this subject area.

This test has the same number of questions as the real GED Mathematical Reasoning test: 50 items. The questions are in the same formats as the ones on the real exam and are designed to measure the same skills. Some of the questions simply ask you to make calculations. Others describe real-life situations that you must decide how to solve using mathematics. Many of the questions on this test are based on graphs or diagrams. Most of the questions are in multiple-choice format, but you will also see questions that ask you to indicate a point on a graph, write your answer in a box, select an answer from a drop-down menu, or "drag" an answer into the correct position in a math expression or equation. On the real GED® test, you will indicate your answers by clicking on the computer screen. For this paper-and-pencil practice test, mark your answers directly on the page.

To get a good idea of how you will do on the real exam, take this test under actual exam conditions. Complete the test in one session and follow the given time limit. If you do not complete the test in the time allowed, you will know that you need to work on improving your pacing.

Try to answer as many questions as you can. There is no penalty for wrong answers, so guess if you have to. In multiple-choice questions, if you can eliminate one or more answer choices, you can increase your chances of guessing correctly.

After you have finished the test, check your answers in the Answers and Explanations section that follows the pretest. Then use the Evaluation Chart at the end of the Answers and Explanations section to determine the skills and content areas in which you need more practice.

Now turn the page and begin the Mathematical Reasoning Pretest.

Mathematics Formula Sheet

Area

parallelogram $A = bh$

trapezoid $A = (\frac{1}{2})h(b_1 + b_2)$

Surface Area and Volume

rectangular/right prism $SA = ph + 2B$ $V = Bh$

cylinder $SA = 2\pi rh + 2\pi r^2$ $V = \pi r^2 h$

pyramid $SA = (\frac{1}{2})ps + B$ $V = (\frac{1}{3})Bh$

cone $SA = \pi rs + \pi r^2$ $V = (\frac{1}{3})\pi r^2 h$

sphere $SA = 4\pi r^2$ $V = (\frac{4}{3})\pi r^3$

$(p = \text{perimeter of base } B; \pi \approx 3.14)$

Algebra

slope of a line $m = (y_2 - y_1)/(x_2 - x_1)$

slope-intercept form of the equation of a line $y = mx + b$

point-slope form of the equation of a line $y - y_1 = m(x - x_1)$

standard form of a quadratic equation $ax^2 + bx + c = y$

quadratic formula $x = \dfrac{-b \pm \sqrt{b^2 - 4ac}}{2a}$

Pythagorean Theorem $a^2 + b^2 = c^2$

simple interest $I = prt$

$(I = \text{interest}, p = \text{principal}, r = \text{rate}, t = \text{time})$

Mathematical Reasoning

50 questions | **90 minutes**

1. The number of fans produced by a manufacturer in a week can be no more than five times the number of lamps produced by the same manufacturer during the same week. If the number of fans produced this week by the manufacturer was 20, what is the minimum number of lamps produced by the manufacturer this week?

    A. 4
    B. 5
    C. 15
    D. 20

2. If a number x has an absolute value of 4, then how many units away from 0 is x on the number line? Indicate your answer in the box.

3. If two coins are flipped, what is the probability that both coins will land on tails?

    A. 0.05
    B. 0.25
    C. 0.30
    D. 0.50

4. A line l passes through point (–2, 5) and has the same y-intercept as the line $y = 3x - 4$. What is the equation for the line l?

    A. $y = -\dfrac{9}{2}x - 4$

    B. $y = -\dfrac{9}{2}x + 3$

    C. $y = -\dfrac{1}{2}x - 4$

    D. $y = -\dfrac{1}{2}x + 3$

5. If $2(x-8)=-4x+2$, then $x=$

   A. -7
   B. -5
   C. 3
   D. 9

6. Which of the following is equivalent to the expression $5x-20$?

   A. $5(x-20)$
   B. $4(x-5)$
   C. $5(x-4)$
   D. $5(x-15)$

7. Which of the following is a factor of x^4-5x^2?

   A. x^2
   B. x^4
   C. $5x^2$
   D. $-x^3$

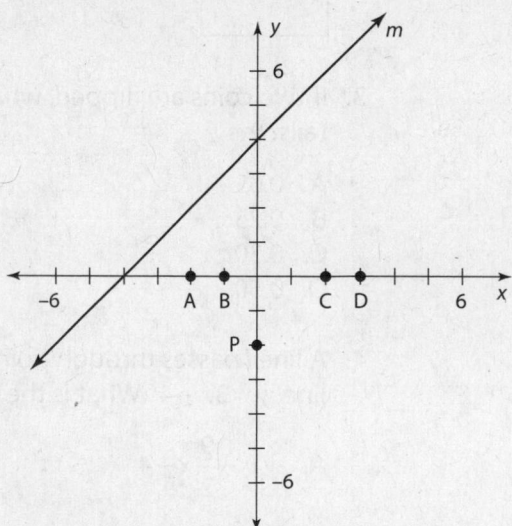

8. If a line is perpendicular to line m in the figure above, and it passes through point P, which of the following points must it also pass through?

   A. Point A
   B. Point B
   C. Point C
   D. Point D

Item 9 contains two numbered blanks, each marked "Select. . . ." Following are two choices for each blank. Indicate the choice that is correct and belongs in each blank. (**Note:** On the real GED® test, the choices will appear as a "drop-down" menu. When you click on a choice, it will appear in the blank.)

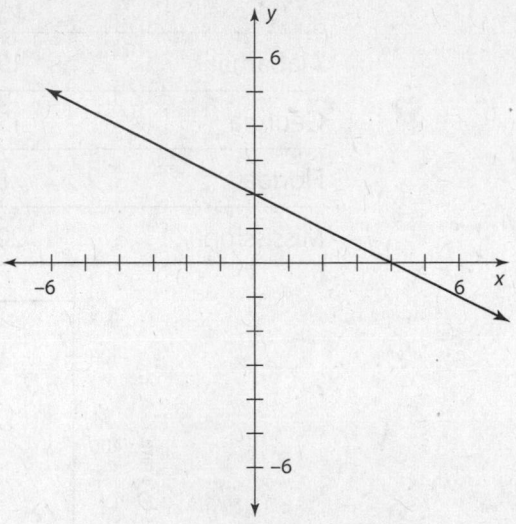

9. The figure above shows the graph of a function *f*. For this function, the value of *y* is positive when *x* is [Select 1... ▼] than [Select 2... ▼].

Select 1... ▼
greater
less

Select 2... ▼
2
4

10. A gallon of paint will cover about 400 square feet in a single coat. To the nearest tenth, how many gallons will be required to cover a circular region with a radius of 40 feet? Indicate your answer in the box.

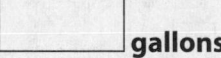 **gallons**

11. The following chart represents the number of a company's full-time and part-time employees in four states. Complete a bar graph that represents the total number of employees in each state. (**Note:** On the real GED® test, you will click on each bar and "drag" it to its proper location on the graph.)

	Part-Time	Full-Time
Alabama	100	300
Georgia	150	150
Florida	80	130
Mississippi	200	250

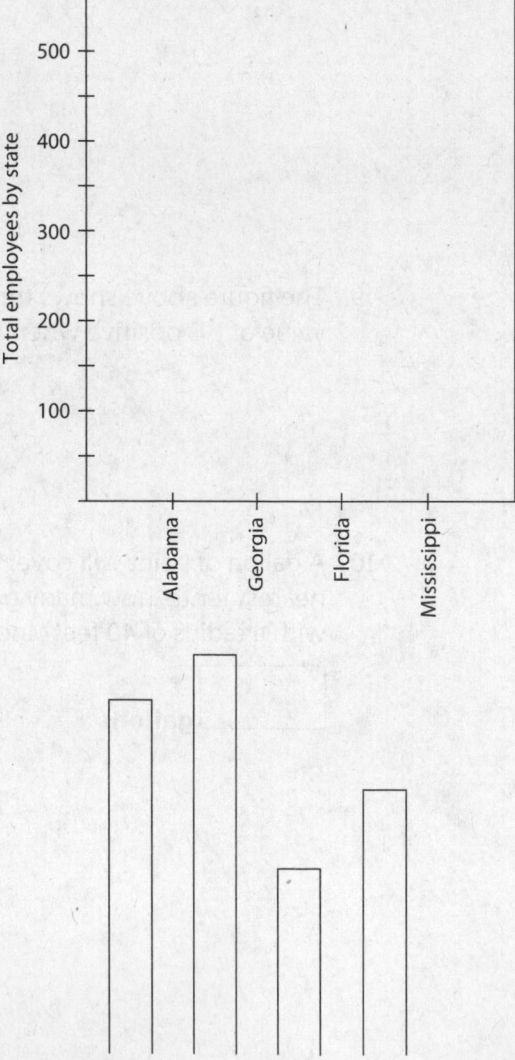

12. What is the slope of a line that passes though the points (−1, 4) and (3, 9)?

    A. $\dfrac{2}{13}$

    B. $\dfrac{1}{3}$

    C. $\dfrac{7}{8}$

    D. $\dfrac{5}{4}$

13. Machine part A must always be four inches smaller in diameter than machine part B's diameter. If machine part A's diameter is 16 inches and machine part B's diameter is x inches, which of the following can be used to solve for x?

    A. $16 = 4x$

    B. $16 = x - 4$

    C. $16 = x + 4$

    D. $16 = \dfrac{x}{4}$

14. If $2x - 2 < 8 + x$, then $x <$

    A. 2
    B. 4
    C. 9
    D. 10

15. A storage room contains a table, two bookshelves, and a large mirror. If the table weighs 37 pounds, each of the bookshelves weighs 42 pounds, and the mirror weighs 18 pounds, how much, in total, do the items in the storage room weigh? Indicate your answer in the box.

    ☐ **pounds**

16. To the nearest tenth of a cubic meter, what is the volume of a cylinder with a height of 4 meters and a radius of 6 meters? Indicate your answer in the box.

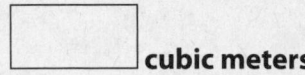 **cubic meters**

17. What is the completely simplified form of the expression $2(1-3x)-(5x+1)$?

    A. $-11x+1$
    B. $-8x+1$
    C. $-11x+3$
    D. $-8x+3$

18. A function of the form $y = mx + b$ passes through the points indicated on the table. What is the y-intercept of this function?

x	0	2	4	8
y	−8	−4	0	8

    A. −8
    B. −4
    C. 4
    D. 8

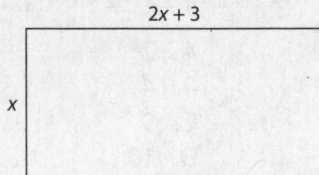

19. If x is a positive rational number, which two of the following numbers or expressions can be added together to equal the area of the given rectangular region? (**Note:** On the real GED® test, you will click on the expressions you choose and "drag" each one into a box below.)

☐ + ☐

20. What is the value of $-2x+5$ when $x=-3$?

    A. -6
    B. -1
    C. 0
    D. 11

21. Which of the following represents the product of $3x+1$ and x^2-1?

    A. $3x^2-1$
    B. x^2-1
    C. $4x^2-3x-1$
    D. $3x^3+x^2-3x-1$

22. Five students took the same mathematics course last semester. Their scores on the first exam and the final exam are listed in the following table. If these points are plotted on the coordinate grid that follows, what would be their locations? (**Note:** On the real GED® test, you will click on the grid to plot the points.)

Student	Exam 1 Score	Final Exam Score
1	53	70
2	65	64
3	85	99
4	78	82
5	60	72

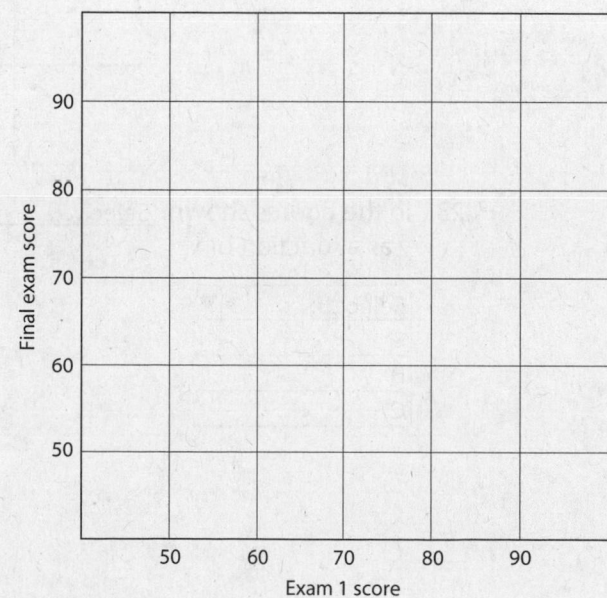

Item 23 contains a blank marked "Select...." Beneath it are three choices. Indicate the choice that is correct and belongs in the blank. (**Note:** On the real GED® test, the choices will appear as a "drop-down" menu. When you click on a choice, it will appear in the blank.)

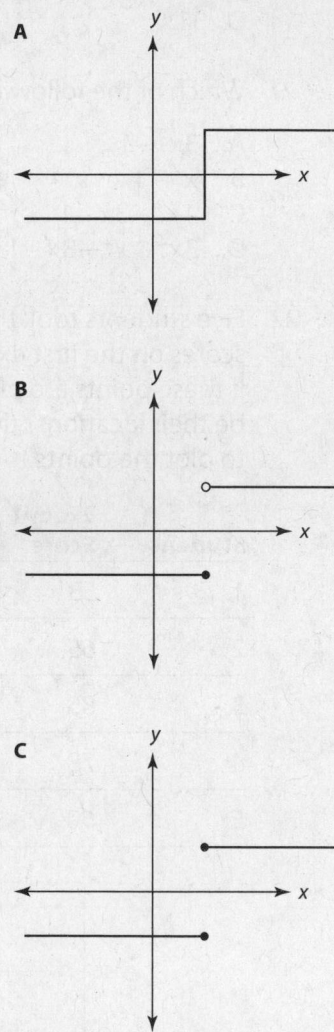

23. In the figures shown, 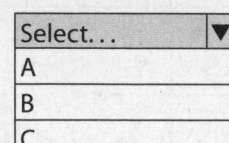 shows a graph that represents *y* as a function of *x*.

Select... ▼
A
B
C

PRETEST

24. Which of the following is equivalent to $2 \times \dfrac{2^5}{2^2}$?

    A. 2^2
    B. 2^4
    C. 2^8
    D. 2^{11}

25. A shipping box measures 14 inches wide, 10 inches tall, and 18 inches long. In cubic inches, what is the volume of this box?

    A. 42
    B. 54
    C. 2520
    D. 2744

26. Which of the following is a solution to the equation $x^2 - 6x + 1 = 0$?

    A. -6
    B. $3 - 2\sqrt{2}$
    C. 3
    D. $6 + 2\sqrt{3}$

27. Four data entry specialists—Tom, Jason, Henrietta, and Alton—are observed for a two-hour testing period. During this period, Tom completed 28 forms, while Jason completed 31. Further, if h represents the number of hours, $f = 13.1h$ represents the number of forms Henrietta completed during the testing period and $f = 17h$ represents the number of forms Alton completed during the testing period.

    Which specialist completed the forms at the fastest average rate?

    A. Tom
    B. Jason
    C. Henrietta
    D. Alton

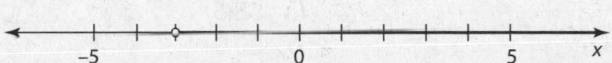

28. Which of the following inequalities is represented by the graph?

    A. $2x < -6$
    B. $2x \leq -6$
    C. $3x \geq -9$
    D. $3x > -9$

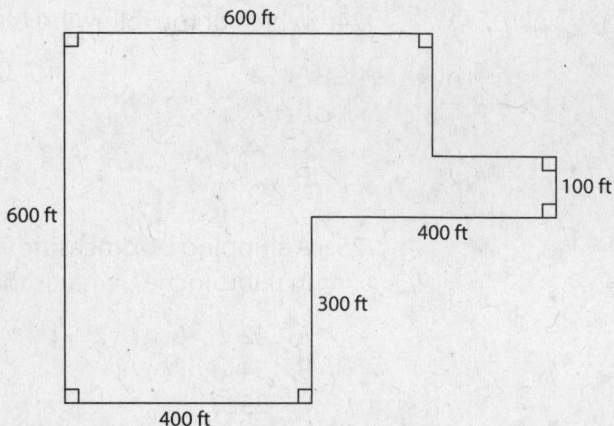

29. The figure represents the property line of a piece of land that is being prepared for sale. If the property is to be completely fenced in prior to the sale, how many feet of fencing will be required?

    A. 1600 feet
    B. 2400 feet
    C. 2800 feet
    D. 3200 feet

30. The mean of the data set 5, 10, 2, 1, and x is 5. What is the value of x?

    A. 5
    B. 7
    C. 13
    D. 18

31. In a group of 20 students, 40% scored 85 on a recent exam while the remaining students scored 90. To the nearest tenth, what was the average score for all 20 students?

    A. 87.5
    B. 88.0
    C. 88.5
    D. 89.0

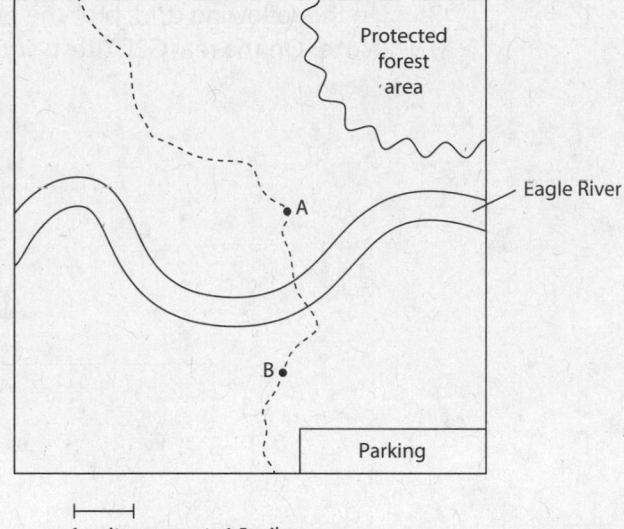

1 unit represents 1.5 miles

32. The map shows a hiking trail through a city park. On the map, the distance along the trail between points A and B is 2.5 units. To the nearest tenth of a mile, what is the true distance between the two points?

    A. 1.7
    B. 2.1
    C. 3.8
    D. 5.0

33. What is the value of $g(h) = -2h^2 - h + 5$ when $h = -3$?

    A. −7
    B. −10
    C. 38
    D. 44

34. A line has a slope of 2 and passes through the point (−8, 1). Which of the following represents the equation for this line?

    A. $y = 2x - 7$
    B. $y = 2x + 8$
    C. $y = 2x + 9$
    D. $y = 2x + 17$

35. On the following grid, plot the point indicated by the ordered pair (−5, 5).
    (**Note:** On the real GED® test, you will click on the grid to plot the point.)

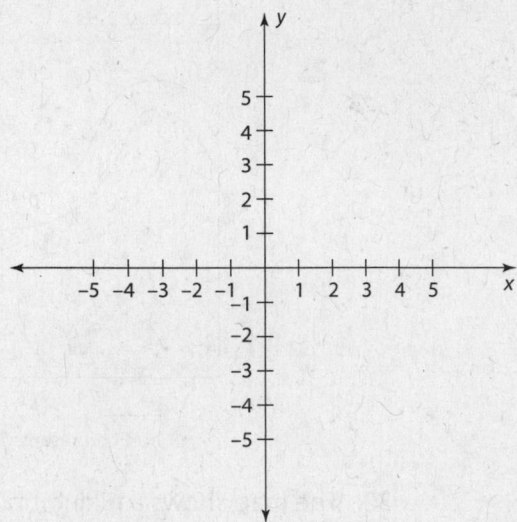

36. A line in the *x-y* coordinate plane is represented by the equation
    $3x - 8y = 2$. What is the slope of this line?

    A. $-\dfrac{1}{4}$

    B. $\dfrac{3}{8}$

    C. $-\dfrac{2}{3}$

    D. 4

37. What is the sum of $\dfrac{2}{3}$ and $\dfrac{1}{6}$?

    A. $\dfrac{1}{3}$

    B. $\dfrac{1}{6}$

    C. $\dfrac{2}{3}$

    D. $\dfrac{5}{6}$

38. Airfare for a plane ticket varies based on the time purchased, among other factors. On a particular flight from Chicago O'Hare Airport to Atlanta Hartsfield Airport, 65 passengers each paid $127.99, 24 passengers each paid $198.50, and 4 each paid $301.70.

    What was the total fare paid by all passengers on this flight?

    A. $14,290.15
    B. $17,224.75
    C. $18,129.85
    D. $58,421.67

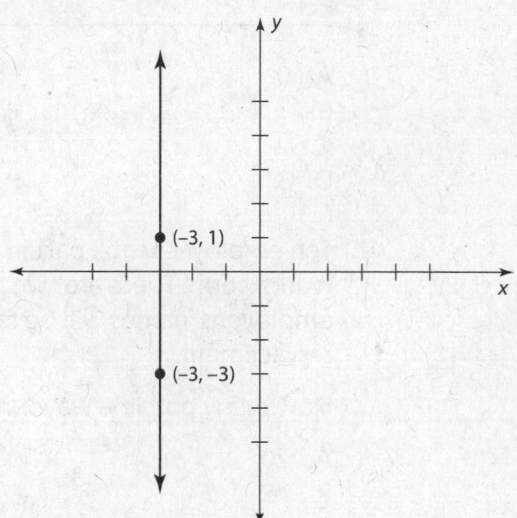

39. The figure shows a line graphed in the *x-y* coordinate plane and indicates two points through which it passes. What is the equation of this line?

    A. $y = -3$
    B. $x = -3$
    C. $y = -3x$
    D. $x = -3y$

40. In a survey, participants were asked how many televisions they currently own. The results of this survey are shown in the following table. What is the median of this data set?

Number of Televisions Owned	Number of Participants
0	5
1	8
2	6
3	1

A. 0
B. 1
C. 2
D. 3

41. Ten employees took part in a raffle to determine who gets a new workstation. There are two new workstations available, and two employees' names will be randomly chosen, one at a time, without replacement.

How many possible ways are there to choose the two employees?

A. 20
B. 45
C. 90
D. 100

42. The distance between Earth and the moon is 2.4×10^8 miles. A rocket has been sent to explore the moon. If the rocket has currently covered $\frac{1}{10}$ of this distance, how many miles has it traveled?

A. 2.4×10^{-2}
B. 2.4×10^{-1}
C. 2.4×10^6
D. 2.4×10^7

43. Assuming x is nonzero, which of the following is equivalent to $\left(x^2 - 5x\right) \div x$?

    A. $x - 5$

    B. $x - \dfrac{5}{x}$

    C. $-4x$

    D. $x^2 - 4x$

44. In a company with 26 offices, 10 of the offices are located in the Southeast, 8 in the Midwest, 6 in the West, and 2 in the Northeast. If an office is randomly selected, then to the nearest ten thousandth, what is the probability it is located in the Southeast or the West?

    A. 0.0769
    B. 0.0888
    C. 0.3846
    D. 0.6154

45. The volume of a perfectly spherical weather balloon is approximately 381.7 cubic feet. To the nearest tenth of a foot, what is the approximate radius of this weather balloon?

    A. 4.5
    B. 5.1
    C. 7.2
    D. 9.4

46. A placekicker kicks a football from the ground ($y = 0$). The vertical path of the football follows a parabolic path described by the equation: $y = 5t - 4.4t^2$ where t is the time in seconds. After how much time will the football hit the ground?

    A. 0 s
    B. 0.88 s
    C. 1.14 s
    D. 2.0 s

47. A linear function has the equation: $f(x) = -\dfrac{1}{3}x + 2$. If $g(x)$ is a linear function that is perpendicular to $f(x)$ and $g(x)$ passes through the point (3, 1), which statement is true?

    A. The slope and y-intercept of $f(x)$ are greater than those of $g(x)$.
    B. The slope of $f(x)$ is greater than that of $g(x)$, and its y-intercept is greater.
    C. The slope and y-intercept of $f(x)$ are smaller than those of $g(x)$.
    D. The slope of $f(x)$ is smaller than that of $g(x)$, but its y-intercept is greater.

48. A line has the equation $y = 5x + 4$. What is the slope of a line perpendicular to it?

    A. $-\dfrac{1}{5}$

    B. $-\dfrac{1}{4}$

    C. 4

    D. 5

49. Mrs. Barnes wants to wrap a cylindrical container with a radius of 4 inches and a height of 12 inches. To wrap the container, she has only whole sheets of 8.5 inch by 11 inch paper. How many whole sheets will she need?

    A. 2
    B. 3
    C. 4
    D. 5

50. A wind-up toy car can travel 5 yards in about 3 minutes. If the car travels at a constant speed, then how many minutes will it take to travel 40 meters? State your answer to the nearest minute. (1 yard = 0.92 meters)

    A. 20
    B. 22
    C. 24
    D. 26

THIS IS THE END OF THE MATHEMATICAL REASONING PRETEST.

Answers and Explanations

1. **Correct answer: A.** Letting *F* represent the number of fans and *L* the number of lamps, you are given that $F \leq 5L$. Substituting in 20 fans, $20 \leq 5L$ or $4 \leq L$. Thus, 4 or more lamps are produced.

2. **Correct answer: 4.** The absolute value of a number can be viewed as its distance from zero on the number line. If the absolute value of a number is 4, then the number is 4 units from zero.

3. **Correct answer: B.** The sample space for this experiment S = {HH, TT, HT, TH}. One of the four outcomes consists of two tails.

4. **Correct answer: A.** The line $y = 3x - 4$ is in $y = mx + b$ form where *b* is the *y*-intercept. If line *l* shares the same *y*-intercept, then it must pass through the point (0, −4) and have an equation of the form $y = mx - 4$ for some *m*. Given that *l* also passes through (−2, 5), $l = \dfrac{5 - (-4)}{-2 - 0} = -\dfrac{9}{2}$.

5. **Correct answer: C.** On the left side of the equation, the 2 must be distributed over $(x - 8)$. This yields the equation $2x - 16 = -4x + 2$. After adding 4*x* and 16 to both sides, $6x = 18$ and $x = 3$.

6. **Correct answer: C.** Both 5*x* and 20 contain a common factor of 5. After factoring out the 5, the remaining factor is $x - 4$.

7. **Correct answer: A.** The first term can be written as $x^4 = x^2(x^2)$ to show that both terms share a factor of x^2.

8. **Correct answer: A.** In the figure, line *m* passes through the points (0, 4) and (−4, 0) indicating it has a slope of 1. Any line perpendicular to *m* will therefore have a slope of −1 (the negative reciprocal of 1). If a line passes through point P(0, −2) with a slope of −1, it must pass through point A (−2, 0).

9. **Correct answer: for this function, the value of *y* is positive when *x* is less than 4.**

   When the graph of any function is above the *x*-axis, it indicates the values of *y* are positive. Similarly, when the graph is below the *x*-axis, the *y* values are negative. The graph of this function is above the *x*-axis at all *x*-values less than 4.

10. **Correct answer: 12.6.** The area of the circular region is $40^2 p \approx 5026.55$ square feet. This will require $\dfrac{5026.55}{400} \approx 12.6$ gallons of paint.

11. **Correct answer:**

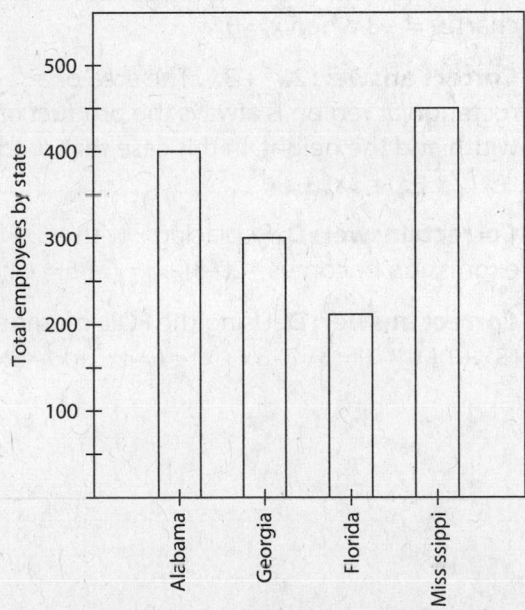

The total number of workers for each state can be found by adding the number of part-time and full-time workers in those states. For Alabama, Georgia, Florida, and Mississippi, those totals are 400, 300, 210, and 450, respectively. These totals are represented in the chart as the height of the bars.

12. **Correct answer: D.** $m = \dfrac{9 - 4}{3 - (-1)} = \dfrac{5}{4}$

13. **Correct answer: B.** If the diameter of machine part A must be 4 smaller, or 4 fewer than machine part B's diameter, then it must have a diameter of $x - 4$.

14. **Correct answer: D.** Subtracting x and adding 2 to both sides, $x < 10$.

15. **Correct answer: 139 pounds.** The total weight is $37 + 2(42) + 18 = 139$.

16. **Correct answer: 452.4.** Using the formula, the volume is pr^2h where r represents radius and h represents height. Using the given values, the volume is $\pi(6^2)(4) \approx 452.4$.

17. **Correct answer: A.**
    $2(1-3x)-(5x+1)=2-6x-5x-1=-11x+1$

18. **Correct answer: A.** The y-intercept is the y value when the value of x is zero. Based on this chart, $y = -8$ when $x = 0$.

19. **Correct answer:** $2x^2 + 3x$. The area of a rectangular region is always the product of the width and the height. In this case that product is $x(2x+3) = 2x^2 + 3x$.

20. **Correct answer: D.** Replacing x with -3, the expression becomes $-2(-3)+5=6+5=11$.

21. **Correct answer: D.** Using the FOIL method, $(3x+1)(x^2-1)=3x^3-3x+x^2-1=3x^3+x^2-3x-1$.

22. **Correct answer:**

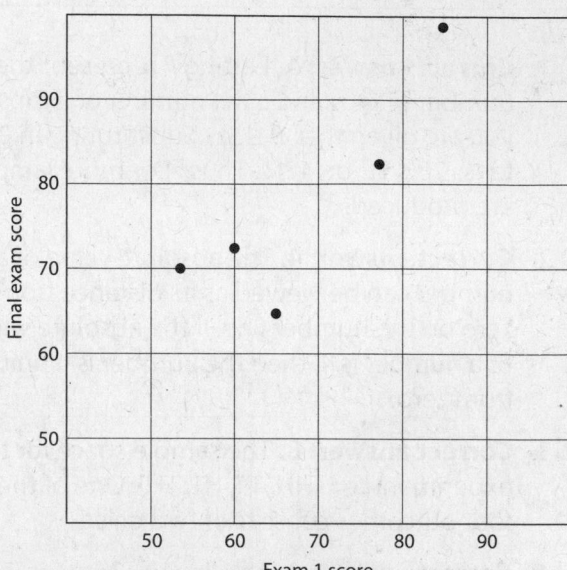

Each point represents the two scores for a single student where the exam 1 score acts as the x-coordinate and the final exam score acts as the y-coordinate.

23. **Correct answer: B.** In the figures, B shows a graph that represents y as a function of x. When y is shown as a function of x, there is only one possible y value for each possible x value. In figures A and C, one x value had many possible y values (plot A) or two possible y values (plot C).

24. **Correct answer: B.** Using the rules of exponents, $2 \times \dfrac{2^5}{2^2} = 2 \times 2^{5-2} = 2 \times 2^3 = 2^{3+1} = 2^4$.

25. **Correct answer: C.** The volume is found using the formula $l \times w \times h$ where l is the length, w is the width, and h is the height. In this case the volume is $14 \times 10 \times 18 = 2520$ cubic inches.

26. **Correct answer: B.** Using the quadratic formula, the solutions are:
$$\frac{-(-6)\pm\sqrt{36-4(1)(1)}}{2(1)} = \frac{6\pm\sqrt{32}}{2} = \frac{6\pm4\sqrt{2}}{2} = 3\pm2\sqrt{2}$$

27. **Correct answer: D.** Finding the average rate for each person, Tom completed $\frac{28}{2} = 14$ forms per hour, Jason completed $\frac{31}{2} = 15.5$ forms per hour, Henrietta completed 13.1 forms per hour, and Alton completed 17 forms per hour.

28. **Correct answer: D.** The open circle indicates the point is not included in the solution, so the graph shows the solution set $x > -3$ which is equivalent to $3x > -9$ if both sides are multiplied by 3.

29. **Correct answer: C.** Starting from the bottom, moving counterclockwise, and including the missing side lengths, the individual side lengths are 400, 300, 400, 100, 200, 200, 600, and then finally on the left 600. The total amount of fencing needed would therefore be $400 + 300 + 400 + 100 + 200 + 200 + 600 + 600 = 2800$ feet.

30. **Correct answer: B.** Using the general formula for the mean, it must be that $\frac{5+10+2+1+x}{5} = 5$. Cross multiplying and adding terms results in the equation $25 = 18 + x$ which has a solution of $x = 7$.

31. **Correct answer: B.** Forty percent of 20 is 8 students. Therefore, 8 students scored an 85 while 12 scored a 90. The mean score is then $\frac{8(85) + 12(90)}{20} = 88$.

32. **Correct answer: C.** According to the map, 1 unit of the given length represents 1.5 miles. For each of the 2.5 units, there are 1.5 miles for a total of $2.5 \times 1.5 = 3.75$ miles between the two points.

33. **Correct answer: B.**
$g(-3) = -2(-3)^2 - (-3) + 5 = -2(9) + 3 + 5 = -18 + 8 = -10$

34. **Correct answer: D.** Using the point-slope formula and simplifying, the equation of the line is:
$y - 1 = 2(x - (-8))$
$y - 1 = 2(x + 8)$
$y - 1 = 2x + 16$
$y = 2x + 17$

35. **Correct answer:**

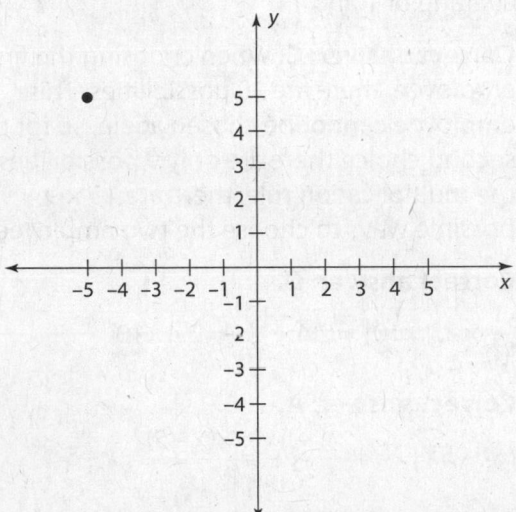

The ordered pair is of the form (x, y). Since the x value is -5 and the y value is 5, the point will be located 5 units to the left of 0 on the x-axis and 5 units above 0 on the y-axis.

36. **Correct answer: B.** Solving for y will put the equation in the form $y = mx + b$ where m is the slope:
$-8y = 2 - 3x \Rightarrow y = -\frac{1}{4} + \frac{3}{8}x$, so $m = \frac{3}{8}$

37. **Correct answer: D.** A common denominator must be found before adding:
$\frac{2}{3} + \frac{1}{6} = \frac{4}{6} + \frac{1}{6} = \frac{5}{6}$

38. **Correct answer: A.** The total fare paid by passengers on this flight is $(65 \times 127.99) + (24 \times 198.5) + (4 \times 301.7) = 14{,}290.15$.

39. **Correct answer: B.** Any vertical line will have an equation of the form $x = c$ for some constant c. In this case, the x value is always -3, so the equation is $x = -3$.

40. **Correct answer: B.** There are 20 total data values, so the median will be the average of the 10th and 11th data values on the list if they are placed in order. The first 5 data values are 0 while the next 8 are 1. The 10th and 11th data values therefore must be 1, and the average of 1 and 1 is 1.

41. **Correct answer: C.** When choosing the first employee, there are 10 possibilities. This employee cannot be chosen again, so for the second choice there are only 9 possibilities. By the multiplication rule, there are $10 \times 9 = 90$ possible ways to choose the two employees.

42. **Correct answer: D.**
$$\frac{1}{10} \times 2.4 \times 10^8 = 2.4 \times \frac{10^8}{10} = 2.4 \times 10^7$$

43. **Correct answer: A.**
$$\left(x^2 - 5x\right) \div x = \frac{x^2 - 5x}{x} = \frac{x(x-5)}{x} = x - 5$$

44. **Correct answer: D.**
$$P\left(SE \text{ or } W\right) = P(SE) + P(W) = \frac{10}{26} + \frac{6}{26} \approx 0.6154$$

45. **Correct answer: A.** Using the formula for the volume of a sphere, $381.7 = \frac{4}{3}\pi r^3$ where r is the radius. Solving this equation for r:

$$\frac{3}{4}(381.7) = 286.275 = \pi r^3$$

$$\frac{286.275}{\pi} = 91.124 = r^3$$

$$r = \sqrt[3]{91.124} = 4.5$$

46. **Correct answer: C.** The left side of the equation should be set to zero (the height of the ground). The right side can be factored into the terms $t(5 - 4.4t)$. By the zero product rule, the solutions are then $t = 0$ and $t = 1.14$ s. The solution $t = 0$ represents when the ball was kicked, so $t = 1.14$ s is when the ball hits the ground.

47. **Correct answer: D.** The function $f(x)$ is written in slope intercept form, so its slope is the coefficient of the x term or $-\frac{1}{3}$. The function $g(x)$ is said to be perpendicular to $f(x)$, so its slope is the negative reciprocal of $f(x)$, which is 3. $g(x)$ passes through the point $(3, 1)$. Therefore, by the point-slope formula, the equation of $g(x)$ is:

$$(y - 1) = 3(x - 3)$$
$$y - 1 = 3x - 9$$
$$y = 3x - 8$$
$$\therefore g(x) = 3x - 8$$

So the slope of $g(x)$ is 3 and the y-intercept is -8. Compared to $g(x)$, the slope of $f(x)$ is smaller ($-\frac{1}{3}$ vs. 3) and its y-intercept is greater (2 vs. -8).

48. **Correct answer: A.** The line $y = 5x + 4$ has a slope of 5. A line perpendicular to it will have a slope that is the negative reciprocal of –5, which is $-\dfrac{1}{5}$.

49. **Correct answer: D.** The surface area of the cylindrical container can be calculated as:

$A = 2pr^2 + 2prh$

$A = 2p(4)^2 + 2p(4)(12)$

$A = 2p(16) + 2p(48)$

$A = 2p(64)$

$A = 128p = (128)(3.14)$

$A = 401.92$

The area of a sheet of 8.5 inch by 11 inch paper is: $A = (8.5)(11) = 93.5$. So the number of whole sheets required is:

$n_{sheets} = \dfrac{A_{cylinder}}{A_{sheet}} = \dfrac{401.92}{93.5} = 4.30$. Therefore,

5 whole sheets will be necessary to wrap the container.

50. **Correct answer: D.** At the given speed, the car can travel 1 yard (or 0.92 meter) in $\dfrac{3}{5} = 0.6$ minutes. Therefore, the car can travel 40 meters in $\dfrac{0.6 \text{ min}}{0.92 \text{ m}}(40\text{m}) = 26$ min.

Evaluation Chart

Check the Answers and Explanations section of the Mathematical Reasoning Pretest to see which answers you got correct and which ones you missed. For each question that you missed, find the item number in the chart below. Check the column on the left to see the test content area for that item. If you missed questions in a particular content area, you need to pay particular attention to that area as you study for the GED® test. The pages of this book that cover that content area are listed in the column on the right.

Content Area	Item Number	Pages to Review
1. Whole Numbers and Operations	15, 38	307–315
2. Exponents, Roots, and Number Properties	24	317–328
3. Decimal Numbers and Operations	42	329–339
4. Fractions and Operations	37	341–358
5. Ratios, Rates, and Proportions	27, 50	359–364
6. Percents and Applications	31	365–372
7. The Number Line and Negative Numbers	2	373–377
8. Probabililty and Counting	3, 41, 44	379–385
9. Statistics and Data Analysis	11, 30, 31, 40	387–404
10. Algebraic Expressions	6, 7, 17, 21, 43	405–428
11. Solving Equations and Inequalities	1, 5, 13, 14, 20, 26, 46	429–451
12. Graphing Equations	4, 8, 12, 22, 23, 28, 34, 35, 36, 39, 47, 48	453–470
13. Functions	9, 18, 33	471–485
14. Geometry	10, 16, 19, 25, 29, 32, 45, 49	487–500

Science

This Science Pretest is designed to introduce you to this section of the GED® test and to give you a good idea of your current skill level in this subject area.

This test has the same number of questions as the real GED Science test: 40 items. The questions are in the same formats as the ones on the real exam and are designed to measure the same skills. Many of the questions are based on short reading passages on science topics. Some are based on scientific illustrations, diagrams, or other graphics. Most of the questions are in multiple-choice format, but you will also see questions that ask you to draw a line or indicate a point on a diagram, fill in a blank, or write a short answer. On the real GED® test, you will indicate your answers by clicking on the computer screen. For this paper-and-pencil practice test, mark your answers directly on the page. Write your short-answer responses on a separate sheet of paper.

To get a good idea of how you will do on the real exam, take this test under actual exam conditions. Complete the test in one session and follow the given time limit. If you do not complete the test in the time allowed, you will know that you need to work on improving your pacing.

Try to answer as many questions as you can. There is no penalty for wrong answers, so guess if you have to. In multiple-choice questions, if you can eliminate one or more answer choices, you can increase your chances of guessing correctly.

After you have finished the test, check your answers in the Answers and Explanations section that follows the pretest. Then use the Evaluation Chart at the end of the Answers and Explanations section to determine the skills and content areas in which you need more practice.

Now turn the page and begin the Science Pretest.

Science

40 questions | **90 minutes**

Use the table for Items 1 and 2:

Surface Temperature Ranges per Star Class

Class	Color	Temperature (K)
O	Blue	> 25,000 K
B	Blue-white	11,000–25,000 K
A	White	7500–11,000 K
F	White	6000 7500 K
G	Yellow	5000–6000 K
K	Orange	3500–5000 K
M	Red	< 3500 K

1. Using the information in the table, which color star is produced by the widest range of surface temperatures?

   A. white
   B. yellow
   C. orange
   D. blue-white

2. Write the appropriate class from the table in the blank.

   The Sun is classified as a Class _____ star because it has a surface temperature of approximately 5778 K.

Use the following passage for Items 3 through 5:

Blood calcium levels are tightly regulated in the human body by the hormones calcitonin and parathyroid hormone (PTH). When calcium levels become too high or low, the thyroid or parathyroid gland produces the appropriate hormone to return the body to homeostasis. The diagram shows the feedback mechanism for regulating blood calcium levels.

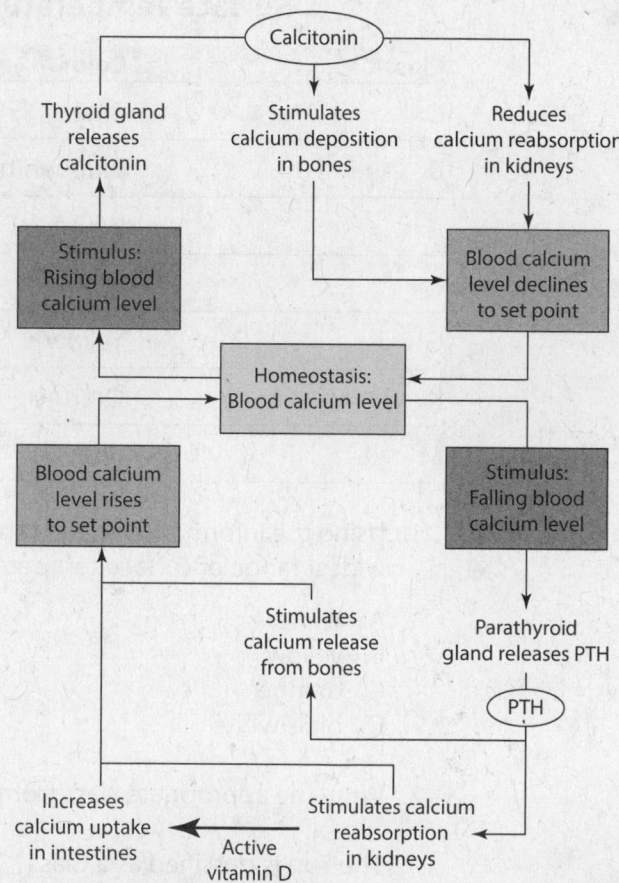

3. Which food is most likely to cause the greatest increase in calcitonin production when eaten?

  A. rice, because it is an easily digested carbohydrate
  B. orange, because it is a good source of vitamin C
  C. yogurt, because it is high in bone-strengthening minerals
  D. squash, because it is a rich source of vitamins and fiber

4. The ability to maintain blood calcium homeostasis depends on the interactions of several different body systems. Draw a line to connect each body system to the role it plays in maintaining calcium homeostasis.

Role in Regulating Blood Calcium Levels	Body System
Bones store calcium to be released when needed	Digestive
Intestines absorb calcium from digested foods	Endocrine
Kidneys remove excess calcium from the blood	Excretory
Thyroid and parathyroid glands produce regulatory hormones calcitonin and PTH	Skeletal

PRETEST

5. **Short answer**

Osteoporosis is a disease in which decreased bone mineral density leads to an increased risk of bone fractures. One risk factor for developing osteoporosis is a diet low in calcium.

Explain how a diet low in calcium can affect the body's ability to regulate blood calcium levels and ultimately contribute to the development of osteoporosis.

Include multiple pieces of evidence from the passage and diagram to support your answer.

Write your response in the space provided. This task may take approximately 10 minutes to complete.

Use the passage and diagram for Items 6 through 8:

The following diagram identifies homologous structures in the forelimbs of seven different species.

The term *homologous* means similar. Scientists use homologous structures as evidence of common ancestry. Through the process of natural selection, structures inherited from a common ancestor become modified to allow each descendant species to best adapt to its unique environment.

Homologous Structures

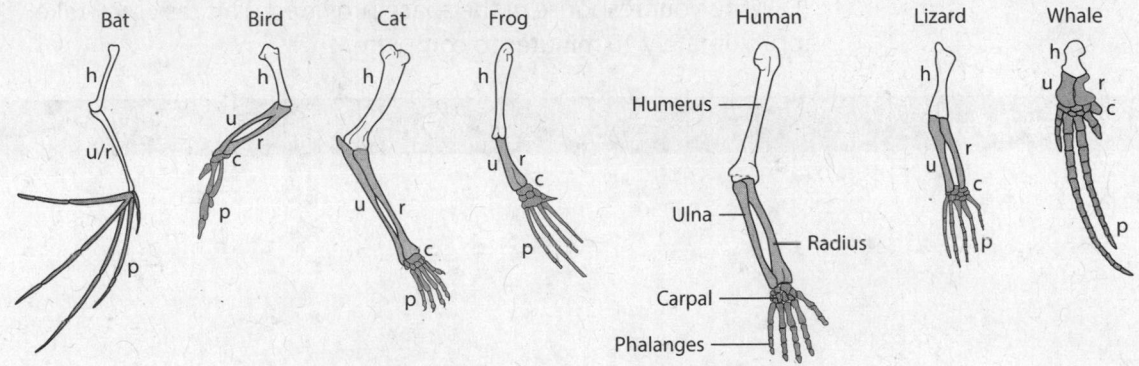

6. The homologies in the seven species' forelimbs result from similarities in

    A. metabolism.
    B. genetic code.
    C. environments.
    D. reproductive strategies.

7. Considering the homologies shown in the diagram, humans likely share the most recent ancestor with which species?

    A. cat
    B. bat
    C. bird
    D. whale

PRETEST

8. **Short answer**

Consider the different functions of the forelimbs shown in the diagram. Each forelimb is adapted to best support one of four functions: flying, grasping, swimming, or walking.

Explain how natural selection can lead to adaptation in forelimbs. Give specific examples of structural adaptations and the functions they support.

Include multiple pieces of evidence from the text and diagram. Discuss specific species as examples to support your answer.

Write your response in the space provided. This task may take approximately 10 minutes to complete.

Cut Copy Paste Undo Redo

Use the passage for Items 9 and 10:

Photosynthesis is the chemical process of using the energy in sunlight to produce glucose. Respiration is the chemical process of converting glucose to energy that can be used by the cell. The chemical equations for both processes are shown below.

Photosynthesis

light energy

$$6CO_2 + 6H_2O \rightarrow C_6H_{12}O_6 + 6O_2$$

Respiration

$$C_6H_{12}O_6 + 6O_2 \rightarrow energy + 6CO_2 + 6H_2O$$

9. Write the appropriate number from the photosynthesis equation in each of the blanks.

   Photosynthesis requires _____ molecules of carbon

   dioxide and _____ molecules of water to produce

   1 molecule of glucose.

10. Which statement correctly describes the relationship between the processes of photosynthesis and respiration?

    A. The reactants of photosynthesis are also used as the reactants for respiration.
    B. The energy produced by respiration is used to fuel the photosynthesis reaction.
    C. Photosynthesis and respiration are two different processes for producing glucose.
    D. The chemical products of photosynthesis are used as the reactants for respiration.

PRETEST

Use the maps for Items 11 and 12:

Heat Maps of U.S. Hazard Areas

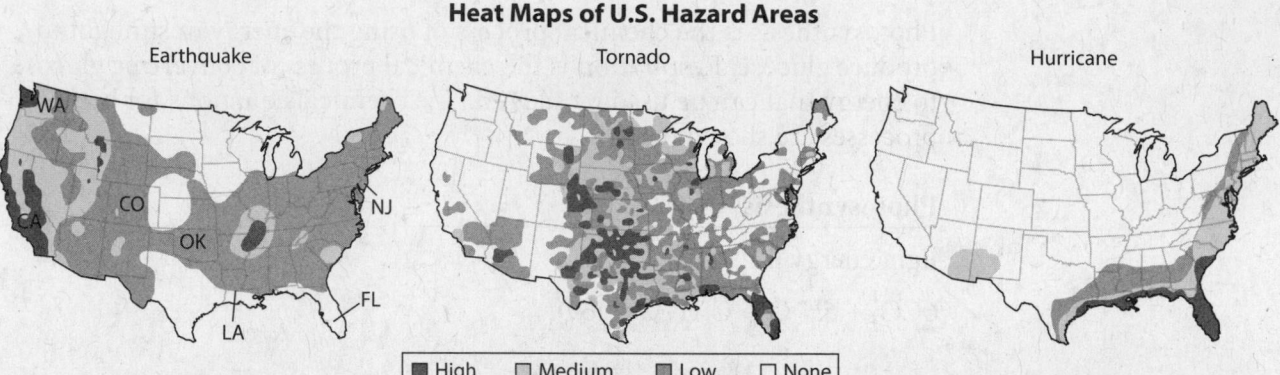

In areas where natural hazards occur frequently, specific precautions are often taken to reduce the impact when natural hazards do occur. Examine the areas in the maps with the highest incidence of each type of natural hazard.

11. Draw a line to connect each state to the precaution that would be most useful.

Precautions Against Natural Hazards	State
Dikes/levees	California
Underground storm shelters	Florida
Steel-plate walls	Oklahoma

12. Using the information in the maps, which state most likely lies closest to a tectonic plate boundary?

A. Colorado
B. Louisiana
C. New Jersey
D. Washington

Use the passage for Items 13 and 14:

The carbon cycle describes the constant exchange of carbon among the atmosphere, land, and ocean. The following diagram depicts carbon cycle processes. The numbers on the diagram represent the approximate number of gigatons of carbon located in different portions of the cycle.

The Carbon Cycle

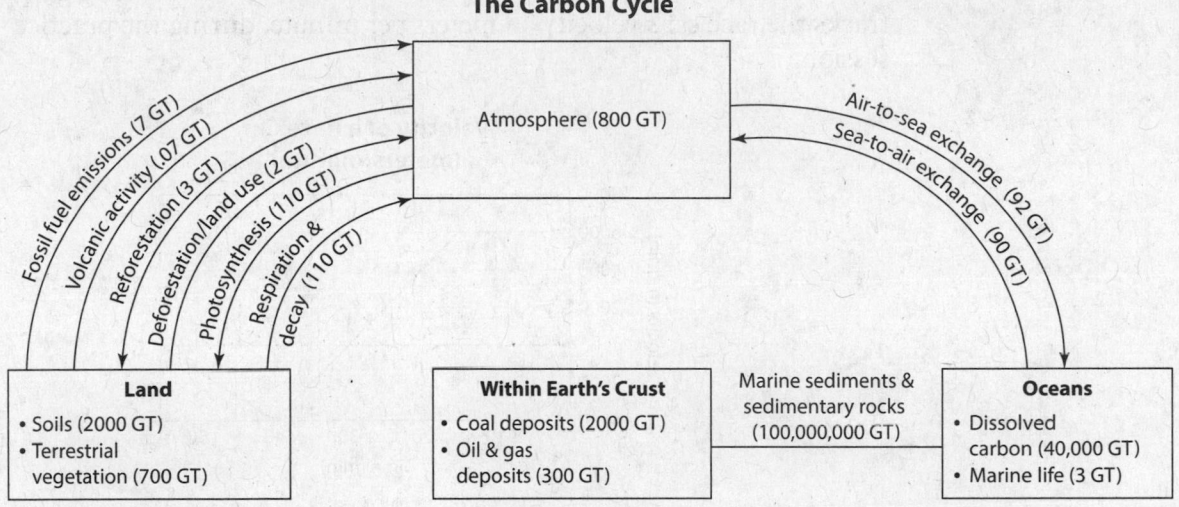

13. On the diagram, indicate the process that removes the greatest proportion of carbon from the atmosphere.

14. Using the information in the diagram, how many gigatons (GT) of carbon are estimated to be stored in fossil fuel deposits?

    A. 7 GT
    B. 300 GT
    C. 2000 GT
    D. 2300 GT

Use the passage for Items 15 through 17:

Velocity is defined as an object's speed in a given direction. Velocity is positive when an object is moving forward, and negative when the object is moving in reverse. Acceleration is the change in an object's velocity over time.

A race car driver is practicing on a linear track. The following graph tracks the race car's velocity, in meters per minute, during the practice session.

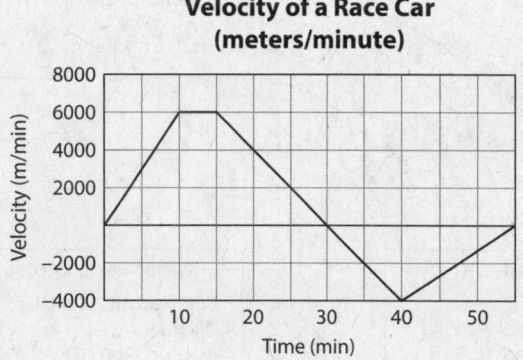

Velocity of a Race Car (meters/minute)

15. Using the information in the passage, mark an **X** on the graph at the point where the race car changes direction from forward to reverse. (**Note:** On the real GED® test, you will click on the graph to mark the point.)

Use the prompt for Item 16:

Acceleration can be calculated using the following formula:

$$\text{acceleration} = \frac{\text{final velocity} - \text{initial velocity}}{\text{time}}$$

16. According to the graph, what is the race car's acceleration between 0 and 10 minutes?

A. 600 m/min
B. 600 m/min^2
C. 600 m^2/min^2
D. 600 (m/min)^2

Use the passage for Item 17:

Newton's Second Law of Motion states that an object's acceleration is proportional to the total net force acting to the object, or force = mass × acceleration.

17. An object traveling at a constant velocity has no acceleration. According to the graph, the race car's velocity was constant between 10 and 15 minutes. Which statement best describes the forces acting on the race car during this period?

A. The forces acting on the race car were balanced.
B. Gravity was the only force acting on the race car.
C. No forces were acting on the race car during this period.
D. The race car's force was greater than the force of friction.

Use the chart and picture for Item 18:

Relationships Within an Ecosystem

Commensalism	Relationship in which one species benefits and the other is not helped or harmed
Mutualism	Relationship in which both species receive a benefit
Parasitism	Relationship in which one species benefits and the other is harmed
Predation	Relationship in which one species serves as food for another species

18. The bee and flower shown in the picture are an example of which type of relationship?

   A. commensalism
   B. mutualism
   C. parasitism
   D. predation

Use the following passage and diagram for Item 19:

Centrifugation is the process of spinning a solution at high speed to separate the solution's components by density. Centrifugation is often used to isolate the specific components of a blood sample for further analysis.

Centrifugation of a Blood Sample

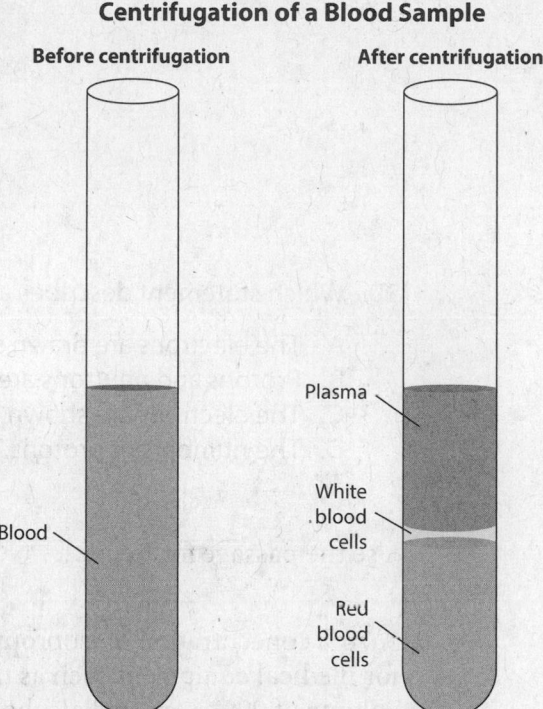

19. According to the diagram, which component has the highest density?

A. plasma
B. whole blood
C. red blood cells
D. white blood cells

Use the diagram for Item 20:

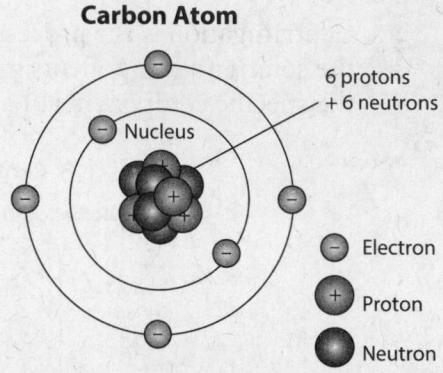

Carbon Atom

20. Which statement describes a weakness in the model of a carbon atom?

    A. The electrons are drawn smaller than the protons.
    B. Protons and neutrons are shown in the atom's nucleus.
    C. The electrons are shown on fixed paths around the nucleus.
    D. The numbers of protons, neutrons, and electrons are the same.

Use the passage for Item 21:

A 70% concentration of isopropyl alcohol is often used as a disinfectant for medical equipment such as thermometers and stethoscopes. The initial volume of 90% isopropyl alcohol needed to produce a batch of 70% isopropyl alcohol can be calculated using the following formula:

(90%)(initial volume) = (70%)(final volume)

21. How many milliliters of 90% isopropyl alcohol are needed to create 1 liter of 70% isopropyl alcohol?

    A. 0.00129 mL
    B. 0.78 mL
    C. 1.29 mL
    D. 780 mL

Use the chart and graph for Item 22:

Earth's Atmosphere

Composition of Earth's Atmosphere

Substance	Concentration in Parts per Million (PPM)
Nitrogen (N_2)	780,840.0
Oxygen (O_2)	209,460.0
Argon (Ar)	9,340.0
Carbon dioxide (CO_2)	360.0
Neon (Ne)	18.2
Helium (He)	5.24
Methane (CH_4)	1.5
Krypton (Kr)	1.14
Hydrogen (H_2)	0.5

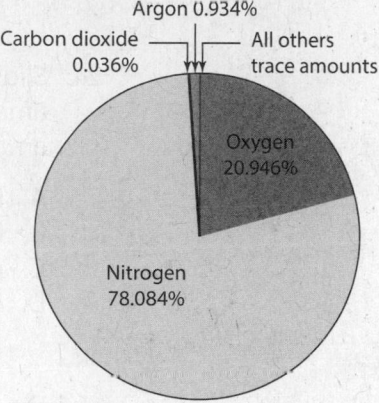

Composition of Earth's Atmosphere by Percent Volume

Argon 0.934%
Carbon dioxide 0.036%
All others trace amounts
Oxygen 20.946%
Nitrogen 78.084%

22. The concentration of substances in a mixture can be expressed in multiple formats. Using the information in the table and graph, what percent of the atmosphere's total volume is made up of hydrogen?

   A. 0.00005%
   B. 0.5%
   C. 5.0%
   D. 50.0%

Use the passage for Item 23:

Ocean currents are streams of water that flow in continuous, directed paths within the ocean. Currents moving through the upper 400 meters of the ocean are classified as surface currents. Currents that flow at greater depths are classified as deep water currents.

23. Which type(s) of currents can be better understood by studying the paths of global wind patterns?

   A. surface currents
   B. deep water currents
   C. both surface and deep water currents
   D. neither surface nor deep water currents

Use the passage for Item 24:

Work is done when a force applied to an object causes the object to move a distance. The amount of work done can be determined by multiplying the force applied by the distance moved ($W = f \times d$).

24. Sliding a box up a ramp into the back of a moving van requires the same amount of work as lifting the box from the ground into the van. If the amount of work is the same, what benefit does using a ramp provide?

   A. increasing the force required to move the box
   B. decreasing the force required to move the box
   C. decreasing the total distance moved by the box
   D. increasing the total distance moved by the box

Use the diagram for Item 25:

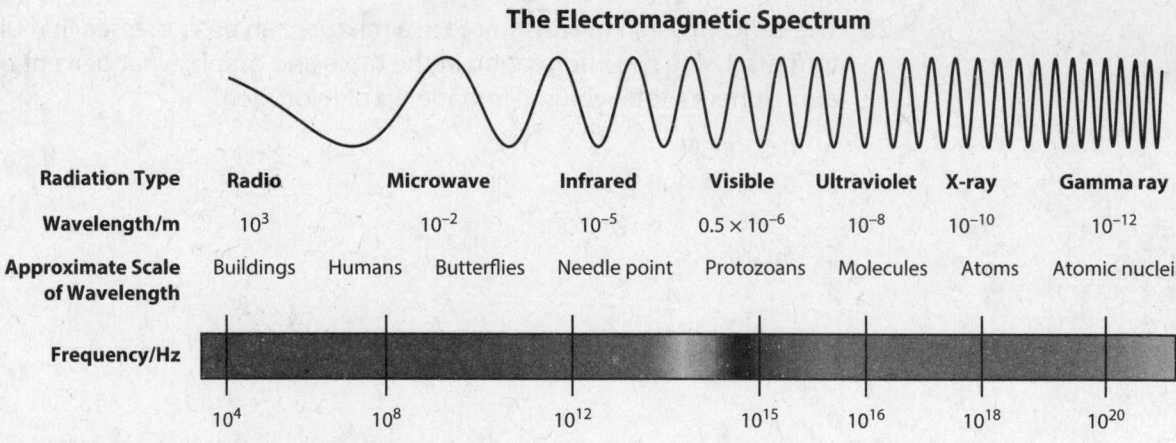

The Electromagnetic Spectrum

Radiation Type	Radio	Microwave	Infrared	Visible	Ultraviolet	X-ray	Gamma ray
Wavelength/m	10^3	10^{-2}	10^{-5}	0.5×10^{-6}	10^{-8}	10^{-10}	10^{-12}
Approximate Scale of Wavelength	Buildings Humans	Butterflies	Needle point	Protozoans	Molecules	Atoms	Atomic nuclei
Frequency/Hz	10^4	10^8	10^{12}	10^{15}	10^{16}	10^{18}	10^{20}

25. Which type of radiation can have a wavelength larger than a human?

   A. radio
   B. microwave
   C. visible light
   D. gamma ray

Use the diagram for Item 26:

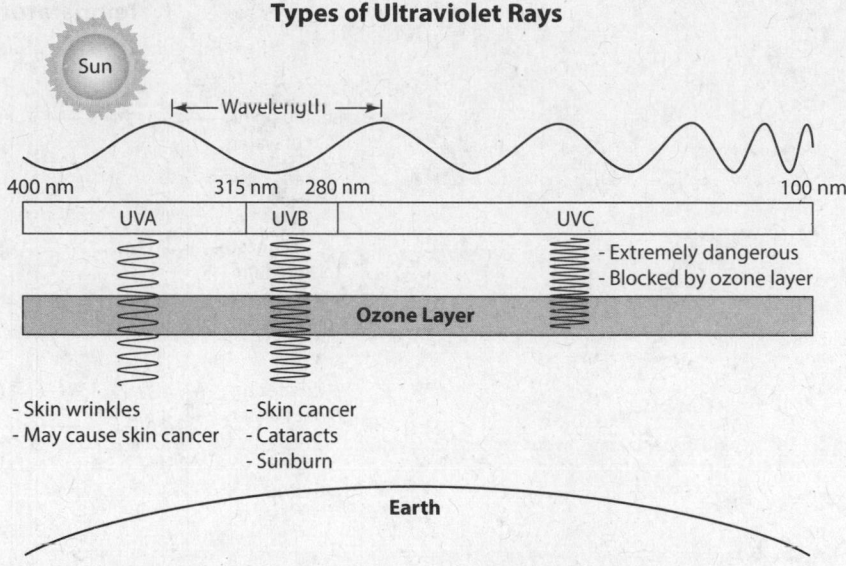

26. Sunscreen lotions and sprays are designed to provide a barrier against UVA and UVB rays only. What information in the diagram explains why sunscreens are not designed to protect against UVC rays?

    A. UVC is extremely dangerous.
    B. UVA and UVB cause skin cancer.
    C. UVC is blocked by the ozone layer.
    D. UVA and UVB have higher wavelengths.

27. Energy stored in chemical bonds is called chemical energy. Which of the following objects stores chemical energy?

    A. lightbulb
    B. solar panel
    C. alkaline battery
    D. electrical outlet

Use the diagram for Item 28:

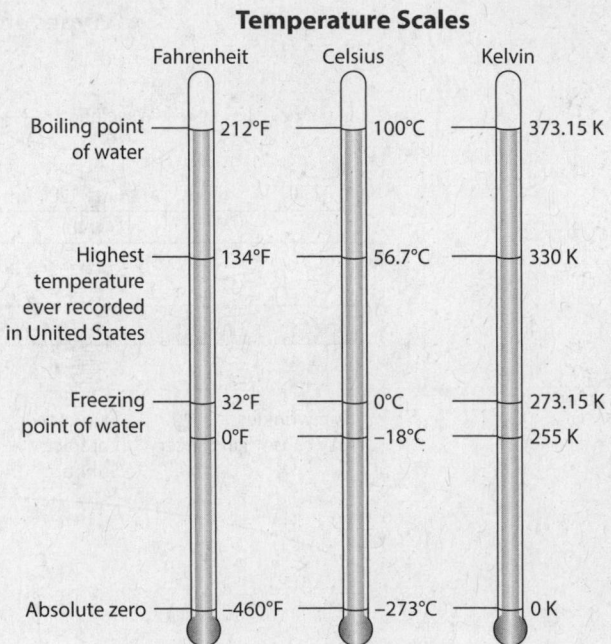

Temperature Scales

28. Restaurant health and safety guidelines require poultry to be cooked to a minimum internal temperature of 165 degrees. On which temperature scale is this guideline based?

A. Kelvin
B. Celsius
C. Fahrenheit
D. none of these

Use the table for Item 29:

Chemical processes can be categorized as endothermic or exothermic. Examples of each type of process are listed in the following table.

Endothermic Processes	Exothermic Processes
Melting ice cubes	Making ice cubes
Cooking an egg	A candle flame
Producing sugar by photosynthesis	Burning sugar
Evaporation of water	Condensation of rain from water vapor

29. Which generalization can be made based on the examples in the table?

   A. A reaction that releases heat is endothermic.
   B. A reaction that releases energy is exothermic.
   C. Exothermic reactions have a net increase in energy.
   D. Endothermic reactions neither absorb nor release heat.

Use the passage for Item 30:

The European woodwasp is an invasive species that is thought to have been accidentally introduced into the United States in a wood shipment in 2004. The European woodwasp feeds on pine trees. It can also carry a fungus that kills pine trees.

30. The introduction of the European woodwasp is most likely to disrupt pine forest ecosystems in which way?

   A. increased competition among consumers
   B. loss of habitat for tree-dwelling organisms
   C. water contamination by decaying pine trees
   D. disease transmission to other insect species

Use the diagram for Item 31:

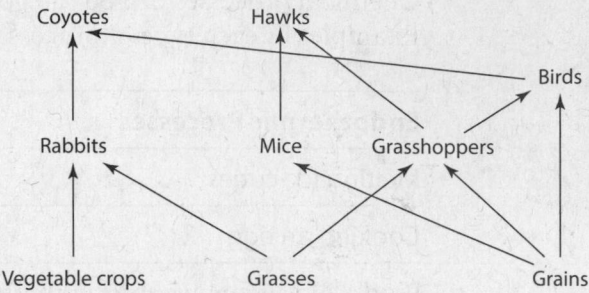

Food Web in a Grassland Ecosystem

31. Which of the following members of the ecosystem would be considered a secondary consumer?

   A. mice because they feed on a producer
   B. rabbits because they have two food sources
   C. grasshoppers because they have two predators
   D. birds because they feed on a primary consumer

Use the diagram for Item 32:

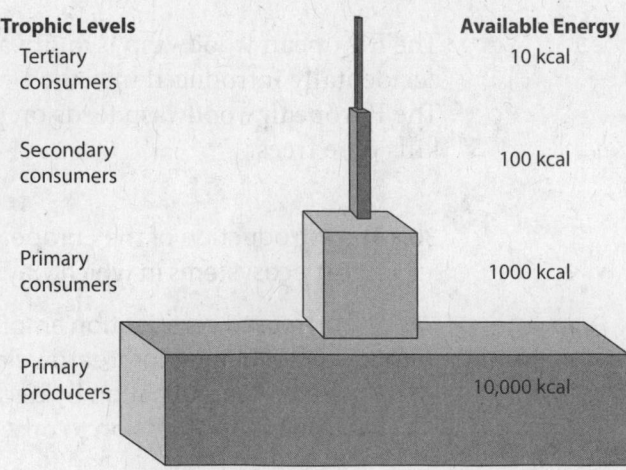

Energy Transfer in a Food Chain

32. What percentage of the energy available at the producer level is transferred all the way to the tertiary consumer level?

   A. 0%
   B. 0.1%
   C. 10%
   D. 25%

Use the passage for Item 33:

A genetic carrier is an individual who has one copy of the gene for a recessive genetic disease and one healthy gene. Since two copies of the disease gene are required to produce the disease, a carrier does not have the disease but can pass on the gene to children.

33. After undergoing genetic screening, a pregnant woman learns that she is a carrier for two genetic diseases: cystic fibrosis and spinal muscular atrophy. Her husband is not a carrier for either disease. What is the probability that the couple's child will be a carrier for at least one of the two diseases?

   A. 0%
   B. 50%
   C. 75%
   D. 100%

Use the passage and the diagram for Item 34:

Mitosis is the process of dividing a cell's nuclear material to produce two identical daughter cells. During mitosis, the cell contains two copies, or pairs, of each chromosome. These chromosome pairs line up and then separate, so that each new daughter cell will receive one complete set of chromosomes. The diagram shows the major stages of mitosis.

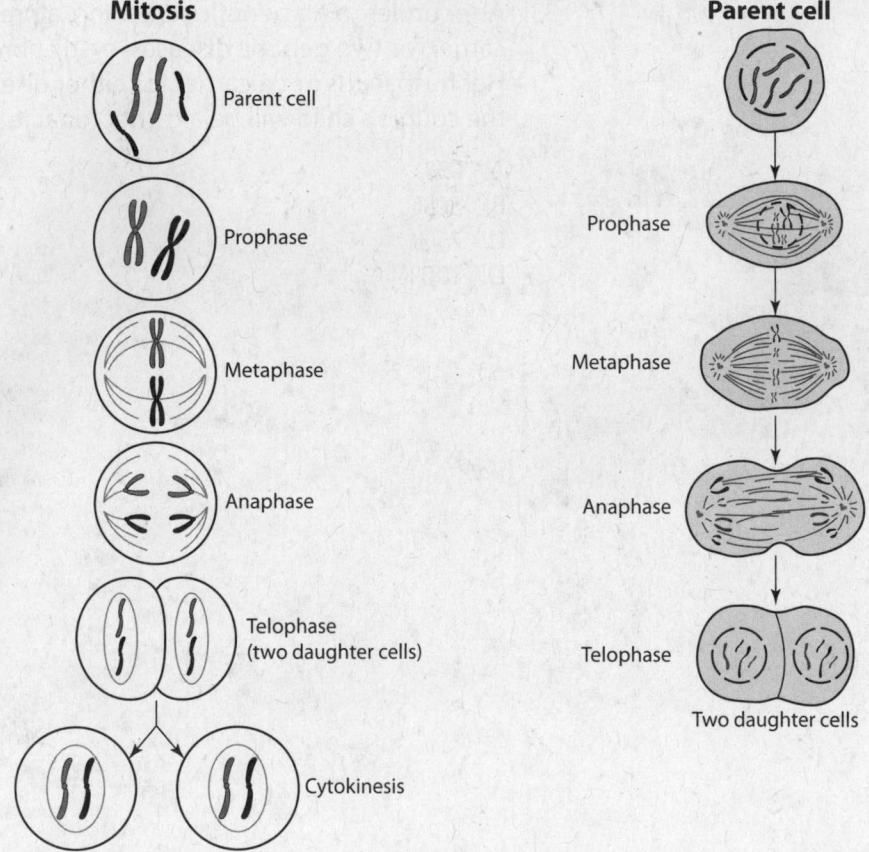

34. According to the diagram, chromosome pairs separate during which stage of mitosis?

   A. prophase
   B. anaphase
   C. telophase
   D. metaphase

35. Essential functions of life are those functions that must be carried out by all living things. Which function is not essential to all life?

   A. growth
   B. metabolism
   C. reproduction
   D. thermoregulation

36. If the longest day of the year in New York, USA, occurs on June 21, when does the shortest day of the year occur in Perth, Australia?

   A. March 21
   B. June 21
   C. September 21
   D. December 21

37. The equation for photosynthesis is shown below.

   $$6CO_2 + 6H_2O + Energy \rightarrow C_6H_{12}O_6 + 6O_2$$

   Which of these correctly identifies the products in the equation?

   A. glucose, oxygen
   B. carbon dioxide, water
   C. oxygen, carbon dioxide
   D. oxygen, water, glucose

38. A driver applies the brakes of a car to exert a constant force. Which type of velocity-time graph would describe the car's acceleration?

   A. Straight line graph with a slope of zero.
   B. Exponential line that curves downward with a generally negative slope.
   C. Straight line graph with a negative slope.
   D. Exponential line that curves upward with a generally positive slope.

39. While conducting an examination of a patient, an optometrist applies drops to the patient's eyes. The drops cause the pupils to enlarge. Which part of the eye is affected by the drops?

   A. lens
   B. iris
   C. retina
   D. cornea

40. During labor, a baby's head puts pressure on the opening of the uterus. Pressure receptors in the uterus send signals to the brain, which releases the hormone oxytocin. Oxytocin stimulates uterine smooth muscle contractions, which cause the baby to exert more pressure on the uterine opening. Which BEST describes this physiological situation?

   A. This is a negative feedback mechanism leading to homeostasis.
   B. This is a negative feedback mechanism leading to extremes.
   C. This is a positive feedback mechanism leading to homeostasis.
   D. This is a positive feedback mechanism leading to extremes.

THIS IS THE END OF THE SCIENCE PRETEST.

Answers and Explanations

1. **Correct answer: D.** According to the table, stars with surface temperatures between 11,000 and 25,000 K appear blue-white. Range is calculated as the difference between the highest and lowest temperature. For blue-white stars, this would be 25,000 K to 11,000 K, for a range of 14,000 K.

2. **Correct answer: G.** The temperature range for a Class G star is 5000 K to 6000 K. The surface temperature of the sun is within this range.

3. **Correct answer: C.** Dairy products like yogurt are rich in calcium. Blood calcium levels are more likely to rise after eating calcium-rich foods, causing the thyroid gland to release more calcitonin.

4. Bones make up the skeletal system. The intestines are part of the digestive system. The kidneys are part of the excretory system. The thyroid and parathyroid glands and the hormones they produce are part of the endocrine system.

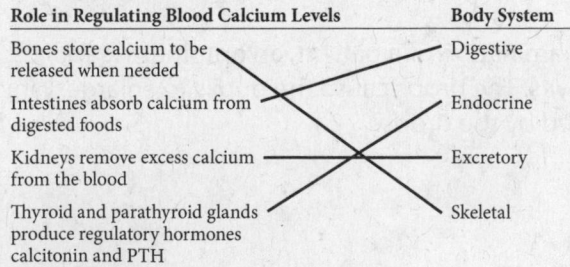

Role in Regulating Blood Calcium Levels	Body System
Bones store calcium to be released when needed	Digestive
Intestines absorb calcium from digested foods	Endocrine
Kidneys remove excess calcium from the blood	Excretory
Thyroid and parathyroid glands produce regulatory hormones calcitonin and PTH	Skeletal

5. **Short-answer reponse:**

   3-Point Response
   - A clear and well-developed explanation of how a low-calcium diet affects the feedback mechanism for blood calcium regulation
   - A clear and well-developed explanation of how chronically unbalanced blood calcium levels could contribute to the development of osteoporosis
   - Complete support from the passage and diagram

Sample Paper
A diet low in calcium limits the supply of calcium available to the body, causing the body to spend a disproportionate amount of time in the part of the regulatory pathway that works to raise blood calcium levels. In this part of the pathway, low blood calcium signals the parathyroid gland to release PTH. PTH then stimulates calcium levels in the blood to increase by causing the release of calcium from bones, reabsorption in the kidneys, and increased uptake from food in the intestines. When the ability to uptake calcium in the intestines is limited by a low-calcium diet, the body has to rely more heavily on the bones as a source of calcium. Over time, releasing more calcium from the bones than is being deposited can lead to a decrease in bone mineral density and the development of osteoporosis.

2-Point Response
- An adequate or partially articulated explanation of how a low-calcium diet affects the feedback mechanism for blood calcium regulation
- An adequate or partially articulated explanation of how chronically unbalanced blood calcium levels could contribute to the development of osteoporosis
- Partial support from the passage and/or diagram

Sample Paper
If blood calcium levels are always low, the body will always be trying to raise calcium levels. One way to raise blood calcium is to remove calcium from bones. Removing calcium can be harmful to bones and could eventually cause osteoporosis.

1-Point Response
- A minimal or implied explanation of how a low-calcium diet affects the feedback mechanism for blood calcium regulation

- A minimal or implied explanation of how chronically unbalanced blood calcium levels could contribute to the development of osteoporosis
- Minimal or implied support from the passage and/or diagram

Sample Paper
The body will not have enough calcium. The body will have to take calcium from bones. Bones with less calcium could get osteoporosis.

0-Point Response
- No explanation of how a low-calcium diet affects the feedback mechanism for blood calcium regulation
- No explanation of how chronically unbalanced blood calcium levels could contribute to the development of osteoporosis
- No support from the passage or diagram

6. **Correct answer: B.** Homologous structures in different species are inherited from the same ancestral species. Species that share a common ancestor will have similarities in their DNA, which stores the genetic code. The species' similar genetic codes produce the homologous structures.

7. **Correct answer: A.** The bones in the cat forelimb look most similar in shape and size to the bones in the human arm. This suggests that the common ancestor of the human and cat lived more recently than the ancestor humans share with the other species in the diagram.

8. **Short-answer response:**

3-Point Response
- A clear and well-developed explanation of how natural selection leads to adaptation in forelimbs
- Well-developed examples from the given diagram identifying structural features that

support the forelimb's unique function in specific species
- Complete support from the passage and diagram

Sample Paper
The process of natural selection allows species to become better adapted to survive in their environment over time. Though the forelimb structures of the species in the diagram originated from the same ancestor, each species' structures have been modified over time in response to the species' unique environments. The forelimb of the whale has reduced humerus, radius, and ulna bones, and elongated second and third phalanges. These adaptations allow the whale's fin to cut through water to support the function of swimming. The forelimbs of the bat and bird have a reduced humerus and carpals and specialized phalanges. These adaptations allow the species' wings to fan out to support the function of flying.

2-Point Response
- An adequate or partially articulated explanation of how natural selection leads to adaptation in forelimbs
- Partial examples from the given diagram identifying structural features that support the forelimb's unique function in specific species
- Partial support from the passage and/or diagram

Sample Paper
Species that have a common ancestor can live in different environments. The species' forelimb structures change over time so each species can survive in its own environment. The whale's forelimb structure is adapted for swimming. The bat's and bird's forelimb structure is adapted for flying.

1-Point Response
- A minimal or implied explanation of how natural selection leads to adaptation in forelimbs
- One or incomplete examples from the given diagram identifying structural features that support the forelimb's unique function in specific species
- Minimal or implied support from the passage and/or diagram

Sample Paper
Different species need to be able to do different things, so their forelimbs have to be a little different. Whales swim with fins. Bats and birds fly with wings.

0-Point Response
- No explanation of how natural selection leads to adaptation in forelimbs
- No examples from the given diagram identifying structural features that support the forelimb's unique function in specific species
- No support from the passage and/or diagram

9. **Correct answer: 6 and 6.** In a chemical equation, the coefficient (number) in front of each substance identifies the number of molecules. According to the photosynthesis equation, 6 molecules of CO_2 (carbon dioxide) and 6 molecules of H_2O (water) are used to produce 1 molecule of $C_6H_{12}O_6$ (glucose) and 6 molecules of O_2 (oxygen).

10. **Correct answer: D.** In a chemical equation, reactants are to the left of the arrow and products are to the right. The products of photosynthesis are glucose and oxygen, and are shown on the right side of the photosynthesis equation. Glucose and oxygen are also the reactants for respiration, and are shown on the left side of the respiration equation.

11. California has a high incidence of earthquakes. Constructing buildings with steel-plate walls is a precaution used in areas with frequent earthquakes. Florida has a high incidence of hurricanes. Dikes, or levees, are walls built as a precaution against storm surge in areas with frequent hurricanes. Oklahoma has a high incidence of tornadoes. Constructing underground shelters is a precaution used in areas with frequent tornadoes.

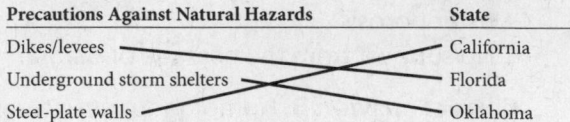

Precautions Against Natural Hazards	State
Dikes/levees	California
Underground storm shelters	Florida
Steel-plate walls	Oklahoma

12. **Correct answer: D.** Earthquakes occur most frequently along the boundaries of tectonic plates. When the pressure built up at a plate boundary becomes too great, energy is released in the form of an earthquake. According to the earthquake map, Washington has a high incidence of earthquakes, indicating that it lies near a plate boundary.

13. **Correct answer: photosynthesis.** Plants and other photosynthetic organisms absorb carbon dioxide from the atmosphere to use as a reactant in photosynthesis. According to the diagram, photosynthesis removes 110 gigatons of carbon from the atmosphere, far more than any other process in the diagram.

The Carbon Cycle

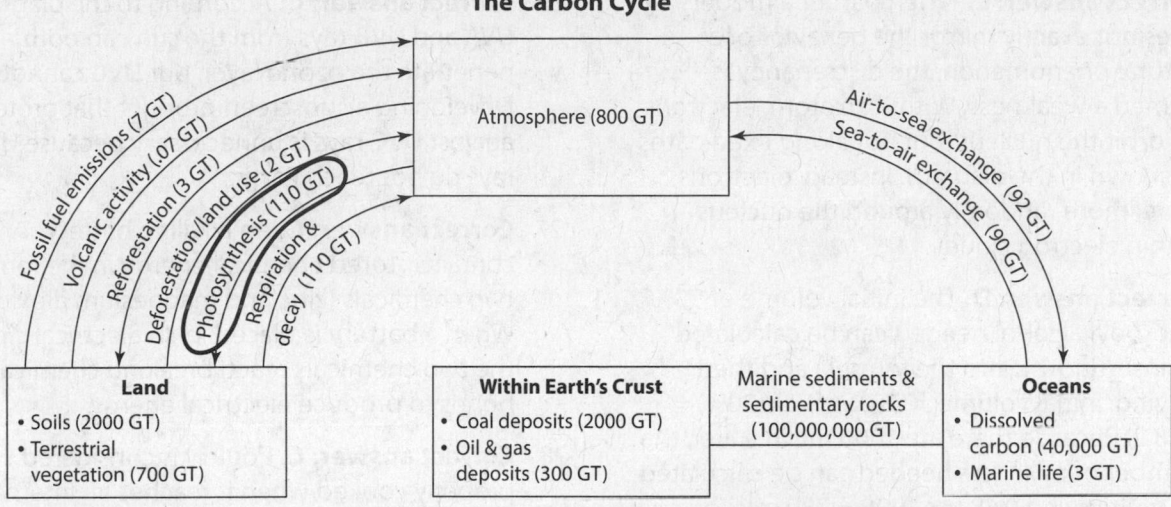

14. **Correct answer: D.** Fossil fuels are fuels derived from the fossil remains of dead organisms. Coal, oil, and natural gas are all fossil fuels. The diagram shows coal deposits storing 2000 GT of carbon, and oil and gas deposits storing 300 GT, for a total of 2300 GT of carbon stored in fossil fuel deposits

15. **Correct answer: The graph should be marked where the line crosses the *x*-axis at 30 minutes.** Above the *x*-axis, velocity is positive, indicating that the race car is moving forward. Below the *x*-axis, velocity is negative, indicating that the race car is moving in reverse. The race car changes direction when the graph crosses the *x*-axis.

Velocity of a Race Car (meters/minute)

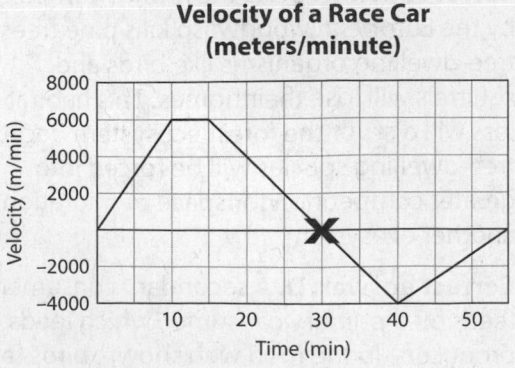

16. **Correct answer: B.** The units of velocity used in the graph are meters per minute (m/min). The units of time are minutes (min). Acceleration is calculated as change in velocity (m/min) divided by time (min), which results in units of m/min/min, or (m/min^2).

17. **Correct answer: A.** According to the equation for Newton's Second Law ($f = ma$), when an object's acceleration is zero, the total net force acting on the object must also be zero. A total net force of zero means that all forces acting on the race car are balanced.

18. **Correct answer: B.** In mutualism, both species receive a benefit from engaging in the relationship. In this case, the bee receives a food source (nectar) from the flower. The flower receives assistance with reproduction as the bee transfers the flower's pollen to the next flower it lands on.

19. **Correct answer: C.** A substance's density describes how tightly packed the substance's molecules are. When a solution is separated into its components, the component with the highest density will sink to the bottom and the component with the lowest density

will remain at the top. In the diagram, red blood cells are at the bottom of the test tube, indicating that they have the highest density.

20. **Correct answer: C.** When part of a model does not exactly mirror the behavior of a natural phenomenon, the discrepancy is termed a weakness. Within an atom, electrons do orbit the nucleus, but not along fixed paths as shown in the diagram. Instead, electrons travel more randomly around the nucleus within electron clouds.

21. **Correct answer: D.** The initial volume of 90% isopropyl alcohol needed can be calculated by inserting 1 L into the formula and then solving: initial volume = (70% × 1 L)/(90%) = 0.78 L. Because there are 1000 mL in a liter, the number of milliliters needed can be calculated by multiplying 0.78 L × 1000 = 780 mL.

22. **Correct answer: A.** The table identifies the atmospheric concentration of hydrogen to be 0.5 PPM. As shown in the pie graph, the concentration in percent volume can be determined by dividing the concentration in PPM by 10,000. Therefore, 0.5 PPM ÷ 10,000 = 0.00005% hydrogen concentration in the atmosphere.

23. **Correct answer: A.** As wind moves along the ocean's surface, the gas particles in the air drag the water particles on the ocean's surface in the same direction. This causes global wind patterns and surface ocean currents to travel along the same paths.

24. **Correct answer: B.** A ramp is a simple machine that reduces the amount of force required to move an object by increasing the total distance over which the object is moved. Increasing the distance allows the same amount of work to be done, but with less force.

25. **Correct answer: A.** The distance between consecutive peaks of a wave identifies its wavelength. As indicated on the diagram, an average radio wave has a wavelength that is

larger than a human. Radio waves have the longest average wavelength (10^3 meters) on the electromagnetic spectrum.

26. **Correct answer: C.** According to the diagram, UVA and UVB rays from the sun can both penetrate the ozone layer, but UVC cannot. Developing a sunscreen product that protects against UVC rays is unnecessary because UVC rays do not reach Earth.

27. **Correct answer: C.** An alkaline battery contains stored chemical energy in the form of two chemicals (zinc and magnesium dioxide). When a battery is placed in an electrical circuit, the two chemicals react, breaking chemical bonds to produce electrical energy.

28. **Correct answer: C.** Poultry is considered properly cooked when it reaches an internal temperature of 165 degrees Fahrenheit. According to the diagram, 165°F falls between the highest air temperature recorded in the United States and the boiling point of water. 165°F is considered hot enough to kill harmful bacteria that may be present in poultry.

29. **Correct answer: B.** The processes in the exothermic column all release energy into the environment, usually in the form of heat. A candle flame produces heat. Burning sugar produces a net release of energy. Making ice cubes and condensing water vapor both require the temperature of water to decrease, which occurs by the release of heat into the environment.

30. **Correct answer: B.** As the fungus carried by the European woodwasp kills pine trees, tree-dwelling organisms like birds and squirrels will lose their homes. This habitat loss will disrupt the forest ecosystem because tree-dwelling species will be forced into greater competition for space or migration to another ecosystem.

31. **Correct answer: D.** A secondary consumer feeds on a primary consumer, which feeds on producers. In the food web shown, birds feed

on grasshoppers, which feed on grasses and grains. The grasses and grains are producers, the grasshoppers are primary consumers, and the birds are secondary consumers.

32. **Correct answer: B.** In an ecosystem, approximately 10% of the energy available at any trophic level is passed up to the organisms in the next trophic level. In this energy pyramid, primary consumers receive 10% (1000 kcal) of the producers' 10,000 kcal. Secondary consumers receive 10% of the primary consumers' 1000 kcal, or 1% of the producers' 10,000 kcal. Tertiary consumers receive 10% of the secondary consumers' 100 kcal, or 0.1% of the producers' 10,000 kcal.

33. **Correct answer: C.** The father passes on only healthy genes to the child. The mother could have passed on 4 different gene combinations to her child, as shown in the following diagram. The 3 gene combinations highlighted in gray include at least one diseased gene, meaning the child has a ¾, or 75%, chance of being a carrier for at least one disease.

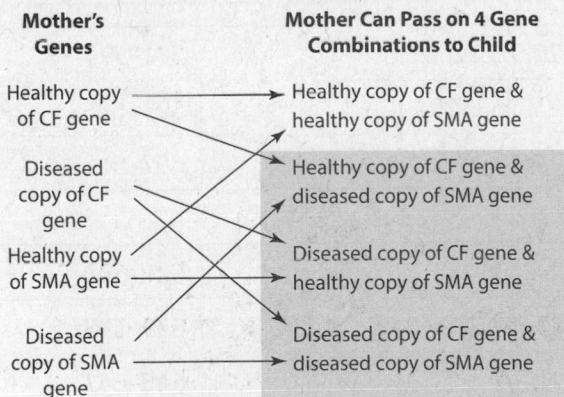

Mother's Genes	Mother Can Pass on 4 Gene Combinations to Child
Healthy copy of CF gene	Healthy copy of CF gene & healthy copy of SMA gene
Diseased copy of CF gene	Healthy copy of CF gene & diseased copy of SMA gene
Healthy copy of SMA gene	Diseased copy of CF gene & healthy copy of SMA gene
Diseased copy of SMA gene	Diseased copy of CF gene & diseased copy of SMA gene

34. **Correct answer: B.** Chromosome pairs separate during anaphase. This is illustrated in the third row of the diagram, in which the x-shaped chromosomes appear to be pulled apart and toward opposite sides of the cell.

35. **Correct answer: D.** Thermoregulation is the ability to maintain a stable body temperature even in a fluctuating environment. Though many organisms, like humans, can thermoregulate, others cannot. Lizards, for example, must absorb heat from the environment. Since all living things are not able to do it, thermoregulation is not an essential function of life.

36. **Correct answer: B.** Seasons in opposing hemispheres are due to the tilt of the Earth's axis and the proximity of the hemisphere to the sun. In summer, the Northern Hemisphere is tilted toward the sun, so New York has its longest day on the summer solstice, in this case June 21. On the same June 21, the Southern Hemisphere is tilted away from the sun, so Perth, Australia, has its shortest day.

37. **Correct answer: A.** Glucose and oxygen are products of the photosynthesis reaction.

38. **Correct answer: C.** The car is decelerating at a constant force, so the velocity is decreasing at a constant rate. Therefore, the velocity-time graph describing this situation would be a straight line with a negative slope.

39. **Correct answer: B.** The iris contains the muscles that contract and relax to regulate the size of the pupil. When the iris contracts, the pupil gets smaller. Conversely, when the iris relaxes, the pupil enlarges. The drops cause the iris to relax, thereby enlarging the pupil.

40. **Correct answer: D.** The stimulus (pressure) leads to hormone secretion that evokes a response (muscle contraction) that furthers the increased stimulus (more pressure). This is a positive feedback mechanism leading to extremes and is stopped only when the baby is delivered and the pressure is finished.

PRETEST

Evaluation Chart

Check the Answers and Explanations section of the Science Pretest to see which answers you got correct and which ones you missed. For each question that you missed, find the item number in the chart below. Check the column on the left to see the test content area for that item. If you missed questions in a particular content area, you need to pay particular attention to that area as you study for the GED® test. The pages of this book that cover that content area are listed in the column on the right.

Content Area	Item Number	Pages to Review
Part 1 Life Science		
1. Structures and Functions of Life	19, 34	523–531
2. Life Functions and Energy Intake	9, 10, 35, 37	533–535
3. Heredity	33	537–545
4. Evolution	6, 7, 8	547–552
5. Ecosystems	18, 30, 21, 32	553–563
6. The Human Body and Health	3, 4, 5, 39, 40	565–575
Part 2 Physical Science		
7. Chemical Interactions	20, 21, 22, 29	581–594
8. Energy	25, 26, 27, 28	595–605
9. Motion and Force	15, 16, 17, 24, 38	607–614
Part 3 Earth and Space Science		
10. Space Systems	1, 2, 36	621–627
11. Earth Systems	12, 13, 23	629–643
12. Interactions Between Earth's Systems and Living Things	11, 14	645–653

Social Studies

This Social Studies Pretest is designed to introduce you to this section of the GED® test and to give you a good idea of your current skill level in this subject area.

This test has the same number of questions as the real GED Social Studies test: 45 items in various formats and one essay question. The question formats are the same as the ones on the real exam and are designed to measure the same skills. Many of the questions are based on historical documents or on short reading passages on social studies topics. Some are based on graphics such as a map, a diagram, or an illustration. You will also see questions based on paired passages.

Most of the questions are in multiple-choice format, but you will also see questions in other formats, such as fill-in-the-blank items and simulated click-and-drag and drop-down items. On the real GED® test, you will indicate your answers by clicking on the computer screen. For this paper-and-pencil practice test, mark your answers directly on the page. Write your essay on a separate sheet of paper.

To get a good idea of how you will do on the real exam, take this test under actual exam conditions. Complete the test in one session and follow the given time limit. If you do not complete the test in the time allowed, you will know that you need to work on improving your pacing.

Try to answer as many questions as you can. There is no penalty for wrong answers, so guess if you have to. In multiple-choice questions, if you can eliminate one or more answer choices, you can increase your chances of guessing correctly.

After you have finished the test, check your answers in the Answers and Explanations section that follows the pretest. Then use the Evaluation Chart that follows the Answers and Explanations section to determine the skills and content areas in which you need more practice.

Now turn the page and begin the Social Studies Pretest.

Social Studies

45 questions | **90 minutes**

Use the passage for Items 1 and 2:

The United States operates under a federal form of government, in which power is shared between different levels of government, with the national government holding the greatest amount of power. In the United States, the state and local levels of government also hold power; however, their power is less than that of the national government. The federal, or national, government has power over issues that affect the entire country. States have power over local issues. Some powers, such as collecting taxes, are shared. The Tenth Amendment to the Constitution says that powers that have not been given to the national government, and have not been withheld from the state government, are reserved for the states. Local and state governments are also able to act if a higher level has not done so.

1. Which of these situations is an example of a lower level of government acting when a higher level has not?

   A. President Abraham Lincoln's Emancipation Proclamation freed slaves in the southern states.
   B. The Constitution of the United States limits the amount of power held by the government.
   C. Following the ratification of the Twenty-sixth Amendment, 18-year-olds in the United States were allowed to vote.
   D. Women in Wyoming were allowed to vote before this right was given by the Nineteenth Amendment to the Constitution.

2. Under Federalism, which power belongs only to the national government?

   A. assessing and collecting taxes
   B. setting up an army and a navy
   C. regulating trade within a state
   D. establishing a local school system

Use the passage and the map for Items 3 and 4:

Throughout history, various types of government have been present around the world. The main differences between these types of government are based on whether the power is held by a single person, a small group of people, or by many people. Until the early 20th century, monarchy was the most common type of government. During the 20th century, the people of the world faced World Wars I and II and witnessed the rise and fall of Soviet communism. Some nations invaded others; others formed alliances to defend themselves. Many countries were divided, expanded, or even created as a result of wars.

The map below shows the types of national governments that were present at the end of the 20th century.

World Governments, 1999

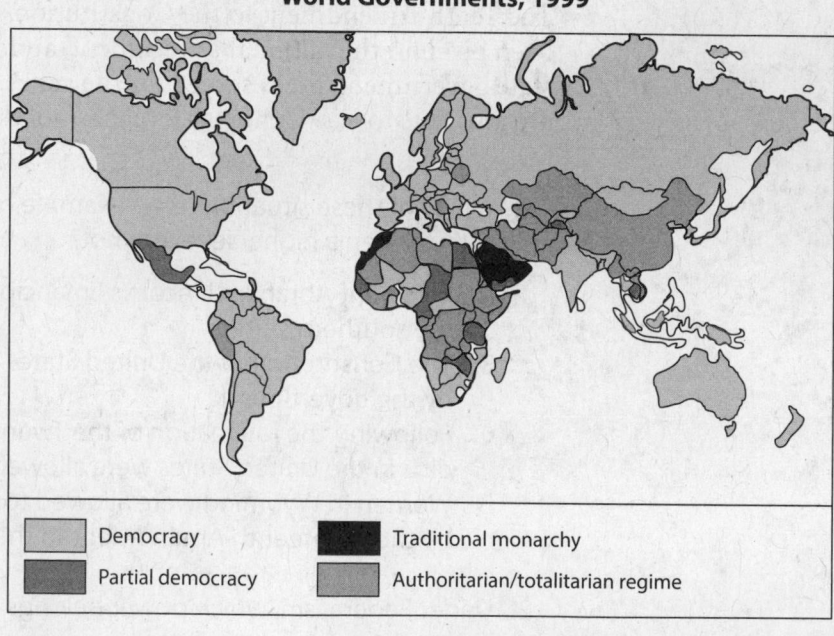

☐	Democracy	■	Traditional monarchy
☐	Partial democracy	☐	Authoritarian/totalitarian regime

3. Based on the data in the map, which type of government was most common at the end of the 20th century?

   A. authoritarian
   B. colonial dependency
   C. democracy
   D. monarchy

4. What inference can be drawn based on the passage and the map?

    A. The type of government that is originally established within a country remains through the course of its history.

    B. Changes to a country's type of government may occur as a result of events that occur around the world.

    C. Only countries with the same type of government become allies with one another.

    D. The location of a country determines the type of government found there.

Use the passage for Item 5:

History provided many ideas for the founders of the United States when they were creating government institutions. The writers of the U.S. Constitution were well aware of the variety of types of government that had been established in other countries.

For example, they knew that cities in ancient Greece, such as Athens, had been organized into small, independent entities known as city-states, each ruled by a small group of powerful, wealthy men. After some time, the citizens protested and wanted to participate in making the laws by which they lived. A political system was developed in which male landowners were permitted to participate directly in the government, creating an early form of democracy.

The U.S. founders also knew that ancient Rome had been a kind of republic. Certain upper-class citizens were permitted to elect representatives in the government, and eventually, lower-class citizens were allowed to vote as well. Over time, those voters brought about changes in government, including demands that the laws be written down to prevent leaders from changing them at will.

As former British subjects, the founders were also well aware of English political history. In early England, under monarchical rule, the king or queen had ultimate power. By the 1200s, this began to change, and eventually a Parliament was established. This group of men represented the interests of particular groups of citizens. Parliament required the king to seek its approval prior to making decisions, thus limiting the power of the monarch.

5. Which conclusion can be made regarding the development of the government of the United States?

   A. Ideas from several historical types of government were incorporated into the structure of U.S. democracy.
   B. The founding fathers modeled the United States government after a single, successful historical type of government.
   C. Ancient governments embodied political systems that were outdated by the time the government of the United States was established.
   D. The early leaders of the United States looked to ancient governments as examples of how not to create a lasting form of government.

Use the passage for Item 6:

The United States Constitution divides our national government into three separate branches: the legislative, executive, and judicial branches. Each branch has its own area of responsibility. The legislative branch includes Congress, and makes laws for the country. This branch also raises money, approves the printing of money, and can declare war. The executive branch is responsible for approving and carrying out the laws, and includes the president, the vice president, and the departments that are needed to enforce the laws, including the military. The judicial branch includes the Supreme Court. The judges in this court are nominated by the president and are responsible for interpreting the laws and determining whether or not they have been followed. This division of power prevents any one part of the government from dominating another.

6. For each of the responsibilities below, indicate the correct column of the chart where it belongs. (**Note:** On the real GED® test, you will click on the items you choose and "drag" each one into position in the chart.)

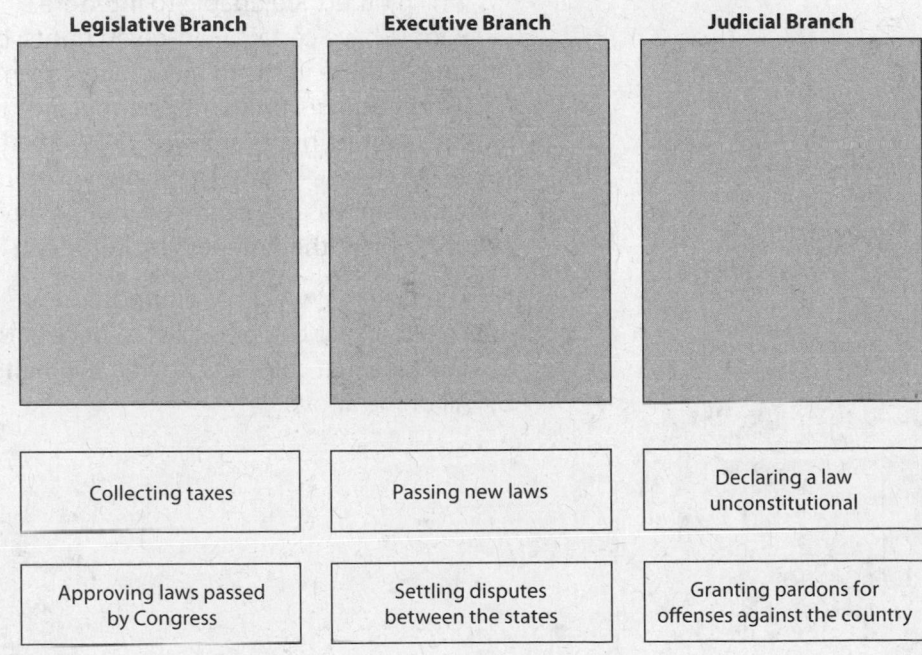

Legislative Branch	Executive Branch	Judicial Branch

Collecting taxes	Passing new laws	Declaring a law unconstitutional
Approving laws passed by Congress	Settling disputes between the states	Granting pardons for offenses against the country

Use the passage for Item 7:

The ideas of the Scottish philosopher John Locke influenced the structure of the government of the United States. Locke's natural rights philosophy theorized how people would act in a state of nature, in which there was no government. Locke believed that the rights to life, liberty, and property were God-given rights that could not be denied; however, in a state of nature, without government, some people would deprive others of these natural rights. He believed that people should have the freedom to make their own choices, as long as those choices do not interfere with the liberty of others. The purpose of government, Locke believed, is to protect people's natural rights.

7. Which statement best explains Locke's ideas about natural rights and government?

   A. The only way for people to be given any rights is through the formation of a strong government.
   B. Government is unnecessary because people have natural rights with which others are unable to interfere.
   C. People have certain God-given rights; however, forming a government causes these rights to be unfairly taken away.
   D. By forming governments, people give up some of their rights; however, their natural rights are then protected by the government.

8. Mercantilism was one of the economic drivers of exploration and colonization of the Americas by European countries. What is mercantilism?

   A. The idea that wealth is limited
   B. The idea that colonies exist to benefit the ruling country
   C. The idea that colonies provide raw materials and new markets
   D. All of the above

Use the passage for Item 9:

Popular sovereignty, one of the principles upon which the Constitution of the United States was built, is a political theory under which government is created by the will of the people. According to this principle, people have the right to make political decisions for themselves.

9. Which document applied the concept of popular sovereignty?

   A. The Taft-Hartley Act of 1947 prohibited certain types of strikes by unionized workers.
   B. The Twenty-second Amendment states that the President of the United States may not be elected more than twice.
   C. The Kansas-Nebraska Act of 1854 allowed each new U.S. territory to determine whether or not slavery would be permitted within its borders.
   D. The Townshend Acts, created in 1767, taxed items imported by the colonies, including tea, glass, lead, paper, and paints.

Use the passage and the numbered list for Item 10:

If the President of the United States is incapacitated, resigns, dies, or is removed from office, the Vice President then takes the office of President. The Presidential Succession Act of 1947, signed by President Harry Truman, set the order of succession if the Vice President were unable to take the office. The original act of 1792 set the Senate President pro tempore and the Speaker of the House in line for the office; however, these official offices had been removed by Congress in 1886. The 1947 act reinserted these officials into the list, but placed the Speaker of the House ahead of the Senate President pro tempore in the succession order. The following list shows the order of succession set by this act.

The Line of Succession to the Presidency of the United States

1. Vice President
2. Speaker of the House
3. President pro tempore of the Senate
4. Secretary of State
5. Secretary of the Treasury
6. Secretary of Defense
7. Attorney General
8. Secretary of the Interior
9. Secretary of Agriculture
10. Secretary of Commerce
11. Secretary of Labor
12. Secretary of Health and Human Services
13. Secretary of Housing and Urban Development
14. Secretary of Transportation
15. Secretary of Energy
16. Secretary of Education
17. Secretary of Veterans Affairs
18. Secretary of Homeland Security

10. Fill in the blank.

    According to the table, the person who would follow the President pro tempore of the Senate in the line of succession is

    _____.

Use the following passages for Item 11:

All Legislative Powers herein granted shall be vested in a Congress of the United States, which shall consist of a Senate and House of Representatives. . . . The Senate of the United States shall be composed of two Senators from each state, chosen by the legislature thereof, for six years; and each Senator shall have one vote. . . . The Vice President of the United States shall be President of the Senate, but shall have no vote, unless they be equally divided. The Senate shall choose their other officers, and also a President pro tempore, in the absence of the Vice President, or when he shall exercise the office of President of the United States. The Senate shall have the sole power to try all impeachments. When sitting for that purpose, they shall be on oath or affirmation. When the President of the United States is tried, the Chief Justice shall preside: And no person shall be convicted without the concurrence of two thirds of the members present.

—Excerpted from Article I of the U.S. Constitution

If each [chamber] is substantially framed upon the same plan, the advantages of the division are shadowy and imaginative. . . . In this view, the organization of the senate becomes of inestimable value. It represents the voice, not of a district, but of a state; . . . not of the interest of one state, but of all; not of the chosen pursuits of a predominant population in one state, but of all the pursuits in all of the states. . . . It is a most important and valuable part of the system, and the real balance-wheel, which adjusts, and regulates its movements.

—Joseph Story, Justice on the Supreme Court (1822–1845)

11. Based on these passages, which statement is true?

    A. The Justices of the Supreme Court believed that officials in the Senate and the House of Representatives should be chosen in the same way.
    B. Story believed that having two Senators from each state fairly represented the interests of all states, without favoring a particular group of citizens.
    C. The Chief Justice of the Supreme Court believed that the Senate should be organized in such a way as to regulate the actions of the President and members of the House.
    D. Story believed that each state should have the same number of representatives in both the Senate and the House in order to fairly represent the interests of the citizens.

Use the passage for Item 12:

The number of Justices on the Supreme Court has varied between five and ten, and was fixed at nine shortly after the Civil War by the Judiciary Act of 1869. At least six Justices must be present in order to hear a case. In general, a decision is reached when a majority of the Justices agree. So, when all nine Justices are present and vote on a case, five votes are required for a majority decision. Under certain circumstances, the Senate hears a case, with the Chief Justice of the Supreme Court presiding.

12. In which case would more than a majority rule have been required?

   A. The Supreme Court case that established the rights of the arrested, *Miranda v. Arizona* (1966)
   B. The Senate impeachment trial of President Bill Clinton on charges brought by the House of Representatives (1999)
   C. The Supreme Court case concerning student rights, *Tinker v. Des Moines ISD* (1969)
   D. The Supreme Court review of the legal challenge to separate but equal schools, *Brown v. Board of Education* (1954)

Use the passage for Item 13:

The U.S. Constitution mandates that the members of the House of Representatives will choose a Speaker, who serves as their leader. This person is ceremonially ranked as the highest official in the legislative branch of the government. The role of Speaker of the House includes being the administrative head of the House of Representatives, presiding over debates, appointing committee members, and administering the oath of office to other members. Although it is not required, the Speaker is almost always elected according to party lines, making him or her a member of whichever party is currently in the majority. There is a majority leader in the House; however, this person is actually the second highest officer of the party, with the Speaker being the highest ranking officer in that party. Generally, the Speaker does not vote to pass a bill unless necessary for the bill to pass.

13. Which statement regarding the Speaker of the House can be supported by the information?

    A. The vote of the Speaker of the House is inconsequential when passing legislation.
    B. The Speaker of the House does not need to be an elected member of the House of Representatives.
    C. The term limit for the Speaker of the House is the same as that of the President of the United States, and so they may agree with each other on major issues.
    D. The Speaker of the House and the President of the United States may represent different political parties and oppose each other on major issues.

Use the following passages for Item 14:

The Congress, whenever two thirds of both Houses shall deem it necessary, shall propose Amendments to this Constitution, or, on the Application of the Legislatures of two thirds of the several States, shall call a Convention for proposing Amendments, which, in either Case, shall be valid to all Intents and Purposes, as Part of this Constitution, when ratified by the Legislatures of three fourths of the several States, or by Conventions in three fourths thereof, as the one or the other Mode of Ratification may be proposed by the Congress.

—*Excerpted from Article V of the U.S. Constitution*

If in the opinion of the people the distribution or modification of the constitutional powers be in any particular wrong, let it be corrected by an amendment in the way which the Constitution designates.

—*George Washington*

14. Which describes Washington's point of view regarding amendments to the Constitution?

   A. The laws and powers established by the Constitution are fair and should be followed, regardless of public opinion.
   B. There are errors in the Constitution, and the representatives in Congress must correct these mistakes so that the people believe that the powers are fair.
   C. It is the opinion of citizens of the United States that the powers set forth in the Constitution are unfair and need to be corrected by amending the document.
   D. When the citizens of the United States believe that an aspect of the Constitution should be changed, Congress should vote on whether or not to amend this document.

Use the passage and the chart for Items 15 and 16:

Following the writing of the U.S. Constitution, many Americans, including Thomas Jefferson and James Madison, demanded that a Bill of Rights be added to the document. This Bill of Rights, which includes the first ten Amendments to the U.S. Constitution, is summarized in the chart below.

Bill of Rights

Amendment I	Freedom of religion, speech, press, assembly, and petition
Amendment II	Right to keep and bear arms in order to maintain a well-regulated militia
Amendment III	No quartering of soldiers in any house without the consent of the owner
Amendment IV	Freedom from unreasonable searches and seizures
Amendment V	Right to due process of law; freedom from self-incrimination and double jeopardy
Amendment VI	Rights of accused persons, such as the right to a speedy and public trial by jury
Amendment VII	Right of trial by jury in civil cases
Amendment VIII	Freedom from excessive bail, cruel and unusual punishments
Amendment IX	Rights in addition to those stated in the Constitution
Amendment X	Powers reserved to the states

15. Based on the information about the Bill of Rights, which conclusion can be drawn?

    A. People wanted to ensure that the federal government did not hold more power than the state governments.
    B. In order to clarify the intentions of political leaders, the rights of the federal government needed to be specifically stated.
    C. There was concern among many citizens that a strong federal government would fail to recognize the rights of individuals.
    D. Most leaders feared that the state governments had been given too much power, and federal rights needed to be outlined.

16. Which of the following is an example of a freedom that is guaranteed by the Bill of Rights?

   A. An editorial article in a major newspaper publicly criticizes the performance of a government official.
   B. A thief is apprehended after breaking into several private homes and stealing personal property.
   C. An eighteen-year-old girl registers to vote in an upcoming presidential election.
   D. A television ad encourages people to join one of the branches of the armed forces.

Use the table for Item 17:

The following table summarizes the decisions of the U.S. Supreme Court in specific cases.

Decisions by the United States Supreme Court

Case	Decision
Shelley v. Kraemer (1948)	Property deeds that limit property rights to Caucasians, and exclude members of other races, are unenforceable
Lau v. Nichols (1973)	The failure of a school system to offer English language instruction to students of Chinese descent was considered unlawful discrimination
Cleveland Board of Education v. LaFleur (1974)	Mandatory maternity leave rules for pregnant teachers in a public school violate due process that is guaranteed by the Constitution

17. In what way could the decisions in these cases be categorized?

   A. Decisions regarding organizations
   B. Decisions regarding racial equality
   C. Decisions regarding personal rights
   D. Decisions regarding educational opportunities

Use the passage for Item 18:

The Magna Carta, written in the year 1297, has been noted as one of the most important legal documents ever written. Originally written to protect the rights and property of a group of English barons from their tyrannical king, this document inspired the colonists during the American Revolution to believe they were entitled to some of the same rights, which were eventually included in the Constitution of the United States and the Bill of Rights. One principle that was included in the Magna Carta that remains evident in our country today includes the statement "No freeman shall be taken, imprisoned, disseised, outlawed, banished, or in any way destroyed, nor will We proceed against or prosecute him, except by the lawful judgment of his peers and by the law of the land."

18. Which Amendment to the Constitution is an example of how this portion of the Magna Carta influenced the United States government?

   A. Amendment V states, "No person shall . . . be deprived of life, liberty, or property, without due process of law."
   B. Amendment VIII states, "Excessive bail shall not be required . . . nor cruel and unusual punishments inflicted."
   C. Amendment XIII states, "Neither slavery nor involuntary servitude, except as a punishment for crime . . . shall exist within the United States."
   D. Amendment XXIV states, "The right of citizens . . . to vote in any primary or other election . . . shall not be denied . . . by reason of failure to pay poll tax or other tax."

Use the passage for Item 19:

Leaders often look to the constitutions of other countries when establishing the governments of their own countries. Many countries, such as the Czech Republic, have used the United States Constitution and European parliamentary systems as examples when adopting the principles by which their government will be ruled.

In 1985, while his country remained under Soviet domination, Vaclav Havel, who later became the first president of the Czech Republic, wrote, "Without free, self-respecting, and autonomous citizens, there can be no free and independent nations. Without internal peace, that, peace among citizens and between the citizens and their state, there can be no guarantee of external peace. . . . A state that denies its citizens their basic rights becomes a danger to its neighbors as well." After becoming president of the newly independent country, Havel said, "The idea of human rights and freedoms must be an integral part of any meaningful world order."

19. Which statement most likely explains Havel's point of view?

   A. Worldwide democracy is necessary for peace.
   B. A single type of government will lead to conflict between countries.
   C. A constitution that provides freedom and power to the people will lead to a country's failure.
   D. People who have too many freedoms are a danger to their own societies, as well as those around them.

PRETEST: Social Studies | **143**

PRETEST

Use the map for Item 20:

The following map shows the westward expansion of the United States in 1850.

Westward Expansion, 1850

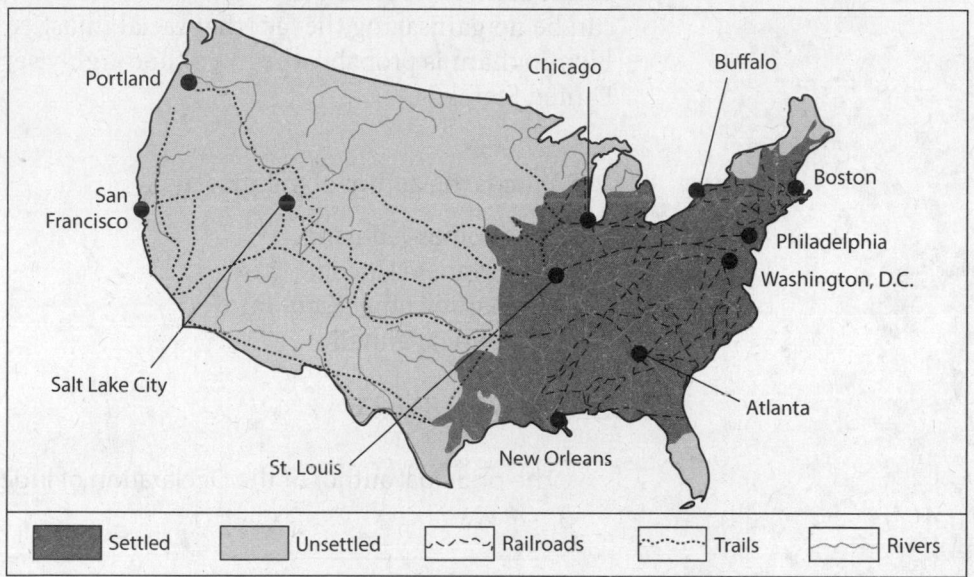

20. Which statement explains how geography influenced this expansion?

A. Many western settlements were built along established railroads.
B. Many people forged trails and built western settlements along rivers.
C. Settlers built railroads that followed the major waterways across the nation.
D. Proximity to the ocean was important to people building railroads.

Use the passage for Item 21:

April 16, 1963

In any nonviolent campaign there are four basic steps: collection of the facts to determine whether injustices exist; negotiation; self purification; and direct action. We have gone through all these steps in Birmingham. There can be no gainsaying the fact that racial injustice engulfs this community. Birmingham is probably the most thoroughly segregated city in the United States.

21. Who is the author of the passage?

   A. Thomas Jefferson
   B. Abraham Lincoln
   C. Martin Luther King, Jr.
   D. John F. Kennedy

22. Fill in the blank.

   The principal author of the Declaration of Independence was

   _____.

23. Fill in the blank.

   The _____ Era, which officially ended in 1877, refers to the period of transformation policies in the South following the Civil War.

24. Which amendment stated, "The right of citizens of the United States to vote shall not be denied or abridged by the United States or by any State on account of sex."

   A. The Thirteenth Amendment
   B. The Fourteenth Amendment
   C. The Fifteenth Amendment
   D. The Nineteenth Amendment

25. The following sentence contains a blank marked "Select. . . ." Beneath it is a list of choices. Indicate the choice that is correct and belongs in the blank. (**Note:** On the real GED® test, the choices will appear as a "drop-down" menu. When you click on a choice, it will appear in the blank.)

    | Select... ▼ | (1820–1906) was a prominent leader of the American woman suffrage movement at the turn of the twentieth century.

Select... ▼
Susan B. Anthony
Dolly Madison
Clara Barton
Jackie Kennedy

26. Fill in the blank.

    In 1848, gold was discovered at John Sutter's mill, beginning the mass

    movement known as the _____.

27. What is the political and economic theory that is based on social ownership and cooperative control?

    A. capitalism
    B. socialism
    C. feudalism
    D. egalitarianism

28. Which classical civilization was characterized by polytheistic religion, the construction of massive structures still standing today, and a written language of hieroglyphs?

    A. the Romans
    B. the Greeks
    C. the Egyptians
    D. the Babylonians

Use the table for Items 29 and 30:

Political Divisions of the U.S. Senate and House of Representatives, from the 100th Congress to the 113th Congress

Congress	Years	Senate*				House of Representatives*			
		Democrats	Republicans	Other Parties	Vacant	Democrats	Republicans	Other Parties	Vacant
100th	1987–1989	55	45	—	—	258	177	—	—
101st	1989–1991	55	45	—	—	260	175	—	—
102nd	1991–1993	56	44	—	—	267	167	1	—
103rd	1993–1995	57	43	—	—	258	176	1	—
104th	1995–1997	48	52	—	—	204	230	1	—
105th	1997–1999	45	55	—	—	207	226	2	—
106th	1999–2001	45	55	—	—	211	223	1	—
107th	2001–2003	50	50	—	—	212	221	2	—
108th	2003–2005	48	51	1	—	204	229	1	1
109th	2005–2007	44	55	1	—	202	232	1	—
110th	2007–2009	49	49	2	—	233	202	—	—
111th	2009–2011	55	41	2	2	256	178	—	1
112th	2011–2013	51	47	2	—	193	242	—	—
113th	2013–2015	53	45	2	—	200	234	—	1

* There are a total of 100 senators in the Senate and 435 representatives in the House of Representatives.

29. Which of the following Congresses saw the lowest number of Republicans in the Senate?

    A. The 103rd Congress
    B. The 110th Congress
    C. The 111th Congress
    D. The 113th Congress

30. During which of the following sessions did the Democrats have a majority in the House of Representatives?

    A. The 100th Congress
    B. The 105th Congress
    C. The 107th Congress
    D. The 113th Congress

31. Below is a list of characteristics of U.S. political parties. For each one, indicate the correct column of the chart where it belongs. (**Note:** On the real GED® test, you will click on the items you choose and "drag" each one into position in the chart.)

Characteristics of U.S. Political Parties

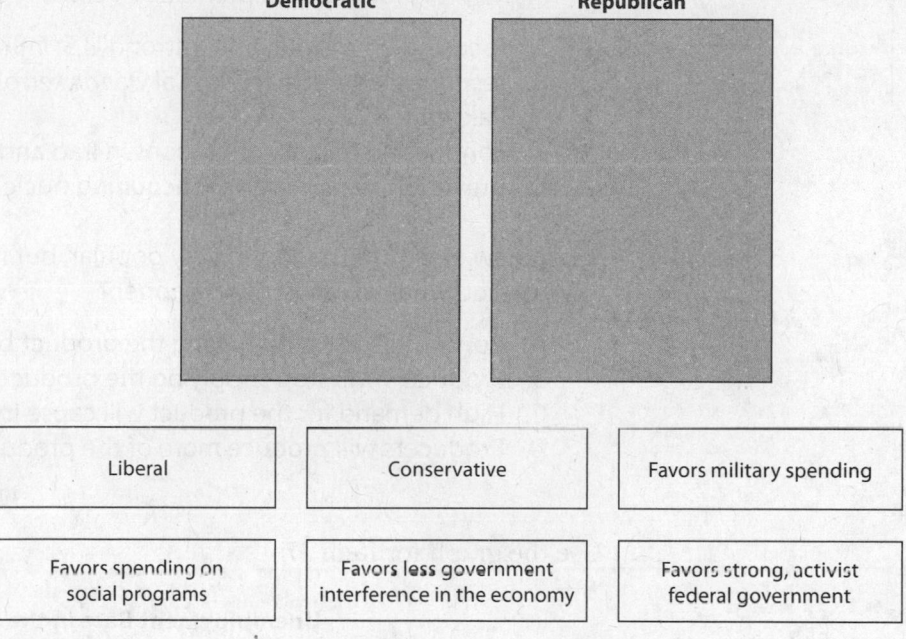

Democratic	Republican

Liberal	Conservative	Favors military spending

Favors spending on social programs	Favors less government interference in the economy	Favors strong, activist federal government

32. Which of the following provided incentives for the use of alternative fuels and energy conservation?

A. The Nuclear Waste Act of 1982
B. The Energy Policy Act of 1922
C. The Natural Gas Act of 1936
D. The Recovery Act of 2009

33. Which was the first European power to settle colonies in the St. Lawrence River valley of eastern Canada and in the Mississippi River valley?

A. France
B. Spain
C. Portugal
D. Great Britain

34. Fill in the blank.

   The League of Nations was formed at the peace conference following the

   end of _____.

35. Which of the following is not characteristic of United States foreign policy in the years following September 11, 2001?

   A. focusing on maintaining a strong U.S. influence in Latin America
   B. responding to threats from al Qaeda terrorists in Afghanistan and Pakistan
   C. conducting military operations in Iraq and Afghanistan
   D. preventing terrorists from acquiring nuclear weapons

36. A new electronic gadget is very popular, but its price is high. In a free market, what will most likely happen?

   A. Consumers will stop buying the product because of its high price.
   B. Producers will stop supplying the product because of weak demand.
   C. High demand for the product will cause its price to go up.
   D. Producers will produce more of the product, and its price will go down.

Use the graph for Item 37:

Unemployment Rate in the United States

37. At which of the following times was the unemployment rate 5.5%?

   A. January 1997
   B. January 1999
   C. January 2001
   D. January 2004

38. Which of the following is not a characteristic of the Fair Credit Reporting Act (FCRA)?

    A. limits on information revealed in a credit report
    B. restrictions on people's access to their credit reports
    C. penalties for people with low personal credit scores
    D. all of the above

39. How did World War II affect the U.S. economy?

    A. It created much-needed jobs.
    B. It bolstered the stock market.
    C. Both A and B
    D. Neither A nor B

40. What is the name of the period from about 1760 to 1840 that saw the development of steam power, a transition from rural to urban living, and a rapid increase in the use of machines to produce goods?

    A. The Industrial Revolution
    B. The Reconstruction Era
    C. The Scientific Revolution
    D. None of the above

Use the chart for Items 41 and 42:

Climate Change and Human Health

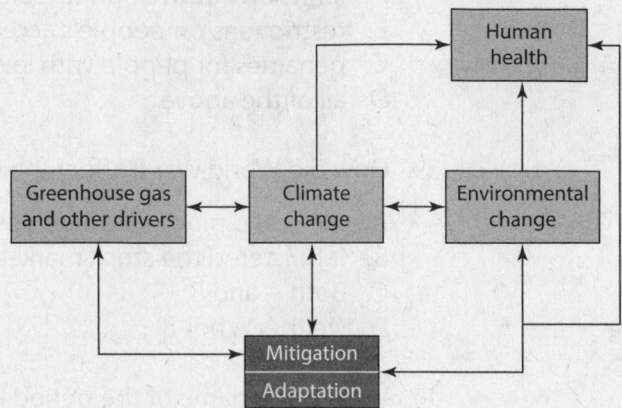

41. Which of the following does not directly influence human health?

   A. climate change
   B. environmental change
   C. greenhouse gas and other drivers
   D. All of the above

42. The following sentence contains a blank marked "Select...." Beneath it is a list of choices. Indicate the choice that is correct and belongs in the blank. (**Note:** On the real GED® test, the choices will appear as a "drop-down" menu. When you click on a choice, it will appear in the blank.)

   Select... ▼ is a factor that directly affects both climate change and environmental change.

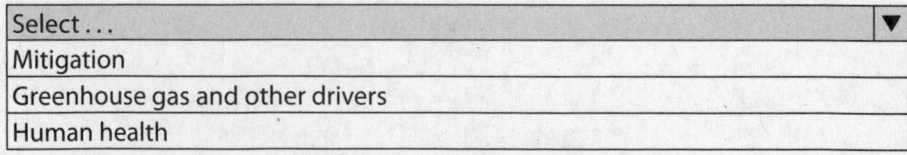

Use the map for Item 43:

Regions of the United States

43. In which region does South Dakota belong?

A. Middle Atlantic
B. The Northeast
C. The Midwest
D. Mountain

44. Scientists believe that people migrated from Siberia to Alaska more than 13,000 years ago by

A. sailing across the central Pacific Ocean
B. crossing a land bridge spanning the Strait of Gibraltar
C. crossing a land bridge spanning the Bering Strait
D. drifting on rafts in the Pacific Ocean currents

Use the following passage for Item 45:

To the People of the State of New York:

AFTER an unequivocal experience of the inefficiency of the subsisting federal government, you are called upon to deliberate on a new Constitution for the United States of America. The subject speaks its own importance; comprehending in its consequences nothing less than the existence of the UNION, the safety and welfare of the parts of which it is composed, the fate of an empire in many respects the most interesting in the world. It has been frequently remarked that it seems to have been reserved to the people of this country, by their conduct and example, to decide the important question, whether societies of men are really capable or not of establishing good government from reflection and choice, or whether they are forever destined to depend for their political constitutions on accident and force. If there be any truth in the remark, the crisis at which we are arrived may with propriety be regarded as the era in which that decision is to be made; and a wrong election of the part we shall act may, in this view, deserve to be considered as the general misfortune of mankind.

This idea will add the inducements of philanthropy to those of patriotism, to heighten the solicitude which all considerate and good men must feel for the event. Happy will it be if our choice should be directed by a judicious estimate of our true interests, unperplexed and unbiased by considerations not connected with the public good. But this is a thing more ardently to be wished than seriously to be expected. The plan offered to our deliberations affects too many particular interests, innovates upon too many local institutions, not to involve in its discussion a variety of objects foreign to its merits, and of views, passions and prejudices little favorable to the discovery of truth.

Among the most formidable of the obstacles which the new Constitution will have to encounter may readily be distinguished the obvious interest of a certain class of men in every State to resist all changes which may hazard a diminution of the power, emolument, and consequence of the offices they hold under the State establishments; and the perverted ambition of another class of men, who will either hope to aggrandize themselves by the confusions of their country, or will flatter themselves with fairer prospects of elevation from the subdivision of the empire into several partial confederacies than from its union under one government.

It is not, however, my design to dwell upon observations of this nature. I am well aware that it would be disingenuous to resolve indiscriminately the opposition of any set of men (merely because their situations might subject them to suspicion) into interested or ambitious views. Candor will oblige us to admit that even such men may be actuated by upright intentions; and it cannot be doubted that much of the opposition which has made its appearance, or may hereafter make its appearance, will spring from sources, blameless at least, if not respectable—the honest errors of minds led astray by preconceived jealousies and fears. So numerous indeed and so powerful are the causes which serve to give a false bias to the judgment, that we, upon many occasions, see wise and good men on the wrong as well as on the right side of questions of the first magnitude to society. This circumstance, if duly attended to, would furnish a lesson of moderation to those who are ever so much persuaded of their being in the right in any controversy. And a further reason for caution, in this respect, might be drawn from the reflection that we are not always sure that those who advocate the truth are influenced by purer principles than their antagonists. Ambition, avarice, personal animosity, party opposition, and many other motives not more laudable than these, are apt to operate as well upon those who support as those who oppose the right side of a question. Were there not even these inducements to moderation, nothing could be more ill-judged than that intolerant spirit which has, at all times, characterized political parties. For in politics, as in religion, it is equally absurd to aim at making proselytes by fire and sword. Heresies in either can rarely be cured by persecution.

—Excerpted from Federalist No. 1 by Alexander Hamilton

45. **Extended response**

Determine and evaluate the purpose of this passage. In Alexander Hamilton's view, which should have more power: the central (federal) government or the states? What reason did he give for his opinion? In your response, incorporate relevant and specific examples from the text to support your claim.

Write your response in the box on the following page. This task may require 25 minutes to complete.

PRETEST

✂ **Cut**   📋 **Copy**   📋 **Paste**   ↶ Undo   ↷ Redo

THIS IS THE END OF THE SOCIAL STUDIES PRETEST.

Answers and Explanations

1. **Correct answer: D.** Women in Wyoming were allowed to vote before this right was given by the 19th Amendment to the Constitution. The state government of Wyoming passed a law permitting women in Wyoming to vote before the national government granted this right through an Amendment to the Constitution. Once the Amendment was ratified, women in all of the states were allowed to vote.

2. **Correct answer: B.** Setting up an army and a navy. Setting up an army and a navy is an issue that affects the entire country, so this is a power that belongs solely to the national government. Regulating trade within a state and establishing a local school system are powers that belong to lower forms of government. Collecting taxes is a power that is shared between the levels of government.

3. **Correct answer: C.** Democracy.

4. **Correct answer: B.** Changes to a country's type of government may occur as a result of events that occur around the world.

5. **Correct answer: A.** Ideas from several historical types of government were incorporated into the structure of U.S. democracy. The United States Constitution established a government in which the people participate in making the laws and elect representatives, and the power of the leader is limited by a group of people who represent the interests of the citizens.

6. The completed chart should look like this:

Legislative Branch	Executive Branch	Judicial Branch
Collecting taxes	Approving laws passed by Congress	Declaring a law unconstitutional
Passing new laws	Granting pardons for offenses against the country	Settling disputes between the states

7. **Correct answer: D.** By forming governments, people give up some of their rights; however, their natural rights are then protected by the government. Locke believed that the purpose of government is to protect people's natural rights. Although some rights are given up when a government is formed, people's natural rights are protected.

8. **Correct answer: D.** All of the above. This answer correctly identifies that all of the answers are true.

9. **Correct answer: C.** The Kansas-Nebraska Act of 1854 allowed each new U.S. territory to determine whether or not slavery would be permitted within its borders. Popular sovereignty allows people to make decisions for themselves. The Kansas-Nebraska Act of 1854 is an example of this concept, because each new territory decided for itself whether to be a slave or free state.

10. **Correct answer: Secretary of State.** The table shows the order in which people would become President, should the previous person be unable to serve in that office. According to the 1947 act, the Secretary of State follows the President pro tempore of the Senate in the order of officials who would take the office of President.

11. **Correct answer: B.** Story believed that having two Senators from each state fairly represented the interests of all states, without favoring a particular group of citizens. Story explained that the way the Senate is organized is "of inestimable value," meaning that it is extremely beneficial. He goes on to explain that the voice of each state is represented, and that everyone's interests, not just those of a "predominant population," are represented.

12. **Correct answer: B.** the Senate impeachment trial that acquitted President Bill Clinton of charges brought by the House of Representatives (1999). As stated in Article I of the Constitution, the Senate, not the

Supreme Court, tries all impeachments. While the majority decides Supreme Court cases, a two-thirds vote is required to decide impeachments in the Senate.

13. **Correct answer: D.** The Speaker of the House and the President of the United States may represent different political parties and oppose each other on major issues. The majority party in the House is not always the same party that the President represents. The speaker and the President may be members of different parties, which can lead to opposing viewpoints.

14. **Correct answer: D.** When the citizens of the United States believe that an aspect of the Constitution should be changed, elected representatives in Congress should vote on whether or not to amend this document. Washington explained that when the people think that there is a problem with a power established by the Constitution, the problem should be corrected by amending the Constitution in the way that the document specifies. This process includes having the elected officials propose and vote on changes.

15. **Correct answer: C.** There was concern among many citizens that a strong federal government would fail to recognize the rights of individuals. The amendments in the Bill of Rights specify the rights of individuals and states. It can be inferred that when the federal government was first established, there were concerns that certain rights of individuals might not be recognized by that government unless they were stated in writing and appended to the Constitution.

16. **Correct answer: A.** An editorial article in a major newspaper publicly criticizes the performance of a government official. The First Amendment guarantees freedom of speech and freedom of the press. People have the right to state their opinion, either orally or in writing, and the press has the right to publish such opinions.

17. **Correct answer: C.** Decisions regarding personal rights. In each of these cases, the Supreme Court determined that the personal rights of an individual, or group of individuals, were being violated.

18. **Correct answer: A.** Amendment V states, "No person shall . . . be deprived of life, liberty, or property, without due process of law." The excerpt from the Magna Carta promises that no person will be prosecuted without being judged by his peers and the law. Amendment V guarantees the right to due process of the law.

19. **Correct answer: A.** Worldwide democracy is necessary for peace. Havel's statements that free citizens are necessary for free nations, and that freedom is "an integral part of any meaningful world order" support the idea that democracy is needed if there is to be peace between nations. The fact that Havel turned to the U.S. Constitution as an model for his own country's government also shows that he believed in the importance of democracy.

20. **Correct answer: B.** Many people forged trails and built western settlements along rivers. Many of the trails settlers traveled to reach the western frontier led along rivers and through mountain passes. The map shows several trails that follow the paths of rivers.

21. **Correct answer: C.** Martin Luther King, Jr. This passage is from King's "Letter from a Birmingham Jail." The repeated references to "Birmingham," the mention of a "nonviolent campaign," and the date are clues to identifying the passage.

22. Blank should be filled in with: Thomas Jefferson.

23. Blank should be filled in with: Reconstruction.

24. **Correct answer: D.** The Nineteenth Amendment, passed in 1920, granted women the right to vote.

25. **Correct answer: Susan B. Anthony.** Anthony was known for cofounding the first women's

temperance society and authoring a women's rights journal. Her actions helped paved the way for the passing of the Nineteenth Amendment, which gave women the right to vote.

26. **Correct answer: California Gold Rush.**

27. **Correct answer: B.** Socialism. The socialist system is characterized by public ownership of the means of production, centralized redistribution of goods and resources, and democratic rule.

28. **Correct answer: C.** The Egyptians. Although the first two characteristics could describe the Romans and Greeks, the ancient Egyptians were the only one of the three to use a hieroglyphic writing system.

29. **Correct answer: C.** The 111th Congress. The 111th Congress had 41 Republican senators, compared to 43 in the 103rd Congress, 49 in the 110th Congress, and 45 in the 113th Congress.

30. **Correct answer: A.** The 100th Congress. There were 258 Democrats versus 177 Republicans in House of Representatives in the 100th Congress.

31. The completed chart should appear as follows:

Characteristics of U.S. Political Parties

Democratic	Republican
Liberal	Conservative
Favors spending on social programs	Favors military spending
Favors strong, activist federal government	Favors less government interference in the economy

32. **Correct answer: B.** The Energy Policy Act of 1922. This act sought to increase energy efficiency and energy conservation. The correct answer can be found by the process of elimination; none of the other choices could

plausibly be concerned with "alternative fuels and energy conservation."

33. **Correct answer: A.** France. France sent colonists to settle the St. Lawrence River valley in Canada (today's Quebec) and areas of the Mississippi River valley down to New Orleans.

34. **Correct answer: World War I.** The League of Nations was created in 1919 during the Paris Peace Conference that ended World War I. The goal of the international cooperative organization was to arbitrate conflicts between nations and establish peace around the world.

35. **Correct answer: A.** Focusing on maintaining a strong U.S. influence in Latin America. U.S. foreign policy following the terrorist attacks of September 11, 2001, was generally preoccupied with antiterrorist efforts and relationships with Middle Eastern countries.

36. **Correct answer: D.** In a free market, when demand for a product is high, most likely producers will begin producing more of it, and as more of the product becomes available, its price will go down.

37. **Correct answer: A.** January 1997. By reading the graph, you can determine that of the years listed, 1997 was the only one with a 5.5% unemployment rate.

38. **Correct answer: D.** All of the above. The purpose of the FCRA is to protect the privacy and security of consumers.

39. **Correct answer: C.** Both A and B. World War II helped the United States recover from the Great Depression by forcing the creation of jobs producing war materials.

40. **Correct answer: A.** The Industrial Revolution. Beginning in Great Britain in the mid eighteenth century, the Industrial Revolution was marked by the beginning of large-scale production in factories run by water and steam power and by the building of railroads.

41. **Correct answer: C.** Greenhouse gas and other drivers. In the diagram, the arrows pointing away from the box go directly to Climate change and Mitigation/Adaptation. Although Greenhouse gas does affect Climate change, which affects Human health, the cause/effect relationship is not a direct one.

42. **Correct answer: Mitigation.** In the diagram, the box with Mitigation and Adaptation is the only one with arrows pointing to both Climate change and Environmental change.

43. **Correct answer: C.** The Midwest. This question tests your ability to read a map and distinguish the difference between region and place.

44. **Correct answer: C.** Scientists believe that prehistoric people crossed a land bridge that spanned what is now the Bering Strait. The land bridge is thought to have appeared due to the formation of large glaciers during the Pleistocene era; with so much of Earth's water "tied up" in ice, sea levels dropped and portions of the seabed were exposed.

45. **Extended response.** In response to this prompt, your essay should address Alexander Hamilton's view that the federal government should be dominant over the states. For example, Hamilton fears that without a strong central government, a certain "class of men" will "hope to aggrandize themselves by . . . subdivision of the empire into several partial confederacies." Additionally, you should incorporate background knowledge into the response. Your response should present the arguments of the Anti-federalists and the Federalists in the development of American constitutional democracy. You should cite multiple ideas from the source text that bolster your position.

If possible, ask an instructor to evaluate your essay. Your instructor's opinions and comments will help you determine what skills you need to practice in order to improve your essay writing.

You may also want to evaluate your essay yourself using the checklist that follows. Be fair in your evaluation. The more items you can check, the more confident you can be about your writing skills. Items that are not checked will show you the essay-writing skills that you need to work on.

My essay:

☐ Creates a sound, logical argument based on the passage.

☐ Cites evidence from the passage to support the argument.

☐ Analyzes the issue and/or evaluates the validity of the arguments in the passage.

☐ Organizes ideas in a sensible sequence.

☐ Shows clear connections between main ideas.

☐ Uses largely correct sentence structure.

☐ Follows Standard English conventions in regard to grammar, spelling, and punctuation.

Evaluation Chart

Check the Answers and Explanations section of the Social Studies Pretest to see which answers you got correct and which ones you missed. For each question that you missed, find the item number in the chart below. Check the column on the left to see the test content area for that item. If you missed questions in a particular content area, you need to pay particular attention to that area as you study for the GED® test. The pages of this book that cover that content area are listed in the column on the right.

Content Area	Item Number	Pages to Review
1. Civics and Government	1, 2, 3, 4, 5, 6, 7, 9, 10, 11, 12, 13, 14, 15, 16, 17, 18, 19, 29, 30, 31, 32, 45	671–699
2. United States History	20, 21, 22, 23, 24, 25, 26, 33, 35	705–750
3. World History	8, 27, 28, 34, 40	757–787
4. Economics	8, 36, 37, 38, 39	791–802
5. Geography	41, 42, 43, 44	807–816

Reasoning Through Language Arts (RLA)

The Reasoning Through Language Arts (RLA) Test

The Reasoning Through Language Arts (RLA) section of the GED® test measures your ability to read carefully, write clearly, and understand and use Standard English grammar.

There are 64 questions on the RLA test. You will have 150 minutes to complete the entire test, including 45 minutes for writing an extended response (essay) and a 10-minute break.

Many questions on the RLA test refer to reading passages. About 75 percent of these passages will be informational texts (nonfiction). The rest will be literary texts (fiction). There will not be any poetry selections. These questions test your reading comprehension ability.

Most of the RLA questions are multiple choice with four answer choices. All of the multiple-choice questions refer to reading passages. These questions measure how well you have understood what you read.

Other RLA questions use interactive formats such as drag and drop, fill in the blank, and drop-down. See "Introducing the GED® Test" at the beginning of this book for an explanation and samples of these formats. Some of these questions will test your mastery of basic English usage and vocabulary as well as your reading comprehension skills.

Your writing abilities will be assessed through short-answer and extended-response questions. For the extended-response item, you will have 45 minutes to write a persuasive essay to explain why you think one of two reading passages makes a stronger argument than the other.

The Reasoning Through Language Arts (RLA) Review

The following section of this book presents a comprehensive review of the skills that are tested on the RLA test. You will see examples of all of the kinds of passages that are included on the test and sample questions like the ones you will encounter on test day. Pay careful attention to the explanations for each example. They will help you become familiar with all the RLA question types, and you will learn test-taking strategies that can raise your score. If you have already taken the RLA pretest at the start of this book, make sure to study those sections that cover the types of questions you missed or found difficult.

This Reasoning Through Language Arts (RLA) review section is organized as follows:

Reasoning Through Language Arts (RLA)

Answers and explanations for all of the practice questions in this section are located at the end of the section.

CHAPTER 1

Testing Basic English Usage

Standard English

What is Standard English, and who sets the rules for it? **Standard English** is the accepted way that English should be spoken and written. It has been established by lexicographers (people who create dictionaries) and by the English language faculty at prestigious universities. Rules for basic English usage have been in effect for many, many years.

Why should you follow the rules of Standard English? There are several reasons to do so. When you speak English well, it is a sign that you are educated. When you do not follow the rules, people may make judgments about you. For instance, a prospective employer might notice that you make a lot of grammatical mistakes when speaking—that your English usage is not good. That might be a reason that you do not get a job.

When people use correct English, it helps them communicate. This could be over the phone, through an e-mail, or by texting.

Another good reason to use correct English is that what you say and/or write needs to be clear to the person listening to you or reading your communication. Faulty English may be misinterpreted.

You will be tested on the use of Standard English in the GED® Reasoning Through Language Arts test. There will be several questions asking you to edit a passage for errors in language usage. You will need to learn and practice the rules of basic English usage to do well on this part of the exam.

"Drop-Down" Questions

As you know, you will take the GED® test on a computer. This allows for the use of certain types of questions other than multiple choice.

The questions on language usage will all be "drop-down" questions. On the screen, you will see a passage in which, at several places, missing words have been replaced by the word "Select. . . ." When you click on the "Select . . ." arrow, you will see four answer choices. Each choice will show a possible way of filling the gap with words that make sense in the context of the passage. But three of the four will have grammar, usage, or spelling errors in them. Only one will be correct. You should click on the correct choice. Here is an example of a drop-down question:

1. The following letter contains a blank marked "Select...." Beneath the blank is a set of choices. Indicate the choice that is correct and belongs in the blank. (**Note:** On the real GED® test, the choices will appear as a "drop-down" menu. When you click on a choice, it will appear in the blank.)

Dear New Vista Green Member:

By joining our time-share club, you are guaranteed the best price for units as long as you commit to stay here for at least one Select... ▼ per year. Of course you have the option of staying here much more frequently than that.

When you click on the blank, you will see the following answer choices:

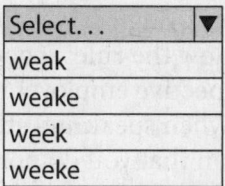

Select... ▼
weak
weake
week
weeke

Editing Mechanics

After any text is written, it usually needs to be edited in order to make sure that there are no mistakes. That is what you will be doing in this part of the GED® test. This chapter will review some common mistakes that people make when writing.

Capitalization

- The first word in a sentence is always capitalized.

  Many books have been written about ecology.

- Every main word in the titles of movies, plays, books, stories, magazines, newspapers, and songs begins with a capital letter.

  The Spy Who Came in from the Cold

  Detroit Free Press

- Words in titles that are not capitalized are short words, such as the articles *a*, *an*, and *the*; the short conjunctions *and*, *but*, *or*, and *for*; and short prepositions like *in*, *from*, *to*, and *into*:

  Your Child from Birth to Age Three

  Acquainted with the Night

  I Have a Dream

- Proper nouns (names, companies, places, and holidays, for example) are always capitalized. In place names like the Great Lakes or Indian Ocean, both parts of the name are capitalized:

    The National Hockey League is holding its championship games in Metropolitan Stadium near Lake Erie.

- Titles such as mayor, principal, aunt, and governor are capitalized when they appear before a name. Titles are not usually capitalized when they follow a name or are used without a name, unless they belong to a high office holder.

    Secretary of State Hillary Clinton met with Queen Elizabeth.

    The President met with a group of senators, congressmen and congresswomen, and presidents of top American companies.

- Do not capitalize the names of seasons: spring, summer, fall, winter.

EXERCISE 1

Capitalization

Directions: Rewrite the following sentences, putting in capital letters where they belong and taking out those capitals that are incorrect. The number of errors in each sentence is in parentheses.

1. The nurses' association is meeting in New York City. (2 errors)

    _____

    _____

2. The department of justice has an office in the Capitol building. (3 errors)

    _____

    _____

3. The Mayor spoke at the Labor Day Parade. (2 errors)

    _____

    _____

4. The City of Monterey, California, is located on the Pacific ocean. (2 errors)

    _____

    _____

Answers are on page 297.

Punctuation

End Marks

End marks are the punctuation marks that go at the end of a sentence. There are three common end marks:

- (.) The **period**, used after most statements—and also after abbreviations
- (!) The **exclamation point**, used after commands or statements that show excitement or strong emotion
- (?) The **question mark**, used for questions

Commas

Commas are used:

- After introductory dependent clauses beginning with words like *if, when, because, after, before, although,* or other conjunctions:

  Whenever danger threatens, small animals hide in their burrows.

- After two or more introductory phrases:

  At the back of the restaurant, there is a private room for parties.

- To separate three or more items in a list:

  The children rushed down the stairs, out the door, and into the yard.

- To separate two or more words describing a word that follows:

  The telephone operator had a pleasant, cheerful, clear voice.

- To separate two independent clauses joined by the words *and, but, not, for,* or *yet*:

  Bruce usually felt at home in the wilderness, yet tonight he was afraid for some unknown reason.

- To set off transitional or parenthetical expressions:

  My mother, on the other hand, is not feeling well.

  Of course, this is not the right time to discuss vacations.

- To set off modifying phrases:

  Christiana Ferrell, the new art teacher, is starting on Monday.

EXERCISE 2

Punctuation

Directions: Indicate the correct end mark after each sentence.

1. They were able to solve the problem without too much trouble

2. Do we have some time before the show begins

3. Watch your fingers when you use that knife

Correct the following paragraph for errors in comma usage:

On ice-covered lakes and seas ships called icebreakers are needed. These ships are used in the Great Lakes Atlantic Ocean and Baltic Sea. An icebreaker which has powerful engines has sides that are plated with metal. When the icebreaker lifts its front onto the ice the weight crushes the ice.

Answers are on page 297.

Sentence Fragments

A sentence always has two parts: a subject and a predicate. The predicate contains a verb. If one of these components is missing, the sentence is incomplete. It is a sentence fragment.

Threw the ball.

Can you tell what this fragment is missing? It is missing a subject. The sentence is incomplete because it does not tell who threw the ball. Here is one way to correct the fragment:

Josh threw the ball.

Now the reader knows it was Josh who threw the ball.

Here is another example of a sentence fragment:

The big red rooster.

In this case the predicate, including the verb, is missing. The reader does not know what the rooster did. Here is a corrected version:

The big red rooster charged into the hen house.

A predicate was added containing the verb *charged* and a prepositional phrase *into the hen house*.

EXERCISE 3

Sentence Fragments

Directions: Write **S** in front of complete sentences and **F** in front of fragments.

_____ **1.** Waited for a long time at the rail station.

_____ **2.** Wanted to go to the party with her friend.

_____ **3.** Nina went to the concert alone.

_____ **4.** She bought a ticket to the art museum to see the show.

_____ **5.** Looked all over the house for the watch his grandfather had given him.

Answers are on page 297.

Run-On and Fused Sentences

A sentence contains one complete thought. **Run-on and fused sentences** are sentences that contain two complete thoughts. A run-on sentence in which the two complete thoughts are separated only by a comma is called a **comma splice**; a fused sentence has two complete thoughts with no punctuation at all.

Here is an example of a fused sentence:

Harry went skating he loves to ice skate.

Here is an example of a comma splice:

Harry went skating, he loves to ice skate.

Both examples are run-on sentences.

The fastest way to fix a run-on sentence or a fused sentence is to put a period after the first complete thought and capitalize the first letter of the second complete thought.

Harry went skating. He loves to ice skate.

A second way to fix the problem is to put a semicolon between the two complete thoughts. In this case there is no need to capitalize the first word of the second complete thought. The two sentences joined this way should be closely related, as is the case here:

Harry went skating; he loves to ice skate.

EXERCISE 4

Run-On and Fused Sentences

Directions: Some of the following sentences are fused sentences or commas splices. If a sentence is correct as written, write **C** in the space. In each fused sentence or comma splice, underline the word that should begin another sentence.

_____ **1.** The children from the day camp enjoyed riding the roller coaster.

_____ **2.** A small group of coyotes may gather together in the evening they make eerie, howling sounds together.

_____ **3.** The doctor performed an emergency operation and saved the man's life.

_____ **4.** I looked in my backpack for my locker key, I couldn't find it.

_____ **5.** Mosquitoes are dangerous creatures most people aren't aware of how harmful they can be.

Answers are on page 297.

Misplaced and Dangling Modifiers

Misplaced modifiers modify the wrong word or seem to modify more than one word in a sentence. To correct a sentence with a misplaced modifier, move the modifier as close as possible to the word it modifies.

> *Misplaced:* Leaves fell gently down on the grass with bright autumn colors.

> *Clear:* Leaves with bright autumn colors fell gently down on the grass.

Dangling modifiers seem to modify no word at all. To correct a sentence with a dangling modifier, you must supply a word that the dangling phrase can logically modify.

> *Dangling:* Following their trail closely, the lions were located.

> *Clear:* Following their trail closely, the safari leader located the lions.

EXERCISE 5

Misplaced and Dangling Modifiers

Directions: Underline the misplaced or dangling modifier and rewrite the sentence so that its meaning is clear.

1. We ate dinner at an elegant restaurant with the Carsons slowly.

2. Joanna had a hot dish of cereal this morning before she left for work.

3. After running home, the television was turned on to watch the baseball game.

Answers are on page 297.

Parallel Structure

When writing or speaking, it is important to employ parallel structure. This means that the various components of a sentence are parallel or are in the same form.

> *Not parallel:* The hostess prepared for her party by cooking, cleaning, and to decorate.

Here the infinitive form of *to decorate* is not parallel to the gerund forms of *cooking* and *cleaning.* Here is how the sentence could be corrected:

> *Parallel:* The hostess prepared for her party by cooking, cleaning, and decorating.

It is not just verbs that need to be presented in a parallel manner.

> *Not parallel:* They spent the spring, summer, and the fall together studying frog behaviors.

> *Parallel:* They spent spring, summer, and fall together studying frog behaviors.

EXERCISE 6

Parallel Structure

Directions: Put **C** before the correct sentence of each pair.

_____ **1a.** It is more important to be healthy than to have wealth.

_____ **1b.** It is more important to be healthy than wealthy.

_____ **2a.** Marion is happy as long as she has clothes, food, and books.

_____ **2b.** Marion is happy as long as she has clothes, food to eat, and can read books.

Answers are on page 298.

Improving Awkward Sentences

Writers create awkwardness when they choose words poorly or arrange them so that the meaning of the sentence is not expressed well. You can usually tell just by reading a sentence whether or not it sounds right. Read this awkward sentence:

> Shout for joy was what Renee did after the track meet she won.

There are many better ways to write this sentence. Here are two good ways:

> Renee shouted for joy after she won the track meet.

> After she won the track meet, Renee shouted for joy.

Here is another example:

> *Awkward*: In the Bronx, General Colin Powell grew up, a section of New York City, in an immigrant family from Jamaica.

> *Clear*: General Colin Powell grew up in the Bronx, a section of New York City, in an immigrant family from Jamaica.

The second version is clear in what it is saying. The first version is confusing. Always make sure that the sentence flows in a logical manner and can be understood easily.

EXERCISE 7

Improving Awkward Sentences

Directions: In each pair, mark the version of the sentence that is clearer with a **C**.

_____ **1a.** One day, he almost made the mistake of running and diving into the deep end when the pool was empty.

_____ **1b.** He almost made the mistake one day of running and diving when the pool was empty into the deep end.

_____ **2a.** The explorer described her trip down the Amazon River in our social studies class in a canoe.

_____ **2b.** In our social studies class, the explorer described her trip down the Amazon River in a canoe.

Answers are on page 298.

Eliminating Informal or Nonstandard Words

Spoken English often differs from written English. Spoken English tends to be more casual and informal. But when you are editing a text, you need to eliminate these less formal and nonstandard words or expressions in order to make the written text more formal.

For instance, many people might say something like the following:

> The home team should try and win the game.

This may or may not sound correct to your ear, but the correct and formal way to say this is the following:

> The home team should try to win the game.

The meaning of the first sentence is unclear. It seems to suggest that the home team should try and also win the game, which is not the intended meaning.

Contractions are also not used as much in written Standard English. It is best to use two complete words, so *isn't* should be *is not* and *aren't* should be *are not*.

Slang should not be used in formal written Standard English. For example, the expression *wassup?* Should be changed to *What is going on?* or *What is happening?*

EXERCISE 8

Eliminating Informal or Nonstandard Words

Directions: Rewrite the following sentences into formal Standard English.

1. He's going to the movie tonight.

2. I can see you are worked up.

3. Where's it at, man?

Answers are on page 298.

Subject-Verb Agreement

In any sentence that you write, the verb must agree with the subject. To make sure that the verb and subject agree, you must first know whether the subject is singular (one person or thing) or plural (more than one person or thing).

In the sentence: *The bird spreads its wings*, the word *bird* is singular. Note how the verb changes when there is more than one bird:

The birds spread their wings.

Regular verbs generally have *s* (or *es*) at the end of the verb if the subject is singular. When the subject is plural, the verb does not end in *s* (or *es*).

Singular	Plural
She dances a lot.	They dance a lot.
He likes ice cream.	They like ice cream.

In simple sentences, it is relatively easy to figure out what the subject of the sentence is. But it is not quite as easy if the sentence is complex.

Intervening Prepositional Phrases

Sometimes people mistakenly think that a noun inside a prepositional phrase is the subject of a sentence.

The author of the stories uses a pen name.

In this sentence, the subject is the word *author*. However, the noun *stories* in the prepositional phrase "of the stories" is closer to the verb *uses*, so some people might mistakenly think that *stories* is the subject. *Stories* is plural, and if you think it is the subject, you might mistakenly change the verb *use* to the plural form, like this:

The author of the stories use a pen name.

Now the singular subject *stories* does not agree with the plural verb *use*. As a result, this sentence is incorrect.

Make sure to watch out for this kind of error when you take the GED® test.

Agreement with Linking Verbs

A noun that follows a linking verb and that renames the subject is called a **predicate nominative**. Sometimes a predicate nominative will be different in number from the subject. But even when that is the case, the linking verb should still agree in number with the subject. Do not change the linking verb to agree with the predicate nominative. In the following sentence, the subject is *act* (singular) and the predicate nominative is *clowns* (plural):

The first act was clowns doing funny tricks.

If you mistakenly changed the linking verb *was* to agree with the predicate nominative *clowns*, you would write, "The first act were clowns doing funny tricks."

This sentence is incorrect. The verb *were* should be *was* to agree with the singular subject *act*.

Agreement with Compound Subjects

Verb agreement becomes more difficult the more complex a sentence is. When the subject of a sentence is compound (more than one), you must pay attention to the conjunction that joins the compound parts and to the meaning of the entire subject. Only then can you know which verb form agrees with a particular compound subject.

Usually compound subjects joined by *and* or by *both . . . and* are considered plural. However, when the parts of the compound subject are actually parts of one unit or when they refer to the same person or thing, the subject is considered singular.

The shark and the porpoise are diving.

In this case, the compound subject *The shark and the porpoise* takes a plural verb.

Peas and carrots is a good side dish.

Here the subject, *peas and carrots*, is one unit and takes a singular verb.

With compound subjects joined by *or* or *nor* (or *either . . . or* or *neither . . . nor*), always make the verb agree with the subject that is nearer to the verb.

Neither the shark nor the porpoises are diving.

Either the shark or the porpoise is diving.

Neither the sharks nor the porpoise is diving.

Agreement in Adjective Clauses

A word group that describes another word in a sentence and that has its own subject and verb is called an **adjective clause**. The verb in an adjective clause must agree with its subject. The subject of an adjective clause is often a relative pronoun such as *that* or *which*. The number of the relative pronoun subject depends on the number of its antecedent in the main clause.

Opera is one of the entertainment forms that combine music, drama, and lavish costumes and stage sets.

Here the antecedent of *that* is *forms*, a plural noun. Therefore, *that* takes the plural verb *combine*.

Opera is the only one of the entertainment forms that is quite unfamiliar to me.

The antecedent of *that* is *one*, a third-person singular pronoun, and it takes the singular verb *is*.

Agreement with Collective Nouns

A noun that names a group is called a **collective noun**. Consider a collective noun singular when it refers to a group as a whole. In this case it would take a singular verb. Consider a collective noun plural when it refers to each member of a group individually. It would then take a plural verb.

Group	Individual
The committee is preparing a plan.	The committee are eating lunch.
The majority is in favor.	The majority are voting yes.

EXERCISE 9

Subject-Verb Agreement

Directions: Read the sentences. Write **C** in front of the sentences in which the subject and verb agree. Write **I** in front of the sentences in which the subject and verb do not agree.

_____ 1. All of the oceans in the world have whales.

_____ 2. A good field guide is one of the items that helps birdwatchers.

_____ 3. The northern oriole is an eastern United States bird that winters in Latin America.

_____ 4. Blue corn is one of those crops that is not common throughout the United States.

_____ 5. Careful planning and good luck was responsible for the successful moon landings.

_____ 6. So far neither soil analysis nor photo scans has established a noticeable trend.

_____ 7. The Riverdale Thunder are a new team.

_____ 8. Overfishing in some waters sometimes eliminate an entire species.

Answers are on page 298.

Verb Tenses

When editing, you should ensure not only that all the verbs agree with their subjects, but also that all the verbs are in the correct tense. It is a good idea to review the various verb tenses for the GED® test.

The **simple future tense** is always formed by inserting the word *will* before the verb.

> I will take a ride to town.

> You will find the book interesting.

The **simple past tense** for regular verbs is formed by adding *ed*, or *d*, if the verb ends in *e*. If a verb ends in *y*, change the *y* to *i* and add *ed*.

> I walked home through the woods.

> I hurried off to see the game.

The **continuous tenses** show action continuing in the past, present, or future.

> *Continuous past:* Marco Polo was bringing treasures from China to Italy.

> *Continuous present:* He is working on his essay for tomorrow's class.

> *Continuous future:* We will be talking about the test before you take it.

The **present perfect tense** is formed by using *has* or *have* with the past participle of a verb: *has started*, *have watched*. This tense is used to express an action or condition that occurred at some indefinite time in the past.

> We have washed the car.

The perfect tense can also be used to express the idea that an action or a condition began in the past and continues into the present.

> I have kept a daily account of my expenses since I began to work.

> My bank account has grown all year.

The **past perfect tense** is formed by using *had* with the past participle of a verb: *had found*, *had placed*. This tense is used to indicate that one past action or condition began and ended before another past action started.

> By the time the ticket office opened, a long line had formed.

The **future perfect tense** is formed by using *will have* with the past participle of a verb: *will have walked*, *will have seen*.

> By December I will have lived here six months.

English has a great number of irregular verbs, and these must be memorized. Here are some common irregular verbs:

Present	Simple	Past	Past Participle
I, you, we, they	have	had	had
He, she, it	has	had	had
I, you, we, they	do	did	done
He, she, it	does	did	done
I	am	was	been
He, she, it	is	was	been
You, we, they	are	were	been
I, you, we, they	read	read	read
He, she, it	reads	read	read
I, you, we, they	feel	felt	felt
He, she, it	feels	felt	felt
I, you, we, they	think	thought	thought
He, she, it	thinks	thought	thought

EXERCISE 10

Verb Tenses

Directions: Rewrite the sentences so that the verbs are in the correct tense.

1. I was in the shower when the phone rings.

2. Since the day when I wrote that poem, I wrote two short stories.

3. By the time I remembered that the roast was in the oven, it overcooks.

4. While he was speaking yesterday, the senator is shouting loudly to make a point.

Answers are on page 298.

Pronoun Usage

The correct use of pronouns is an important subject to review for the GED®
test. There will definitely be questions that will require you to choose the
correct pronoun.

A **pronoun** is a word that takes the place of a noun, a group of words
acting as a noun, or another pronoun.

A **personal pronoun** refers to a specific person or thing. Personal
pronouns are singular or plural. They are in the subjective or objective case.

	Singular Subject	Singular Object	Plural Subject	Plural Object
First person	I	me	we	us
Second person	you	you	you	you
Third person	he	him	they	them

He went swimming.

Betty saw her first.

We need to get some lunch.

You can do that homework later.

Call us when you can.

The **possessive pronouns** take the place of the possessive forms of nouns.

	Singular	Plural
First person	my*, mine	our*, ours
Second person	your*, yours	your*, yours
Third person	his*, his	their*, theirs
	her*, hers	
	its*	

*The starred possessive pronouns are used to modify another noun. *This is my dog.* The
possessive pronouns that are not starred are used alone: *This dog is mine.*

My name is Susanna.

Their party started late.

Our decision was a personal one.

This piece of cake is yours.

Its color was a light blue.

Reflexive and intensive pronouns are formed by adding -*self* or -*selves* to certain of the personal pronouns.

Singular	Plural
myself	ourselves
yourself	yourselves
himself	themselves
herself	
itself	

A reflexive pronoun refers to a noun or another pronoun and indicates that the same person or thing is involved.

> **I** promised **myself** to exercise more. (*Myself* refers to *I*.)
>
> **He** bought **himself** a new jacket. (*Himself* refers to *he*.)

A **relative pronoun** is used to begin a special subject-verb word group called a subordinate clause.

Subject: who, which, that

Object: whom

Possessive: whose

> The woman who was teaching the course was late.
>
> The man for whom the award was named was waiting in the hallway.
>
> That dog, whose owner was on vacation, would not eat its food.
>
> Her invention, which is very useful, can be found in many kitchens.
>
> Solutions that make our lives easier are always welcome.

Pronoun-Antecedent Agreement

The noun to which a pronoun refers is called its **antecedent**. The antecedent may be a noun, another pronoun, or a phrase or clause acting as a noun. A pronoun must always agree with its antecedent in number and gender. People are sometimes confused about which word is the antecedent of a pronoun in a sentence. In the following examples, the pronouns are in bold type and their antecedents are underlined.

> Abraham Lincoln gave **his** Gettysburg address in 1863.
>
> A lion and her cubs spend a good part of **their** day playing.
>
> You had better take care of **your** new phone.
>
> We are hoping to start out on **our** trip tomorrow.
>
> Linda went to Mexico during **her** school holiday.

EXERCISE 11

Pronoun Usage

Directions: Put a **C** in front of sentences that are correct and an **I** in front of sentences that are incorrect.

_____ **1.** Veronica asked Beverly and me to watch her dance in the final awards competition.

_____ **2.** She and me have been going to ballet lessons for years, but she is much better than I am.

_____ **3.** I thought Ted had gone to the play with they, but he was in the house playing video games.

_____ **4.** Lucille and Danny lost ourselves in their hobbies.

_____ **5.** Learning to swim turned out to be surprisingly difficult for my brother and I when we first tried.

_____ **6.** Participants in this marathon must train in all weather, for you cannot predict what the weather will be like here in April.

Correct the following paragraph for errors in pronoun usage:

Mariana wanted to learn to play the piano, but you knew how difficult learning the piano is for a beginner. Still she worked hard at it and oftentimes gave up your free time. She spent less time at the mall with your friends. In the end, she was pleased with yourself.

Answers are on pages 298–299.

Apostrophes and Possessive Nouns

Nouns Not Ending in *s*

Use an apostrophe and *s* to form the possessive of a singular or plural noun not ending in *s*, whether common or proper.

> boy's desk
>
> women's department
>
> Picasso's paintings

Plural Nouns Ending in *s*

Use an apostrophe alone to form the possessive of a plural noun ending in *s*, whether common or proper.

> the teachers' association
>
> the Beatles' albums

Singular Nouns Ending in *s*

The possessive of a singular noun ending in *s* (or an *s* or *z* sound), whether common or proper, depends on the number of syllables in the noun.

If the noun has only one syllable, use an apostrophe and *s*. If the noun has more than one syllable, you can usually use an apostrophe alone. (Note that some grammar styles dictate always using an apostrophe and *s*, no matter how many syllables.)

> the bus's tires
>
> Yeats's poetry
>
> the fox's paws
>
> Dickens' novels
>
> Sophocles' tragedies
>
> the duchess' piano

Compound Nouns

Put only the last word of a compound noun in the possessive form.

> her sister-in-law's birthday
>
> the court of law's rule
>
> my great-grandfather's coat

Joint Possession and Separate Possession

If two or more persons (or partners in a company) possess an item or items jointly, use the possessive form for the last person named.

Johnson & Johnson's laboratory

Rodgers and Hammerstein's musicals

If two or more persons (or companies) possess an item or items individually, put each one's name in the possessive form.

Keats's and Shelley's poetry

Beethoven's and Mozart's music

EXERCISE 12

Apostrophes and Possessive Nouns

Directions: Rewrite the underlined nouns so they are in a correct possessive form.

1. In Italian, <u>Florence</u> name is Firenze and <u>Venice</u> name is Venezia.

2. My sister and I went to several readings that featured <u>T. S. Eliot</u> poetry.

3. My father and my brother just started a new business and named it <u>Bailey</u> and <u>Bailey</u> Art Supplies.

4. David wrote an irate letter to the newspaper about the <u>editor in chief</u> column.

5. I could not find <u>Chris</u> new watch in the bureau where he said he put it.

6. The <u>ceremonies</u> leaders marched into the room one after the other.

Answers are on page 299.

Transitional Words and Expressions

Transitional words and expressions help create a smooth coherence in a sentence or paragraph. But probably more important, they show the relationship between two ideas:

- They can show order or time: meanwhile, so far, finally, at last, then, lastly, first, when, next.

  It was a four-hour hike; finally we reached the lake.

- They can show contrast or comparison: but, however, in contrast, on the other hand, similarly, unlike.

  We were late to the concert, but Jimmy and Bernard were early.

- They can show cause and effect: as a result, consequently, therefore, since, thus, because.

  The grill was out of gas; consequently, we did not have a cookout.

- They can provide an example or emphasis: in fact, for example, specifically, of course, that is, for instance.

  The fish were really jumping; for example, I caught one in two minutes.

- They can add to an idea: also, additionally, besides, furthermore, in addition.

  This product is an effective cream; additionally, it is affordable.

EXERCISE 13

Transitional Words and Expressions

Directions: Fill in each blank with a transition word or expression from the box.

as a result,	however,	for example,	in addition,

1. My French teacher speaks Portuguese and Italian; _____ she can read Spanish.

2. Science was a difficult subject for me in high school; _____ I avoided science courses in college.

3. Rome has many interesting buildings; _____ the Colosseum is a huge ancient arena.

4. Sam wanted some ice cream; _____ the store was out of it.

Answers are on page 299.

Frequently Confused Words

Some words are frequently confused with another word. For example, the word *its* and *it's* are often mixed up. *Its* is a singular third person possessive pronoun.

> Its nose is so cold to the touch.

It's is the contraction of *it is*.

> It's too late to get to the concert.

An easy way to figure out which form should be used is to ask yourself if the words *it is* would make sense in a sentence. If they do not make sense, use *its*.

Here are some other words that are often confused:

- *Their*; *there*; *they're*. *Their* is a plural third person possessive pronoun.

> The boys are eating their dinner.

There is an adverb.

> We should be there soon.

They're is the contraction of they are.

> They're about two hours away.

- *Who's*; *whose*. *Who's* is a contraction of *who is*.

> Who's the one who wants to go swimming?

Whose is a possessive pronoun.

> Whose ticket is this?

- *To*; *too*; *two*. *To* is a preposition indicating direction.

> I am going to the bakery.

Too means also.

> Jeremy has a new bike, too.

Two is a number.

> There are two tickets left.

- *Knew*; *new*. *Knew* is the past tense of the verb *to know*.

> He knew the deal would not go through.

New means latest or novel.

> The new model is much sleeker than the old one.

• *Passed*; *past*. *Passed* is the past tense of *pass* or an adjective that means *approved*.

> He passed the exam.

> The law was passed.

Past is a noun meaning history as in "the past" or an adjective meaning something bygone.

> The past seems so romantic to me.

> His past performance proves he is capable of handling the job.

EXERCISE 14

Frequently Confused Words

Directions: Fill in the blank with the correct word from the parentheses.

1. This _____ week has been exceedingly busy. (past, passed)

2. I will get to the additional work when I know _____ time to do it. (it's, its)

3. I wanted to start a _____ club, but no one was interested. (new, knew)

4. Robert tried _____ kinds of medicine for his rash. (to, too, two)

5. _____ going to the picnic today? (Who's, Whose)

6. _____ is no reason to change your outfit before the party. (Their, There, They're)

Answers are on page 299.

Testing Basic English Usage

Directions: The following passages contain several blanks, each marked "Select. . . ." Beneath each passage is a set of words, phrases, or sentences. Indicate the one from each set that is correct and belongs in the blank. (**Note:** On the real GED® test, each set will appear as a "drop-down" menu. When you click on your choice, it will appear in the blank.)

PASSAGE 1

To: Linda Jones

From: Ken Smith

Re: Fur Ball Fundraiser

Hi Linda,

You will never guess how successful this year's Fur Ball was this `Select 1... ▼` weekend. Thanks to a large turnout, many generous bids for auction items, and great organizers, some $4500 was cleared. This will be a great assistance to the shelter, which, as you know, has been suffering through cutbacks lately due to less city funding.

I want to thank you personally for donating the photograph of Honey. It was a great draw, and it brought in $550 on its own. People were anxious to actually have an original Moreno photograph. It was a fine thing for you to do, and we will be pleased to place you on `Select 2... ▼` for this past year.

I hope you enjoyed `Select 3... ▼`. The band and comedians were kind enough to donate their time, and the dinner was partially donated by the hotel, which made our lives a lot easier in terms of turning a profit.

Please drop by and say hello to all of our feline and canine residents as well as to me sometime soon. We would all `Select 4... ▼` of our latest plans for improving our facility.

Best wishes,

Ken

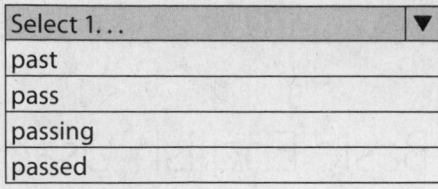

Select 1... ▼
past
pass
passing
passed

Select 2... ▼
our "wall of Contributors"
our "Wall of contributors"
our "Wall Of contributors"
our "Wall of Contributors"

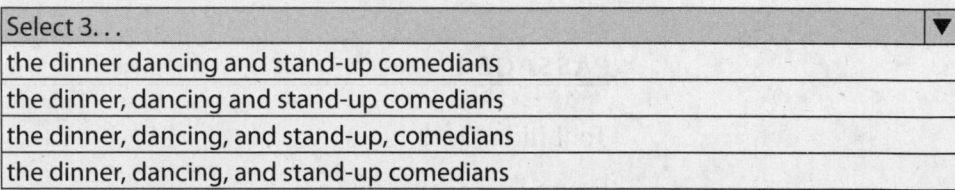

Select 3... ▼
the dinner dancing and stand-up comedians
the dinner, dancing and stand-up comedians
the dinner, dancing, and stand-up, comedians
the dinner, dancing, and stand-up comedians

Select 4... ▼
love to show you around and telling you
love showing you around and tell you
love to show you around and tell you
love to show you around and was telling you

PASSAGE 2

Dear Mr. Locke:

[Select 1... ▼] I am looking for summer employment or at the very least an internship.

My teacher, David Bianco, suggested I contact you about the possibility of finding a position with [Select 2... ▼] firm for the summer. He told me that you have been very receptive in the past about hiring students who are in his department.

I have experience working in offices and am an excellent keyboarder. Last summer I worked as a receptionist in a law firm, where there were more than 10 employees, and thoroughly [Select 3... ▼] myself. I am hoping that working at the [Select 4... ▼] office would prove an excellent experience and that I would learn a great deal.

Please let me know if you would like me to come by for an interview. I am enclosing my resume.

[Select 5... ▼]

Most sincerely,

Anita White

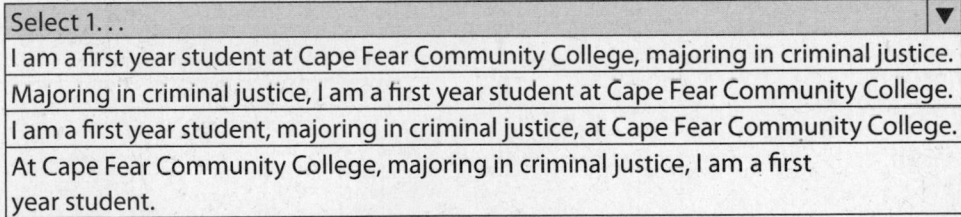

Select 1... ▼
I am a first year student at Cape Fear Community College, majoring in criminal justice.
Majoring in criminal justice, I am a first year student at Cape Fear Community College.
I am a first year student, majoring in criminal justice, at Cape Fear Community College.
At Cape Fear Community College, majoring in criminal justice, I am a first year student.

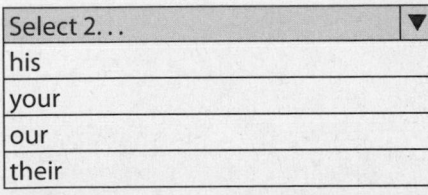

Select 2... ▼
his
your
our
their

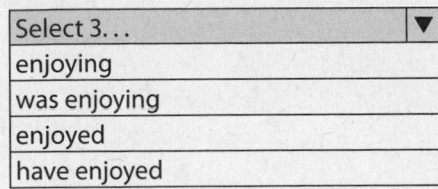

Select 3... ▼
enjoying
was enjoying
enjoyed
have enjoyed

Select 4... ▼
public defenders's
public defender's
public's defender's
public's defender

Select 5... ▼
I can't wait to hear from ya.
I look forward to hearing from you.
Hope to see you soon.
Bye now.

PASSAGE 3

To: All Employees

From: HR

Re: Upcoming Conference

A conference will be held at the Hudson Hotel [Select 1... ▼] Attendance is required. It will start promptly at 8:30 a.m., Saturday, and conclude at 8:30 p.m. following a group dinner. The Sunday portion runs from 11 a.m. to 4 p.m. Both days include lunch as well.

Mr. Charles Harding will be the leader of the conference. [Select 2... ▼] We expect all employees to be open-minded in their perception of the subject, which so often gets overlooked in the workplace.

If there [Select 3... ▼] any questions, contact Mary Suede at extension 231.

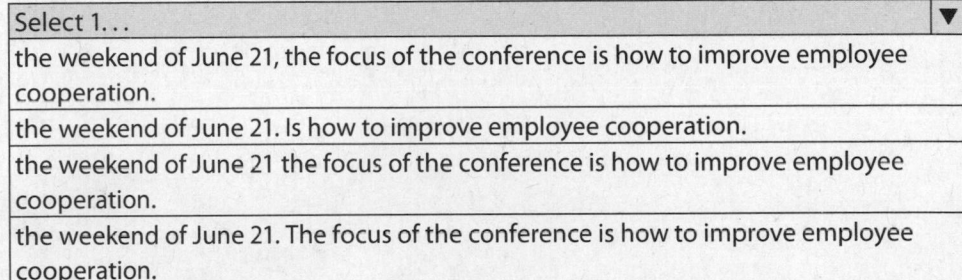

Select 1... ▼
the weekend of June 21, the focus of the conference is how to improve employee cooperation.
the weekend of June 21. Is how to improve employee cooperation.
the weekend of June 21 the focus of the conference is how to improve employee cooperation.
the weekend of June 21. The focus of the conference is how to improve employee cooperation.

Select 2... ▼
Employees will be asked to break into little groups, so that they can, in small groups, perform the exercises that are key to better cooperation in the workplace.
Employees will break into small groups to perform key exercises designed to improve cooperation in the workplace.
We ask that employees break into small groups, that way we can have them perform key exercises, which are designed to improve cooperation in the workplace.
After employees break into small groups, they will perform all the key exercises, which have been designed and used to improve cooperation in the workplace.

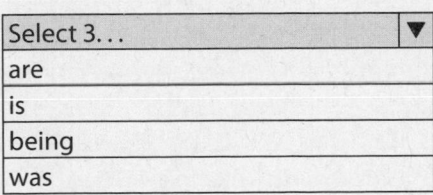

Select 3... ▼
are
is
being
was

Answers are on pages 299–300.

CHAPTER 2

Testing Reading Comprehension

Reading Comprehension on the GED® Test

The GED® test will measure your reading comprehension skills by asking questions that are tied to passages. Many of the questions will involve making inferences and drawing conclusions as well as providing evidence that support the conclusions. The GED® test will be based on the Common Core State Standards that focus largely on historic texts or foundational political documents of the United States. Other passages will come from the literature of the nineteenth and early twentieth centuries.

In this section you will learn how to interpret texts that may be somewhat more complicated than what you are used to reading. You will learn how to make inferences and how to recognize evidence that supports inferences. You will also learn about how to make connections between ideas found in texts.

Question Types

As you learned elsewhere in this book, because the GED® test is given on a computer, while most questions are of the traditional multiple-choice variety, there are other types of questions that are more interactive.

Multiple-Choice Questions

When taking the GED on a computer, just click on the correct answer of a multiple-choice question. There will always be four answer choices.

"Drag-and-Drop" Questions

"Drag-and-drop" questions will ask you to choose the appropriate information and drag it into the answer space. On the real GED® test, you will click on the correct answer(s) and drag them to the space indicated.

For instance, after reading a text, a question may look like this one:

Indicate each word that describes Anthony and belongs in the character web.

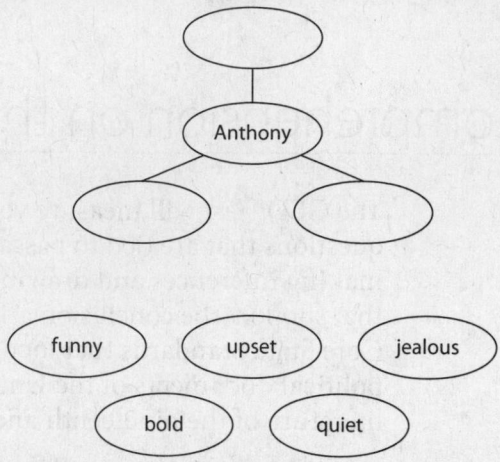

To answer the question, you need to click, one at a time, on the three words that best describe the character and drag each word into the character web.

Fill-in-the-Blank Questions

Another kind of question you may be asked on the GED® test is the fill-in-the-blank question. After reading a text, you might see this question:

Directions: Fill in the blank with the correct answer.

What city is the capital of the United States? _____

In this case you would simply input the answer to the question by typing in the blank.

Basic Critical Reading Skills

The Common Core State Standards stress critical reading skills, and the questions on the GED® test reflect this focus. The questions also vary in degree of difficulty. A few questions test your basic reading skills. Most questions on the GED® test measure your critical reading skills.

Identifying the Main Idea in a Text

The main idea of a text is what it is mostly about. The details that may also be included are usually provided mainly in order to expand on or support the main idea.

In some texts, the main idea is stated directly. In other words, in these texts the main idea is *explicit*. The sentence in which the main idea is stated is called the topic sentence. When the main idea is stated in this way, you do not have to analyze the details of the text to figure out what the main idea is.

Directions: Read the passage and decide which sentence expresses the main idea.

1   A visit to the town of Williamsburg in Virginia is a trip into our colonial American past. This is because the people there live, dress, cook, and travel just as they did 300 years ago. There are no TV sets, cars, or tall apartment houses. Instead there are small wooden or stone houses heated with wood stoves, and horses and wagons for travel. Williamsburg is a "theme" park in which volunteers re-create life as it was lived in colonial times. In the governor's palace, visitors can watch men and women in colonial dress prepare and serve a supper just as it was done in 1725.

Which sentence in the passage expresses the main idea?

A. "A visit to the town of Williamsburg in Virginia is a trip into our colonial American past."
B. "There are no TV sets, cars, or tall apartment houses."
C. "Instead there are small wooden or stone houses heated with wood stoves, and horses and wagons for travel."
D. "In the governor's palace, visitors can watch men and women in colonial dress prepare and serve a supper just as it was done in 1725."

Choice A expresses the main idea. It is what the passage is mostly about. The other choices are details that support the main idea. They tell more about it.

Finding Details in a Text

A few questions on the GED® test may ask you about specific details included in the text. In this case, you need to scan the passage and find those details in order to answer the question.

Directions: Read the passage. Then answer the question.

1   Invisible ink has a very long history. During the Middle Ages, lovers would send notes in invisible ink. Spies throughout the ages have used invisible ink to send secret messages. The oldest known ink for these secret messages is lemon juice, although milk is also satisfactory. Notes written in either become visible when you heat the paper.

2   At one time, department stores sold diaries with pages made from specially coated paper. A special pen came with each diary. Anything written in the diary would fade from view after a few moments. Along with the specially coated paper and pens came a development fluid called Inspection Fluid. When this was sprayed on a page, all the writing became visible once more.

3   The most sophisticated invisible ink was developed by the U.S. Navy. The writer used a special chemical to write with. The only way to read the message was by inserting it in a machine that focused powerful beams of lights on the writing. Only a person who owned one of these machines could read the message.

Which of the following is the earliest form of invisible ink?

A. blood
B. lemon juice
C. milk
D. water

To answer this question, you need to scan through the passage and find the information you need. You could look for the answer choice words, *blood*, *lemon juice*, *milk*, and *water* and see what the text says about each one. In his way, you could figure out that the correct answer is choice B.

Analyzing Implicit Main Ideas

Most texts on the GED® test will not contain explicit main ideas. The main idea will be *implicit*, meaning that you will have to figure it out based on the overall text and the details that are included. You will have to use your critical reading skills to answer this kind of question.

Directions: Read the passage and decide on its main idea.

1   In the seventeenth century, a woman was obliged to obey her husband, and all legal and public affairs were under his control. A woman's domain was the home, although, when necessary, widows operated businesses. Women were barred from the professions and from public life. They could not serve in government or hold religious office, and they were invisible so far as art or literature was concerned.

2   Colonial America provided two famous exceptions to this rule: Anne Hutchinson and Anne Bradstreet. Anne Hutchinson of Rhode Island became an active and controversial Protestant preacher in the 1630s and continued to preach publicly until her death in 1643. Anne Bradstreet of Massachusetts had a book of her poems published in London in 1650. She is generally considered to be the first important American poet.

What is the main idea of this passage?

A. During colonial times in America women were barred from public life.
B. During the colonial times in America women had to obey their husbands.
C. Two women obtained public recognition in male-dominated colonial America.
D. All legal and public affairs were under the control of men in colonial America.

The text talks about what colonial America was like for women. It gives details about what women were allowed and not allowed to do. It also tells about two women who were able to bypass these rules and do something notable. Choice A and choice B are details in the passage that support the main idea. So is choice D. The overall passage is about these two women and what they accomplished, so choice C is the main idea.

The GED® test may also ask you to identify a detail that supports a main idea. It is important to learn to distinguish between details that support the main idea and those that do not.

Directions: Read the following text, which is adapted from *Peter Pan* by J. M. Barrie:

1   When the children flew away, Mr. Darling felt in his bones that all the blame was his for having chained Nana [the dog] up, and that from first to last she had been wiser than he. Of course, as we have seen, he was quite a simple man; indeed he might have passed for a boy again if he had been able to take his baldness off; but he had also a noble sense of justice and a lion's courage to do what seemed right to him; and having thought the matter out with anxious care after the flight of the children, he went down on all fours and crawled into the kennel. To all Mrs. Darling's dear invitations to him to come out, he replied sadly but firmly, "No, my own one, this is the place for me."

2   In the bitterness of his remorse he swore that he would never leave the kennel until his children came back. Of course this was a pity, but whatever Mr. Darling did he had to do in excess, otherwise he soon gave up doing it. And there never was a more humble man than the once proud George Darling, as he sat in the kennel of an evening talking with his wife of their children and all their pretty ways.

The main idea is that Mr. Darling felt he was to blame for his children flying off. Which detail from the passage supports the main idea? Mr. Darling

A. was a simple man.
B. did things to excess.
C. would not come out of the kennel.
D. looked young except for his baldness.

In order to answer this question, you need to look at each answer choice and see which detail clearly relates to the main idea. Choices A, B, and D are details that tell about Mr. Darling, but they do not relate to his feelings, which are the main idea. Only choice C supports the main idea.

Making Inferences and Drawing Conclusions

One of the most important skills to develop for the GED® test is learning how to make inferences and draw conclusions. A large proportion of the questions on the GED® test will involve making inferences.

When you make an inference or draw a conclusion, you use evidence that is available to you in the text and make a calculated guess that is supported by that evidence.

For instance, if you read a story about people swimming in the ocean and relaxing in the water, you might infer that the water temperature is probably fairly warm and the waves are probably fairly calm. That might not be true, but it is the best guess that you can make based on the evidence.

Directions: Read the passage and answer the question.

1   The pitcher plant eats flies and other insects. It produces a sweet nectar that flies love. The nectar contains a drug that makes the fly drunk and less able to escape. The plant also has slippery spines that prevent the fly from crawling out. In addition, it has a little pool of liquid in the bottom of its pitcher-shaped leaves, and any fly that slips and lands in this water will drown.

Based on the information in the passage, what inference can you make?

A. Flies loathe the taste of sweet liquids.
B. Flies rarely escape from the pitcher plant.
C. Flies' population is increasing thanks to the pitcher plant.
D. Flies love to slide down the slippery spines of the pitcher plant.

First you need to analyze each possible answer choice and to figure out which is most likely true based on what the text tells you. The text describes the various features of pitcher plants that enable them to trap flies.

Choice A cannot be correct because the text says that the flies love the sweet liquid in the pitcher plant. Choice C is not supported by anything in the text. Choice D contradicts the text because it says that the slippery spines of the pitcher plant prevent the fly from crawling out. But choice B is a conclusion that is supported by the evidence in the text. Because pitcher plants are so good at trapping flies, few flies ever escape from a pitcher plant.

Identifying Textual Evidence

Some questions on the GED® test will ask you to identify evidence that supports an inference. The following example presents a text and an inference based on that text. See if you can identify the evidence that supports that inference.

Directions: Read the passage, and then answer the question.

1   Our modern diet consists of many kinds of meat and a variety of fruits and vegetables. We obtain protein, fat, carbohydrates, vitamins, and minerals from these foods. However, we do not really need such a wide variety of foods. We could eat a more restricted diet and still stay healthy. Some people, for example, eat only vegetables. Others eat fish or chicken along with their vegetables, but no other meat.

2   Some restrictive diets can provide all the nutrients we need. But one diet seems much too narrow to provide what we need to stay

healthy. This was the diet of the Inuit people of the Far North. A hundred years ago, the Inuit diet consisted only of meat and fish. Even the old name for the Inuit, "Eskimo," means "eaters of raw meat." Most nutritionists assume that such a diet is harmful to health. Yet the Inuit thrived on it until recently. Their diet was one of the most limited diets the world has ever known. Very few plants grow in the cold Arctic lands where the Inuit live. They had to survive on meat and fish or starve.

3   Nutritionists have been puzzled by Inuit resistance to disease—their diet lacked the carbohydrates, vitamins, and minerals we obtain from plants. Why did they have so little sickness? There have been many different theories. Perhaps some of the whales they ate had plants in their stomachs that provided the Inuit with vital minerals. But few people believe this.

4   Today, few Inuit follow the old ways of life. They eat store-bought foods rather than freshly caught seal meat and whale meat, and they suffer the same kinds of health problems as people in other modern societies. Perhaps we will never know why the old Inuit diet was so successful.

Based on the text, you might infer that nutritionists do not fully comprehend what makes a diet healthy. Which quotation is evidence for this inference?

A. "We obtain protein, fat, carbohydrates, vitamins, and minerals from these foods."
B. "Most nutritionists assume that such a diet is harmful to health."
C. "Nutritionists have been puzzled by Inuit resistance to disease—their diet lacked the carbohydrates, vitamins, and minerals we obtain from plants."
D. "They eat store-bought foods rather than freshly caught seal meat and whale meat, and they suffer the same kinds of health problems as people in other modern societies."

The first step in figuring out the answer is to analyze each sentence and see if it relates to the inference that has been made. Choice A makes a statement about what people obtain from food. This has nothing to do with the inference about nutritionists, so it can be eliminated. Choice B does mention nutritionists, but it does not present any evidence that nutritionists don't fully understand why a diet is healthy. Choice C also mentions nutritionists. It says that nutritionists have been puzzled by the Inuit resistance to disease even though the Inuit diet lacked the usual variety of carbohydrates, vitamins, and minerals from plants. This relates directly to the inference.

But before making a final choice, you need to look at all of the options. Choice D tells what the Inuit people eat today. That does not relate to the inference. So you can conclude that choice C is the correct answer. It provides evidence to support the inference that nutritionists do not fully comprehend what makes a diet healthy.

Inferences can be made regarding both nonfiction and fiction texts.

Directions: Read the following text, which is excerpted from *Swiss Family Robinson* by Johann David Wyss. Then answer the questions.

1   Early next morning we were awake, and went to our various jobs. My wife milked the goats and cow, while we gave the animals their food, after which we went down to the beach, to collect more wood for building our tree house.

2   To the larger beams we harnessed the cow and donkey so they could pull them. We ourselves dragged up the rest. Fritz and I then climbed the tree, and finished the preparations I had begun the night before. All useless branches we cut off, leaving a few about six feet from the floor, from which we would sling our hammocks, and others still higher, to support a temporary roof of sailcloth to keep us dry when it rained.

3   My wife tied the planks to a rope that passed through the block I had fixed to the branch above us, and by this means Fritz and I hauled them up. These we put side by side on the foundation of branches, so as to form a smooth, solid floor. Around this platform we built a wall of planks, and then throwing the sailcloth over the higher branches, we drew it down and firmly nailed it. Our house was enclosed on three sides. On the back side the great trunk protected us, while the front was left open to allow the fresh sea breeze which blew directly in.

4   We then hauled up our hammocks and bedding and slung them from the branches we had left for that purpose. A few hours of daylight still remaining, we cleared the floor of leaves and chips, and then climbed down to build a table and a few benches from the remainder of the wood. After working so hard all day, Fritz and I flung ourselves on the grass, while my wife arranged supper on the table we had made.

What is true of the narrator?

A. He is shortsighted about his goals.
B. He does not delegate work to others.
C. He is self-absorbed about his project.
D. He is able to do a great deal with a little.

To answer this question, you will need to look back in the text to see what the author of the story indicates about the narrator. The story tells about a family who have been shipwrecked on a deserted island, and their efforts to create a new home. It is clear that the narrator does not have a lot of tools to work with. He harnesses the cow and the donkey to pull up the beams for a treehouse.

Next, look through the answer choices and see which best describes the narrator. There is no evidence that choice A is true; the narrator does not seem shortsighted about anything. Choice B is not what the text portrays;

the narrator has his son working with him. Certainly choice C cannot be correct; rather than being self-absorbed, the narrator is occupied with seeing to the needs of his family. Choice D is an inference that is based on the evidence in the text. The narrator is able to do a great deal with very little.

Which quotation from the text best supports the inference that the entire family worked well together?

A. "My wife milked the goats and cow, while we gave the animals their food, after which we went down to the beach, to collect more wood for building our tree house."
B. "Fritz and I then climbed the tree, and finished the preparations I had begun the night before."
C. "Our house was enclosed on three sides."
D. "On the back side the great trunk protected us, while the front was left open to allow the fresh sea breeze which blew directly in."

Two of the sentences talk about working together; the other two, choices C and D, do not. Therefore, they could not be evidence about the family working well together. Choice B tells how the narrator and his son worked together, so this is a tempting choice. But it does not include the wife. Choice A tells about all three members of the family and how they worked together. That is the evidence you need to support the inference.

Drawing conclusions and making inferences are vital skills for solving questions about both fiction and nonfiction texts. Learning to find supporting evidence is essential whether you are analyzing a main idea, the motivation of a character, the viewpoint of the author, or the underlying premise of a text.

Making Connections Between Ideas

Within a text, different ideas typically connect to each other and affect the development of the text's main idea, theme, or argument. The main idea of one paragraph may be influenced, revised, or even contradicted by the main idea of a following paragraph. Identifying the main idea of each paragraph in a text can help you make generalizations and inferences about the entire text as well.

Learning to make connections between ideas in a text is an important skill. Your ability to connect ideas will be measured on the GED® test.

Directions: Read the following text and identify the main ideas in each paragraph. Then answer the questions.

1   What were the people like who came to our country hundreds of years ago and settled in what would become the thirteen colonies? Why did they come here? What did they care about?

2   Some early American settlers came here because they wanted the freedom to practice their own religion. They were willing to leave their native lands and suffer great hardship to worship in their own

way. Others came because they were merchants and wanted to earn money as traders. Many people who worked on the farms of rich English landlords dreamed of owning their own farms. They felt sure that the combination of hard work and fertile American soil would assure any farmer success. The people who came here in search of religious freedom, farmland, or opportunities to trade were often poor. They were still better off, however, than the many people who came to America with virtually nothing.

3   The very poorest folk were, of course, the slaves. These African men and women were captured, often as the result of tribal warfare, and sold to slave boat captains. Those who survived the horrendous journey across the Atlantic worked mainly in the South as field hands. Some history books do not sufficiently emphasize the number of slaves in early America. There were more slaves than merchants, more slaves than farm owners, more slaves than craftsmen, more slaves than people seeking freedom from religious oppression. One out of every five people who lived here in 1750 was a slave. In Virginia, almost half the population consisted of slaves, and in South Carolina, more than half.

4   In addition to slaves, America had many indentured servants. An indentured servant agreed to work for a master for four years, usually in return for the passage to America. Indentured servants differed from slaves because they were freed after four years. But during that time, some of them were treated almost as badly as slaves. Indentured servants could even be sold at auctions just like slaves, and, like slaves, they had no control over who bought them.

5   In addition, there is one other group of Americans that is rarely discussed in our history books—the men and women who were shipped to the colonies, particularly Georgia, as punishment for their crimes. Once they obtained their freedom, many of them became hard-working, skilled, and honest people.

6   America was settled by a diverse collection of people. It is time we honored everyone who came from overseas to help build this country.

How does the main idea of paragraph 3 influence the development of the text?

A. It develops the main idea that people coming to the colonies were seeking religious freedom.
B. It adds to the main idea by showing that many different kinds of people came to the colonies.
C. It expands the main idea by stating that some people coming to the colonies came against their will.
D. It increases the importance of the main idea by showing that people came to the colonies from many different places.

Paragraph 3 talks about how African Americans came to the colonies as slaves. This is additional information about the early settler population. Unlike the people discussed earlier in the text who came of their own free will, the slaves were forced to come to the colonies.

Choice A is not correct. The idea that some settlers came in search of religious freedom is found in paragraph 2. Choice B is not correct. Although paragraph 3 shows that many different kinds of people came to the colonies, this idea is not what the paragraph contributes to the main idea. Choice D is truc, but this is not the main point of paragraph 3. Choice C is the correct answer. The idea that some people came to the colonies against their will is what paragraph 3 adds to the main idea of the overall text.

What does the text suggest about America today?

A. It offers great economic opportunities.
B. It is a melting pot of different kinds of people.
C. Its role in history is still unknown.
D. Its history is similar to that of other countries.

The text talks about the various kinds of people who came to the colonies. If you generalize this information and apply it to the country today, it is likely you would come up with choice B as the answer. This is a generalization you can make based on the information in the text. Choice A has nothing to do with the information in the text. Choices C and D do not make much sense either.

Testing Reading Comprehension

Directions: Read the following text, which is excerpted from an essay by the naturalist John Burroughs. Then answer the questions that follow.

1   We often hear it said of a man that he was born too early, or too late, but is it ever true? If he is behind his times, would he not have been behind at whatever period he had been born? If he is ahead of his times, is not the same thing true? In the vegetable world the early flowers and fruit blossoms are often cut off by the frost, but not so in the world of man. Babies are in order at any time. Is a poet, or a philosopher, ever born too late? or too early? If Emerson had been born a century earlier, his heterodoxy would have stood in his way; but in that case he would not have been a heretic. Whitman would have had to wait for a hearing at whatever period he was born. He said he was willing to wait for the growth of the taste for himself, and it finally came. Emerson's first thin volume called "Nature" did not sell the first edition of five hundred copies in ten years, but would it have been different at any other time? A piece of true literature is not superseded. The fame of man may rise and fall, but it lasts. Was Watt too early with his steam-engine, or Morse too early with his telegraph? Or Bell too early with his telephone? Or Edison with his phonograph or his incandescent light? Or the Wright brothers with their flying-machine? Or Henry Ford with his motor car? Before gasoline was discovered they would have been too early, but then their inventions would not have materialized.

2   The world moves, and great men are the springs of progress. But no man is born too soon or too late.

1. Which quotation from the text supports the idea that Burroughs believes people are born when they are meant to be born?

   A. "If he is behind his times, would he not have been behind at whatever period he had been born?"
   B. "Babies are in order at any time."
   C. "A piece of true literature is not superseded."
   D. "But no man is born too soon or too late."

2. What is true of the author?

   A. He has little imagination.
   B. He is reflective by nature.
   C. He thinks that life is too short.
   D. He worries about meaningless things.

3. What does the text suggest about life?

   A. People are born randomly in time.
   B. Time does not matter in the long run.
   C. It is unimportant when people are born.
   D. There is a reason that people are born when they are.

Directions: Read the following text, which is excerpted from *Love of Life* by Jack London. Then answer the questions that follow.

1   He was lost and alone, sick and injured too badly to walk upright. He crawled on. There came frightful days of snow and rain. He did not know when he made camp, when he broke camp. He traveled in the night as much as in the day. He rested wherever he fell and crawled on whenever the dying life in him flickered up and burned less dimly. He did not try. It was the life in him, unwilling to die, that drove him on. He didn't suffer. His nerves had become blunted and numb, while his mind was filled with weird visions and delicious dreams.

2   There were some members of a scientific expedition on the whaleship, Bedford. From the deck they saw a strange object on the shore. It was on the beach, moving towards the water. They couldn't tell what it was. Being scientists, they took a boat to see. They saw something alive; but it hardly looked like a man. It was blind, unconscious, and crawled on the beach like a giant worm. Most of its effort to crawl was useless, but it kept trying. It turned and twisted, moving about 20 feet an hour.

3   Three weeks afterwards the man lay in a bunk on the whaleship, and with tears streaming down his wasted cheeks told who he was and what he had undergone. He also babbled words that made no sense: about his mother, of sunny Southern California, and a home among the orange groves and flowers.

4   The days were not many after that when he sat at table with the scientific men and ship's officers. He was happy over the sight of so much food, watching it anxiously as it went into the mouths of others. With the disappearance of each mouthful, an expression of deep regret came into his eyes. He was quite sane, yet he hated those men at mealtimes because they ate so much food. He was haunted by a fear that it would not last. He inquired of the cook, the cabin-boy, the captain concerning the food stores. They reassured him countless times; but he could not believe them and pried cunningly about the food storage chest to see with his own eyes.

5   It was noticed that the man was getting fat. He grew stouter with each day. The scientific men shook their heads and theorized. They limited the man at his meals, but still his girth increased and his body grew fatter under his shirt.

6   The sailors grinned. They knew. And when the scientific men followed the man, they knew, too. They saw him bent over after breakfast, and like

a mendicant, with outstretched palm, stop a sailor. The sailor grinned and passed him a fragment of sea biscuit. He clutched it avariciously, looking at it as a miser looks at gold, and thrust it inside his shirt. Similar were the donations from other grinning sailors.

7   The scientific men respected the man's privacy. They left him alone. But they secretly examined his bunk. It was lined with seamen's crackers; the mattress was stuffed with crackers; every nook and cranny was filled with crackers. Yet he was sane. He was taking precautions against another possible famine—that was all. He would recover from it, the scientific men said; and he did, 'ere the Bedford's anchor rumbled down in San Francisco.

4. Which quotation from the text best supports the idea that the scientists were not disturbed by the man hiding food in his bunk?

   A. "They saw something alive, but it hardly looked like a man."
   B. "The scientific men shook their heads and theorized."
   C. "They saw him bent over after breakfast, and like a mendicant, with outstretched palm, stop a sailor."
   D. "He was taking precautions against another possible famine—that was all."

5. What is the main idea of the passage?

   A. how scientists study behavior
   B. how a starving man recuperated
   C. what kind of food a starving person ate
   D. why scientists picked up a starving person

6. Why did the man store biscuits in his mattress?

   A. He enjoyed stealing.
   B. He wanted to feed the wildlife on shore.
   C. He knew that biscuits were in short supply.
   D. He wanted to be prepared in case the ship ran out of food.

7. What generalization can be made based on the story?

   A. Humans are resilient.
   B. Scientists are emotional.
   C. Humans have many needs.
   D. Scientists enjoy helping others.

Directions: Read the following text, which is excerpted from *Lincoln* by Emil Ludwig. Then answer the questions that follow.

1   The postmastership seems to have become his main source of income; he holds it four years and finds it advantageous in many ways. He is appointed because people trust him, and because he can write and read so well; now

he can enjoy a first reading of all the newspapers brought by the post-coach. That is an old privilege of western postmasters, and the subscriber is apt to expect, when he receives his journal, that the postmaster will be so obliging as to give him an abstract of the contents. The recipient of a letter, too, generally gets the postmaster to read it aloud to him; or, if he is one of the lucky ones who can read, he will not be such a curmudgeon as to keep all the news to himself. This is very agreeable to our anecdotalist and student of human nature; and as he goes his rounds, carrying all the undelivered letters in his hat, he gets to know folk more intimately.

2   All this brings him day after day into touch with the varied thoughts of the people. He learns about classes, temperaments, grades of life, types of character; and during the next few years, in this remote settlement, he gains by direct observation such treasures of human experience as no formal process of education on the grand scale could ever have supplied.

3   Still, he remains an omnivorous reader. All is grist that comes to his mill: besides the newspapers which pass through his hands as postmaster, he gets books from wayfarers, some of them light reading. When by a lucky chance an emigrant in a covered wagon wants to get rid of a barrel full of rubbish, Lincoln good-naturedly buys it. A few days later, emptying his new acquisition, he finds amid the plunder the four volumes of a famous work, Blackstone's "Commentaries on the Laws of England," the most notable law book of the day. This supplies him with a hundred important ideas and teaches him where to look for additions to his knowledge. He borrows more books from judges and lawyers and immerses himself in study, withdrawing for a time from his comrades.

4   But he soon gets acquainted with a vagabond of artistic temperament, an inspired loafer who spends most of his time on the river bank with rod and line and knows by heart long passages of Shakespeare and Burns. He quotes them feelingly to Lincoln, and lends him the originals, thus opening new worlds to his friend. Lincoln, however, is most eager to get hold of history books. In them he discovers that the fathers of his country were more or less opposed to slavery; that Washington and Adams, Jefferson and Madison, Franklin and Hamilton—in their various ways the best men in the land, and some of them slave owners—wanted to check the spread of the system. Ever ready to store up anecdotes in his mind, he cannot fail to note and to remember that Washington would not have a runaway Negress hunted and recaptured, but left it to her free choice whether she would stay away or return.

5   However, the reading of books and desultory conversations do not provide a living. The store, naturally, does not flourish, and the day comes when store and contents are seized by creditors. Berry decamps, and Lincoln has to shoulder the whole burden of debt, eleven hundred dollars in all. Daily bread can be earned readily enough, and in addition to such casual earnings he has his salary as postmaster. Enough for current expenses; but how on earth is he to free himself from the crushing load of his debts?

8. What can the reader conclude about Lincoln?

    A. He loved learning.
    B. He was competitive.
    C. He was light hearted.
    D. He longed for excitement.

9. Which quotation supports the idea that Lincoln was interested in the subject of slavery?

    A. "He is appointed because people trust him, and because he can write and read so well; now he can enjoy a first reading of all the newspapers brought by the post-coach."
    B. "All is grist that comes to his mill: besides the newspapers which pass through his hands as postmaster, he gets books from wayfarers, some of them light reading."
    C. "In them he discovers that the fathers of his country were more or less opposed to slavery; that Washington and Adams, Jefferson and Madison, Franklin and Hamilton—in their various ways the best men in the land, and some of them slave owners—wanted to check the spread of the system."
    D. "The store, naturally, does not flourish, and the day comes when store and contents are seized by creditors."

10. How does paragraph 4 develop the main idea of the text? It shows that Lincoln

    A. did not like poetry.
    B. was not very sociable.
    C. was particular about whom he talked to.
    D. was open to knowing all kinds of people.

11. Based on the text, what generalization can be made? People who want to

    A. be trusted do not read other people's mail.
    B. stand out must learn to keep away from trouble.
    C. get ahead must work hard to learn what they need to know.
    D. become successful must study how to be good businessmen.

12. Which detail supports the main idea?

    A. Lincoln's store closes.
    B. Lincoln has a lot of debt.
    C. Lincoln knew about slavery.
    D. Lincoln obtains books to read.

Answers are on pages 300–301.

CHAPTER 3

Structure and Author's Choices

Sequence of Events

When you read texts, it is important to take note of the order in which events occur. The GED® test will ask you about the sequence of events to make sure you are following the way in which a text unfolds. The GED® test may use a "drag-and-drop" question type for this kind of question.

Directions: Read the following text, which is excerpted from *White Fang* by Jack London. Then answer the question.

1   In midsummer White Fang had an experience. Trotting along in his silent way to investigate a new teepee which had been erected on the edge of the village while he was away with the hunters after moose, he came full upon Kiche. He paused and looked at her. He remembered her vaguely, but he remembered her, and that was more than could be said for her. She lifted her lip at him in the old snarl of menace, and his memory became clear. His forgotten cubhood, all that was associated with that familiar snarl, rushed back to him. Before he had known the gods, she had been to him the center-pin of the universe. The old familiar feelings of that time came back upon him, surged up within him. He bounded toward her joyously, and she met him with shrewd fangs that laid his cheek open to the bone. He did not understand. He backed away, bewildered and puzzled.

2   But it was not Kiche's fault. A wolfmother was not made to remember her cubs of a year or so before. So she did not remember White Fang. He was a strange animal, an intruder; and her present litter of puppies gave her the right to resent such intrusion.

3   One of the puppies sprawled up to White Fang. They were half-brothers, only they did not know it. White Fang sniffed the puppy curiously, whereupon Kiche rushed upon him, gashing his face a second time. He backed farther away. All the old memories and associations died down again and passed into the grave from which they had been resurrected. He looked at Kiche licking her puppy and stopping now and then to snarl at him. She was without value to him. He had learned to get along without her. Her meaning was forgotten. There was no place for her in his scheme of things, as there was no place for him in hers.

Indicate the order in which the following events took place.

Order of Events

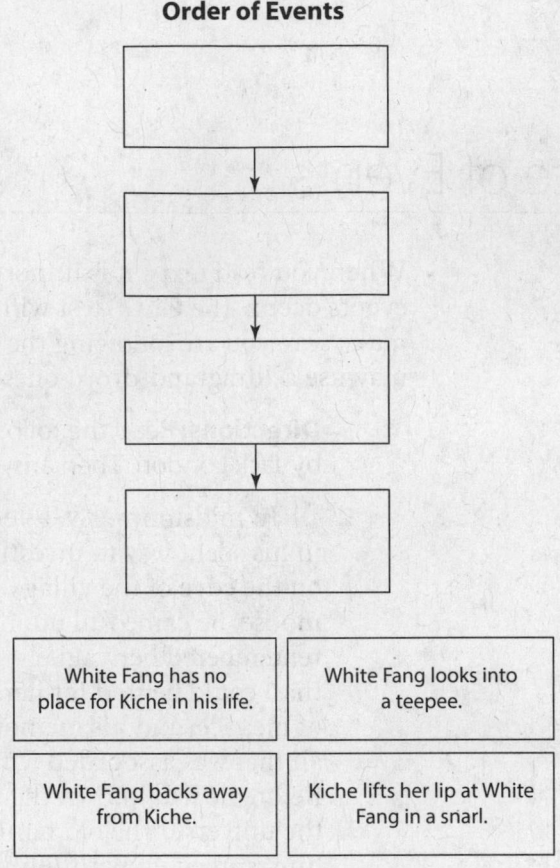

White Fang has no place for Kiche in his life.	White Fang looks into a teepee.
White Fang backs away from Kiche.	Kiche lifts her lip at White Fang in a snarl.

To complete this task, you will need to return to the text and see in what order the events took place. You can then select the event that happened first. In this case it is "White Fang looks into a teepee." Then look through the other possibilities. See which happens next. Go back to the text and trace the action. You will see that the next event is "Kiche lifts her lip at White Fang in a snarl." The third event is "White Fang backs away from Kiche," which makes sense. Finally, "White Fang has no place for Kiche in his life" is the last event.

After you have figured out the order of the events, indicate that order by following the given directions. On the real GED® test you, will "drag and drop" each event into the proper box on the computer screen. The completed chart will look like this.

Order of Events

```
┌─────────────────────────┐
│  White Fang looks into   │
│       a teepee.          │
└─────────────────────────┘
            │
            ▼
┌─────────────────────────┐
│  Kiche lifts her lip at  │
│   White Fang in a snarl. │
└─────────────────────────┘
            │
            ▼
┌─────────────────────────┐
│   White Fang backs away  │
│       from Kiche.        │
└─────────────────────────┘
            │
            ▼
┌─────────────────────────┐
│  White Fang has no place │
│    for Kiche in his life.│
└─────────────────────────┘
```

Structural Relationships

Authors make many decisions as they write. One of them is what information to include and where to place it. Each part of a text builds on the preceding part. Each sentence, paragraph, or section fits into the overall structure and contributes to the development of ideas.

The GED® test will ask you questions about how a particular sentence or paragraph helps to develop and contribute to the overall point of the text. Some questions will also ask how the structure of a paragraph or section of a text shapes its meaning, emphasizes certain ideas, and reinforces an author's purpose.

Some questions may also ask how one paragraph develops or refines a key concept or how one idea is distinguished from another.

Lastly, some questions may ask how the structure of a paragraph or section emphasizes a key idea or supports the author's purpose.

Directions: Read the following message to the troops from General Dwight David Eisenhower before the D-Day invasion of Europe (1944). Then answer the questions.

1   Soldiers, Sailors and Airmen of the Allied Expeditionary Force! You are about to embark upon a great crusade, toward which we have striven these many months. The eyes of the world are upon you. The hopes and prayers of liberty loving people everywhere march with you. In company with our brave Allies and brothers in arms on other fronts, you will bring about the destruction of the German war machine, the elimination of Nazi tyranny over the oppressed peoples of Europe, and security for ourselves in a free world.

2   Your task will not be an easy one. Your enemy is well trained, well equipped and battle hardened, he will fight savagely.

3   But this is the year 1944! Much has happened since the Nazi triumphs of 1940–41. The United Nations have inflicted upon the Germans great defeats, in open battle, man to man. Our air offensive has seriously reduced their strength in the air and their capacity to wage war on the ground. Our home fronts have given us an overwhelming superiority in weapons and munitions of war, and placed at our disposal great reserves of trained fighting men. The tide has turned! The free men of the world are marching together to victory!

4   I have full confidence in your courage, devotion to duty and skill in battle. We will accept nothing less than full victory!

5   Good Luck! And let us all beseech the blessings of Almighty God upon this great and noble undertaking.

How does paragraph 1 convey a key idea of the message? It says that

A. the world is not free.
B. the Germans have been winning.
C. the effort of the troops is vitally important to the world.
D. the Nazis are no longer as strong as they were.

Paragraph 1 talks about how the troops are going on a crucial mission and how much support they have from people around the world. Choice A is clearly incorrect. While part of the world, General Eisenhower says, is not free, this is not true of the entire world. Choice B is not correct. Although General Eisenhower does mention the German war machine, this is not the point of the paragraph. Choice D is not correct either. Choice C is the correct answer.

Why did General Eisenhower include the sentence "The tide has turned!" in his message?

A. to give the troops hope
B. to announce that the war was ending
C. to explain why the invasion will be difficult
D. to suggest that the invasion was about to take place

Choice A is the correct answer. This is the intent of the sentence. Choice B is not suggested by the paragraph or by the message as a whole. Choices C and D are not the reasons why the sentence was included.

Author's Language

It is important to notice what words an author chooses because those words can influence a text in many ways. They can help you understand relationships between ideas, can give you clues to unknown words, can suggest subtle distinctions, and can create tone. The words that an author uses can lend color and interest to a text, making it fuller and more meaningful.

Transitional Words

Authors often use transitional words to show relationships between ideas in a text. Such words as *however, nevertheless, consequently,* and *otherwise* help you understand how one idea links to another and make the intent or purpose of the author clearer.

Directions: Read the following text. Then answer the question.

1   The loggerhead turtle mates in the ocean and returns to shore to lay her eggs. She crawls up the beach and, using her two back flippers, digs a small hole about 18 inches in depth, deposits about a hundred eggs, and slowly wends her way back to the sea. The round and white eggs, resembling ping pong balls, rest in this warm cavity under the sand for about three months before hatching.

2   The period after hatching is more dangerous for the tiny turtles than battles are for most soldiers. The little hatchlings must cross the beach to return to the ocean. In doing so, they must avoid such predators as gulls and other birds eager for a meal. In order to escape from these predators, the baby turtles scurry into the ocean late at night. However, another problem may prevent them from finding their way safely to the ocean. When they leave their nest and try to find the ocean, their instinct directs them to head for the brightest object they see. Long ago this worked well because the brightest object at night was the sea sparkling with moonlight. But today the brightest object might be a lamppost on the beach or a car's headlights. Turtles who are diverted from their course by these bright objects may never find their way into the ocean. Even if they find the ocean, they still may fall prey to birds, fish, and crabs. Few turtle hatchlings live to be adults, but if they do, they may survive for up to twenty years.

Why does the author use the word *However* in paragraph 2 to introduce the problem that bright artificial lights pose for hatchlings?

A. to compare the hatchling turtles to soldiers facing danger in battle
B. to explain that lamplights and car headlights can be brighter than the moon
C. to emphasize that man-made items now add to the natural obstacles that hatchlings face
D. to illustrate the relationship between the hatchlings and predators such as gulls and crabs

The answer is choice C. The author uses the word *However* to emphasize the idea that today's lampposts and car headlights add an extra layer of difficulty to the natural obstacles that turtle hatchlings face in their struggle for survival.

Context Clues

If in your reading you encounter an unknown word or phrase, one way to figure out its meaning is to look for context clues in the nearby text. Context clues are hints to the meaning of a word or expression. They can be found in the same sentence as the unknown word or in the surrounding sentences.

Directions: Read the following text. Then answer the question.

1   There was a portentous feeling to the night. Something would happen soon—something dramatic and unforgettable. It was very quiet now. But that wouldn't last. Miguel had heard that the rebels might emerge from the nearby mountains and attack at any moment. The boy lay awake, wondering what the night might bring.

Based on context clues, what does *portentous* mean?

A. calm
B. noisy
C. boring
D. threatening

There are several context clues that can help you determine the meaning of *portentous*. The text says that something dramatic and unforgettable was going to happen; that rebels might emerge and attack. An attack is something to fear, so the only answer choice that makes sense is choice D, *threatening*. The other answer choices do not fit with the context of the passage.

Directions: Read the following text, which comes from a short story by Washington Irving titled *The Devil and Tom Walker*.

1   Tom looked in the direction that the stranger pointed, and beheld one of the great trees, fair and flourishing without, but rotten at the core, and saw that it had been nearly hewn through, so that the first high wind was likely to blow it down. . . . He now looked round, and

found most of the tall trees marked with the name of some great man of the colony, and all more or less scored by the ax.

Based on the context of the text, what does *hewn through* mean?

A. pushed over
B. in blossom
C. cut in two
D. shaking in the wind

Choice C is correct. There are several context clues to help you figure out the meaning of the phrase *hewn through*. The passage says that the tree was rotten at the core, that it was likely to blow down, and that the nearby trees were all marked with an ax. The only logical conclusion is that *hewn through* means something like "cut in two."

One way to test an answer choice is to substitute it for the unknown word or phrase. If your choice makes sense in the sentence, then you have chosen wisely.

Connotation

The exact dictionary definition of a word is called its denotative meaning. But many words also have what is called a connotative meaning. The connotative meaning of a word is what the word suggests (connotes). The connotative meaning often includes emotional associations based on how and when the word is used. The connotative meaning of a word is in addition to its dictionary meaning.

For example, the words *clever* and *brilliant* both have the dictionary meaning of "smart," but their connotative meanings are completely different. *Clever* suggests being "sharp" or mentally adept, while *brilliant* suggests a gifted intelligence.

Unlike denotative meanings, connotative meanings are subjective; that is, they relate to the reader's own emotional associations with the word. When you are reading, look for words that have connotative meanings. Consider how they influence the meaning of the text.

Directions: Read the following text, and then answer the question.

1   "Yes," said the real estate broker to the prospective home buyers, "this little town has a lot to recommend it. It has got quiet streets, plenty of parks and playgrounds, and excellent shopping. But it's a lot more than just a pleasant place to live. I think that when you settle here and get to know your neighbors, you'll find that it's a real community."

What is the connotation of the word *community*?

A. a town that has a large number of inhabitants
B. a suburb with good transportation links to a nearby city
C. a remote village with only one main street
D. a place where people are friendly and share common interests

Choice D is the correct answer. The word *community* can mean simply "a place where people live." But the word also has a specific connotation. By using the word *community*, the speaker is conveying the idea that the people in the town are friendly with each other, they share common interests, and they are cooperative and willing to work together to make the town a good place for everyone to live.

Tone

Tone and mood are important aspects of a text. The author's language and word choice can create a particular tone or mood that colors all the other aspects of the text. Tones can be mysterious, frightening, ironic, inspiring, or amusing.

When you read, look for words the author chooses in order to create a particular tone or mood.

Directions: Read the following excerpt from Herman Melville's *Moby Dick* and think about its tone. Then answer the question.

1   Queequeg and I had just left the Pequod, and were sauntering away from the water, for the moment each occupied with his own thoughts, when the above words were put to us by a stranger, who, pausing before us, levelled his massive forefinger at the vessel in question. He was but shabbily apparelled in faded jacket and patched trowsers; a rag of a black handkerchief investing his neck. A confluent small-pox had in all directions flowed over his face, and left it like the complicated ribbed bed of a torrent, when the rushing waters have been dried up.

2   "Have ye shipped in her?" he repeated.

3   "You mean the ship Pequod, I suppose," said I, trying to gain a little more time for an uninterrupted look at him.

4   "Aye, the Pequod—that ship there," he said, drawing back his whole arm, and then rapidly shoving it straight out from him, with the fixed bayonet of his pointed finger darted full at the object.

5   "Yes," said I, "we have just signed the articles."

6   "Anything down there about your souls?"

7   "About what?"

8   "Oh, perhaps you hav'n't got any," he said quickly. "No matter though, many chaps that hav'n't got any,—good luck to 'em; and are all the better off for it. A soul's a sort of fifth wheel to a wagon."

9   "What are you jabbering about, shipmate?" said I.

10 "*He's* got enough, though, to make up for all deficiencies of that sort in other chaps," abruptly said the stranger, placing a nervous emphasis upon the word *he*.

11   "Queequeg," said I, "let's go; this fellow has broken loose from somewhere, he's talking about something and somebody we don't know."

12   "Stop!" cried the stranger. "Ye said true—ye hav'n't seen Old Thunder yet, have ye?"

13   "Who's Old Thunder?" said I, again riveted with the insane earnestness of his manner.

14   "Captain Ahab."

15   "What! The captain of our ship, the Pequod?"

16   "Aye, among some of us old sailor chaps, he goes by that name. Ye hav'n't seen him yet, have ye?"

17   "No, we hav'n't. He's sick they say, but is getting better, and will be all right again before long."

18   "All right again before long!" laughed the stranger, with a solemnly derisive sort of laugh. "Look ye; when Captain Ahab is all right, then this left arm of mine will be all right; not before."

What is the tone of the passage?

A. tragic
B. peaceful
C. ominous
D. lighthearted

The tone is ominous, choice C. The conversation between the stranger and Queequeg and the narrator has a mysterious and ominous tone that foreshadows the tragedy of the book. The stranger talks about whether they have souls and how captain Ahab can make up for their deficiencies. The tone here is not yet tragic, but only ominous. Choices B and D are incorrect.

It is important to be able to recognize how the tone of a text can be changed simply by replacing one word with another.

"Senators, I stand before you to urge you to vote for my bill. A yes vote is the right thing to do under these circumstances."

How would the tone be affected if the word *urge* were replaced by the word *beg*? The tone becomes

A. desperate.
B. formal.
C. angry.
D. lighthearted.

Choice A is the correct answer. The word *urge* is fairly neutral, but the word *beg* has the connotation that the speaker is pleading and is afraid of being turned down. So the change in words would have a large impact on the tone of the sentence.

Figurative Language

Writers often achieve their effects by using language in an unusual or particularly striking fashion. For example, consider this sentence:

Adrien eats more than an elephant.

Of course, this isn't literally true. This is just the writer's way of saying that Adrien eats a lot. This sentence is an example of exaggeration or hyperbole. That is a type of figurative language.

Figurative language helps enliven a passage; it adds color to what would otherwise be an ordinary text.

There are many other types of figurative language, but they all have this in common: words are used to say one thing and mean another. Figurative language is not meant to be taken literally. When you read figurative language, you must figure out what the writer is telling you. Some types of figurative language are:

- Alliteration (using the same sound or combinations of letters repeatedly in a group of words)

- Simile (comparing one thing to another using the words *like* or *as*)

- Metaphor (comparing one thing to another without using the words *like* or *as*)

- Personification (giving human characteristics to something that is nonhuman)

- Onomatopoeia (using words that sound like what they signify)

- Hyperbole (making an unbelievable exaggeration)

It is useful to be able to tell the difference between the various kinds of figurative language. The GED® test will measure your understanding of figurative language.

Directions: Read the text and answer the question.

1   We had been sequestered inside the barn all afternoon. It was hot, really hot, and the sweat dropped off our foreheads and ran down our shirts as we worked. When the sun finally set and I opened the door, the evening air swept over us like a fresh April shower, leaving us ready to enjoy the evening.

What is the meaning of the expression *like a fresh April shower*?

A. The evening air felt humid and sticky.
B. The evening air was bitterly cold.
C. The evening air was warm and still.
D. The evening air was cool and renewing.

The correct answer is choice D. Here the author uses a simile, "like a fresh April shower" to compare one thing, the "evening air," with another, "a fresh April shower."

Structure and Author's Choices

Directions: Read the following text, which is excerpted from a speech by U.S. Congresswoman Patsy Mink on making English the official language of the United States. Then answer the questions.

1   Mr. Chairman, this bill that we are considering is entitled "The English Language Empowerment Act." I see nothing in this bill that empowers anybody in terms of becoming better acquainted with English or more proficient. There is not a penny being spent for education to promote English. We look at the education budget, and it is being cut. What this bill really is doing is to confine, to restrict the programs and opportunities for people who are not proficient in English and to prevent those people from participating in all the fullness and richness of this society. It really degrades the whole notion of our open society, accessible to everybody legally within its borders.

2   The moment we say something cannot be printed in anything else other than English, we are punishing that small sector of our society who are not a threat to our democracy. Less than 5 percent of our people in the census said they were not proficient in English. They are not a threat at all. Yet we are seeking to deny access to the Government by refusing to allow Government agencies to print documents explaining how to get into programs, how to apply for business loans, how to really make themselves much more a part, an integral part, of this society.

3   If we want to empower all these individuals in our community, regardless of what their ethnic origin is or where they came from, it seems to me that we have to find ways in which to embrace them, not to leave them out. This bill excludes opportunity contained in all the bills that we have passed; it says they are repealed. If we said anything previously about opening up government and creating access for people who are not proficient in English, those are repealed. There is a repealer paragraph in this bill.

4   Mr. Chairman, this is not an empowerment. It is denial.

1. How does paragraph 2 influence the passage?

   A. It stresses the punitive aspect of the bill.
   B. It emphasizes the fact that there is no funding in the bill.
   C. It focuses the passage on the need to promote the use of English.
   D. It adds more information about people who do not speak English well.

2. In paragraph 1, what is the meaning of *degrades*?

   A. assists
   B. hampers
   C. lowers
   D. questions

3. How does the last sentence influence the tone of the passage?

   A. It makes the tone more insistent.
   B. It has a calming effect on the tone.
   C. It creates a sense of disbelief.
   D. It changes the tone from tongue-in-cheek to ironic.

4. In paragraph 3, what effect does the word *embrace* have on the intent of the passage? It shows that the speaker wants to

   A. hug people with limited English skills.
   B. protect people with limited English skills.
   C. reject people with limited English skills.
   D. welcome people with limited English skills.

Directions: Read the following text, which is excerpted from *The Garden Party and Other Stories* by Katherine Mansfield. Then answer the questions.

1   "And so you go back to the office on Monday, do you, Jonathan?" asked Linda.

2   "On Monday the cage door opens and clangs to upon the victim for another eleven months and a week," answered Jonathan.

3   Linda swung a little. "It must be awful," she said slowly.

4   "Would ye have me laugh, my fair sister? Would ye have me weep?"

5   Linda was so accustomed to Jonathan's way of talking that she paid no attention to it.

6   "I suppose," she said vaguely, "one gets used to it. One gets used to anything."

7   "Does one? Hum!" The "Hum" was so deep it seemed to boom from underneath the ground. "I wonder how it's done," brooded Jonathan; "I've never managed it."

8   "It seems to me just as imbecile, just as awful, to have to go to the office on Monday," said Jonathan, "as it always has done and always will do. To spend all the best years of one's life sitting on a stool from nine to five, scratching in somebody's ledger! It's a strange use to make of one's . . . one and only life, isn't it? Or do I fondly dream?" He rolled over on the grass and looked up at Linda. "Tell me, what is the difference between my life and that of an ordinary prisoner. The only difference I can see is that I put myself in

jail and nobody's ever going to let me out. That's a more intolerable situation than the other. For if I'd been—pushed in, against my will—kicking, even—once the door was locked, or at any rate in five years or so, I might have accepted the fact and begun to take an interest in the flight of flies or counting the warden's steps along the passage with particular attention to variations of tread and so on. But as it is, I'm like an insect that's flown into a room of its own accord. I dash against the walls, dash against the windows, flop against the ceiling, do everything, in fact, except fly out again. And all the while I'm thinking, like that moth, or that butterfly, or whatever it is, 'The shortness of life! The shortness of life!' I've only one night or one day, and there's this vast dangerous garden, waiting out there, undiscovered, unexplored."

5. How does the mention of jail influence the story? It suggests that Jonathan

   A. should be punished.
   B. feels stuck in his situation.
   C. spent time in jail when he was younger.
   D. thinks he has done something very wrong.

6. Which of the following best describes the tone of the excerpt?

   A. inspirational
   B. lighthearted
   C. theatrical
   D. tranquil

7. Indicate the order in which the following events took place. (**Note:** On the real GED® test, you will click and drag each choice to its proper location in the diagram.)

Order of Events

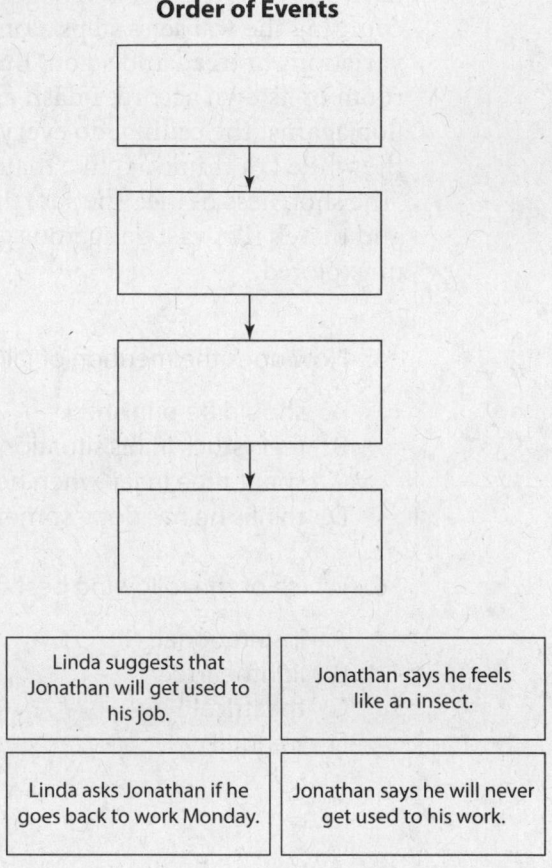

| Linda suggests that Jonathan will get used to his job. | Jonathan says he feels like an insect. |
| Linda asks Jonathan if he goes back to work Monday. | Jonathan says he will never get used to his work. |

8. Read the sentence from paragraph 6, " 'I suppose,' she said vaguely, 'one gets used to it.' " What does the author suggest by using the word *vaguely*?

   A. that Linda is trying to be supportive of Jonathan
   B. that Linda does not understand what Jonathan is saying
   C. that Linda is not all that interested in Jonathan's problem
   D. that Linda is trying to understand why Jonathan says what he does

Directions: Read the following text, which is excerpted from "The Snow-Walkers" from *In The Catskills* by John Burroughs. Then answer the questions.

1   He who marvels at the beauty of the world in summer will find equal cause for wonder and admiration in winter. It is true the pomp and the pageantry are swept away, but the essential elements remain—the day and the night, the mountain and the valley, the elemental play and succession and the perpetual presence of the infinite sky. In winter the stars seem to have rekindled their fires, the moon achieves a fuller triumph, and

the heavens wear a look of a more exalted simplicity. On the other hand, summer is more wooing and seductive, more versatile and human, appeals to the affections and the sentiments, and fosters inquiry and the art impulse. Winter is of a more heroic cast, and addresses the intellect. The severe studies and disciplines come easier in winter. One imposes larger tasks upon himself, and is less tolerant of his own weaknesses.

2   The tendinous part of the mind, so to speak, is more developed in winter; the fleshy, in summer. I should say winter had given the bone and sinew to Literature, summer the tissues and blood.

3   The simplicity of winter has a deep moral. The return of nature, after such a career of splendor and prodigality, to habits so simple and austere, is not lost either upon the head or the heart. It is the philosopher coming back from the banquet and the wine to a cup of water and a crust of bread.

4   And then this beautiful masquerade of the elements, the novel disguises our nearest friends put on! Here is another rain and another dew, water that will not flow, nor spill, nor receive the taint of an unclean vessel. And if we see truly, the same old beneficence and willingness to serve lurk beneath all.

9. How does the transition phrase *on the other hand* in paragraph 1 influence the text?

   A. It introduces a critical analysis.
   B. It suggests that the essay has many topics.
   C. It helps the author focus on what he plans to say.
   D. It prepares the reader for information that is new.

10. In paragraph 1, what is the meaning of *essential*?

   A. basic
   B. complex
   C. irrelevant
   D. problematic

11. To what does the author compare the return to winter?

   A. to a return to water and bread
   B. to a return to wine and a banquet
   C. to a return to pomp and pageantry
   D. to a return to versatility and humanity

12. Read the sentence from paragraph 3, "The simplicity of winter has a deep moral." Why does the author include this sentence?

   A. to focus on winter's beauty
   B. to emphasize his love of winter
   C. to suggest that winter is a difficult period
   D. to show what can be learned from the season

Answers are on pages 301–302.

CHAPTER 4

Literary Texts

You are probably familiar with many kinds of literary texts. Realistic fiction presents characters and situations that are familiar from real life. Science fiction describes things that might happen in the future. There are also fables, fairy tales, and legends. But the literary passages that you will find on the GED® test come mainly from classic literature of the late 19th and early 20th centuries.

These works of literature are rich in the language they use, the plots they develop, and the characters that they draw. Some of the writing may seem somewhat dated to you, but a careful reading of the text will help you understand what is happening in each passage. As you read, you should try to be aware of the elements that make up fiction. They are:

- Theme
- Plot or events of a story
- Characters
- Setting
- Narrator and character viewpoint

Using Textual Evidence to Analyze Elements of Fiction

Theme

The theme of a story is the central idea behind its events and characters. There are many different kinds of themes. For example, the theme of a story might be how a wronged person can obtain justice, or how difficult it is to make peace between enemies, or how a journey can bring wisdom to a traveler.

A theme is rarely stated directly. You must figure it out from what happens in the story, how its characters behave, and how the author describes the characters and events. You must base your choice of theme on the evidence in a text.

Directions: Read the following excerpt from Sherwood Anderson's short story "Paper Pills." As you read, try to identify the theme of the passage. Then answer the question.

1   He was an old man with a white beard and huge nose and hands. . . . [H]e was a doctor and drove a jaded white horse from house to house through the streets of Winesburg. Later he married a girl who had money. She had been left a large fertile farm when her father died. The girl was quiet, tall, and dark, and to many people she seemed very beautiful. Everyone in Winesburg wondered why she married the doctor. Within a year after the marriage she died.

2   Winesburg had forgotten the old man, but in Doctor Reefy there were the seeds of something very fine. Alone in his musty office in the Heffner Block above the Paris Dry Goods Company's store, he worked ceaselessly, building up something that he himself destroyed. Little pyramids of truth he erected and after erecting knocked them down again that he might have the truths to erect other pyramids.

3   Doctor Reefy was a tall man who had worn one suit of clothes for ten years. It was frayed at the sleeves and little holes had appeared at the knees and elbows. In the office he wore also a linen duster with huge pockets into which he continually stuffed scraps of paper. After some weeks the scraps of paper became little hard round balls, and when the pockets were filled he dumped them out upon the floor. For ten years he had but one friend, another old man named John Spaniard who owned a tree nursery. Sometimes, in a playful mood, old Doctor Reefy took from his pockets a handful of the paper balls and threw them at the nursery man. "That is to confound you, you blathering old sentimentalist," he cried, shaking with laughter.

4   The story of Doctor Reefy and his courtship of the tall dark girl who became his wife and left her money to him is a very curious story. It is delicious, like the twisted little apples that grow in the orchards of Winesburg. In the fall one walks in the orchards and the ground is hard with frost underfoot. The apples have been taken from the trees by the pickers. They have been put in barrels and shipped to the cities where they will be eaten in apartments that are filled with books, magazines, furniture, and people. On the trees are only a few gnarled apples that the pickers have rejected. They look like the knuckles of Doctor Reefy's hands. One nibbles at them and they are delicious. Into a little round place at the side of the apple has been gathered all of its sweetness. One runs from tree to tree over the frosted ground picking the gnarled, twisted apples and filling his pockets with them. Only the few know the sweetness of the twisted apples.

5   The girl and Doctor Reefy began their courtship on a summer afternoon. He was forty-five then and already he had begun the practice of filling his pockets with the scraps of paper that became hard balls and were thrown away. The habit had been formed as he sat in his buggy behind the jaded white horse and went slowly

along country roads. On the papers were written thoughts, ends of thoughts, beginnings of thoughts.

6   One by one the mind of Doctor Reefy had made the thoughts. Out of many of them he formed a truth that arose gigantic in his mind. The truth clouded the world. It became terrible and then faded away and the little thoughts began again.

7   The tall dark girl came to see Doctor Reefy because she was in the family way and had become frightened. She was in that condition because of a series of circumstances also curious . . . .

8   After the tall dark girl came to know Doctor Reefy it seemed to her that she never wanted to leave him again. She went into his office one morning and without her saying anything he seemed to know what had happened to her.

9   In the office of the doctor there was a woman, the wife of the man who kept the bookstore in Winesburg. Like all old-fashioned country practitioners, Doctor Reefy pulled teeth, and the woman who waited held a handkerchief to her teeth and groaned. Her husband was with her and when the tooth was taken out they both screamed and blood ran down on the woman's white dress. The tall dark girl did not pay any attention. When the woman and the man had gone the doctor smiled. "I will take you driving into the country with me," he said.

10   For several weeks the tall dark girl and the doctor were together almost every day. The condition that had brought her to him passed in an illness, but she was like one who has discovered the sweetness of the twisted apples, she could not get her mind fixed again upon the round perfect fruit that is eaten in the city apartments. In the fall after the beginning of her acquaintanceship with him she married Doctor Reefy and in the following spring she died. During the winter he read to her all of the odds and ends of thoughts he had scribbled on the bits of paper. After he had read them he laughed and stuffed them away in his pockets to become round hard balls.

Which of the following sentences from the story best represents its theme?

A. "For several weeks the tall dark girl and the doctor were together almost every day."
B. "The tall dark girl did not pay any attention."
C. "The knuckles of the doctor's hands were extraordinarily large."
D. "Only the few know the sweetness of the twisted apples."

To answer this question, you need to consider what happens in the story. The characters say very little and the story is very short, so you can be sure that author has chosen his words carefully. We first meet Dr. Reefy, we are told he is an old man who had been "forgotten" by the town. The author brings particular attention to his large knuckles and nose, as if he is misshapen somehow, and yet the author says inside him are the "seeds of something very fine." And we also learn that he had a beloved and beautiful wife who died, and that the story of how they met and fell in love is "is delicious, like the twisted little apples that grow in the orchards of Winesburg." These apples, like Dr. Reefy, are twisted and abandoned. By the middle of the story, it is clear that the author is drawing a connection between Dr. Reefy and the twisted apples. The story also poses the question of why the tall girl falls in love with Dr. Reefy. We then find out that she came to him "in the family way" (pregnant) but that he is sweet and not judgmental, offering to take her riding and sharing his thoughts with her.

Finally, near the end of the story, the author is fairly specific, writing, "she was like one who has discovered the sweetness of the twisted apples, she could not get her mind fixed again upon the round perfect fruit that is eaten in the city apartments." The best choice, then, is D, meaning that few people can understand the essential value and sweetness of some people that others view as outsiders.

Remember, on the GED® test, you will not only be asked to analyze the theme, you will be asked to tell which sentence from the passage most suggests the theme.

Directions: Read the following excerpt from the first chapter of Edith Wharton's novel *Ethan Frome*. Think about how it establishes the theme of the novel. Then answer the question.

1   I had the story, bit by bit, from various people, and, as generally happens in such cases, each time it was a different story.

2   If you know Starkfield, Massachusetts, you know the post-office. If you know the post-office you must have seen Ethan Frome drive up to it, drop the reins on his hollow-backed bay and drag himself across the brick pavement to the white colonnade: and you must have asked who he was.

3   It was there that, several years ago, I saw him for the first time; and the sight pulled me up sharp. Even then he was the most striking figure in Starkfield, though he was but the ruin of a man. It was not so much his great height that marked him, for the "natives" were easily singled out by their lank longitude from the stockier foreign breed: it was the careless powerful look he had, in spite of a lameness checking each step like the jerk of a chain. There was something bleak and unapproachable in his face, and he was so stiffened and grizzled that I took him for an old man and was surprised to hear that he was not more than fifty-two. I had this from Harmon Gow, who had driven the stage from Bettsbridge to Starkfield in pre-trolley days and knew the chronicle of all the families on his line.

4   "He's looked that way ever since he had his smash-up; and that's twenty-four years ago come next February," Harmon threw out between reminiscent pauses.

5   The "smash-up" it was—I gathered from the same informant—which, besides drawing the red gash across Ethan Frome's forehead, had so shortened and warped his right side that it cost him a visible

effort to take the few steps from his buggy to the post-office window. He used to drive in from his farm every day at about noon, and as that was my own hour for fetching my mail I often passed him in the porch or stood beside him while we waited on the motions of the distributing hand behind the grating. I noticed that, though he came so punctually, he seldom received anything but a copy of the Bettsbridge Eagle, which he put without a glance into his sagging pocket. At intervals, however, the post-master would hand him an envelope addressed to Mrs. Zenobia—or Mrs. Zeena-Frome, and usually bearing conspicuously in the upper left-hand corner the address of some manufacturer of patent medicine and the name of his specific. These documents my neighbour would also pocket without a glance, as if too much used to them to wonder at their number and variety, and would then turn away with a silent nod to the post-master.

6   Everyone in Starkfield knew him and gave him a greeting tempered to his own grave mien; but his taciturnity was respected and it was only on rare occasions that one of the older men of the place detained him for a word. When this happened he would listen quietly, his blue eyes on the speaker's face, and answer in so low a tone that his words never reached me; then he would climb stiffly into his buggy, gather up the reins in his left hand and drive slowly away in the direction of his farm.

7   "It was a pretty bad smash-up?" I questioned Harmon, looking after Frome's retreating figure, and thinking how gallantly his lean brown head, with its shock of light hair, must have sat on his strong shoulders before they were bent out of shape.

8   "Wust kind," my informant assented. "More'n enough to kill most men. But the Fromes are tough. Ethan'll likely touch a hundred."

9   "Good God!" I exclaimed. At the moment Ethan Frome, after climbing to his seat, had leaned over to assure himself of the security of a wooden box—also with a druggist's label on it—which he had placed in the back of the buggy, and I saw his face as it probably looked when he thought himself alone. "That man touch a hundred? He looks as if he was dead and in hell now!"

10   Harmon drew a slab of tobacco from his pocket, cut off a wedge and pressed it into the leather pouch of his cheek. "Guess he's been in Starkfield too many winters. Most of the smart ones get away."

11   "Why didn't he?"

12   "Somebody had to stay and care for the folks. There warn't ever anybody but Ethan. Fust his father—then his mother—then his wife."

13   "And then the smash-up?"

14   Harmon chuckled sardonically. "That's so. He had to stay then."

15   "I see. And since then they've had to care for him?"

16   Harmon thoughtfully passed his tobacco to the other cheek. "Oh, as to that: I guess it's always Ethan done the caring."

17   Though Harmon Gow developed the tale as far as his mental and moral reach permitted there were perceptible gaps between his facts, and I had the sense that the deeper meaning of the story was in the gaps. But one phrase stuck in my memory and served as the nucleus about which I grouped my subsequent inferences: "Guess he's been in Starkfield too many winters."

What is the theme suggested by the passage?

A. Difficult life events can stifle personal desires.
B. Physical injuries can cause mental damage.
C. Love can help you conquer all challenges.
D. Small towns allow for close personal relationships.

To answer this question, first note that the novel is named after a character, and that character is immediately introduced. It seems clear that something about that character's actions or decisions will form the backbone of the novel. We read that Ethan Frome was seriously injured in an accident—a "smash-up"—twenty-four years ago, and that he bears permanent injuries from the accident. We also learn that he rarely speaks to other people, but comes into town to pick up medicine for a Zenobia Frome, his wife. That might lead you to find choice B attractive, because Ethan's behavior is a bit out of the ordinary. However, notice that the author repeats a phrase twice in the space of just a few paragraphs, and draws particular attention to it: "Guess he's been in Starkfield too many winters." The narrator says Ethan looks like he is in "hell." We can guess by this that Ethan probably did not wish to remain in Starkfield, or that he had once had some other plans for how he wanted his life to turn out. We also learn that Ethan was—or at least felt—compelled to take care of family members who needed him. These details make it clear that choice A is the best selection.

Here is another example.

Directions: Read the following excerpt from the short story "The Open Boat," by Stephen Crane. Then answer the question.

1   It would be difficult to describe the subtle brotherhood of men that was here established on the seas. No one said that it was so. No one mentioned it. But it dwelt in the boat, and each man felt it warm him. They were a captain, an oiler, a cook, and a correspondent, and they were friends, friends in a more curiously iron-bound degree than may be common. The hurt captain, lying against the water-jar in the bow, spoke always in a low voice and calmly, but he could never command a more ready and swiftly obedient crew than the motley three of the dingey. It was more than a mere recognition of what was best for the common safety. There was surely in it a quality that was personal and heartfelt. And after this devotion to the commander of the boat there was this comradeship that the correspondent, for instance, who had been taught to be cynical of men, knew even at the

time was the best experience of his life. But no one said that it was so. No one mentioned it.

2　"I wish we had a sail," remarked the captain. "We might try my overcoat on the end of an oar and give you two boys a chance to rest." So the cook and the correspondent held the mast and spread wide the overcoat. The oiler steered, and the little boat made good way with her new rig. Sometimes the oiler had to scull sharply to keep a sea from breaking into the boat, but otherwise sailing was a success.

3　Meanwhile the lighthouse had been growing slowly larger. It had now almost assumed color, and appeared like a little grey shadow on the sky. The man at the oars could not be prevented from turning his head rather often to try for a glimpse of this little grey shadow.

4　At last, from the top of each wave the men in the tossing boat could see land. Even as the lighthouse was an upright shadow on the sky, this land seemed but a long black shadow on the sea. It certainly was thinner than paper. "We must be about opposite New Smyrna," said the cook, who had coasted this shore often in schooners. "Captain, by the way, I believe they abandoned that life-saving station there about a year ago."

5　"Did they?" said the captain. . . .

6　Slowly the land arose from the sea. From a black line it became a line of black and a line of white, trees and sand. Finally, the captain said that he could make out a house on the shore. "That's the house of refuge, sure," said the cook. "They'll see us before long, and come out after us."

7　The distant lighthouse reared high. "The keeper ought to be able to make us out now, if he's looking through a glass," said the captain. "He'll notify the life-saving people."

8　"None of those other boats could have got ashore to give word of the wreck," said the oiler, in a low voice. "Else the lifeboat would be out hunting us."

9　Slowly and beautifully the land loomed out of the sea. The wind came again. It had veered from the north-east to the south-east. Finally, a new sound struck the ears of the men in the boat. It was the low thunder of the surf on the shore. "We'll never be able to make the lighthouse now," said the captain. "Swing her head a little more north, Billie," said he.

10　"'A little more north,' sir," said the oiler.

11　Whereupon the little boat turned her nose once more down the wind, and all but the oarsman watched the shore grow. Under the influence of this expansion doubt and direful apprehension was leaving the minds of the men. The management of the boat was still most absorbing, but it could not prevent a quiet cheerfulness. In an hour, perhaps, they would be ashore.

What is the theme suggested by the passage?

A. People facing death often develop a false sense of their chances of rescue.

B. People who go through dangerous situations together feel a special bond.

C. People tend to look after their own safety more than others' in times of trouble.

D. People respect the orders of an authority figure, even if the authority figure is hurt.

To answer this question, ask yourself what is going on in the passage. There are several men in a lifeboat who do not know each other very well. Each is identified only by his job—correspondent, oiler, captain, cook. It is true that the characters seem hopeful of rescue, although it is far from certain, so choice A may seem possible. The men in the boat do seem to respect the injured captain, so choice D may seem like a good choice. But based on the first paragraph of the passage, choice C is not correct because it is clear from the first paragraph that a "brotherhood" based on the need for "common safety" had developed among the people in the boat. The author also refers to them repeatedly as "the men"—a unit. Based on the details in the passage, choice B is the best option.

Plot or Events in a Story

The plot is what happens in a story. The plot is made up of various events that build a story line. In a typical plot, there is a central problem; something needs to be accomplished, or maybe something goes wrong. The story may also provide a resolution: how the problem is resolved or fixed.

The GED® test will ask you questions about the problems facing a character.

Directions: Read the following passage. Then answer the questions.

1   Pat's house was full of animals. The neighbors called it a zoo. There were the usual pets, a couple of cats and some kittens, an older dog, some goldfish and a parrot. But Pat also kept a lizard, a turtle, a spider and a snake indoors. Outside she had a pen full of rabbits.

2   One day Pat's mother came home and found a mouse in a shoe box. Pat had brought it home from school to keep for the weekend.

3   "That's it," her mother said, sounding more upset than Pat had ever heard her. "This zoo has got to go. I want to live in a house where there are more people than animals."

4   Pat's mother let her keep the dog and the two cats. Pat had to find a home for the rest of her pets. Pat missed her animal friends. For a while she felt very sad. But Pat was not a person to just sit around and feel sorry for herself. There was a pet hospital a few blocks away. Pat spoke to the veterinarian and asked if she could help out. She offered

to clean out the cages and walk the dogs that needed exercise. They were happy to give her the job. Every day after school, before Pat went home to her own pets, she helped the sick animals at the hospital. Pat was happy, the animals were happy and so was her mother.

What was Pat's problem?

A. She wanted more animals for her zoo.
B. She could not keep the mouse in the box.
C. Her mother was not able to take care of all of the animals.
D. Her mother wanted to find other homes for some of her pets.

To answer this question you need to figure out what Pat's central problem is. Choice A does not seem to be the problem. There is nothing in the text to suggest that choice B or C is correct either. Choice D is the correct answer. She had to get rid of some pets.

Now that you know what the problem is, you need to find the quotation that supports it.

Which quotation from the story supports the central problem?

A. "Pat's house was full of animals."
B. "Outside she had a pen full of rabbits."
C. " 'This zoo has got to go.' "
D. "Pat was happy, the animals were happy and so was her mother."

Only choice C is directly related to the problem that Pat faces. Her mother said she didn't want so many animals. The other choices are details, but they do not support the central problem.

Which quotation from the story supports the resolution?

A. "Pat missed her animal friends."
B. "For a while she felt very sad."
C. "There was a pet hospital a few blocks away."
D. "she helped the sick animals at the hospital."

To answer this question, first figure out what the resolution is. Then look for the quotation that most closely supports it. Choice D is the only quotation that supports the resolution. The other choices tell details, but do not relate to the resolution.

Characters

One of the most important elements of fiction is the characters in a story. They shape the story and give it meaning. Story characters are often multifaceted and deserve careful study.

There are many ways that an author develops the characters in a story. Authors may describe a character directly by telling what the person is like, or they may prefer to have the reader figure out what the character is like based on the way the character acts and speaks, what others say about the character, and how the character interacts with others.

The GED® test will ask you questions about what words best describe a character. Read the following example and answer the question.

Directions: Read the following text, which is excerpted from *Winesburg, Ohio* by Sherwood Anderson. Then answer the question.

1   George came down the little incline from the New Willard House at seven o'clock. Tom Willard carried his bag. The son had become taller than the father.

2   On the station platform everyone shook the young man's hand. More than a dozen people waited about. George was embarrassed. Gertrude Wilmot, a tall thin woman of fifty who worked in the Winesburg post office, came along the station platform. She had never before paid any attention to George. Now she stopped and put out her hand. In two words she voiced what everyone felt. "Good luck," she said sharply and then turning went on her way.

3   When the train came into the station George felt relieved. He scampered hurriedly aboard. George glanced up and down the car to be sure no one was looking, then took out his pocket-book and counted his money. His mind was occupied with a desire not to appear green. Almost the last words his father had said to him concerned the matter of his behavior when he got to the city. "Be a sharp one," Tom Willard had said. "Keep your eyes on your money. Be awake. That's the ticket. Don't let anyone think you're a greenhorn."

4   After George counted his money he looked out of the window and was surprised to see that the train was still in Winesburg.

5   The young man, going out of his town to meet the adventure of life, began to think but he did not think of anything very big or dramatic.

6   He thought of little things—Turk Smollet wheeling boards through the main street of his town in the morning, Butch Wheeler the lamp lighter of Winesburg hurrying through the streets on a summer evening and holding a torch in his hand, Helen White standing by a window in the Winesburg post office and putting a stamp on an envelope.

7   The young man's mind was carried away by his growing passion for dreams. One looking at him would not have thought him particularly sharp. With the recollection of little things occupying his mind he closed his eyes and leaned back in the car seat. He stayed that way for a long time and when he aroused himself and again looked out of the car window the town of Winesburg had disappeared and his life there had become but a background on which to paint the dreams of his manhood.

Indicate each word that describes George and belongs in the character web. (**Note:** On the real GED® test, you will click on the words you choose and "drag" each one into position in the character web.)

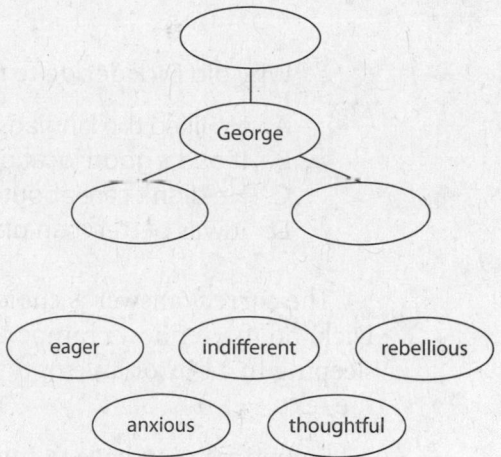

To answer this question, check through the various words and see which seem to apply best. George is setting out for a new life, and he seems excited to do so, so the word *eager* applies. But even though George is somewhat of a dreamer, the word *indifferent* does not apply; George is alert to the risk of being thought a greenhorn, and he has sharp impressions of life in Winesburg. George does not seem *rebellious*, but rather traditional, so that word too can be eliminated. He counts his money and doesn't want to appear green, so you can infer that he is somewhat *anxious*. And because he thinks about his past and the future, he can also be called *thoughtful*.

Motivation

When you analyze a character, you will also need to analyze the character's **motivation**—the reasons for his or her actions in the story. Sometimes you must infer a character's motivation by "reading between the lines"; other times the author states it directly.

Directions: Read the following text, which is excerpted from *Ragged Dick* by Horatio Alger, Jr. Then answer the question.

1   Dick followed the landlady up two narrow staircases, uncarpeted and dirty, to the third landing, where he was ushered into a room about ten feet square. It could not be considered a very desirable apartment. It had once been covered with an oilcloth carpet, but this was now very ragged, and looked worse than none. There was a single bed in the corner, covered with an indiscriminate heap of bed-clothing, rumpled and not overclean. There was a bureau, with the veneering scratched and in some parts stripped off, and a small glass, eight inches by ten, cracked across the middle; also two chairs in rather a disjointed condition. Judging from Dick's appearance, Mrs. Mooney thought he would turn from it in disdain.

2   It must be remembered that Dick's past experience had not been of a character to make him fastidious. In comparison with sleeping in a box, or an empty wagon, even this little room seemed comfortable. He decided to hire it if the rent proved reasonable.

Why did Dick decide to rent the apartment?

A. He liked the landlady.
B. It had a good location.
C. He didn't care about things being clean.
D. It was better than places he stayed before.

The correct answer is choice D. The author of the story explains that to Dick, no matter how cramped the apartment was, it was still better than sleeping in a box or an empty wagon. The other choices are not indicated by the text.

Sometimes you have to infer a motivation. Read the next example and try to figure out Rosedale's motivation for his actions.

Directions: Read the following text, which is excerpted from *The House of Mirth* by Edith Wharton. Then answer the question.

1   "My goodness—you can't go on living here!" Rosedale exclaimed.

2   Lily smiled. "I am not sure that I can; but I have gone over my expenses very carefully, and I rather think I shall be able to manage it."

3   "Be able to manage it? That's not what I mean—it's no place for you!"

4   "It's what I mean; for I have been out of work for the last week."

5   "Out of work—out of work! What a way for you to talk! The idea of your having to work—it's preposterous." He brought out his sentences in short violent jerks, as though they were forced up from a deep inner crater of indignation. "It's a farce—a crazy farce," he repeated, his eyes fixed on the long vista of the room reflected in the glass between the windows.

6   Lily continued to meet his arguments with a smile. "I don't know why I should regard myself as an exception—" she began.

7   "Because you ARE; that's why; and your being in a place like this is a damnable outrage. I can't talk of it calmly."

8   She had in truth never seen him so shaken out of his usual glibness; and there was something almost moving to her in his inarticulate struggle with his emotions.

9   He rose with a start which left the rocking-chair quivering on its beam ends, and placed himself squarely before her.

10   "Look here, Miss Lily, I'm going to Europe next week: going over to Paris and London for a couple of months—and I can't leave you

like this. I can't do it. I know it's none of my business—you've let me understand that often enough; but things are worse with you now than they have been before, and you must see that you've got to accept help from somebody. You spoke to me the other day about some debt to Trenor. I know what you mean—and I respect you for feeling as you do about it."

11   A blush of surprise rose to Lily's pale face, but before she could interrupt him he had continued eagerly: "Well, I'll lend you the money to pay Trenor; and I won't—I—see here, don't take me up till I've finished. What I mean is, it'll be a plain business arrangement, such as one man would make with another. Now, what have you got to say against that?"

Why does Rosedale offer to pay Lily's debt?

A. He cares about Lily.
B. He wants to show off.
C. He owes Lily some money.
D. He is a good friend of Trenor.

The passage does not provide a clear-cut answer, so you have to make your best guess based on the evidence in the text. According to the passage, Rosedale does not think Lily should be living where she is living because it is not good enough for her. He also doesn't like the idea of her working. You are also told that he is struggling with his emotions. On the strength of those clues, choice A seems to be the most logical conclusion: Rosedale cares about Lily. The other choices do not fit with the evidence in the passage.

Character Traits

It is important to notice the words an author uses to describe a person's character traits.

Directions: Read the following text, which is excerpted from *The Scarlet Letter* by Nathaniel Hawthorne. Then answer the questions.

1   The young woman was tall, with a figure of perfect elegance on a large scale. She had dark and abundant hair, so glossy that it threw off the sunshine with a gleam, and a face which, besides being beautiful from regularity of feature and richness of complexion, had the impressiveness belonging to a marked brow and deep black eye. She was lady-like, too, after the manner of the feminine gentility of those days; characterized by a certain state and dignity, rather than by the delicate, evanescent, and indescribable grace, which is now recognized as its indication. And never had Hester Prynne appeared more lady-like, in the antique interpretation of the term, than as she issued from the prison. Those who had before known her, and had expected to behold her dimmed and obscured by a disastrous cloud, were astonished, and even startled, to perceive how her beauty shone

out, and made a halo of the misfortune and ignominy in which she was enveloped. It may be true, that, to a sensitive observer, there was something exquisitely painful in it. Her attire, which, indeed, she had wrought for the occasion, in prison, and had modelled much after her own fancy, seemed to express the attitude of her spirit, the desperate recklessness of her mood, by its wild and picturesque peculiarity.

How does the author describes Hester Prynne?

A. uninteresting and dull looking
B. elegant, feminine, and dignified
C. flirtatious
D. timid

Choice B is the correct answer. The author states directly that Hester was "a figure of perfect elegance," "lady-like [. . .] after the manner of the feminine gentility of those days," and "characterized by a certain state and dignity."

In this case, the author tells you specifically about a person's character traits. In other cases, however, the author may tell you only how a person looks or what the person says or does, and you will have to interpret those hints in order to infer what the person thinks or feels.

Directions: Read the following text, which is excerpted from *Babbitt* by Sinclair Lewis. Then answer the questions.

1   His name was George F. Babbitt. He was forty-six years old now, in April, 1920, and he made nothing in particular, neither butter nor shoes nor poetry, but he was nimble in the calling of selling houses for more than people could afford to pay. . . .

2   He looked blurrily out at the yard. It delighted him, as always; it was the neat yard of a successful business man of Zenith, that is, it was perfection, and made him also perfect. He regarded the corrugated iron garage. For the three-hundred-and-sixty-fifth time in a year he reflected, "No class to that tin shack. Have to build me a frame garage. But by golly it's the only thing on the place that isn't up-to-date!" While he stared he thought of a community garage for his acreage development, Glen Oriole. He stopped puffing and jiggling. His arms were akimbo. His petulant, sleep-swollen face was set in harder lines. He suddenly seemed capable, an official, a man to contrive, to direct, to get things done.

Which excerpt from the text suggests that George Babbitt is a materialistic person?

A. "he made nothing in particular, neither butter nor shoes nor poetry"
B. "His petulant, sleep-swollen face was set in harder lines."
C. "It delighted him . . . it was perfection, and made him also perfect."
D. "He suddenly seemed capable, an official, a man to contrive, to direct, to get things done."

From the passage, it is clear that George Babbitt sells real estate. In this passage, we only get a short glimpse of him, but two things become apparent: he is a middle-aged man who shows his age somewhat (with his "jiggling" and "sleep-swollen face"). The author seems to implicitly criticize Babbitt's profession, noting he "was nimble in the calling of selling houses for more than people could afford to pay." About half of the passage is about how Babbitt looks, and the other half is about what he does and says. He actually does not do much but look over his property as he wakes up. But notice how he reacts to his home, his garage, and his yard. It is clear that he feels these possessions are important parts of how he sees himself. The author is explicit, in fact, in telling the reader that Babbitt adores his yard: "It delighted him, as always; it was the neat yard of a successful business man of Zenith, that is, it was perfection, and made him also perfect." Someone who values physical possession excessively is considered materialistic. Someone who feels his yard or garage can make him a "perfect" person is materialistic. So choice C is the best option.

Interaction Between Characters

Characters in fiction interact with each other, and when they do they reveal something about themselves and the other characters. Also, the way in which characters with different traits interact and react to each other can be what triggers or determines the events of the story. It is important to watch for the ways that characters in fiction interact with each other.

Directions: Read the following text, which is excerpted from *The Fate of Man* by Mikhail Sholokhov. Then answer the question.

1   After a year I came back from Kuban, sold my house and went to Voronezh. First I worked as a carpenter, then I went to a factory and learned to be a mechanic. Soon I got married. My wife had been raised in a children's home. She was an orphan. Yes, I lucked out there! Good-tempered, cheerful, always anxious to please. And smart she was, too. No comparison with me. She had known real trouble since she was a kid—maybe that affected her character. Just looking at her from the side, she wasn't all that striking. But, you see, I wasn't looking at her from the side, I was looking at her full face. And for me there was no more beautiful woman in the whole world, and there never will be.

2   I'd come home from work tired and ill-tempered. But she'd never fling your rudeness back at you. She'd be so gentle and quiet, couldn't do enough for you, always trying to get you a bit of somethin' nice, even when there wasn't enough to go around. It made your heart lighter just to look at her, and after a while you'd put your arm around her and say: "Sorry I was rude to you, Irina my love, I had a rotten day at work today." And again there'd be peace between us, and my mind would be at rest. And you know what that means to your world, my friend? In the morning I'd be out of bed like a shot and off to the factory, and any job I laid hands on would go smooth as clockwork.

What effect did Irina's character have on her husband?

A. She pushed him to work harder and get ahead.
B. Her kindness brought him out of his bad moods.
C. He felt sorry for her and was never unkind to her.
D. He was as anxious to please her as she was to please him.

Irina's effect on her husband was that she helped him overcome his bad mood. Choice B is the correct answer. The text clearly shows this with several examples.

Setting

The setting of a story is where and when it takes place. Sometimes the author does not tell you the setting in so many words. You must figure it out. Read the next few lines and figure out the setting.

> The sand had gotten in his bathing suit and in his hair. The hot sun was burning his skin. Sonny was tired, but he did not wish to leave. The sound of the waves was like beautiful music to Sonny. But his mother said that they had to go home for lunch, and then go shopping, for dinner.

The hot sun, the sand, and the waves all show Sonny was at the beach. You can also guess that it is the middle of the day. The story says that Sonny had to go home for lunch. These five sentences tell you where and when the story is set.

Setting often has a strong influence on a story. It helps determine the plot and define the characters.

Directions: Read the following text, which is excerpted from *To Build a Fire* by Jack London. Then answer the question.

1   The man flung a look back along the way he had come. The Yukon lay a mile wide and hidden under three feet of ice. On top of this ice were as many feet of snow. It was all pure white, rolling in gentle undulations where the ice-jams of the freeze-up had formed. North and south, as far as his eye could see, it was unbroken white, save for a dark hairline that curved and twisted from around the spruce-covered island to the south, and that curved and twisted away into the north, where it disappeared behind another spruce-covered island. This dark hairline was the trail—the main trail—that led south five hundred miles to the Chilcoot Pass, Dyea, and salt water; and that led north seventy miles to Dawson, and still on to the north a thousand miles to Nulato, and finally to St. Michael on Bering Sea, a thousand miles and a half thousand more.

2   But all this—the mysterious, far reaching hairline trail, the absence of sun from the sky, the tremendous cold, and the strangeness and weirdness of it all—made no impression on the man. It was not because he was long used to it. He was a newcomer in the

land, a cheechako, and this was his first winter. The trouble with him was that he was without imagination. He was quick and alert in the things of life, but only in things, not in the significances. Fifty degrees below zero meant eighty-odd degrees of frost. Such fact impressed him as being cold and uncomfortable, and that was all. It did not lead him to meditate on his frailty as a creature of temperature, and upon man's frailty in general, able only to live within certain narrow limits of heat and cold; and from there on it did not lead him to the conjectural field of immortality and man's place in the universe. Fifty degrees below zero stood for a bite of frost that hurt and that must be guarded against by the use of mittens, ear flaps, warm moccasins, and thick socks. Fifty degrees below zero was to him just precisely fifty degrees below zero. That there should be anything more to it than that was a thought that never entered his head.

How does the setting influence the story?

A. It explains why the man is alone.
B. It tells when the story takes place.
C. It helps to define the man's character.
D. It determines what will happen next.

When reading this passage, you almost have the feeling that the setting is another character. And the interaction between the setting and the man gives the author a way to vividly define the man's character (choice C). Choice A is incorrect. There is nothing in the setting that explains why the man is alone. Choice B is also incorrect. Nothing in the setting tells you when the story takes place. Choice D is also incorrect because the setting provides no hint about what will happen next.

Character and Narrator Viewpoint

The characters and the narrator (if there is a narrator) all have a point of view. Each one sees the story from a different perspective, and how they feel about what is happening influences the plot. It is up to the reader to determine what point of view characters have based on what they say and do. Read the following passage and think about the point of view of each character.

Directions: Read the following excerpt from *Adventures of Huckleberry Finn,* by Mark Twain. Then answer the question.

1   The Widow Douglas she took me for her son, and allowed she would sivilize me; but it was rough living in the house all the time, considering how dismal regular and decent the widow was in all her ways; and so when I couldn't stand it no longer I lit out. I got into my old rags and my sugar-hogshead again, and was free and satisfied. But Tom Sawyer he hunted me up and said he was going to start a band of robbers, and I might join if I would go back to the widow and be respectable. So I went back.

2   The widow she cried over me, and called me a poor lost lamb, and she called me a lot of other names, too, but she never meant no harm by it. She put me in them new clothes again, and I couldn't do nothing but sweat and sweat, and feel all cramped up. Well, then, the old thing commenced again. The widow rung a bell for supper, and you had to come to time. When you got to the table you couldn't go right to eating, but you had to wait for the widow to tuck down her head and grumble a little over the victuals, though there warn't really anything the matter with them,—that is, nothing only everything was cooked by itself. In a barrel of odds and ends it is different; things get mixed up, and the juice kind of swaps around, and the things go better.

What is the point of view of the speaker in the passage?

A. He is a lonely orphan and craves adult attention and care.
B. He is a natural risk-taker who enjoys breaking the law.
C. He wants to live his life by his own rules, not the rules of others.
D. He feels guilty that he cannot live up the expectations of the widow.

Hints in the passage indicate that the speaker (who is Huckleberry Finn, by the way) is indeed an orphan, and probably fairly young. Choice A might seem appealing. There is a mention of a friend wanting him to join a "band of robbers," so choice B might seem like a possibility. Huckleberry does seem to respect the Widow Douglas, so choice D might be an option. However, if you look at everything Huck says, it is evident that while he thinks the Widow Douglas is a good person, he is not really interested in her mission to "sivilize" him and he chafes at her attempts. He even runs away, and is only lured back by his friend's offer to start a band of robbers (which seems most likely to be a boyish game instead a criminal plan). All the evidence in the passage points to Huck wanting to be "free" to do as he pleases. Choice C, then, is the best answer.

Directions: Read the following text, which is excerpted from *The Sheik* by Edith Hull. Then answer the question.

1   The voice seemed to come from the dark shadows at the end of the garden. The singer sang slowly, his voice lingering caressingly on the words; the last verse dying away softly and clearly, almost imperceptibly fading into silence.

2   For a moment there was utter stillness; then Diana lay back with a little sigh. "The Kashmiri Song. It makes me think of India. I heard a man sing it in Kashmere last year, but not like that. What a wonderful voice!"

3   Arbuthnot looked at her curiously, surprised at the sudden ring of interest in her tone, and the sudden animation of her face.

4   "You say you have no emotion in your nature, and yet that unknown man's singing has stirred you deeply. How do you reconcile the two?" he asked, almost angrily.

5   "Is an appreciation of the beautiful emotion?" she challenged, with uplifted eyes. "Surely not. Music, art, nature, everything beautiful appeals to me. But there is nothing emotional in that. It is only that I prefer beautiful things to ugly ones. For that reason even pretty clothes appeal to me," she added, laughing.

6   "You are the best-dressed woman in Biskra," he acceded. "But is not that a concession to the womanly feelings that you despise?"

7   "Not at all. To take an interest in one's clothes is not an exclusively feminine vice. I like pretty dresses. I admit to spending some time in thinking of colour schemes to go with my horrible hair, but I assure you that my dressmaker has an easier life than my brother's tailor."

8   She sat silent, hoping that the singer might not have gone, but there was no sound except a cicada chirping near her. She swung round in her chair, looking in the direction from which it came. "Listen to him. Jolly little chap! They are the first things I listen for when I get to Port Said. They mean the East to me."

9   "Maddening little beasts!" said Arbuthnot irritably.

10   "They are going to be very friendly little beasts to me during the next four weeks. . . . . You don't know what this trip means to me. I like wild places. The happiest times of my life have been spent camping in America and India, and I have always wanted the desert more than either of them. It is going to be a month of pure joy. I am going to be enormously happy."

What is Diana's viewpoint towards the desert?

A. She is bored by it.
B. She is fearful of it.
C. She thinks it is ugly.
D. She finds it exciting.

Choice D is the correct answer. This is what she feels towards the East and the desert. A close reading of the text will tell you that.

Literary Texts

Directions: Read the following text, which is excerpted from *Tom Sawyer* by Mark Twain. Then answer the questions that follow.

1   "TOM! Where are you?"

2   No answer was forthcoming.

3   "TOM! Come here!"

4   Still no answer was heard.

5   "What's gone with that boy, I wonder? You TOM!"

6   No answer was heard yet again.

7   The woman pulled her spectacles down and looked over them about the room; then she put them up and looked out under them. She seldom or never looked THROUGH them for so small a thing as a boy; they were her best pair, the pride of her heart, and were built for "style," not service— she could have seen through a pair of stove-lids just as well; she looked perplexed for a moment, and then said, not fiercely, but still loud enough for the furniture to hear:

8   "Well, I if you don't come right away I'll—"

9   She did not finish, for by this time she was bending down and checking under the bed with the broom, and so she needed breath to punctuate her search; she didn't find anything but the cat.

10   She went to the open door and stood in it and looked out among the tomato vines and weeds in the garden: no Tom there. So she lifted up her voice at an angle calculated for distance and shouted:

11   "Y-o-u-u TOM, answer me at once!"

12   There was a slight noise behind her and she turned just in time to seize a small boy by the slack of his shirt and stop his flight.

13   "There! I might 'a' thought of that closet. What you been doing in there?"

14   "Nothing."

15   "Nothing! Look at your hands and look at your mouth; what IS that stuff?"

16   The lad said nothing; instead he looked down at his feet.

17   "Well, I know; it's jam—that's what it is—and you know too. Forty times I've said if you didn't let that jam alone you would be punished."

18   "I'm sorry, Aunt. I couldn't help myself."

19   The threat of punishment hovered in the air—the peril was intense—

20   Then quite suddenly Tom spoke in a voice filled with deep concern. "My! Watch out; look behind you, aunt!"

21   His aunt whirled round, and snatched her skirts out of danger and just in that instant the lad fled, scrambling up the high board-fence, and disappearing over it, far out of sight of his aunt.

22   His aunt Polly stood surprised a moment, and then broke into a gentle laugh.

23   "Hang the boy, can't I never learn anything? Ain't he played me tricks enough like that for me to be looking out for him by this time? But old fools is the biggest fools there is. Can't learn an old dog new tricks, as the saying is. But my goodness, he never plays them alike, two days, and how is a body to know what's coming? He 'pears to know just how long he can torment me before I get my dander up, and he knows if he can make out to put me off for a minute or make me laugh, it's all down again. He's sure is mischievous, but laws-a-me; he's my own sister's boy, and I ain't got the heart to really punish him, somehow. Every time I let him off, my conscience does hurt me so, and every time I punish him my old heart most breaks. Well-a-well, man that is born of woman is of few days and full of trouble, and I reckon it's so."

1. Which quotation from the text best supports the theme of the story?

   A. "The woman pulled her spectacles down and looked over them about the room; then she put them up and looked out under them."
   B. "She went to the open door and stood in it and looked out among the tomato vines and weeds in the garden: no Tom there."
   C. "There was a slight noise behind her and she turned just in time to seize a small boy by the slack of his shirt and stop his flight."
   D. "He 'pears to know just how long he can torment me before I get my dander up, and he knows if he can make out to put me off for a minute or make me laugh, it's all down again."

2. What is Tom's viewpoint?

   A. He dislikes his aunt.
   B. He enjoys annoying his aunt.
   C. He wants to change the way that he acts.
   D. He thinks that his aunt should be stricter.

3. Which excerpt supports the idea that Tom is someone who can move very quickly?

   A. There was a slight noise behind her and she turned just in time to seize a small boy by the slack of his shirt and stop his flight.
   B. "I'm sorry, Aunt. I couldn't help myself."
   C. Then quite suddenly Tom spoke in a voice filled with deep concern. "My! Watch out; look behind you, aunt!"
   D. His aunt whirled round, and snatched her skirts out of danger and just in that instant the lad fled, scrambling up the high board-fence, and disappearing over it, far out of sight of his aunt.

4. Why does Aunt Polly feel badly about punishing Tom?

   A. He is very young.
   B. He is her sister's son.
   C. He cries a lot when he is punished.
   D. He does not understand right from wrong.

Directions: Read the following text, which is excerpted from *Mr. Travers's First Hunt* by Richard Harding Davis. Then answer the questions that follow.

1   Young Travers, who had been engaged to a girl down on Long Island, only met her father and brother a few weeks before the day set for the wedding. The father and son talked about horses all day and until one in the morning, for they owned fast thoroughbreds, and entered them at race-tracks. Old Mr. Paddock, the father of the girl to whom Travers was engaged, had often said that when a young man asked him for his daughter's hand he would ask him in return, not if he had lived straight, but if he could ride straight.

2   Travers was invited to their place in the fall when the fox-hunting season opened, and spent the evening most pleasantly and satisfactorily with his fiancée in a corner of the drawing-room.

3   But as soon as the women had gone, young Paddock joined him and said, "You ride, of course?" Travers had never ridden; but he had been prompted how to answer by Miss Paddock, and so said there was nothing he liked better.

4   "That's good," said Paddock. "I'll give you Monster tomorrow morning at the meet. He is a bit nasty at the start of the season; and ever since he killed Wallis, the second groom, last year, none of us care much to ride him. But you can manage him, no doubt."

5   Mr. Travers dreamed that night of taking large, desperate leaps into space on a wild horse that snorted forth flames, and that rose at solid stone walls as though they were haystacks.

6   He came downstairs the next morning looking very miserable indeed. Monster had been taken to the place where they were to meet, and Travers viewed him on his arrival there with a sickening sense of fear as he saw him pulling three grooms off their feet.

7   Travers decided that he would stay with his feet on solid earth just as long as he could, and when the hounds were sent off and the rest had started at a gallop, he waited until they were all well away. Then he scrambled up onto the saddle and the next instant he was off after the others, with a feeling that he was on a locomotive that was jumping the ties. Monster had passed the other horses in less than five minutes.

8   Travers had taken hold of the saddle with his left hand to keep himself down, and sawed and swayed on the reins with his right. He shut his eyes whenever Monster jumped, and never knew how he happened to stick on; but he did stick on, and was so far ahead that no one could see in the misty morning just how badly he rode. As it was, for daring and speed he led the field.

9   There was a broad stream in front of him, and a hill just on its other side. No one had ever tried to take this at a jump. It was considered more of a swim than anything else, and the hunters always crossed it by the bridge. Travers saw the bridge and tried to jerk Monster's head in that direction; but Monster kept right on as straight as an express train over the prairie.

10   Travers could only gasp and shut his eyes. He remembered the fate of the second groom and shivered. Then the horse rose like a rocket, lifting Travers so high in the air that he thought Monster would never come down again; but he did come down, on the opposite side of the stream. The next instant he was up and over the hill, and had stopped panting in the very center of the pack of hounds that were snarling and snapping around the fox.

11   And then Travers hastily fumbled for his cigar case, and when the others came pounding up over the bridge and around the hill, they saw him seated nonchalantly on his saddle, puffing critically at a cigar, and giving Monster patronizing pats on the head.

12   "My dear girl," said old Mr. Paddock to his daughter as they rode back, "if you love that young man of yours and want to keep him, make him promise to give up riding. A more reckless and more brilliant horseman I have never seen. He took that jump at that stream like a centaur. But he will break his neck sooner or later, and he ought to be stopped."

13   Young Paddock was so delighted with his prospective brother-in-law's great riding that that night in the smoking-room he made him a present of Monster before all the men.

14   "No," said Travers, gloomily, "I can't take him. Your sister has asked me to give up what is dearer to me than anything next to herself, and that is my riding. She has asked me to promise never to ride again, and I have given my word."

15   A chorus of sympathy rose from the men.

16   "Yes, I know," said Travers to her brother, "it is rough, but it just shows what sacrifices a man will make for the woman he loves."

5. Which of the following best describes Travers' problem?

    A. He is fearful of asking young Paddock how to ride.
    B. He worries that his fiancée does not really care for him.
    C. He wants to impress his fiancée's family, but he is afraid.
    D. He wants to impress young Paddock, but he does not know how.

6. How does Travers give the impression that he is an excellent rider?

    A. by getting Monster to do several jumps
    B. by showing that he is skilled in handling the horse
    C. by bragging a lot about his riding ability after the hunt
    D. by managing to stay on Monster as the horse goes wildly onward

7. Which of the following best explains why Travers did not take the bridge over the stream?

   A. He preferred to jump over it.
   B. His fiancée warned him not to.
   C. He couldn't get Monster to go over to it.
   D. He wanted to show off his courage and skill.

8. In paragraph 4, what is one probable reason that young Paddock chose Monster for Travers to ride?

   A. He wants to test Travers.
   B. He wants to upset his sister.
   C. He wants to please Travers.
   D. He thinks Travers deserves the best horse.

Directions: Read the following text, which is excerpted from *Hearts and Hands* by O. Henry. Then answer the questions that follow.

1   At Denver there was an influx of passengers into the coaches on the eastbound express. In one coach there sat a very pretty young woman dressed in elegant taste and surrounded by all the luxurious comforts of an experienced traveler. Among the newcomers were two young men, one of handsome presence with a bold, frank look and manner, the other a ruffled, glum-faced person, heavily built and roughly dressed. The two were handcuffed together.

2   As they passed down the aisle of the coach, the only vacant seat offered was a reversed one facing the attractive young woman. Here the linked couple seated themselves. The young woman's glance fell upon them with a distant, swift disinterest. Then with a lovely smile brightening her face and a tender pink coloring her rounded cheeks, she held out a little gray-gloved hand. When she spoke her voice, full, sweet, and deliberate, proclaimed that its owner was accustomed to speak and be heard.

3   "Well, Mr. Easton, if you *will* make me speak first, I suppose I must. Don't you ever recognize old friends when you meet them in the West?"

4   The younger man roused himself sharply at the sound of her voice, seemed to struggle with a slight embarrassment which he threw off instantly, and then clasped her fingers with his left hand.

5   "It's Miss Fairchild," he said, with a smile. "I'll ask you to excuse the other hand; it's otherwise engaged just at present."

6   He slightly raised his right hand, bound at the wrist by the shining "bracelet" to the left one of his companion. The glad look in the girl's eyes slowly changed to a bewildered horror. The glow faded from her cheeks. Her lips parted in a vague distress. Easton, with a little laugh, as if amused, was about to speak again, when the other man interrupted him. The glum-faced man had been watching the girl's countenance with veiled glances from his keen, shrewd eyes.

7   "You'll excuse me for speaking, miss, but I see you're acquainted with the marshal here. If you'll ask him to speak a word for me when we get to the pen he'll do it, and it'll make things easier for me there. He's taking me to Leavenworth prison. It's seven years for counterfeiting."

8   "Oh!" said the girl, with a deep breath and returning color. "So that is what you are doing out here? A marshal!"

9   "My dear Miss Fairchild," said Easton, calmly, "I had to do something. Money has a way of taking wings unto itself, and you know it takes money to keep in step with our crowd in Washington. I saw this opening in the West, and—well, a marshalship isn't quite as high a position as that of ambassador, but—"

10   "The ambassador," said the girl, warmly, "doesn't call any more. He needn't ever have done so. You ought to know that. And so now you are one of these dashing Western heroes, and you ride and shoot and go into all kinds of dangers. That's different from the Washington life. You have been missed from the old crowd."

11   The girl's eyes, fascinated, went back, widening a little, to rest upon the glittering handcuffs.

12   "Don't you worry about them, miss," said the other man. "All marshals handcuff themselves to their prisoners to keep them from getting away."

13   "Will we see you again soon in Washington?" asked the girl.

14   "Not soon, I think," said Easton. "My butterfly days are over, I fear."

15   "I love the West," said the girl. She looked out the car window. She began to speak truly and simply, without the gloss of style and manner: "Mamma and I spent the summer in Denver. She went home a week ago, because Father was slightly ill. I could live and be happy in the West. I think the air here agrees with me. Money isn't everything. But people always misunderstand things and remain stupid—"

16   "Say, Mr. Marshal," growled the glum-faced man. "This isn't quite fair. I haven't had a smoke all day. Haven't you talked long enough? Take me in the smoker now, won't you? I'm half dead for a pipe."

17   The bound travelers rose to their feet, Easton with the same slow smile on his face.

18   "I can't deny a petition for tobacco," he said lightly. "It's the one friend of the unfortunate. Good-bye, Miss Fairchild. Duty calls, you know." He held out his hand for a farewell.

19   "It's too bad you are not going East," she said, reclothing herself with manner and style. "But you must go on to Leavenworth, I suppose?"

20   "Yes," said Easton, "I must go on to Leavenworth."

21   The two men sidled down the aisle into the smoker.

22   The two passengers in a seat nearby had heard most of the conversation. Said one of them: "That marshal's a good sort of chap. Some of these Western fellows are all right."

23   "Pretty young to hold an office like that, isn't he?" asked the other.

24   "Young!" exclaimed the first speaker, "why—Oh, didn't you catch on? Say—did you ever know an officer to handcuff a prisoner to his right hand?"

9. How does the setting influence the story?

    A. The train allows the characters to talk freely.
    B. The train provides a means for a chance meeting.
    C. The train helps the characters focus on their problems.
    D. The train helps the marshal understand what is going on.

10. Which is the most likely description of Easton's relationship to the ambassador?

    A. He left Washington because he fought with him.
    B. He wanted to become ambassador instead of him.
    C. He was a good friend of the ambassador and misses him.
    D. He was jealous about his seeing Miss Fairfield in Washington.

11. Which best describes Miss Fairchild's initial reaction upon seeing Easton with handcuffs?

    A. She was angry.
    B. She was horrified.
    C. She was uninterested.
    D. She thought it was funny.

12. What is the marshal's viewpoint toward Easton?

    A. He is worried that Easton will try to escape.
    B. He wants to spare Easton from an embarrassment.
    C. He feels that Easton should tell Miss Fairchild the truth.
    D. He thinks Easton should have been punished more severely.

Answers are on pages 302–303.

CHAPTER 5

Informational Texts

Many of the reading passages that appear on the GED® test are informational (nonfiction) texts. That is, they relate to real people and real events and are not taken from literature. Informational texts can include letters, speeches, reports, newspaper and magazine articles, and general texts on nonfiction topics in areas such as science or social studies. A certain number of the informational texts will be historical documents. Reading and analyzing informational texts is different from analyzing literary texts. You will be asked to use different reading skills and to answer different kinds of questions.

Foundational Texts

Many of the historical documents that appear on the GED® test are what are called **foundational texts**; that is, they are documents related in some basic way to the history of the United States. You may encounter selections from the Bill of Rights, the U.S. Constitution, and other similar texts dating from the early history of this country.

Here is an example of a foundational text.

Directions: Read the following text, which is excerpted from the Bill of Rights of the United States Constitution. Then answer the question.

Amendment I

1 Congress shall make no law respecting an establishment of religion, or prohibiting the free exercise thereof; or abridging the freedom of speech, or of the press; or the right of the people peaceably to assemble, and to petition the Government for a redress of grievances.

Amendment II

2 A well regulated Militia, being necessary to the security of a free State, the right of the people to keep and bear Arms, shall not be infringed.

Amendment III

3 No Soldier shall, in time of peace be quartered in any house, without the consent of the Owner, nor in time of war, but in a manner to be prescribed by law.

Amendment IV

4   The right of the people to be secure in their persons, houses, papers, and effects, against unreasonable searches and seizures, shall not be violated, and no Warrants shall issue, but upon probable cause, supported by Oath or affirmation, and particularly describing the place to be searched, and the persons or things to be seized.

What is the main idea of Amendment IV?

A. People may be subjected to unreasonable searches under certain circumstances.
B. People have the right to be free from unreasonable searches.
C. Unreasonable searches are permitted if done in certain ways.
D. The government has the right to administer unreasonable warrants.

Choice B is the correct answer. A thorough reading of this amendment will tell you the main idea.

Inferring Relationships Between Ideas

In nonfiction texts in particular, writers connect ideas in certain ways in order to make a point or advance a thesis. Some of the ways that ideas are connected are:

• Cause and effect

• Compare and contrast

• Parallel ideas

Cause and Effect

Ideas are often connected to each other by cause and effect. This means that one idea (or event or trend) is the cause of a second idea (or event or trend). The second idea is the effect that results from the first idea.

This kind of relationship is often found in nonfiction, and in particular, speeches.

Directions: Read the following passage, and then answer the question.

1   Fellow citizens, I come here today to plead my case. Today in our state people do not have enough jobs. But the unemployment problem will not be solved until we get our weak economy moving again. Other politicians talk about strengthening the economy, but they have no plan to make it happen. That is why I am proposing new measures that will positively affect the economy and the job outlook. They will impact your well-being directly.

2   Vote for me this November because I promise to do what is needed to stabilize the economy and create more jobs.

What cause-and-effect relationship exists in the passage?

A. between job growth and politicians
B. between a weak economy and a lack of jobs
C. between politicians and a strong economy
D. between a lack of jobs and a strong economy

Choice B is the correct answer. The speaker claims that there is a direct cause-and-effect relationship between the lack of jobs and a weak economy. It is an explicit relationship. It is stated in the text.

Read the next passage and look for a cause-and-effect relationship.

Directions: Read the following passage, and then answer the question.

1   Baking a perfect loaf of French bread, or baguette, is a complicated process. But you will decide it is well worth the effort once you enjoy a sandwich made with your fresh, delicious bread. If you are trying to make French bread for the first time, it is important that you follow all the recipe directions exactly. Make sure you have all the necessary ingredients and equipment handy before you start. One mistake many inexperienced bakers make is not kneading the bread dough long enough. It might not seem necessary, but kneading the dough is critical. The kneading process is what allows gluten to form, and gluten is what gives French bread its light texture. However, there is such a thing as too much kneading. If you knead dough for longer than is recommended in the recipe, your bread will have a dense, unappealing texture.

What cause-and-effect relationship exists in this passage?

A. between kneading dough and the formation of gluten
B. between baking French bread and enjoying sandwiches
C. between following the recipe and baking perfect bread
D. between kneading bread and producing a dense texture

Sandwiches, recipes, and textures are all mentioned in this passage, but the only direct cause-and-effect relationship noted is between kneading dough and the formation of gluten. Kneading causes the formation of gluten. Choice A is correct.

Compare and Contrast

Oftentimes an author uses a compare-and-contrast relationship between ideas in a passage. In making this kind of relationship, the author explains how two ideas are alike or different.

Directions: Read the following passage, and then answer the question.

1   Animals hunt in different ways. Some animals hunt with their noses. Dogs can smell food even if it's far away. Bats hunt with their ears. Bats can catch insects in the dark.

2   Falcons hunt with their sharp eyes. They fly high above the earth. They can see a small movement in the grass. They zoom down and catch a little mouse.

3   Rattlesnakes hunt in a different way. They can tell if there is something warm near them. They go through the grass very quietly. They find a mouse. They can't see it, but they can feel the heat from the mouse. One quick bite from the snake and the mouse becomes lunch.

What ideas are being contrasted in the passage? The different ways animals

A. see
B. hear
C. hunt
D. move

Choice C is the correct answer. These are the ideas that are being contrasted. That is how they are related.

Parallel Ideas

A parallel relationship is a way of equating two ideas so that they are presented in an equal or parallel form. It is often used to make a dramatic point and is found frequently in speeches.

One famous example of parallelism is found in President John F. Kennedy's Inaugural Address, given in 1960:

> Ask not what your country can do for you—ask what you can do for your country.

Here two ideas are linked together in a parallel form; this gives them a dramatic sense as well as a rhythmic quality.

Following are two other examples of parallelism. It is good to be able to recognize it when it occurs.

The first is from "Of Studies" by the English philosopher Francis Bacon (1561–1626):

> Read not to contradict and confute; nor to believe and take for granted; nor to find talk and discourse; but to weigh and consider.

The second is a quotation from the French Novelist Albert Camus (1913–1960):

> Those who write clearly have readers; those who write obscurely have commentators.

Author's Viewpoint and Purpose

The **author's viewpoint** is what the author thinks about the topic that she or he is presenting. The author's viewpoint may be directly stated, or it may be concealed. If it is concealed, it is up to the reader to look for hints that indicate the author's viewpoint.

Directions: Read the passage, and then answer the question.

1   The Romanian capital of Bucharest was officially founded in 1495 by Prince Vlad Tepes. This beautiful city, on the banks of the Dambovita River, became prominent as the city from which he governed. While Prince Vlad was notorious for his cruel treatment of his enemies—his reputation inspired the Irish writer Bram Stoker to create the fictitious Count Dracula—he was a wise and brave defender of the people over whom he ruled.

Which statement below best reflects the author's view of Vlad Tepes? He thinks that

A. Prince Vlad was a poor ruler.
B. Vlad Tepes was not to be feared by anyone.
C. Vlad Tepes has been unfairly portrayed.
D. Count Dracula was not nearly as terrifying as Vlad Tepes.

Choice C is correct. In describing Prince Vlad as a wise and brave ruler, the author is suggesting that Vlad's reputation as a cruel and violent man is one-sided and only part of the story. Clues like this will help you figure out the author's viewpoint.

The **author's purpose** is what the author hopes to accomplish by writing a text. An author may want to entertain, express feelings, inform, or persuade.

Directions: Read the passage, and then answer the question.

1   Until fairly recently in human history, the most popular medical remedy for all manner of ailments was bloodletting. Leeches were placed on the patient's skin and allowed to drain from twelve to eighty ounces of blood. Bloodletting was routinely used to treat outbreaks of yellow fever in the eighteenth century. George Washington's troops, for example, were regularly leeched, though the process could not have helped soldiers who were already weakened by cold and an inadequate diet.

2   Finally, in the last century, a French doctor decided to find out if bleeding really did help. He observed 134 patients with a variety of diseases and concluded that bloodletting was no help at all. After that, the practice dwindled. Today there are only two or three conditions for which modern medicine might use bloodletting. Bloodletting can be used to reduce a bloody swelling or an abnormal buildup of iron in the blood.

Why did the author write this passage?

A. to inform readers about a subject
B. to persuade readers to do something
C. to explain to readers how to solve a problem
D. to give directions on how to perform a task

Choice A is clearly the correct answer. The author's purpose is to inform readers about the topic of medical bloodletting. The author is not making any attempt to persuade readers to do something, to explain how to solve a problem, or to give directions on how to perform a task.

An author will often make his or her purpose clear to the reader, but not always. An author who wants to persuade a reader to do something may hide the real purpose of what is being said. That is why it is important to ask yourself, "Why did the author write this text? What is the author's purpose for writing this?" Once you understand the author's purpose, it is much easier to understand the meaning of a text.

Directions: Read the following letter. Then answer the question.

1 Dear Rosa:

2   The Spring Book Sale is a great event. It has been held for the past 10 years, and we hope the tradition will continue for at least another 10 years. Alice Mann was the person to organize the first book fair. Without her selfless work, the library would be in much more difficult financial straits than it is today.

3   The event is fun for everyone who participates, including those who volunteer at the booths. Although some people complain that it's a lot to ask of people to give up a Saturday for a cause like raising money for the local library, I think you would agree that it is a rewarding experience.

4   This year we are looking for someone to coordinate the fair. I understand you have experience doing such a thing. Would you consider taking on the post? I will give you a call later in the week to discuss this in greater detail.

5 Best wishes,

6 Tonia Rogers

What is the author's purpose for writing this letter?

A. to tell about the history of the Spring Book Fair
B. to ask if Rosa would coordinate this year's fair
C. to point out how much fun it is to volunteer for the Spring Book Fair
D. to explain that the Spring Book Fair benefits the library's finances

Although all of the choices are mentioned in the letter, the true purpose of the letter is to ask Rosa to coordinate the fair. You have to look beyond the many topics that are discussed to realize why Tonia Rogers wrote the letter.

Analyzing Arguments

Persuasive texts, such as speeches, use arguments to try to convince the reader to believe something or to do something. Learning to recognize and analyze arguments is an important skill when reading this kind of text. There will be many questions on the GED about the kinds of arguments that are used in a text. You will need to recognize whether or not arguments are based on sound reasoning, or whether they merely reflect the writer's opinion.

Directions: Read the following text, which is excerpted from President Franklin Delano Roosevelt's First Inaugural Address, given during the Great Depression of the 1930s. Then answer the questions.

I am certain that my fellow Americans expect that on my induction into the Presidency I will address them with a candor and a decision which the present situation of our Nation impels. This is preeminently the time to speak the truth, the whole truth, frankly and boldly. Nor need we shrink from honestly facing conditions in our country today. This great Nation will endure as it has endured, will revive and will prosper. So, first of all, let me assert my firm belief that the only thing we have to fear is fear itself—nameless, unreasoning, unjustified terror which paralyzes needed efforts to convert retreat into advance. In every dark hour of our national life a leadership of frankness and vigor has met with that understanding and support of the people themselves which is essential to victory. I am convinced that you will again give that support to leadership in these critical days.

What argument is President Roosevelt making?

A. At no time in history have Americans faced such grave problems.
B. The American people are unable to master their fears.
C. The United States will surely overcome its current problems.
D. The American people do not want President Roosevelt to be honest about the country's difficulties.

Choice C is the correct answer. Roosevelt argues that whenever the United States has faced problems, the American people have met the challenge.

Which quotation from the text supports the argument?

A. "I am certain that my fellow Americans expect that on my induction into the Presidency I will address them with a candor and a decision which the present situation of our Nation impels."
B. "This is preeminently the time to speak the truth, the whole truth, frankly and boldly."
C. "This great Nation will endure as it has endured, will revive and will prosper."
D. "In every dark hour of our national life a leadership of frankness and vigor has met with that understanding and support of the people themselves which is essential to victory."

Choice C is the correct answer. This is the only sentence that supports the main argument of the passage.

Fact Versus Opinion

When analyzing arguments, you need to decide which claims are based on fact and which ones are based on opinion. Claims based on fact can be proven; claims based on opinion cannot be proven. Here are some examples:

Opinion	Fact
You are nervous.	You have an exam today.
Terri is a great ice skater.	Terri won an award for ice skating.
Joan has been helpful to me.	Joan gave me a new computer.

These are obvious examples of fact and opinion. Sometimes it is more difficult to discern which is which, especially in a longer, more complicated passage.

When analyzing more complicated passages, it is often helpful to separate what is factual from what is based on opinion.

Directions: Read the following text, which is based on the autobiographical writings of the 19th-century African American social reformer Frederick Douglass. Then answer the question.

1   When African Americans traveled by train in the pre–Civil War era, they were consigned to separate and inferior compartments, a demeaning experience which infuriated Douglass. Whenever he traveled by train, he made a point of occupying the most luxurious compartment in the white section.

2   On one memorable occasion, Douglass was traveling by train through Massachusetts, comfortably seated in a carriage reserved exclusively for Caucasian passengers. The conductor ordered him to leave and Douglass, when told that the reason was the color of his skin, gave no sign of complying but simply leaned back comfortably in his chair. Soon six rough-looking trainmen appeared, and when Douglass still gave no sign of leaving, they seized him. Douglass simply wrapped his arms and legs around the seat. The six men heaved and struggled. Finally they managed to work their opponent free, but not before large chunks of the seat were ripped out.

3   In the days that followed, Douglass stayed in the nearby town of Lynn, where his ejection from the train was the exclusive topic of conversation. Indeed, Lynn's railway superintendent, fearing further disturbances, commanded that all trains should bypass his town until he could learn what Douglass would do next. Accordingly, for the next few days, trains dashed through Lynn without stopping.

Which statement is based on opinion?

A. African Americans were given train seats separate from Caucasian passengers.
B. The conductor ordered Douglass to leave his seat, but Douglass did not do so.
C. The trainmen tried to seize Douglass and take him out of his seat.
D. In the town of Lynn, people talked about nothing but the incident.

Choice D is the statement that is based on opinion rather than fact. This is the author's opinion. The other statements describe specific things that actually happened.

Source Reliability

When analyzing arguments, you first need to know if the information that is being presented is true. To do that, you need to be able to judge whether or not the source of that information is reliable. Many writers use information from sources that are not reliable. For example, when writers gather information from random Internet websites, some (or even much) of that information may not be true. When you are analyzing a writer's argument, look to see whether the writer's information comes from a trustworthy source.

You are reading an article about the American Revolutionary War. The author cites several sources that she has used for information. Which source is the most reliable?

A. letters written by a colonial spy during the Revolutionary War
B. an Internet site that has interesting facts about the Revolutionary War
C. a book entitled *What Else You Didn't Know About the Revolutionary War*
D. a magazine that features modern writers who are Revolutionary War history buffs

Choice A is the best source. Some of the others might also be reliable, but the letters were written by someone who was actually there when the events took place. Documents like that are the most trustworthy kind of information source. That is why they are called **primary sources**. Other kinds of primary sources include official government documents, speeches, and other texts written at the time of, or as part of, the events to which they relate.

Primary sources are reliable because they consist of eyewitness accounts or firsthand knowledge of ideas or events. **Secondary sources**, by contrast, are texts that analyze those ideas or events, but were written later by people who were not directly involved. Secondary sources include history textbooks and other academic works, magazine articles, plays and movies, and the like. Secondary sources are reliable only to the extent that they faithfully reflect the primary sources on which they are based. Also, the authors of secondary sources pick and choose which primary sources they wish to follow, and their choices may not always accurately portray reality. Finally, secondary sources may be unreliable because they may describe events in the light of the author's personal opinions.

Read the next example and decide why it is reliable.

Directions: Read the following text, which is excerpted from the *Memoirs* of General Ulysses S. Grant, the commander of the Union armies in the Civil War. Grant is describing his meeting with the Confederate commander General Robert E. Lee at the end of the war. Then answer the question.

What General Lee's feelings were I do not know. As he was a man of much dignity, with an impassable face, it was impossible to say whether he felt inwardly glad that the end had finally come, or felt sad over the result, and was too manly to show it. Whatever his feelings, they were entirely concealed from my observation; but my own feelings, which had been quite jubilant on the receipt of his letter, were sad and depressed. I felt like anything rather than rejoicing at the downfall of a foe who had fought so long and valiantly, and had suffered so much for a cause, though that cause was, I believe, one of the worst for which a people ever fought, and one for which there was the least excuse. I do not question, however, the sincerity of the great mass of those who were opposed to us.

Why are General Grant's *Memoirs* reliable?

A. They include stories that General Grant heard from friends of General Lee.
B. They are based on the author's research into General Lee's background.
C. They were written by a Northerner during the Civil War era.
D. They were written by a person who was an eyewitness.

Choice D is the correct answer. The *Memoirs* are reliable because they were written by a person who was an eyewitness of the events described. They are a primary source written by General Grant about General Lee.

Read the next example and decide who is a primary source.

Directions: Read the following passage, and then answer the question.

1   Yesterday evening Angela Lawrence reported an accident outside of her apartment building. "I was coming back from the store when I heard a loud crashing noise," Lawrence told this reporter. "There were two cars involved. It looked pretty bad. I dialed 911 and told them and they said they would send the police and an ambulance. I stayed here until they arrived."

2   Emergency fire vehicles reached the scene at 8:05 p.m. and tended to the accident victims. They had to use the jaws of life to extract one of the passengers, but it appears that the motorist only sustained minor injuries.

3   "It was a bad accident," said Police Chief Winston Albert. "We were able to get everyone out of the cars and, miraculously, there were no critical injuries. The EMTs worked very hard helping everyone and transported the accident victims to the hospital. Things might have been worse if they hadn't responded so quickly."

4   Lawrence's daughter, Marianne Lawrence, said that she looked out the window when she heard the crash. "It was a loud noise," she said. "I knew something was wrong. When I saw my mother on the street, I ran out of the house and watched what was going on. The police arrived first and then the ambulance. They really worked to get everyone out of the cars and into the ambulance. I hear that there were no critical injuries, so that was good news. The cars were wrecked, both of them, though."

5   This reporter was told by Chief Albert that the cause of the accident was a jammed gas pedal.

Three eyewitnesses are cited in the article: Angela Lawrence, Lawrence's daughter Marianne, and Police Chief Albert. Which of the following statements best describes these eyewitness accounts?

A. None of them is a primary source.
B. All of them are primary sources.
C. Police Chief Albert and Angela Lawrence are primary sources; Marianne Lawrence is not.
D. Marianne Lawrence is a primary source; Police Chief Albert and Angela Lawrence are not.

Choice B is the correct answer. All of these people were eyewitnesses, so their statements are primary sources.

Evaluating Claims

An author who is writing to persuade you may make many claims. While some of those claims may be valid, others might be based on faulty reasoning or invalid sources or may simply be misleading. It is up to you as a reader to decide which claims are valid and which are not.

Directions: Read the following passage, and then answer the question.

1 Good evening, Council members.

2   I want to tell you a story about myself. Four years ago, my wife bought me a bicycle. She thought I needed to get more exercise. At first I was resistant, but with her support I started to ride on the weekends. I realized how wonderful it was to be out of doors and also to be exercising. Slowly I started to benefit from that exercise with a more toned body, greater stamina, and improved circulation.

3   Then something hit me. My job is only two miles from my home. I decided to try biking to work as often as I could and I just loved it.

It still do love it. I get up in the morning, have my breakfast, and then just take off. To be honest, when it's raining or snowing I take the car, but even in winter, when it is clear, I cycle to work and the fresh cold air clears my head and makes me feel so good.

4   Did you know that according to the U.S. Census, some 500,000 people bike to work each day? I believe that number is growing at a fast pace. In addition, according to a website called Environmental Benefits of Cycling and Walking, there are about 2.8 million bike commuters. I would estimate that at least a third of these people are under the age of 16! They bike to and from school. Many of those counted are in high school and others are in college.

5   So that's why I am making the following proposal.

6   We as a community should create bike paths along the busiest roads. This would make bike travel so much safer for the bikers and for vehicle drivers as well. It would also promote an activity that helps people get and stay in shape.

7   I have drawn up a petition which has been signed by 412 people, and that's without even trying. I know that I could garner more than 1000 signatures if need be.

Which claim is most valid?

A. Some 500,000 people bike to work each day.
B. Bike paths make travel safer for vehicle drivers was well as for bikers.
C. At least a third of the 2.8 million bike commuters are under the age of 16.
D. The speaker can easily get more than 1000 signatures on the petition.

Choice A is the most valid claim. It is backed up by the U.S. Census. The other claims are not backed up by any authority.

Rhetorical Techniques

Writers and orators use many verbal techniques to capture an audience's attention. These are called **rhetorical techniques**.

There are several different kinds of rhetorical techniques. Some of the most common are the use of alliteration, analogies, enumerations, repetition and parallelism, juxtaposition of opposites, and qualifying statements. These techniques are used by writers and speakers to make their words more attractive and interesting to you. Writers or speakers who are trying to convince you of something will use rhetorical techniques to make their arguments more persuasive.

- **Alliteration** is the repetition of letters in words to draw attention to what is being said.

- **Analogy** is the comparison of one situation to another to make a point.

- **Enumeration** is making a list of different items or breaking the items into categories.

- **Repetition** and **parallelism** occur when a writer repeats related statements in a parallel or equivalent way.

- **Juxtaposition of opposites** is a way to show how things are different from one another.

- **Qualifying statements** show that a statement may or may not be true as stated.

Directions: Read the following passage, which comes from President Barack Obama's Keynote Address at the Democratic Convention in 2004 when he was a senator from Illinois. Then answer the question.

That is the true genius of America, a faith—a faith in simple dreams, an insistence on small miracles; that we can tuck in our children at night and know that they are fed and clothed and safe from harm; that we can say what we think, write what we think, without hearing a sudden knock on the door; that we can have an idea and start our own business without paying a bribe; that we can participate in the political process without fear of retribution, and that our votes will be counted—at least most of the time.

What rhetorical technique does President Obama employ?

A. analogy
B. alliteration
C. qualifying statements
D. repetition and parallelism

Choice D is the correct answer. The presentation of ideas in repeated, parallel forms is used to make a dramatic statement.

Author's Response to Conflicting Viewpoints and Bias

People engaged with ideas or events often have conflicting viewpoints. An author who wants to describe those different viewpoints can deal with them in different ways. She or he can try to be objective and avoid taking sides. But an author who supports a particular viewpoint may wish to argue in favor of that side. One way to do so is to favor evidence that supports that side. An author who unfairly presents only evidence that favors one particular side, and limits or omits evidence that supports the other side, is said to be **biased**. When you are analyzing a text, you need to recognize when the author is biased in favor of one particular viewpoint.

Directions: Read the following example, and then answer the question.

1   Scientists are divided on the topic of the effects of the blue light that is emitted from electronic devices, including television sets. Many argue that the blue light upsets the body's melatonin levels, which interfere with sleep. Others say that simple common sense practices can offset the problem of loss of melatonin.

2   Researchers at the University of Basel in Switzerland recently studied the effects of evening use of computer monitors. Thirteen volunteers were studied in a controlled setting where they were exposed to five hours of computer light in the evening and night time hours. Some used blue light LED monitors; others used white, non-LED backlit screens. Those exposed to blue light showed a significant, measurable decrease in cognitive performance, attention span, and alertness as compared to the volunteers using white screens. Most important, the results showed a significant inhibition of the normal nighttime rise of endogenous (naturally produced) melatonin in the blue light user group.

3   In another study by engineers at Rensselaer Polytechnic Institute (RPI) in Troy, New York, the findings of the Basel researchers were confirmed. Extensive use of the electronic devices interfered with the body's normal night time increase in the release of melatonin. In fact, usage of these devices two hours before retiring to sleep lowered melatonin by 22 percent in the experimental group. It is precisely this group, adolescents and young adults, who are the most prone to sleep disruption and the consequent pattern of behavior changes. The task being performed on the device, as well as how close it was held to the retina, affected the level of melatonin suppression by as much as a factor of 10 in the lux level, a measure of the intensity of light perceived by the eye.

4   Even though these studies show some negative effects of electronic devices, there is also proof, which I find encouraging, that those effects can be mitigated by using tinted goggles or by attaching tinted screens over monitors. The advancement of technology is too important to be held back by these side effects.

Which of the following best expresses the position of the writer?

A. The writer is against all advances in electronic technology.
B. The writer believes that problems with electronic devices can be resolved.
C. The writer thinks that electronic devices should be banned.
D. The writer wants scientists to stop studying the effects of blue light.

Choice B is the correct answer. According to the writer, studies indicate that electronic devices have some harmful effects. But on the other hand, there are ways to control these effects so that users are not harmed. The writer neither claims that electronic devices are harmless nor calls for bans on their use. Instead, evidence on both sides is presented objectively, without bias toward one side or the other.

Comparing Texts

One task that you will encounter on the GED RLA test is to compare two passages. The passages will both be nonfiction and will usually have a similar theme or topic, but each text will approach that topic from a different angle. The questions may be about the similarities or differences between the passages in terms of perspective, tone, structure, purpose, or overall impact.

Directions: Read the following passages, and then answer the questions.

Passage A

1   I have been studying the subject of school-uniform requirements and have finally come to a conclusion based on what I have found. According to the literature and studies that I have read, it is wise to require schoolchildren to wear uniforms so that the playing field will be level for all students.

2   The studies I have read show that when children are required to wear an issued uniform, they all look basically alike. If a uniform is not required, some children will wear more expensive clothes and others will wear hand-me-downs. Studies show that these differences in dress lead to divisions among the students. Children whose clothes are similar—both the well-to-do and the poorer children—will seek each other out. Children in one group will not associate with children in another group. The resulting class-conscious division can be detrimental to the future of a child's development. That is the conclusion that I have come to after thinking long and hard about this subject.

Passage B

1   I believe in my heart that children should be allowed to express themselves. Even at a young age, being allowed to select the clothes they wear helps children to develop their sense of individualism and identity. This is why I am opposed to requiring uniforms in schools. Simply dressing children in the same way will not keep some children from associating exclusively with peers who are most like themselves socially and economically.

2   Uniforms just make children feel lost because they do not have the ability to show who they are or who they would like to be. Requiring uniforms would nip in the bud any sense of creative spirit and would only cause resentment in children who might not feel that way otherwise. I feel it is un-American to require school uniforms and I am opposed to it completely. This is not something that we should be doing to our children!

3   The truth is that uniforms do not make children equal, as some educators believe; they just stunt their growth.

How is the tone of Passage A different from the tone of Passage B?

A. Passage A has an angrier tone than Passage B.
B. Passage A has a sadder tone that Passage B.
C. Passage A has a more inspirational tone than Passage B.
D. Passage A has a more thoughtful tone than Passage B.

Choice D is the correct answer. The author of Passage A makes it clear that she or he has done a great deal of research and has thought about the subject in great depth. The tone of Passage A is much more thoughtful than the tone of Passage B, which is more argumentative and less sensitive.

How are Passage A and Passage B similar in purpose? Both passages

A. want to convince readers that a particular idea is correct.
B. employ rhetorical techniques to capture attention and get their point across.
C. want to impress readers by presenting scientific evidence.
D. support their viewpoint through the use of anecdotes.

Choice A is the only option that is correct. Both passages want to convince readers that they are correct. Passage B does use some rhetorical techniques, but Passage A does not. The author of Passage A is probably trying to impress readers by citing studies, but this is not true of the author of Passage B. Neither passage includes an anecdote, so choice D is not correct.

You may also be asked to compare passages of different genres or to compare a graphic representation with a text. These questions will ask you about the way in which information is presented.

Directions: Read the following passages, and then answer the questions.

Passage A

Report: Why Many Students Attend Community College

This report was compiled at the request of the President of Hanover County Community College.

We started our study on students studying at Hanover County Community College six months ago. This is the analysis that we have developed.

Of the 98 students interviewed:

- 69 students said they were happy they chose a community college over a four-year college.

- 18 students said they felt they should have gone directly into a four-year college.

The reasons given for choosing a community college were:

- Finances—the cost of a community college is less than the cost of a four-year college.

- Ability to live at home—45 of the 98 students interviewed live at home.

- Ability to take courses when they wanted—42 students said they liked the idea of being able to take night courses instead of day courses because it fit their lifestyle better.

- Combining school and work—55 students were employed, some full time, some part time.

Of the 98 students interviewed:

- 49 students said that would go on to get their bachelor's degree.

- 25 students said that they would not seek further education.

- 24 students said they had not made a decision on whether to seek a higher degree.

Passage B

Community Colleges Get the Job Done

by Clarence Williams

More and more students are turning to community colleges instead of four-year schools, and they say it is the practical thing to do.

"I attend Hanover Community College and I am studying criminal justice. I just couldn't have afforded a four-year college. But I feel I am getting a good foundation here, and then I will transfer. It's just less of a big deal to go to a community college and live at home than it would be to go to a school that would cost a lot and wouldn't provide an education in the basics that was any better," said second-year student Jeffrey Bailey, who will graduate this spring with an associate's degree in criminal justice.

"I am planning to go to State next fall. I feel that I am prepared for that big jump now. I've saved up some money, and I even got a scholarship. I am in good shape," he said.

He echoes the sentiments of many of the students at Hanover Community College. Recently the college authorized a study of its students, which shows that of 98 students who were interviewed, 69 said they were happy with their choice of a community college over a four-year school.

The study was commissioned by Hanover Community College but done by an outside agency. Other findings showed that a majority of the students at Hanover Community College are planning to go on to get a bachelor's degree.

"We are definitely filling a niche in our community. We offer good education in the basics and a way to get educated without breaking the bank," said college spokesman Dean Arthur D'Elia.

He added that there are some 500 students enrolled in the school this year compared to 350 three years ago.

How is the intended audience of Passage A different from the intended audience of Passage B?

A. The intended audience of Passage A is students, while the intended audience of Passage B is college teachers and administrators.

B. The intended audience of Passage A is the general public, while the intended audience of Passage B is students.

C. The intended audience of Passage A is college teachers and administrators, while the intended audience of Passage B is the general public.

D. The intended audience of Passage A is high school students, while the intended audience of Passage B is college teachers and administrators.

Choice C is the correct answer. Passage A is a report on the students at Hanover Community College and was intended for college teachers and administrators. Passage B is a newspaper story intended for the general public.

How does the genre of each passage affect your opinion of the information it contains?

A. Passage A is less credible than Passage B.
B. Passage A is more factual than Passage B.
C. Passage A is more emotional than Passage B.
D. Passage A is harder to understand than Passage B.

Choice B is the correct answer. Passage A is a report based strictly on facts; Passage B is a newspaper article that weaves facts into a story designed to attract reader interest.

Directions: Read the following passages, and then answer the question.

Passage A

1   The expiration dates on packaged foods can be confusing. They are not always accurate since it depends on how a product is refrigerated, packaged, and whether it has been opened or not.

2   But expiration dates do exist and people use them as a guide for how long a product will last. If, however, your refrigerator is not as cold as it should be, or if you leave your quart of milk out on the table for a half hour each day, the expiration date will not be accurate and bacteria will start growing at a greater speed, which means that your food will spoil much faster.

3   There are even expiration dates on water. These are usually one or two years after the water was bottled. Manufacturers of bottled water say that the taste of water will degenerate after a certain period. This may seem a bit odd. After all, water is water, but that is the belief of the people in the industry.

4   There are many ways that food can spoil. Microbes can grow in milk, making it taste terrible; mold can grow on cheese, but some people just cut off the moldy part and still use the cheese.

5   Some food may taste fine but still contain deadly microbes. Other foods may taste bad but still be safe to eat, as long as you don't mind the taste.

Passage B

How to Interpret Expiration Dates

What Does It Say?	What Does This Mean?	Can It Be Eaten?
Use by	The manufacturer won't guarantee the food's quality after this date.	It may still be edible, but may be less appealing.
Sell by	Tells the store when to take the product off the shelf.	The food will still be good for a few days.
Expires	Throw the food out after this date.	Should not be eaten.

How does the table in Passage B complement the information in Passage A?

A. It details the ways in which foods can be preserved.
B. It tells which foods can be eaten even if they are spoiled.
C. It tells how long foods will last when properly refrigerated.
D. It gives specific information about different types of expiration dates.

Choice D is the correct answer. Passage A describes expiration dates and their uses in general; the table in Passage B lists three different kinds of expiration dates and tells what each one means.

Informational Texts

Directions: Read the following text, which is excerpted from *The Hurricane* by John James Audubon. Then answer the questions.

1   Various portions of our country have at different periods suffered severely from the influence of violent storms of wind, some of which have been known to traverse nearly the whole extent of the United States, and to leave such deep impressions in their wake as will not easily be forgotten. Having witnessed one of these awful phenomena, in all its grandeur, I will attempt to describe it. The recollection of that astonishing revolution of the ethereal element even now bringing with it so disagreeable a sensation, that I feel as if about to be affected by a sudden stoppage of the circulation of my blood.

2   I had left the village of Shawaney, situated on the banks of the Ohio, on my return from Henderson, which is also situated on the banks of the same beautiful stream. The weather was pleasant, and I thought not warmer than usual at that season. My horse was jogging quietly along, and my thoughts were, for once at least in the course of my life, entirely engaged in commercial speculations. I had forded Highland Creek, and was on the eve of entering a tract of bottom land or valley that lay between it and Canoe Creek, when on a sudden I remarked a great difference in the aspect of the heavens. A hazy thickness had overspread the country, and I for some time expected an earthquake, but my horse exhibited no propensity to stop and prepare for such an occurrence. I had nearly arrived at the verge of the valley, when I thought fit to stop near a brook, and dismounted to quench the thirst which had come upon me.

3   I was leaning on my knees, with my lips about to touch the water, when from my proximity to the earth, I heard a distant murmuring sound of an extraordinary nature. I drank, however, and as I rose on my feet, looked toward the southwest, where I observed a yellowish oval spot, the appearance of which was quite new to me. Little time was left me for consideration, as the next moment a smart breeze began to agitate the taller trees. It increased to an unexpected height, and already the smaller branches and twigs were seen falling in a slanting direction towards the ground. Two minutes had scarcely elapsed, when the whole forest before me was in fearful motion. Here and there, where one tree pressed against another, a creaking noise was produced, similar to that occasioned by the violent gusts which sometimes sweep over the country. Turning instinctively toward the direction from which the wind blew, I saw, to my great astonishment, that the noblest trees of the forest bent their lofty heads for a while, and, unable to stand against the blast, were falling into pieces. First, the branches were broken off with a crackling noise; then went the upper part of the massy trunks; and in many places whole trees of gigantic size were falling entire to

the ground. So rapid was the progress of the storm, that before I could think of taking measures to insure my safety, the hurricane was passing opposite the place where I stood. Never can I forget the scene which at that moment presented itself. The tops of the trees were seen moving in the strangest manner, in the central current of the tempest, which carried along with it a mingled mass of twigs and foliage, that completely obscured the view. Some of the largest trees were seen bending and writhing under the gale; others suddenly snapped across; and many, after a momentary resistance, fell uprooted to the earth. The mass of branches, twigs, foliage, and dust that moved through the air, was whirled onward like a cloud of feathers, and on passing, disclosed a wide space filled with fallen trees, naked stumps, and heaps of shapeless ruins, which marked the path of the tempest. This space was about a fourth of a mile in breadth, and to my imagination resembled the dried-up bed of the Mississippi, with its thousands of planters and sawyers, strewn in the sand, and inclined in various degrees. The horrible noise resembled that of the great cataracts of Niagara, and as it howled along in the track of the desolating tempest, produced a feeling in my mind which it is impossible to describe.

1. What is the author's viewpoint towards the storm?

   A. He is terrified that he will be injured by the storm.
   B. He is in awe of the power of the storm.
   C. He fears that the storm may have killed people.
   D. He loves being in storms because he finds them exciting.

2. Which quotation expresses an opinion?

   A. "I had left the village of Shawaney, situated on the banks of the Ohio, on my return from Henderson, which is also situated on the banks of the same beautiful stream."
   B. "I had forded Highland Creek, and was on the eve of entering a tract of bottom land or valley that lay between it and Canoe Creek, when on a sudden I remarked a great difference in the aspect of the heavens."
   C. "I had nearly arrived at the verge of the valley, when I thought fit to stop near a brook, and dismounted to quench the thirst which had come upon me."
   D. "The mass of branches, twigs, foliage, and dust that moved through the air, was whirled onward like a cloud of feathers, and on passing, disclosed a wide space filled with fallen trees, naked stumps, and heaps of shapeless ruins, which marked the path of the tempest."

3. What primary cause-and-effect relationship is found in the text? Between the

   A. storm and the trees
   B. author and the trees
   C. storm and the stream
   D. author and the stream

4. Why is this text reliable?

   A. It was written by an eyewitness to the storm.
   B. It is excerpted from a story in a much longer book.
   C. It describes something that many people have experienced.
   D. It was written long before people understood what causes storms.

Directions: Read the following passages, and then answer the questions.

PASSAGE A

The following text is excerpted from the speech given by Chief Joseph of the Nez Perce Native American tribe upon surrendering to the U.S. federal government in 1877.

1   Tell General Howard I know his heart. What he told me before, I have it in my heart. I am tired of fighting. Our Chiefs are killed; Looking Glass is dead, Ta Hool Hool Shute is dead. The old men are all dead. It is the young men who say yes or no. He who led on the young men is dead. It is cold, and we have no blankets; the little children are freezing to death. My people, some of them, have run away to the hills, and have no blankets, no food. No one knows where they are—perhaps freezing to death. I want to have time to look for my children, and see how many of them I can find. Maybe I shall find them among the dead. Hear me, my Chiefs! I am tired; my heart is sick and sad. From where the sun now stands I will fight no more forever.

PASSAGE B

The following text is excerpted from a speech given by Chief Seattle of the Suquamish Native American tribe to Governor Isaac Stevens in the Washington Territory in 1854.

1   White Chief says the Big Chief at Washington sends us greetings of friendship and good will. This is kind of him for we know he has little need of our friendship in return. His people are many. They are like the grass that covers vast prairies. My people are few. They resemble the scattering trees of a storm-swept plain. The Great—and I presume—good White Chief sends us word that he wishes to buy our lands but is willing to allow us enough land to live comfortably. This indeed appears just, even generous, for the Red Man no longer has rights that he need respect, and the offer may be wise also, as we are no longer in need of an extensive country. . . .

2   To us the ashes of our ancestors are sacred and their resting place is hallowed ground. You wander far from the graves of your ancestors and seemingly without regret. Your religion was written upon tables of stone by the iron finger of your God so that you could not forget. The Red Man could never comprehend nor remember it. Our religion is the tradition of our ancestors—the dreams of our old men, given in solemn hours of night by the

Great Spirit; and the visions of our sachems; and it is written in the hearts of our people. . . .

3   However, your proposition seems fair, and I think that my people will accept it and will retire to the reservation you offer them. . . . But should we accept it, I here and now make this condition—that we will not be denied the privilege of visiting at any time the tombs of our ancestors, friends and children. Every part of this soil is sacred in the estimation of my people. Every hillside, every valley, every plain and grove, has been hallowed by some sad or happy event in days long vanished. The very dust upon which you stand responds more lovingly to my people's footsteps than to yours, because it is rich with the dust of their ancestors, and our feet are conscious of their sympathetic touch.

5. In passage A, what is Chief Joseph's viewpoint on war?

    A. He has been fighting in war long enough.
    B. He has never waged war against anyone.
    C. He believes that war is his only alternative.
    D. He wants the young men of his tribe to wage war.

6. In passage B, what is Chief Seattle's view of the relations between whites and Native Americans at the time when he spoke?

    A. Native Americans had little power and were few in number compared to whites.
    B. Native Americans and whites were on friendly terms and trusted one another.
    C. Native Americans were used to being treated with respect by white Americans.
    D. Native Americans would never surrender their land to whites and live on reservations.

7. How is the purpose of Chief Joseph's speech different from the purpose of Chief Seattle's speech?

    A. Chief Joseph wants to fight for more land, but Chief Seattle is willing to settle for less land.
    B. Chief Joseph wants to ensure that his people are safe, but Chief Seattle wants to please the federal government.
    C. Chief Joseph is trying to provoke the federal government, but Chief Seattle wants to reach a settlement with the federal government.
    D. Chief Joseph is surrendering after being beaten in war, but Chief Seattle is agreeing to go willingly into a reservation.

8. In what way is the perspective of Chief Joseph similar to the perspective of Chief Seattle? They both

    A. are concerned about their people's future welfare.
    B. want to thank the federal government for its help.
    C. are angry with the federal government regarding its treatment of their people.
    D. believe they need more land than what the federal government will give them.

Directions: Read the following passages, and then answer the questions.

PASSAGE A

The following text is excerpted from a speech given by Patrick Henry, a delegate to the Virginia Convention in 1775, in regard to the American colonies and their relationship to Great Britain.

1   Sir, we have done everything that could be done to avert the storm which is now coming on. We have petitioned; we have remonstrated; we have supplicated; we have prostrated ourselves before the throne, and have implored its interposition to arrest the tyrannical hands of the ministry and Parliament.

2   Our petitions have been slighted; our remonstrances have produced additional violence and insult; our supplications have been disregarded; and we have been spurned, with contempt, from the foot of the throne. In vain, after these things, may we indulge the fond hope of peace and reconciliation. There is no longer any room for hope.

3   If we wish to be free—if we mean to preserve inviolate those inestimable privileges for which we have been so long contending—if we mean not basely to abandon the noble struggle in which we have been so long engaged, and which we have pledged ourselves never to abandon until the glorious object of our contest shall be obtained, we must fight! I repeat it, sir, we must fight! An appeal to arms and to the God of Hosts is all that is left us!

4   They tell us, sir, that we are weak—unable to cope with so formidable an adversary. But when shall we be stronger? Will it be the next week, or the next year? Will it be when we are totally disarmed, and when a British guard shall be stationed in every house? Shall we gather strength by irresolution and inaction? Shall we acquire the means of effectual resistance, by lying supinely on our backs, and hugging the delusive phantom of hope, until our enemies shall have bound us hand and foot?

5   Sir, we are not weak, if we make a proper use of the means which the God of nature hath placed in our power. Three millions of people, armed in the holy cause of liberty, and in such a country as that which we possess, are invincible by any force which our enemy can send against us. Besides, sir, we shall not fight our battles alone. There is a just God who presides over the destinies of nations, and who will raise up friends to fight our battles for us.

6   The battle, sir, is not to the strong alone; it is to the vigilant, the active, the brave. Besides, sir, we have no election. If we were base enough to desire it, it is now too late to retire from the contest. There is no retreat but in submission and slavery! Our chains are forged! Their clanking may be heard on the plains of Boston! The war is inevitable—and let it come! I repeat it, sir, let it come!

7   It is in vain, sir, to extenuate the matter. Gentlemen may cry, "Peace! Peace!"—but there is no peace. The war is actually begun! The next gale that sweeps from the north will bring to our ears the clash of resounding arms! Our brethren are already in the field! Why stand we here idle? What is it that gentlemen wish? What would they have? Is life so dear, or peace so sweet, as to be purchased at the price of chains and slavery? Forbid it, Almighty God! I know not what course others may take; but as for me, give me liberty, or give me death!

PASSAGE B

1773

May 10	The Tea Act
Dec. 16	The Boston Tea Party

1774

March 31	Boston Port Act, one of the "Intolerable Acts"
May 20	Administration of Justice Act, one of the "Intolerable Acts"
May 20	Massachusetts Government Act, one of the "Intolerable Acts"
June 2	Quartering Act of 1774, one of the "Intolerable Acts"
June 22	Quebec Act, one of the "Intolerable Acts"
Sept. 5–Oct. 26	The First Continental Congress meets in Philadelphia and issues Declaration and Resolves
Oct. 10	Battle of Point Pleasant, Virginia (disputed as to whether it was a battle of the American Revolution or the culmination of Lord Dunmore's War)
Oct. 20	The Association (prohibition of trade with Great Britain)
Oct. 24	Galloway's Plan rejected

1775

March 23	Patrick Henry's "Give me liberty or give me death" speech
Apr. 18	The rides of Paul Revere and William Dawes
Apr. 19	Minutemen and British troops clash at Lexington and Concord; "The shot heard 'round the world."

9. What is Patrick Henry's main argument?

   A. War has really already started against Great Britain.
   B. Not enough has been done to avert war with Great Britain.
   C. The colonies have other options than to go to war with Great Britain.
   D. The colonies are not strong enough to win a war against Great Britain.

10. Which rhetorical technique does Patrick Henry use in paragraph 7 of Passage A?

   A. anecdote
   B. alliteration
   C. qualifying statements
   D. repetition and parallelism

11. Which quotation from Passage A supports Patrick Henry's claim that the colonies are not weak?

   A. "Sir, we have done everything that could be done to avert the storm which is now coming on."
   B. "An appeal to arms and to the God of Hosts is all that is left us!"
   C. "Three millions of people, armed in the holy cause of liberty, and in such a country as that which we possess, are invincible by any force which our enemy can send against us."
   D. "The battle, sir, is not to the strong alone; it is to the vigilant, the active, the brave."

12. How does the timeline in Passage B complement Patrick Henry's speech in Passage A? It indicates

   A. the reasons that caused each event in the timeline to take place.
   B. the reasons that caused the American colonies to go to war with Great Britain.
   C. how his speech caused other events that led to war.
   D. when his speech was given in relation to other events leading to war.

Answers are on pages 303–304.

CHAPTER 6

RLA Essay Writing

The GED Reasoning Through Language Arts (RLA) test includes two extended-response items. For each one, you will read two nonfiction texts. Then you will analyze and assess their arguments and write a fairly long essay stating your opinion about which text offers the soundest arguments and why. Your essay should be designed to persuade a reader that your opinion is correct. You will need to present evidence to back up your claims.

The following section will focus on what makes an effective persuasive essay.

Elements of a Persuasive Essay

The purpose of persuasive writing is to gain acceptance for an idea, a point of view, or a recommended course of action. The chief means of gaining this acceptance is to present as strong an argument as possible.

An **argument** is an ordered presentation of support for a position that you want others to accept. An argument is made up of an opening statement of position, any background information that your reader may need to follow the argument, the evidence that you use to support and defend your position—including a response to opposing arguments, if needed—and a concluding statement.

In general terms, your persuasive essay should include the following elements.

Opening Statement

In persuasive writing, the purpose of the opening paragraph is to launch your argument with a clear, concise statement of your position. Give your opinion with conviction, but do not antagonize your audience with overly emotional words or phrases.

Supporting Evidence

In the following paragraphs, develop your argument in a logical manner and present evidence to support your position. Your supporting evidence can consist of facts or arguments from a text that you are analyzing. Organize the evidence for maximum effect by using order of importance or another appropriate method of development. Because you will be typing your essay into a computer, you will be able to write down your ideas quickly, and then go back to refine your essay. As you write, you will be able to view the passages that you are writing about, which will help you recall their arguments and the evidence they contain.

When writing, keep in mind the importance of achieving coherence in your essay. Make sure to include transition words because you want your audience to follow every step of your thinking. Some common transition words and phrases are:

To Present Evidence

First, second, third

Most important

For example

For instance

The facts show

According to

To State Your Opinion

In my opinion

I believe that

From my point of view

In my experience

To Deal with Conflicting Opinions or Arguments

Although

Conversely

In opposition to

Even though

In contrast to

Still

Remember that in persuasive writing, your strongest weapon is your supporting evidence. Your personal commitment to your argument is important, but your readers will judge your ideas on how well they are supported by evidence.

Answering Opposing Arguments

Your argument will be stronger if you anticipate questions or doubts in your audience's mind and respond to them. Depending on your topic, you may present and answer opposing arguments in a paragraph just before the concluding paragraph or as you develop each of your main points.

Concluding Statement

Conclude your persuasive essay with a short restatement of your central argument. Your concluding statement should summarize your position and briefly review the reasons for your choice.

Scoring Rubric

Each of your essays will be scored on a 0 to 12 point system. The essays are graded based on sets of writing standards called **rubrics**. There are three rubrics, worth 2 points each. Your score on each one will be double-weighted so that the maximum point score is 12. The first rubric will assess your analysis of arguments and the use of evidence in your essay. The second rubric will assess the development of your ideas and the organizational structure of your essay. The third rubric will assess the clarity of your writing and the command of Standard English conventions in your essay. Your essay does not have to be perfect grammatically. But it does need to be logical and coherent and include evidence from the passages for your position.

Here are simplified versions of the rubrics. Read through them so that you know what the readers scoring your essay are looking for.

Score	Description
Trait 1: Creation of Arguments and Use of Evidence	
2	Creates an argument based on the source text(s), with a purpose that relates to the prompt
	Supports the argument with evidence from the source text(s)
	Analyzes issues and/or evaluates arguments in the source texts (e.g., identifies claims that are not supported, makes reasonable inferences about underlying assumptions, identifies unsound reasoning, evaluates source credibility, etc.)

(continued)

Score	Description
1	Creates an argument that has some relation to the prompt
	Supports the argument with some evidence from the source text(s)
	Makes some attempt to analyze issues and/or evaluate arguments in the source texts
0	May try to create an argument OR response lacks any relation to the prompt
	Presents little or no evidence from the source text(s)
	Makes very little attempt to analyze issues and/or evaluate arguments in the source texts; may show little or no understanding of given argument(s)
Trait 2: Development of Ideas and Organizational Structure	
2	Presents well-developed, generally logical ideas; elaborates on most ideas
	Organizes ideas in a sensible sequence; clearly links main points and details
	Structures the response to clearly convey the message and purpose; makes use of transition words
	Uses a formal style and appropriate tone, showing awareness of the audience
	Chooses words that express ideas clearly
1	Presents ideas in a way that indicates vague or simplistic reasoning; elaborates on only some ideas
	Sequence of ideas has some logic, but connections between main ideas and details may be poor or missing
	Organization of ideas may be inconsistent or not fully effective at conveying the argument; few transition words are used
	Style and tone may be inconsistent or not always appropriate for the audience or purpose of the response
	May sometimes misuse words and/or choose words that do not make the meaning clear

Score	Description
0	Develops ideas without consistency or logic; offers little or no elaboration on main ideas
	Organization of ideas is unclear or shows no logic; details may be missing or unrelated to the main idea
	Creates an organizational structure that is ineffective or cannot be followed; does not use transition words or uses them inappropriately
	Uses an inappropriate style and/or tone and shows little or no awareness of the audience
	May frequently misuse words, overuse slang, repeat ideas, or express ideas unclearly

Trait 3: Clarity and Command of Standard English Conventions

Score	Description
2	Uses largely correct sentence structure in regard to the following:
	• Sentence structure varies within a paragraph or paragraphs
	• Subordination, coordination, and parallelism are used correctly
	• Wordiness and awkwardness are avoided
	• Transitional words are used as appropriate
	• There are no run-on sentences, fused sentences, and sentence fragments
	Applies Standard English conventions competently in regard to the following:
	• Frequently confused words and homonyms, including contractions
	• Subject-verb agreement
	• Pronoun usage, including pronoun-antecedent agreement, unclear pronoun references, and pronoun case
	• Placement of modifiers and correct word order
	• Capitalization
	• Use of apostrophes with possessive nouns
	• Punctuation
	May make some errors in usage and mechanics, but these do not interfere with meaning overall

(continued)

Score	Description
1	Uses inconsistent sentence structure; may include some repetitive or awkward sentences that interfere with clarity; control over sentence structure and fluency is inconsistent
	Control of Standard English grammar and punctuation is inconsistent
	May make frequent errors in usage and mechanics that occasionally interfere with meaning
0	Sentence structure is consistently flawed and may obscure meaning; control over sentence structure and fluency is minimal
	Control of Standard English grammar and punctuation is minimal
	Makes severe and frequent errors in usage and mechanics that interfere with meaning OR response is insufficient to demonstrate level of mastery over usage and mechanics

Nonscorable Responses

- Response contains only text copied from source texts or prompt
- Response shows no evidence that test-taker has read the prompt or is off-topic
- Response is incomprehensible
- Response is not in English
- Response has not been attempted (blank)

Writing a Persuasive Essay

On the essay portion of the GED® test, when you are given two conflicting arguments, your job is to persuade your readers that one of the two arguments is stronger than the other. So your first task is to evaluate the strength of each argument. You studied how to analyze arguments in the preceding chapter. You learned how to:

- Separate facts from opinion
- Determine if sources are reliable
- Evaluate claims

Now you need to use these skills to analyze the arguments in the passages in the essay portion. If you determine that one of the two arguments better reflects the facts, or is based on more reliable sources, or makes more valid claims, that is the evidence you need for your essay. You can use it to show why you think one argument is stronger than the other, and to persuade your readers that your opinion is correct.

Directions: Read the following two passages.

Passage A

The following text is excerpted from a speech given in Des Moines, Iowa, in 1941 by the American aviator Charles Lindbergh.

1   When this war started in Europe, it was clear that the American people were solidly opposed to entering it. Why shouldn't we be? We had the best defensive position in the world; we had a tradition of independence from Europe; and the one time we did take part in a European war left European problems unsolved, and debts to America unpaid.

2   National polls showed that when England and France declared war on Germany, in 1939, less than 10 percent of our population favored a similar course for America. But there were various groups of people, here and abroad, whose interests and beliefs necessitated the involvement of the United States in the war.

3   To use a specific example; in 1939, we were told that we should increase our air corps to a total of 5000 planes. Congress passed the necessary legislation. A few months later, the administration told us that the United States should have at least 50,000 planes for our national safety. But almost as fast as fighting planes were turned out from our factories, they were sent abroad, although our own air corps was in the utmost need of new equipment; so that today, two years after the start of war, the American army has a few hundred thoroughly modern bombers and fighters—less in fact, than Germany is able to produce in a single month.

4   Ever since its inception, our arms program has been laid out for the purpose of carrying on the war in Europe, far more than for the purpose of building an adequate defense for America. Now at the same time we were being prepared for a foreign war, it was necessary, as I have said, to involve us in the war. This was accomplished under that now famous phrase "steps short of war."

5   England and France would win if the United States would only repeal its arms embargo and sell munitions for cash, we were told. And then this refrain began, a refrain that marked every step we took toward war for many months—"the best way to defend America and keep out of war," we were told, was "by aiding the Allies."

6   First, we agreed to sell arms to Europe; next, we agreed to loan arms to Europe; then we agreed to patrol the ocean for Europe; then we occupied a European island in the war zone. Now, we have reached the verge of war.

7   The war groups have succeeded in the first two of their three major steps into war. The greatest armament program in our history is under way.

8   We have become involved in the war from practically every standpoint except actual shooting. Only the creation of sufficient "incidents" yet remains; and you see the first of these already taking place, according to plan— a plan that was never laid before the American people for their approval.

9   Men and women of Iowa; only one thing holds this country from war today. That is the rising opposition of the American people. Our system of democracy and representative government is on test today as it has never been before. We are on the verge of a war in which the only victor would be chaos and prostration.

10   We are on the verge of a war for which we are still unprepared, and for which no one has offered a feasible plan for victory—a war which cannot be won without sending our soldiers across the ocean to force a landing on a hostile coast against armies stronger than our own.

11   We are on the verge of war, but it is not yet too late to stay out. It is not too late to show that no amount of money, or propaganda, or patronage can force a free and independent people into war against its will. It is not yet too late to retrieve and to maintain the independent American destiny that our forefathers established in this new world.

12   The entire future rests upon our shoulders. It depends upon our action, our courage, and our intelligence. If you oppose our intervention in the war, now is the time to make your voice heard.

13   Help us to organize these meetings; and write to your representatives in Washington. I tell you that the last stronghold of democracy and representative government in this country is in our House of Representatives and our Senate.

14   There, we can still make our will known. And if we, the American people, do that, independence and freedom will continue to live among us, and there will be no foreign war.

Passage B

The following text is excerpted from President Franklin Delano Roosevelt's press conference on December 17, 1940.

1   Now we have been getting stories, speeches, et cetera, in regard to this particular war that is going on, which go back a little bit to that attitude. It isn't merely a question of doing things the traditional way; there are lots of other ways of doing them.

2   There is another one which is also somewhat banal—we may come to it, I don't know—and that is a gift; in other words, for us to pay for all these munitions, ships, plants, guns, et cetera, and make a gift of

them to Great Britain. I am not at all sure that that is a necessity, and I am not at all sure that Great Britain would care to have a gift from the taxpayers of the United States. I doubt it very much.

3   Well, there are other possible ways, and those ways are being explored. All I can do is to speak in very general terms, because we are in the middle of it. I have been at it now three or four weeks, exploring other methods of continuing the building up of our productive facilities and continuing automatically the flow of munitions to Great Britain. I will just put it this way, not as an exclusive alternative method, but as one of several other possible methods that might be devised toward that end.

4   It is possible—I will put it that way—for the United States to take over British orders, and, because they are essentially the same kind of munitions that we use ourselves, turn them into American orders. We have enough money to do it. And thereupon, as to such portion of them as the military events of the future determine to be right and proper for us to allow to go to the other side, either lease or sell the materials, subject to mortgage, to the people on the other side. That would be on the general theory that it may still prove true that the best defense of Great Britain is the best defense of the United States, and therefore that these materials would be more useful to the defense of the United States if they were used in Great Britain, than if they were kept in storage here.

5   Now, what I am trying to do is to eliminate the dollar sign. That is something brand new in the thoughts of practically everybody in this room, I think—get rid of the silly, foolish old dollar sign.

6   Well, let me give you an illustration: Suppose my neighbor's home catches fire, and I have a length of garden hose four or five hundred feet away. If he can take my garden hose and connect it up with his hydrant, I may help him to put out his fire. Now, what do I do? I don't say to him before that operation, "Neighbor, my garden hose cost me $15; you have to pay me $15 for it." What is the transaction that goes on? I don't want $15—I want my garden hose back after the fire is over. All right. If it goes through the fire all right, intact, without any damage to it, he gives it back to me and thanks me very much for the use of it. But suppose it gets smashed up—holes in it—during the fire; we don't have to have too much formality about it, but I say to him, "I was glad to lend you that hose; I see I can't use it any more, it's all smashed up." He says, "How many feet of it were there?" I tell him, "There were 150 feet of it." He says, "All right, I will replace it." Now, if I get a nice garden hose back, I am in pretty good shape.

7   In other words, if you lend certain munitions and get the munitions back at the end of the war, if they are intact haven't been hurt—you are all right; if they have been damaged or have deteriorated or have been lost completely, it seems to me you come out pretty well if you have them replaced by the fellow to whom you have lent them.

8   I can't go into details; and there is no use asking legal questions about how you would do it, because that is the thing that is now under study; but the thought is that we would take over not all, but a very large number of, future British orders; and when they came off the line, whether they were planes or guns or something else, we would enter into some kind of arrangement for their use by the British on the ground that it was the best thing for American defense, with the understanding that when the show was over, we would get repaid sometime in kind, thereby leaving out the dollar mark in the form of a dollar debt and substituting for it a gentleman's obligation to repay in kind. I think you all get it.

On the GED® test, the essay question might ask something similar to the following:

> While Charles Lindbergh argues that the United States is being dragged into a war in Europe that it does not really want, U.S. President Franklin Roosevelt urges the United States to help England as a protective measure for the United States.
>
> In your response, analyze both speeches to determine which position is best supported. Use relevant and specific evidence from both sources to support your response.
>
> Write your response in the box. This task may require approximately 45 minutes to complete.

The first thing to do is to analyze each speech to identify the arguments that the speaker uses. Let's list the arguments that Charles Lindbergh uses in his speech.

Charles Lindbergh's Arguments

Americans were clearly opposed to getting involved in the war when it started.

The United States has the best defensive position.

The United States is independent from Europe.

Our one attempt to intervene in a European war did not end well.

Certain groups of people want us to become involved in the war for their own interests.

The United States built 5000 planes, but they were sent abroad and are no longer available to us.

We have only a few hundred modern bombers, fewer than Germany is able to produce in a month.

Try analyzing these various arguments. The first argument, that Americans were opposed to the war, appears to be based on fact. Lindbergh mentions national polls showing that fewer than 10 percent of Americans favored declaring war. But the claims about America's defensive position and its independence from European affairs are opinions, not facts. It is a fact that America's previous intervention in a European war (in World War I) did not resolve political problems in Europe. But Lindbergh's claim that certain groups of people want to involve America in a new war for their own interests seems doubtful; he offers no evidence to support it. Lindbergh's claims that the United States has sent many of its military planes overseas and has few bombers left for defense may be facts, but are they valid reasons why the United States should stay out of the war?

Now let's list President Roosevelt's arguments.

President Roosevelt's Arguments

The United States could take over producing munitions for Great Britain.

We have enough money to do it.

The best defense of the United States is the defense of Great Britain.

Our defense materials are more useful for the defense of the United States if they are used in Great Britain rather than keeping them in storage in the United States.

As an example, if a neighbor's home catches on fire and I have a hose, I don't make my neighbor pay for the hose, but I let him use it to put out the fire. Afterward if the hose is fine, he returns it to me, but if it is broken and unusable, he gets me another one.

The hose my neighbor uses is like the munitions that Great Britain would replace after using the ones made in this country.

We should do this to defend the United States, and Great Britain will somehow repay us after the war is over.

Again, let's analyze these arguments. President Roosevelt says that the United States could take over producing munitions for Great Britain, and that "we have enough money to do it." He offers no evidence for either claim, but you know that the United States is a rich country, so there is no particular reason to disbelieve him. Roosevelt then claims that the best defense of the United States is the defense of Great Britain. This is his opinion, and it is the heart of his argument. At the time he spoke, it was up to the American people to decide whether or not they agreed with him. Roosevelt then argues that it makes sense to ship munitions to the British as a defense measure, and that the British will somehow find a way to repay. He supports his argument with the analogy of lending a hose to a neighbor whose house is on fire. Do you consider that to be a valid analogy? Is it a strong argument in support of aiding the British, or a weak argument?

Now let's look at some sample student responses. In this first essay, the student writer tries to persuade readers that Charles Lindbergh's arguments are stronger than those of President Roosevelt.

> I believe that Charles Lindbergh's arguments are stronger and more effective than President Roosevelt's. Lindbergh points out that the American people don't want to be involved in the war. He also says that the United States has a great defensive position, so it has no reason to fear attack. If you don't want to go to war, and if you don't need to go to war to defend yourself, then you should not go to war.
>
> Obviously President Roosevelt wants to go to war to help England. He argues that America's best defense is helping to defend Great Britain by manufacturing planes and munitions for them. He uses the analogy of a person loaning someone his hose when his house is on fire. But I do not think the analogy works. These are very different situations; one is about a fire and a hose and the other is about war and using American factories to build planes and munitions so that Great Britain can use them.
>
> Lindbergh, on the other hand, thinks this kind of thing is just a way around getting the United States into the war. He feels that the government is actually doing something that the people of the United States did not really vote for, getting involved with the European war.

This essay is reasonably good, but it has some areas that could be improved.

While the opening of the essay is strong and the reasons given for preferring Lindbergh's arguments are adequate, the writer falls short by not including more of Lindbergh's arguments. The writer points out that most Americans do not want to go to war, and as you have seen, that argument is based on evidence. But the claim about America's strong defensive position is really an opinion, and thus not necessarily a strong argument. And the writer neglects to include Lindbergh's factual claims that the prior intervention in Europe did not end well and that the United States is militarily unprepared for war.

The writer then opposes Roosevelt's claims by denying the validity of the analogy about the neighbor whose house is on fire. Roosevelt's analogy is an explanation, but it is not a claim based on hard evidence, and the writer has the right to disagree with it.

Finally, the conclusion of the essay is lacking. It does not review the writer's argument in favor of Lindbergh and the evidence supporting that argument. It should repeat the idea that Lindbergh did a better job of arguing for his position and that in the writer's opinion, Roosevelt failed to argue his position as well as Lindbergh did.

Here is another sample essay about the two passages. In this case, the student writer tries to persuade readers that President Roosevelt's arguments are stronger.

I feel that President Franklin Roosevelt's arguments far outweigh those of Charles Lindbergh. Lindbergh's argument is that the United States should only take care of itself and not its neighbors. However, Roosevelt's analogy about the neighbor whose house is on fire is a much better way to view the situation. If your neighbor's house is on fire, the right thing to do is to offer your help, especially if the fire might spread to your house too. Roosevelt's argument is that people, and nations, should care for one another in times of need.

Lindbergh's arguments are based on the past and a prejudice against war of any kind. He makes it clear that he wants the United States to be isolated. He does not think the United States should help England at all. But as Roosevelt argues, this aid to England actually is the United States' best defense. By making England stronger with planes and munitions built in America, it allows England to fight a better battle against the enemy. Lindbergh would rather stockpile the planes, which does not make sense in terms of defense.

In closing, I would like to say that the two opposing views show strong ideological differences; one is pushing for isolationism and the other for a sense of community among like-minded nations. I feel President Roosevelt's arguments are stronger.

This essay is better than the first one. Can you figure out why? The writer may be faulted for focusing a bit too much on personal opinions, but he or she backs up the opinion expressed in the essay with references to the various arguments and gives reasons why some are stronger than others.

RLA Essay Writing

Directions: Read the following text, which is excerpted from a speech by Secretary of Defense Leon Panetta.

1   One of my priorities as Secretary of Defense has been to remove as many barriers as possible for talented and qualified people to be able to serve this country in uniform. Our nation was built on the premise of the citizen-soldier. In our democracy, I believe it is the responsibility of every citizen to protect the nation. And every citizen who can meet the qualifications of service should have that opportunity.

2   To that end, I've been working closely with General Dempsey and the Joint Chiefs of Staff. We've been working for well over a year to examine, how can we expand the opportunities for women in the armed services?

3   It's clear to all of us that women are contributing in unprecedented ways to the military's mission of defending the nation. Women represent 15 percent of the force, over 200,000. They're serving in a growing number of critical roles on and off the battlefield. The fact is that they have become an integral part of our ability to perform our mission.

4   Over more than a decade of war, they have demonstrated courage and skill and patriotism. A hundred and fifty-two women in uniform have died serving this nation in Iraq and Afghanistan. Female service members have faced the reality of combat, proven their willingness to fight and, yes, to die to defend their fellow Americans.

5   However, many military positions, particularly in ground combat units, still remain closed to women because of the 1994 direct ground combat definition and assignment rule. Military and civilian leaders in this department have been taking a hard look at that rule based on the experiences of the last decade.

6   Every time I visited the war zone, every time I've met with troops, reviewed military operations, and talked to wounded warriors, I've been impressed with the fact that everyone—men and women alike—everyone is committed to doing the job. They're fighting and they're dying together. And the time has come for our policies to recognize that reality.

7   The chairman and the Joint Chiefs of Staff and I believe that we must open up service opportunities for women as fully as possible. And therefore today, General Dempsey and I are pleased to announce that we are eliminating the direct ground combat exclusion rule for women and we are moving forward with a plan to eliminate all unnecessary gender-based barriers to service. In a few moments after we speak, we'll both sign a memo that will rescind the '94 barrier.

8   Our purpose is to ensure that the mission is carried out by the best-qualified and the most-capable service members, regardless of gender and regardless of creed and beliefs. If members of our military can meet the qualifications for a job—and let me be clear, I'm not talking about reducing the qualifications for the job—if they can meet the qualifications for the job, then they should have the right to serve, regardless of creed or color or gender or sexual orientation.

9   For this change and policy to succeed, it must be done in a responsible, measured, and a coherent way. I'll let General Dempsey describe our plan of action in greater detail. But the bottom line is that further integration of women will occur expeditiously, even as we recognize the need to take time to institutionalize changes of this importance.

10   The steps we are announcing today are significant. And in many ways, they are an affirmation of where we have been heading as a department for more than 10 years. Nevertheless, it will take leadership and it will take professionalism to effectively implement these changes. I am confident in our ability to do that, because I am confident in the leadership that General Dempsey and the Joint Chiefs of Staff have demonstrated throughout this process.

11   When I look at my grandsons and my granddaughters—you know, I've got six grandchildren, three grandsons and three granddaughters—I want each of them to have the same chance to succeed at whatever they want to do. In life, as we all know, there are no guarantees of success. Not everyone is going to be able to be a combat soldier. But everyone is entitled to a chance.

12   By committing ourselves to that principle, we are renewing our commitment to the American values our service members fight and die to defend. As Secretary, when I've gone to Bethesda to visit wounded warriors, and when I've gone to Arlington to bury our dead, there is no distinction that's made between the sacrifices of men and women in uniform. They serve, they're wounded, and they die right next to each other. The time has come to recognize that reality.

13   By opening up more opportunities for people to serve in uniform, we are making our military stronger and we are making America stronger. We deeply honor all of those past generations, combat soldiers and Marines, who fought and died for our freedom. And in many ways, their sacrifice has ensured that the next greatest generation will be one of men and women who will fight and die together to protect this nation. And that is what freedom is all about.

Read the following text, which is excerpted from a letter signed Sentry, appearing on an Internet website.

1   I'm a female veteran. I deployed to Anbar Province, Iraq. When I was active duty, I was 5'6", 130 pounds, and scored nearly perfect on my PFTs. I naturally have a lot more upper-body strength than the average woman: not only can I do pull-ups, I can meet the male standard. I would love to have

been in the infantry. And I still think it will be an unmitigated disaster to incorporate women into combat roles. I am not interested in risking men's lives so I can live my selfish dream.

2   We're not just talking about watering down the standards to include the politically correct number of women into the unit. This isn't an issue of "if a woman can meet the male standard, she should be able to go into combat." The number of women that can meet the male standard will be minuscule—I'd have a decent shot according to my PFTs, but dragging a 190-pound man in full gear for 100 yards would DESTROY me—and that minuscule number that can physically make the grade AND has the desire to go into combat will be facing an impossible situation that will ruin the combat effectiveness of the unit. First, the close quarters of combat units make for a complete lack of privacy and EVERYTHING is exposed, to include intimate details of bodily functions. Second, until we succeed in completely reprogramming every man in the military to treat women just like men, those men are going to protect a woman at the expense of the mission.

3   Third, women have physical limitations that no amount of training or conditioning can overcome. Fourth, until the media in this country is ready to treat a captured/raped/tortured/mutilated female soldier just like a man, women will be targeted by the enemy without fail and without mercy.

4   Regarding physical limitations, not only will a tiny fraction of women be able to meet the male standard, the simple fact is that women tend to be shorter than men. I ran into situations when I was deployed where I simply could not reach something. I wasn't tall enough. I had to ask a man to get it for me. I can't train myself to be taller. Yes, there are small men . . . but not nearly so many as small women. More, a military PFT doesn't measure the ability to jump. Men, with more muscular legs and bones that carry more muscle mass than any woman can condition herself to carry, can jump higher and farther than women. That's why we have a men's standing jump and long jump event in the Olympics separate from women's. When you're going over a wall in Baghdad that's 10 feet high, you have to be able to reach the top of it in full gear and haul yourself over. That's not strength per se, that's just height and the muscular explosive power to jump and reach the top. Having to get a boost from one of the men so you can get up and over could get that man killed.

5   Without pharmaceutical help, women just do not carry the muscle mass men do. That muscle mass is also a shock absorber. Whether it's the concussion of a grenade going off, an IED, or just a punch in the face, a woman is more likely to go down because she can't absorb the concussion as well as a man can. And I don't care how the PC forces try to slice it, in hand-to-hand combat the average man is going to destroy the average woman because the average woman is smaller, period. Muscle equals force in any kind of strike you care to perform. That's why we don't let female boxers face male boxers.

6   Lastly, this country and our military are NOT prepared to see what the enemy will do to female POWs. The Taliban, AQ, insurgents, jihadis, whatever you want to call them, they don't abide by the Geneva Conventions

and treat women worse than livestock. Google Thomas Tucker and Kristian Menchaca if you want to see what they do to our men (and don't google it unless you have a strong stomach) and then imagine a woman in their hands. How is our 24/7 news cycle going to cover a captured, raped, mutilated woman? After the first one, how are the men in the military going to treat their female comrades? ONE Thomasina Tucker is going to mean the men in the military will move heaven and earth to protect women, never mind what it does to the mission. I present you with Exhibit A: Jessica Lynch. Male lives will be lost trying to protect their female comrades. And the people of the U.S. are NOT, based on the Jessica Lynch episode, prepared to treat a female POW the same way they do a man.

7   I say again, I would have loved to be in the infantry. I think I could have done it physically, I could've met almost all the male standards (jumping aside), and I think I'm mentally tough enough to handle whatever came. But I would never do that to the men. I would never sacrifice the mission for my own desires. And I wouldn't be able to live with myself if someone died because of me.

While Secretary Leon Panetta argues that women should be allowed to serve in the same capacity in the armed forces as men, Sentry argues that women will cause men to die if they are treated as equals.

In your response, analyze both texts to determine which position is best supported. Use relevant and specific evidence from both sources to support your response.

Write your response in the box on the following page. This task may require approximately 45 minutes to complete.

A sample response appears on page 304.

Reasoning Through Language Arts (RLA)

Chapter 1 Testing Basic English Usage

Exercise 1: Capitalization

1. The Nurses' Association is meeting in New York City.
2. The Department of Justice has an office in the Capitol Building.
3. The mayor spoke at the Labor Day parade.
4. The city of Monterey, California, is located on the Pacific Ocean.

Exercise 2: Punctuation

1. They were able to solve the problem without too much trouble.
2. Do we have some time before the show begins?
3. Watch your fingers when you use that knife!

   Corrected paragraph: On ice-covered lakes and seas, ships called icebreakers are needed. These ships are used in the Great Lakes, Atlantic Ocean, and Baltic Sea. An icebreaker, which has powerful engines, has sides that are plated with metal. When the icebreaker lifts its front onto the ice, the weight crushes the ice.

Exercise 3: Sentence Fragments

__F__ 1. Waited for a long time at the rail station.

__F__ 2. Wanted to go to the party with her friend.

__S__ 3. Nina went to the concert alone.

__S__ 4. She bought a ticket to the art museum to see the show.

__F__ 5. Looked all over the house for the watch his grandfather had given him.

Exercise 4: Run-On and Fused Sentences

__C__ 1. The children from the day camp enjoyed riding the roller coaster.

_____ 2. A small group of coyotes may gather together in the evening they make eerie, howling sounds together.

__C__ 3. The doctor performed an emergency operation and saved the man's life.

_____ 4. I looked in my backpack for my locker key, I couldn't find it.

_____ 5. Mosquitoes are dangerous creatures most people aren't aware of how harmful they can be.

Exercise 5: Misplaced and Dangling Modifiers

1. We ate dinner at an elegant restaurant with the Carsons slowly.

   We ate dinner slowly at an elegant restaurant with the Carsons.

2. Joanna had a hot dish of cereal this morning before she left for work.

   Joanna had a dish of hot cereal this morning before she left for work.

3. After running home, the television was turned on to watch the baseball game.

   After running home, we turned on the television to watch the baseball game.

Exercise 6: Parallel Structure

_____ 1a. It is more important to be healthy than to have wealth.

__C__ 1b. It is more important to be healthy than wealthy.

__C__ 2a. Marion is happy as long as she has clothes, food, and books.

_____ 2b. Marion is happy as long as she has clothes, food to eat, and can read books.

Exercise 7: Improving Awkward Sentences

__C__ 1a. One day, he almost made the mistake of running and diving into the deep end when the pool was empty.

_____ 1b. He almost made the mistake one day of running and diving when the pool was empty into the deep end.

_____ 2a. The explorer described her trip down the Amazon River in our social studies class in a canoe.

__C__ 2b. In our social studies class, the explorer described her trip down the Amazon River in a canoe.

Exercise 8: Eliminating Informal or Nonstandard Words

1. He is going to the movie tonight.

2. I can see you are upset.

3. Where is it?

Exercise 9: Subject-Verb Agreement

__C__ 1. All of the oceans in the world have whales.

__I__ 2. A good field guide is one of the items that helps birdwatchers.

__C__ 3. The northern oriole is an eastern United States bird that winters in Latin America.

__I__ 4. Blue corn is one of those crops that is not common throughout the United States.

__I__ 5. Careful planning and good luck was responsible for the successful moon landings.

__I__ 6. So far neither soil analysis nor photo scans has established a noticeable trend.

__I__ 7. The Riverdale Thunder are a new team.

__I__ 8. Overfishing in some waters sometimes eliminate an entire species.

Exercise 10: Verb Tenses

1. I was in the shower when the phone rang.

2. Since the day when I wrote that poem, I have written two short stories.

3. By the time I remembered that the roast was in the oven, it had overcooked.

4. While he was speaking yesterday, the senator was shouting loudly to make a point.

Exercise 11: Pronoun Usage

__C__ 1. Veronica asked Beverly and me to watch her dance in the final awards competition.

__I__ 2. She and me have been going to ballet lessons for years, but she is much better than I am.

__I__ 3. I thought Ted had gone to the play with they, but he was in the house playing video games.

__I__ 4. Lucille and Danny lost ourselves in their hobbies.

__I__ 5. Learning to swim turned out to be surprisingly difficult for my brother and I when we first tried.

ANSWERS AND EXPLANATIONS

_____ 6. Participants in this marathon must train in all weather, for you cannot predict what the weather will be like here in April.

Corrected paragraph: Mariana wanted to learn to play the piano, but she knew how difficult learning the piano is for a beginner. Still she worked hard at it and oftentimes gave up her free time. She spent less time at the mall with her friends. In the end, she was pleased with herself.

Exercise 12: Apostrophes and Possessive Nouns

1. In Italian, **Florence's** name is Firenze and **Venice's** name is Venezia.

2. My sister and I went to several readings that featured **T. S. Eliot's** poetry.

3. My father and my brother just started a new business and named it **Bailey** and **Bailey's** Art Supplies

4. David wrote an irate letter to the newspaper about the **editor in chief's** column.

5. I could not find **Chris's** new watch in the bureau where he said he put it.

6. The **ceremonies'** leaders marched into the room one after the other.

Exercise 13: Transitional Words and Expressions

1. My French teacher speaks Portuguese and Italian; **in addition,** she can read Spanish.

2. Science was a difficult subject for me in high school; **as a result,** I avoided science courses in college.

3. Rome has many interesting buildings; **for example,** the Colosseum is a huge ancient arena.

4. Sam wanted some ice cream; **however,** the store was out of it.

Exercise 14: Frequently Confused Words

1. This **past** week has been exceedingly busy.

2. I will get to the additional work when I know **it's** time to do it.

3. I wanted to start a **new** club, but no one was interested.

4. Robert tried **two** kinds of medicine for his rash.

5. **Who's** going to the picnic today?

6. **There** is no reason to change your outfit before the party.

Practice: Testing Basic English Usage

PASSAGE 1

Select 1 correct answer: past. This adjective is the correct choice. It indicates that something happened a while ago.

Select 2 correct answer: our "Wall of Contributors." This is the proper way to capitalize a formal name.

Select 3 correct answer: the dinner, dancing, and stand-up comedians. Commas go after every item in a series.

Select 4 correct answer: love to show you around and tell you. These verbs are parallel to one another. Both are in the infinitive form.

PASSAGE 2

Select 1 correct answer: I am a first year student at Cape Fear Community College, majoring in criminal justice. This is the best way to write this sentence in order to eliminate a dangling or misplaced modifier or illogical word order.

Select 2 correct answer: your. This pronoun agrees with its antecedent, _you._ The other choices do not.

Select 3 correct answer: enjoyed. This is the proper verb form and agrees with the subject _I._

Select 4 correct answer: public defender's. This is the proper possessive form for this term.

Select 5 correct answer: I look forward to hearing from you.

PASSAGE 3

Select 1 correct answer: the weekend of June 21. The focus of the conference is how to improve employee cooperation. This is a run-on sentence and needs to be made into two sentences since it is two complete thoughts.

Select 2 correct answer: Employees will break into small groups to perform key exercises designed to improve cooperation in the workplace. This sentence is the one that is the least awkward and repetitive.

Select 3 correct answer: are. This is the correct verb. Its subject is the noun.

Chapter 2 Testing Reading Comprehension

Practice: Testing Reading Comprehension

1. **Correct answer: D.** Choice A asks a question about whether a man born behind time would be behind time whenever he was born. This is not evidence for the inference. Choice B states a fact about babies and does not support the inference. Choice C does not support the inference either since it is talking about literature, not man.

2. **Correct answer: B.** Based on the text, choice A cannot be correct; the author obviously has a good imagination. There is no evidence that choice C is correct. To the author, these questions have great meaning, so choice D is not correct.

3. **Correct answer: D.** Based on the text, you can apply the reasoning that there is a reason for people being born when they are. Choice A is contrary to what the author suggests. Choices B and C also contradict the author's beliefs.

4. **Correct answer: D.** This is the only sentence that gives evidence that the inference about the scientists is accurate. Choice A discusses what the scientists saw when they first saw the man on the beach. Choice B tells about what the scientists did, and choice C tells how the scientists saw the man begging for food from a sailor.

5. **Correct answer: B.** This is what the passage is mostly about. Choice A is about the scientists who did study the man's behavior, but this is a detail, not the main idea. Choices C and D are also details, not the main idea.

6. **Correct answer: D.** There is no evidence in the text that the man enjoyed stealing, and there is no mention of wildlife on the shore, so choice B is incorrect. Choice C is contrary to what is stated in the text; there was plenty of food.

7. **Correct answer: A.** The story is about a person who nearly starves and whether he

will be permanently scarred. In the end, he recovers. He comes back. There is nothing in this story that would suggest that choice B is correct. If anything, the opposite is true. The scientists are curious, not emotional. Choice C is a possible answer, but this is not what the story is about. Choice D is a broad statement that may be true of some scientists, but certainly not true of all scientists.

8. **Correct answer: A.** This text clearly shows that Lincoln loved to read and learn new things. Choice B may have been true, but this is not what the text suggests about him. The text shows Lincoln as quite serious, so choice C is incorrect. Again, he may have longed for excitement, but there is no evidence of that in the text.

9. **Correct answer: C.** This is the only sentence that is concerned with slavery. Choice A tells about why Lincoln was hired as postmaster. Choice B tells what Lincoln read as a postmaster. Choice D recounts the fact that Lincoln's store did not do well financially.

10. **Correct answer: D.** This paragraph shows that Lincoln knew all types of people and gained information from them. Choice A contradicts what the paragraph is about. It says that his acquaintance would recite Shakespeare and Burns. Choice B is not indicated by the paragraph; Lincoln seems to enjoy the company of this person. Choice C is not indicated either.

11. **Correct answer: C.** This generalization can be made based on the information in the text. Choice A does not make sense in the context of the text. Choice B is irrelevant; there is no mention of trouble. Choice D is not a generalization that can be made based on the text; it appears that Lincoln was not a good businessman.

12. **Correct answer: D.** If you analyze the passage, you will figure out that the main idea is that Lincoln loved to learn about things and read a great many books to become educated. Choice D supports this main idea. The other choices are details from the passage, but they do not support the main idea.

Chapter 3 Structure and Author's Choices

Practice: Structure and Author's Choices

1. **Correct answer: A.** This is what the paragraph does. It does not discuss funding (choice B), nor does it focus on the need to promote the use of English. Choice D is incorrect also.

2. **Correct answer: C.** Context clues help the reader figure out the answer. None of the other answer choices fits within the context of the sentence and paragraph.

3. **Correct answer: A.** This is the effect of the final sentence. It is strong and direct. It does not lessen the tone; nor does it create a sense of disbelief (choices B and C). It is certainly not ironic.

4. **Correct answer: D.** The connotations of the word *embrace* tell you that the speaker wants to welcome people with limited English skills. The literal meaning of *embrace* is not being used here; rather the word is being used figuratively, so choice A is incorrect.

5. **Correct answer: B.** This is how the image influences the story. Jonathan's words indicate that he feels there is no solution to his situation. Choices A, C, and D are not correct because there is no mention of punishment, wrongdoing, or spending time in a jail.

6. **Correct answer: C.** The overly dramatic references to prison and insects dashing

against the wall give a tone of the theatrical to the excerpt. Choice A is incorrect; there is nothing inspiring in Jonathan's words. Choice B is not correct either because Jonathan is hardly lighthearted on the subject of his job. Although there might be tranquility in lying on the grass, his words do not convey that sense, so choice D is incorrect.

7. **The correct order of events:**

   Linda asks Jonathan if he goes back to work Monday.

   Linda suggests that Jonathan will get used to his job.

   Jonathan says he will never get used to his work.

   Jonathan says he feels like an insect.

8. **Correct answer: C.** The author subtly suggests through the use of the word that Linda is not

all that focused on what Jonathon is saying; she just isn't that interested. The other choices are not suggested by the text.

9. **Correct answer: D.** This phrase introduces new information in the text.

10. **Correct answer: A.** Context can help the reader realize the word means *basic*. Choice B is an antonym of *essential*. Choices C and D do not fit into the context of the paragraph.

11. **Correct answer: A.** If the reader concentrates on the images that the author creates, it becomes clear that he is comparing winter to the return to water and bread from the wine and a banquet of summer.

12. **Correct answer: D.** The author has a great sensitivity and awareness of the seasons and learns from each one. The other choices are incorrect.

Chapter 4 Literary Texts

Practice: Literary Texts

1. **Correct answer: D.** The story is about how Tom annoys his aunt, but then when she gets angry, he makes her laugh. Choice D is the only sentence that relates to this theme.

2. **Correct answer: B.** You can eliminate the other choices by reading the text closely. There is no sign he dislikes his aunt, so choice A is incorrect. There is no evidence that he wants to behave, either, making choice C incorrect. Certainly choice D is incorrect.

3. **Correct answer: D.** This is the only sentence that supports the idea that Tom is physically speedy. The other sentences describe other aspects of Tom's character.

4. **Correct answer: B.** This fact is found in the text itself. The other choices are not correct and there is no evidence to support them.

5. **Correct answer: C.** Choice B does not seem likely. While he might be fearful of asking how to ride, that is not his predicament. Choice D is incorrect also.

6. **Correct answer: D.** This is how Travers gets the respect of the other riders. Choice A is not correct; Travers was not responsible for getting Monster to do jumps. Choices B and C are incorrect also.

7. **Correct answer: C.** The passage says he tried to get Monster to the bridge, but the horse would not comply. The other choices are not indicated.

8. **Correct answer: A.** Although we cannot be sure what young Paddock's motivation was, this is the closest to the truth. Clearly Monster was not the best horse, so choice D is not correct. It is doubtful that he was trying to please Travers with what he had to say about the horse. Choice B is not likely, either.

9. **Correct answer: B.** This is how the setting influences the story. Without the train, Easton would most likely not have run into Miss Fairchild. The other choices are incorrect.

10. **Correct answer: D.** Putting the hints together, the reader can figure out that this is the

relationship between the two men. There is no evidence that choice A is true; nor is there any evidence that choices B or C are true either.

11. **Correct answer: B.** When Miss Fairchild first sees Easton with handcuffs, she does not know what to think. The text tells you this. The other choices are not correct.

12. **Correct answer: B.** From the start when Miss Fairchild begins to talk to Easton, the marshal tries to keep her from learning about the truth. This is his viewpoint toward his charge. There is no evidence in the text to support choice A, B, or C.

Chapter 5 Informational Texts

Practice: Informational Texts

1. **Correct answer: B.** A close reading of the text will show that Audubon is in awe of the power of the storm. He may be somewhat fearful, but he is not terrified by it, so choice A is incorrect. There is no mention of the storm killing people. There is no evidence in the passage for choice D.

2. **Correct answer: D.** It expresses an opinion of Audubon: he thinks that the whirling forest debris looks like "a cloud of feathers."

3. **Correct answer: A.** The storm has a strong effect on the trees, ripping them apart and knocking them over.

4. **Correct answer: A.** This is a primary source since it was written by a person who experienced the storm. The other choices are no guarantees of reliability.

5. **Correct answer: A.** Chief Joseph says that he no longer wants to do battle. Choice B is not correct because Chief Joseph has just finished waging a war. Choice C is incorrect because

Chief Joseph says that he is now ready to stop fighting. Choice D is incorrect because Chief Joseph makes no attempt to urge other members of his tribe to continue the war.

6. **Correct answer: A.** Chief Seattle says that Native Americans had little power and were few in number compared to whites. The other choices are directly contradicted by the passage.

7. **Correct answer: D.** Chief Joseph is announcing his surrender after being beaten in war. Chief Seattle is agreeing to go willingly with his people into a reservation.

8. **Correct answer: A.** While Chief Joseph and Chief Seattle have different purposes, they share the same concern. Chief Seattle thanks the federal government, but Chief Joseph does not, so choice B is incorrect. Chief Joseph may well be angry about what has happened to his people, but Chief Seattle is not, so choice C is incorrect. Neither chief makes a claim for more land, so choice D is not correct.

9. **Correct answer: A.** Henry claims that the American colonies are already in a state of war with Great Britain. There is no evidence in the text for the other choices.

10. **Correct answer: D.** Henry asks several questions. The questions are parallel in form. The fact that he asks question after question is a form of repetition. The other choices are not correct. Henry does not use anecdotes or alliteration.

11. **Correct answer: C.** This quotation directly supports Henry's claim that the colonies are not weak. The other quotations are about other subjects.

12. **Correct answer: D.** The purpose of a timeline is to show the order of events. It allows you to place Henry's speech within the sequence of events leading to the outbreak of war between the American colonies and Great Britain.

Chapter 6 RLA Essay Writing

Practice: RLA Essay Writing

SAMPLE ESSAY RESPONSE

The issue of whether or not women should be allowed to serve in combat positions in the military has been controversial for a long time. It is time for that controversy to end. Women should have the right to be given equal opportunity to serve in combat positions.

Secretary Panetta says, "I'm not talking about reducing the qualifications for the job—if they can meet the qualifications for the job, then they should have the right to serve, regardless of creed or color or gender or sexual orientation." That is a key piece of his argument for many reasons, and it also knocks a hole in Sentry's argument. She talks about "watering down" standards for holding combat positions. That is clearly not something that Secretary Panetta intends. Also, Secretary Panetta mentions creed, color, and sexual orientation. He does not go into detail, but I believe he is reminding us that the U.S. Armed Forces used to discriminate against African Americans and homosexuals. These prejudices were also strongly held. Discrimination against women is no different, and no less wrong.

Sentry also argues that even if women could meet the physical qualifications necessary for combat positions, just the presence of a woman in combat would change the way her fellow soldiers fight, meaning that they would want to protect her, and would risk their lives for her because it is their nature to do so. I believe that male soldiers already protect each other and risk their lives for each other. Whether that fellow soldier is a male or female would make no difference. It is true perhaps that our current culture encourages men to protect women. But cultures evolve, and soldiers going into combat receive rigorous training.

It is not that Sentry's argument isn't persuasive. Her direct experience in combat makes her statements especially forceful. However, she is just one person. Secretary Panetta has heard directly from multiple veterans and listened to the opinions of top military and civilian leaders. He has based his opinion and decision on a much larger body of information than Sentry has.

It might not happen overnight, but U.S. military culture can and should evolve. All Americans deserve equal opportunity—including the brave female service members who serve our country.

Mathematical Reasoning

The Mathematical Reasoning Test

The Mathematical Reasoning section of the GED® test measures your ability to solve problems using essential concepts of high school mathematics. The test is 90 minutes long and includes 50 items in a variety of formats. There is a short section in which a calculator is not allowed, but for most of the test a calculator is allowed. The calculator is available on the computer screen. You will also be provided with a list of essential mathematical formulas that you can use to solve problems.

About half of the test focuses on quantitative problem solving, and about half focuses on basic algebraic problem solving. There are also some geometry questions. Some of the questions simply require mathematical calculations, but others present hypothetical real-world situations, and you must decide which problem-solving technique will enable you to arrive at the correct answer. Many questions refer to diagrams, charts, coordinate grids, or other graphics.

Most Mathematical Reasoning questions are multiple choice with four answer choices. However, some questions use interactive formats such as drag and drop and drop-down. In some questions, you will be asked to type your answer in a box on the computer screen. Other questions may ask you to click on the screen in order to plot points on a coordinate grid. See "Introducing the GED® Test" at the beginning of this book for an explanation and samples of these formats.

The Mathematical Reasoning Review

The following section of this book presents a comprehensive review of the skills that are tested on the Mathematical Reasoning test. There are short review sections on all of the essential mathematical concepts that you need to know. Each review section ends with an exercise that you can use to test your mastery of the concept. You will also see sample questions like the ones you will encounter on test day. Pay careful attention to the explanations for each question. They will help you become familiar with all the Mathematical Reasoning question types, and you will learn test-taking strategies that can raise your score. If you have already taken the Mathematical Reasoning Pretest at the start of this book, make sure to study those sections that cover the types of questions you missed or found difficult.

This Mathematical Reasoning review section is organized as follows:

Answers and explanations for all of the practice questions in this section are located at the end of the section.

CHAPTER 1

Whole Numbers and Operations

After years of having a calculator available for things like addition, subtraction, division, and multiplication, it is easy to forget some of the steps needed to do these types of problems by hand. For most of the GED® test math section, you won't have to worry about this—there is an onscreen calculator. However, there are a handful of questions for which the calculator is not available. These questions are designed to make sure that you remember how to do things like add large numbers or perform long division. To make sure you're ready, let's go through and review these operations.

Addition

To add two or more numbers, line up the numbers in columns by place value. This means that the ones place of the first number is lined up with the ones place of the next number. After this, add each column from right to left. In addition, the solution is called the **sum**.

EXAMPLE 1

112 + 26

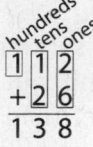

EXAMPLE 2

Add: 56 + 11 + 2.

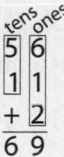

When the total in one column is larger than 10, "carry" the tens digit over to the next column to the left.

EXAMPLE 3

Add: 242 + 18 + 195.

$$\begin{array}{r} \overset{1}{2}\overset{1}{4}2 \\ 18 \\ +195 \\ \hline 455 \end{array}$$ ← Total in the first column was 15 so carry the 1

Although the examples simply go in the same order as in the question, addition is **commutative**. This means that the order in which numbers are added does not matter.

Subtraction

To subtract, line up numbers in columns the same way as with addition and then subtract each column from right to left. In subtraction, the solution is called the **difference**.

EXAMPLE 4

Subtract: 2055 − 13.

$$\begin{array}{r} 2055 \\ -13 \\ \hline 2042 \end{array}$$

If there are not enough ones to subtract, regroup 1 ten as 10 ones. In other words, subtract 1 from the number in the tens place and place a 1 in front of the number in the ones place. Then subtract the ones. If there are not enough numbers in other columns, use regrouping in the same way.

EXAMPLE 5

Subtract: 1758 − 909.

$$\begin{array}{r} \overset{0}{\cancel{1}}\,{}^{1}7\,\overset{4}{\cancel{5}}\,{}^{1}8 \\ -909 \\ \hline 849 \end{array}$$ ← Place a 1 next to the 8 to make it 18 and regroup this from the 5

Your final answer in any subtraction question can always be double-checked by comparing the top term with the sum of the difference and the bottom term. For instance, in the example above, 849 + 909 = 1758, which is the original number on the top line. If the numbers added up to something else, you would know that there was a mistake in the subtraction.

Multiplication

Multiplication is a bit more complicated than addition and subtraction. Remember that the solution to a multiplication problem is called the **product**.

Let's look at the process of multiplication step-by-step.

EXAMPLE 6

Multiply: 185×6.

In this example, multiply each of the digits in 185 by 6, from right to left. If the result in any case is larger than 10, then the tens digit will be carried over to the next column.

$$
\begin{array}{r}
{}^{5}\;{}^{3}\;\;\\
1\;8\;5 \\
\times \qquad 6 \\
\hline
1\;1\;1\;0
\end{array}
$$

STEPS

① Multiply: $5 \times 6 = 30$, carry the 3.
② Multiply: 8×6, add 3, carry the 5.
③ Multiply: 1×6, and add the 5.

When the second number has more than one digit, the steps stay the same but you need to indent and then add to find the final answer.

EXAMPLE 7

Multiply: 289×24.

$$
\begin{array}{r}
{}^{1}\;{}^{1}\;\\
{}^{3}\;{}^{3}\;\\
2\;8\;9 \\
\times \quad 2\;4 \\
\hline
1\;1\;5\;6 \\
5\;7\;8\;0 \\
\hline
6\;9\;3\;6
\end{array}
$$

STEPS

① Multiply every digit by 4 and carry when needed.
② Indent with a zero on the second row.
③ Multiply every digit by 2 and carry when needed.
④ Add to get the final answer.

As in addition, the order in which numbers are multiplied does not matter.

Division

Division is calculated in a process that is commonly called "long division." Remember that the solution of a division problem is called the **quotient**.

Let's look at the division process step-by-step.

EXAMPLE 8

Divide: $1638 \div 7$.

```
      2 3 4
  7 | 1 6 3 8
    - 1 4 ↓
        2 3
      - 2 1 ↓
          2 8
        - 2 8
            0
```

STEPS

① Divide by 7 into the smallest number possible. Since 1 can't be evenly divided by 7, divide 16 by 7.

② Multiply the 2 and 7 and then subtract.

③ Bring down the 3 and divide the resulting 23 by 7.

④ Repeat the process of dividing, multiplying, subtracting, and carrying until there are no numbers to carry down.

The number left after the last subtraction is called the remainder

If at any point in the process you reach a number that is too small to be divided, write a zero and then bring down the next number. Look at the next example.

EXAMPLE 9

Divide: $2018 \div 4$.

```
      5 0 4
  4 | 2 0 1 8
    - 2 0 ↓
        0 1
      - 0 ↓
          1 8
        - 1 6
            2
```

← Since 1 can't be divided by 4, write a zero in the answer before bringing down the next number

Calculators and the GED® Mathematical Reasoning Test

The GED® Mathematical Reasoning test includes an on-screen version of the TI-30XS calculator. Even though you may not need it for every question, the calculator is available for a majority of the math questions.

Make sure you are completely familiar with this calculator before the test by either using one to practice or reviewing as much about the calculator as you can. Even though we will review all of the steps for using the calculator, you may find it useful to check the website of the GED Testing Service at http://gedtestingservice.com/testers/calculator. There you will find demonstration videos and guides.

Basic Operations on the TI-30XS

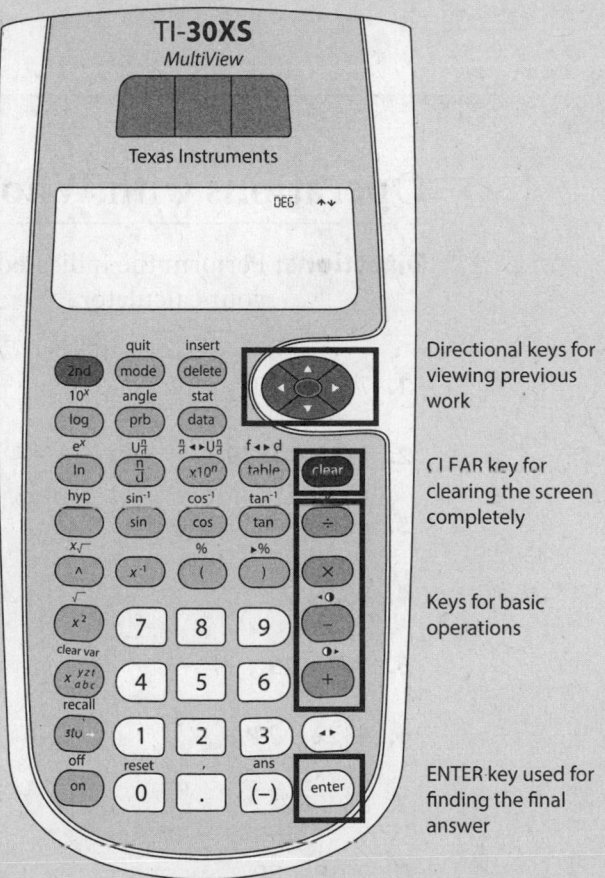

To get a final answer for any operation, you will hit the ENTER key. There is no need to clear your screen in between problems, but if you wish to do so, you may use the CLEAR key at any time. If you do not clear your screen, the up and down arrows allow you to view your previous work.

For addition, subtraction, multiplication, and division you will type in the first number, the operation key, and then the second number, and then press the ENTER key.

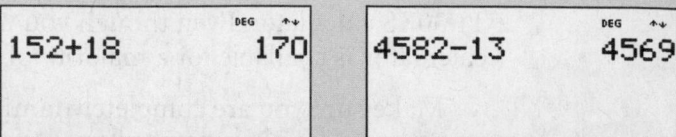

Important: When performing subtraction, make sure to press the subtraction key on the right of the calculator and not the negative key on the bottom of the calculator. Otherwise, you will get an error.

EXERCISE 1

Operations with Whole Numbers

Directions: Perform the indicated operation and check your final answer on your calculator.

1. 76 + 1088

2. 2133 − 1849

3. 65 + 14 + 930

4. 852 ÷ 7

5. 168 × 19

6. 4322 − 24

7. 85 − 72

8. 2018 × 89

9. 1084 + 9417

10. 1528 ÷ 12

11. 890 − 104

12. 72 + 215

13. 1999 + 631

14. $810 \div 2$

15. $9380 \div 20$

16. 75×15

17. 49×82

18. $4003 - 209$

19. $4429 \div 6$

20. 1600×28

Answers are on page 501.

Word Problems Involving Basic Operations

When working on word problems involving the basic operations, there are some key phrases or ideas that can help you keep track of whether you should multiply, add, divide, or subtract.

- **Addition:** Find a total, find a sum, determine how many "altogether"
- **Subtraction:** Find the difference, determine how many are left over
- **Multiplication:** Find a total when given groups, find the product, find how many "altogether" (when working with groups)
- **Division:** Find an amount or rate "per," split into equal parts, share, find how many in each group given a total

The list does not show every possibility, and there are many other ways that these operations are indicated in word problems. The best way to get comfortable with the wording is to work plenty of problems. With that in mind, let's go through a few examples together.

EXAMPLE 10

Nathan runs errands for a small fee. In the past four days, he has earned $13, $45, $20, and $32 running errands. In total, how much money has Nathan made during this time period?

Because this problem is asking for a total, add the given numbers:

$13 + 45 + 20 + 32 = 110$

Nathan has earned a total of $110 during this time period.

EXAMPLE 11

An office begins the month with 20 reams of paper. If the office used 3 reams the first week and 8 the second, how many reams of paper remain?

In this question, you are asked how many reams of paper remain after some are used. Every time a ream of paper is used, there is one less remaining. In other words, this problem requires subtraction.

There are $20 - 3 - 8 = 17 - 8 = 9$ reams of paper remaining.

EXAMPLE 12

A storage area can hold 110 large storage bins. If each storage bin can hold 30 hardcover books, how many hardcover books can be stored in the storage area?

Like example 10, this problem is also asking for a total. What makes it different is that the total involves groups: groups of books in storage bins. Anytime you are finding a total involving groups, you will multiply.

Each bin can hold 30 books, and there are 110 bins in the storage area. So, $110 \times 30 = 3300$ books can be stored in the storage area.

EXAMPLE 13

In the past 30 days, a website has received a total of 37,500 visitors. If the site received the same number of visitors each day, how many did it receive each day?

Here, you are asked to divide the total number of visitors evenly, over the 30 days. Dividing up groups is represented by division. Therefore, you can say that there were $37,500 \div 30 = 1250$ visitors to the website each day.

EXAMPLE 14

Kate has 30 scented candles. She plans to give 6 of the candles to her friend Lisa. She then plans to sell the remaining candles for $8 each in order to raise money for charity. If she sells all of the remaining candles, how much money will she raise?

There is a lot more going on in this problem than in the ones we have seen so far. First, some of the candles are given away (subtraction), and then you are asked to find a total based on the remaining group of candles (multiplication). The order in which these things happen matters because selling 24 candles would be different from selling 30.

After Kate gives Lisa 6 candles, she has $30 - 6 = 24$ candles remaining. She will sell each of these for $8, so the total will be $\$8 \times 24 = \$192$ raised.

EXERCISE 2

Word Problems

Directions: Solve each of the following word problems. Pay close attention to the language used in the problem to determine which operation makes the most sense.

1. Rich has five paychecks left before his summer job ends. If he saves $35 from each of these remaining paychecks, how much will he have saved when his job ends?

2. Two brothers and a sister share the cost of renting a 3-bedroom apartment. Because the sister is still in college, the brothers let her pay only $300 a month toward the rent. The two brothers split the remainder evenly. If the total rent for the apartment is $1400 a month, how much does each brother pay?

3. Since the start of the year, a small company has made $45,690 in sales. If the company makes $39,115 in sales over the remainder of the year, what will be its total sales for the year?

4. On Monday, the balance in a checking account was $1,250. On Tuesday, two bills were paid from this account: an electric bill of $142 and a cable bill of $95. Assuming there were no other transactions, what is the balance of the checking account at the end of the day on Tuesday?

5. A towing company charges drivers $200 to tow a car to the company's lot and $40 a day to store it. If a car was towed to the lot 26 days ago, how much has its driver accumulated in fees?

Answers are on page 501.

CHAPTER 2

Exponents, Roots, and Number Properties

Exponents

Exponents are a common shorthand used in mathematics. You have probably seen terms like 4^2 or 3^4. Both of these are written with exponents. These are read as "four to the second power" and "three to the fourth power" respectively. This is why you sometimes hear people call exponents "powers."

base → 2^6 ← exponent

In a term like the one shown, the exponent tells you how many times to multiply the base by itself. For example, $4^2 = 4 \times 4 = 16$ and $3^4 = 3 \times 3 \times 3 \times 3 = 81$. The following are a few special rules and some terminology you should be familiar with in regard to exponents.

- Any number with an exponent of 0 is equal to 1.

  This means that $4^0 = 1$, $\left(\dfrac{2}{3}\right)^0 = 1$, and $1215^0 = 1$. (The only exception is 0^0, which is considered an indeterminate form. This will not be on the GED® test, however!)

- Any number to the power of 1 is just that number.

  For example, $8^1 = 8$ and $\left(\dfrac{1}{2}\right)^1 = \dfrac{1}{2}$.

- Any number to the power of 2 is said to be "squared." Any number to the power of 3 is said to be "cubed."

  For example, 5^2 can be read as "five squared" and 5^3 can be read as "five cubed."

Negative Exponents

Negative exponents have a special meaning. They can be thought of as a way to rewrite a fraction. As a general rule, for any number A that is not zero:

$$A^{-n} = \frac{1}{A^n}$$

In other words, any number with a negative exponent can be rewritten as a fraction with 1 above the fraction bar and the same number with a positive exponent below the fraction bar. Here are some examples.

EXAMPLE 1

$$5^{-2} = \frac{1}{5^2} = \frac{1}{5 \times 5} = \frac{1}{25}$$

EXAMPLE 2

$$3^{-1} = \frac{1}{3^1} = \frac{1}{3}$$

EXAMPLE 3

$$2^{-4} = \frac{1}{2^4} = \frac{1}{2 \times 2 \times 2 \times 2} = \frac{1}{16}$$

EXERCISE 1

Exponents

Directions: Evaluate each of the following expressions containing exponents.

1. 3^2

2. 1^5

3. 12^1

4. 7^3

5. 2^2

6. 18^0

7. 8^{-2}

8. 6^{-1}

9. 4^{-3}

10. 1^{-4}

Answers are on pages 501–502.

The Rules of Exponents

Expressions with exponents have rules that allow you to simplify them. These are commonly called the rules or laws of exponents. These rules apply whether the exponents are negative or positive, or even if they are not whole numbers.

Rule 1: When Multiplying Two Terms with the Same Base, Add the Exponents

$$A^n \times A^m = A^{n+m}$$

Remember that this rule applies only if the base numbers are the same. For example, $2^3 \times 2^{-1}$ can be simplified using rule 1 because in both terms the base is 2. But $3^2 \times 4^{10}$ cannot be simplified in that way because the base is 3 in one term but 4 in the other.

EXAMPLE 4

Using the laws of exponents, write a numerical expression that is equivalent to $4^4 \times 4^2$.

Because the two terms with exponents have the same base, you can apply rule 1: $4^4 \times 4^2 = 4^{4+2} = 4^6$.

EXAMPLE 5

Using the laws of exponents, write a numerical expression that is equivalent to $\left(\frac{1}{2}\right)^3 \times \left(\frac{1}{2}\right)^6$.

Again, the two terms have the same base, so

$$\left(\frac{1}{2}\right)^3 \times \left(\frac{1}{2}\right)^6 = \left(\frac{1}{2}\right)^{3+6} = \left(\frac{1}{2}\right)^9.$$

Rule 2: When Dividing Two Terms with the Same Base, Subtract the Exponents

$$A^m \div A^n = \frac{A^m}{A^n} = A^{m-n}$$

On the GED® test, you may see division written with the usual division symbol, or you may see it written as a fraction. Both of these are shown in this rule, and both mean the same thing.

EXAMPLE 6

Using the laws of exponents, write a numerical expression that is equivalent to $\dfrac{3^5}{3^2}$.

The two terms have the same base and are being divided, so apply rule 2: $\dfrac{3^5}{3^2} = 3^{5-2} = 3^3$.

EXAMPLE 7

Using the laws of exponents, write a numerical expression that is equivalent to $4^5 \div 4$.

Both terms have the same base, but the second 4 does not appear to have an exponent. However, recall that any number to the power of 1 is that same number. Therefore, 4 can be thought of as 4^1. Thus, $4^5 \div 4 = 4^{5-1} = 4^4$.

Rule 3: To Take a Term with an Exponent to a Power, Multiply the Powers

$$\left(A^m\right)^n = A^{m \times n}$$

For this rule, you do not need to worry about the base. Just remember that when a power is taken to a power, the exponents are multiplied.

For example, $\left(3^2\right)^4 = 3^8$ and $\left(\left(\dfrac{1}{3}\right)^5\right)^3 = \left(\dfrac{1}{3}\right)^{15}$.

When simplifying some expressions, you may need to use more than one of the rules provided above. In these cases, the order in which you apply the rules does not matter so long as anything within parentheses is simplified first.

EXAMPLE 8

Simplify the expression $\left(4^3 \times 4^2\right)^2$ using the laws of exponents.

Working inside the parentheses first, $\left(4^3 \times 4^2\right)^2 = \left(4^5\right)^2 = 4^{10}$.

Rules of Exponents

Directions: For each of the following, select the expression that is equivalent to the one given.

1. $2^3 \times 2^5$

   A. $\dfrac{1}{2^2}$

   B. 2

   C. 2^2

   D. 2^8

2. $\dfrac{5}{5^4}$

   A. $\dfrac{1}{5^5}$

   B. $\dfrac{1}{5^3}$

   C. 5^4

   D. 5^5

3. $\left(\dfrac{1}{6}\right)^2 \times \dfrac{1}{6}$

   A. $\dfrac{1}{6}$

   B. $\left(\dfrac{1}{6}\right)^2$

   C. $\left(\dfrac{1}{6}\right)^3$

   D. $\left(\dfrac{1}{6}\right)^4$

4. $\left(8^4\right)^4$

   A. $\dfrac{1}{8^4}$

   B. 1

   C. 8^8

   D. 8^{16}

5. $\dfrac{3^2}{3^2}$

   A. 0

   B. $\dfrac{1}{6}$

   C. 1

   D. 3^4

6. $\left(3^2 \times 3\right)^3$

   A. 3^3

   B. 3^6

   C. 3^7

   D. 3^9

7. $\dfrac{1}{7^2 \times 7^5}$

   A. $\dfrac{1}{7^{10}}$

   B. 7^{10}

   C. $\dfrac{1}{7^7}$

   D. 7^7

8. $\left(\dfrac{4^8}{4^3}\right)^3$

   A. 4^5
   B. 4^8
   C. 4^{15}
   D. 4^{21}

9. $18 \times 18 \times 18^2$
   A. 1
   B. 18
   C. 18^2
   D. 18^4

10. $\left(9^3\right)^4 \times 9$

    A. 9^2
    B. 9^4
    C. 9^8
    D. 9^{13}

Answers are on page 502.

Square Roots and Cube Roots

Square roots and cube roots are two ways of "undoing" exponents. For example, because $6^2 = 36$, the square root of 36 is 6. Also, because $2^3 = 8$, the cube root of 8 is 2. The symbol used for any type of root is called a radical. For a square root, the symbol is $\sqrt{}$. For the cube root, the symbol is $\sqrt[3]{}$. For the first two examples, you could have written $\sqrt{36} = 6$ and $\sqrt[3]{8} = 2$.

Numbers for which the square root or the cube root is a whole number are referred to as "perfect squares" or "perfect cubes." It is a good idea to know some of the common perfect squares and perfect cubes. The most common of these are listed here:

Selected Perfect Squares

$\sqrt{4} = 2$	$\sqrt{9} = 3$
$\sqrt{16} = 4$	$\sqrt{25} = 5$
$\sqrt{36} = 6$	$\sqrt{49} = 7$
$\sqrt{64} = 8$	$\sqrt{81} = 9$
$\sqrt{100} = 10$	$\sqrt{121} = 11$
$\sqrt{144} = 12$	$\sqrt{81} = 9$

Selected Perfect Cubes

$\sqrt[3]{8} = 2$	$\sqrt[3]{27} = 3$
$\sqrt[3]{64} = 4$	$\sqrt[3]{125} = 5$

Expressions involving square roots and cube roots can be simplified by using your knowledge of the perfect squares and cubes. The next two examples show how this works.

EXAMPLE 9

Simplify: $\sqrt{72}$.

Anytime you need to simplify a square root term, try to rewrite the number under the radical as an expression containing a perfect square. For example, $72 = 2 \times 36$ and 36 is a perfect square. Therefore, $\sqrt{72} = \sqrt{2 \times 36} = 6\sqrt{2}$.

Because the square root of 36 is 6, the 36 under the radical can be rewritten as 6 in front of the radical. The final answer is read as "6 times the square root of 2."

EXAMPLE 10

Simplify: $\sqrt{12}$.

Because 12 can be rewritten as the product of 3 and 4, you can simplify this term as $\sqrt{12} = \sqrt{4 \times 3} = 2\sqrt{3}$.

The same process can be applied to perfect cubes and cube roots. For example, $\sqrt[3]{32} = \sqrt[3]{8 \times 4} = 2\sqrt[3]{4}$.

Note that not all expressions with square roots or cube roots can be simplified. If the number cannot be rewritten as an expression containing a perfect square or a perfect cube, then the radical cannot be simplified.

EXERCISE 3

Square Roots and Cube Roots

Directions: Simplify each of the following using your knowledge of perfect squares and perfect cubes.

1. $\sqrt{32}$

2. $\sqrt{18}$

3. $\sqrt{40}$

4. $\sqrt{300}$

5. $\sqrt{24}$

6. $\sqrt[3]{16}$

7. $\sqrt[3]{128}$

8. $\sqrt[3]{24}$

9. $\sqrt[3]{375}$

10. $\sqrt[3]{800}$

Answers are on page 502.

Exponents and Roots on the TI-30XS

Here are the basics of how to calculate exponents and roots on the TI-30XS calculator.

Exponents

To calculate the value of any exponent, type in the base first followed by the caret key (∧) located in the left-hand column of the calculator. For example, to find 3^4:

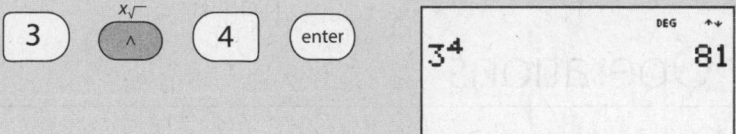

This works for any power, but there is a shortcut key that can be used for squaring numbers.

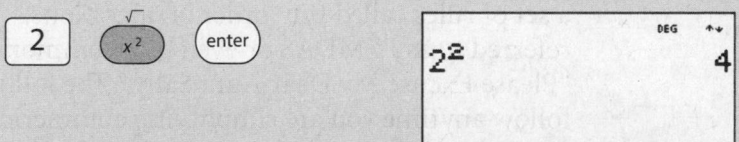

Roots

The radical symbols on the calculator are both above the regular buttons in green writing. This means that you must utilize the 2nd key to access them. For cube roots, the calculator will give a decimal approximation, but for square roots, the calculator will give the simplified version by default. In order to get the decimal approximation, you will need to press (◄►) (the toggle key).

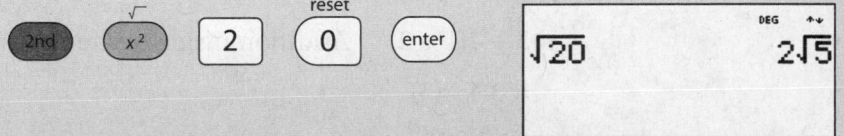

(finds the simplified answer)

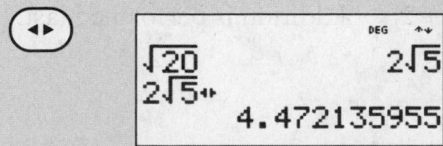

(converts to a decimal approximation)

Cube roots are found using a different key, as you can see in the following example. Notice that the 3 from the root symbol is typed in first.

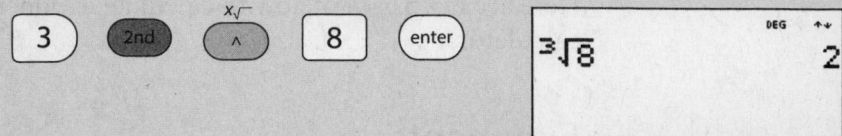

Go back and try the practice problems with the calculator. For square roots, make sure to practice getting the decimal approximation as well as the simplified versions of the answers.

Order of Operations

Which of the following is equal to $3 + 4(1 + 2)$? Is it 15, or is it 9? Which answer you get depends on the order in which you did the operations, but only one answer is correct. Getting the correct answer depends on following a set of rules called the "order of operations." You may have heard this referred to as PEMDAS or even by a common saying used to remember it: "Please Excuse My Dear Aunt Sally." The following is the process you should follow anytime you are simplifying a numerical expression.

- **Parentheses.** Complete any operations inside of parentheses first. If there is more than one set, start with the innermost parentheses.

- **Exponents.** Find the value of any exponents.

- **Multiplication and division.** Perform any multiplication or division from left to right.

- **Addition and subtraction.** Perform any addition or subtraction from left to right.

The example was the expression $3 + 4(1 + 2)$. Following the order of operations:

$3 + 4(1 + 2)$ Addition inside of the parentheses is performed first.

$= 3 + 4(3)$

Multiplication is performed next because there are no terms with exponents. (Remember that multiplication can be written as $4(3)$ *or* 4×3).

$3 + 4(1 + 2)$ Addition is performed last.

$= 15$

Let's go through a couple more examples to make sure it all makes sense.

EXAMPLE 11

Find the value of $45 - \dfrac{4^2}{2}$.

Just as there are different ways to write multiplication, there are different ways to write division. The term $\dfrac{4^2}{2} = 4^2 \div 2$. However, before the division can be completed, the term with the exponent must be calculated (this is the first step because there are no parentheses):

$$45 - \frac{4^2}{2} = 45 - \frac{16}{2} = 45 - 8 = 37$$

EXAMPLE 12

Find the value of $2(2 + 5)^2 - 6$.

$$2(2 + 5)^2 - 6 = 2(7)^2 - 6 = 2(49) - 6 = 98 - 6 = 92$$

EXERCISE 4

Order of Operations

Directions: Find the value of each of the following numerical expressions.

1. $8 \div 2^2 + 1$

2. $\dfrac{18 - 2}{2}$

3. $4 + 2(8 + 6) - 1$

4. $3(6 - 5)^3$

5. $4 \times 3 - 2$

6. $3 - 1 + 2^2 \times 5$

7. $(8 + 1 - 5)^3$

8. $(2 + 4) \div 2 - 1$

9. $5^2 + \dfrac{6 - 4}{2}$

10. $16 + 4(3 + 2)$

Answers are on page 502.

The Distributive Property

Using the order of operations, you know that $2(1 + 5) = 2(6) = 12$, but a test question may ask you simply to rewrite this expression instead of calculate its final value. This can be done using the **distributive property**. If A, B, and C are any numbers, then:

$$A(B + C) = A(B) + A(C)$$

and

$$A(B - C) = A(B) - A(C).$$

This property says that with an expression such as $2(1 + 5)$, you can first add the terms inside the parentheses as previously shown, or you can multiply each term inside the parentheses by the 2 to get $2(1 + 5) = 2(1) + 2(5)$. If you calculate the value, you will see that the result is 12, just as before. The distributive property will very useful later on when you work with algebraic expressions.

Some important things to note: The distributive property only works if the operation inside the parentheses is addition or subtraction. It will not work with any other operations.

However, the property will work no matter how many terms are added or subtracted within the parentheses. So the expression $4(5 + 6 - 1 + 2)$ is equivalent to $4(5) + 4(6) - 4(1) + 4(2)$. Notice that the 4 is multiplied by ("distributed to") each term inside the parentheses and that the terms keep the same operation (addition or subtraction).

CHAPTER 3

Decimal Numbers and Operations

Decimals appear in a wide variety of questions on the GED® test either in basic calculations or in word problems, especially those that involve money. In this chapter, you will review how to work with decimals.

Decimals and Place Value

The following chart shows how to refer to each place value in a decimal. Using this table, a number such as 5.38 is read "5 and thirty-eight hundredths," while 0.237 is read as "two hundred thirty-seven thousandths." Notice that the place value of the last number determines how it is read.

Hundred Thousands	Ten Thousands	Thousands		Hundreds	Tens	Ones		Tenths	Hundredths	Thousandths	Ten Thousandths
___	___	___	,	___	___	___	.	___	___	___	___

Rounding Decimals

Often, you will need to be able to round a decimal to a specific place. For example, a GED® test question may say "to the nearest hundredth meter, what is the radius of the circle?" This indicates that the final answer must be rounded to the nearest hundredth.

When rounding decimals, look at the number immediately to the right of the place you are rounding to. If that number is 5 or larger, add 1 to the place you are rounding. If that number is smaller than 5, keep the place the same. Remove all numbers to the right of the place you are rounding to.

EXAMPLE 1

Round 1.09256 to the nearest thousandth.

$1.09\boxed{2}\underline{5}6$

The number in the thousandths place is 2. The number immediately to the right of this number is 5. Therefore, the 2 is rounded up to 3 to get 1.093.

EXAMPLE 2

Round 8.63 to the nearest tenth.

8.⬛63

Because the number to the right of the 6 is 3, the 6 stays the same and the final result is 8.6.

Comparing Decimals

Some questions on the GED® test will ask you to determine which decimal in a group or pair is largest or smallest. You may also have to order the decimals from largest to smallest or the other way around. A common mistake is to think that a decimal with more numbers is always the largest. But for example, 0.12 is smaller than 0.3.

In order to compare two decimals, it is helpful to rewrite the decimals so that they have the same number of digits. Any zero written on the end of a decimal number does not change its value. So 0.3 is the same as 0.30, and that is the same as 0.300.

By rewriting 0.3 as 0.30 and comparing it to 0.12, you can see that 0.12 is smaller because 12 is smaller than 30. This works anytime you are comparing two decimal numbers.

To indicate that one number is larger or smaller than another, mathematics uses the symbols > and <. In each case, the open part of the symbol always points to the larger number. Which one you use just depends on the order in which the numbers are written.

EXAMPLE 3

Use > or < to indicate which number is larger.

0.098 _____ 0.22

Rewriting the decimals so that they each have three digits, you are comparing 0.098 and 0.220. Because 220 is larger than 98, 0.22 must be larger. Using one of the symbols:

0.098 < 0.22.

This is read as "Ninety-eight thousandths is **less than** twenty-two hundredths."

EXAMPLE 4

Use > or < to indicate which number is larger.

0.001 _____ 0.0009

Again rewriting, the decimals are 0.0010 and 0.0009, and because 10 is larger than 9:

0.001 > 0.0009

When the open part of the symbol faces left, it is read as "greater than." Therefore, this statement is read as "one thousandth is **greater than** nine ten thousandths."

EXERCISE 1

Comparing Decimals

Directions: Use >, <, or = to compare the given decimals.

1. 25.099 _____ 25.915

2. 0.108 _____ 0.0108

3. 0.00054 _____ 0.0019

4. 8.6 _____ 8.09

5. 0.40 _____ 0.4

6. 0.1053 _____ 0.0153

7. 2.00501 _____ 2.51

8. 0.133 _____ 1.33

9. 1.69401 _____ 1.694

10. 14.9 _____ 14.988

Answers are on page 502.

Scientific Notation

When working with decimals that have a lot of digits, you can write them in a kind of shorthand called scientific notation. Scientific notation is based on the idea that multiplying or dividing a decimal by 10 is the same as moving the decimal point one place.

For example, take the decimal 0.52. If this decimal is multiplied by 10, the result is 5.2. In other words, multiplying by 10 moves the decimal point one place to the right. If 0.52 is divided by 10, the result is 0.052. Here, dividing by 10 moved the decimal point one place to the left.

Dividing by 10 is the same as multiplying by the fraction $\frac{1}{10} = 10^{-1}$. This concept is used anytime a decimal is rewritten using scientific notation. In general, numbers written with scientific notation are written as

$$\underline{} . \underline{} \times 10^{\overline{}},$$

where the numbers in the blank spaces depend on the original number. The first part of the notation is typically a number between 1 and 10, while the power on the 10 is either positive or negative. The sign indicates whether the decimal is moved left or moved right.

EXAMPLE 5

Write 0.000381 using scientific notation.

Start with the number 3.81 and count how many places you would have to move the decimal point to the left in order to get the original number back. If you count carefully, you will see that you would have to move the decimal point in 3.81 four decimal places to the left. Therefore:

$$0.000381 = 3.81 \times 10^{-4}$$

EXAMPLE 6

Write 1.9×10^{-6} as a decimal.

Starting with 1.9, move the decimal point 6 places to the left (because the −6 is negative). Remember to place zeroes between the decimal point and the start of the number.

$$1.9 \times 10^{-6} = 0.0000019$$

Scientific notation can also be used to represent very large numbers. In this case, the power on the 10 is positive, indicating the decimal is moved to the right. Look at the next two examples.

EXAMPLE 7

Write 19,750,000 using scientific notation.

As before, start with a number smaller than 10. In this case, that would be 1.975. How many places to the right would you have to move the decimal point in order to get the original number? The answer is 7, so $19,750,000 = 1.975 \times 10^7$.

EXAMPLE 8

What number is represented by 9.6×10^4

Because the power on the 10 is a positive 4, move the decimal point four places to the right.

$9.6 \times 10^4 = 96,000$

Scientific Notation on the Calculator

When you are working with very large numbers or very small numbers, your calculator may give you the final answer in scientific notation. As an example, the following is the output when multiplying 56,895 by 225,893.

```
                         DEG    ↑↓
56895*225893
1.285218224*10¹⁰
```

Now that you know how scientific notation works, you could easily convert this to a whole number if you needed to for a final answer.

There may be times where you want to enter a number in the calculator using scientific notation. Luckily, it can be entered just as it looks—like a multiplication problem. If you don't remember how to enter exponents, you can find those instructions on page 325.

The following shows how 1.5×10^{-6} is entered.

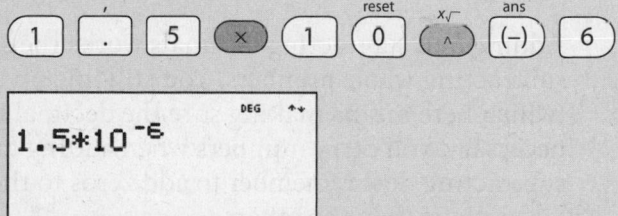

```
             DEG    ↑↓
1.5*10 ⁻⁶
```

Notice that the (−) key was pressed and not the subtraction key! Pressing the subtraction key will result in an error.

Scientific Notation

Directions: Write each of the following numbers in scientific notation.

1. 0.0025

2. 7,836,000,000

3. 0.000001

4. 0.605

5. 360,000,000

Write the number represented by each of the following.

6. 2.4×10^{-9}

7. 1.3×10^{8}

8. 4.08×10^{-2}

9. 9.0×10^{-4}

10. 5.6×10^{5}

Answers are on page 503.

Adding and Subtracting Decimals

Adding and subtracting decimals works the same way as adding and subtracting whole numbers. You still line up the numbers by place value (which here means making sure the decimal points line up), and when necessary, you carry numbers when adding and regroup numbers when subtracting. Just remember to add zeros to the end of any decimals that have fewer digits than the others.

EXAMPLE 9

Find the sum of 8.1, 0.026, 30, and 0.45.

$$
\begin{array}{r}
8.1 \\
0.026 \\
30 \\
+\ 0.45 \\
\end{array}
\qquad
\begin{array}{c}
\text{Place} \\
\text{zeros} \\
\text{on end} \\
\end{array}
\longrightarrow
\qquad
\begin{array}{r}
8.100 \\
0.026 \\
30.000 \\
+\ 0.450 \\
\hline
38.576 \\
\end{array}
$$

EXAMPLE 10

Subtract: 15.26 − 1.325.

$$
\begin{array}{r}
15.26 \\
-\ 1.325 \\
\hline
\end{array}
\qquad
\begin{array}{c}
\text{Place} \\
\text{zeros} \\
\text{on end} \\
\end{array}
\longrightarrow
\qquad
\begin{array}{r}
1\overset{4}{5}.\overset{1}{2}\overset{5}{6}\overset{1}{0} \\
-\ 1.325 \\
\hline
13.935 \\
\end{array}
$$

Multiplying Decimals

When multiplying decimals, you do not need to line up the numbers by place value. Instead, you multiply as if the two numbers were whole numbers and then count the number of digits to the right of the decimal point ("decimal digits") in both numbers to determine the number of decimal digits in the final answer.

EXAMPLE 11

Multiply 5.18 and 0.2.

$$
\begin{array}{r}
\overset{1}{5}.18 \\
\times\ 0.2 \\
\hline
1.036 \\
\end{array}
$$
There are a total of 3 decimal digits in both numbers, so the answer will have 3 decimal digits

EXAMPLE 12

Multiply 0.0062 and 0.099.

$$
\begin{array}{r}
\overset{5}{}\ \overset{1}{} \\
\overset{5}{}\ \overset{1}{} \\
0.0062 \\
\times\ 0.099 \\
\hline
00558 \\
0005580 \\
\hline
6138 \\
\end{array}
\longrightarrow 0.0006138
$$

There are a total of 7 decimal digits in both numbers, so the answer will have 7 decimal digits

In example 12, notice that the final answer needs to have 7 decimal digits but there are only 4 digits left after multiplying. In situations like this, add zeros at the beginning of the number until there are enough decimal digits.

Dividing Decimals

When dividing decimals, there are three possibilities: you may be dividing a decimal by a whole number, a whole number by a decimal, or a decimal by a decimal. For each of these, the process is slightly different. While that may sound complicated, the steps are actually all very similar.

Dividing a Decimal by a Whole Number

When dividing a decimal by a whole number, the process is exactly the same as when you divide a whole number by another whole number. As you compute your answer, make sure that the decimal point in the answer is directly above the decimal point in the number you are dividing.

EXAMPLE 13

Divide: $12.56 \div 4$.

① Place a decimal point directly above the decimal point in 12.56.

② Do regular long division.

$$
\begin{array}{r}
. \\
4\overline{)12.56}
\end{array}
$$

$$
\begin{array}{r}
3.14 \\
4\overline{)12.56} \\
\underline{12} \\
05 \\
\underline{4} \\
16 \\
\underline{16} \\
0
\end{array}
$$

Dividing a Whole Number by a Decimal

When dividing a whole number by a decimal, the process is a little different. First, rewrite the decimal as a whole number. Do this by moving the decimal point to the right. Then, in the whole number, move the decimal point (which is understood to be located after the last digit) the same number of places to the right. Fill up the empty places with zeros. Then divide. Again, make sure that the decimal point in the answer is directly above the decimal point in the number you are dividing.

EXAMPLE 14

Divide: 18 ÷ 1.4.

① Move the decimal point of both numbers to the right one space since this will make 1.4 a whole number.

$$1.4\overline{\smash{)}18.0} \longrightarrow 14\overline{\smash{)}180}$$

② Do regular long division.

```
        1 2 . 8
  14 ) 1 8 0 . 0
        1 4
        ----
          4 0
          2 8
          ----
          1 2 0
          1 1 2
          -----
              8
```

Notice in the division that a zero is added after the decimal point in 180. Adding a decimal point with zeroes after it doesn't change the number (180 is the same as 180.0), but it gives you "room" to finish the division. In fact, you can keep adding zeroes after the decimal point to get a more and more accurate answer. For example, suppose for the problem in example 14 you are asked for an answer to the nearest thousandths place. You can do this by adding two more zeroes on the end of 180.0 and continuing with the division.

```
        1 2 . 8 5 7
  14 ) 1 8 0 . 0 0 0
        1 4
        ----
          4 0
          2 8
          ----
          1 2 0
          1 1 2
          -----
              8 0
              7 0
              ----
              1 0 0
                9 8
                ---
                  2
```

Dividing a Decimal by a Decimal

To divide a decimal by a decimal, the process is nearly the same. In the decimal by which you are dividing, move the decimal point to the right until you have a whole number. Then, in the decimal that is being divided, move the decimal point the same number of places to the right. Then divide, remembering to place the decimal point in the answer directly above the decimal point in the decimal that is being divided.

EXAMPLE 15

Divide: 1.021 ÷ 0.03.

① Move the decimal point of both numbers to the right two places since this will make 0.03 a whole number.

② Do regular long division.

$$0.03\overline{)1.021} \longrightarrow 3\overline{)102.1}$$

```
      3 4 . 0
  3 ) 1 0 2 . 1
      9
      1 2
      1 2
        0 1
          0
          1
```

Finally, you may need to deal with decimals even when you are dividing two whole numbers. Consider 4 divided by 9. Since 9 is larger than 4, the final answer will have to be smaller than 1, but how would you use division here?

The key is to add a decimal point and zeroes to the end of the 4. Remember that adding zeroes after a decimal point does not change the value of the number.

EXAMPLE 16

Divide: 4 ÷ 9.

```
      . 4 4
  9 ) 4 . 0 0
      3 6
        4 0
        3 6
          4
```

Later, this method will be used to convert fractions to decimals.

EXERCISE 3

Operations with Decimals

Directions: Perform each of the following calculations by hand and then check your final answer using your calculator.

1. 18.03 + 12.1 + 0.0036

2. 15.4295 + 0.8826

3. 0.029 + 0.0041 + 3

4. 8.11 + .011

5. 16.5 + 206.9

6. 20 − 0.15

7. 1.023 − 0.0014

8. 15.6 − 2.9

9. 230.8 − 150.1

10. 0.554 − 0.099

11. 25 × 1.5

12. 1.22 × 6.4

13. 18.5 × 1.7

14. 2.63 × 9.13

15. 5.0001 × 26

16. 15 ÷ 0.3

17. 2.14 ÷ 0.05

18. 2 ÷ 16

19. 7.016 ÷ 3.9

20. 50.22 ÷ 10

Answers are on page 503.

CHAPTER 4

Fractions and Operations

Fractions are a way of representing a "part" of some larger "whole" when the whole has been divided into an equal number of parts.

- The top of a fraction (the number above the bar) is called the **numerator**. It represents the number of parts "taken out" of the whole.

- The bottom part of a fraction (the number below the bar) is called the **denominator**. It represents the number of equal parts in the whole.

For example, the fraction $\frac{3}{5}$ represents 3 parts out of a whole that has been divided into 5 parts. The numerator is 3 and the denominator is 5.

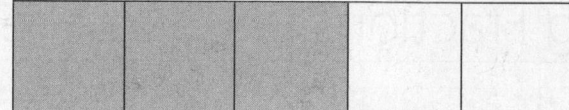

Equivalent Fractions

Two different fractions can represent the same part of a whole. For example, in the following figures, you can see that $\frac{2}{4} = \frac{1}{2}$. These are called **equivalent fractions**.

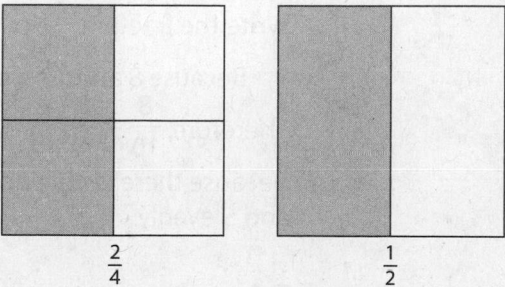

$$\frac{2}{4} \qquad \frac{1}{2}$$

If the numerator and denominator of any fraction are multiplied or divided by the same number, the result will be an equivalent fraction. For example, if you divide the numerator and denominator of $\frac{2}{4}$ each by 2, the result will be the equivalent fraction $\frac{1}{2}$.

EXAMPLE 1

Write a fraction that is equivalent to $\frac{1}{4}$ but has a denominator of 12.

The denominator of $\frac{1}{4}$ is 4. Multiplying 4 by 3 will give a denominator of 12, but to produce an equivalent fraction, the numerator must be multiplied by the same number. Therefore, $\frac{1}{4} = \frac{1 \times 3}{4 \times 3} = \frac{3}{12}$.

EXAMPLE 2

What number should replace the question mark? $\frac{4}{5} = \frac{16}{?}$

To get from 4 to 16, the numerator must have been multiplied by 4. Therefore to make an equivalent fraction, the denominator must be multiplied by 4 as well: $\frac{4}{5} = \frac{16}{20}$. These are equivalent fractions.

Reducing Fractions to Lowest Terms

Fractions are said to be reduced, or written in lowest terms, if there is no whole number that will evenly divide both the numerator and the denominator. Examples of fractions written in lowest terms are $\frac{1}{2}, \frac{3}{4}, \frac{11}{16}$, and $\frac{7}{8}$.

For most questions on the GED® test involving fractions, you will be expected to reduce fractions to lowest terms. To reduce fractions, see if there is any whole number that evenly divides both the numerator and the denominator, and then divide it out.

EXAMPLE 3

Write the fraction $\frac{8}{10}$ in lowest terms.

Because 8 and 10 are even numbers, both can be divided by 2. Therefore, $\frac{8}{10} = \frac{8 \div 2}{10 \div 2} = \frac{4}{5}$. You know the fraction $\frac{4}{5}$ is in lowest terms because there is no whole number other than 1 that will divide both 4 and 5 evenly.

EXAMPLE 4

Write the fraction $\frac{27}{81}$ in lowest terms.

The numerator 27 is the same as 9×3 and the denominator is $9 \times 9 = 81$. This means that the numerator and the denominator can each be divided by 9.

$$\frac{27}{81} = \frac{27 \div 9}{81 \div 9} = \frac{3}{9}$$

In $\frac{3}{9}$, however, the numerator and the denominator can each be divided by 3. This means that the fraction is not yet reduced to lowest terms.

So $\frac{27}{81}$ reduced to lowest terms is $\frac{1}{3}$.

Reducing Fractions on the Calculator

Fractions can be entered on the calculator using the $\frac{n}{d}$ key. Press this key before entering your fraction, and then press the ENTER key to reduce the fraction to lowest terms.

EXERCISE 1

Equivalent Fractions

Directions: For each of the following, write an equivalent fraction as indicated by either dividing or multiplying the numerator and the denominator by the same number.

1. Write a fraction that is equivalent to $\frac{5}{9}$ but has a denominator of 45.

2. Write a fraction that is equivalent to $\frac{1}{7}$ but has a numerator of 21.

3. What number should replace the question mark: $\frac{1}{2} = \frac{?}{24}$

4. What number should replace the question mark: $\dfrac{18}{60} = \dfrac{?}{30}$

5. What number should replace the question mark: $\dfrac{35}{45} = \dfrac{7}{?}$

Write each of the following fractions in lowest terms. Check your answer using your calculator.

6. $\dfrac{22}{42}$

7. $\dfrac{10}{50}$

8. $\dfrac{12}{16}$

9. $\dfrac{3}{90}$

10. $\dfrac{14}{48}$

Answers are on page 503.

Fractions and Decimals

Fractions and decimals can represent the same number. By dividing the numerator by the denominator, you can see what number or decimal is equivalent to the fraction.

EXAMPLE 5

Find the decimal that represents $\dfrac{3}{5}$.

Because $3 \div 5 = 0.6$, $\dfrac{3}{5} = .06$.

EXAMPLE 6

Find the decimal that represents $\dfrac{1}{20}$.

$1 \div 20 = 0.05$. Therefore, $\dfrac{1}{20} = 0.05$.

Decimals can be converted to fractions by using their place value and numbers like 10, 100, 1000, and 10,000. The place value tells you which number to use.

EXAMPLE 7

Write 0.05 as a fraction in lowest terms.

You read this decimal as "five hundredths" because the 5 is in the hundredths place. So the equivalent fraction is $\frac{5}{100}$, which can be reduced to $\frac{1}{20}$.

EXAMPLE 8

Write 0.480 as a fraction in lowest terms.

You read this decimal as "four hundred eighty thousandths." As before, use the place value to write the equivalent fraction, and then reduce.

$$\frac{480}{1000} = \frac{12}{25}$$

Converting Between Fractions and Decimals on the Calculator

Converting from a fraction to a decimal is simply done by the usual division operation on any calculator. However, the TI-30XS used on the GED® test can easily convert from a decimal to a fraction with a special fraction-to-decimal function. This is located in green above the (table) button, so the 2nd key must be pressed to access it. The following steps show how to use this with the previous example of 0.480.

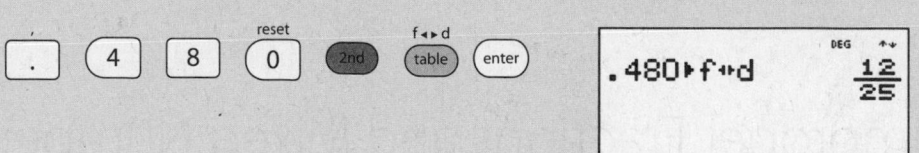

Converting Between Fractions and Decimals

Directions: For each of the following fractions, find the equivalent decimal. Round your answer to the nearest hundredths place.

1. $\dfrac{3}{4}$

2. $\dfrac{2}{5}$

3. $\dfrac{1}{4}$

4. $\dfrac{21}{100}$

5. $\dfrac{7}{15}$

For each of the following decimal numbers, find an equivalent fraction and write it in lowest terms.

6. 0.028

7. 0.225

8. 0.16

9. 0.31

10. 0.90

Answers are on page 504.

Improper Fractions and Mixed Numbers

In the fraction $\dfrac{5}{2}$ the numerator is greater than the denominator. A fraction of this kind is called an **improper fraction**. The decimal equivalent of $\dfrac{5}{2}$ is 2.5, which is greater than 1. Improper fractions will always have decimal equivalents that are greater than 1.

Another way to represent an improper fraction like $\frac{5}{2}$ is as a mixed number. **Mixed numbers** show the whole number part of the fraction and the fractional part separately. For example, $\frac{5}{2}$ becomes $2\frac{1}{2}$ when written as a mixed number.

To write an improper fraction as a mixed number, determine how many times the denominator can divide the numerator evenly. Then, write any remaining part as a fraction with the original denominator.

EXAMPLE 9

Write $\frac{23}{7}$ as a mixed number.

The denominator 7 can divide the numerator 3 times with 2 left over. Therefore, $\frac{23}{7} = 3\frac{2}{7}$.

EXAMPLE 10

Write $\frac{11}{8}$ as a mixed number.

The denominator 8 can divide 11 once with 3 left over: $\frac{11}{8} = 1\frac{3}{8}$.

Converting from a mixed number back to an improper fraction is a quick process illustrated in the following examples.

EXAMPLE 11

Write $6\frac{2}{3}$ as an improper fraction.

$$6\frac{2}{3} = \frac{18 + 2}{3} = \frac{20}{3}$$

EXAMPLE 12

Write $2\frac{1}{5}$ as an improper fraction.

$$2\frac{1}{5} = \frac{10 + 1}{5} = \frac{11}{5}$$

Converting Between Mixed Numbers and Improper Fractions on the Calculator

Improper fractions can be typed into the calculator using the $\frac{n}{d}$ key. Just above this key is the mixed numbers function. By pressing the 2nd key followed by the $\frac{n}{d}$ key, you can enter mixed numbers. Here is an example using a calculator to convert $8\frac{2}{3}$ to an improper fraction.

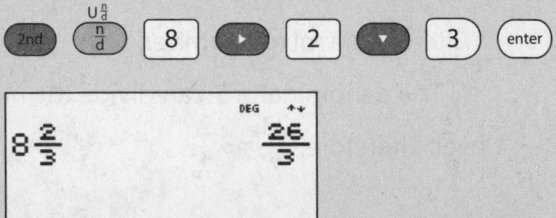

$$8\frac{2}{3} \qquad \frac{26}{3}$$

The $\frac{n}{d} \blacktriangleleft\blacktriangleright U\frac{n}{d}$ function located above the $(x10^n)$ key can be used to convert between improper fractions and whole numbers. Here is an example converting $\frac{25}{9}$ to a mixed number.

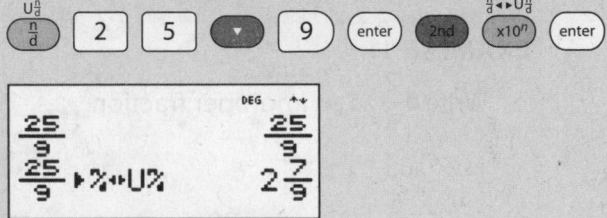

$$\frac{25}{9} \qquad \frac{25}{9}$$
$$\frac{25}{9} \blacktriangleright \% \blacktriangleleft U\% \qquad 2\frac{7}{9}$$

EXERCISE 3

Mixed Numbers

Directions: Rewrite each of the following improper fractions as mixed numbers and check your answer with your calculator.

1. $\dfrac{19}{5}$

2. $\dfrac{21}{2}$

3. $\dfrac{95}{20}$

4. $\dfrac{28}{6}$

5. $\dfrac{45}{8}$

Rewrite each of the following mixed numbers as improper fractions and check your answers with your calculator.

6. $2\dfrac{1}{8}$

7. $9\dfrac{3}{5}$

8. $4\dfrac{1}{16}$

9. $5\dfrac{5}{7}$

10. $16\dfrac{2}{3}$

Answers are on page 504.

Comparing Fractions

Ordering fractions from greatest to smallest or smallest to greatest is a skill that is commonly tested on the GED® test. To order fractions correctly, you need to be able to compare fractions with each other.

Suppose you want to determine which is larger, $\dfrac{1}{5}$ or $\dfrac{3}{5}$. Remember that fractions represent parts of a whole. In that case, $\dfrac{3}{5}$ must be larger because 3 is more "parts" than 1 ($\dfrac{3}{5}$ has a larger numerator than $\dfrac{1}{5}$). This works because both fractions have a denominator of 5.

To compare fractions with different denominators, such as $\dfrac{1}{2}$ and $\dfrac{3}{7}$, you will need to find equivalent fractions with a common denominator. A **common denominator** is one number that can be used as a denominator for both equivalent fractions.

For example, $\dfrac{1}{2}$ and $\dfrac{3}{7}$ can each be written as equivalent fractions with a denominator of 14: $\dfrac{1}{2}=\dfrac{7}{14}$ and $\dfrac{3}{7}=\dfrac{6}{14}$. Now you can compare the two fractions and see that $\dfrac{1}{2}=\dfrac{7}{14}$ is the greater fraction.

To find a common denominator for two different fractions, follow these steps:

- Determine if one of the denominators can be divided by the other. If so, this larger denominator is a common denominator.

- Otherwise, multiply the two denominators and use the result as a common denominator.

The following examples use the same symbols that were used when comparing decimals.

EXAMPLE 13

Use <, >, or = to compare the fractions: $\dfrac{3}{4}, \dfrac{7}{8}$.

Looking at the denominators, 8 can be divided by 4, so 8 is the common denominator. Rewrite $\dfrac{3}{4}$ using this denominator.

$$\frac{3}{4} = \frac{3 \times 2}{4 \times 2} = \frac{6}{8}$$

Because the numerator of $\dfrac{7}{8}$ is greater than the numerator of $\dfrac{6}{8}$, it is the greater fraction. Therefore, $\dfrac{3}{4} < \dfrac{7}{8}$.

EXAMPLE 14

Use <, >, or = to compare the fractions: $\dfrac{3}{5}, \dfrac{8}{9}$.

Neither denominator can be divided by the other, so the common denominator is their product: $5 \times 9 = 45$. Both fractions have to be rewritten using this denominator.

$$\frac{3}{5} = \frac{3 \times 9}{5 \times 9} = \frac{27}{45}$$

$$\frac{8}{9} = \frac{8 \times 5}{9 \times 5} = \frac{40}{45}$$

Because 27 is less than 40, $\dfrac{27}{45} < \dfrac{40}{45}$ and $\dfrac{3}{5} < \dfrac{8}{9}$.

Comparing Fractions and Decimals

As shown in the preceding section, rewriting two fractions with a common denominator makes it easier to compare them. The same idea applies when comparing fractions and decimals. Because every fraction can be written as a decimal, converting the fraction to a decimal lets you compare the two numbers on the same footing.

EXAMPLE 15

Fill in the blank with <, >, or = to make a true statement: $\frac{2}{5}$ _____ 0.455.

Written as a decimal, $\frac{2}{5} = 2 \div 5 = 0.4 = 0.400$. This decimal is smaller than 0.455, so $\frac{2}{5} < 0.455$.

EXAMPLE 16

Fill in the blank with <, >, or − to make a true statement: $\frac{3}{10}$ _____ 0.29.

Because $\frac{3}{10} = 3 \div 10 = 0.3 = 0.30$, and 0.30 is greater than 0.29:

$\frac{3}{10} > 0.29$.

EXERCISE 4

Comparing Fractions

Directions: Use >, <, or = to compare the given fractions.

1. $\frac{2}{3}$ _____ $\frac{1}{9}$

2. $\frac{7}{15}$ _____ $\frac{3}{5}$

3. $\frac{9}{20}$ _____ $\frac{1}{6}$

4. $\frac{5}{18}$ _____ $\frac{4}{9}$

5. $\frac{1}{2}$ _____ $\frac{1}{3}$

Use >, <, or = to compare the given fractions and decimals.

6. 0.22 _____ $\frac{1}{3}$

7. $\frac{1}{2}$ _____ 0.18

8. 0.578 _____ $\frac{51}{100}$

9. 0.8821 _____ $\frac{15}{17}$

10. $\frac{5}{13}$ _____ 0.42

Answers are on page 504.

Adding and Subtracting Fractions

The rules for adding and subtracting fractions depend on whether or not the fractions share the same denominator. When the fractions share the same denominator, you will just add or subtract the numerators from left to right. When they do not, you must find a common denominator before doing anything else.

EXAMPLE 17

Find the sum: $\frac{2}{7} + \frac{3}{7}$. Write your answer in lowest terms.

The fractions have the same denominator, so the sum is found by just adding the numerators.

$$\frac{2}{7} + \frac{3}{7} = \frac{5}{7}$$

EXAMPLE 18

Find the difference: $\frac{5}{8} - \frac{1}{4}$. Write your answer in lowest terms.

Because these fractions do not have the same denominator, use the techniques to find a common denominator. The denominator 8 can be divided by 4, so 8 is the common denominator. Once both fractions are rewritten with that denominator, you can subtract the numerators in the same way as you added in example 17. To rewrite $\frac{1}{4}$, the numerator and the denominator must be multiplied by 2.

$$\frac{5}{8} - \frac{1}{4} = \frac{5}{8} - \frac{1 \times 2}{4 \times 2} = \frac{5}{8} - \frac{2}{8} = \frac{3}{8}$$

EXAMPLE 19

Find the sum: $\frac{1}{6} + \frac{1}{10}$. Write your answer in lowest terms.

Neither denominator will divide the other, so the common denominator is $6 \times 10 = 60$. Both fractions must be rewritten before they can be added.

$$\frac{1}{6} + \frac{1}{10} = \frac{1 \times 10}{6 \times 10} + \frac{1 \times 6}{10 \times 6} = \frac{10}{60} + \frac{6}{60} = \frac{16}{60}$$

The answer $\frac{16}{60}$ is not written in lowest terms, because 16 and 60 can each be divided evenly by 4. To reduce the fraction, divide the numerator and denominator each by 4 to reach your final answer.

$$\frac{16}{60} = \frac{16 \div 4}{60 \div 4} = \frac{4}{15}$$

EXERCISE 5

Adding and Subtracting Fractions

Directions: Calculate the indicated sums or differences and write your final answer in lowest terms.

1. $\dfrac{2}{5} + \dfrac{1}{5}$

2. $\dfrac{8}{13} + \dfrac{3}{13}$

3. $\dfrac{4}{9} + \dfrac{5}{6}$

4. $\dfrac{1}{12} + \dfrac{1}{4}$

5. $\dfrac{5}{21} + \dfrac{2}{7}$

6. $\dfrac{3}{4} - \dfrac{1}{4}$

7. $\dfrac{5}{8} - \dfrac{1}{8}$

8. $\dfrac{9}{14} - \dfrac{2}{7}$

9. $\dfrac{8}{25} - \dfrac{1}{5}$

10. $\dfrac{1}{3} - \dfrac{1}{4}$

Answers are on pages 504–505.

Multiplying Fractions

When multiplying two fractions, you do not need to worry about common denominators. Whether or not the two fractions have the same denominator, the process is always the same: multiply the numerators and multiply the denominators. In fact, by cross canceling, you can reduce the fraction before you even multiply!

EXAMPLE 20

Multiply: $\dfrac{2}{9} \times \dfrac{1}{4}$.

① 2 and 4 can be divided evenly by 2, so cross cancel.

② Multiply across.

$$\dfrac{2}{9} \times \dfrac{1}{4} \longrightarrow \dfrac{\overset{1}{2}}{9} \times \dfrac{1}{\underset{2}{4}}$$

$$\dfrac{\overset{1}{2}}{9} \times \dfrac{1}{\underset{2}{4}} = \dfrac{1 \times 1}{9 \times 2} = \dfrac{1}{18}$$

EXAMPLE 21

Multiply: $\dfrac{3}{10} \times \dfrac{16}{33}$.

① 3 and 33 can be evenly divided by 3, while 10 and 16 can be evenly divided by 2.

② Multiply across.

$$\dfrac{3}{10} \times \dfrac{16}{33} \longrightarrow \dfrac{\overset{1}{3}}{\underset{5}{10}} \times \dfrac{\overset{8}{16}}{\underset{11}{33}}$$

$$\dfrac{\overset{1}{3}}{\underset{5}{10}} \times \dfrac{\overset{8}{16}}{\underset{11}{33}} = \dfrac{1 \times 8}{5 \times 11} = \dfrac{8}{55}$$

Dividing Fractions

When dividing fractions, simply "flip and multiply." This works because multiplication and division are closely related. Any division problem can be written as a multiplication problem. For example, multiplying by $\dfrac{1}{3}$ is the same as dividing by 3. When a fraction is "flipped," the resulting fraction is called its **reciprocal**. The numbers 3 and $\dfrac{1}{3}$ are reciprocals, as are $\dfrac{2}{5}$ and $\dfrac{5}{2}$. When you "flip and multiply," you are actually just rewriting the division as multiplication by the reciprocal.

EXAMPLE 22

Divide: $\dfrac{1}{9} \div \dfrac{3}{4}$.

The first fraction stays the same, but the second fraction is flipped. Then you multiply instead of divide.

$$\dfrac{1}{9} \div \dfrac{3}{4} = \dfrac{1}{9} \times \dfrac{4}{3} = \dfrac{4}{27}$$

Note that you cannot cross cancel until you reach the multiplication step!

EXAMPLE 23

Divide: $\dfrac{5}{8} \div \dfrac{15}{10}$.

Keep the first fraction the same and multiply by the reciprocal of the second.

$$\frac{5}{8} \div \frac{15}{10} = \frac{5}{8} \times \frac{10}{15}$$

It is now possible to cross cancel before multiplying to find the final answer.

$$\frac{\overset{1}{\cancel{5}}}{\underset{4}{\cancel{8}}} \times \frac{\overset{5}{\cancel{10}}}{\underset{3}{\cancel{15}}} = \frac{1 \times 5}{4 \times 3} = \frac{5}{12}$$

EXERCISE 6

Multiplying and Dividing Fractions

Directions: Multiply or divide the following fractions as indicated. Write your answer in lowest terms.

1. $\dfrac{4}{5} \times \dfrac{3}{4}$

2. $\dfrac{1}{9} \times \dfrac{1}{10}$

3. $\dfrac{2}{7} \times \dfrac{2}{18}$

4. $\dfrac{2}{3} \times \dfrac{1}{3}$

5. $\dfrac{2}{15} \times \dfrac{3}{8}$

6. $\dfrac{2}{11} \div \dfrac{3}{4}$

7. $\dfrac{4}{5} \div \dfrac{2}{5}$

8. $\dfrac{15}{16} \div \dfrac{1}{8}$

9. $\dfrac{1}{2} \div \dfrac{3}{4}$

10. $\dfrac{8}{9} \div \dfrac{10}{19}$

Answers are on page 505.

Operations with Fractions, Whole Numbers, and Mixed Numbers

Sometimes you may need to add or subtract two mixed numbers, divide a whole number by a fraction, or multiply a mixed number by a whole number. In these cases, the following facts can help you with your calculations:

- The reciprocal of any whole number is a fraction with 1 in the numerator and the whole number in the denominator. The following pairs are all reciprocals: $\frac{1}{5}$ and 5, 9 and $\frac{1}{9}$, $\frac{1}{2}$ and 2.
- Mixed numbers can always be converted to improper fractions. Once converted, the regular rules of operations with fractions apply.
- Any fraction with the same number in the numerator and the denominator equals 1. (This rule does not apply if the number is zero.) All of the following are equal to 1: $\frac{6}{6}, \frac{2}{2}, \frac{1}{1}$.
- Any whole number can be rewritten as a fraction with a denominator of 1. For example, $5 = \frac{5}{1}$ and $\frac{10}{1} = 10$.

Let's see how these facts can help with a few examples.

EXAMPLE 24

Divide: $\frac{1}{2} \div 3$.

Use the "flip and multiply" technique. Remember that the reciprocal of 3 is $\frac{1}{3}$:

$$\frac{1}{2} \div 3 = \frac{1}{2} \times \frac{1}{3} = \frac{1}{6}$$

EXAMPLE 25

Multiply: $10 \times \frac{4}{5}$.

Rewrite 10 as a fraction with a denominator of 1. Then multiply as you would with any other fractions (including cross canceling).

$$10 \times \frac{4}{5} = \frac{10}{1} \times \frac{4}{5} = \frac{2}{1} \times \frac{4}{1} = \frac{8}{1} = 8$$

EXAMPLE 26

Add: $2\frac{1}{4} + \frac{2}{9}$.

First, convert $2\frac{1}{4}$ to an improper fraction. Then you can add fractions as usual. Remember that you need like denominators when adding and subtracting fractions.

$$2\frac{1}{4} + \frac{2}{9} = \frac{9}{4} + \frac{2}{9} = \frac{9 \times 9}{4 \times 9} + \frac{2 \times 4}{9 \times 4} = \frac{81}{36} + \frac{8}{36} = \frac{89}{36}$$

How you format your final answer depends on the question being asked. When working with mixed numbers, you usually will need to write your final answer as a mixed number. In this example, the final answer would be:

$$\frac{89}{36} = 2\frac{17}{36}$$

EXERCISE 7

Operations with Fractions, Whole Numbers, and Mixed Numbers

Directions: Find the sum, difference, product, or quotient as indicated. If the original problem contains a mixed number, write your final answer as a mixed number. Otherwise, write your final answer in lowest terms.

1. $5 - \dfrac{2}{5}$

2. $\dfrac{1}{9} \times 3$

3. $4 \div \dfrac{1}{2}$

4. $3\dfrac{1}{4} \div \dfrac{2}{3}$

5. $8\dfrac{1}{3} - 6\dfrac{3}{5}$

6. $4 + \dfrac{2}{7}$

7. $18 \div \dfrac{3}{2}$

8. $2 \times \dfrac{6}{7}$

9. $10 \times \dfrac{2}{3}$

10. $6 - \dfrac{1}{15}$

Answers are on page 505.

Operations with Fractions on the Calculator

Any of the basic operations with fractions can be performed on the calculator, and the final answer will automatically be given in reduced form. Remember that to enter fractions in the calculator, you use the $\frac{n}{d}$ key and that mixed numbers can be entered using the $U\frac{n}{d}$ function (see the mixed numbers section for more details).

For example, here is how you would use the calculator to find $\frac{1}{8} \div \frac{2}{3}$.

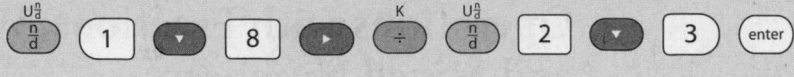

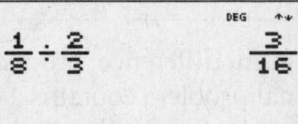

CHAPTER 5

Ratios, Rates, and Proportions

Ratios and Rates

A **ratio** is a way of showing how two or more things compare in terms of size, number, or amount. For example, if a club has 3 members who are men for every 2 members who are women, you would say that the ratio of men to women club members is 3 to 2.

There are three common ways to write ratios. Using the ratio of men to women as an example:

- As a statement: as in the preceding example, "the ratio of men to women is 3 to 2"
- In a fraction: $\dfrac{3}{2}$
- In ratio notation: 3:2

Ratios are always written in lowest terms. Therefore, the ratio 6:10 (said "six to ten") must be simplified to 3:5.

A ratio that compares two quantities with different units is called a **rate**. Rates are common in everyday life. A very common example is the speed limit on major highways: 65 miles per hour. This is a ratio of 65 miles for each hour.

Word Problems with Ratios and Rates

On the GED® test, ratios and rates often come up in word problems. You may also be asked to simplify a given ratio. Let's look at a couple of examples.

EXAMPLE 1

A craftsman uses 48 nails to attach 200 feet of siding. As a fraction, what is the ratio of nails to feet of siding?

The problem is asking for the ratio of nails to feet of siding, so the order matters. As a fraction, the ratio is $\dfrac{48}{200} = \dfrac{6}{25}$.

EXAMPLE 2

The list shows the price of different quantities of ketchup at three different stores.

Sam's Grocery	$3.25 for 24 ounces
Outlet Mart	$6.99 for 64 ounces
B & E Gas and Grocery	$1.58 for 12 ounces

To the nearest hundredth, which store has the lowest price per ounce?

Each price per quantity can be written as a ratio. To find the price "per ounce," you will need to simplify each ratio until it has a denominator of 1.

Sam's Grocery: $\dfrac{3.25 \text{ dollars}}{24 \text{ ounces}}$

Outlet Mart: $\dfrac{6.99 \text{ dollars}}{64 \text{ ounces}}$

B & E Gas and Grocery: $\dfrac{1.58 \text{ dollars}}{12 \text{ ounces}}$

To make the denominator of each ratio 1, divide each by its denominator.

Sam's Grocery: $\dfrac{3.25 \text{ dollars} \div 24 \text{ dollars}}{24 \div 24 \text{ ounces}} = \dfrac{0.14 \text{ dollars}}{1 \text{ ounce}}$

Outlet Mart: $\dfrac{6.99 \text{ dollars} \div 64 \text{ dollars}}{64 \div 64 \text{ ounces}} = \dfrac{0.11 \text{ dollars}}{1 \text{ ounce}}$

B & E Gas and Grocery: $\dfrac{1.58 \text{ dollars} \div 12 \text{ dollars}}{12 \div 12 \text{ ounces}} = \dfrac{0.13 \text{ dollars}}{1 \text{ ounce}}$

Now that you have found the rate per unit (the rate where the denominator is 1), you can see that Outlet Mart has the lowest price per ounce.

EXERCISE 1

Ratios and Rates

Directions: Match the ratio on the left with its equivalent ratio on the right. There is only one correct answer for each of the problems 1 through 3. Not all of the answers on the right will be used.

1. 3:4   **A.** $\dfrac{18}{81}$

2. 2:9   **B.** $\dfrac{12}{6}$

3. 8:6   **C.** $\dfrac{15}{20}$

           D. $\dfrac{18}{24}$

           E. $\dfrac{16}{12}$

Write each of the following ratios or rates as fractions in their lowest terms.

4. A writer types 500 words every 2 hours.

5. The new trail has 3 miles for every 2 miles of the old trail.

6. The temperature increases 15 degrees every 5 hours.

7. The school has 400 freshmen for every 100 seniors.

Solve each of the following word problems.

8. A company's workforce is composed of 10 men for every 12 women. What is the ratio of men to women at this company?

9. The Andersons and the Lamberts are on road trips. The Andersons traveled 300 miles in 6 hours, while the Lamberts traveled 200 miles in 5 hours. Which family traveled at a faster average rate?

10. Miguel's garden is four times larger than Tama's garden. Write the fraction that represents the ratio of the size of Miguel's garden to the size of Tama's garden.

Answers are on pages 505–506.

Proportions

Proportions are equations involving equal ratios or rates. Often, problems with proportions will require you to find a missing value, usually shown as x or some other letter. You can do this through a process called cross multiplying.

EXAMPLE 3

What is the value of x if $\dfrac{3}{4} = \dfrac{x}{12}$?

Cross multiplying means multiplying diagonally across the equals sign. When you cross multiply in this problem, you get:

$(3 \times 12) = (4 \times x)$ *or* $36 = 4x$

You can then find the unknown value by dividing both sides by 4: $x = 9$.

EXAMPLE 4

What is the value of b if $\dfrac{b}{2} = \dfrac{5}{10}$?

Cross multiply: $10b = 10$.

Divide both sides by the number in front of b: $b = 1$.

EXERCISE 2

Proportions

Directions: Find the unknown value that makes each of the statements below true.

1. $\dfrac{4}{8} = \dfrac{n}{18}$

2. $\dfrac{5}{a} = \dfrac{15}{30}$

3. $\dfrac{4}{5} = \dfrac{x}{20}$

4. $\dfrac{2}{9} = \dfrac{m}{81}$

5. $\dfrac{x}{16} = \dfrac{2}{8}$

Answers are on page 506.

Word Problems with Proportions

There are many real-life applications of proportions, and these can show up in word problems on the GED® test. Let's look at some examples.

EXAMPLE 5

A car is traveling at a rate of 60 miles per hour. If this rate is maintained, how long will it take the car to travel 180 miles?

Set up the proportion $\dfrac{60}{1} = \dfrac{180}{h}$ where h represents the number of hours. Note that both numerators are in miles and both denominators are in hours. In proportions like this one, the numerators and denominators must each be in the same units.

Cross multiply: $60h = 180$.

Divide by the number in front of h: $h = 3$.

The car will take 3 hours to travel 180 miles.

EXAMPLE 6

The ratio of links to images on a website is 3:10. If there are 500 images on the website, how many links does it contain?

The proportion is $\dfrac{3}{10} = \dfrac{L}{500}$, where L is the number of links.

Cross multiply: $1500 = 10L$.

Divide both sides by 10: $150 = L$.

There are 150 links on the website.

Word Problems with Proportions

1. There are 40 men in a sporting league and the ratio of men to women in the league is 5:3. How many women are in the league?

2. It took a bicyclist 4 hours to cover 30 miles of hilly terrain. At this rate, how many hours will it take her to cover 15 more miles?

3. A factory makes a party snack mix containing 20 pounds of peanuts for every 2 pounds of cashews. If a new batch of the mix contains 100 pounds of peanuts, how many pounds of cashews does it contain?

4. If a data entry specialist can enter 40 patient records in 3 hours, how long will it take him to enter 60 records?

5. A hiking map is drawn so that each inch represents 10 miles. If a popular trail is 16 miles long, how long will it be on the hiking map?

Answers are on page 506.

CHAPTER 6

Percents and Applications

Percents, fractions, and decimals are all ways to represent a part of a whole. With percents, that whole has been divided into 100 equal parts. Percents come up constantly in everyday life in situations involving, for example, sales taxes, bank interest, and tips on restaurant meals. On the GED® test, questions about percents tend to involve uses like these and require a firm understanding of how percents work.

Converting Between Fractions, Decimals, and Percents

The first thing it is important to know is how to convert between fractions, decimals, and percents.

Converting a Percent to a Fraction

Because a percent represents a portion taken from 100 equal parts, any percent can be written as a fraction by writing its value over 100 and simplifying.

EXAMPLE 1

Write 35% as a fraction.

Write 35 over 100 and simplify.

$$35\% = \frac{35}{100} = \frac{7}{20}$$

EXAMPLE 2

Write 2% as a fraction.

Write 2 over 100 and simplify.

$$2\% = \frac{2}{100} = \frac{1}{50}$$

Converting a Percent to a Decimal

Similarly, converting a percent to a decimal involves dividing by 100. If you imagine a decimal point on the end of a whole number such as 12, you can divide by 100 by moving that decimal point two places to the left.

EXAMPLE 3

Write 12% as a decimal.

Divide by 100 (or move the decimal point two places to the left): 12% = 0.12.

EXAMPLE 4

Write 4% as a decimal.

Divide by 100 (or move the decimal point two places to the left): 4% = 0.04.

These conversions even work when you are dealing with fractional or decimal percentages. For example:

0.5% = 0.005 (move the decimal point two places to the left)

$\frac{1}{8}$% = 0.125% = 0.00125 (because 1 ÷ 8 = 0.125)

Converting a Decimal to a Percent

Going in the other direction, a decimal can be written as a percent by moving the decimal point two places to the right. This has the same effect as multiplying by 100. Since any fraction can also be quickly written as a decimal, this also allows you to convert fractions to percents as well.

EXAMPLE 5

Write 0.226 as a percent.

Multiply by 100 (or move the decimal two places to the right): 0.226 = 22.6%.

EXAMPLE 6

Write $\frac{3}{5}$ as a percent.

As a decimal, $\frac{3}{5}$ = 0.6 because 3 ÷ 5 = 0.6. Multiply by 100: 0.6 = 60%.

EXERCISE 1

Converting Between Percents, Decimals, and Fractions

Directions: Write the following percents as decimals and as fractions. Make sure the fraction you give is in its lowest terms.

1. 30%

2. 22%

3. 49%

4. 1%

5. 8%

Write each of the following as a percent. Round to the nearest tenth of a percent if necessary.

6. 0.044

7. 0.9

8. 0.001

9. $\dfrac{3}{8}$

10. $\dfrac{7}{10}$

Answers are on page 506.

Working with Percents

Understanding the relationship between percents, decimals, and fractions can be very helpful in solving many types of problems. As you work through the following examples, pay close attention to the wording because it will be similar to the wording you will find in application problems later.

EXAMPLE 7

What percent of 50 is 4?

The question is asking "What is x if $50 \times x = 4$?" Solve for x.

$x = \dfrac{4}{50} = 4 \div 50 = 0.08$ and $0.08 = 8\%$

EXAMPLE 8

What is 16% of 34?

The word "of" in the question implies multiplication. In fact, to find any percent of any number, always multiply by the decimal form of the percent.

$0.16 \times 34 = 5.44$

EXAMPLE 9

What Is 150% of 20?

Multiplication will work here too. The decimal equivalent of 150% is 1.5 (imagine there is a decimal point on the end of 150 and move it two places to the left), so 150% of 20 is $1.5 \times 20 = 30$.

Examples 8 and 9 illustrate two important rules you should know:

• Less than 100% of a number will always be a smaller number.

• More than 100% of a number will always be a larger number.

You may be wondering what 100% of a number is. Because *percent* means "a part out of 100," 100% means 100 out of 100 or, in other words, everything, so 100% of any number is the number itself.

For many types of percent problems you may encounter, the following proportion is very useful.

$$\frac{\text{part}}{\text{whole}} = \frac{\text{percent}}{100}$$

When working with these types of percent problems, the goal is to decide which parts of the ratio you have and which parts you need to find.

EXAMPLE 10

30 is 60% of what number?

Here you have the part and the percent and you are trying to find the whole. Set up a ratio and let n represent the unknown number,

$$\frac{30}{n} = \frac{60}{100}$$

Now cross multiply to find the value of n.

Cross multiply: $3000 = 60n$

Divide by 60: $n = 50$.

EXERCISE 2

Working with Percents

Directions: Solve each of the following problems. Round your answer to the nearest tenth or the nearest tenth of a percent, as necessary.

1. What percent of 60 is 15?

2. What percent of 1000 is 200?

3. What percent of 35 is 45?

4. What is 60% of 250?

5. What is 3% of 18?

6. What is 0.5% of 90?

7. What is 360% of 20?

8. 18 is 40% of what number?

9. 100 is 10% of what number?

10. 75 is 150% of what number?

Answers are on pages 506–507.

Word Problems with Percents

When solving application problems on the GED® test, you will use the very same techniques you use when working with percents in general. The problems may require you to determine the total cost of an item after tax, calculate the commission a salesperson will earn, or determine a percent increase over time. The next two examples show you some of the types of percent application problems you can expect on the test.

EXAMPLE 11

Mary, Jackson, and Bob go out for lunch. Including tax, Mary's bill was $12.99, Jackson's bill was $11.20, and Bob's bill was $18.50. If they plan to tip 20% of the total, how much will they tip?

This question has two parts—finding the total bill and then finding the amount of the tip. Recall that to find a total, you must add:

Total bill is $12.99 + $11.20 + $18.50 = $42.69.

The next step is to find the tip. The question states that they wish to "tip 20% of the total." From working with percents before, you know that "of" implies multiplication:

Tip is 0.2 × $42.69 = $8.54.

EXAMPLE 12

When Geri started her running program, she ran 3 miles in the first week. Now she is able to run 4.5 miles in a week. What is the percent increase in the number of miles she is able to run?

Problems involving percent increase or percent decrease can always be solved using the formula

$$100\% \times \frac{\text{change}}{\text{original value}},$$

where the *change* is the new value minus the original value. In this example, the percent increase would be

$$100\% \times \frac{4.5 - 3}{3} = 100\% \times \frac{1.5}{3} = 100\% \times 0.5 = 50\%.$$

EXERCISE 3

Word Problems with Percents

1. For each sale that she makes, a salesperson is paid a 3% commission. How much will her commission be on a sale of $140?

2. A home office takes up 15% of the square footage of a home. If the home office is 390 square feet, what is the square footage of the home?

3. A company that accepts credit cards is charged $0.02 a transaction in addition to a 1% fee on the value of the transaction. How much will the company be charged for a transaction of $580.00?

4. Eric has been working to conserve energy around his home. His electric bill last month was $125, while his bill this month was $98. What is the percent decrease in his electric bill over the past month?

5. An office manager estimates that she spends 40% of her 30-minute lunch break driving to and from a restaurant. If this is true, how many minutes of her lunch break are spent driving?

Answers are on page 507.

Simple Interest

Typically, interest is earned when money is loaned or invested. One kind of interest is called **simple interest**. Simple interest is earned only on the **principal**, or amount loaned or invested. Questions on the GED® test about interest will deal only with simple interest. (Another kind of interest, called compound interest, is earned on the principal and also on the interest that accumulates over time. Questions on the GED® test about interest will not deal with compound interest.)

All simple interest problems can be solved with the simple interest formula $I = Prt$. In this formula, I is the interest earned, P is the principal, r is the rate of interest expressed as a decimal, and t is the time in years.

EXAMPLE 13

A simple interest loan of $500 is made for 2 years at a rate of 5% per year. What is the total amount of interest that will be paid on this loan?

This is one of the more straightforward types of interest problems you may see. You are given the principal ($500), the time in years (2), and the rate (0.05). Therefore, to find the total amount of interest that will be paid, just plug these numbers into the formula.

$I = 500 \times 0.05 \times 2 = 50$

The interest to be paid will be $50.

Note that sometimes you may be asked to find the total payment due on a loan. The total payment includes the original amount borrowed as well as any interest. In example 13, the total payment due is $500 + $50 = $550.

EXAMPLE 14

Jason deposits $2,500 in a savings account that will pay 3% simple interest in one year. Interest is paid in monthly installments. What will be the total value of the account after 6 months?

There are two parts to this question. First, you must calculate the interest that will be paid during 6 months. Then you need to calculate the total value of the account, including the $2,500 initial deposit. You need to be careful because the time given is in months while the interest formula uses time in years.

In terms of years, 6 months represents $\frac{6}{12} = \frac{1}{2}$ year. Additionally, be sure to express the rate (3%) as a decimal (0.03). Using this to find the interest:

$$I = 2500 \times 0.03 \times \left(\frac{1}{2}\right) = 37.50$$

If the interest earned in 6 months is $37.50, then the total value of the account after 6 months will be $2,500 + $37.50 = $2,537.50.

EXAMPLE 15

Jennifer made purchases worth $3,000 using a store credit card. She paid off the charge after 4 months and paid $36 in simple interest. What was the yearly interest rate on the credit card?

In this question, you are given the principal ($3,000), the time $\left(\frac{4}{12} = \frac{1}{3}\right)$, and the interest paid ($36). Plugging these into the interest formula, you have:

$$36 = 3000 \times r \times \frac{1}{3}$$

Multiplying the fraction and 3000, this simplifies to:

$$36 = 3000 \times r$$

To find the rate, r, in this equation, divide both sides by 1000:

$$\frac{36}{1000} = 0.036 = r$$

The yearly interest rate on the card was 3.6%. Not bad at all for a credit card!

In problems like these where you are missing one of the values from the formula, you will always follow the same steps. Simplify (as when you multiplied $\frac{1}{3}$ and 3000) and then divide.

Simple Interest

1. A loan of $2,000 is made for 3 months at a yearly simple interest rate of 16%. What is the total amount due at the end of the 3 months?

2. A shop owner took out a 6-month loan at a yearly simple interest rate of 8% to purchase inventory. If the owner paid $860 in interest, what was the original amount of the loan?

3. Jamal invests $900 in a bond that pays 4% annual simple interest. How much interest will he earn on the investment after 2 years?

4. Which will earn more interest over 1 year: an investment of $5,000 at 3% simple interest or an investment of $6,000 at 2.6% simple interest?

5. A repair shop took a short-term 1-year loan to purchase new equipment. The original loan amount was $10,000, but at the end of the year the shop had to repay a total of $11,950. What was the simple interest rate on the loan?

Answers are on page 507.

CHAPTER 7

The Number Line and Negative Numbers

So far, you have seen how to work with positive whole numbers, fractions, and decimals. In this chapter, you will see how to work with negative numbers. Any of the number types you have worked with so far can be negative as well as positive. But whether a fraction or a whole number is negative or positive, its basic properties stay the same.

The Number Line

One common way to picture the set of all possible numbers is the **number line**. The number line includes all negative and positive numbers in order from left to right. This means that every number on the line is greater than the number to its left but smaller than the number to its right. You can imagine that in between any two whole numbers are all the fractions and decimals that have values that are between those two numbers.

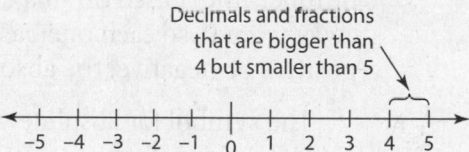

EXAMPLE 1

The following figure shows four numbers marked on the number line: $-\dfrac{3}{4}, 4, \dfrac{5}{2}, 1.90$. Determine which of these numbers is represented by the letter B.

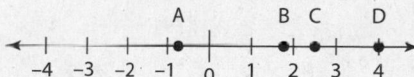

Point B appears to be slightly to the left of the line marking 2. Therefore, it must be slightly smaller than 2. Therefore, point B must represent 1.90.

Just as an exercise in ordering numbers (which the GED may ask you to do), let's figure out the values of the other points. If you convert any fractions to decimals, then you can easily see which is larger and which is smaller.

$$-\frac{3}{4}=-(3\div 4)=-0.75$$

$$\frac{5}{2}=5\div 2=2.5$$

Looking at the number line, point A is slightly to the right of −1. This means that point A is slightly greater than −1. Another way to think about this is that point A is slightly less negative than −1. The only value you have that makes sense for this is $-\frac{3}{4}$.

Point C is halfway between 2 and 3. So it must be greater than 2 but smaller than 3. The only candidate is 2.5.

Finally, point D is right on the line for 4, so its value is 4. The figure below shows what you just found.

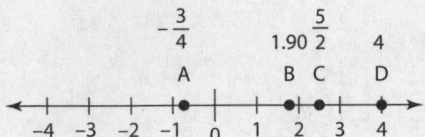

Absolute Value

The **absolute value** of a number represents its distance from 0 on the number line. Based on this definition, the points 3 and −3 are both 3 units away from 0, so each one has an absolute value of 3. In fact, for any number, positive or negative, the absolute value is the positive value of that number.

The symbol for absolute value is two bars. For example, the absolute value of −5 is written as $|-5|$ while the absolute value of 10 is written as $|10|$.

EXAMPLE 2

Find the absolute value of the following numbers: −15, 12, −2, and 1.

$$|-15|=15$$
$$|12|=12$$
$$|-2|=2$$
$$|1|=1$$

EXAMPLE 3

Which of the following points has the greatest absolute value?

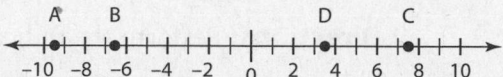

The correct answer is point A. Remember that absolute value is the distance from 0, and point A is the farthest from 0. Therefore, it has the greatest absolute value.

Adding and Subtracting Negative Numbers

When adding and subtracting negative and positive numbers, different rules apply depending on whether or not the numbers share the same sign.

- **To add a negative and a positive number,** find their absolute values, and then subtract the smaller from the greater one. Your answer will have the same sign as the number with the greater absolute value.

  $(-8) + (+3) = -5$

  The absolute values are 8 and 3. Subtract $8 - 3$. The answer is -5 because -8 has the greater absolute value.

- **To add two negative numbers**, add their absolute values, and then put a minus sign in front of the total.

  $(-3) + (-8) = -11$

  The absolute values are 3 and 8. Add: $3 + 8$. The answer is -11 because both numbers added are negative.

- **To subtract a negative number from a positive number**, add their absolute values, and then put a positive sign in front of the total.

  $5 - (-3) = 5 + (+3) = 8$

  The absolute values are 5 and 3. Add: $5 + 3 = 8$. The answer is $+8$ (positive).

- **To subtract a positive number from a negative number**, add their absolute values, and then put a minus sign in front of the total.

  $(-5) - (+3) = 5 + 3 = -8$

  The absolute values are 5 and 3. Add: $5 + 3 = 8$. The answer is -8 (negative).

- **To subtract one negative number from another**, reverse the sign on the second number, and then add.

  $(-3) - (-8) = (-3) + (+8) = 5$

Adding and Subtracting Negative Numbers

Directions: Perform the indicated operation.

1. 5 + (−2)

2. 19 − 25

3. −44 + (−20)

4. −18 − 5

5. (−10) + (−2)

6. 4 − 8

7. −15 + 29

8. 6 + (−1)

9. −2 + 3

10. −8 − 14

Answers are on page 507.

Multiplying and Dividing Negative Numbers

When multiplying and dividing signed numbers, follow these rules:

• Opposite signs result in a negative answer.

• Same signs result in a positive answer.

In multiplication and division, the sizes of the numbers have nothing to do with the sign of the answer. The sign of the answer depends only on the signs of the numbers that are being multiplied or divided.

EXAMPLE 4

$4 \times 4 = 16$	Same signs → positive answer
$(-3) \times (-3) = 9$	Same signs → positive answer
$(-2) \times 5 = -10$	Opposite signs → negative answer
$3 \times (-2) = -6$	Opposite signs → negative answer

EXAMPLE 5

$10 \div 2 = 5$	Same signs → positive answer
$(-7) \div (-1) = 7$	Same signs → positive answer
$(-18) \div 3 = -6$	Opposite signs → negative answer
$8 \div (-4) = -2$	Opposite signs → negative answer

EXERCISE 2

Multiplying and Dividing Negative Numbers

Directions: Perform the indicated operation.

1. $6 \times (-4)$

2. $(-5) \times (5)$

3. $(-1) \times 10$

4. $8 \times (-2)$

5. $(-6) \times (-3)$

6. $-6 \div 3$

7. $-3 \div (-1)$

8. $16 \div (-4)$

9. $-14 \div (-7)$

10. $9 \div (-3)$

Answers are on pages 507–508.

Negative Numbers on the Calculator

Any of the operations done in this chapter can also be done on the calculator. When entering negative numbers, make sure to use the (–) key instead of the subtraction key. For example, to find $-5 + 26$, you would type:

CHAPTER 8

Probability and Counting

Finding probabilities is all about determining the likelihood or the chances of some event occurring. You are already familiar with some types of probability. For example, you know that a 10% chance of rain today means that it probably will not rain, while a 80% chance means that it probably will. In this chapter, you will learn how to calculate some simple probabilities.

Basic Probability

When working with probabilities, think in terms of experiments. A probability experiment is just a situation that has some type of result. When a 6-sided die is rolled, that is an experiment. If someone tries to guess a whole number between 1 and 10, that is also an experiment.

In probability, all of the possibilities of an experiment are called outcomes. In the experiment where someone guesses a whole number between 1 and 10, one possible outcome is 2. Because someone could guess any one of the whole numbers between 1 and 10, there are ten possible outcomes.

A question might ask for the probability that someone guesses a number "greater than 6." In probability, this is called an event. An **event** is a grouping of one or more outcomes that you might be interested in. For example, the outcomes that make up the event "greater than 6" are 7, 8, 9, and 10.

The following formula is used to find the probability that an event will occur:

$$\text{probability of an event} = \frac{\text{number of outcomes that make up the event}}{\text{total number of possible outcomes in the experiment}}$$

Using this formula, the probability that someone will guess a number greater than 6 is $\frac{4}{10} = \frac{2}{5}$. In the experiment, there are a total of 10 possible numbers to guess, and 4 of them are larger than 6.

Let's review some important rules about probabilities:

- A probability can never be smaller than 0 or larger than 1 (smaller than 0% or larger than 100%).

- Probabilities can be represented as fractions, decimals, or percents.

EXAMPLE 1

The accounting department of a large firm has 45 male employees and 100 female employees. If one of the employees is randomly selected to be in charge of refilling the copier, what is the probability that the chosen person is male? Write your answer as a whole number percent.

The specified event is that a randomly selected person from this group will be a male. There are 45 male employees, so 45 possibilities that this could happen. There are a total of 45 + 100 = 145 employees in the department. Because each employee has an equal chance of being picked, this represents all of the possible outcomes. Therefore, the probability is:

$$\frac{45}{145} = 0.31 \text{ or } 31\%.$$

EXAMPLE 2

A single fair, six-sided die is rolled. What is the probability that it will land on a number smaller than 3? Write your answer as a reduced fraction.

There are a total of 6 possibilities when rolling the die and only 2 (the numbers 1 and 2) are smaller than 3, so the probability is $\frac{2}{6} = \frac{1}{3}$.

EXERCISE 1

Basic Probability

Directions: Answer each of the following questions. Write your answer as a decimal rounded to the nearest hundredths place.

1. A shipment of 500 computer monitors is known to have 10 defective monitors. If one of the monitors is selected randomly, what is the probability that the selected monitor is defective?

2. A high school club has 10 members who are seniors and 8 members who are juniors. If a member is randomly selected to be the club president, what is the probability that the person will NOT be a senior?

3. A game is played in which a card is drawn from a special deck that contains red, green, and blue cards. If a blue card is drawn, the player can advance to the next level. The deck has 100 cards, of which 30 are red, 15 are blue, and 55 are green. If a player draws a card at random, what is the probability that the player will advance to the next level?

4. Beth is trying to guess the number that her friend Harry is thinking. All she knows is that the number is between 1 and 20 (including 1 and 20). If she guesses randomly, what is the probability that she will guess the right number?

5. A drawer contains 6 spoons and 3 forks. If someone picks one utensil out of the drawer without looking, what is the probability of picking a spoon?

Answers are on page 508.

Compound Probabilities

"And" Events

When two events occur at the same time or one after the other, this is called the intersection of two "and" events. In some cases, the probability of an intersection occurring can be found just by multiplying the probability of the two events. But when the first event affects the probability of the second event, a different method is needed. Let's look at the simple case first.

EXAMPLE 3

In a survey of 1000 people, 450 are currently working full-time, 300 are taking college classes, and 120 are taking college classes and working full-time. If a person from this survey is selected at random, what is the probability that he or she is working full-time and taking college classes?

In this example, you are told that there are 120 people in the group who are taking college classes and working full-time. In other words, you are given the number of outcomes in the event. So the same formula can still be used. The probability is $\frac{120}{1000} = 0.12$.

EXAMPLE 4

Suppose that a bag contains 10 red and 12 green marbles. You will randomly select one marble from the bag and then put it back in the bag, and then randomly select a second marble from the bag. What is the probability that your first selection will be a red marble and your second selection will be a green marble?

First, identify the two "and" events. The first event is selecting a red marble, and the second event is selecting a green marble. You want to find the probability of selecting a red marble, returning it to the bag, and then selecting a green marble. So first identify the probability of the first event. Because there are 10 red marbles in the bag and a total of 22 marbles, the probability based on the probability formula would be $\frac{10}{22} = 0.45$. The probability of the second event follows the same rule and would be $\frac{12}{22} = 0.54$. The probability of both events occurring is calculated using the formula:

probability of two independent events = probability of first event × probability of second event

The more difficult case is when the first event affects the probability of the second event. Suppose that that same bag contains 10 red and 12 green marbles. The experiment is to select two marbles, one at a time, without returning the first selected marble back to the bag. What is the probability that both selected marbles will be green?

Use this formula:

probability of first event × probability of second event after the first has occured

The probability that the first selected marble is green is $\frac{12}{22} = \frac{6}{11}$ because there are 12 green marbles and 22 total marbles. But what is the probability that the second selected marble is green? Because the first marble is no longer in the bag, there are now only 21 marbles in the bag. Also, there are only 11 green marbles in the bag because the first selected marble was a green one. So the probability that the second selected marble is green is $\frac{11}{21}$. Now, using these fractions and the formula, the probability that both selected marbles are green is $\left(\frac{6}{11}\right) \times \left(\frac{11}{21}\right) = 0.29$.

EXAMPLE 5

Two employees at a small company are to be randomly selected for a team-building exercise. If there are 20 senior employees and 30 junior employees at the company, what is the probability that both of the selected employees will be senior employees?

Probability that the first employee will be senior is $\frac{20}{50} = \frac{2}{5}$.

Probability that the second employee will be senior is $\frac{19}{49}$.

(Remember, one employee has already been selected, and that employee was one of the senior ones.)

Probability that both will be senior is $\left(\frac{2}{5}\right) \times \left(\frac{19}{49}\right) = 0.16$.

"Or" Probabilities

Finding the probability of one event *or* the other occurring is not as complicated as the examples you just saw. The basic formula for this type of probability is:

probability of first event + probability of second event − probability of both events

EXAMPLE 6

If a fair, six-sided die is rolled, what is the probability that the number that comes up is greater than 2 or even?

probability of first event (greater than 2): $\dfrac{4}{6}$ (there are 4 numbers greater than 2)

probability of second event (even): $\dfrac{3}{6}$ (there are three even numbers: 2, 4, and 6)

probability of both events: $\dfrac{2}{6}$ (there are two numbers that are both even and greater than 2)

Therefore, the probability of one or the other event is: $\dfrac{4}{6}+\dfrac{3}{6}-\dfrac{2}{6}=\dfrac{5}{6}$.

EXERCISE 2

Compound Probability

Directions: Answer each of the following probability questions. Give your answers as fractions in their lowest terms.

1. In a group of 10 third and 8 fourth graders, two students must be randomly selected to be the leaders for the day. If the first student selected is a fourth grader, what is the probability that the second student selected is a third grader?

2. At a hospital, out of 10 doctors, 3 are on duty on Saturday, 4 on Sunday, and 2 on both days. If one of these doctors is randomly selected, what is the probability that she or he is on duty on Saturday or Sunday?

3. There are 4 chocolate chip cookies and 3 oatmeal cookies in a cookie jar. If a child randomly takes 2 cookies, what is the probability that both are chocolate chip?

4. In a raffle, two names of contestants are drawn one at a time. The first person drawn wins a prize of $500 and the second person drawn wins a prize of $100. Contestants can enter their names into the contest only once, and a total of 400 people have entered. After the winner of the first prize is chosen, what is the probability of winning the second prize?

5. The table below shows data from a survey of 46 students at a local high school. The numbers each represent the total number of students in the given category.

	Lives Within 5 Miles of School	Lives More than 5 Miles from School
Plans to attend college	10	25
Does not plan to attend college	8	3

If one of the surveyed students is selected at random, what is the probability that she or he lives within 5 miles of the school and plans to attend college?

Answers are on page 508.

Counting

Counting and probability are closely related because you will almost always have to count something in order to find a probability. On the GED® test, some questions may ask you to just do some counting without finding a probability. In these questions, the focus is on the number of possibilities, given a particular situation. Finding this number can be done using the **multiplication rule.** By this rule, the numbers of possibilities at each step of a process are multiplied to find the number of possibilities overall.

EXAMPLE 7

A soup shop allows customers to design their own soup. Customers choose one base, one main vegetable, and one main meat. If there are 3 possible bases, 10 possible main vegetables, and 4 possible meats, how many different types of soups can be made?

To make any soup, there are three steps: choose a base, choose a vegetable, and choose a meat. Using the multiplication rule, there are $3 \times 10 \times 4 = 120$ possible soups.

EXAMPLE 8

A group of 4 students must line up for a photo. If each possible lineup is a different photo, how many different photos are possible?

This one is trickier, but think of the photo as representing four spots that need to be filled. There are 4 students who could be in the first spot, 3 in the second, 2 in the third, and 1 in the fourth. This has to be true because a student cannot be in two spots in a single photo.

By the multiplication rule, the number of possible photos is: $4 \times 3 \times 2 \times 1 = 24$.

EXERCISE 3

Counting

1. Carlos has three dress shirts, two dress pants, and three pairs of dress socks. How many different outfits does he have for an occasion that requires formal dress?

2. A special at a pizza parlor lets customers pick one topping from a choice of 10 and one crust from a choice of 3. How many different kinds of pizza are possible with this special?

3. In a club of 20 members, a club president, vice president, and secretary must be chosen to form a club cabinet. If members can hold only one position, how many possibilities are there for the club cabinet?

4. Yin is designing a flyer and must choose among 8 fonts and 6 templates to determine the overall design. With these fonts and templates, how many different designs are possible?

5. A stage manager is trying to seat important guests in the front row of a theater. She would like to seat a diplomat in the first seat, a singer in the second seat, and a movie director in the third seat. If there are 3 diplomats, 2 singers, and 2 directors attending the show, how many different front row plans are possible?

Answers are on page 508.

CHAPTER 9

Statistics and Data Analysis

Data can be any collection of information. The heights of trees in a certain area, voters' opinion on a hot topic, the income of residents in a certain state—all are examples of data. Understanding data is important to virtually every career field. **Statistics** is the science of studying and understanding data. While statistics is a huge field, questions on the GED® test focus entirely on summarizing data, either by making certain calculations (such as finding the mean) or by creating charts (such as pie charts).

Analyzing Data Sets

The mean, median, and mode are all measures of the same thing: the "central tendency" of a data set. The idea is that by describing the central tendency in a collection of data values, you can tell what the typical data value in that collection looks like. Deciding which of the three measures best summarizes the data depends on the nature of the data itself.

The Mean

The **mean** is the average of a data set. It is calculated by adding all of the values in the set and dividing by the total number of values. For example, the mean of 18, 4, 2, 9, and 6 is 7.8.

$$18+4+2+9+6=39 \text{ and } 39 \div 5 = 7.8$$

The mean is affected by extreme values, called **outliers**. These are values that are much greater than, or smaller than, most of the other values in the set. If a data set includes one or two outliers, then the mean is "pulled" toward those outliers and may not accurately represent the true center. In the following figure, you can see the effect of changing one value in the data set to an outlier.

DATA SET 1	DATA SET 2
1, 3, 5, 7	1, 3, 5, 70
mean is 4	mean is 19.75

In some data sets, the same values appear numerous times. In such cases, when you are asked to calculate the mean, you may not be given a list of every individual value. Instead, you may be given the values and told the *frequency* of each one (how many times it appears in the data set). When calculating a mean with frequencies, multiply each number by its frequency, add the results, and then divide by the total frequency.

EXAMPLE 1

Jake has been playing a video game and has kept track of his scores. The following frequency table shows his scores for the last 30 games.

Score	Frequency
1200	2
1800	10
2000	12
3000	6

What was his average score for these 30 games?

Step 1: Multiply each value by its frequency and add the results.

$$1200 \times 2 + 1800 \times 10 + 2000 \times 12 + 3000 \times 6 = 62{,}400$$

Step 2: Divide by the total frequency (the total number of values).

The total frequency is 30, so the mean is $62{,}400 \div 30 = 2080$.

The Median

The **median** is the middle value of a data set when all of the numbers are listed in order from least to greatest or greatest to least. How it is calculated depends on how many values are in the data set. If there is an odd number of values in the data set, then to find the median, put all of the values in order and select the middle value. If there is an even number of values in the data set, put all of the values in order and find the average of the two middle values. That average is the median.

DATA SET 1	DATA SET 2
(odd number of values)	(even number of values)
2, 9, (12), 12, 18	6, (13, 15,) 20
median is 12	median is 14
	(the average of 13 and 15)

The median is less affected by outliers. Looking at data set 2 in the preceding figure, the median would be 14 whether the last value is 20 or 200 because the two middle values would still be 13 and 15.

The Mode

For some data sets, such as the eye colors of students in a class, finding a mean or a median is not possible or doesn't make sense. This is even true for some numerical data sets. If you collected the zip code of everyone in your workplace, would it make sense to find an average? What would that represent?

For data sets like these, the mode can be a way to measure the central tendency. The **mode** is simply the most commonly occurring value. In the data set 3, 3, 3, 1, 4, 9, for example, the mode is 3. If two different data values occur with the same frequency, both data values are modes. If all of the values in a data set are different, the set does not have a mode.

Weighted Averages

When more importance (or "weight") is placed on certain numbers in a calculation of the mean, you are finding what is called a weighted average. This is common in some grading schemes in which exams may count more than homework. A weighted average is calculated by multiplying each value by its weight and then adding the results.

EXAMPLE 2

The final grade in a science course is determined by a student's performance on two exams, a final, and quizzes. Each exam is worth 25%, the final is worth 30%, and the quizzes 20%. Given Sara's grades, which follow, what will be her final grade in the course?

Exam 1	85
Exam 2	75
Final Exam	72
Quizzes	80

Using the weights, the final score will be:

$$0.25 \times 85 + 0.25 \times 75 + 0.30 \times 72 + 0.20 \times 80 = 77.6$$

The Range

In statistics, there are many ways to measure the extent to which a data set is spread out. One of these measures is called the **range**. The range is calculated by taking the largest value in the data set and subtracting the smallest value. For example, the range for the data set 1, 9, 2, 5, 6 is $9 - 1 = 8$.

Analyzing Data Sets

Directions: For the following questions, calculate the indicated value. Round your answers to the nearest hundredth if necessary.

1. At a certain summer camp there are ten 9-year-olds, six 12-year-olds, and three 11-year-olds. What is the average age of the campers?

Use the following to answer questions 2 through 4.

The employees of the Marla Community Hospital held a charity event to raise money. The following are the amounts raised by the six hospital departments that participated.

$451.00

$690.00

$318.00

$500,00

$405.00

$320.00

2. What was the mean amount raised by the departments?

3. What was the median amount raised by the departments?

4. What was the range of the amounts raised by the departments?

5. On each of her exams this semester, Emily has scored between 60 and 70. If she scores a 90 on her next exam, which of the following must be true?

A. Her mean score will decrease.
B. Her mean score will stay the same.
C. Her mean score will increase.
D. Her mean score may increase or decrease depending on how many exams she has taken.

Answers are on pages 508–509.

Summarizing Data with Pictures

The mean, median, and mode all represent specific numerical summaries of a data set. Graphical summaries, by contrast, are charts or graphs that are designed to give an overview of a whole data set. Statisticians use many different types of graphical summaries, and each has its own special features. The following types of charts and graphs commonly appear on the GED® test.

Bar Charts

Bar charts are a useful way to compare data for different categories. The categories might be numerical, such as the ages of different people, or non-numerical, such as different brands of automobiles. When working with bar charts, you need to pay close attention to the labels on the bars and also to the scaling on the horizontal or vertical axis. You will need to understand the scaling to answer questions.

The sample bar chart shows the total sales of a certain electronics company in 2012, broken down by department. The heights of the bars tell you the sales totals for each department. For example, the bar for the software department reaches a point midway between 20 and 30 on the scale shown on the vertical axis. Because the label says that the scale shows sales in thousands of dollars, the bar for software indicates that sales by the software department totaled approximately $25,000. Note how you can see at a glance that the hardware and training departments earned far more in sales than the software and support departments. Bar charts are a good way to illustrate contrasts of this kind.

The bars in bar charts can be horizontal instead of vertical, as you can see in the following example. This bar chart illustrates the same data as the chart with vertical bars. The only difference is that the bars are horizontal and the scale appears along the horizontal axis at the bottom.

2012 Total Sales

Department

Software

Support

Hardware

Training

10 20 30 40 50 60 70 80 90 100

Sales in thousands of dollars

Circle Graphs

Circle graphs are also known as pie charts. These graphs use a circle to show how the parts of a whole relate to each other. The circle represents the whole. The size of each segment of the circle indicates the size of that category and the share of the whole that it represents.

A–Z Used Books July Expenses

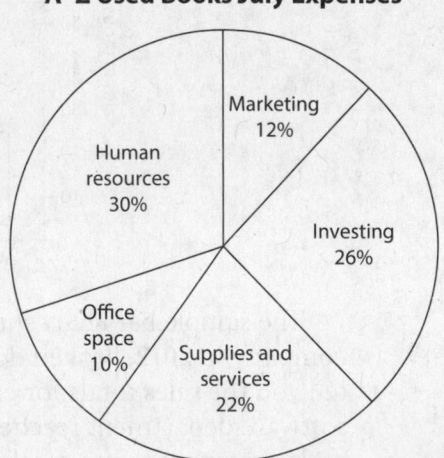

Marketing
12%

Human
resources
30%

Investing
26%

Office
space
10%

Supplies and
services
22%

The graph shows the breakdown of expenses for a small business in July. Note that the size of each section of the circle corresponds to the size of the percent. For example, human resources accounted for 30% of expenses in July, so a section corresponding to 30% of the circle is labeled "Human resources." Note too that the total percents add up to 100.

EXAMPLE 3

Suppose that the total expenses in July for A–Z Used Books were $14,780. Based on the graph, how much did the company spend on marketing during this month?

The circle graph indicates that 12% of the July expenses was spent on marketing. Therefore, you need to find 12% of $14,780. Multiply:

$0.12 \times 14{,}780 = 1773.6$

In July, $1,773.60 was spent on marketing.

EXERCISE 2

Bar Charts and Circle Graphs

Directions: The following bar graph shows the enrollment for a weeklong seminar offered monthly to college juniors and seniors who are looking for jobs while in school. Use this information to answer questions 1 through 5.

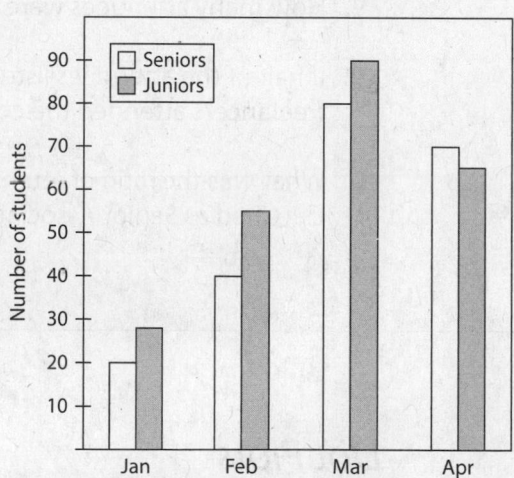

1. In which month was total enrollment greatest?

2. How many seniors were enrolled in February?

3. In which month did the number of seniors exceed the number of juniors enrolled?

4. What was the total enrollment in the seminar in April?

5. In which month was the largest difference in the number of seniors and juniors enrolled?

The following circle graph shows the job classifications for 1800 attendees at a technology conference. Use this to answer questions 6 through 10.

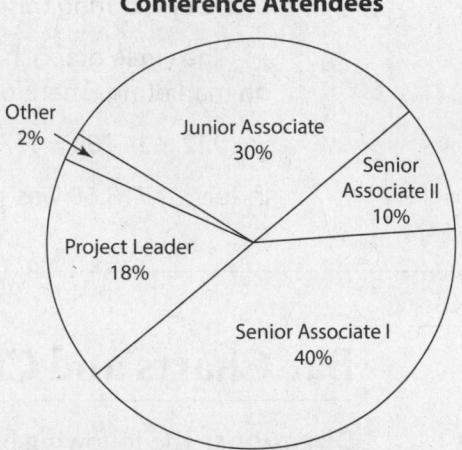

Conference Attendees

6. How many conference attendees were classified as Project Leaders?

7. What was the most common job classification among the attendees?

8. How many attendees were classified as a Senior Associate I or II?

9. If half of the attendees listed as "other" were freelancers, how many freelancers attended the conference?

10. What was the ratio of attendees classified as Senior Associate I to those classified as Senior Associate II?

Answers are on page 509.

Dot Plots

Dot plots are very detailed graphs that can be used on a wide variety of data sets. On a dot plot, each individual data value is represented as a dot above a number line and any repeated value is "stacked" on top of the others. This type of graph can be used to show how the data are spread out without losing any information about the individual data values.

The following dot plot shows the results of a survey in which a random sample of adults were asked how many Internet-connected devices are owned by members of their household.

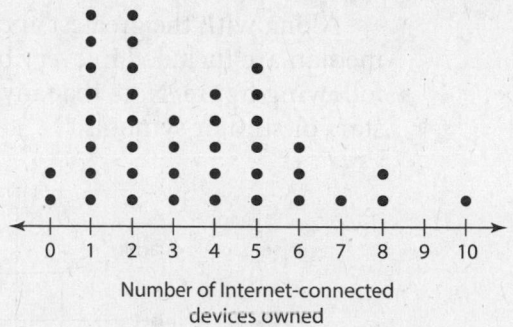

Number of Internet-connected
devices owned

Each dot represents an individual response. Because there are two dots above 0, you know that two people stated that there are no Internet-connected devices owned by members of their household. Similarly, only one person stated there were 10 such devices in his or her household.

EXAMPLE 4

Based on the preceding dot plot, how many people in the survey stated that members of their household owned more than 5 Internet-connected devices?

Count the number of dots for responses of 6, 7, 8, 9, and 10 Internet-connected devices:

$3 + 1 + 2 + 1 = 7$

Box Plots

Box plots show a data set broken up into four sections. These sections are based on the median and two new measures: the first quartile and the second quartile. These quartiles are defined as follows.

Given any data set, you can arrange it in order from smallest to largest in order to calculate the median. Because the median is the middle value, you can say that about 50% (or half) of the data set is smaller than the median and about 50% (or half) of the data set is greater than the median.

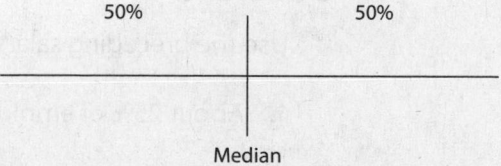

The quartiles break these two halves into quarters. About 25% of the data values are smaller than the first quartile. About 75% of the data values are smaller than the second quartile.

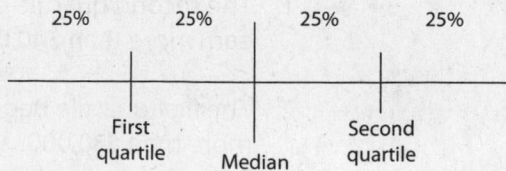

Along with the greatest and smallest data values, the quartiles and median are included in every box plot. The general shape is shown in the following figure. Note that any very small or very large outliers are shown by stars or similar symbols.

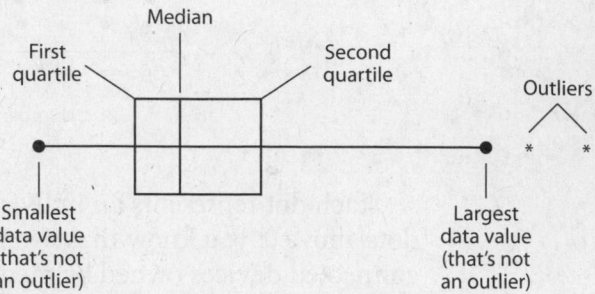

As with bar charts, you may see some box plots drawn horizontally. Either way, the basic structure remains the same. As you answer questions about any box plot, remember that it is presenting the data in order, broken up into fourths or quarters.

The following box plot shows the salaries, in thousands of dollars, for all full-time employees at a printing company.

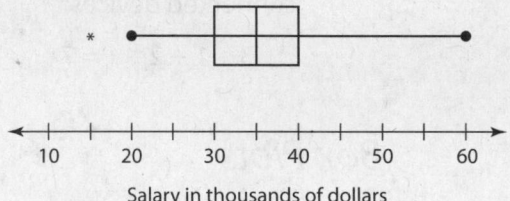

Salary in thousands of dollars

Using this plot, you can see that the smallest salary earned by any employee is $15,000 while the largest is $60,000. The box that covers the space from the first to the second quartile represents the middle 50% of the data. In this example, that means that 50% of the employees earn between $30,000 and $40,000 a year. The median is $35,000 (the line in the middle of the box), so you can also say that 50% of employees earn less than $35,000 in salary.

EXAMPLE 5

Use the preceding salary box plot to complete the following sentences.

1. About 25% of employees earn more than _____.

2. About 75% of employees earn more than _____.

Here are the solutions:

1. The second quartile ends at $40,000, so about 25% of employees earn more than $40,000.

2. The first quartile begins at $30,000, so about 75% of employees earn more than $30,000.

Histograms

At first, histograms seem not too different from bar graphs. However, the information contained in a histogram is much more detailed. Because histograms can be complicated, let's start by analyzing an example.

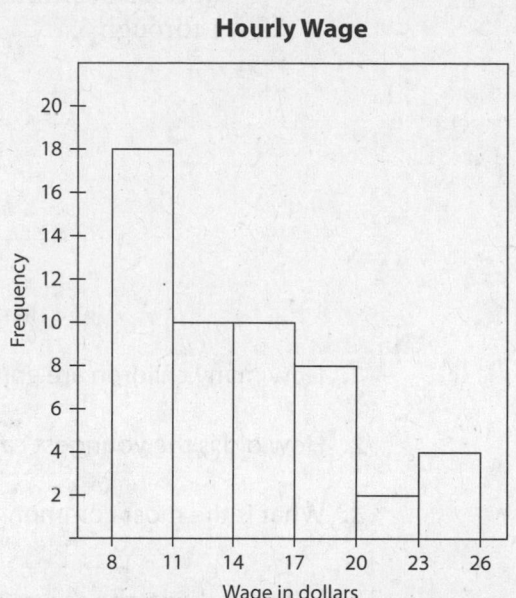

Hourly Wage

This histogram shows the distribution of hourly wages based on survey data. The wage levels are broken up into ranges that are shown on the wage scale at the bottom. The height of each bar represents the frequency for each range, or how many data values are in that range. Thus there are 18 people who have an hourly wage of $8 up to $11, and there are 10 people who have an hourly wage of $11 up to $14. In each range, the last value is not included. For example, if a person makes $11 per hour, that person is counted in the $11-to-$14 range and not in the $8-to-$11 range.

With histograms, no information about individual data values is shown. In this example, there is no way to tell how many people have an hourly wage of exactly $9. You can only see how many are in a given range.

EXAMPLE 6

Based on the preceding histogram showing hourly wages, how many people were surveyed? What percentage of them earn less than $14 per hour?

Because the groups do not overlap and the height of the bars tells you how many people are in each group, add up the heights of all the bars: 18 + 10 + 10 + 8 + 2 + 4 = 52. There were 52 people surveyed.

To find the percentage that earn less than $14 an hour, you need to add the frequencies of the bars that cover that range of values (the part) and divide by 52 (the whole).

$$\frac{18+10}{52} = 0.538$$

53.8% of those surveyed earn less than $14 an hour.

Histograms and Dot Plots

Directions: The following dot plot shows the ages of children enrolled in a weeklong summer day camp. Use this plot to answer questions 1 through 3.

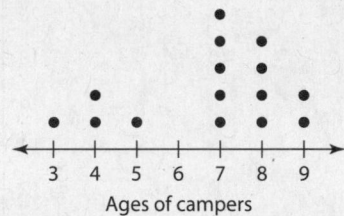

Ages of campers

1. How many children are enrolled in the day camp?

2. How old is the youngest camper?

3. What is the most common age among the campers?

The box plot shows the scores on a factory's in-house certification exam. The data are divided into two groups. The people in Group 1 studied on their own, while those in Group 2 were assigned a mentor who guided their study plans. Use this data to answer questions 4 through 6.

In-House Certification Exam

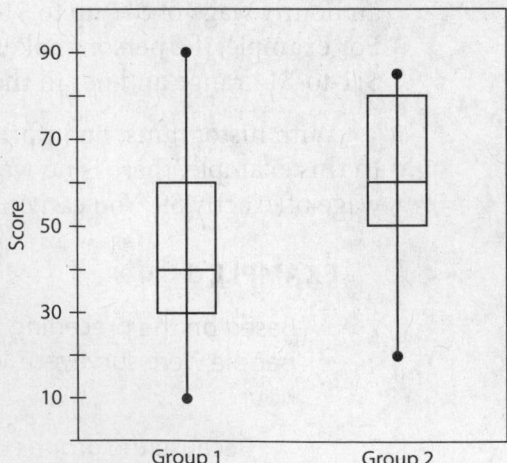

4. In which group was the person with the lowest score?

5. What was the median score for those in Group 2?

6. What percentage of people in Group 1 scored higher than 60?

Amanda searched a local website and collected data on the asking prices for all the homes for sale in her town. The data she collected is represented in the following histogram. Use this histogram to answer questions 7 through 10.

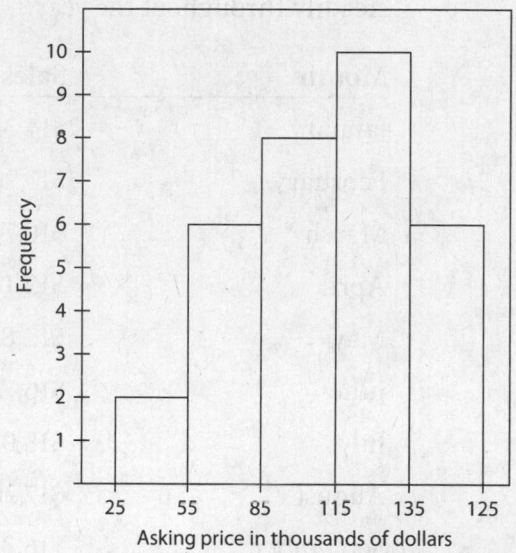

7. How many asking prices for homes are included in the histogram?

8. How many homes had an asking price of less than $135,000?

9. What percentage of homes had an asking price of $115,000 or more?

10. What percentage of homes had an asking price of less than $55,000?

Answers are on page 509.

Relationships Between Data Sets

Line graphs and scatter plots are both used to illustrate relationships between two sets of data. In line graphs, one data set is the time when data values in the other set are occurring. In scatter plots, the two data sets can be anything! Both types of graphs are common on the GED® test.

Line Graphs

The following table shows the sales that a company made each month last year. Looking at this table, it is clear that the company's best month was July, but what was the overall trend? Did sales fall in the winter? Did sales rise steadily throughout the year?

Month	Sales
January	$14,350
February	$11,900
March	$10,777
April	$12,100
May	$12,800
June	$16,720
July	$18,000
August	$17,200
September	$16,350
October	$16,300
November	$15,000
December	$15,100

Displaying this data in a line graph will help you answer those types of questions. In a line graph, the data is plotted against time, and lines are drawn connecting the data values so that the trends are easier to see. The sales data is plotted in the following line graph.

EXAMPLE 7

The preceding line graph shows the monthly sales for a company last year. Based on this graph, between which two months did the company see the largest increase in sales?

The steepest section of the graph is between May and June. Steep sections of line graphs represent sudden changes in time periods.

Scatter Plots

A mechanic wants to know if there is a relationship between the age of a car and the typical repair bill at his shop. He finds the bills for ten randomly selected cars that he has worked on. The following table shows the data he has collected.

Age of Car (in years)	7	10	2	1	8	4	6	1	1	3
Repair Bill	$200	$850	$100	$285	$900	$180	$699	$120	$90	$150

This is an example of paired data. Each repair bill is paired with the age of the car. Data like these can be plotted on a scatter plot just like points in the (x, y) plane. For example, one bill was for $200 on a 7-year-old car.

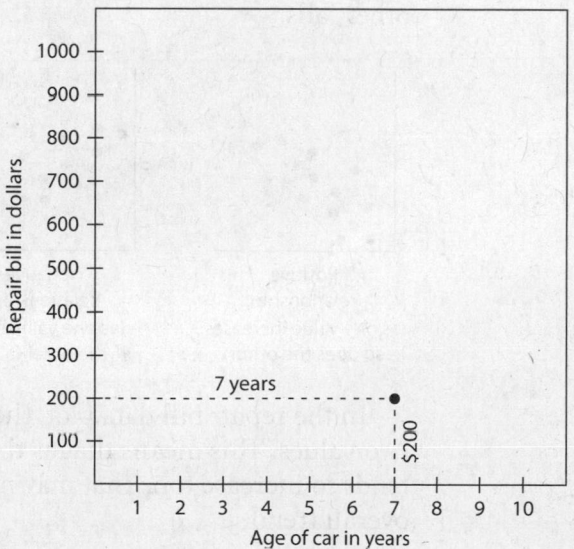

Each pair of data values is plotted in a similar way to complete the scatter plot.

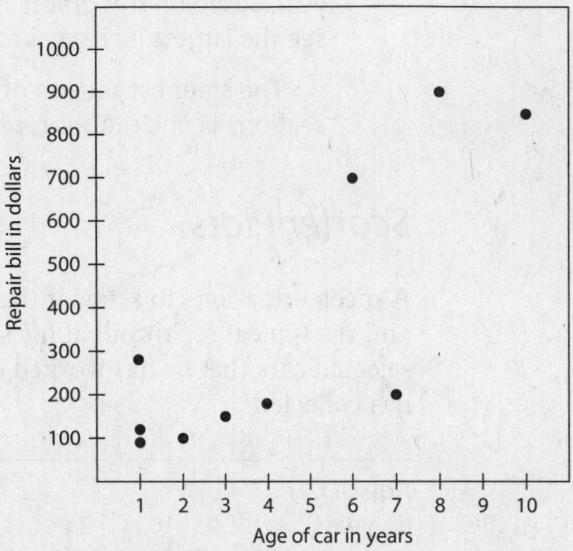

When analyzing a scatter plot, look at the overall pattern. If the points tend to locate along an imaginary line that rises from left to right, we say that there is a positive relationship between the two values. That is, as one value increases, so does the other. If the points tend to locate along an imaginary line that falls from left to right, we say that there is a negative relationship between the two values. That is, as one value rises, the other falls.

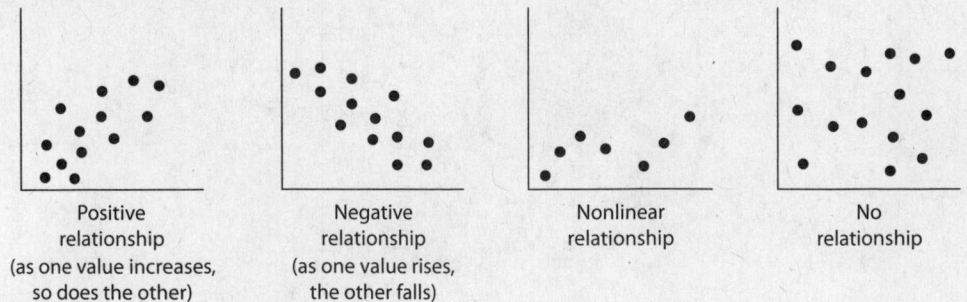

In the repair bill data plot, there is a positive relationship between the two values. This means that as the age of the car increases, the repair bill tends to increase too. That may not be true in every single case, but it is the overall trend.

Relationships Between Data Sets

Directions: Casey is a runner and has kept track of her weekly mileage for the past two months. Use the following graph to answer questions 1 through 3.

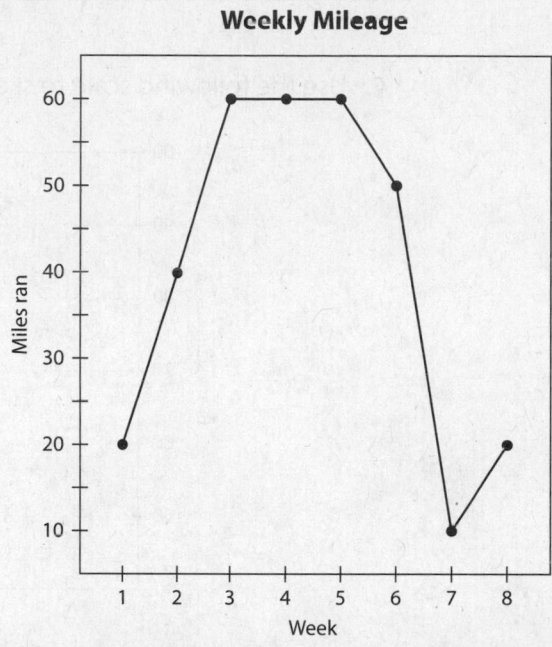

Weekly Mileage

1. In week 6, Casey twisted her ankle and had to run less the following week. How much did her mileage drop from week 6 to week 7?

2. During which weeks did Casey run more than 40 miles?

3. If Casey burns 110 calories for each mile she runs, how many calories did she burn running in week 2?

Kaitlyn, a middle school teacher, wants to see if her students' quiz scores (graded from 0 to 30) are related to their exam scores (graded from 0 to 100). She collected the following data from 8 students. Use this to answer questions 4 and 5.

Quiz Score	5	8	22	28	30	30	17	25
Exam Score	65	70	88	95	90	92	75	80

4. Use the following scale to sketch a scatter plot of this data.

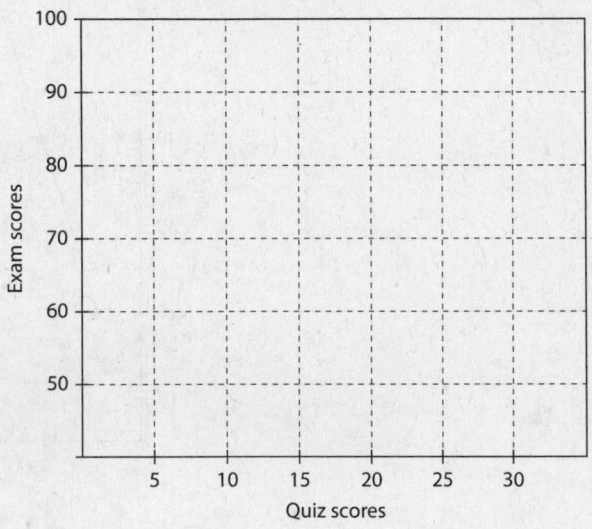

5. Based on the scatter plot you sketched, which of the following statements is true for the students whose scores were included in the data set?

A. In general, students with higher quiz scores tend to have lower exam scores.

B. In general, students with higher quiz scores tend to have higher exam scores.

C. In general, there is no relationship between quiz scores and exam scores.

D. There is a nonlinear relationship between quiz scores and exam scores.

Answers are on page 509.

CHAPTER 10

Algebraic Expressions

Algebra involves working with unknown values called **variables**. These variables are the common x, y, z, or other letters that you think of when you think of algebra. (By contrast, a simple number with a known value is called a **constant**.) The power of using variables is that applications can be generalized. That is, instead of solving similar problems over and over again with different numbers, you can follow a set of general rules using variables in place of the numbers. Those rules are what you study when you study algebra.

Variables, Terms, and Expressions

In algebra, **terms** are numbers, variables, and combinations such as 7, $3x$, y, and $2x^2$.

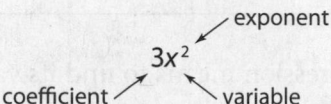

In a term such as $3x$, the 3 and the x are actually being multiplied together. This term is read "$3x$," but it really means "3 times x." The 3 in this case is called the **coefficient**. Any term with a variable has a coefficient. In a term such as y, the coefficient is understood to be 1 because 1 times y is just y.

When terms are combined with operations or grouping symbols such as parentheses, the result is called an **algebraic expression**. As you work through different types of algebraic expressions, you may notice that sometimes multiplication is written differently. As explained previously, the term $3x$ is actually a multiplication of 3 and x. Multiplication in algebra is also commonly shown with parentheses. For example, the expression $4(x-1)$ represents 4 times the expression $(x - 1)$.

Some types of expressions occur often enough to be given special names. In the following table, each of these is shown so that you can be familiar with vocabulary you may see on the GED® test.

Linear expression	Example: $5x + 2$, $3y$, $2y - 10$
	In linear expressions, terms may be added or subtracted and any variables have an exponent of 1 (remember, if you don't see the exponent, it is 1).
Polynomial	Example: $2x^2$, $3x^4 - 10$, $9x^2 - 5x + 1$
	Polynomials are expressions in which terms and numbers may be added and subtracted and any exponent on a term can be any positive whole number. Linear expressions are actually a special type of polynomial.
Rational expression	Example: $\dfrac{1}{x}$, $\dfrac{x-5}{2}$, $\dfrac{y^2+6}{y^2-1}$
	Rational expressions are fractions that include a polynomial as either the numerator or the denominator.

Evaluating Expressions

To evaluate an expression means to find its value if the variables were replaced with numbers. For linear and polynomial expressions, this means carefully applying the order of operations. With rational expressions, you follow the same order of operations, but there can be some extra considerations when giving a final answer.

EXAMPLE 1

Evaluate the expression $3x^3 + 5x^2 - 10$ for $x = 2$.

To evaluate the expression, replace each x term with a 2 and then compute. Be sure to follow the order of operations!

$$3(2)^3 + 5(2)^2 - 10 = 3(8) + 5(4) - 10 = 24 + 20 - 10 = 34$$

EXAMPLE 2

Evaluate the expression $3(x^2 + 2)^2$ for $x = -1$.

$$3((-1)^2 + 2)^2 = 3((1) + 2)^2 = 3(3)^2 = 3(9) = 27$$

When working with rational expressions, remember that in mathematics, division by zero is said to be "undefined." So, any number that makes the denominator of a rational expression zero makes the whole expression undefined.

For example, the expression $\dfrac{3}{x-1}$ is undefined when $x = 1$.
Because the denominator is $x - 1$, evaluating this for $x = 1$ would
give $1 - 1 = 0$.

EXAMPLE 3

Evaluate the expression $\dfrac{x^2 - 5}{x}$ for $x = 4$.

$$\frac{(4)^2 - 5}{4} = \frac{16 - 5}{4} = \frac{11}{4}$$

In algebra, the final answer is almost always left as a simplified fraction
(even if it is an improper fraction).

EXAMPLE 4

Evaluate the expression $\dfrac{x-5}{x+5}$ for $x = -5$.

Replacing each x with -5 yields the numerical expression
$\dfrac{-5-5}{-5+5} = \dfrac{-10}{0}$, which is undefined. The final answer here would be
"The expression is undefined with $x = -5$."

EXERCISE 1

Evaluating Expressions

Directions: Evaluate each of the expressions for the given value of the
variable. If a rational expression is undefined, write your final
answer as "undefined."

1. $5y - 10$ for $y = -6$

2. $16x - 4$ for $x = -1$

3. $9(x-1)$ for $x = 0$

4. $-2x^4 + x^2 - 1$ for $x = 2$

5. $x^2 + 5x - 12$ for $x = 3$

6. $2(x-5)^2 + 3x$ for $x = 4$

7. $-x^3 - 1$ for $x = 3$

8. $\dfrac{w-7}{w+1}$ for $w = 0$

9. $\dfrac{a^2 - 6a}{a}$ for $a = 1$

10. $\dfrac{x^2 + 6}{x^2 - 4}$ for $x = 2$

Answers are on pages 509–510.

Combining Like Terms

In algebra, **like terms** are terms that have the same variable and the same exponent. Because plain numbers do not include any variable, they are always considered like terms. Following are some more examples.

$5x, -10x, \frac{1}{2}x$ — Like terms because each term has a variable of x and an exponent of 1

$8y^2, y^2, -2y^2$ — Like terms because each term has a variable of y and an exponent of 2

Like terms can be combined by adding their coefficients. This process is often part of finding the final answer to a problem. Answers to many algebra problems must be simplified, and an algebraic expression is considered simplified when there are no remaining parentheses and all of the like terms have been combined.

EXAMPLE 5

Simplify the expression $3x^2 - 4x + 2x^2 - 1$.

In this expression, the terms $3x^2$ and $2x^2$ are like terms, so they can be combined by adding the coefficients 3 and 2. There are no other like terms, so once these are combined the expression is completely simplified.

$$3x^2 - 4x + 2x^2 - 1 = 5x^2 - 4x - 1$$

EXAMPLE 6

Simplify the expression $2w - 6w + w$.

There are three like terms in this expression. Remember that a variable without a coefficient has a default coefficient of 1. So the coefficient of the final answer is found by adding the coefficients of the like terms: $2 - 6 + 1 = -3$.

$$2w - 6w + w = -3w$$

In some cases, you will need to use the distributive property. Remember that with the distributive property, when terms inside parentheses are multiplied by a number outside the parentheses, each term inside the parentheses must be multiplied by the number outside the parentheses.

EXAMPLE 7

Simplify the expression $5x - 6(x + 2)$.

Distribute the -6: $5x - 6x + (-6)(2) = 5x - 6x - 12$

Combine like terms: $5x - 6x - 12 = -x - 12$

When working with parentheses, the order of operations still applies. If there is an exponent on the parentheses, you need to calculate that value before applying the distributive property. The expression $2(x+1)^2$ does not equal $2x^2 + 4$. Instead, you first need to multiply $(x + 1) \times (x + 1)$. (This is called "expanding" the term.) Expanding uses a method called FOIL, which will be discussed later in this chapter.

EXERCISE 2

Combining Like Terms

Directions: Simplify each of the expressions below.

1. $8x - 2x + 10$

2. $14y + 1 + 3y - 5$

3. $-2z^2 - 15z^2 + z^2$

4. $-2(x - 2) + x$

5. $16y^4 + 5(1 - y^4)$

Answers are on page 510.

Adding and Subtracting Polynomials

Combining two polynomials by either adding them or subtracting them is actually just a form of combining like terms. However, when subtracting polynomials, just remember to distribute the negative!

EXAMPLE 8

Find the sum of $x^2 + 2x - 5$ and $9x^2 - 6x + 1$.

First, write both polynomials with a "+" symbol between them. Then combine like terms to find the answer.

Set up: $\qquad\qquad x^2 + 2x - 5 + 9x^2 - 6x + 1$

Combine like terms
to find the answer: $\qquad x^2 + 2x - 5 + 9x^2 - 6x + 1 = 10x^2 - 4x - 4$

Notice that it doesn't matter if the like terms are not next to each other. For example, x^2 and $9x^2$ can be combined even though there are two terms between them.

EXAMPLE 9

Find the difference of $x^4 + x^2 - 1$ and $6 - x^4 + 3x^2$.

"Find the difference" always means subtract. To set up a subtraction problem with two polynomials, write the first polynomial as it is, then write the second polynomial in parentheses with a "−" in front. Next, distribute the negative to every term inside the parentheses. Finally, combine like terms. Remember the rules you learned in Chapter 7 for subtracting signed numbers.

Set up: $\qquad\qquad x^4 + x^2 - 1 - (6 - x^4 + 3x^2)$

Distribute
the negative: $\qquad x^4 + x^2 - 1 - (6 - x^4 + 3x^2) = x^4 + x^2 - 1 - 6 + x^4 - 3x^2$

Combine like terms: $\quad x^4 + x^2 - 1 - 6 + x^4 - 3x^2 = 2x^4 - 2x^2 - 7$

When the negative is distributed to the terms inside the parentheses, the sign for *every* one of those terms changes. Let's study another example to see how this works.

EXAMPLE 10

Find $(16y - 2) - (18y + 16 - y^2)$.

In this subtraction problem, the parentheses around $16y - 2$ can be dropped because there is nothing in front of them. However, the parentheses around $18y + 16 - y^2$ cannot be dropped until the negative in front of them is distributed.

Distribute the negative: $(16y - 2) - (18y + 16 - y^2) = 16y - 2 - 18y - 16 + y^2$

Combine like terms: $\qquad 16y - 2 - 18y - 16 + y^2 = -2y - 18 + y^2$

EXAMPLE 11

Find $(3x^2 - x) + (4x + x^2)$.

When two polynomials are added, both sets of parentheses can be dropped in the first step because distributing a "+" does not change any of the signs.

Rewrite without parentheses: $(3x^2 - x) + (4x + x^2) = 3x^2 - x + 4x + x^2$

Combine like terms: $3x^2 - x + 4x + x^2 = 4x^2 + 3x$

On the GED® test, problems asking you to add or subtract polynomials are sometimes written using words like *sum* or *difference* and other times are written using parentheses as in the last two examples. Either way, the solution steps are the same.

EXERCISE 3

Adding and Subtracting Polynomials

Directions: Find the sum or the difference as indicated.

1. $\left(x^2 - 2\right) + \left(x^2 - 1\right)$

2. $\left(x^5 - x + 2\right) + \left(x + 6\right)$

3. $\left(3x^2 - 2x + 5\right) + \left(-x^2 - 5x + 1\right)$

4. $\left(x^4 - 2x\right) + \left(3x - x^2\right)$

5. $\left(12x^2 + 3x\right) + \left(4x + x^2 - 1\right)$

6. $\left(x^3 - 4\right) - \left(x^3 + 10\right)$

7. $\left(3x + x^2\right) - \left(x^2 + 2x\right)$

8. $\left(3x^2 - 10x + 2\right) - \left(6x^2 - 5x + 1\right)$

9. $\left(x^2 - 9x\right) - \left(6x + 2\right)$

10. $\left(4x^3 + x\right) - \left(2x^2 + 4x\right)$

Answers are on page 510.

Multiplying Polynomials

The method used to multiply polynomials depends on the number of terms that make up the polynomials. In all cases, you need to remember how to work with the laws of exponents (see Chapter 2), use the distributive property (see Chapter 2), and simplify by combining like terms. As you work through the examples in this section, remember that in algebra, multiplication can be indicated by parentheses, as in $2x(3x)$, or by a dot between the terms, as in $2x \cdot 3x$.

Multiplying Single Terms

Recall that according to the laws of exponents, when you multiply two exponents with the same base, the exponents are added. This still applies in multiplication involving variables. When multiplying single terms, you will multiply the coefficients and then add the exponents if the variables are the same.

EXAMPLE 12

Multiply $3x^2 \cdot 2x$.

$$3x^2 \cdot 2x = 6x^{2+1} = 6x^3$$

Remember that if there is no exponent written, the exponent is understood to be 1.

EXAMPLE 13

Multiply $y^2 \cdot \left(-2y^4\right)$.

$$y^2 \cdot \left(-2y^4\right) = -2y^{2+4} = -2y^6$$

The rules of exponents cannot be used if the bases are different. Here the bases are the variables. If the variables are different, only the coefficients are multiplied.

EXAMPLE 14

Multiply $3x \cdot 8y$.

$$3x \cdot 8y = 24xy$$

EXERCISE 4

Multiplying Polynomials (Single Terms)

Directions: Multiply the given terms.

1. $4x^2 \cdot x$

2. $x^2 \cdot x^4$

3. $10x^2 \cdot 3x^2$

4. $-6x \cdot \dfrac{1}{2}x$

5. $2x \cdot 3y^2$

Answers are on page 510.

Multiplying Single Terms and Larger Polynomials

Using the distributive property, you can multiply any polynomial by a single term by distributing the single term to every term in the polynomial. After that, it is just a matter of applying the rules of exponents and simplifying.

EXAMPLE 15

Multiply $3x(4x^2 - 1)$.

$$3x(4x^2 - 1) = 3x \cdot 4x^2 - 3x \cdot 1 = 12x^3 - 3x$$

EXAMPLE 16

Multiply $(-2x^3) \cdot (x^2 - x + 4)$.

$$(-2x^3) \cdot (x^2 - x + 4) = -2x^3 \cdot x^2 - (-2x^3) \cdot x + (-2x^3) \cdot 4 = -2x^5 + 2x^4 - 8x^3$$

Multiplying Polynomials (Single Terms and Larger Terms)

Directions: Multiply the given polynomials.

1. $-6x(x+9)$

2. $\frac{1}{2}x(x^2-2x+4)$

3. $x^4(x-5-x^2)$

4. $5x^2(-x^2-10)$

5. $4x^3(x^4-x^2+6x-9)$

Answers are on page 510.

Multiplying Two Binomials

A **binomial** is a polynomial with two terms. Some examples of binomials are $x-4$, $2x^2+1$, $3x-5$, and x^2-x. There are certain steps to follow when multiplying two binomials. They are commonly referred to by the shorthand term FOIL.

Let's use the example of multiplying $3x+1$ and $x-2$ to understand the steps of FOIL.

Step 1: F—multiply the First two terms

$$(3x+1)(x-2) = 3x^2$$

Step 2: O—multiply the Outer two terms

$$(3x+1)(x-2) = 3x^2 - 6x$$

Step 3: I—multiply the Inner two terms

$$(3x+1)(x-2) = 3x^2 - 6x + x$$

Step 4: L—multiply the Last two terms

$$(3x + 1)(x - 2) = 3x^2 - 6x + x - 2$$

Now you can just combine like terms to find the final answer.

$$(3x + 1)(x - 2) = 3x^2 - 6x + x - 2 = 3x^2 - 5x - 2$$

EXAMPLE 17

Multiply $(x-5)(2x+1)$.

Apply FOIL and simplify.

$$(x-5)(2x+1)=2x^2+x-10x-5=2x^2-9x-5$$

Multiplying Two Binomials

Directions: Multiply the given binomials.

1. $(x-1)(x+2)$

2. $(5x-2)(x+5)$

3. $(-2x+2)(4x-1)$

4. $(x^2+1)(x^2-1)$

5. $(x^2-6)(2x-9)$

Answers are on page 510.

Multiplying Polynomials with More than Two Terms

Some questions on the GED® test may ask you to multiply two polynomials with many terms, such as x^2-9x+2 and $4x^2-6x+1$. In questions like these, keep your work organized (there will be a lot of terms to keep track of), and remember to "distribute every term."

EXAMPLE 18

Multiply $(x+5)(x^2-2x+1)$.

There are two terms in the first polynomial: x and 5. In order to multiply these two polynomials, each term in the second polynomial must be multiplied by x and then again by 5.

$$(x+5)(x^2-2x+1) = \underbrace{x(x^2)+x(-2x)+x(1)}_{\text{Multiply each term by }x.}+\underbrace{5x^2+5(-2x)+5(1)}_{\text{Multiply each term by 5.}}$$

Now simplify the expression to get the final answer.

$$x^3-2x^2+x+5x^2-10x+5=x^3+3x^2-9x+5$$

EXAMPLE 19

Multiply $(2x-1)(4x^2+3x+2)$.

As in example 18, distribute the $2x$ and the -1 to each term in the second polynomial.

$$(2x-1)(4x^2+3x+2)=2x(4x^2)+2x(3x)+2x(2)-1(4x^2)-1(3x)-1(2)$$

Again, simplify to find the final answer.

$$2x(4x^2)+2x(3x)+2x(2)-1(4x^2)-1(3x)-1(2)=8x^3+6x^2+4x-4x^2-3x-2$$
$$=8x^3+2x^2+x-2$$

EXERCISE 7

Multiplying Polynomials with More than Two Terms

Directions: Multiply the given polynomials.

1. $(x-3)(x^2+5x+1)$

2. $(2x+1)(-x^2-x+4)$

3. $(x+3)(9x^2-6x+2)$

4. $(x^2-x)(x^3+x+1)$

5. $(x^3-4)(x^2+2x-1)$

Answers are on page 510.

Factoring

Factors are terms or expressions that are multiplied together to produce a more complex expression. You can simplify many complex expressions by dividing them into their factors. This process is called **factoring**. Not every polynomial can be factored, but when it can, factoring can be used to simplify complex expressions and even solve some equations.

Factoring Using the Greatest Common Factor

The greatest common factor (GCF) between two terms is the largest factor that both terms share. To understand this better, consider the terms $4x^2$ and x^3. You can rewrite these terms showing all of their factors.

$$4x^2 = 2 \cdot 2 \cdot x \cdot x$$

$$x^3 = x \cdot x \cdot x$$

As you look at these rewritten terms, you can see that they each share x as a factor. However, they also each share 2 x's, or $x \cdot x = x^2$, as a factor. Because this is the largest term that both of them share, the GCF is x^2. Using this knowledge, you can factor the expression $x^3 + 4x^2$ and rewrite it as $x^2(4 + x)$. The factors of the expression are x^2 and $(4 + x)$. In a way, factoring using the GCF is like undoing a distributive property problem.

EXAMPLE 20

Factor the polynomial $9x^2 - 3x$.

Find the shared factors: $9x^2 = 3x \cdot 3x$ and $-3x = -1 \cdot 3x$

Rewrite using the GCF: $3x(3x - 1)$

Once you have rewritten the polynomial with the GCF, you have completely factored the expression and this is your final answer.

EXAMPLE 21

Factor the polynomial $15x^4 - 10x^2$.

Find the shared factors: $15x^4 = 5x^2 \cdot 3x^2$ and $-10x^2 = 5x^2 \cdot (-2)$

Rewrite using the GCF: $5x^2(3x^2 - 2)$

EXAMPLE 22

Factor the polynomial: $8x^3 + 4x - x^4$.

Find the shared factors: $8x^3 = x \cdot 8x^2, 4x = x \cdot 4$, and $-x^4 = x(-x^3)$

Rewrite using the GCF: $x(8x^2 + 4 - x^3)$

Note that you can always check your answer by distributing. If you did the problem correctly, distributing the GCF should give you the same polynomial you started with.

EXERCISE 8

Factoring Using the Greatest Common Factor

Directions: Factor the given polynomial expression using the GCF.

1. $3x^2 + 9$

2. $4x^3 - 16x^2$

3. $18x + 9$

4. $x^5 - x^2 - 2x$

5. $10x^3 + 14x^2$

Answers are on page 511.

Factoring by Reversing FOIL

Many (not all) polynomials that are made up of an x^2 term, an x term, and a number term can be factored into two binomials by undoing the steps of FOIL. The steps in this type of factoring are best shown in an example. Let's go through the steps and factor $x^2 + 2x - 15$.

Step 1: Find all the pairs of factors for the number term.

In this case, the number term is −15. There are many pairs of numbers that when multiplied together make 15. They are:

−1(15), 1(−15), −3(5), 3(−5)

Step 2: Pick the pair of factors that add up to the coefficient of the x term.

The coefficient of the x term is 2. Checking each pair of factors, the pair that adds to 2 is −3 and 5.

Step 3: Use these to factor the polynomial into two binomials.

These types of polynomials will always factor into (x + or − some number) (x + or − another number). The numbers used are those from step 2. For this polynomial, those numbers are −3 and 5. So the factored form is $(x - 3)(x + 5)$.

EXAMPLE 23

Factor $x^2 - 6x - 7$.

Step 1: The pairs of factors for −7 are −7(1) and 7(−1).

Step 2: The pair of factors that add to −6 are −7 and 1.

Step 3: The factored form is therefore $(x - 7)(x + 1)$.

EXAMPLE 24

Factor $x^2 + 9x + 20$.

Step 1: The pairs of factors for 20 are 20(1), 2(10), and 4(5).

Step 2: The pair of factors that add to 9 are 4 and 5.

Step 3: The factored form is therefore $(x+4)(x+5)$.

If the *x* term in the polynomial is negative but the number term is positive, look for negative factors of the number. Remember that when you multiply two negatives, you get a positive.

EXAMPLE 25

Factor $x^2 - 6x + 8$.

Step 1: Because the *x* term is negative and the number term is positive, look for negative factors to make positive 8. These are −1(−8) and −2(−4).

Step 2: The pair of factors that add to −6 are −2 and −4.

Step 3: The factored form is therefore $(x-2)(x-4)$.

You can always check your final answer by using FOIL on the factored form. If your answer is correct, you should get the same polynomial you started with.

EXERCISE 9

Factoring by Reversing FOIL

Directions: Factor the given polynomial.

1. $x^2 - 7x + 12$

2. $x^2 - x - 2$

3. $x^2 - 3x - 18$

4. $x^2 - 6x - 40$

5. $x^2 - 5x + 6$

Answers are on page 511.

Difference of Squares

Any polynomial that is the difference between x^2 and a perfect square can be factored into two binomials. The two binomials are written in the same way as when you were reversing FOIL except this time, the numbers are the positive and negative square roots of the perfect square. A list of perfect squares can be found on 323.

EXAMPLE 26

Factor $x^2 - 25$.

This is a difference of squares because $25 = 5^2$. Therefore, the polynomial can be factored into $(x + 5)(x - 5)$.

EXAMPLE 27

Factor $x^2 - 16$.

The number term is equal to 4^2, so $x^2 - 16 = (x + 4)(x - 4)$.

It is important to note that this technique will work with a **difference** of squares, but it will not work with a **sum** of squares. The expression $x^2 + 25$, for instance, cannot be factored.

EXERCISE 10

Difference of Squares

Directions: Factor the given polynomial.

1. $x^2 - 1$

2. $x^2 - 4$

3. $x^2 - 81$

4. $x^2 - 36$

5. $x^2 - 9$

Answers are on page 511.

Rational Expressions

Working with rational expressions is a lot like working with fractions. In both cases, you look for like denominators and simplify by eliminating factors. To find common denominators, you will need to know how to multiply polynomials. To simplify, you will need to know how to factor.

Simplifying Rational Expressions

When you studied fractions in Chapter 4, you saw that $\frac{3}{9} = \frac{1}{3}$ because $\frac{3}{9} = \frac{3 \times 1}{3 \times 3}$. To simplify this fraction, you divided the numerator and the denominator each by 3. One way to think of this is that you "cancelled out" the 3 because it was a factor of both the numerator and the denominator. Thinking this way, to simplify an algebraic expression, you can cancel out any factors shared by the numerator and the denominator.

EXAMPLE 28

Simplify the expression $\frac{2x^2 + 4x}{4x^2}$.

A $2x$ can be factored out of both the numerator and the denominator. Once it is factored out, canceling this term will give the simplified expression.

$$\frac{2x^2 + 4x}{4x^2} = \frac{2x(x+2)}{2x(2x)} = \frac{x+2}{2x}$$

EXAMPLE 29

Simplify the expression $\frac{x^2 - x - 6}{x^2 + x - 2}$.

The numerator and the denominator can both be factored by reversing FOIL.

$$\frac{x^2 - x - 6}{x^2 + x - 2} = \frac{(x-3)(x+2)}{(x-1)(x+2)}$$

Now you can see that the numerator and the denominator share a factor of $x+2$, so the simplified form is:

$$\frac{x-3}{x-1}$$

EXAMPLE 30

Simplify the expression $\frac{x^2 + 4x}{(x+4)^2}$.

It is hard to see what factors the numerator and denominator may share, but factoring the numerator may make it easier to see if there are any shared factors.

$$\frac{x^2 + 4x}{(x+4)^2} = \frac{x(x+4)}{(x+4)^2} = \frac{x(x+4)}{(x+4)(x+4)} = \frac{x}{x+4}$$

Simplifying Rational Expressions

Directions: Simplify the given rational expression.

1. $\dfrac{x+5}{x^2+3x-10}$

2. $\dfrac{x^2-7x}{x^2}$

3. $\dfrac{x^3-x^2}{x^2}$

4. $\dfrac{x^2+x-2}{x^2-1}$

5. $\dfrac{2x}{2x-8}$

Answers are on page 511.

Adding and Subtracting Rational Expressions

When you were adding and subtracting fractions, you were able to add the numerators whenever the denominators were the same. The same holds true when adding and subtracting rational expressions. And just as with fractions, if the denominators are not the same, you must find a common denominator before completing the problem.

EXAMPLE 31

Add $\dfrac{3x+5}{x-1}+\dfrac{2x-9}{x-1}$.

The denominators are the same, so add numerators and simplify if needed.

$$\frac{3x+5}{x-1}+\frac{2x-9}{x-1}=\frac{3x+5+2x-9}{x-1}=\frac{5x-4}{x-1}$$

EXAMPLE 32

Subtract $\dfrac{x-1}{x+7}-\dfrac{x-6}{x+7}$.

Once again, the denominators are the same, so subtract numerators and simplify (if needed).

$$\frac{x-1}{x+7}-\frac{x-6}{x+7}=\frac{x-1-(x-6)}{x+7}=\frac{x-1-x+6}{x+7}=\frac{5}{x+7}$$

When two rational expressions do not share the same denominator, you will need to find a common denominator. One trick to do this is first to check if one of the denominators is a factor of the other. If so, the larger expression is the common denominator. If not, you can always multiply the two expressions to find a common denominator.

EXAMPLE 33

Add $\dfrac{x+1}{x^2-4}+\dfrac{x-1}{x-2}$.

The denominator of the first fraction, x^2-4, can be factored into $(x+2)(x-2)$. The denominator of the second fraction is a factor of x^2-4, Thus x^2-4 is the common denominator. You need to rewrite the second fraction with this denominator. Because the denominator of the second fraction is missing only an $(x+2)$, multiply both the numerator and the denominator of the second fraction by this value.

$$\frac{x+1}{x^2-4}+\frac{x-1}{x-2}=\frac{x+1}{x^2-4}+\frac{(x-1)\cdot(x+2)}{(x-2)\cdot(x+2)}=\frac{x+1}{x^2-4}+\frac{x^2+x-2}{x^2-4}$$

Now the numerators can be added across. Do not forget to simplify your final answer if it is possible.

$$\frac{x+1}{x^2-4}+\frac{x^2+x-2}{x^2-4}=\frac{x+1+x^2+x-2}{x^2-4}=\frac{x^2+2x-1}{x^2-4}$$

This final expression cannot be simplified any further, so it is the final answer.

EXAMPLE 34

Subtract $\dfrac{x-2}{x}-\dfrac{x+1}{x-3}$.

Neither denominator is a factor of the other, so a common denominator is $x(x-3)=x^2-3x$. Both fractions must be rewritten by multiplying both the numerator and the denominator by the "missing" piece.

$$\frac{x-2}{x}-\frac{x+1}{x-3}=\frac{(x-2)\cdot(x-3)}{x\cdot(x-3)}-\frac{(x+1)\cdot x}{(x-3)\cdot x}=\frac{x^2-5x+6}{x^2-3x}-\frac{x^2+x}{x^2-3x}$$

Now, subtract and simplify.

$$\frac{x^2-5x+6}{x^2-3x}-\frac{x^2+x}{x^2-3x}=\frac{x^2-5x+6-\left(x^2+x\right)}{x^2-3x}=\frac{x^2-5x+6-x^2-x}{x^2-3x}=\frac{-6x+6}{x^2-3x}$$

Adding and Subtracting Rational Expressions

Directions: Add or subtract as indicated.

1. $\dfrac{1-x}{x}+\dfrac{2}{x^2}$

2. $\dfrac{2x-1}{x+5}+\dfrac{x-1}{x^2-25}$

3. $\dfrac{1}{x}+\dfrac{1}{x^3}$

4. $\dfrac{1}{x-3}+\dfrac{x+1}{x-2}$

5. $\dfrac{x+5}{x-6}+\dfrac{2x}{x-6}$

6. $\dfrac{1}{x}-\dfrac{1}{2x}$

7. $\dfrac{x-1}{x^2-4}-\dfrac{1}{x-2}$

8. $\dfrac{x+3}{x-5}-\dfrac{x+1}{x+2}$

9. $\dfrac{6x}{x-1}-\dfrac{3x}{x-1}$

10. $\dfrac{4}{x^4}-\dfrac{3}{x}$

Answers are on pages 511–512.

Multiplying Rational Expressions

When multiplying rational expressions, a common denominator is not necessary. Instead, the expressions are always multiplied straight across. Sometimes you will need to simplify the result before you have a final answer. As before, you will use cross canceling to simplify before multiplying to make things easier.

EXAMPLE 35

Multiply $\dfrac{2}{x}\cdot\dfrac{x-6}{x^2}$.

Multiply across:

$$\dfrac{2}{x}\cdot\dfrac{x-6}{x^2}=\dfrac{2(x-6)}{x^3}=\dfrac{2x-12}{x^3}.$$

EXAMPLE 36

Multiply $\dfrac{x-1}{x+2} \cdot \dfrac{x-1}{x+4}$.

Multiply across:

$$\dfrac{x-1}{x+2} \cdot \dfrac{x-1}{x+4} = \dfrac{(x-1)(x-1)}{(x+2)(x+4)} = \dfrac{x^2-2x+1}{x^2+6x+8}$$

In examples 35 and 36, the last expression could not be simplified, so it was the final answer. Sometimes you will need to simplify, but this will be before you use FOIL or distribute.

EXAMPLE 37

Multiply $\dfrac{x^2-4}{x-1} \cdot \dfrac{x+2}{x-2}$.

Before multiplying, notice that $x^2-4=(x+2)(x-2)$. This means that there are terms that can be cross canceled. That should be your first step.

$$\dfrac{(x+2)\cancel{(x-2)}}{(x-1)} \cdot \dfrac{x+2}{\cancel{x-2}} = \dfrac{x+2}{x-1} \cdot \dfrac{x+2}{1}$$

Multiply across: $\dfrac{x+2}{x-1} \cdot \dfrac{x+2}{1} = \dfrac{x^2+4x+4}{x-1}$

Dividing Rational Expressions

Rational expressions are divided with the same "flip and multiply" rule you used with fractions. Rewrite the division as a multiplication problem in which the first expression is multiplied by the reciprocal of the second.

EXAMPLE 38

Divide $\dfrac{x-5}{x} \div \dfrac{2}{x^2}$.

Rewrite as multiplication: $\dfrac{x-5}{x} \div \dfrac{2}{x^2} = \dfrac{x-5}{x} \cdot \dfrac{x^2}{2}$

Cross cancel if possible: $\dfrac{x-5}{x} \cdot \dfrac{x^2}{2} = \dfrac{x-5}{1} \cdot \dfrac{x}{2}$

Multiply across: $\dfrac{x-5}{1} \cdot \dfrac{x}{2} = \dfrac{(x-5)x}{2} = \dfrac{x^2-5x}{2}$

EXAMPLE 39

Divide $\dfrac{x-5}{x+1} \div \dfrac{x-6}{x+4}$.

Rewrite as multiplication: $\dfrac{x-5}{x+1} \div \dfrac{x-6}{x+4} = \dfrac{x-5}{x+1} \cdot \dfrac{x+4}{x-6}$

Cross cancel if possible: There are no terms here that can be cross canceled.

Multiply across: $\dfrac{x-5}{x+1} \cdot \dfrac{x+4}{x-6} = \dfrac{(x-5)(x+4)}{(x+1)(x-6)} = \dfrac{x^2-x-20}{x^2-5x-6}$

Multiplying and Dividing Rational Expressions

Directions: Multiply or divide the expressions as indicated.

1. $\dfrac{2}{x} \cdot \dfrac{1}{x+1}$

2. $\dfrac{x}{x-5} \cdot \dfrac{x}{x+5}$

3. $\dfrac{x-1}{4x} \cdot \dfrac{x+2}{x}$

4. $\dfrac{x^2+2}{x+1} \cdot \dfrac{x+1}{x-5}$

5. $\dfrac{x-3}{x+4} \cdot \dfrac{x-2}{2x-6}$

6. $\dfrac{1}{x^2} \div \dfrac{4}{x}$

7. $\dfrac{x}{x-2} \div \dfrac{5x}{x-6}$

8. $\dfrac{x+4}{x-1} \div \dfrac{x+2}{x^2-1}$

9. $\dfrac{x^3}{x-5} \div \dfrac{x}{x+2}$

10. $\dfrac{x+1}{x+3} \div \dfrac{x+1}{x+4}$

Answers are on page 512.

Writing Expressions

Writing algebraic expressions is a way to represent, or model, real-life situations using variables. As you learn to write expressions to represent a given situation, you need to watch for some key phrases. While there are many possible clues to indicate which operation makes sense, the following phrases will often appear.

- **Addition:** increased by, the sum, more than (as in "5 more than"), added to

- **Subtraction:** decreased by, the difference, less than (as in "6 less than"), subtracted from

- **Multiplication:** the product, double (times 2), triple (times 3), multiplied by
- **Division:** the quotient, divided by, halved (divided by 2)
- **Exponents:** *squared* or *square* refers to taking a variable to the second power; *cubed* or *cube* refers to the third power

EXAMPLE 40

A number is doubled and then decreased by 5. Write an algebraic expression to represent the value of the resulting number.

You are not given the variable in the question, so your first step is to choose a variable to represent the unknown value. Let's use n.

If n is doubled, it is multiplied by 2, resulting in $2n$. It was then decreased by 5, which means 5 is subtracted from it. Therefore the final expression is $2n - 5$.

EXAMPLE 41

To find the volume of a square chest, the width is squared and then multiplied by the height. If the height is 3 feet and the width is w feet, write an expression that represents the volume of this chest in terms of w.

The width is squared, so you can represent it by w^2. Multiplying this by 3 gives you the final expression $3w^2$.

EXAMPLE 42

Gary pays \$3.50 in tolls and \$0.53 per mile to drive to and from work each day. If m represents the number of miles he drives each day, write an expression to represent his cost in terms of m.

The word "per" is a clue that you should multiply; it indicates the cost for *each* mile driven. The tolls are paid only once, so you can add them on at the end.

The expression that represents his cost: $0.53m + 3.5$.

EXAMPLE 43

Five friends go out to lunch and plan to split the bill evenly. If the final bill is \$$b$, write an expression that represents the amount each friend will pay in terms of b.

If the bill is divided evenly, it will be divided by 5. Because the bill is \$$b$, the cost to each friend will be $\dfrac{b}{5}$ dollars.

Writing Expressions

Directions: Write an expression to represent the given situation.

1. A company has k employees where k is a whole number. A bonus of $2,000 is to be divided evenly among all the employees. Write an expression to represent the amount each employee will receive in terms of k.

2. In the past two weeks, the amount in a student's checking account has increased by $505. If the amount two weeks ago was x, write an expression to represent the current amount in terms of x.

3. Ryan collects action figures and adds two to his collection every month. If he starts with y action figures, then in terms of y, how many will he have in 3 months?

4. A cell phone plan charges $30.00 a month for service plus $0.15 a minute for any calls. If Janelle makes a total of m minutes of calls in a month, what expression will represent Janelle's total bill in terms of m?

5. A staple gun is used to secure fabric by placing a staple every n feet. Write an expression that represents the number of staples used to secure 20 feet of fabric.

Answers are on page 512.

CHAPTER 11

Solving Equations and Inequalities

One of the biggest topics in algebra is solving equations and inequalities. Both come in many forms, but the goal always remains the same: find values that make the given statement true. In fact, that is exactly what it means to "solve for x." In this chapter, you will study the most common types of equations you will see on the GED® test.

Linear Equations

The difference between a linear equation and a linear expression is just an equals sign. Technically, a linear equation is a linear expression set equal to a number or equal to another linear expression. To solve any linear equation, the goal is to get a statement of the form:

"the variable" = "a number"

In order to do this, any operation that has been applied to the variable must be undone. The one rule to remember is that any operation performed on one side of the equation must be performed on the other side of the equation as well.

With one-step equations, only one operation is being done to the variable. This means that it takes only one step to undo this operation and get the final answer (the variable by itself).

Consider the equation $2x = 8$. Here, the x is being multiplied by 2. To "undo" this and get the x by itself, you can divide both sides by 2 and get $x = 4$. Similarly, in the equation $x + 5 = 2$, a 5 is being added to the x. To "undo" this, you subtract 5 from both sides and get $x = -3$. In both of these cases, you solved the equation because you found the value of x that made the statement true.

EXAMPLE 1

Solve for x: $\qquad\qquad\qquad\qquad\qquad\qquad\qquad\qquad$ $x - 11 = 14$

Undo the subtraction by adding 11 to both sides: $\quad$ $x - 11 + 11 = 14 + 11$

Final answer: $\qquad\qquad\qquad\qquad\qquad\qquad\qquad\qquad$ $x = 25$

EXAMPLE 2

Solve for x: $\qquad\qquad\qquad\qquad\qquad\qquad\qquad\qquad$ $5x = 15$

Undo the multiplication by dividing both sides by 5: $\quad$ $\dfrac{5x}{5} = \dfrac{15}{5}$

Final answer: $\qquad\qquad\qquad\qquad\qquad\qquad\qquad\qquad$ $x = 3$

EXAMPLE 3

Solve for x: $\dfrac{2}{3}x = 8$

Undo the multiplication by dividing both sides by $\dfrac{2}{3}$: $\dfrac{\frac{2}{3}x}{\frac{2}{3}} = \dfrac{8}{\frac{2}{3}}$

Final answer: $x = 8 \cdot \dfrac{3}{2} = \dfrac{24}{2} = 12$

The work in example 3 may seem complicated, but remember that dividing by a fraction is the same as multiplying by its reciprocal. On the left, $\dfrac{2}{3}$ divided by itself is 1 (any number divided by itself is 1) and 8 divided by $\dfrac{2}{3}$ is, by definition, 8 times $\dfrac{3}{2}$. The overall process of undoing the operation still held true.

You may find that for the other examples, you were able to tell the answer simply by looking at the equation. Even so, it is still a good idea to practice these techniques so that you can use them for the more complicated equations later in the chapter.

EXERCISE 1

One-Step Equations

Directions: Solve each of the following equations for x. If your answer is a fraction, write it in its lowest terms.

1. $3x = 2$

2. $5x = 25$

3. $\dfrac{x}{4} = 5$

4. $x - 7 = 10$

5. $x + 3 = -1$

Answers are on page 513.

Two-Step Equations

As you might guess, in a two-step equation, two operations are being done to the variable that you must undo before you can find its value. At this stage, the methods stay the same, but the order of the steps is important.

Step 1: Undo any addition or subtraction.

Step 2: Undo any multiplication or division.

EXAMPLE 4

Solve for x:	$4x - 1 = 7$
Undo the subtraction:	$4x - 1 + 1 = 7 + 1$
	$4x = 8$
Undo the multiplication:	$\dfrac{4x}{4} = \dfrac{8}{4}$
Final answer:	$x = 2$

EXAMPLE 5

Solve for x:	$\dfrac{x}{7} + 3 = -5$
Undo the addition:	$\dfrac{x}{7} + 3 - 3 = -5 - 3$
	$\dfrac{x}{7} = -8$
Undo the division:	$7\left(\dfrac{x}{7}\right) = 7(-8)$
Final answer:	$x = -56$

EXERCISE 2

Two-Step Equations

Directions: Solve each of the following equations for x. If your final answer is a fraction, write it in its lowest terms.

1. $2x - 5 = 11$

2. $-x + 4 = -8$

3. $\dfrac{1}{2}x - 3 = -1$

4. $\dfrac{x}{4} + 2 = -2$

5. $3x - \dfrac{1}{2} = 4$

Answers are on page 513.

Multiple-Step Equations

Some linear equations have variables on both sides of the equation or have unsimplified expressions on one or both sides. In these situations, the equation has to be simplified before you can apply the usual process of undoing operations.

Consider the equation $2x - 4 = x + 2$. Before you can get the equation into the final answer form "variable = number," you need to get all of the x-terms on one side and all of the numbers on the other. To make that happen, you can move values around by adding them or subtracting them from both sides. For example, subtracting x from both sides will bring all of the x's to one side of the equation.

$$2x - 4 - x = x + 2 - x$$
$$x - 4 = 2$$

Now this is a one-step equation, and you can solve it like the ones you solved previously. In general, this will be the process.

Step 1: Simplify one or both sides.

Step 2: Bring all variables to one side of the equation.

Step 3: Undo any addition or subtraction.

Step 4: Undo any multiplication.

Whether or not you need steps 1 and 2 depends on the equation. In some cases, you will only need to simplify. In other cases, you will only need to move variables.

EXAMPLE 6

Solve for x: $3(x-6)+1=-2$

Before you can move terms, you need to simplify the left side using the distributive property.

Simplify: $3x-18+1=-2$

$$3x-17=-2$$

Undo the subtraction: $3x-17+17=-2+17$

$$3x=15$$

Undo the multiplication: $\dfrac{3x}{3}=\dfrac{15}{3}$

Final answer: $x=5$

EXAMPLE 7

Solve for *x*: $4x - 9 = 5x + 1$

Both sides are simplified, so you can start off by moving terms around.

Bring all variables to one side: $4x - 9 - 5x = 5x + 1 - 5x$

$$-x - 9 = 1$$

Undo the subtraction: $-x - 9 + 9 = 1 + 9$

$$-x = 10$$

Undo the multiplication: $\dfrac{-x}{-1} = \dfrac{10}{-1}$

Final answer: $x = -10$

EXAMPLE 8

Solve for *x*: $2(x + 3) = 4x - 1$

Simplify first by using the distributive property on the left side of the equation. Then you can move terms to get the *x*'s on one side.

Simplify: $2x + 6 = 4x - 1$

Bring all variables to one side: $2x + 6 - 4x = 4x - 1 - 4x$

$$-2x + 6 = -1$$

Undo the addition: $-2x + 6 - 6 = -1 - 6$

$$-2x = -7$$

Undo the multiplication: $\dfrac{-2x}{-2} = \dfrac{-7}{-2}$

Final answer: $x = \dfrac{7}{2}$

EXERCISE 3

Multiple-Step Equations

Directions: Solve each of the following equations for *x*. If your final answer is a fraction, write it in its lowest terms.

1. $-2(x + 4) = x - 5$

2. $3x + 1 = x + 7$

3. $-x + 4 = x + 9$

4. $3(x + 1) = 9x$

5. $-9x + 4 = -3(2x + 6)$

Inequalities

So far, the only type of relationship you have seen between two expressions or terms is equality, as shown in an equation. However, it is possible that two expressions relate in such a way that one side is smaller than the other or vice-versa. This type of relationship is called an **inequality**. Some examples include $x - 3 > 2$, $x + 4 \leq 3$, and $4x < -6$.

As with equations, solving an inequality means finding values that make the statement true. With equations, there is often just one value that works, and you show it by stating something like "$x = 2$." In the case of inequalities, there are many values that will make the statement true, and these solutions are written either algebraically (as seen in the following chart) or graphically (discussed later in this chapter).

Example	Meaning
$x < 3$	x is "less than" 3
	Any whole number or decimal value for x that is smaller than 3 will make this statement true.
$x \leq -2$	x is "less than or equal to" -2
	Any whole number or decimal value for x that is equal to or smaller than -2 will make this statement true.
$x > 10$	x is "greater than" 10
	Any whole number or decimal value for x that is greater than 10 will make this statement true.
$x \geq 4$	x is "greater than or equal to" 4
	Any whole number or decimal value for x that is equal to or greater than 4 will make this statement true.

Solving Inequalities

The steps in solving a linear inequality are exactly the same as those used in solving linear equations. There is, however, one very important new rule to follow.

Anytime you multiply or divide by a negative number, the inequality changes direction.

Let's start with an example to show how this works.

EXAMPLE 9

Solve for x: $\qquad\qquad -4x \geq 16$

In order to undo the multiplication, divide both sides by -4. However, because this is negative number, the direction of the inequality will change.

Undo the multiplication: $\quad \dfrac{-4x}{-4} \leq \dfrac{16}{-4}$

Final answer: $\qquad\qquad x \leq -4$

As you can see, other than the change in direction of the inequality, the solution steps are generally the same as those for equations.

EXAMPLE 10

Solve for x: $\qquad\qquad x - 5 < 2$

Undo the subtraction: $\quad x - 5 + 5 < 2 + 5$

Final answer: $\qquad\qquad x < 7$

EXAMPLE 11

Solve for x: $\qquad\qquad 2x - 2 \leq -10$

Undo the subtraction: $\quad 2x - 2 + 2 \leq -10 + 2$

$\qquad\qquad\qquad\qquad 2x \leq -8$

Undo the multiplication: $\quad \dfrac{2x}{2} \leq \dfrac{-8}{2}$

Final answer: $\qquad\qquad x \leq -4$

Graphing Solutions

Using the number line, all of the values of x that make a given inequality true can be shown by shading the region representing those numbers. In this process, an open circle is used if the inequality uses a $<$ or $>$ while a closed circle is used if the inequality uses a $\leq$ or $\geq$.

EXAMPLE 12

Solve the inequality and graph its solution set on the number line.

$\qquad\qquad\qquad -3x + 7 > -2$

Undo the addition: $\qquad -3x + 7 - 7 > -2 - 7$

$\qquad\qquad\qquad\qquad -3x > -9$

Undo the multiplication: $\quad \dfrac{-3x}{-3} < \dfrac{-9}{-3}$

(Notice that the direction changes because the 3 is negative.)

Final answer: $\qquad\qquad x < 3$

This solution is graphed on a number line by placing an open circle on 3 and shading in all of the values to the left (because these values are all smaller than 3).

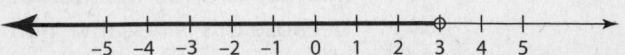

Some other examples of graphed solution sets are shown here.

Solution Set	Graph
$x > 2$	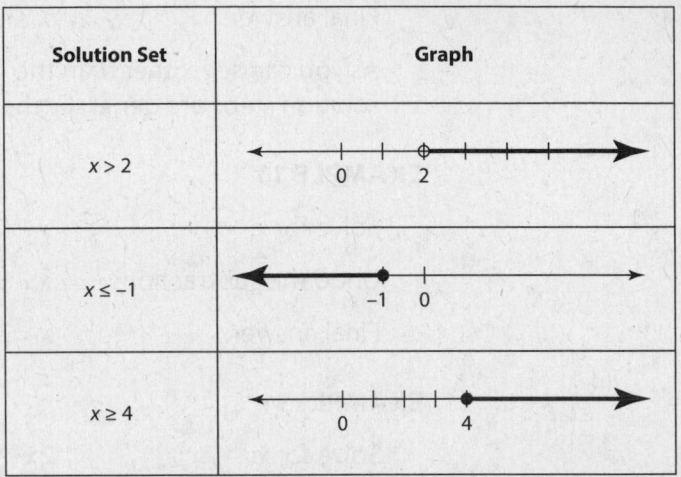
$x \leq -1$	
$x \geq 4$	

EXERCISE 4

Solving Inequalities

Directions: Solve the following inequalities.

1. $x + 3 > 8$

2. $x - 10 < 4$

3. $2x - 7 < 5$

4. $-5x + 1 \leq -4$

5. $-\dfrac{1}{2}x \geq 12$

Answers are on page 513.

Writing Linear Equations and Inequalities

In order to solve word problems about real-life situations, you need to be able to write equations or inequalities to represent them. Many of the key phrases you watched for when writing linear expressions will still be useful, but now you also watch for a few new ones. These new key phrases can help you decide if you should use an equals sign or one of the inequality signs in your statements.

Symbol	Key Phrases
=	is, is the same as, equals, was, yields, gives
<	is less than, is smaller than
≤	is less than or equal to, is the same or less, is the same or smaller, at most
>	is greater than, is larger than
≥	is greater than or equal to, is the same or more, is the same or greater, at least

EXAMPLE 13

Mary's age in years is three more than Blake's age. If Blake's age is b years and Mary's age is m years, write an equation that represents Mary's age in terms of Blake's age.

The statement implies that if you add 3 to Blake's age, you will have Mary's age. Therefore, $m = b + 3$.

EXAMPLE 14

Bob makes it a rule never to let the balance in his bank account drop below $100. If the balance in his bank account is $$d$, write an equation or inequality to represent his rule about the balance.

If the balance can never be less than $100, then it must always be $100 or greater. This is represented by the inequality $d \geq 100$.

EXAMPLE 15

A warehouse will only accept crates that weigh under 500 pounds. If a crate weighs c pounds, write an inequality that represents this requirement.

The phrase "under" is the same as "less than." Therefore, $c < 500$.

EXAMPLE 16

In terms of employees, the accounting department of a company is three times as large as the marketing department. If the number of employees in the accounting department is A and the number of employees in the marketing department is M, write an equation to represent this relationship.

"Three times as large" means that you would have to multiply the number of employees in the marketing department by 3 to get the number of employees in the accounting department. As an equation, this can be written as $A = 3M$.

EXERCISE 5

Writing Linear Equations and Inequalities

Directions: Write an equation or inequality to represent the described situation, as indicated.

1. A number x is three less than double a number y. Write an equation that describes the relationship between x and y.

2. In a college course, any calculated grade of 90 and above will receive an A as the final course letter grade. If G represents the calculated grade, write an inequality that shows what set of grades will qualify for an A.

3. The length of a rectangle is larger than 2 times its width. If the rectangle's width is 3 inches, write an inequality to represent the length x of the rectangle.

4. The output of a machine today is m units. That is at least 5 more than its output yesterday. If the output yesterday was 300 units, write an inequality to represent the value of m.

5. On Wednesday, Tony worked at a local fair and made $34 less than what he makes per day at his usual job. If he made $$w$ on Wednesday and $$r$ each day at his usual job, write an equation that represents the relationship between w and r.

Answers are on page 513.

Word Problems with Equations and Inequalities

Solving word problems really just requires being able to write an equation to represent the situation and then being able to solve it. Often you will not be given a variable to work with, so your first step is to choose a variable to represent the value you are trying to find.

EXAMPLE 17

The product of a number and 3 is 42. What is the value of the number?

If the number is *x*, this relationship can be represented by $3x = 42$. Solving the equation:

$$\frac{3x}{3} = \frac{42}{3}$$

$$x = 14$$

The number is 14.

EXAMPLE 18

A consultant charges a company $50 an hour in addition to a one-time analysis fee of $450. If the company paid the consultant $1,050, how many hours did she work?

If *h* represents the number of hours worked, then the consultant's total charge is $50h + 450$. Because the total payment was $1,050, it must be that $50h + 450 = 1050$. Solving this equation:

$$50h + 450 = 1050$$

$$50h + 450 - 450 = 1050 - 450$$

$$\frac{50h}{50} = \frac{600}{50}$$

$$h = 12$$

The consultant worked for 12 hours.

EXAMPLE 19

The average of the numbers *x*, 15, 9, 8, and 2 is 12. What is the value of *x*?

This question requires the use of the average formula. To find the average, add the numbers and then divide the sum by the number of numbers. If the average is 12, then

$$\frac{x + 15 + 9 + 8 + 2}{5} = 12,$$

which is equivalent to

$$\frac{x + 34}{5} = 12.$$

Now undo the division by multiplying both sides by 5. Then you can subtract the 34 from both sides.

$$x + 34 = 60$$

$$x = 26$$

The problem in example 19 is a common problem on the GED® test. You may find that you need to use common formulas and your knowledge of word problems to find unknown values in some problems. Just remember that the basic rules for solving equations always apply.

EXERCISE 6

Word Problems with Equations and Inequalities

1. A car rental company charges $125 a week plus 14 cents a mile. If the Chens paid $141.80 for their weeklong rental, how many miles did they drive?

2. Ten less than a number is two more than double the number. What is the value of the number?

3. The average of the numbers 2, 3, 4, and y is 6. What is the value of y?

4. A clerk must enter n new orders into a computer system. The clerk is able to enter orders at a rate of 40 per hour. If it takes her 12 hours to enter the orders, what is the value of n?

5. A coffee shop opened with 6 different types of snacks available. Since then, it has added 2 new choices every week. If the shop now offers 28 snacks, how many weeks has it been open?

Answers are on pages 513–514.

Systems of Two Equations with Two Unknowns

Systems of two equations with two unknowns are often needed to represent real-life situations. To solve a system means to find values for the unknowns that make both equations true at the same time. One common way to do this is a technique called elimination.

The idea of elimination is to multiply one or both equations by a number that will cause one of the variables to be cancelled out when the equations are added. What number is used depends on the equations, and it takes practice to know which one to use. Follow these steps:

Step 1: Multiply one or both of the equations by a number chosen because it will eliminate one of the variables.

Step 2: Add the equations.

Step 3: Solve the equation that results from step 2.

Step 4: Use the result to find the value of the other variable.

EXAMPLE 20

Solve the system of equations:

$$3x - y = 13$$
$$5x + 2y = 18$$

Step 1: Multiply one or both of the equations by a number chosen because it will eliminate one of the variables.

In the first equation, the coefficient of y is -1. In the second equation the coefficient of y is 2. If you multiply the first equation by 2, the coefficients will be -2 and 2, and they will therefore cancel out when the equations are added. So multiply the first equation by 2.

$$2(3x - y) = 2(13) \qquad 6x - 2y = 26$$
$$\qquad\qquad\qquad\rightarrow$$
$$5x + 2y = 18 \qquad\qquad 5x + 2y = 18$$

Step 2: Add the equations.

$$\begin{array}{r} 6x - 2y = 26 \\ + 5x + 2y = 18 \\ \hline 11x \qquad = 44 \end{array}$$

Step 3: Solve the equation from step 2.

$$\frac{11x}{11} = \frac{44}{11}$$

$$x = 4$$

Step 4: Use the result to find the value of the other variable.

If $x = 4$, this value can be plugged into any of the equations to find the value of y. Using the first equation, $3x - y = 13$, so $3(4) - y = 13$. Solving this equation:

$$12 - y = 13$$

$$12 - y - 12 = 13 - 12$$

$$-y = 1$$

$$y = -1$$

The solution to the system of equations is $x = 4$ and $y = -1$.

EXAMPLE 21

Solve the system of equations:

$$3a + 4b = -18$$
$$2a + 6b = -32$$

Step 1: Multiply one or both of the equations by a number chosen because it will eliminate one of the variables.

In the last system, it was easiest to eliminate y because to do so, only one of the equations had to be multiplied. Here it is not obvious that eliminating one variable will be easier than another. If you choose to eliminate the a, then you need to multiply the first equation by 2 and the second by -3. One has to be negative so that the a's will cancel when added together.

$$2(3a + 4b) = 2(-18) \qquad \rightarrow \qquad 6a + 8b = -36$$
$$-3(2a + 6b) = -3(-32) \qquad\qquad -6a - 18b = 96$$

Step 2: Add the equations.

$$\begin{aligned} 6a + 8b &= -36 \\ +\; -6a - 18b &= 96 \\ \hline -10b &= 60 \end{aligned}$$

Step 3: Solve the equation from step 2.

$$\frac{-10b}{-10} = \frac{60}{-10}$$
$$b = -6$$

Step 4: Use the result to find the value of the other variable.

Plugging the value of b into the first equation, $3a - 24 = -18$. Solving this equation:

$$3a - 24 + 24 = -18 + 24$$
$$3a = 6$$
$$\frac{3a}{3} = \frac{6}{3}$$
$$a = 2$$

In this example, you would get the exact same answer if you chose to eliminate b rather than a. Trying to do this would be a good way to make sure you understand how elimination works.

EXERCISE 7

Solving Systems of Equations

Directions: Solve the following systems of equations using the elimination method.

1. $x - y = -2$
   $2x + 3y = 1$

2. $3x + 2y = 20$
   $-4x + y = -12$

3. $x - 3y = -6$
   $8x + 5y = 10$

4. $-6x + 4y = 18$
   $2x + 2y = 14$

5. $x + y = 0$
   $-x + 2y = -6$

Answers are on page 514.

Word Problems and Systems of Equations

Systems of equations are needed to represent many real-life situations. Writing the equations to represent these situations requires the same skills as writing an equation with one variable.

EXAMPLE 22

A high school club sold tickets to a basketball game in order to raise money. Club members raised $205 by selling 35 tickets. For people with a family member in the club, the tickets cost $5. For everyone else, tickets cost $8. How many tickets did club members sell to people with family members in the club?

The unknown values are the number of each type of ticket sold. Let F be the number sold to people with family members in the club and T be the number sold to everyone else. The club sold a total of 35 tickets, so it must be that $F + T = 35$.

In order to find the value of either F or T, you need one more equation. The only information you have not used is the total amount raised, $205. Each family ticket brought in $5, while every other ticket brought in $8. Therefore $5F + 8T = 205$.

The question asks only for F, so you can save some work by eliminating T first.

$$-8(F + T) = -8(35) \qquad -8F - 8T = -280$$
$$5F + 8T = 205 \quad \rightarrow \quad \underline{5F + 8T = 205}$$
$$-3F = -75$$

Solving this equation, $F = 25$. There were 25 tickets sold to family members.

This example illustrates two important points about working with this type of word problem. First, when creating your equations, you need to put like information together. In this case, you put information about the ticket sales together and information about the money together.

Second, these questions tend to ask for only one of the variables. So save yourself some work by eliminating the other variable first. That way, you do not have to solve the whole system.

EXAMPLE 23

A gym is storing 5-pound and 10-pound dumbbells. If there are a total of 10 dumbbells weighing 70 pounds altogether, how many 10-pound dumbbells does the gym have in storage?

The unknowns are the number of 5-pound dumbbells and the number of 10-pound dumbbells. Let's call these x (5-pound) and y (10-pound). There are a total of 10 dumbbells, so $x + y = 10$ weighing a total of 70 pounds. Because each 5-pound dumbbell contributes 5 pounds to this total and each 10-pound dumbbell contributes 10 pounds, $5x + 10y = 70$.

The question asks only for the number of 10-pound dumbbells, which is y. Therefore, eliminate x first.

$$\begin{array}{ll} -5(x + y) = -5(10) & -5x - 5y = -50 \\ 5x + 10y = 70 & \underline{5x + 10y = 70} \\ & 5y = 20 \end{array}$$

Solving this equation, $y = 4$. There are four 10-pound dumbbells in storage.

EXAMPLE 24

A restaurant has two types of tables: family-size tables that seat 8 people and small tables that seat 4 people. To purchase the tables, the owner spent $180 for each family-size table and $100 for each small table for a total of $3,660. If the restaurant can seat a total of 156 people, how many family-size tables does it have?

In this question, the unknowns are the number of each type of table. Let f be the number of family-size tables and s be the number of small tables. You have two kinds of information: the number of people and the cost. You should be able to create an equation for each of these.

Considering the cost, each family-size table contributed $180 and each small table contributed $100 to the total. This gives you the equation $180f + 100s = 3660$. The same idea works for the number of people. Each family-size table seats 8 and each small table seats 4, so $8f + 4s = 156$. Because the question asks for the number of family-size tables, you will save time by eliminating s.

$$\begin{array}{ll} 180f + 100s = 3660 & 180f + 100s = 3600 \\ -25(8f + 4s) = -25(156) & \underline{-200f - 100s = -3900} \\ & -20f = -240 \end{array}$$

Solving this equation for f, you find that the restaurant has 12 family-size tables.

EXERCISE 8

Word Problems and Systems of Equations

1. A piggy bank is filled with only nickels and dimes. If there are 61 coins worth $4.10 in the bank, how many of the coins are nickels?

2. A factory takes 10 man-hours to produce a fan and 15 man-hours to produce an air conditioner. If the factory produced a total of 20 fans and air conditioners in 260 hours, how many of the items produced were fans?

3. At a bake sale, muffins are $1.50 and brownies are $2. If 40 of these items were sold for a total of $70, how many of the items sold were brownies?

4. A cleaning service requires 1 hour to vacuum and 1.5 hours to deep-clean a car. The service requires 1.5 hours to vacuum and 2 hours to deep-clean a truck. If the service spent 14 hours vacuuming and 19.5 hours deep-cleaning trucks and cars, how many of the vehicles were cars?

5. A school spent $1,022 buying graphing and scientific calculators. Each graphing calculator cost $95 and had a shipping weight of 6 ounces. Each scientific calculator cost $12 and had a shipping weight of 3 ounces. If the full shipment of calculators weighed 78 ounces, how many graphing calculators did the school purchase?

Answers are on page 514.

Solving Quadratic Equations with the Square Root Rule

Quadratic equations are a special type of equation in which the highest exponent on any variable is 2. Depending on the form of the equation, quadratic equations can be solved using the square root rule, factoring, or the quadratic formula.

When a quadratic equation has a single squared term and no other variables, the square root rule is the fastest way to solve it. The **square root rule** says that if c is any positive number and $x^2 = c$, then:

$$x = \sqrt{c} \text{ or } x = -\sqrt{c}$$

The square root rule gives two solutions because anytime a negative is squared, it gives a positive. For instance, if you know that a number squared is 4, there is no way to know if the original number was 2 or −2. It could have been either.

EXAMPLE 25

Solve for x: $\qquad\qquad x^2 = 9$

Using the square root rule: $\quad x = \sqrt{9},\ x = -\sqrt{9}$

Simplifying: $\qquad\qquad\quad x = 3,\ -3.$

If there is any number that is multiplied, divided, added, or subtracted with the squared term, the operation can be undone using the same methods you used with linear equations. This method should always be used before using the square root rule.

EXAMPLE 26

Solve for x: $\qquad\qquad 5x^2 = 20$

Undo the multiplication: $\quad \dfrac{5x^2}{5} = \dfrac{20}{5}$

$\qquad\qquad\qquad\qquad\quad x^2 = 4$

Use the square root rule: $\quad x = \sqrt{4},\ x = -\sqrt{4}$

Final answer: $\qquad\qquad\ x = 2,\ -2$

EXAMPLE 27

Solve for x: $\qquad\qquad x^2 - 5 = 3$

Undo the subtraction: $\qquad x^2 - 5 + 5 = 3 + 5$

$\qquad\qquad\qquad\qquad\quad x^2 = 8$

Use the square root rule: $\quad x = \sqrt{8},\ x = -\sqrt{8}$

Final answer: $\qquad\qquad\ x = 2\sqrt{2},\ -2\sqrt{2}$

Finally, it is possible to use the square root rule with more complicated equations. In some cases, it may be that a larger term is squared. Even then, the rule still applies.

EXAMPLE 28

Solve for x: $\qquad\qquad (x-1)^2 = 16$

Because the subtraction is on the inside of the square, use the square root rule first.

Use the square root rule: $\quad x - 1 = \sqrt{16},\ x - 1 = -\sqrt{16}$

$\qquad\qquad\qquad\qquad\quad x - 1 = 4,\ x - 1 = -4$

This step results in two equations, but both can be solved by undoing the subtraction.

Undo the subtraction: $\qquad x - 1 + 1 = 4 + 1,\ x - 1 + 1 = -4 + 1$

Final answer: $\qquad\qquad\ x = 5,\ -3$

Solving Quadratic Equations with the Square Root Rule

Directions: Solve each of the following equations for x. If the final answer involves a root, simplify it completely.

1. $x^2 = 12$

2. $x^2 = 81$

3. $2x^2 = 32$

4. $x^2 - 3 = 15$

5. $(x+2)^2 = 4$

Answers are on page 514.

Solving Quadratic Equations by Factoring

In Chapter 10, you learned how to factor an expression that has an x^2 term, an x term, and a number term. You did this by reversing FOIL. Some quadratic equations are in this form, and you can use factoring to solve them. To do this, you will follow these steps.

Step 1: Move terms to one side of the equation (if necessary).

The equation should be in the form $ax^2 + bx + c = 0$ where a, b, and c are numbers.

Step 2: Factor the quadratic equation.

Step 3: Set each factor equal to zero.

Step 4: Solve the two resulting equations. The result will be the final answer.

EXAMPLE 29

Solve for x: $x^2 - 5x - 36 = 0$

Step 1: All of the terms are on one side of the equation, so you can skip this step.

Step 2: $x^2 - 5x - 36 = 0$

$(x-9)(x+4) = 0$

Step 3: $x - 9 = 0$ and $x + 4 = 0$

Step 4: $x = 9$ and $x = -4$

EXAMPLE 30

Solve for x: $x^2 + x = 2$

Step 1: $x^2 + x - 2 = 2 - 2$

$x^2 + x - 2 = 0$

Step 2: $(x-1)(x+2) = 0$

Step 3: $x - 1 = 0$ and $x + 2 = 0$

Step 4: $x = 1$ and $x = -2$

EXERCISE 10

Solving Quadratic Equations by Factoring

Directions: Solve each of the following equations for x.

1. $x^2 - 3x - 4 = 0$

2. $x^2 - 5x + 6 = 0$

3. $x^2 + 3x + 2 = 0$

4. $x^2 - 9x = -18$

5. $x^2 + 3x = 4$

Answers are on page 514.

Solving with the Quadratic Formula

Another method for solving any quadratic equation is using the **quadratic formula**. While it looks very complicated, using the formula is really just a matter of plugging in numbers and simplifying. (It is also included on the formula sheet for the GED® test, so there is no need to memorize it.)

If a, b, and c are numbers, you can think of any quadratic equation as $ax^2 + bx + c = 0$. The quadratic formula says that when this is the case, the final answer will be:

$$x = \frac{-b \pm \sqrt{b^2 - 4ac}}{2a}$$

The symbol in the numerator of the fraction is called a "plus-minus" symbol. This symbol means that there are actually two answers. One is with the plus sign (+) and one is with the minus sign (–). The steps for using this formula are:

Step 1: Identify a, b, and c.

Step 2: Plug a, b, and c into the formula and simplify.

Step 3: Use the + and the – to show the two final answers.

EXAMPLE 31

Solve for x: $2x^2 - 3x + 1 = 0$

Step 1: $a = 2$, $b = -3$, and $c = 1$

Step 2: $x = \dfrac{-(-3) \pm \sqrt{(-3)^2 - 4(2)(1)}}{2(2)} = \dfrac{3 \pm \sqrt{9-8}}{4} = \dfrac{3 \pm \sqrt{1}}{4} = \dfrac{3 \pm 1}{4}$

Step 3: $x = \dfrac{3+1}{4} = \dfrac{4}{4} = 1$ and $x = \dfrac{3-1}{4} = \dfrac{2}{4} = \dfrac{1}{2}$

Final answer: $x = 1$, $x = \dfrac{1}{2}$

The equation in example 30 could actually be factored into $(2x - 1)(x - 1)$ and solved using that method. Even so, the quadratic formula can work for any type of quadratic equation. If you find yourself having trouble factoring, try using the quadratic formula instead!

EXAMPLE 32

Solve for x: $6x^2 + 11x + 3 = 0$

Step 1: $a = 6$, $b = 11$, and $c = 3$

Step 2: $x = \dfrac{-11 \pm \sqrt{11^2 - 4(6)(3)}}{2(6)} = \dfrac{-11 \pm \sqrt{121 - 72}}{12} = \dfrac{-11 \pm \sqrt{49}}{12} = \dfrac{-11 \pm 7}{12}$

Step 3: $x = \dfrac{-11+7}{12} = \dfrac{-4}{12} = -\dfrac{1}{3}$ and $x = \dfrac{-11-7}{12} = \dfrac{-18}{12} = -\dfrac{3}{2}$

Final answer: $x = -\dfrac{1}{3}$, $x = -\dfrac{3}{2}$

For equations that cannot be factored, the final answers will often contain some square roots as you can see in the following example.

EXAMPLE 33

Solve for x: $x^2 - 8x + 4 = 0$

Step 1: $a = 1$, $b = -8$, and $c = 4$

Step 2: $x = \dfrac{-(-8) \pm \sqrt{(-8)^2 - 4(1)(4)}}{2(1)} = \dfrac{8 \pm \sqrt{64 - 16}}{2} = \dfrac{8 \pm \sqrt{48}}{2} = \dfrac{8 \pm 4\sqrt{3}}{2} = 4 \pm 2\sqrt{3}$

In the last step, the numerator and the denominator share a factor of 2, which cancels out.

Step 3: $x = 4 + 2\sqrt{3}$ and $x = 4 - 2\sqrt{3}$

Final answer: $x = 4 + 2\sqrt{3}$, $x = 4 - 2\sqrt{3}$

The answer in the last step cannot be simplified any further, so those two values are the final answer. When you work with these types of problems, just remember that whole numbers and square roots cannot be combined.

EXERCISE 11

Solving with the Quadratic Formula

Directions: Solve the following equations using the quadratic formula.

1. $x^2 - 3x - 10 = 0$

2. $x^2 + 2x - 3 = 0$

3. $6x^2 + x - 2 = 0$

4. $3x^2 + 4x - 4 = 0$

5. $x^2 - 4x + 2 = 0$

Answers are on page 514.

Writing Quadratic Equations

As you saw when working with linear equations, equations can be written to represent many types of real-life situations. This is also true with quadratic equations. When writing these equations, remember the keywords from writing expressions such as "squared" for an exponent of 2 and others that may mean addition, subtraction, or multiplication.

EXAMPLE 34

The difference between a number x^2 and 5 is equal to 18. Write an equation to represent this relationship.

When a problem says "the difference," it is referring to subtraction. So one side of the equation is $x^2 - 5$. Because this expression is equal to 18, the equation is $x^2 - 5 = 18$.

EXAMPLE 35

The area of a small rug can be found by multiplying its length by its width. If the rug's length and width both measure y and its area is 49 square feet, write an equation to show the relationship between y and 49.

If the area is 49, then the basic form of the equation will be $area = 49$. The area can be found by multiplying the length by the width, which are both y. Therefore, $area = y \cdot y = y^2$. Plugging this into your original statement gives you the equation $y^2 = 49$.

CHAPTER 12

Graphing Equations

Equations involving two variables or unknowns can be represented visually with graphs. These graphs allow you to better understand how the variables move together and understand different properties of the equation. In algebra, equations are usually graphed in the ***x-y* coordinate plane** (sometimes just called the coordinate plane).

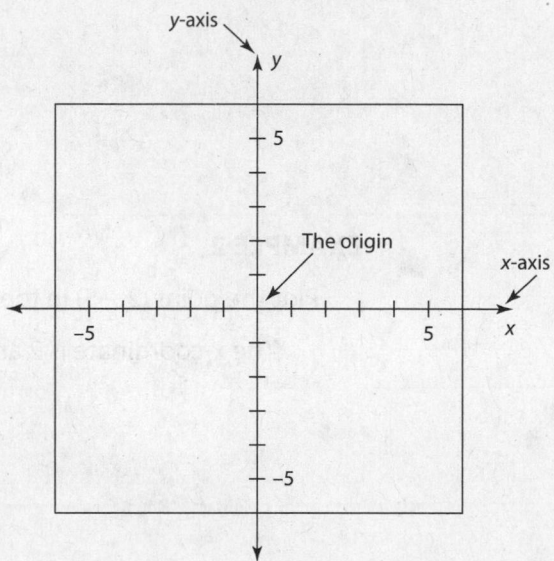

Plotting Points

Graphs of equations are made up of many individual points. To know how to graph a line or other equation, you must be comfortable graphing these points.

(x, y)

x-coordinate   *y*-coordinate

Points in the coordinate plane are called **ordered pairs**. As you can see in the preceding equation, ordered pairs always have an *x* value first and a *y* value second. These values tell you where the point is located in the coordinate plane. Plotting these points is really just about "reading" this ordered pair correctly. Starting from the **origin** [the point (0, 0)], the ***x*-coordinate** gives the distance left to right (negative means left) and the ***y*-coordinate** gives the distance up or down (negative means down).

EXAMPLE 1

Plot the point (−3, 4) in the coordinate plane.

The x-coordinate is −3 and the y-coordinate is 4.

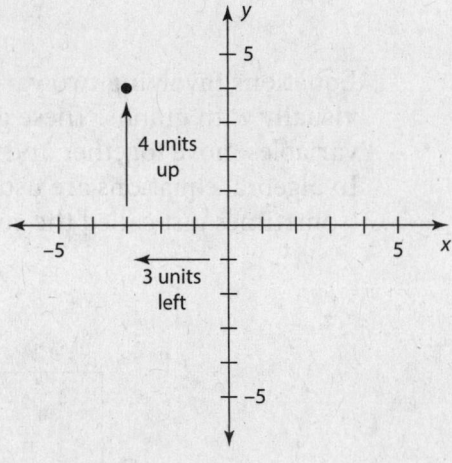

EXAMPLE 2

Plot the point (2, −5) in the coordinate plane.

The x-coordinate is 2 and the y-coordinate is −5.

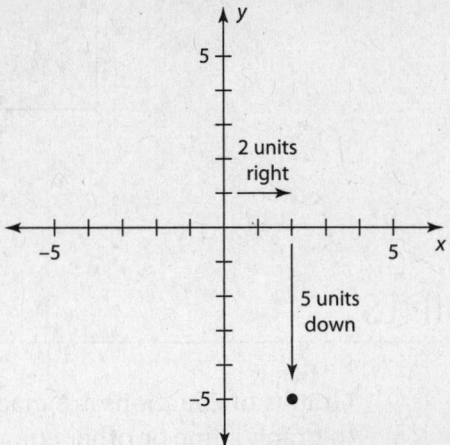

Plotting Points

Directions: Plot each of the following points on the *x-y* coordinate plane below. Label your points with the appropriate letter.

1. A (−2, 6)

2. B (4, 4)

3. C (8, −5)

4. D (−3, −9)

5. E (0, 5)

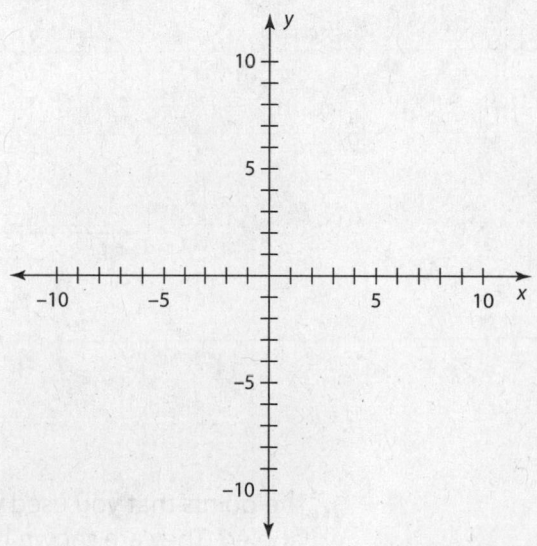

Answers are on page 515.

Graphing Lines

In general, the graph of any equation represents the plot of all points that make the equation true. If you were to plot these points for the equations $y = 2x + 5$, $y = \frac{1}{2}x$, and $y = -x + 1$, the resulting graphs would all be lines. This would be true of any equation where the *x* term has an exponent of 1.

To graph these types of equations (called linear equations), you only need to find two points on the line. Once you find them, you can connect them to make the full graph. To do this, you can pick any two values of x, and then see what the resulting values of y would be for that equation.

EXAMPLE 3

Graph the line represented by the equation $y = 3x + 1$.

It does not matter what values of x you choose, so choose something easy to work with. Let's use $x = 0$ and $x = 1$.

If $x = 0$, then $y = 3(0) + 1 = 1$. This means that the point $(0, 1)$ is on the line.

If $x = 1$, then $y = 3(1) + 1 = 3 + 1 = 4$. This means that the point $(1, 4)$ is on the line.

Now plot these points and sketch the line connecting them. This will be the graph of the equation.

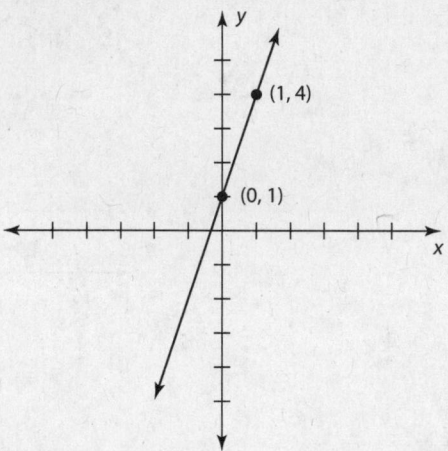

The points that you used when graphing the line do not have to be labeled. They are shown here just to make it easier to understand how the line was created.

EXAMPLE 4

Graph the line represented by the equation $y = -2x + 4$.

If $x = 0$, then $y = -2(0) + 4 = 4$.

If $x = 1$ then $y = -2(1) + 4 = -2 + 4 = 2$.

Points: $(0, 4)$ and $(1, 2)$

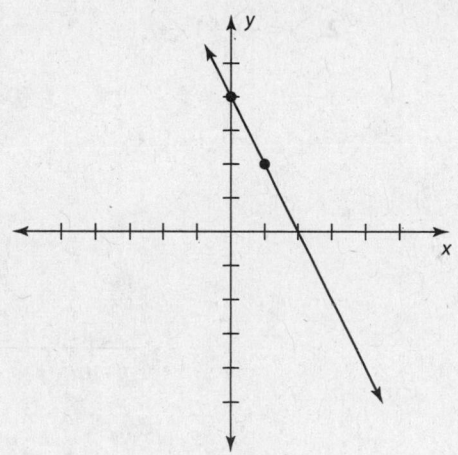

When you pick which *x*-values to plot, remember to save yourself work. If the number multiplying *x* is a fraction, pick a number that will be easy to multiply. For example, if you are graphing the equation $y = \frac{1}{3}x + 2$, using *x* values of 0 and 3 would be easy because 0 cancels out the *x* and 3 is easy to multiply by $\frac{1}{3}$.

EXERCISE 2

Graphing Lines

Directions: Graph the following lines on the *x-y* coordinate plane.

1. $y = -5x - 10$

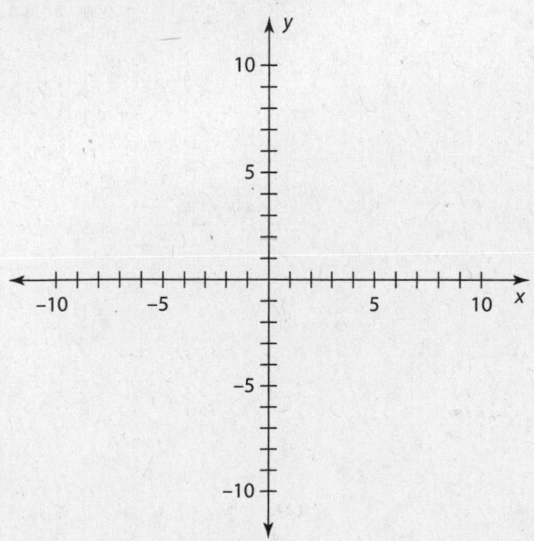

2. $y = -x + 1$

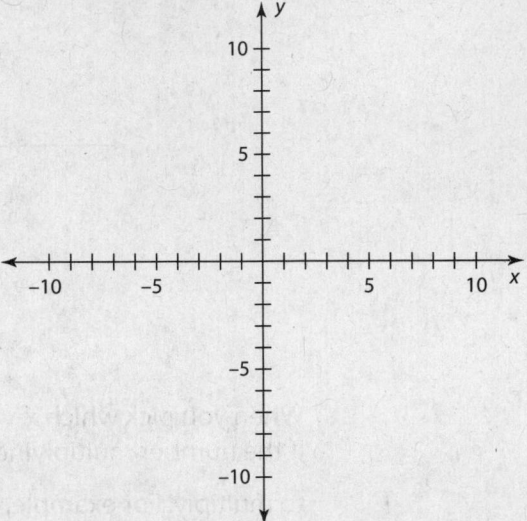

3. $y = \dfrac{1}{2}x + 3$

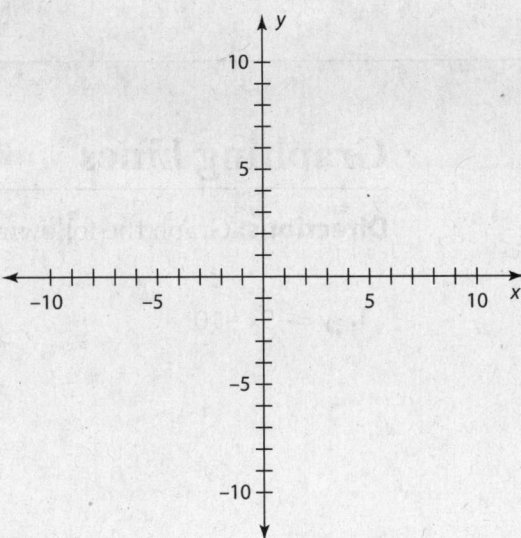

4. $y = 4x - 9$

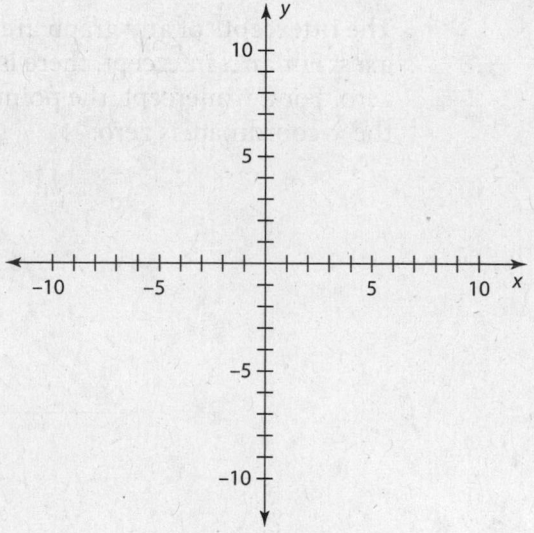

5. $y = x + 7$

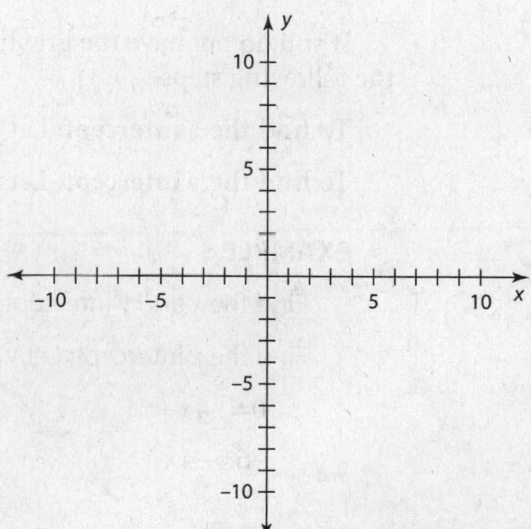

Answers are on pages 515–516.

Intercepts

The **intercepts** of any graph are the points where it crosses the x and the y axes. For an x intercept, there is no height to the point, so the y-coordinate is zero. For a y intercept, the point is not moved left or right from the origin, so the x-coordinate is zero.

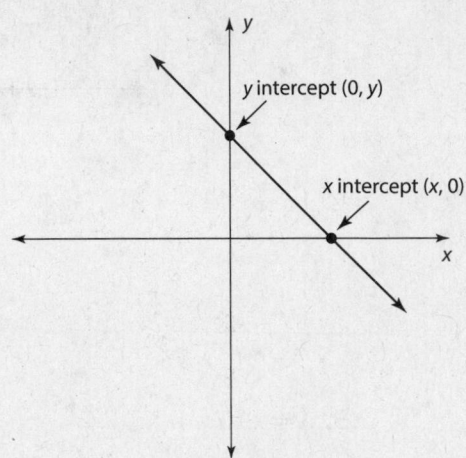

If you do not have the graph, the x and y intercepts can be found using the following steps.

- **To find the x intercept:** Let $y = 0$ and solve for x.

- **To find the y intercept:** Let $x = 0$ and solve for y.

EXAMPLE 5

Find the x and y intercepts of the line $y = -4x + 6$.

Find the x intercept: Let $y = 0$ and solve for x.

$$0 = -4x + 6$$

$$-6 = -4x$$

$$\frac{-6}{-4} = x$$

$$x = \frac{3}{2}$$

The x intercept is $\left(\frac{3}{2}, 0\right)$.

Find the y intercept: Let $x = 0$ and solve for y.

$$y = -4(0) + 6$$
$$y = 6$$

The y intercept is $(0,6)$

You may have noticed that the y intercept was much quicker to find. What you are noticing is that when the equation is written in the form $y = mx + b$ where m and b are numbers, b represents the y intercept. For example, the y intercept of the line $y = \frac{1}{2}x + 14$ is $(0, 14)$.

EXERCISE 3

Intercepts

Directions: Find the x and y intercepts of the following lines.

1. $y = \frac{3}{4}x - 2$

2. $y = x + 5$

3. $y = 8x - 10$

4. $y = 3x - 15$

5. $y = -x + 2$

Answers are on page 516.

Slope

Slope is a way of measuring the steepness of a line. Ignoring the sign, a very steep line will have a very large slope and a very flat line will have a very small slope. The sign of the slope also tells you about the direction of the line. Lines with positive slopes rise from left to right. Lines with negative slopes fall from left to right.

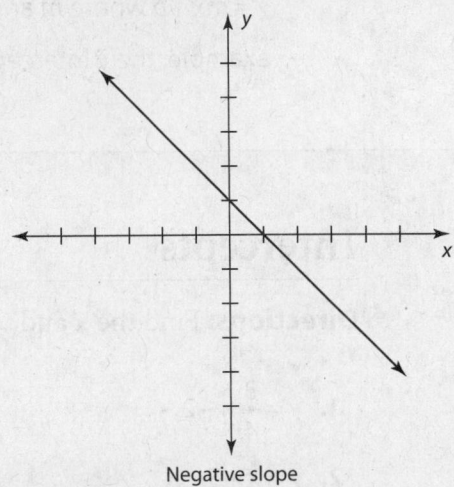

Negative slope

There are two special cases in regard to slope.

- The slope of any horizontal line is zero.
- The slope of any vertical line is undefined.

Calculating the Slope

The slope of a line passing through two points can be found using the **slope formula** (this formula is given on the GED® test formula sheet):

$$m = \frac{y_2 - y_1}{x_2 - x_1}$$

In this formula, m represents the slope and the points are represented by (x_1, y_1) and (x_2, y_2). Another way to define slope is as the change in y over the change in x. For this reason, slope is almost always represented as either a whole number or a reduced fraction.

EXAMPLE 6

Find the slope of a line passing through the points (1, 4) and (2, 7).

Given these two points, $(x_1, y_1) = (1, 4)$ and $(x_2, y_2) = (2, 7)$, and plugging these into the formula

$$m = \frac{y_2 - y_1}{x_2 - x_1} = \frac{7-4}{2-1} = \frac{3}{1} = 3,$$

the slope of the line is 3.

EXAMPLE 7

Find the slope of the line graphed in the *x-y* coordinate plane shown.

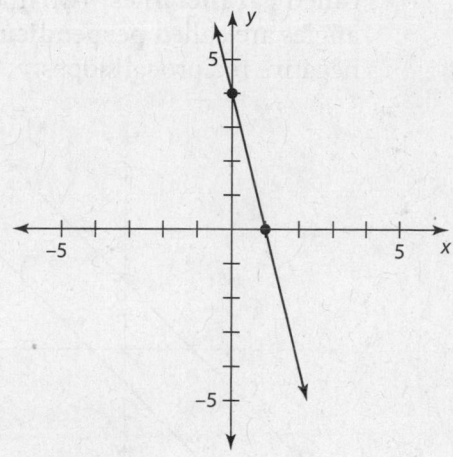

Based on the graph, the line passes through the points (0, 4) and (1, 0). Letting $(x_1, y_1) = (0, 4)$ and $(x_2, y_2) = (1, 0)$, the slope is

$$m = \frac{y_2 - y_1}{x_2 - x_1} = \frac{0 - 4}{1 - 0} = \frac{-4}{1} = -4.$$

In the last section, you saw that when a line is in the form $y = mx + b$, the *b* value is the *y* intercept. It is also true that when a line is in this form, *m* is the slope. For example, the slope of the line $y = \frac{1}{2}x + 4$ is $m = \frac{1}{2}$. For this reason, this form is called the **slope-intercept form** of an equation.

EXAMPLE 8

What is the slope of the line $4x - 3y = 10$?

If you solve this equation for *y* and put it in slope-intercept form, you will be able to "read" the slope from the equation. Solving for *y*:

$$4x - 3y = 10$$

$$4x - 3y - 4x = 10 - 4x$$

$$\frac{-3y}{-3} = \frac{10}{-3} - \frac{4}{-3}x$$

$$y = -\frac{10}{3} + \frac{4}{3}x$$

The coefficient of *x* is $\frac{4}{3}$, therefore the slope is $m = \frac{4}{3}$.

Parallel and Perpendicular Lines

Two lines that pass through different points but have the same slope are called **parallel lines**. Two lines that cross at a single point forming right angles are called **perpendicular lines**. Perpendicular lines always have negative reciprocal slopes.

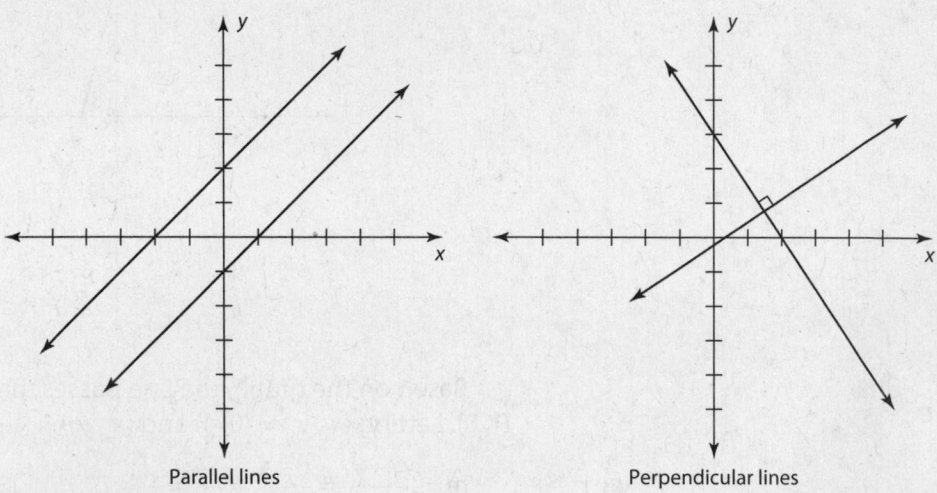

Parallel lines   Perpendicular lines

EXAMPLE 9

Line *n* passes through the points (–2, 5) and (8, 1). What is the slope of a line parallel to line *n*?

Parallel lines always have the same slope, so if you find the slope of line *n*, that will be the same as the slope of any line parallel to *n*.

Slope of line n: $m = \dfrac{1-5}{8-(-2)} = \dfrac{-4}{10} = -\dfrac{2}{5}$

Line *n* and any line parallel to *n* have a slope of $-\dfrac{2}{5}$.

EXAMPLE 10

What is the slope of a line perpendicular to the line $y = \dfrac{1}{4}x - 10$?

This line is in slope-intercept form, so you know the slope is $\dfrac{1}{4}$. Any line perpendicular to this line will have the negative reciprocal slope. To get the negative reciprocal, flip the fraction and change its sign.

$-\dfrac{4}{1} = -4$

The slope of any line perpendicular to the given line is –4.

Interpreting Slope

In general, the slope of a line can be thought of as a rate of change. In applications, the formula $\dfrac{\text{change in } y}{\text{change in } x}$ can be adjusted to whatever x and y represent. If the denominator is 1, then the slope represents the change in y for every one unit of change in x. A rate in this form is called a **unit rate**. Many common ways of measuring speed are unit rates. Some examples include miles per hour when driving and words per minute when typing.

EXAMPLE 11

The price of a certain item P in dollars changes with its age A in years according to the formula $P = -1.3A + 10$. In terms of dollars per year, at what rate is its price declining?

In this formula, P is taking the usual place of y and A is taking the usual place of x. So the slope represents the change in P (price) over the change in A (age). Because the slope is written as a decimal or whole number, it represents a unit rate. In other words, the price is decreasing by $1.30 for each year.

EXAMPLE 12

The following figure represents the additional distance covered by a student on her second day of a weeklong bike tour. Given this graph, what was the student's rate of speed on the second day, in miles per hour?

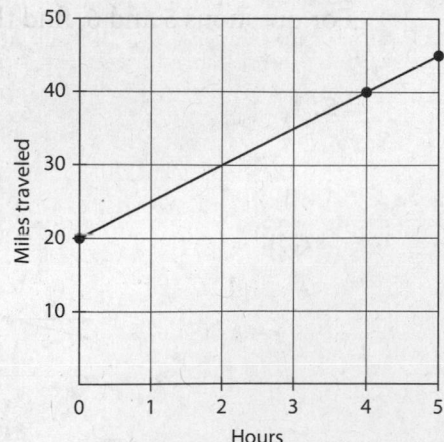

In this example, x represents hours (because it is the horizontal axis) and y represents miles (because it is the vertical axis). Therefore, the slope is

$$\frac{\text{change in } y}{\text{change in } x} = \frac{\text{change in miles}}{\text{change in hours}}$$

If this is simplified so that the denominator is 1, then it will give the change in miles for every 1 hour. In other words, it will be the speed in miles per hour.

To calculate the slope, you need two points. Looking at the graph, the line passes through the points (0, 20) and (5, 45). Therefore the slope is:

$$m = \frac{45-20}{5-0} = \frac{25}{5} = 5.$$

She was traveling at a rate of 5 miles per hour.

EXERCISE 4

Slope

Directions: For questions 1 through 4, find the slope of the line that passes through the given points.

1. (0, −8) and (2, 6)

2. (−4, 2) and (1, 6)

3. (1, 4) and (0, 7)

4. (10, 6) and (−5, −2)

For questions 5 and 6, find the slope of the line graphed in the given figure.

5.

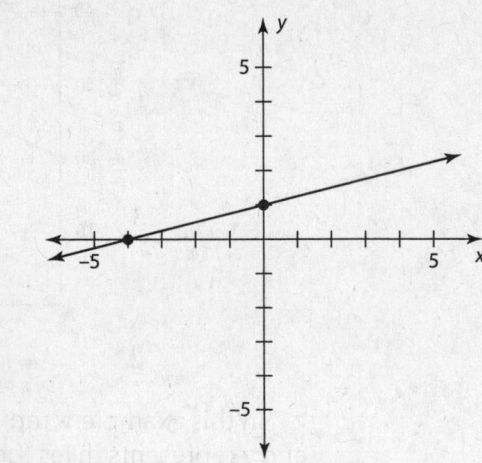

6.

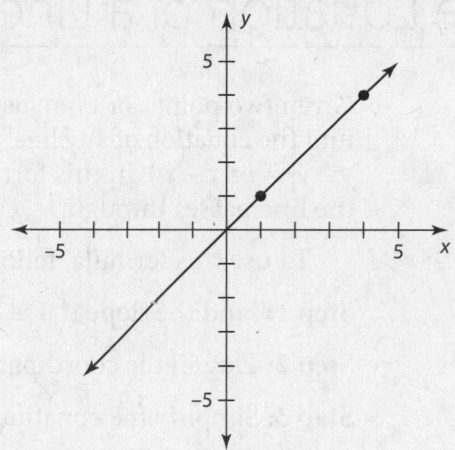

7. What is the slope of any line parallel to the line $-2x + y = 2$?

8. What is the slope of any line perpendicular to the line $y = -\dfrac{3}{2}x + 4$?

The graph shown represents the number of items produced at Smith Manufacturing during the first five hours of the day.

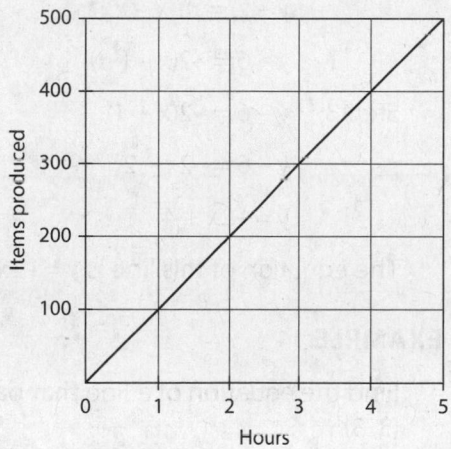

9. How many items did Smith Manufacturing produce each hour?

10. If Jackson Manufacturing produces items according to the formula $N = 150T$, where N is the number of items produced in T hours, then which factory produces items faster?

Answers are on page 516.

Finding the Equation of a Line

Given two points, or even just the slope and a single point, you can find the equation of any line. To do this, use the **point-slope formula** $y - y_1 = m(x - x_1)$. In this formula, m is the slope, and (x_1, y_1) is a point that the line passes through.

To use this formula, follow these steps.

Step 1: Find the slope if it is not given.

Step 2: Plug in the coordinates from the first point.

Step 3: Simplify the equation.

(Usually you will write the equation in $y = mx + b$ form.)

EXAMPLE 13

Find the equation of a line with slope -2 that passes through the point $(-1, 6)$.

Step 1: The slope is given. It is $m = -2$.

Step 2: Using the point $(x_1, y_1) = (-1, 6)$

$$y - y_1 = m(x - x_1)$$
$$y - 6 = -2(x - (-1))$$

Step 3: $y - 6 = -2(x + 1)$

$$y - 6 = -2x - 2$$
$$y = -2x + 4$$

The equation of this line is $y = -2x + 4$.

EXAMPLE 14

Find the equation of a line that passes through the points $(6, 1)$ and $(3, 3)$.

Step 1: Using the slope formula and $(x_1, y_1) = (6, 1)$, $(x_2, y_2) = (3, 3)$

$$m = \frac{3 - 1}{3 - 6} = \frac{2}{-6} = -\frac{2}{3}$$

Step 2: $y - y_1 = m(x - x_1)$

$$y - y_1 = -\frac{2}{3}(x - 6)$$
$$y - 1 = -\frac{2}{3}x + 4)$$
$$y = -\frac{2}{3}x + 5$$

The equation of the line is $y = -\frac{2}{3}x + 5$.

Finding the Equation of a Line

Directions: For questions 1 and 2, find the equation of the line given the indicated slope and point.

1. $m = -5$, point: (1, 3)

2. $m = \dfrac{1}{2}$, point: (-4, 4)

For questions 3 and 4, find the equation of the line that passes through the two points.

3. (1, -4) and (2, -2)

4. (2, 5) and (5, 14)

5. Let n be a line with slope 4.

   (a) Find the equation of a line parallel to line n that passes through the point (0, 2).

   (b) Find the equation of a line perpendicular to line n that passes through the point (-3, 1).

Answers are on page 516.

Graphs and Systems of Equations

One surprising application of the graphs of equations is with systems of equations. With any system of equations, it is possible to sketch the graphs of both and use them to find the solution to the system.

EXAMPLE 15

In the figure are the graphs of two equations from a system of two equations involving the variables x and y. Based on this figure, what is the solution to this system of equations?

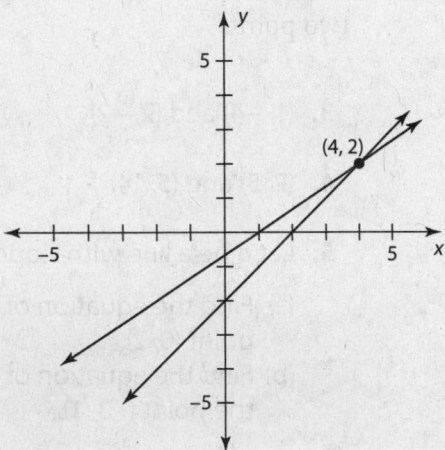

The two lines **intersect**, or cross, at the point (4, 2). In this situation, the x coordinate represents the value of x that makes both equations true and the y coordinate represents the value of y that makes both equations true. Therefore, the solution to the system is $x = 4$ and $y = 2$.

CHAPTER 13

Functions

A **function** is a mathematical rule that relates an input to exactly one output. As an example, "add five" is a function because it takes any number (an input) and gives one output (the number plus 5). In algebra, functions are given names, and the most common are f, g, and h. If the rule that relates the output and input is given, it is shown using function symbols. The function "add five" is shown as follows using this notation. The symbol $f(x)$ is read as "f of x."

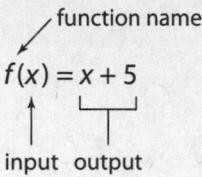

$$f(x) = x + 5$$

input output

Evaluating Functions

In any function rule, the x or other variable acts as a placeholder. To evaluate a function means to substitute a number for this variable. For example, $f(-1)$ (read "f of negative 1") means you should replace each x in the rule with -1.

EXAMPLE 1

If $f(x) = x^2 + 1$, find the value of $f(3)$.

$$f(3) = 3^2 + 1 = 10$$

EXAMPLE 2

If $g(a) = a^2 - 2a + 5$, find the value of $g(-2)$.

$$g(-2) = (-2)^2 - 2(-2) + 5 = 4 + 4 + 5 = 13$$

EXAMPLE 3

What is the value of $h(n) = n + 1$ if $n = 10$?

$$h(10) = 10 + 1 = 11$$

Evaluating Functions

Directions: Evaluate each function as indicated.

For questions 1 and 2, let $f(x) = 5x + 2$ and find the given value.

1. $f(4)$

2. $f(-6)$

For questions 3 to 5, let $g(x) = 2x^2 - x + 3$ and find the given value.

3. $g(0)$

4. $g(-1)$

5. $g(2)$

Answers are on page 517.

Recognizing Functions

In general, any type of mathematical rule can be represented by a table or graph. How can you tell if the rule is a function? Look at a table showing the output y for each input x. With functions, for each input there is only one output *by definition*. If that rule holds in the table, you can say that the rule is a function.

EXAMPLE 4

In the table, y is the value after a rule f is applied to x. Based on this, is f a function of x?

x	−1	2	4	−1
y	0	6	1	2

There is one input that appears twice: $x = -1$. That is acceptable as long as the value of the output y is the same for both. However, in one case when $x = -1$, $y = 0$ and in the other, $y = 2$. Because there are two possible outputs for one input of x, f is not a function of x.

EXAMPLE 5

Does the table represent y as a function of x for the given values of x?

x	5	6	7
y	2	3	4

Here, y is a function of x for these values. Each input has only one possible output.

As you can see in examples 4 and 5, when checking a table, the key is to see if an input does not result in more than one output. When checking a graph, this idea remains the same. However, there is a shortcut that you can use called the **vertical line test**. This rule says that given any graph, if there is anyplace where a vertical line would touch the graph more than once, then the graph does not represent a function. Let's see how this works.

EXAMPLE 6

Determine if the graph represents y as a function of x.

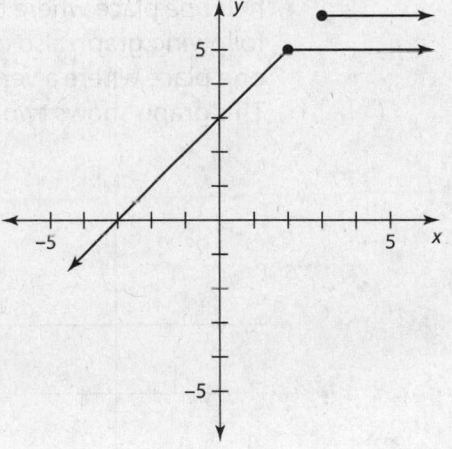

This graph looks like a function until you approach $x = 3$. After that, there are two y outputs for each x input. You can see this by using the vertical line test.

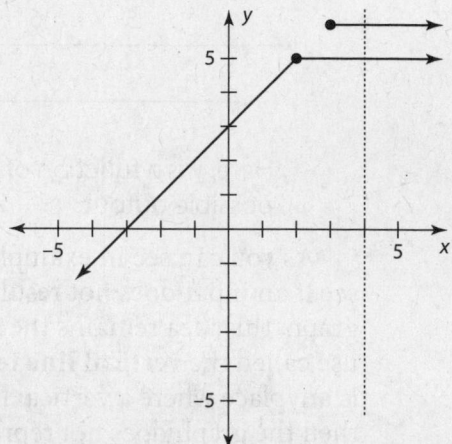

Because the line intersects with two separate lines at the same position, this graph does not show y as a function of x.

Remember that when using the vertical line test, you only need to find *one* place where the line touches two points on the graph. The following graph also does not show y as a function of x, because there is one place where a vertical line passes through two points on the graph. This graph shows two possible outputs for $x = -2$.

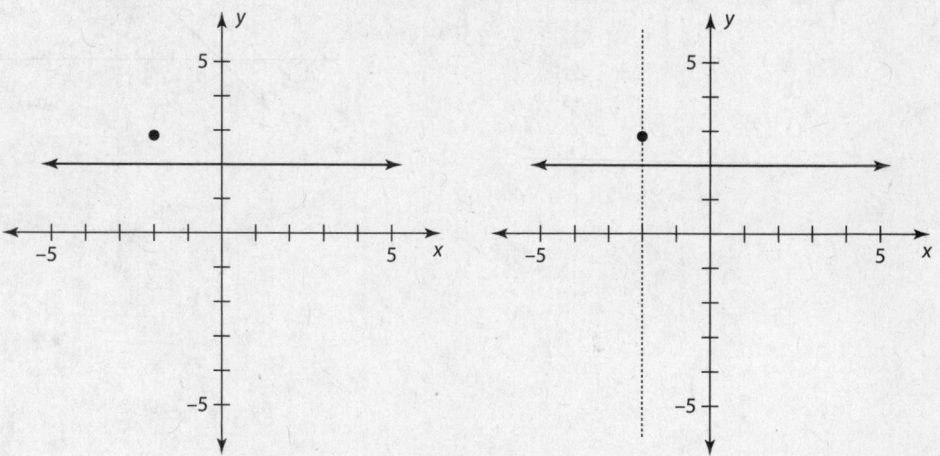

Also, be careful with the symbols used. An open circle means that the function is not defined at that point. Just changing the preceding graph a little bit will make it a function.

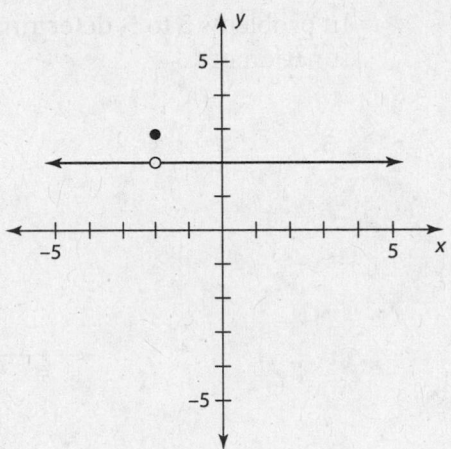

Now that the circle is open, there is only one output for $x = -2$. This is now a graph of a function.

Finally, here are two more examples so you can see that graphs can come in all types. The first graph does show a function because no vertical line could pass through two points. However, the second graph does not show a function. As you can see, it is possible to find places where a vertical line could touch more than one point on the graph.

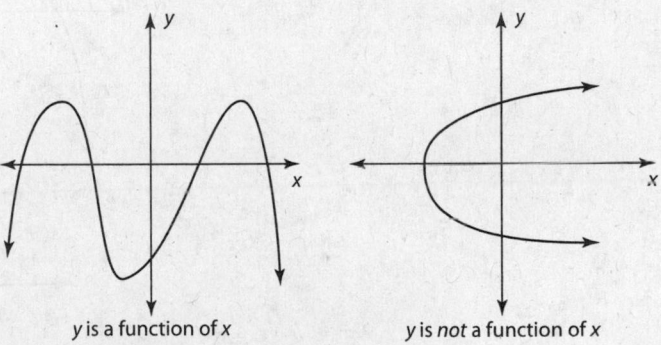

y is a function of *x*   *y* is *not* a function of *x*

EXERCISE 2

Recognizing Functions

Directions: In problems 1 and 2, determine whether the table represents *y* as a function of *x* for the given values.

1.

x	1	0	2
y	3	4	3

2.

x	1	0	0
y	2	-5	6

In problems 3 to 5, determine whether the given graph represents *y* as a function of *x*.

3.

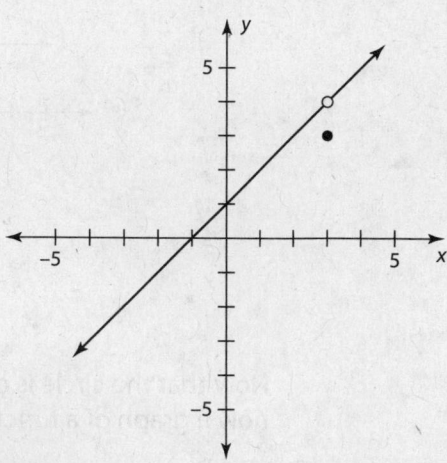

4.

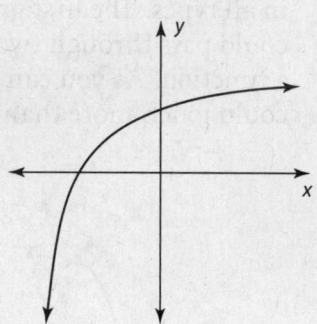

5.

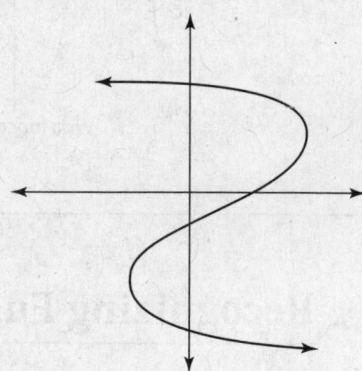

Answers are on page 517.

Properties of Functions

Whether represented by a table, graph, or rule, many functions share similar properties. Because they are so common, it is important to be able to identify and compare these properties given a table or graph.

Recall that for any graph, the y intercept is the point where the graph crosses the y-axis and the x intercept is the point where the graph crosses the x-axis. For a function, there can be either zero or one y intercept and zero or many x intercepts.

EXAMPLE 7

Identify any x intercepts in the graph of a function $f(x)$.

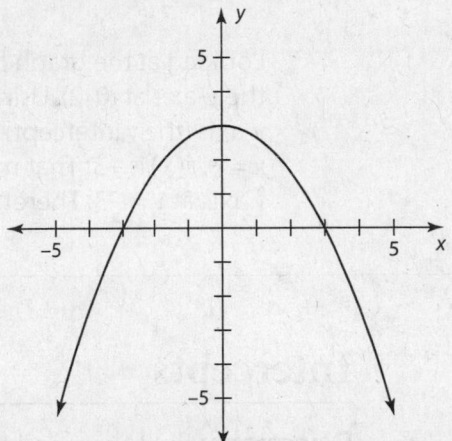

The graph passes through the x axis at $x = -3$ and $x = 3$. Therefore, its x intercepts are $(-3, 0)$ and $(3, 0)$.

EXAMPLE 8

Following is a table of values for a function f and a graph for another function g. Based on this information, which function crosses the y-axis at the highest point?

Table for f

x	0	5	10
$f(x)$	-3	0	3

Graph for *g*:

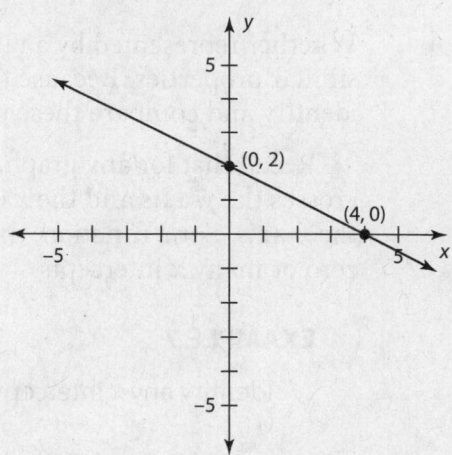

Looking at the graph for *g*, you can quickly see that the graph crosses the *y*-axis at (0, 2). Using a table, the point where the graph crosses the *y*-axis (the *y* intercept) is the *y* value when *x* = 0. From the table, when *x* = 0, *f*(*x*) is −3. That means if you were to graph *f*(*x*), it would cross the *y* axis at *y* = −3. Therefore, *g* crosses the axis at a higher point.

EXERCISE 3

Intercepts

Directions: Find the *x* and *y* intercepts as indicated.

For questions 1 to 3, use the tables to find the *x* and *y* intercepts of the given function.

1.
x	2	1	0
f(*x*)	0	4	6

2.
x	−1	0	2	5	10
g(*x*)	0	4	6	0	0

3.
x	−3	0	2
h(*x*)	5	0	−6

4.

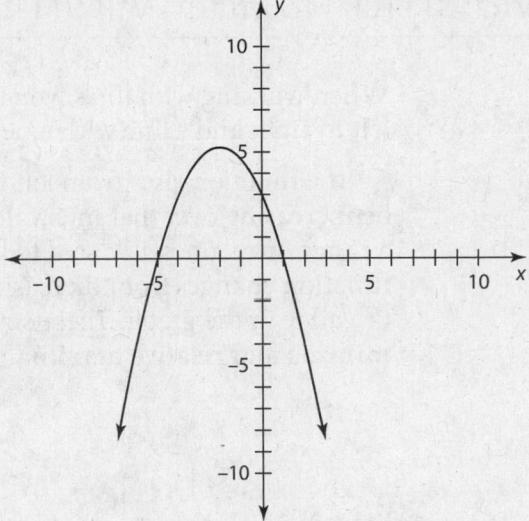

5.

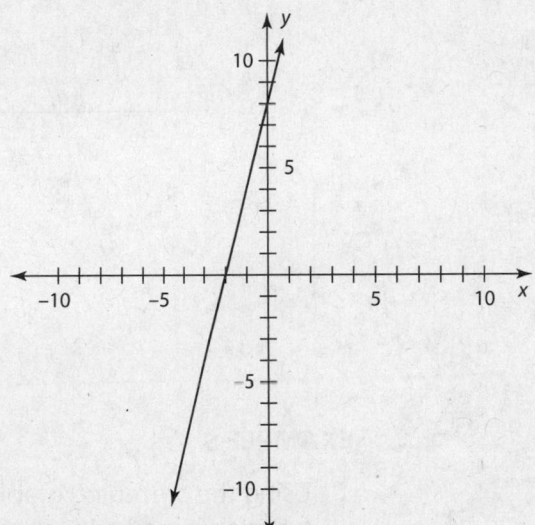

Answers are on page 517.

Relative Maximums and Minimums

When working with lines, you saw that a line with a positive slope rises from left to right and a line with a negative slope falls from left to right.

If a function rises from left to right for a range of x values, it is said to be increasing over that interval. If the function falls from left to right for a range of x values, it is said to be decreasing over that interval. When a function changes from increasing to decreasing, there is often a small peak or valley in the graph. These small peaks and valleys represent **relative minima** and **relative maxima**.

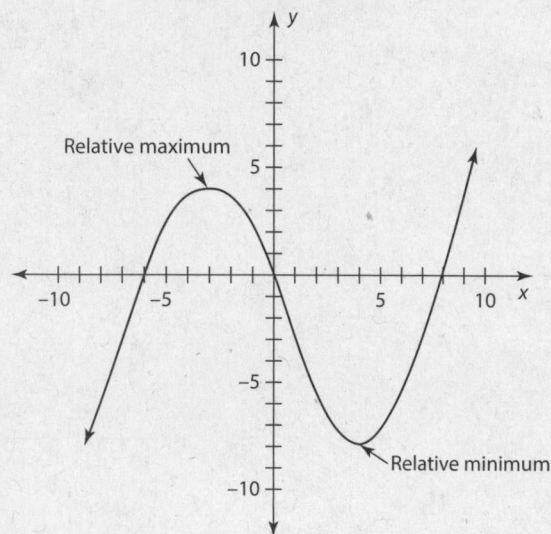

EXAMPLE 9

Using the preceding graph, determine over what values of x the function is increasing or decreasing. Also determine at what x values the function reaches any relative minima or maxima.

In the preceding graph, the function is increasing for all x values up to -3. Then at $x = -3$, it has a relative maximum. After this, the function is decreasing until it reaches $x = 4$. There it has a relative minimum. After this, it increases for all x values greater than 4.

To state the final answer more formally:

The function is increasing for x values less than -3 or greater than 4.

The function is decreasing for x values between -3 and 4.

The function reaches a relative maximum at $x = -3$.

The function reaches a relative minimum at $x = 4$.

As you can see, relative maxima are points where the graph is higher than nearby points, while relative minima are points where the graph is lower than nearby points. Some graphs may not have any relative maxima or minima. For example, the graph of a line does not have either, because it is always increasing or always decreasing.

Positive and Negative Values

Using a graph, it is possible to determine when a function is positive ($f(x) > 0$) or negative ($f(x) < 0$) by paying close attention to the x-axis. Whenever a graph is above the x-axis, it is said to be positive, and whenever it is below the x-axis it is said to be negative.

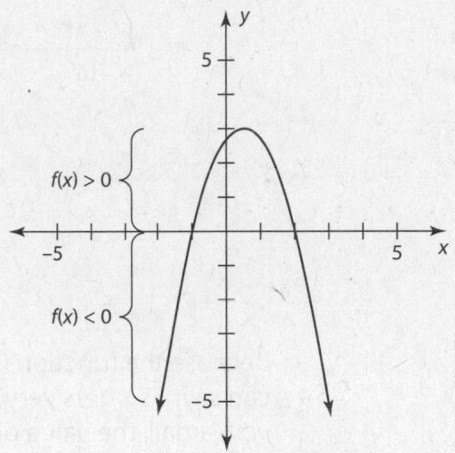

EXAMPLE 10

Determine what values of x make the function above positive and negative.

The function is above the x-axis between $x = -1$ and $x = 2$. Therefore, you can say that the function is positive whenever x is between -1 and 2. Because before $x = -1$ the graph is below the x-axis, you can say that for values smaller than $x = -1$ the function is negative. The same is true for values greater than (to the right of) $x = 2$.

End Behavior and Periodic Functions

Whether a function rises or falls at the far end of a graph is called its **end behavior**. This corresponds to what happens as x gets very small (left-hand side of the graph) or what happens as x gets very large (right-hand side of the graph).

If a graph . . .	Then the function value . . .
falls at the right	gets smaller as x gets very large
rises at the right	gets larger as x gets very large
falls at the left	gets smaller as x gets very small
rises at the left	gets larger as x gets very small

EXAMPLE 11

Based on the graph of $f(x)$, describe what happens to the value of $f(x)$ as x gets very large or very small.

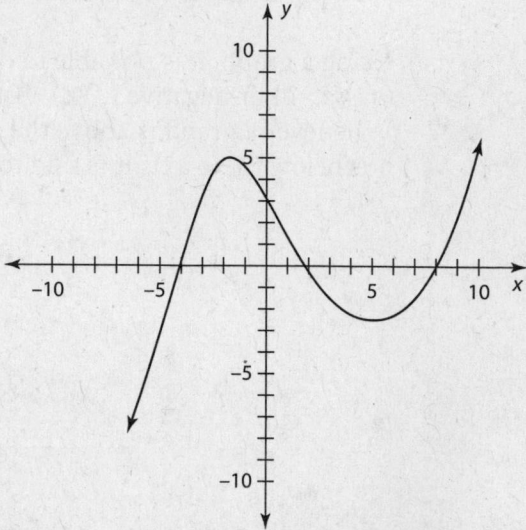

Because the function is falling on the left and rising on the right, you can say: As x gets very large, the value of $f(x)$ also gets large. As x gets very small, the value of $f(x)$ gets very small.

Instead of rising or falling on the ends, some functions have a pattern that repeats over a given range. These functions are called **periodic functions**. How often the pattern repeats is called the function's **period**. For example, the function shown in the following graph is periodic with a period of 2 because its pattern repeats every 2 units.

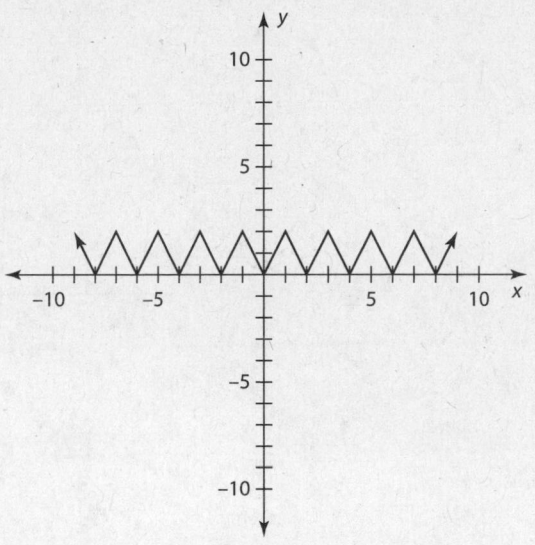

EXAMPLE 12

If the function $g(x)$ is periodic, what is the function's period?

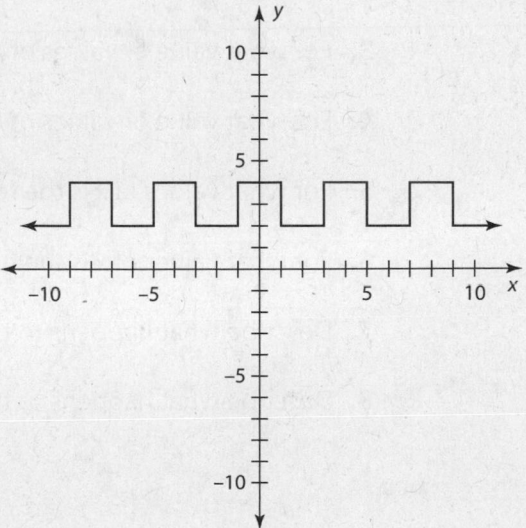

Because the pattern repeats every 4 units, the period of the function is 4.

Other Properties of Functions

Directions: For questions 1 to 8, use the following graph of a function $f(x)$.

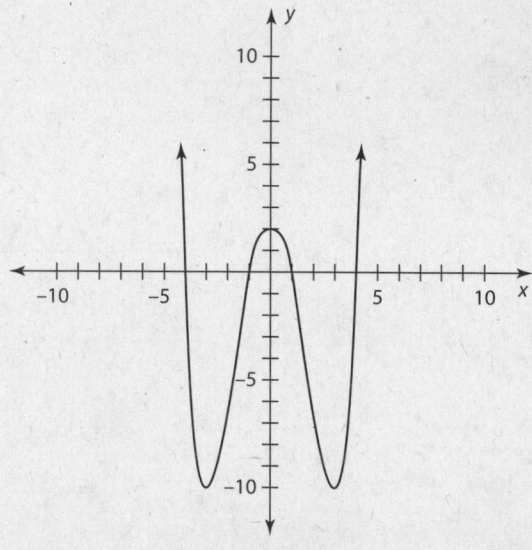

1. For what values of x is the function positive?

2. For what values of x is the function negative?

3. For what value or values of x does the function reach a relative minimum?

4. For what value or values of x does the function reach a relative maximum?

5. For what values of x is the function increasing?

6. For what values of x is the function decreasing?

7. Describe what happens to the value of $f(x)$ as x gets very large.

8. Describe what happens to the value of $f(x)$ as x gets very small.

For questions 9 and 10, the given graphs show periodic functions.
Determine the period of the function from the graph.

9.

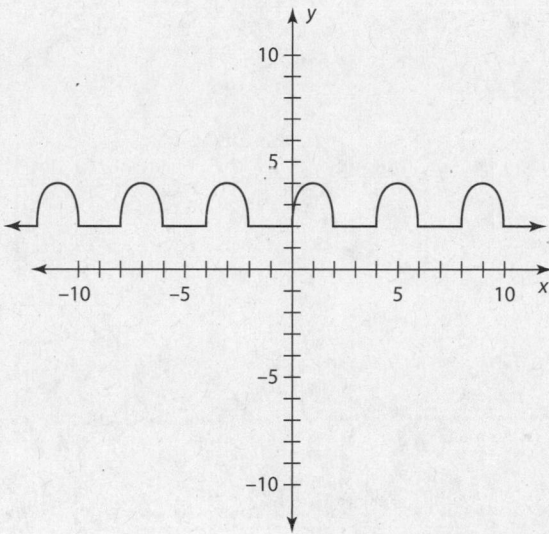

10.

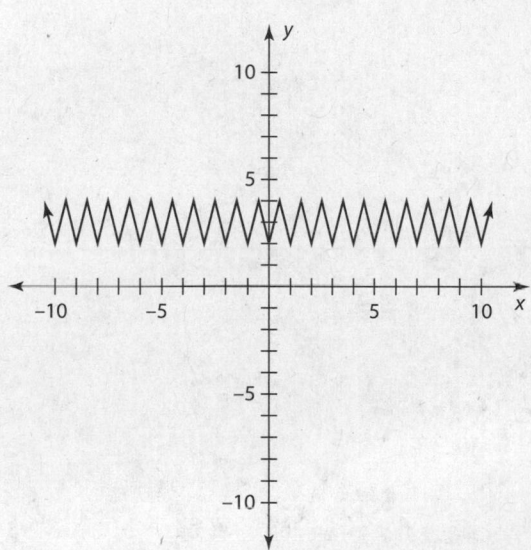

Answers are on page 517.

CHAPTER 14

Geometry

Area, perimeter, and other geometric topics show up in many questions on the GED test. Some geometric formulas you will need to memorize; other formulas will be given to you. Even if you are given a formula, it is important to understand the basic concepts so that you can apply the formula correctly.

Area and perimeter are concepts associated with 2-dimensional figures. **Area** is measured in square units and tells how much space a figure takes up. **Perimeter** is measured in regular units and tells the distance around an object. As you work on area and perimeter, you may find the following facts about specific figures useful.

Polygons

A **polygon** is any closed figure with three or more straight sides. Common polygons are squares, rectangles, and triangles. To find the perimeter of a polygon, you add the lengths of all of its sides.

- **Rectangles** are 4-sided polygons in which opposite sides have the same measure.

- **Squares** are 4-sided polygons in which all sides have the same measure.

- **Triangles** are 3-sided polygons in which the sides can have the same measure or different measures.

EXAMPLE 1

What is the perimeter of the rectangle pictured?

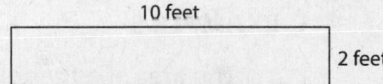

Even though you are given only two sides, you know that in a rectangle, opposite sides have the same measure. Therefore the perimeter is 10 + 2 + 10 + 2 = 24 feet.

EXAMPLE 2

A square has sides that each measure 10 meters. What is the perimeter of this square?

Because a square has four sides of the same length, the perimeter is 10 + 10 + 10 + 10 = 40 meters.

To find the area, there are different formulas for different kinds of polygons. Memorize the following formulas because they will not be given to you on the GED® test.

Shape	Area Formula
Square	$A = \text{length}^2$
Rectangle	$A = \text{length} \times \text{width}$
Triangle	$A = \frac{1}{2}(\text{base})(\text{height})$

EXAMPLE 3

Find the area of the triangle pictured. Round your answer to the nearest tenth.

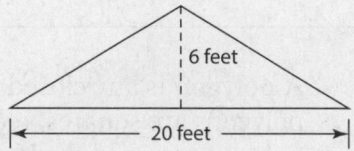

The height of the triangle is 6 feet and the length of the base is 20 feet. Therefore the area is

$$\frac{1}{2}(6)(20) = 60 \text{ square feet.}$$

EXAMPLE 4

Adam has a table with a rectangular top that measures 3 feet by 2 feet. In square feet, what is the area of the table top?

Using the formula, the area is $3 \times 2 = 6$ square feet.

EXAMPLE 5

The area of a triangle is 20 square meters. If the length of its base is 10 meters, what is the height of the triangle?

A question like this one requires you to combine your algebra and geometry skills. Plugging the given information into the area formula, $20 = \frac{1}{2}(10)h$ where h is the height. Now you can use algebra to find h.

Simplify: $20 = 5h$

Undo the multiplication: $\dfrac{20}{5} = \dfrac{5h}{5}$

$h = 4$

The height of the triangle is 4 meters.

EXERCISE 1

Area and Perimeter of Polygons

1. What is the perimeter of a triangle with sides of length 9 feet, 12 feet, and 15 feet?

2. A square has sides of length 8 inches. What is the area of this square? What is its perimeter?

3. Find the area and perimeter of the rectangle pictured.

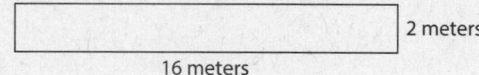

2 meters

16 meters

4. If the area of the rectangle pictured below is 40 square feet, then what is the value of *x*?

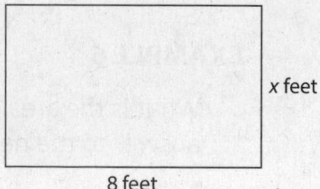

x feet

8 feet

5. The sides of a triangle all have equal length. If the perimeter of this triangle is 36 feet, what is the length of a single side?

Answers are on page 517.

Circles

A **circle** is a figure in which all points on the edge of the circle are the same distance from the central point (called the **origin**).

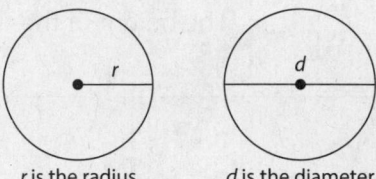

r is the radius   d is the diameter

The **diameter** of a circle is the straight-line distance all the way across the circle passing through the center. The diameter is generally indicated by the letter d. The **radius** of a circle is the straight-line distance from the center of the circle to any point on its edge. The radius is generally indicated by the letter r. The diameter is always twice the length of the radius. Or to put it another way, the radius is always half the length of the diameter. Finally, the distance around the outside of a circle is called its **circumference**. The circumference is generally indicated by the letter C.

Memorize the following formulas for circles:

Area: $A = \pi r^2$

Circumference: $C = 2\pi r$

The Greek letter π (pi) represents a constant that is approximately equal to 3.14. When working with π, you can either use this approximation or use the π button on your calculator for a more exact answer.

EXAMPLE 6

What is the area of a circle with a diameter of 6 meters? Round your answer to the nearest tenth.

If the diameter is 6 meters, then the radius is $6 \div 2 = 3$ meters. Using the area formula, the area is

$$A = \pi(3)^2 = 9\pi = 28.3 \text{ square meters.}$$

EXAMPLE 7

A circular garden with a radius of 10 feet will be completely enclosed with a wire fence. How many feet of fencing will this project require? Round your answer to the nearest tenth.

The distance completely around the circular garden is the circumference. Using the formula, the circumference is

$$C = 2\pi(10) = 20\pi = 62.8.$$

Therefore the project will require 62.8 feet of fencing.

EXAMPLE 8

If the area of a circle is 16π square feet, then what is its diameter?

Using the area formula and the given values, $16\pi = \pi r^2$. Solving for r:

Undo the multiplication: $\dfrac{16\pi}{\pi} = \dfrac{\pi r^2}{\pi}$

$$16 = r^2$$

Using the square root rule: $r = \sqrt{16}, -\sqrt{16}$

$$r = 4, -4$$

The radius can never be negative, so it must be 4 feet. However, the question asks for the diameter. The diameter is $4 \times 2 = 8$ feet.

EXERCISE 2

Circles

Directions: Use the following figure to answer questions 1 and 2.

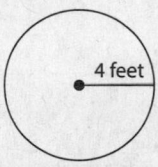

1. To the nearest tenth, what is the area of the given circle?

2. To the nearest tenth, what is the circumference of the given circle?

3. If the diameter of a circle is 40 meters, what is its circumference? Round your answer to the nearest tenth.

4. The area of a circular region is approximately 100 square feet. To the nearest tenth, what is the radius of this circle?

5. If the circumference of a circle is approximately 30π inches, what is the diameter of the circle? Round your answer to the nearest tenth.

Answers are on page 518.

3-Dimensional Objects

Volume and surface area are measures that apply to 3-dimensional figures. The **volume** represents how much space is taken up by an object. The **surface area** is the total area of the outside surfaces of the object. On the GED® test, you will be given all of the formulas you need to find surface area or volume.

Cylinder	Surface area	$SA = 2\pi r^2 + 2\pi rh$, where r is the radius of the base and h is the height.
	Volume	$V = \pi r^2 h$, where r is the radius of the base and h is the height.
Cone	Surface area	$SA = \pi rs + \pi r^2$, where r is the radius of the base and s is the measure along a side from the tip of the cone to the base.
	Volume	$V = \frac{1}{3}\pi r^2 h$, where r is the radius of the base and h is the height.
Sphere	Surface area	$SA = 4\pi r^2$, where r is the radius of the sphere.
	Volume	$V = \frac{4}{3}\pi r^3$, where r is the radius of the sphere.
Rectangular prism	Surface area	$SA = 2ab + 2bc + 2ac$, where a, b, and c are the length, width, and height.
	Volume	$V = lwh$
Right prism	Surface area	$SA = 2B + Ph$, where B is the area of a base, P is the perimeter of the base, and h is the height.
	Volume	$V = Bh$, where B is the area of the base and h is the height.
Pyramid	Surface area	$SA = \frac{1}{2}Ps + B$, where P is the perimeter of the base, s is the slant height, and B is the area of the base.
	Volume	$V = \frac{1}{3}Bh$, where B is the area of the base and h is the height.

Practice working with these formulas. You will find that the process is not much different from working with area and perimeter formulas for 2-dimensional objects. Following are the common 3-dimensional figures you will work with.

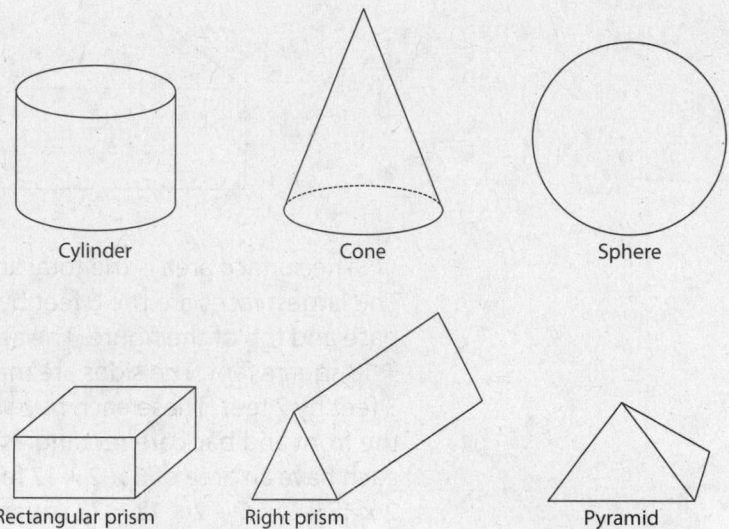

Cylinder   Cone   Sphere

Rectangular prism   Right prism   Pyramid

EXAMPLE 9

The following cylindrical container is designed to hold water. To the nearest tenth, how many cubic feet of water can the container store?

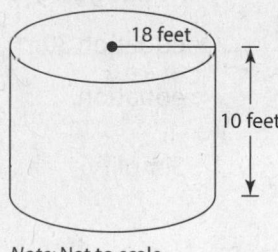

18 feet

10 feet

Note: Not to scale.

The amount the container can hold is the volume of the cylinder. Using the volume formula,

$$V = \pi r^2 h = \pi (18)^2 (10) = \pi (3240) = 10{,}178.8.$$

The container can store up 10,178.8 cubic feet of water.

EXAMPLE 10

The following figure represents a rectangular box that will be completely painted. What is the surface area that the paint will cover?

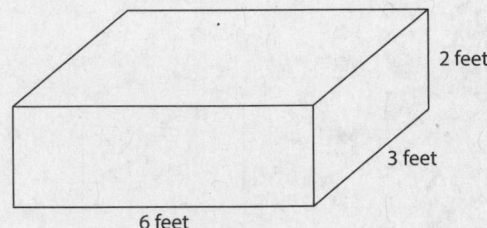

The surface area is the total area of each of the faces of the region. The largest faces are the 6 feet by 3 feet rectangles that make up the base and top of the figure. The area of each of these rectangles is $6 \times 3 = 18$ square feet. The sides are made up of two rectangles measuring 3 feet by 2 feet. These each have an area of $3 \times 2 = 6$ square feet. Finally, the front and back are rectangles that measure 6 feet by 2 feet and thus each have an area of $6 \times 2 = 12$ feet. Therefore the total surface area is $2 \times 18 + 2 \times 6 + 2 \times 12 = 72$ square feet.

EXAMPLE 11

If the volume of a cone is 30π cubic meters and its radius is 3 meters, what is its height?

Plugging the known values into the volume formula yields the equation $30\pi = \frac{1}{3}\pi(3)^2 h$, where h is the height. To find h, solve this equation.

Simplify:

$$30\pi = \frac{1}{3}\pi 9h$$

$$30\pi = 3\pi h$$

Undo the multiplication: $\dfrac{30\pi}{3\pi} = \dfrac{3\pi h}{3\pi}$

$$10 = h$$

The height is 10 meters.

EXERCISE 3

Volume and Surface Area of 3-Dimensional Objects

Directions: Using the formulas for volume and surface area, find the indicated values.

1. The radius of a sphere is 10 meters. What is the volume of this sphere, to the nearest tenth?

2. The volume of the rectangular container pictured is 180 cubic feet. What is the value of x?

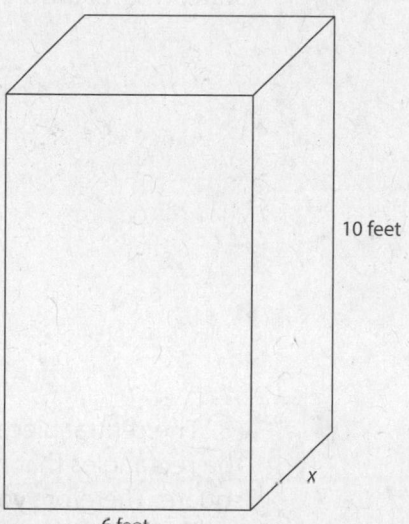

3. If the base of the following pyramid is a square, what is the volume of the pyramid? Round your answer to the nearest tenth.

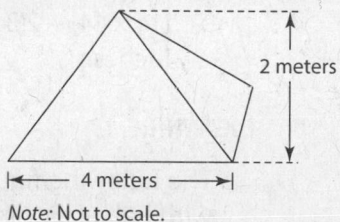

Note: Not to scale.

4. A rectangular locker measuring 6 feet tall, 2 feet deep, and 2 feet wide is about $\frac{1}{2}$ full of books and other materials. In cubic feet, how much space is still available in the locker?

5. A city uses two large cylindrical containers to store salt for the winter. If both containers measure 30 feet tall with diameters of 12 feet, then in cubic feet, what is the total amount of salt the city can store? Round your answer to the nearest tenth.

Answers are on page 518.

Complex Figures

Complex, or composite, figures are 2-dimensional or 3-dimensional objects that are created by combining common objects. Calculating different types of measures for these figures requires you to mentally break up the figure into its component parts.

EXAMPLE 12

The figure represents the shape of a cardboard piece that will be folded along the dashed lines to create a stabilizer inside of a storage container. The base is a square with sides of length 14 inches while the parts that will be folded up are rectangular with the given measures. In its current state, what is the area of this cardboard piece?

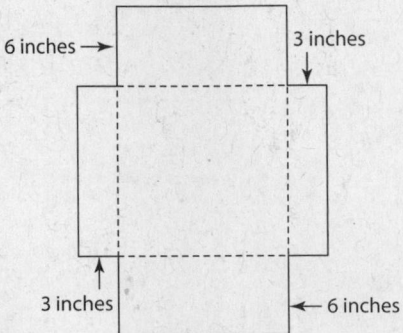

The central piece is the square that has sides of length 14. Each of the rectangles that make up the rest of the figure shares a side with this square. Therefore you can say that the piece is made up of one 14 inch × 14 inch square, two 3 inch × 14 inch rectangles, and two 6 inch × 14 inch rectangles.

The area is therefore

$(14 \times 14) + 2(3 \times 14) + 2(6 \times 14) = 196 + 2(42) + 2(84) = 448$ square inches.

EXAMPLE 13

The following figure was created by combining a rectangular prism with half of a cylinder that is the same length as the prism. What is the volume of this composite figure? Round your answer to the nearest cubic foot.

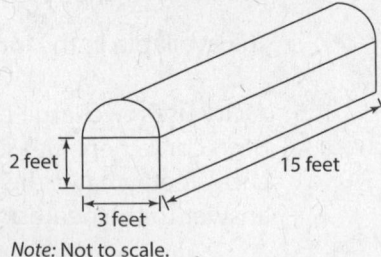

Note: Not to scale.

To find the total volume, break up the object into its component parts. The first is a rectangular $2 \times 3 \times 15$ foot prism. This prism has a volume of $2 \times 3 \times 15 = 90$ cubic feet.

The top part is half of a cylinder. The cylinder matches up with the prism and from that you can see that the diameter is 3 feet. This means that the radius is 1.5 feet. Now you need to find the volume of the cylinder and divide it by 2 because this is just half of the cylinder.

$$V = \pi(1.5)^2(15) = 33.75\pi = 106.03 \text{ and half is } \frac{1}{2} \times 106.03 = 53$$

Therefore the total volume is $90 + 53 = 143$ cubic feet.

EXERCISE 4

Complex Figures

Directions: The following figure represents plans for dividing up a large plot of land. The two regions that will be created are rectangular. Use this information and the figure to answer questions 1 to 3.

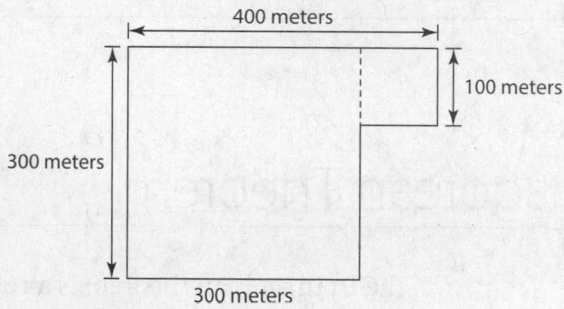

1. The solid line in the figure represents fencing that completely surrounds the property. How many meters of fencing are represented in the figure?

2. What is the total area of the property?

3. When the property is divided up, a new section of fencing will be placed along the dotted line. How many more feet of fencing will this require?

The following figure represents a plastic fastener composed of two solid rectangular pieces. The figure is not drawn to scale. Use this information to answer questions 4 and 5.

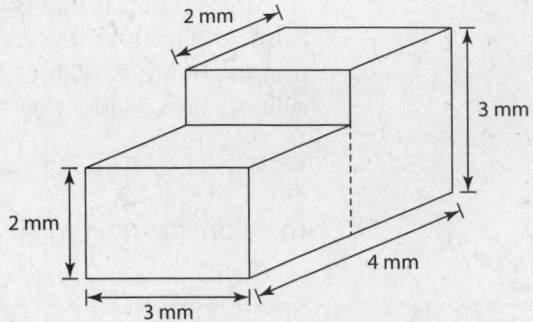

4. Given that the object is solid, how many cubic millimeters of plastic does it contain?

5. If the outside of the object is to be covered in a protective coating, how many square millimeters will need to be covered?

Answers are on page 518.

The Pythagorean Theorem

The Pythagorean theorem is a rule that applies to a type of triangles called right triangles. **Right triangles** are triangles that include a right angle (two sides that are perpendicular and meet to form a perfect corner). The longest side of any right triangle is called its **hypotenuse** (usually labeled *c*) and the two other sides are called **legs** (usually labeled *a* and *b*).

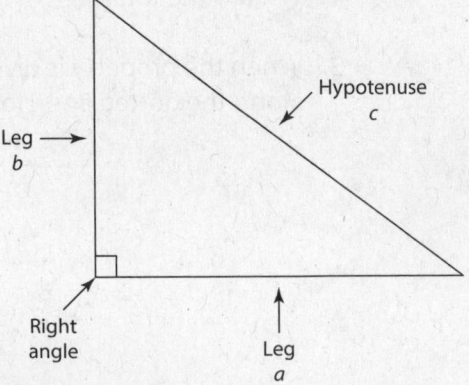

The Pythagorean theorem is a formula that relates the sides and the hypotenuse:

$$a^2 + b^2 = c^2$$

EXAMPLE 14

Given the triangle shown, what is the value of x?

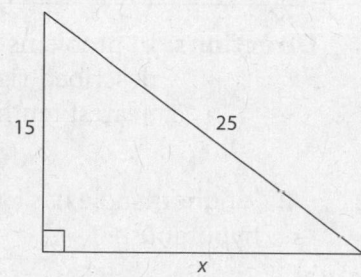

Using the Pythagorean theorem with legs a and b and hypotenuse c, you can write that $15^2 + x^2 = 25^2$. Solving this equation for x gives you the final answer.

Simplify: $225 + x^2 = 625$

Undo the subtraction: $x^2 = 400$

Square root rule: $x = \sqrt{400} = 20$

(You need only the positive part of the square root rule when working with triangles because side lengths cannot be negative.)

EXAMPLE 15

As shown in the figure, a computer monitor measures 12 inches wide by 6 inches high. To the nearest tenth of an inch, what is the diagonal measure of the monitor as indicated by the dashed line?

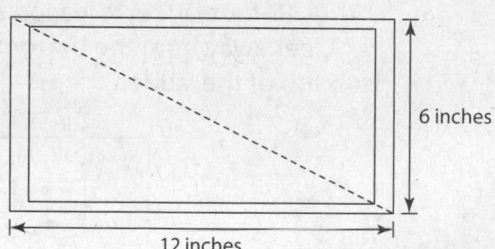

Although the monitor is a rectangle, the two halves created by the diagonal are right triangles with legs of 12 inches and 6 inches. To find the diagonal, which is the hypotenuse, use the Pythagorean theorem.

Pythagorean Theorem: $6^2 + 12^2 = c^2$

Simplify: $180 = c^2$

Square root rule: $c = \sqrt{180} = 13.4$

The diagonal measures about 13.4 inches.

As you work with the Pythagorean theorem, make sure you know whether you are trying to find the length of a leg or the hypotenuse. Also, watch for areas where right triangles are not obviously present, as in example 15.

EXERCISE 5

The Pythagorean Theorem

Directions: In problems 1 and 2, find the length of the missing side of the described right triangle. If necessary, round your answers to the nearest tenth.

1. A right triangle has legs of measure 10 and 15. What is the measure of its hypotenuse?

2. The leg of a right triangle has a length of 3 inches while the hypotenuse has a length of 5 inches. What is the length of the remaining leg?

3. What is the value of x in the figure?

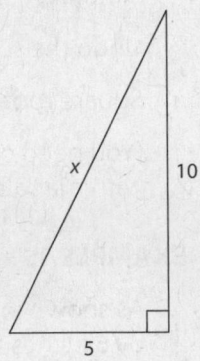

4. A 15-foot ladder is leaned against a building. The base of the ladder is 12 feet away from the bottom of the building. How far from the ground is the top of the ladder?

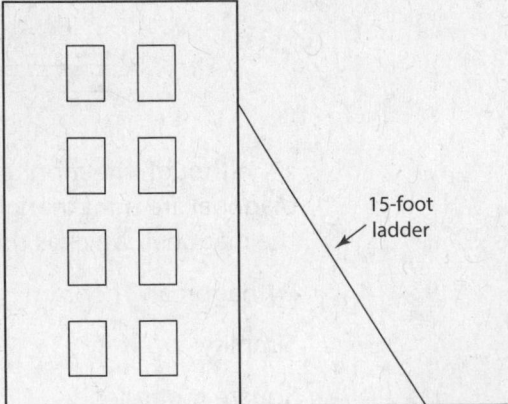

5. A right triangle has a hypotenuse measuring 10 feet and one leg measuring 6 feet. What is the perimeter of this triangle?

Answers are on page 518.

Mathematical Reasoning

Chapter 1 Whole Numbers and Operations

Exercise 1: Operations with Whole Numbers

1. 1164
2. 284
3. 1009
4. 121 remainder 5
5. 3192
6. 4298
7. 13
8. 179,602
9. 10,501
10. 127 remainder 4
11. 786
12. 287
13. 2630
14. 405
15. 469
16. 1125
17. 4018
18. 3794
19. 738 remainder 1
20. 44,800

Exercise 2: Word Problems

1. **$175** He will save $35 for each of 5 paychecks: $5 \times 35 = 175$.

2. **$550** After the $300 is subtracted for the sister who is a college student, the two brothers must pay $1,100: $1,100 \div 2 = 550.

3. **$84,805** $45,690 + 39,115 = 84,805$

4. **$1,013** $1250 - 142 = 1108$ and $1108 - 95 = 1013$

5. **$1,240** The base cost of towing is $200. Each day the car is stored, $40 is charged. $26 \times 40 + 200 = 1240$.

Chapter 2 Exponents, Roots, and Number Properties

Exercise 1: Exponents

1. 9
2. 1
3. 12
4. 343
5. 4
6. 1
7. $\dfrac{1}{64}$

8. $\dfrac{1}{6}$

9. $\dfrac{1}{64}$

10. 1

Exercise 2: Rules of Exponents

1. D

2. B

3. C

4. D

5. C

6. D

7. C

8. C

9. D

10. D

Exercise 3: Square Roots and Cube Roots

1. $4\sqrt{2}$

2. $3\sqrt{2}$

3. $2\sqrt{10}$

4. $10\sqrt{3}$

5. $2\sqrt{6}$

6. $2\sqrt[3]{2}$

7. $4\sqrt[3]{2}$

8. $2\sqrt[3]{3}$

9. $5\sqrt[3]{3}$

10. $2\sqrt[3]{100}$

Exercise 4: Order of Operations

1. **3** $\quad 8\div 2^2 +1 = 8\div 4+1 = 2+1 = 3$

2. **8** $\quad \dfrac{18-2}{2} = \dfrac{16}{2} = 8$

3. **31** $\quad 4+2(8+6)-1 = 4+2(14)-1 = 4+28-1 = 31$

4. **3** $\quad 3(6-5)^3 = 3(1)^3 = 3(1) = 3$

5. **10** $\quad 4\times 3-2 = 12-2 = 10$

6. **22** $\quad 3-1+2^2\times 5 = 3-1+4\times 5 = 3-1+20 = 22$

7. **64** $\quad (8+1-5)^3 = (4)^3 = 64$

8. **2** $\quad (2+4)\div 2-1 = 6\div 2-1 = 3-1 = 2$

9. **26** $\quad 5^2 + \dfrac{6-4}{2} = 25 + \dfrac{6-4}{2} = 25 + \dfrac{2}{2} = 25+1 = 26$

10. **36** $\quad 16+4(3+2) = 16+4(5) = 16+20 = 36$

Chapter 3 Decimal Numbers and Operations

Exercise 1: Comparing Decimals

1. $25.099 < 25.915$

2. $0.108 > 0.0108$

3. $0.00054 < 0.0019$

4. $8.6 > 8.09$

5. $0.40 = 0.4$

6. $0.1053 > 0.0153$

7. $2.00501 < 2.51$

8. $0.133 < 1.33$

9. $1.69401 > 1.694$

10. $14.9 < 14.988$

Exercise 2: Scientific Notation

1. 2.5×10^{-3}
2. 7.836×10^{9}
3. 1.0×10^{-6}
4. 6.05×10^{-1}
5. 3.6×10^{8}
6. 0.0000000024
7. 130,000,000
8. 0.0408
9. 0.0009
10. 560,000

Exercise 3: Operations with Decimals

1. 30.1336
2. 16.3121
3. 3.0331
4. 8.121
5. 223.4
6. 19.85
7. 1.0216
8. 12.7
9. 80.7
10. 0.455
11. 37.5
12. 7.808
13. 31.45
14. 24.0119
15. 130.0026
16. 50
17. 42.8
18. 0.125
19. 1.80 (calculator: 1.798974359)
20. 5.022

Chapter 4 Fractions and Operations

Exercise 1: Equivalent Fractions

1. $\dfrac{25}{45}$ $\quad \dfrac{5 \times 5}{9 \times 5} = \dfrac{25}{45}$

2. $\dfrac{3}{31}$ $\quad \dfrac{1 \times 3}{7 \times 3} = \dfrac{3}{21}$

3. 12 $\quad \dfrac{1 \times 12}{2 \times 12} = \dfrac{12}{24}$

4. 9 $\quad \dfrac{18 \div 2}{60 \div 2} = \dfrac{9}{30}$

5. 9 $\quad \dfrac{35 \div 5}{45 \div 5} = \dfrac{7}{9}$

6. $\dfrac{11}{21}$ $\quad \dfrac{22 \div 2}{42 \div 2} = \dfrac{11}{21}$

7. $\dfrac{1}{5}$ $\quad \dfrac{10 \div 10}{50 \div 10} = \dfrac{1}{5}$

8. $\dfrac{3}{4}$ $\quad \dfrac{12 \div 4}{16 \div 4} = \dfrac{3}{4}$

9. $\dfrac{1}{30}$ $\quad \dfrac{3 \div 3}{90 \div 3} = \dfrac{1}{30}$

10. $\dfrac{7}{24}$ $\quad \dfrac{14 \div 2}{48 \div 2} = \dfrac{7}{24}$

ANSWERS AND EXPLANATIONS

Exercise 2: Converting Between Fractions and Decimals

1. 0.75
2. 0.40
3. 0.25
4. 0.21
5. 0.47
6. $\dfrac{7}{250}$
7. $\dfrac{9}{40}$
8. $\dfrac{4}{25}$
9. $\dfrac{31}{100}$
10. $\dfrac{9}{10}$

Exercise 3: Mixed Numbers

1. $3\dfrac{4}{5}$
2. $10\dfrac{1}{2}$
3. $4\dfrac{15}{20}=4\dfrac{3}{4}$
4. $4\dfrac{4}{6}=4\dfrac{2}{3}$
5. $5\dfrac{5}{8}$
6. $\dfrac{17}{8}$
7. $\dfrac{48}{5}$
8. $\dfrac{65}{16}$

9. $\dfrac{40}{7}$
10. $\dfrac{50}{3}$

Exercise 4: Comparing Fractions

1. $\dfrac{2}{3}>\dfrac{1}{9}$
2. $\dfrac{7}{15}<\dfrac{3}{5}$
3. $\dfrac{9}{20}>\dfrac{1}{6}$
4. $\dfrac{5}{18}<\dfrac{4}{9}$
5. $\dfrac{1}{2}>\dfrac{1}{3}$
6. $0.22<\dfrac{1}{3}$
7. $\dfrac{1}{2}>0.18$
8. $0.578>\dfrac{51}{100}$
9. $0.8821<\dfrac{15}{17}$
10. $\dfrac{5}{13}<0.42$

Exercise 5: Adding and Subtracting Fractions

1. $\dfrac{3}{5}$
2. $\dfrac{11}{13}$
3. $\dfrac{23}{18}$ $\dfrac{4}{9}+\dfrac{5}{6}=\dfrac{4\times2}{9\times2}+\dfrac{5\times3}{6\times3}=\dfrac{8}{18}+\dfrac{15}{18}=\dfrac{23}{18}$
4. $\dfrac{1}{3}$ $\dfrac{1}{12}+\dfrac{1}{4}=\dfrac{1}{12}+\dfrac{1\times3}{4\times3}=\dfrac{1}{12}+\dfrac{3}{12}=\dfrac{4\div4}{12\div4}=\dfrac{1}{3}$

5. $\dfrac{11}{21}$ $\dfrac{5}{21}+\dfrac{2}{7}=\dfrac{5}{21}+\dfrac{2\times3}{7\times3}=\dfrac{5}{21}+\dfrac{6}{21}=\dfrac{11}{21}$

6. $\dfrac{1}{2}$

7. $\dfrac{1}{2}$

8. $\dfrac{5}{14}$ $\dfrac{9}{14}-\dfrac{2}{7}=\dfrac{9}{14}-\dfrac{2\times2}{7\times2}=\dfrac{9}{14}-\dfrac{4}{14}=\dfrac{5}{14}$

9. $\dfrac{3}{25}$ $\dfrac{8}{25}-\dfrac{1}{5}=\dfrac{8}{25}-\dfrac{1\times5}{5\times5}=\dfrac{8}{25}-\dfrac{5}{25}=\dfrac{3}{25}$

10. $\dfrac{1}{12}$ $\dfrac{1}{3}-\dfrac{1}{4}=\dfrac{1\times4}{3\times4}-\dfrac{1\times3}{4\times3}=\dfrac{4}{12}-\dfrac{3}{12}=\dfrac{1}{12}$

Exercise 6: Multiplying and Dividing Fractions

1. $\dfrac{3}{5}$ $\dfrac{4}{5}\times\dfrac{3}{4}=\dfrac{1}{5}\times\dfrac{3}{1}=\dfrac{3}{5}$

2. $\dfrac{1}{90}$ $\dfrac{1}{9}\times\dfrac{1}{10}=\dfrac{1}{90}$

3. $\dfrac{2}{63}$ $\dfrac{2}{7}\times\dfrac{2}{18}=\dfrac{1}{7}\times\dfrac{2}{9}=\dfrac{2}{63}$

4. $\dfrac{2}{9}$ $\dfrac{2}{3}\times\dfrac{1}{3}=\dfrac{2}{9}$

5. $\dfrac{1}{20}$ $\dfrac{2}{15}\times\dfrac{3}{8}=\dfrac{1}{5}\times\dfrac{1}{4}=\dfrac{1}{20}$

6. $\dfrac{8}{33}$ $\dfrac{2}{11}\div\dfrac{3}{4}=\dfrac{2}{11}\times\dfrac{4}{3}=\dfrac{8}{33}$

7. 2 $\dfrac{4}{5}\div\dfrac{2}{5}=\dfrac{4}{5}\times\dfrac{5}{2}=\dfrac{2}{1}\times\dfrac{1}{1}=\dfrac{2}{1}=2$

8. $\dfrac{15}{2}$ $\dfrac{15}{16}\div\dfrac{1}{8}=\dfrac{15}{16}\times\dfrac{8}{1}=\dfrac{15}{2}\times\dfrac{1}{1}=\dfrac{15}{2}$

9. $\dfrac{2}{3}$ $\dfrac{1}{2}\div\dfrac{3}{4}=\dfrac{1}{2}\times\dfrac{4}{3}=\dfrac{1}{1}\times\dfrac{2}{3}=\dfrac{2}{3}$

10. $\dfrac{76}{45}$ $\dfrac{8}{9}\div\dfrac{10}{19}=\dfrac{8}{9}\times\dfrac{19}{10}=\dfrac{4}{9}\times\dfrac{19}{5}=\dfrac{76}{45}$

Exercise 7: Operations with Fractions, Whole Numbers, and Mixed Numbers

1. $\dfrac{23}{5}$ $5-\dfrac{2}{5}=\dfrac{5}{1}-\dfrac{2}{5}=\dfrac{25}{5}-\dfrac{2}{5}=\dfrac{23}{5}$

2. $\dfrac{1}{3}$ $\dfrac{1}{9}\times3=\dfrac{1}{9}\times\dfrac{3}{1}=\dfrac{3}{9}=\dfrac{1}{3}$

3. 8 $4\div\dfrac{1}{2}=\dfrac{4}{1}\times\dfrac{2}{1}=\dfrac{8}{1}=8$

4. $\dfrac{39}{8}$ $3\dfrac{1}{4}\div\dfrac{2}{3}=\dfrac{13}{4}\times\dfrac{3}{2}=\dfrac{39}{8}$

5. $1\dfrac{11}{15}$ $8\dfrac{1}{3}-6\dfrac{3}{5}=\dfrac{25}{3}-\dfrac{33}{5}=\dfrac{125}{15}-\dfrac{99}{15}=\dfrac{26}{15}=1\dfrac{11}{15}$

6. $\dfrac{30}{7}$ $4+\dfrac{2}{7}=\dfrac{4}{1}+\dfrac{2}{7}=\dfrac{28}{7}+\dfrac{2}{7}=\dfrac{30}{7}$

7. 12 $18\div\dfrac{3}{2}=\dfrac{18}{1}\times\dfrac{2}{3}=\dfrac{6}{1}\times\dfrac{2}{1}=\dfrac{12}{1}=12$

8. $\dfrac{12}{7}$ $2\times\dfrac{6}{7}=\dfrac{2}{1}\times\dfrac{6}{7}=\dfrac{12}{7}$

9. $\dfrac{20}{3}$ $10\times\dfrac{2}{3}=\dfrac{10}{1}\times\dfrac{2}{3}=\dfrac{20}{3}$

10. $\dfrac{89}{15}$ $6-\dfrac{1}{15}=\dfrac{6}{1}-\dfrac{1}{15}=\dfrac{90}{15}-\dfrac{1}{15}=\dfrac{89}{15}$

Chapter 5 Ratios, Rates, and Proportions

Exercise 1: Ratios and Rates

1. **C**

2. **A**

3. **E**

4. $\dfrac{250}{1}$ $\dfrac{500}{2}=\dfrac{250}{1}$

5. $\dfrac{3}{2}$

6. $\dfrac{3}{1}$ $\dfrac{15}{5} = \dfrac{3}{1}$

7. $\dfrac{4}{1}$ $\dfrac{400}{100} = \dfrac{4}{1}$

8. **5:6** $10:12 = 5:6$

9. The Andersons traveled at a rate of $\dfrac{300 \text{ miles}}{6 \text{ hours}} = \dfrac{50 \text{ miles}}{1 \text{ hour}}$, while the Lamberts traveled at a rate of $\dfrac{200 \text{ miles}}{5 \text{ hours}} = \dfrac{40 \text{ miles}}{1 \text{ hour}}$.

10. $\dfrac{4}{1}$

Exercise 2: Proportions

1. **9** $8n = 72 \Rightarrow n = 72 \div 8 = 9$

2. **10** $15a = 150 \Rightarrow a = 150 \div 15 = 10$

3. **16** $5x = 80 \Rightarrow x = 80 \div 5 = 16$

4. **18** $9m = 162 \Rightarrow m = 162 \div 9 = 18$

5. **4** $8x = 32 \Rightarrow x = 32 \div 8 = 4$

Exercise 3: Word Problems with Proportions

1. **24 women** $\dfrac{5}{3} = \dfrac{40}{w}$ and
$5w = 120 \Rightarrow w = 120 \div 5 = 24$

2. **2 hours** $\dfrac{4}{30} = \dfrac{h}{15}$ and
$30h = 60 \Rightarrow h = 60 \div 30 = 2$

3. **10 pounds** $\dfrac{20}{2} = \dfrac{100}{c}$ and
$20c = 200 \Rightarrow c = 200 \div 20 = 10$

4. **4.5 hours** $\dfrac{40}{3} = \dfrac{60}{h}$ and
$40h = 180 \Rightarrow h = 180 \div 40 = 4.5$

5. **1.6 inches** $\dfrac{1}{10} = \dfrac{l}{16}$ and
$10l = 16 \Rightarrow l = 16 \div 10 = 1.6$

Chapter 6 Percents and Applications

Exercise 1: Converting Between Percents, Decimals, and Fractions

1. $0.3, \dfrac{3}{10}$

2. $0.22, \dfrac{11}{50}$

3. $0.49, \dfrac{49}{100}$

4. $0.01, \dfrac{1}{100}$

5. $0.08, \dfrac{2}{25}$

6. 4.4%

7. 90%

8. 0.1%

9. **37.5%** $100 \times (3 \div 8) = 37.5$

10. **70%** $100 \times (7 \div 10) = 70$

Exercise 2: Working with Percents

1. **25%** $\dfrac{15}{60} = 0.25$

2. **20%** $\dfrac{200}{1000} = 0.2$

3. **128.6%** $\dfrac{45}{35} = 1.286$

ANSWERS AND EXPLANATIONS

4. **150** $0.6 \times 250 = 150$

5. **0.5** $0.03 \times 18 = 0.5$

6. **0.5** $0.005 \times 90 = 0.45$

7. **72** $3.6 \times 20 = 72$

8. **45** $\dfrac{18}{n} = \dfrac{40}{100}$ and

$40n = 1800 \Rightarrow n = 1800 \div 40 = 45$

9. **1000** $\dfrac{100}{n} = \dfrac{10}{100}$ and

$10n = 10000 \Rightarrow n = 10000 \div 10 = 1000$

10. **50** $\dfrac{75}{n} = \dfrac{150}{100}$ and

$150n = 7500 \Rightarrow n = 7500 \div 150 = 50$

Exercise 3: Word Problems with Percents

1. **$4.20** 0.03×140

2. **2,600 square feet** $\dfrac{390}{x} = \dfrac{15}{100}$ and

$15x = 39,000 \Rightarrow x = 39,000 \div 15 = 2600$

3. **$5.82** $0.01 \times 580.00 + 0.02 = 5.82$

4. **21.6%** $100\% \times \dfrac{125 - 98}{125} = 21.6\%$

5. **12 minutes** $0.4 \times 30 = 12$

Exercise 4: Simple Interest

1. **$2,080.00** $I = 2000(0.16)\left(\dfrac{3}{12}\right) = 80$, total due

is this plus principal

2. **$21,500** $860 = P(0.08)\left(\dfrac{6}{12}\right)$

$860 = 0.04P$

$P = 860 \div 0.04 = 21,500$

3. **$72** $I = 900(0.04)(2) = 72$

4. **$6,000 @2.6%**   The 3% investment will earn
$I = 5000(0.03)(1) = 150$.

The 2.6% investment will earn
$I = 6000(0.026)(1) = 156$.

5. **19.5%**   Interest paid was
$10,000 - $11,950 = $1,950$

$1950 = 10,000(r)(1)$

$r = 1950 \div 10,000 = 0.195$

Chapter 7 The Number Line and Negative Numbers

Exercise 1: Adding and Subtracting Negative Numbers

1. 3

2. −6

3. −64

4. −23

5. −12

6. −4

7. 14

8. 5

9. 1

10. −22

Exercise 2: Multiplying and Dividing Negative Numbers

1. −24

2. 25

3. −10

4. −16

5. 18

6. −2

7. 3

8. −4

9. 2

10. −3

Chapter 8 Probability and Counting

Exercise 1: Basic Probability

1. **0.02** $\dfrac{10}{500}$

2. **0.44** $\dfrac{8}{18}$

3. **0.15** $\dfrac{15}{100}$

4. **0.05** $\dfrac{1}{20}$

5. **0.67** $\dfrac{6}{9}$

Exercise 2: Compound Probability

1. $\dfrac{10}{17}$ After the first student is selected, there are only 17 students left. But the first student was a fourth grader, so there are still 10 third graders remaining.

2. $\dfrac{1}{2}$ $\dfrac{3}{10}+\dfrac{4}{10}-\dfrac{2}{10}=\dfrac{5}{10}$

3. $\dfrac{2}{7}$ $\dfrac{4}{7}\times\dfrac{3}{6}=\dfrac{12}{42}$

4. $\dfrac{1}{399}$ After one person has won, there are 399 people still in the contest.

5. $\dfrac{5}{23}$ $\dfrac{10}{46}$

Exercise 3: Counting

1. **18** $3\times2\times3$

2. **30** 10×3

3. **6,840** $20\times19\times18$ (A person can't be in more than one position, so there is one less for each spot.)

4. **48** 8×6

5. **288** $3\times2\times2\times4\times3\times2\times1$

Chapter 9 Statistics and Data Analysis

Exercise 1: Analyzing Data Sets

1. **10.26 years** $\dfrac{10(9)+6(12)+3(11)}{10+6+3}=\dfrac{195}{19}=10.26$

2. **$447.33** $\dfrac{451+690+318+500+405+320}{6}=\dfrac{2684}{6}=447.3$

ANSWERS AND EXPLANATIONS

3. **$428.00** $\dfrac{405+451}{2}=\dfrac{856}{2}=428$

4. **$372.00** $690-318=372$

5. **C**   This score will be an outlier and will "pull" the mean toward it.

Exercise 2: Bar Charts and Circle Graphs

1. **March** $80+90=170$

2. **40**

3. **April**

4. **135** $70+65=135$

5. **February**   This month had the biggest height difference between the bars.

6. **324** $0.18(1800)=324$

7. **Senior Associate 1**

8. **900** $0.5(1800)=900$

9. **18** $0.02(1800)=36\dfrac{36}{2}=18$

10. **4:1** $\dfrac{0.4(1800)}{0.1(1800)}=\dfrac{720}{180}=\dfrac{4}{1}$

Exercise 3: Histograms and Dot Plots

1. **15**   total number of dots

2. **3**

3. **7**

4. **Group 1**

5. **60**

6. **25%**   Based on the plot, 60 is the third quartile.

7. **32** $2+6+8+10+6$

8. **26** $2+6+8+10$

9. **50%** $\dfrac{16}{32}=0.5$

10. **6.25%** $\dfrac{2}{32}=0.0625$

Exercise 4: Relationships Between Data Sets

1. **40 miles** $50-10=40$

2. **3, 4, 5, and 6**

3. **4400**

4.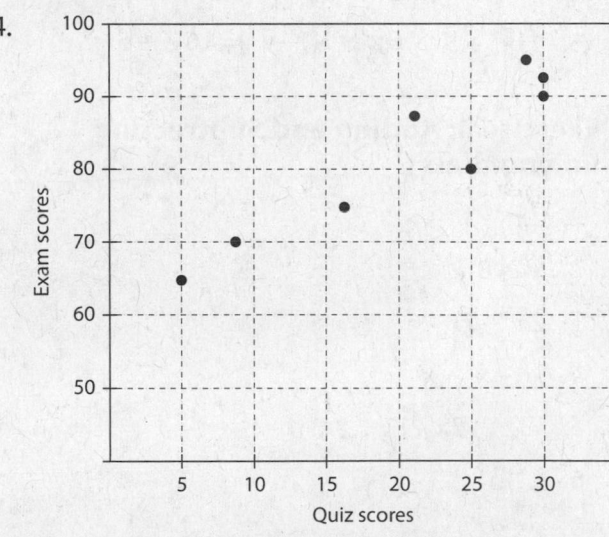

5. **B**   The general trend is positive.

Chapter 10 Algebraic Expressions

Exercise 1: Evaluating Expressions

1. **−40** $5(-6)-10=-40$

2. **−20** $16(-1)-4=-16-4=-20$

3. **−9** $9(0-1)=9(-1)=-9$

4. **−29** $-2(2)^4+2^2-1=-2(16)+4-1=-32+4-1=-29$

5. **12** $3^2+5(3)-12=9+15-12=12$

6. **14** $2(4-5)^2 + 3(4) = 2(-1)^2 + 12 = 2 + 12 = 14$

7. **−28** $-(3)^3 - 1 = -(27) - 1 = -27 - 1 = -28$

8. **−7** $\dfrac{0-7}{0+1} = \dfrac{-7}{1} = -7$

9. **−5** $\dfrac{(1)^2 - 6(1)}{1} = \dfrac{1-6}{1} = \dfrac{-5}{1} = -5$

10. **Undefined** $\dfrac{2^2 + 6}{2^2 - 4} = \dfrac{4+6}{4-4} = \dfrac{10}{0}$

Exercise 2: Combining Like Terms

1. **6x + 10**

2. **17y − 4**

3. **−16z²**

4. **−x + 4** $-2(x-2) + x = -2x + 4 + x$

5. **11y⁴ + 5** $16y^4 + 5(1-y^4) = 16y^4 + 5 - 5y^4$

Exercise 3: Adding and Subtracting Polynomials

1. $2x^2 - 3$

2. $x^5 + 8$

3. $2x^2 - 7x + 6$

4. $x^4 - x^2 + x$

5. $13x^2 + 7x - 1$

6. -14

7. x

8. $-3x^2 - 5x + 1$

9. $x^2 - 15x - 2$

10. $4x^3 - 2x^2 - 3x$

Exercise 4: Multiplying Polynomials (Single Terms)

1. $4x^3$

2. x^6

3. $30x^4$

4. $-3x^2$

5. $6xy^2$

Exercise 5: Multiplying Polynomials (Single Terms and Larger Terms)

1. $-6x^2 - 54x$

2. $\dfrac{1}{2}x^3 - x^2 + 2x$

3. $x^5 - 5x^4 - x^6$

4. $-5x^4 - 50x^2$

5. $4x^7 - 4x^5 + 24x^4 - 36x^3$

Exercise 6: Multiplying Two Binomials

1. $x^2 + x - 2$

2. $5x^2 + 23x - 10$

3. $-8x^2 + 10x - 2$

4. $x^4 - 1$

5. $2x^3 - 9x^2 - 12x + 54$

Exercise 7: Multiplying Polynomials with More than Two Terms

1. **x³ + 2x² − 14x − 3**
$x^3 + 5x^2 + x - 3x^2 - 15x - 3 = x^3 + 2x^2 - 14x - 3$

2. **−2x³ − 3x² + 7x + 4**
$-2x^3 - 2x^2 + 8x - x^2 - x + 4 = -2x^3 - 3x^2 + 7x + 4$

3. **9x³ + 21x² − 16x + 6**
$9x^3 - 6x^2 + 2x + 27x^2 - 18x + 6 = 9x^3 + 21x^2 - 16x + 6$

4. **x⁵ − x⁴ + x³ − x**
$x^5 + x^3 + x^2 - x^4 - x^2 - x = x^5 - x^4 + x^3 - x$

5. **x⁵ + 2x⁴ − x³ − 4x² − 8x + 4**
This is the result of distributing both terms. It can't be simplified further.

Exercise 8: Factoring Using the Greatest Common Factor

1. $3(x^2+3)$
2. $4x^2(x-4)$
3. $9(2x+1)$
4. $x(x^4-x-2)$
5. $2x^2(5x+7)$

Exercise 9: Factoring by Reversing FOIL

1. $(x-3)(x-4)$
2. $(x-2)(x+1)$
3. $(x-6)(x+3)$
4. $(x-10)(x+4)$
5. $(x-2)(x-3)$

Exercise 10: Difference of Squares

1. $(x+1)(x-1)$
2. $(x+2)(x-2)$
3. $(x+9)(x-9)$
4. $(x+6)(x-6)$
5. $(x+3)(x-3)$

Exercise 11: Simplifying Rational Expressions

1. $\dfrac{1}{x-2}$ $\quad \dfrac{x+5}{x^2+3x-10}=\dfrac{x+5}{(x+5)(x-2)}=\dfrac{1}{x-2}$

2. $\dfrac{x-7}{x}$ $\quad \dfrac{x^2-7x}{x^2}=\dfrac{x(x-7)}{x(x)}=\dfrac{x-7}{x}$

3. $x-1$ $\quad \dfrac{x^3-x^2}{x^2}=\dfrac{x^2(x-1)}{x^2}=\dfrac{x-1}{1}=x-1$

4. $\dfrac{x+2}{x+1}$ $\quad \dfrac{x^2+x-2}{x^2-1}=\dfrac{(x+2)(x-1)}{(x+1)(x-1)}=\dfrac{x+2}{x+1}$

5. $\dfrac{x}{x-4}$ $\quad \dfrac{2x}{2x-8}=\dfrac{2(x)}{2(x-4)}=\dfrac{x}{x-4}$

Exercise 12: Adding and Subtracting Rational Expressions

1. $\dfrac{-x^2+x+2}{x^2}$ $\quad \dfrac{x(1-x)}{x(x)}+\dfrac{2}{x^2}=\dfrac{x-x^2}{x^2}+\dfrac{2}{x^2}=\dfrac{-x^2+x+2}{x^2}$

2. $\dfrac{2x^2-10x+4}{x^2-25}$ $\quad \dfrac{(x-5)(2x-1)}{(x-5)(x+5)}+\dfrac{x-1}{x^2-25}=\dfrac{2x^2-11x+5}{x^2-25}+\dfrac{x-1}{x^2-25}=\dfrac{2x^2-10x+4}{x^2-25}$

3. $\dfrac{x^2+1}{x^3}$ $\quad \dfrac{(x^2)1}{(x^2)x}+\dfrac{1}{x^3}=\dfrac{x^2}{x^3}+\dfrac{1}{x^3}=\dfrac{x^2+1}{x^3}$

4. $\dfrac{x^2-x-5}{x^2-5x+6}$ $\quad \dfrac{(x-2)(1)}{(x-2)(x-3)}+\dfrac{(x-3)(x+1)}{(x-3)(x-2)}$

   $\quad =\dfrac{x-2}{x^2-5x+6}+\dfrac{x^2-2x-3}{x^2-5x+6}=\dfrac{x^2-x-5}{x^2-5x+6}$

5. $\dfrac{3x+5}{x-6}$ $\quad \dfrac{x+5}{x-6}+\dfrac{2x}{x-6}=\dfrac{x+5+2x}{x-6}=\dfrac{3x+5}{x-6}$

6. $\dfrac{1}{2x}$ $\quad \dfrac{(2)1}{(2)x}-\dfrac{1}{2x}=\dfrac{2}{2x}-\dfrac{1}{2x}=\dfrac{1}{2x}$

7. $\dfrac{-3}{x^2-4}$ $\quad \dfrac{x-1}{x^2-4}-\dfrac{1(x+2)}{(x-2)(x+2)}=\dfrac{x-1}{x^2-4}-\dfrac{x+2}{x^2-4}=\dfrac{x-1-x-2}{x^2-4}=\dfrac{-3}{x^2-4}$

8. $\dfrac{9x+11}{x^2-3x-10}$ $\dfrac{(x+3)(x+2)}{(x-5)(x+2)}-\dfrac{(x+1)(x-5)}{(x+2)(x-5)}=$

$\dfrac{x^2+5x+6}{x^2-3x-10}-\dfrac{x^2-4x-5}{x^2-3x-10}=\dfrac{x^2+5x+6-x^2+4x+5}{x^2-3x-10}=\dfrac{9x+11}{x^2-3x-10}$

9. $\dfrac{3x}{x-1}$ $\dfrac{6x}{x-1}-\dfrac{3x}{x-1}=\dfrac{3x}{x-1}$

10. $\dfrac{4-3x^3}{x^4}$ $\dfrac{4}{x^4}-\dfrac{3(x^3)}{x(x^3)}=\dfrac{4}{x^4}-\dfrac{3x^3}{x^4}=\dfrac{4-3x^3}{x^4}$

Exercise 13: Multiplying and Dividing Rational Expressions

1. $\dfrac{2}{x^2+x}$ $\dfrac{2}{x}\cdot\dfrac{1}{x+1}=\dfrac{2}{x(x+1)}=\dfrac{2}{x^2+x}$

2. $\dfrac{x^2}{x^2-25}$ $\dfrac{x}{x-5}\cdot\dfrac{x}{x+5}=\dfrac{x^2}{(x-5)(x+5)}=\dfrac{x^2}{x^2-25}$

3. $\dfrac{x^2+x-2}{4x^2}$ $\dfrac{x-1}{4x}\cdot\dfrac{x+2}{x}=\dfrac{(x-1)(x+2)}{4x(x)}=\dfrac{x^2+x-2}{4x^2}$

4. $\dfrac{x^2+2}{x-5}$ $\dfrac{x^2+2}{x+1}\cdot\dfrac{x+1}{x-5}=\dfrac{x^2+2}{1}\cdot\dfrac{1}{x-5}=\dfrac{x^2+2}{x-5}$

5. $\dfrac{x-2}{2x+8}$ $\dfrac{x-3}{x+4}\cdot\dfrac{x-2}{2x-6}=\dfrac{x-3}{x+4}\cdot\dfrac{x-2}{2(x-3)}=\dfrac{1}{x+4}\cdot\dfrac{x-2}{2}=\dfrac{x-2}{2x+8}$

6. $\dfrac{1}{4x}$ $\dfrac{1}{x^2}\div\dfrac{4}{x}=\dfrac{1}{x^2}\cdot\dfrac{x}{4}=\dfrac{1}{x}\cdot\dfrac{1}{4}=\dfrac{1}{4x}$

7. $\dfrac{x-6}{5x-10}$ $\dfrac{x}{x-2}\div\dfrac{5x}{x-6}=\dfrac{x}{x-2}\cdot\dfrac{x-6}{5x}=\dfrac{1}{x-2}\cdot\dfrac{x-6}{5}=\dfrac{x-6}{5x-10}$

8. $\dfrac{x^3+5x+4}{x+2}$ $\dfrac{x+4}{x-1}\div\dfrac{x+2}{x^2-1}=\dfrac{x+4}{x-1}\cdot\dfrac{x^2-1}{x+2}=\dfrac{x+4}{x-1}\cdot\dfrac{(x+1)(x-1)}{x+2}$

$=\dfrac{x+4}{1}\cdot\dfrac{x+1}{x+2}=\dfrac{x^2+5x+4}{x+2}$

9. $\dfrac{x^3+2x^2}{x-5}$ $\dfrac{x^3}{x-5}\div\dfrac{x}{x+2}=\dfrac{x^3}{x-5}\cdot\dfrac{x+2}{x}=\dfrac{x^2}{x-5}\cdot\dfrac{x+2}{1}=\dfrac{x^3+2x^2}{x-5}$

10. $\dfrac{x+4}{x+3}$ $\dfrac{x+1}{x+3}\div\dfrac{x+1}{x+4}=\dfrac{x+1}{x+3}\cdot\dfrac{x+4}{x+1}=\dfrac{1}{x+3}\cdot\dfrac{x+4}{1}=\dfrac{x+4}{x+3}$

Exercise 14: Writing Expressions

1. $\dfrac{2000}{k}$

2. $x+505$

3. $y+6$

4. $0.15m+30$

5. $\dfrac{20}{n}$

Chapter 11 Solving Equations and Inequalities

Exercise 1: One-Step Equations

1. $x = \dfrac{2}{3}$

2. $x = 5$

3. $x = 20$

4. $x = 17$

5. $x = -4$

Exercise 2: Two-Step Equations

1. $x = 8$

2. $x = 12$

3. $x = 4$

4. $x = -16$

5. $x = \dfrac{3}{2}$

Exercise 3: Multiple-Step Equations

1. $x = -1$ $-2(x+4) = x-5$
$$-2x - 8 = x - 5$$
$$-3x = 3$$
$$x = -1$$

2. $x = 3$ $3x + 1 = x + 7$
$$2x = 6$$
$$x = 3$$

3. $x = -\dfrac{5}{2}$ $-x + 4 = x + 9$
$$-2x + 4 = 9$$
$$-2x = 5$$
$$x = -\dfrac{5}{2}$$

4. $x = \dfrac{1}{2}$ $3(x+1) = 9x$
$$3x + 3 = 9x$$
$$3 = 6x$$
$$\dfrac{3}{6} = x$$

5. $x = \dfrac{22}{3}$ $-9x + 4 = -3(2x + 6)$
$$-9x + 4 = -6x - 18$$
$$-3x = -22$$
$$x = \dfrac{22}{3}$$

Exercise 4: Solving Inequalities

1. $x > 5$

2. $x < 14$

3. $x < 6$

4. $x \geq 1$

5. $x \leq -24$

Exercise 5: Writing Linear Equations and Inequalities

1. $x = 2y - 3$

2. $G \geq 90$

3. $x > 6$ $x > (2)(3)$

4. $m \geq 305$ $m \geq 300 + 5$

5. $w = r - 34$

Exercise 6: Word Problems with Equations and Inequalities

1. **120** $125 + 0.14m = 141.80$

2. **–12** $x - 10 = 2x + 2$

3. **15** $\dfrac{2 + 3 + 4 + y}{4} = 6$

ANSWERS AND EXPLANATIONS

4. **480** $\dfrac{n}{40}=12$

5. **11** $6+2w=28$

Exercise 7: Solving Systems of Equations

1. $x=-1, y=1$

2. $x=4, y=4$

3. $x=0, y=2$

4. $x=6, y=1$

5. $x=2, y=-2$

Exercise 8: Word Problems and Systems of Equations

1. **40** $n+d=61$
   $0.05n+0.10d=4.10$

2. **8** $10f+15a=260$
   $f+a=20$

3. **20** $m+b=40$
   $1.5m+2b=70$

4. **5** $c+1.5t=14$
   $1.5c+2=19.5$

5. **10** $95g+12s=1022$
   $6g+3s=78$

Exercise 9: Solving Quadratic Equations with the Square Root Rule

1. $x=2\sqrt{3}, -2\sqrt{3}$

2. $x=9, -9$

3. $x=4, -4$

4. $x=3\sqrt{2}, -3\sqrt{2}$

5. $x=0, -4$

Exercise 10: Solving Quadratic Equations by Factoring

1. **$x=4,-1$** $(x-4)(x+1)=0$

2. **$x=2,3$** $(x-2)(x-3)=0$

3. **$x=-2,-1$** $(x+2)(x+1)=0$

4. **$x=3,6$** $x^2-9x+18=(x-6)(x-3)=0$

5. **$x=-4,1$** $x^2+3x-4=(x+4)(x-1)=0$

Exercise 11: Solving with the Quadratic Formula

1. **$x=5,-2$** $x=\dfrac{3\pm\sqrt{9-4(1)(-10)}}{2}=\dfrac{3\pm\sqrt{49}}{2}=\dfrac{3\pm7}{2}$

2. **$x=-3,1$** $x=\dfrac{-2\pm\sqrt{4-4(1)(-3)}}{2}=\dfrac{-2\pm\sqrt{16}}{2}=\dfrac{-2\pm4}{2}=-1\pm2$

3. **$x=\dfrac{1}{2},\dfrac{2}{3}$** $x=\dfrac{-1\pm\sqrt{1-4(6)(-2)}}{12}=\dfrac{-1\pm\sqrt{49}}{12}=\dfrac{-1\pm7}{12}$

4. **$x=\dfrac{2}{3},-2$** $x=\dfrac{-4\pm\sqrt{16-4(3)(-4)}}{6}=\dfrac{-4\pm\sqrt{64}}{6}=\dfrac{-4\pm8}{6}=\dfrac{-2\pm4}{3}$

5. **$x=2+\sqrt{2}, 2-\sqrt{2}$** $x=\dfrac{4\pm\sqrt{16-4(1)(2)}}{2}=\dfrac{4\pm\sqrt{8}}{2}=\dfrac{4\pm2\sqrt{2}}{2}=2\pm\sqrt{2}$

Chapter 12 Graphing Equations

Exercise 1: Plotting Points

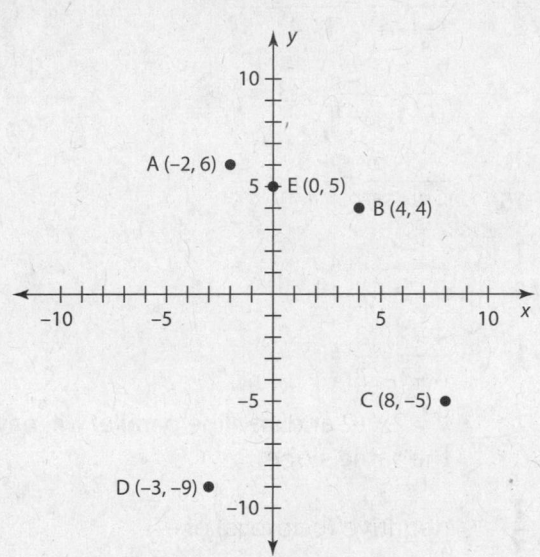

2.

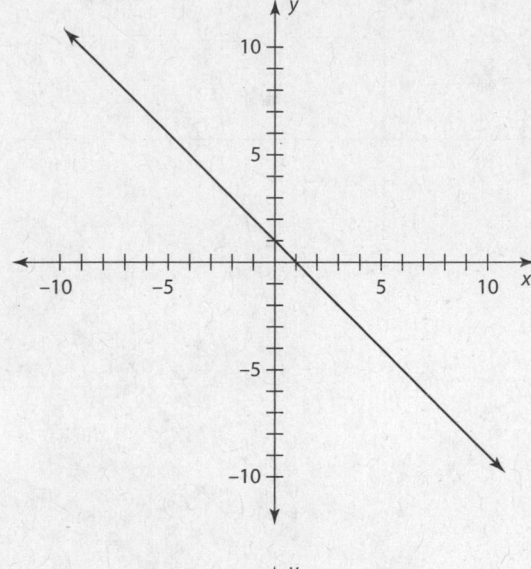

Exercise 2: Graphing Lines

1.

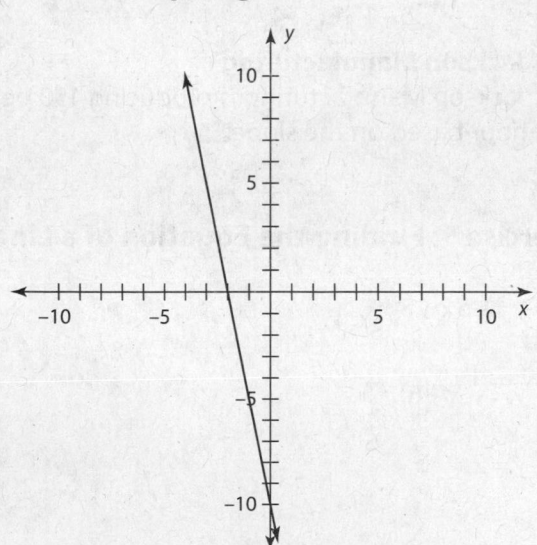

3.

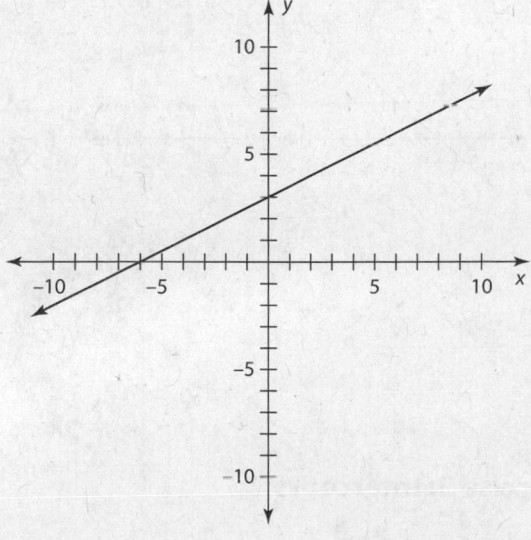

4.

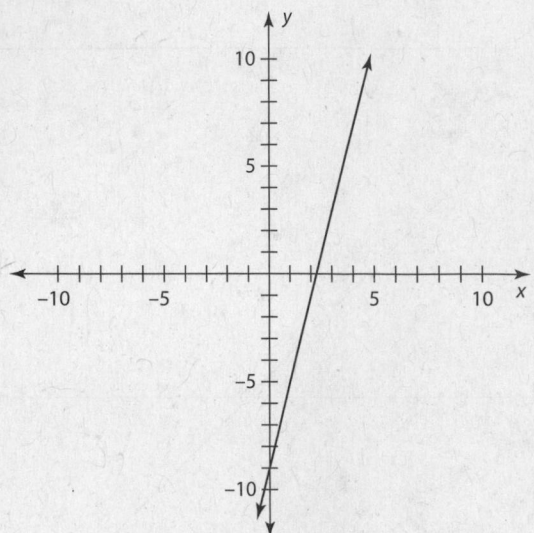

Exercise 4: Slope

1. **7** $\dfrac{6-(-8)}{2-0}=\dfrac{6+8}{2}=\dfrac{14}{2}=7$

2. $\dfrac{4}{5}$ $\dfrac{6-2}{1-(-4)}=\dfrac{4}{1+4}=\dfrac{4}{5}$

3. **–3** $\dfrac{7-4}{0-1}=\dfrac{3}{-1}=-3$

4. $\dfrac{8}{15}$ $\dfrac{-2-6}{-5-10}=\dfrac{-8}{-15}=\dfrac{8}{15}$

5. $\dfrac{1}{4}$ $\dfrac{1-0}{0-(-4)}=\dfrac{1}{4}$

6. **1** $\dfrac{4-1}{4-1}=\dfrac{3}{3}=1$

7. **2** $y=2x+2$ and any line parallel will have the same slope.

8. $\dfrac{2}{3}$ negative reciprocal of $-\dfrac{3}{2}$

9. **100**   The unit rate is the slope.
   $$\dfrac{500-100}{5-1}=\dfrac{400}{4}=100$$

10. **Jackson Manufacturing**
    Jackson Manufacturing is producing 150 per hour based on the slope.

5.

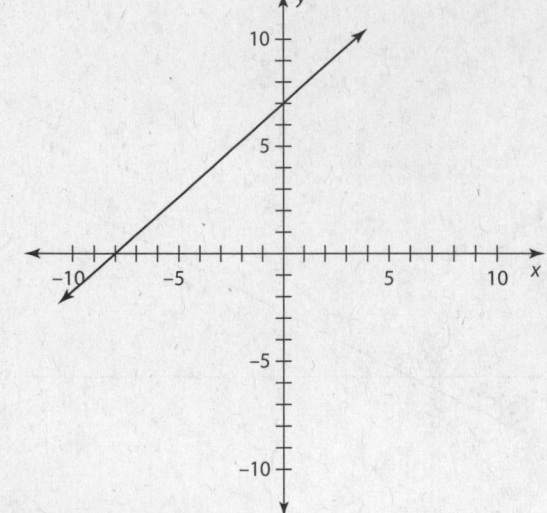

Exercise 5: Finding the Equation of a Line

1. $y=-5x+8$

2. $y=\dfrac{1}{2}x+6$

3. $y=2x-6$

4. $y=3x-1$

5. (a) $y=4x+2$

   (b) $y=-\dfrac{1}{4}x+\dfrac{1}{4}$

Exercise 3: Intercepts

1. x intercept $\dfrac{8}{3}$, y intercept -2

2. x intercept -5, y intercept 5

3. x intercept $\dfrac{5}{4}$, y intercept -10

4. x intercept 5, y intercept -15

5. x intercept 2, y intercept 2

Chapter 13 Functions

Exercise 1: Evaluating Functions

1. **22** $5(4)+2=20+2=22$

2. **−28** $5(-6)+2=-30+2=-28$

3. **3** $2(0)^2-0+3=2(0)+3=3$

4. **6** $2(-1)^2-(-1)+3=2(1)+1+3=2+1+3=6$

5. **9** $2(2)^2-2+3=2(4)-2+3=8-2+3=9$

Exercise 2: Recognizing Functions

1. function

2. not a function

3. function

4. function

5. not a function

Exercise 3: Intercepts

1. x intercept: 2, y intercept: 6

2. x intercept: −1, 5, 10; y intercept: 4

3. x intercept: 0; y intercept: 0

4. x intercept: −5, 1; y intercept: 3

5. x intercept: −2; y intercept: 8

Exercise 4: Other Properties of Functions

1. x smaller than −4, x between −1 and 1, and x larger than 4

2. x between −4 and −1 and x between 1 and 4

3. relative minimums at $x=-3$ and $x=3$

4. relative maximum when $x=0$

5. The function is increasing when x is between −3 and 0 and when x is larger than 3.

6. The function is decreasing when x is smaller than −4 and when x is between 0 and 3.

7. As x gets very large, $f(x)$ also gets large.

8. As x gets very small, $f(x)$ gets very large.

9. 4

10. 1

Chapter 14 Geometry

Exercise 1: Area and Perimeter of Polygons

1. **36 feet** $9+12+15$

2. **Area: 64 square inches** 8×8

   Perimeter: 32 inches $8+8+8+8$

3. **Area: 32 square meters** 16×2

   Perimeter: 36 meters $16+16+2+2$

4. **$x=5$** $8x=40$

5. **12** $3x=36$

Exercise 2: Circles

1. **50.3 square feet** $\pi4^2 = 16\pi$

2. **25.1 feet** $2\pi(4) = 8\pi$

3. **125.7 meters** radius is 20 m; $2\pi(20) = 40\pi$

4. **5.6 feet** $100 = \pi r^2$

   $r^2 = \dfrac{100}{3.14} = 31.85$

   $r = \sqrt{31.85} = 5.6$

5. **30 inches** $30\pi = 2\pi r$

   $r = \dfrac{30\pi}{2\pi} = 15 \Rightarrow d = 30$

Exercise 3: Volume and Surface Area of 3-Dimensional Objects

1. **4188.8 cubic meters** $\dfrac{4}{3}\pi10^3$

2. **3 feet** $6(10)x = 180$

3. **10.7 cubic meters**

   $\dfrac{1}{3}(\text{area of base})(\text{height}) = \dfrac{1}{3}(4 \times 4)(2)$

4. **12 cubic feet** half is left: $\dfrac{1}{2}(6)(2)(2) = 12$

5. **6785.8 cubic feet** Radius is 6.

   Volume of one $\pi(6)^2(30) = 3339.12$; volume of two $= 2 \times 3339.12 = 6782.4$.

Exercise 4: Complex Figures

1. **1400 meters** $300 + 300 + 200 + 100 + 100 + 400$

2. **100,000 square meters** $(300 \times 300) + (100 \times 100)$

3. **100 meters**

4. **30 cubic mm** $(2 \times 3 \times 2) + (3 \times 2 \times 3)$

5. **62 square mm**

   SA of smaller rectangular prism:
   $(2 \times 3) + 2(2 \times 2) + 2(2 \times 3) = 26$

   SA of larger rectangular prism:
   $2(3 \times 2) + (1 \times 3) + (3 \times 3) + 2(3 \times 2) = 36$

   Total SA: $26 + 36 = 62$

Exercise 5: The Pythagorean Theorem

1. **18.0** $c^2 = 10^2 + 15^2$

   $c = \sqrt{325} = 18.0$

2. **4 inches** $a^2 + 3^2 = 5^2$

   $a^2 = 16$

   $a = 4$

3. **11.2** $x^2 = 5^2 + 10^2$

   $x^2 = 125$

   $x = \sqrt{125} = 11.2$

4. **9 feet** $a^2 + 12^2 = 15^2$

   $a^2 + 144 = 225$

   $a^2 = 225 - 144$

   $a^2 = 81$

   $a = \sqrt{81} = 9$

5. **24** To find the perimeter, you must first find the length of the remaining leg.

   $a^2 + 6^2 = 10^2$

   $a^2 = 64$

   $a = \sqrt{64} = 8$

   $P = 10 + 6 + 8 = 24$

Science

The Science Test

The Science section of the GED® test measures your knowledge of key science topics and how well you understand basic scientific practices. There are approximately 40 questions on the Science test, and you will have 90 minutes to complete the entire test. About 40 percent of the questions focus on life science, about 40 percent focus on physical science, and the remaining 20 percent focus on Earth and space science.

Questions on the Science test may ask about the information in a short passage, a graph, a table, or some other graphic presentation of scientific data. Sometimes two or three questions will refer to the same passage, graph, or table. These questions measure your ability to interpret scientific data.

Most Science questions are multiple choice with four answer choices. Others use interactive formats such as drag and drop, fill-in-the-blank, drop-down, and short answer. See "Introducing the GED® Test" at the beginning of this book for an explanation and samples of these formats.

The Science Review

The following section of this book presents a comprehensive review of the knowledge that is tested on the Science test. Each main topic is followed by an exercise to measure how well you have mastered that subject. The exercise questions include examples of the kinds of short passages, charts, tables, and other graphics that you will encounter on test day. These exercises will help you become familiar with all the Science question types. If you have already taken the Science Pretest at the start of this book, make sure to study those sections of the Science review that correspond to the questions you missed or found difficult.

This Science review section is organized as follows:

Science

Part 1   Life Science

Chapter 1   Structures and Functions of Life

Chapter 2   Life Functions and Energy Intake

Chapter 3   Heredity

Chapter 4   Evolution

Answers and explanations for all of the practice questions in this section are located at the end of the section.

PART 1

Life Science

CHAPTER 1

Structures and Functions of Life

Cells, Tissues, and Organs

The **cell theory** explains the relationship between cells and living things. It has three components:

- All living things are made of one or more cells.

- Cells are the smallest unit of structure and function in all living things.

- New cells can only be produced from other cells.

These ideas might seem like common sense today, but until the late 1500s, people had no way of knowing that cells existed. When the first microscope was invented around 1590, scientists started examining what living things are made of. By the 1800s, scientists had learned enough about cells to formulate the cell theory.

Specialized Cells

The following diagram shows just a few of the different types of cells in your body. Look at how different the cells' structures are. Each cell's structure helps it to carry out a unique function within the body. Muscle cells, for example, must be able to contract so the body can move. Nerve cells (neurons) have long appendages for transmitting signals throughout the body. Each type of cell is **specialized** for a particular job.

Human Body Cells

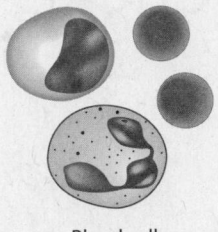

Blood cells

Surface skin cells

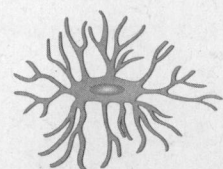

Bone cell

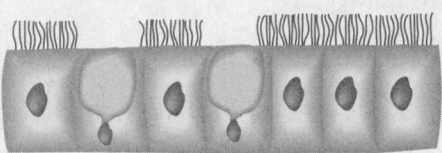

Columnar epithelial and goblet cells

Cardiac muscle cell

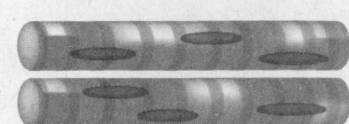

Skeletal muscle cells

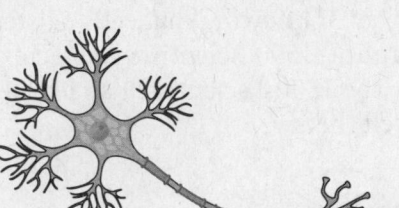

Neuron

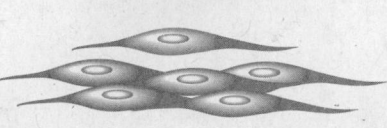

Smooth muscle cells

A group of specialized cells working together make up a **specialized tissue**. The following diagram shows four major types of specialized tissues. Connective tissue protects and connects other body tissues to one another. Bone, cartilage, and blood are connective tissues. Epithelial tissue covers and protects the surface of the body and the organs. Skin is an epithelial tissue.

Four Types of Tissue

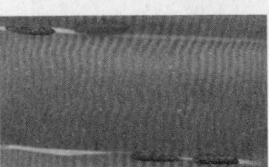

Muscle tissue

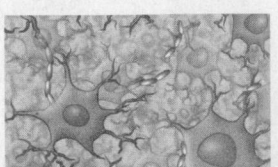

Nervous tissue

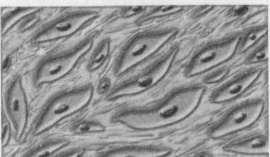

Connective tissue

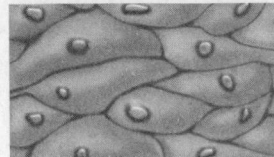

Epithelial tissue

Levels of Organization

Your heart, blood vessels, and blood are all part of your body's cardiovascular system. These different parts work together to move needed substances throughout your body. Your body is also made up of several other **organ systems**, each with a unique job. Just like the cardiovascular system, each organ system is made up of several different **organs** working together.

An organ is composed of a group of tissues working together. Your heart is an organ made of cardiac muscle tissue. Remember that a tissue is composed of a group of specialized cells working together. Your heart tissue is made of cardiac muscle cells. Cardiac muscle cells contract together to make your heart beat.

The following diagram shows the different levels of organization in your body.

Levels of Organization in the Human Body

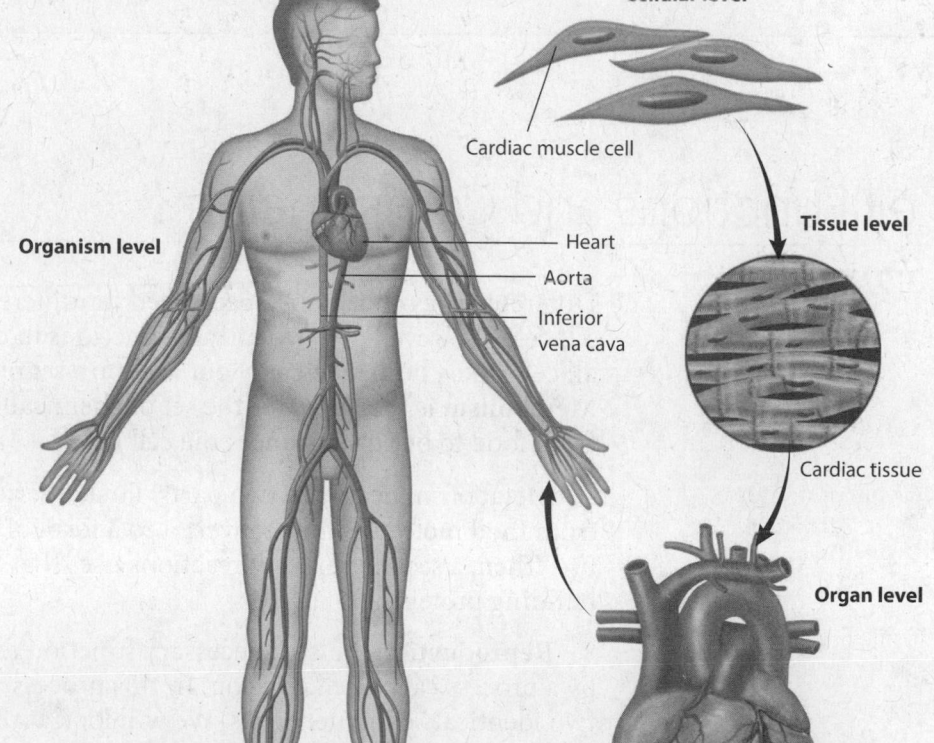

Cellular level

Cardiac muscle cell

Organism level

Heart

Aorta

Inferior vena cava

Tissue level

Cardiac tissue

Organ level

System level

Heart

Cells, Tissues, and Organs

Directions: Choose the best answer for each of the following items.

1. Which statement is supported by the cell theory?

    A. A single cell is not considered a living thing.
    B. Anything that has cells is considered a living thing.
    C. All living things are made of the same types of cells.
    D. A living thing can absorb new cells from the environment.

2. Complete the statement with a term from the section.

    A bone cell is _____ to perform the unique function of

    storing minerals for the body.

Answers are on page 656.

Cell Functions and Components

Different types of cells are specialized for different functions in your body. All cells, however, do have certain functions in common. For example, all cells must be able to carry out a certain set of chemical reactions. **Metabolism** is the name for the set of chemical reactions that use the energy from food to build substances the cell needs.

Metabolism occurs in two parts. First, a series of reactions extract energy from food molecules and convert it to a form of energy that the cell can use. Then, a second series of reactions uses that energy to fuel processes like building proteins.

Reproduction is also a necessary function for all cells. Cells reproduce by a process called cell division. In this process, the "parent" cell divides into two identical "daughter" cells. We will look at this process in more detail later.

Cell Components

The following diagram represents a typical animal cell.

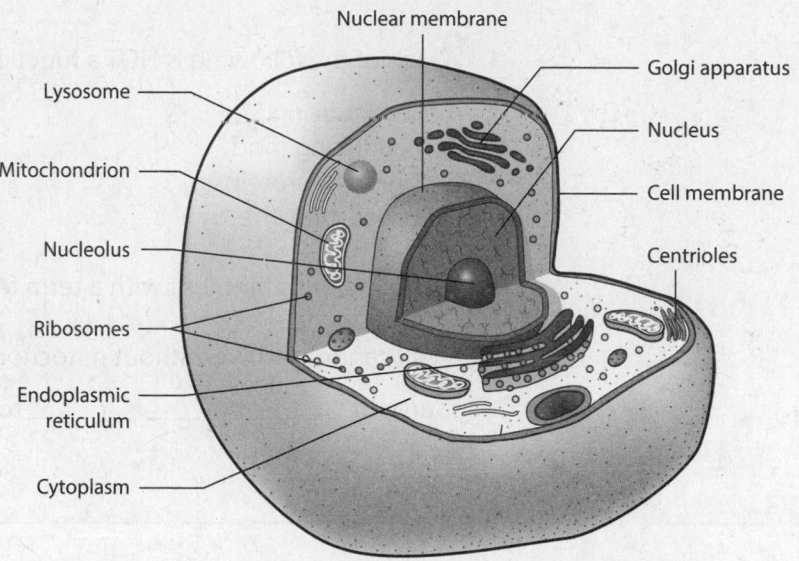

Typical Animal Cell

Just as different cell types have unique functions, the different components of a cell also have unique functions. This table lists the functions of some of the most important cell components.

Cell Component	Function
Cell membrane	Allows some substances into the cell and keeps others out
Mitochondrion	Site of cell metabolism, converts energy into a form the cell can use
Nucleus	Stores cell's DNA
Ribosome	Site where proteins are built

Enzymes are also important molecules found inside cells. Enzymes are proteins that help chemical reactions to occur faster. Without enzymes, a cell would not be able to produce needed substances fast enough.

EXERCISE 2

Cell Functions and Components

Directions: Choose the best answer for each of the following items.

1. Which of the following is NOT a function performed by all cells?

   A. reproducing
   B. producing food
   C. building proteins
   D. converting energy

2. Complete the statement with a term from the section.

   A cell cannot survive without mitochondria, because it would have no

   source of _____ to run cell processes.

Answers are on page 656.

Cell Division

A cell reproduces by a process called cell division. Cell division occurs in three stages. First, the cell's nucleus makes an extra copy of its deoxyribonucleic acid (DNA) molecules, which carry the genetic instructions for forming new cells. Then the nucleus divides into two parts, each containing an identical copy of the DNA. Finally, the "parent" cell divides into two identical "daughter" cells.

Mitosis

Mitosis is the name for the second stage of cell division, when the cell's nucleus divides in two. Mitosis occurs in four predictable phases, each of which is described in the following table. Remember that the cell starts mitosis with two copies of the DNA, and ends mitosis as two identical cells, each containing one copy of the DNA.

Mitosis

Prophase DNA condenses into structures called chromosomes. The cell's nucleus disappears.	Chromosomes
Metaphase Chromosomes line up in the center of the cell.	Chromosomes
Anaphase Chromosomes split into 2 identical chromatids. The sets of identical chromatids travel to opposite sides of the cell.	 Chromatids
Telophase A new nucleus forms around each set of chromatids. The cell is ready to separate into 2 identical cells.	

Meiosis

Meiosis is a special type of cell division that produces reproductive cells. You probably know that reproductive cells (eggs and sperm) unite to produce the first body cell of a new organism. Reproductive cells have half the number of chromosomes found in a regular body cell, so they must be made by a special process.

Meiosis occurs in two stages: meiosis I and meiosis II. Both stages are described in the following list. As in mitosis, the cell makes a copy of its DNA before starting meiosis. You'll notice that the steps of meiosis are similar to the steps of mitosis, but with a few important changes.

Meiosis I

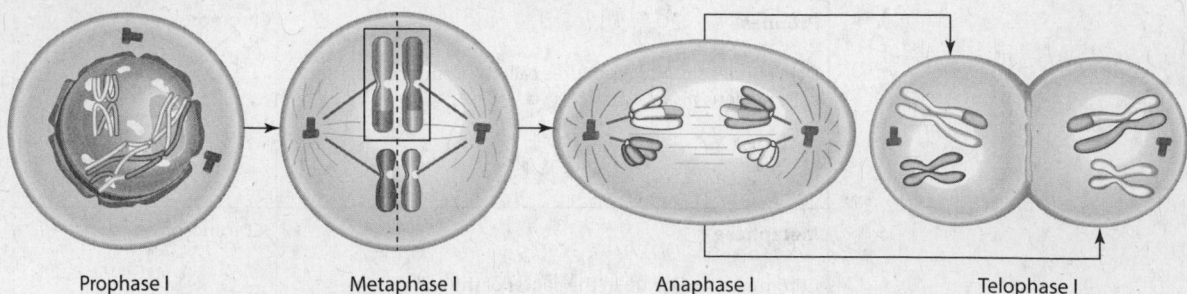

Prophase I   Metaphase I   Anaphase I   Telophase I

- **Prophase I.** DNA condenses into structures called chromosomes and the nucleus disappears. Matching pairs of chromosomes trade segments in a process called crossing over. (We'll discuss chromosomes in more detail and the importance of crossing over in a later section.)

- **Metaphase I.** Chromosomes line up in matching pairs.

- **Anaphase I.** One chromosome from each pair moves to the opposite side of the cell.

- **Telophase I.** The cell splits in two.

Meiosis II

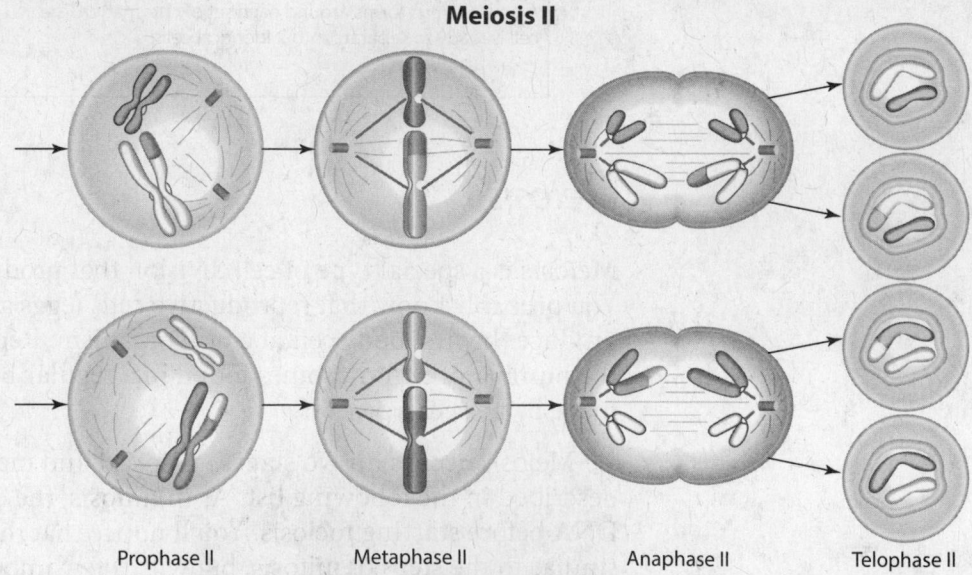

Prophase II   Metaphase II   Anaphase II   Telophase II

- **Prophase II.** Two cells have the same number of chromosomes as the original. Unlike prophase I, during this phase there is no new replication of DNA.

- **Metaphase II.** Individual chromosomes line up in each cell.

- **Anaphase II.** Chromosomes split into chromatids. Chromatids move to opposite sides of the cell.

- **Telophase II.** A nucleus reforms around each set of chromatids. Each cell splits in two again.

Notice that the final result of meiosis is four reproductive cells, each with half the DNA of a regular body cell.

EXERCISE 3

Cell Division

Directions: Choose the best answer for each of the following items.

Question 1 is based on the following diagram.

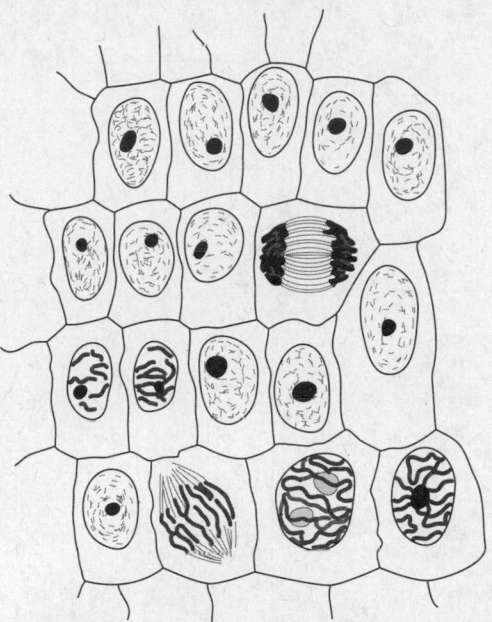

1. A student creates the drawing shown as he observes mitosis in onion root cells under a microscope.
   Place a circle on the diagram to indicate the cell that appears to be transitioning from metaphase to anaphase.

2. Indicate your answer choice by connecting the correct process(es) to each description. Each process may be used more than once.

   a) occurs in humans   **mitosis**

   b) produces 2 body cells

   c) produces 4 reproductive cells
                                                          meiosis
   d) starts with a cell containing 2 copies
      of DNA

   e) involves crossing over of chromosome   **mitosis and meiosis**
      segments

Answers are on page 656.

CHAPTER 2

Life Functions and Energy Intake

Photosynthesis

Just as a lightbulb needs electricity and a car needs gasoline, cells need a source of energy to function. All organisms obtain energy from food. Most organisms are consumers; they eat other organisms for food. Producers, such as plants, take in light energy from the sun and use it to make their own food. The process of converting light energy into food is called **photosynthesis**.

Photosynthesis is a chemical reaction that takes place in the cells of plants' leaves. Look at the leaf diagram. Carbon dioxide enters cells through tiny holes in the leaf. Water absorbed by the plant's roots also travels to the lcaf cells. When light energy enters the cells, carbon dioxide and water react in structures called chloroplasts. The reaction produces glucose (sugar) and oxygen. Glucose travels to the rest of the plant to be used or stored. The oxygen exits the leaf through the tiny holes. The equation accompanying the diagram summarizes the photosynthesis reaction.

Photosynthesis

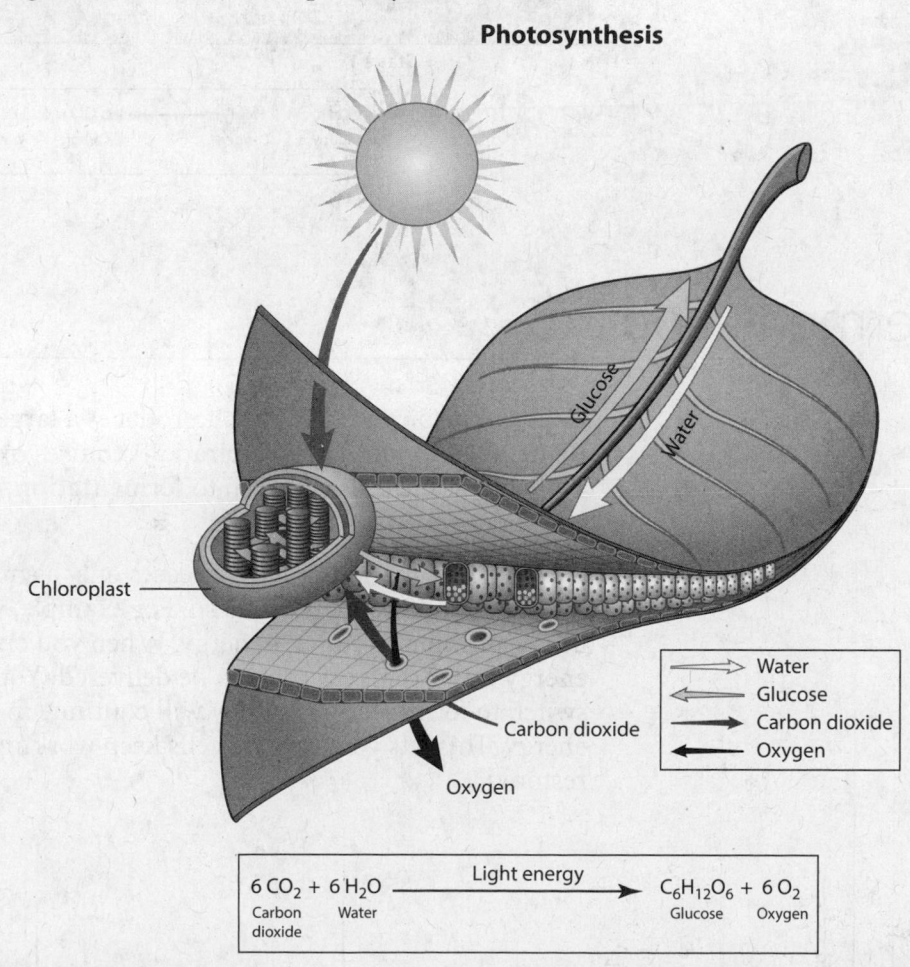

Chloroplast

Water
Glucose
Carbon dioxide
Oxygen

Water
Glucose
Carbon dioxide

Oxygen

$$6\,CO_2 + 6\,H_2O \xrightarrow{\text{Light energy}} C_6H_{12}O_6 + 6\,O_2$$

Carbon dioxide   Water   Glucose   Oxygen

Respiration

Although organisms get energy from food, the energy is not in a form their cells can use. Cells use a process called **respiration** to convert the energy from food into a usable form.

Respiration occurs in two stages, as shown in the diagram. First, glucose from food enters the cell and is broken down into smaller molecules. This process releases a small amount of energy for the cell to use. Next, the smaller molecules react with oxygen inside the cell's mitochondria. This reaction produces carbon dioxide, water, and a large amount of energy. The cell now has the energy it needs to carry out its normal functions. The equation accompanying the diagram summarizes the respiration reaction.

Respiration

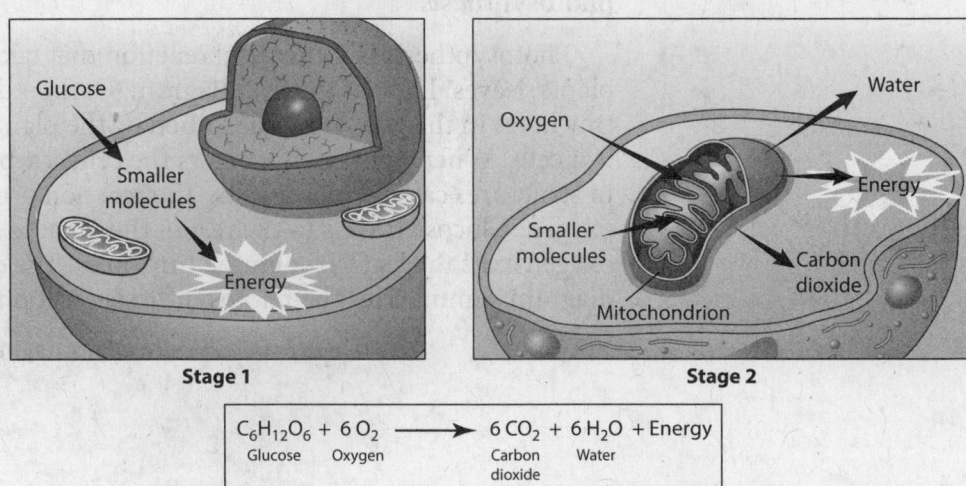

Stage 1 — Glucose, Smaller molecules, Energy

Stage 2 — Oxygen, Water, Energy, Smaller molecules, Carbon dioxide, Mitochondrion

$$C_6H_{12}O_6 + 6\,O_2 \longrightarrow 6\,CO_2 + 6\,H_2O + Energy$$

Glucose   Oxygen   Carbon   Water
dioxide

Fermentation

Cells use respiration because it produces a large amount of usable energy. Remember, though, that respiration requires oxygen. When oxygen is not available, some cells can turn to **fermentation**, an alternate method for converting energy.

The fermentation process releases only a small amount of energy, but it does not need oxygen to do so. For example, your muscle cells normally use respiration to convert energy. When you exercise, however, the cells use energy faster than oxygen can be delivered. Your muscle cells temporarily switch to fermentation so they will continue to have at least a small supply of energy. This lets your muscle cells keep working until the oxygen supply is restored.

EXERCISE 1

Energy for Life Functions

Directions: Choose the best answer for each of the following items.

Question 1 is based on the following passage.

> The owner of a small freshwater aquarium notices bubbles rising from the leaves of one of the aquatic plants. She researches the process of photosynthesis in aquatic plants and makes more observations. She concludes that the bubbles are oxygen gas.

1. Which statement supports her conclusion?

    A. Photosynthesis takes place in the chloroplasts of leaf cells.
    B. Leaves use oxygen to make glucose during photosynthesis.
    C. Plants absorb carbon dioxide and water for photosynthesis.
    D. Leaves release oxygen as they make glucose during photosynthesis.

2. Determine whether the process is *respiration* or *fermentation* and write the correct response in the blank.

    a) _____ provides a lot of energy.

    b) _____ needs oxygen.

    c) _____ provides a little energy.

    d) _____ does not need oxygen.

Answers are on page 657.

CHAPTER 3

Heredity

DNA and Chromosomes

A cell uses the instructions in its deoxyribonucleic acid (**DNA**) to make substances called proteins. Proteins are responsible for producing physical traits such as eye color.

A **gene** is a segment of DNA that codes for a specific protein. Look at the following diagram of DNA. DNA is made up of pairs of four chemical bases. The specific sequence of bases in a gene determines the protein it makes.

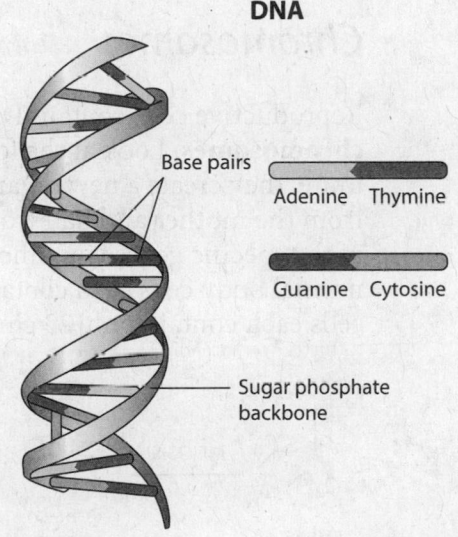

DNA

Base pairs

Adenine   Thymine

Guanine   Cytosine

Sugar phosphate backbone

The process of using a gene to make a protein happens in two major steps shown in the following diagram. First, the gene is transcribed into a molecule called ribonucleic acid (RNA). The RNA carries the gene's sequence to a cell structure called a ribosome, where a protein is built. This process of DNA to RNA to protein is so specific and key in living things that it is referred to as the **central dogma of biology** or **central dogma of molecular biology**.

Central Dogma of Molecular Biology

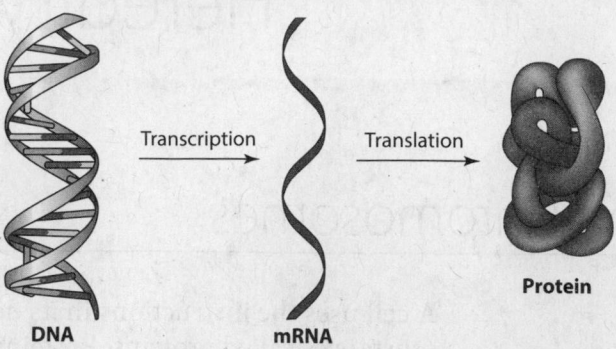

Children typically exhibit a mixture of traits from both of their parents. You might have, for example, your mother's eye color and your father's face shape. When people and other organisms reproduce, they pass on traits to their children through their DNA.

Chromosomes

Reproductive cells contain DNA in the form of structures called **chromosomes**. Look at the following diagram. When an egg and sperm cell unite, they create a new organism with a complete set of chromosomes, half from the mother and half from the father. Your mixture of traits is the result of the specific genes you inherited from each of your parents. In humans, normal body cells each contain 46 chromosomes. By contrast, reproductive cells each contain only 23 chromosomes.

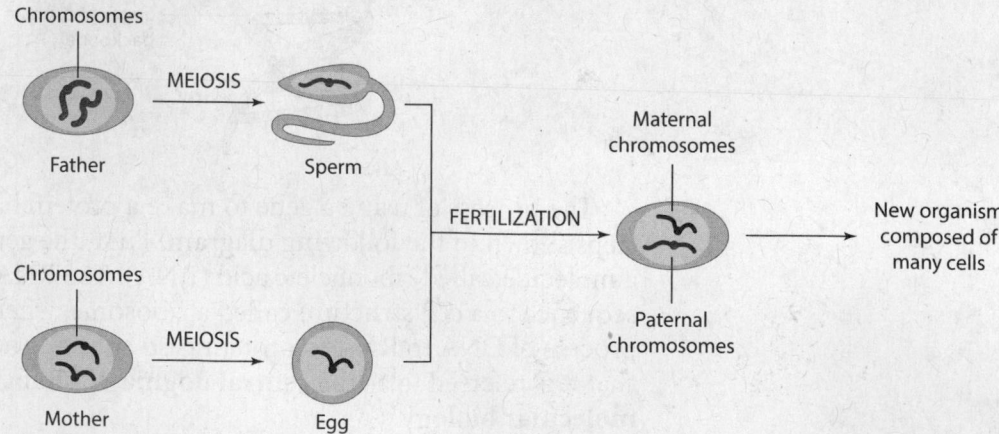

The chromosomes that store DNA are located inside a cell's nucleus. Look at the following diagram of a chromosome. A chromosome consists of two identical chromatids attached to each other. The location where the chromatids attach is called the centromere. Hundreds or even thousands of genes can be stored on one chromosome.

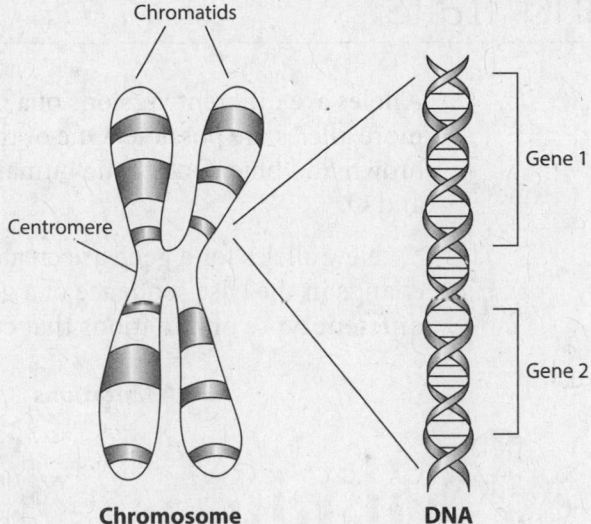

Remember that during meiosis, the chromosome splits apart into individual, but identical, chromatids. This means that the reproductive cells created during meiosis each receive one chromatid, containing one copy of every gene.

EXERCISE 1

DNA and Chromosomes

Directions: Choose the best answer for each of the following items.

1. Complete the statement with terms from the section.

   To produce a trait, DNA in the nucleus is converted to

   _____, which is used to build a _____.

2. A normal human body cell contains 46 total chromosomes. When reproductive cells (egg and sperm cells) unite, how many total chromosomes exist in the new cell they create?

   A. 2
   B. 23
   C. 46
   D. 92

3. Which statement about chromosomes is NOT true?

   A. Chromosomes are stored in the nucleus of a cell.
   B. A chromosome has different genes on each chromatid.
   C. Chromosomes split apart into chromatids during meiosis.
   D. A single chromosome can contain over a thousand genes.

Answers are on page 657.

Alleles and Traits

Alleles are different versions of a gene. Most genes have two alleles, though more alleles are possible. One of the human eye color genes has two alleles: brown and blue. One of the human blood type genes has three alleles: A, B, and O.

New alleles for a gene are created by **mutations**. A mutation is a random change in the base sequence of a gene. The following diagram shows different types of mutations that can lead to new alleles.

DNA Mutations

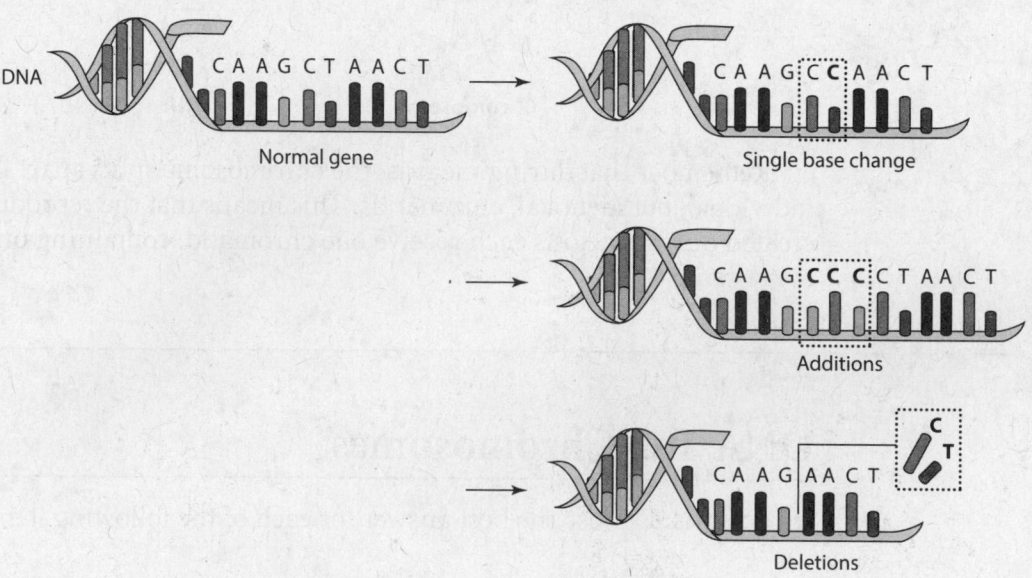

Assortment of Alleles

Recall that at the beginning of meiosis, a cell has two copies of each chromosome. Before the chromosomes are separated and new cells are formed, they go through a process called **crossing over**. Look at the following diagram. An *arm* from each chromosome literally "crosses over" the other, allowing the arms to trade segments. Notice in the diagram that the chromosomes have traded alleles of the "B" gene.

Look at the two chromosomes shown on the right side of the following diagram. Each chromosome is now made up of one original chromatid and one chromatid with a new combination of alleles. When these four unique chromatids separate during meiosis, no two reproductive cells will have the same combination of alleles.

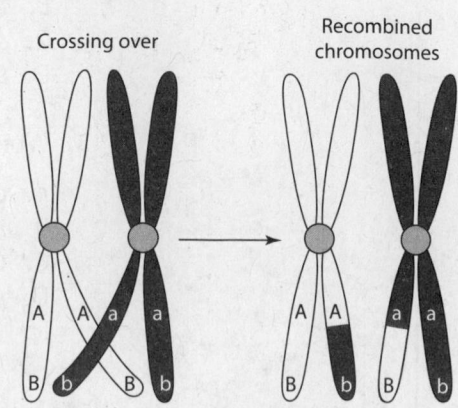

Crossing over   Recombined chromosomes

Environmental Altering of Traits

Some traits, like your blood type, are the direct result of the alleles you inherited from your parents. Your blood type is genetically determined, and it cannot be changed. Other traits are the result of a combination of your alleles and environmental factors. The following table describes three examples of traits that are linked to specific genes but can be altered by the environment.

Trait	Genetics	Environment
Height	Alleles of several genes influence a person's height.	A diet low in needed vitamins and minerals can limit how tall a person will grow.
Handedness	The handedness gene has right- and left-handed alleles.	A person can learn to use the opposite hand, often if his or her dominant hand is injured.
Cancer	Certain alleles make a person more likely to develop certain cancers.	Lifestyle choices (smoking, exercise, diet) can increase or decrease a person's risk for certain cancers.

Expression of Traits

When a gene is actively being used to make a protein, the gene is said to be turned on, or "expressed." The genes for some traits are expressed all the time. Others are only turned on when a specific protein is needed. The study of how genes are turned off and on is called **epigenetics**.

Environmental factors like temperature can also directly affect which genes are expressed. Color spots on the face, ears, feet, and tail of Siamese cats are a good example. In Siamese cats, hair on warm parts of the body stays light-colored, and hair on cool parts of the body is dark-colored. This is because the hair color gene is expressed only in areas below a certain temperature.

Genes Expressed and Not Expressed

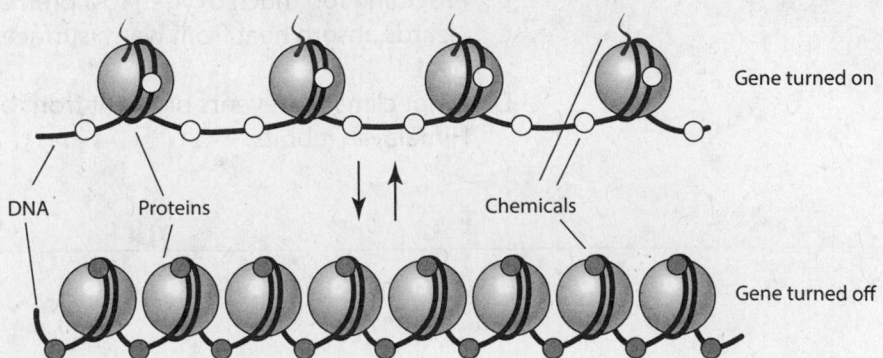

Gene turned on

DNA   Proteins   Chemicals

Gene turned off

Alleles and Traits

Directions: Choose the best answer for each of the following items.

1. The addition of an extra base to a segment of DNA produces a new

   A. trait.
   B. gene.
   C. allele.
   D. chromosome.

Question 2 is based on the following diagram.

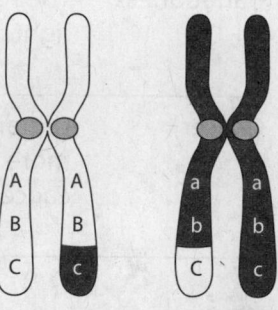

2. Look at the pair of chromosomes shown. What evidence indicates that crossing over has occurred?

   A. The two chromosomes contain different alleles of genes A, B, and C.
   B. The two inside chromatids contain different alleles of genes A, B, and C.
   C. The two outside chromatids contain different alleles of genes A, B, and C.
   D. The first chromosome's two chromatids contain different alleles of gene C.

3. Which of the following is NOT an example of the environment altering the expression of a trait?

   A. A temperature of 80°F in an alligator's nest causes the eggs to hatch as females.
   B. Providing too much oxygen to a premature baby can cause blindness.
   C. Lizards absorb heat from warm surfaces instead of producing body heat.
   D. A hot climate prevents pigment from being produced in the fur of Himalayan rabbits.

Answers are on page 657.

Simple Inheritance

Remember that you have two copies of every gene—one inherited from your mother and one from your father. Your combination of alleles for a specific gene is called your **genotype**. Your physical appearance for a trait is called your **phenotype**. Your genotype determines your phenotype.

In simple inheritance, a gene has two alleles (versions). The two alleles are represented by a capital and lowercase letter. The following diagram shows the possible genotypes and phenotypes for the human eye color gene. (Although there are several different genes that affect human eye color, we will focus only on the blue/brown gene.)

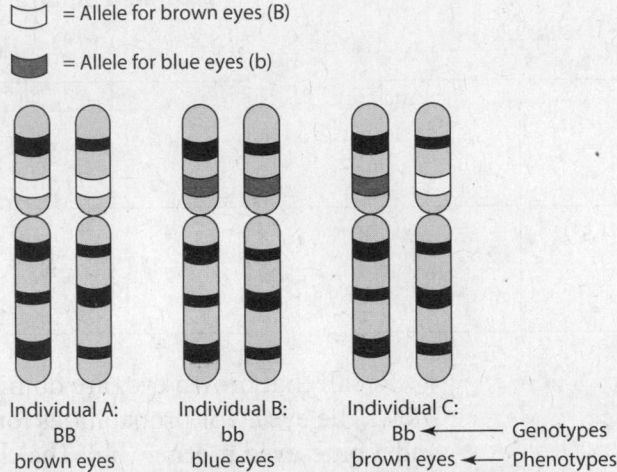

In simple inheritance, a gene has a dominant and a recessive allele. If a person has at least one copy of the dominant allele (represented by a capital letter), he or she will have the dominant phenotype. A recessive phenotype requires two copies of the recessive allele (represented by a lowercase letter). Notice in the diagram that brown eye color is dominant and blue eye color is recessive.

Probability of Inheriting Traits

A **Punnett square** is a chart used to calculate the probability of parents passing on a trait to their child. When using a Punnett square, remember:

- One parent's alleles go along the top and one parent's alleles go along the left side of the Punnett square.

- The parents' alleles are matched up inside each box to show all of the allele combinations (genotypes) that the child could receive.

- The child has a 25 percent chance of inheriting the combination in each box.

Punnett Square

Father's alleles

	B	b
b		
b		

Mother's alleles

	B	b
b	Bb	bb
b	Bb	bb

	B	b
b	Bb 25%	bb 25%
b	Bb 25%	bb 25%

Recall that brown eyes are dominant over blue eyes. The Punnett square shows the eye color probabilities for the child of a brown-eyed father (Bb) and a blue-eyed mother (bb). The child has a 50 percent chance of having brown eyes (Bb) and a 50 percent chance of having blue eyes (bb).

A **pedigree chart** is used to trace the inheritance of a trait through the generations of a family. This type of chart is often used to study genetic disorders such as colorblindness.

The following pedigree chart traces the inheritance of colorblindness through three generations of a family. Notice the meaning of the different symbols in the key. Colorblindness is a recessive trait. The person with the half-shaded symbol is called a "carrier" because she has one copy of the recessive colorblindness allele and one copy of the dominant color vision allele. She is not colorblind, but she can pass the colorblindness allele on to her child.

Pedigree Chart: Inheritance of Colorblindness

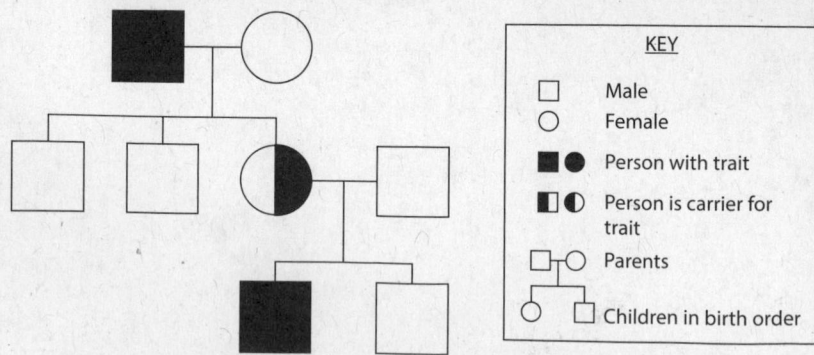

KEY

- ☐ Male
- ○ Female
- ■ ● Person with trait
- ◨ ◖ Person is carrier for trait
- ☐⊸○ Parents
- ○⊥☐ Children in birth order

EXERCISE 3

Simple Inheritance

Directions: Choose the best answer for each of the following items.

Questions 1 through 3 are based on the following information and diagram.

Cystic fibrosis is a genetic disease. The cystic fibrosis allele (c) is recessive to the healthy allele (C). The following pedigree chart shows the inheritance of the cystic fibrosis allele through three generations of a family.

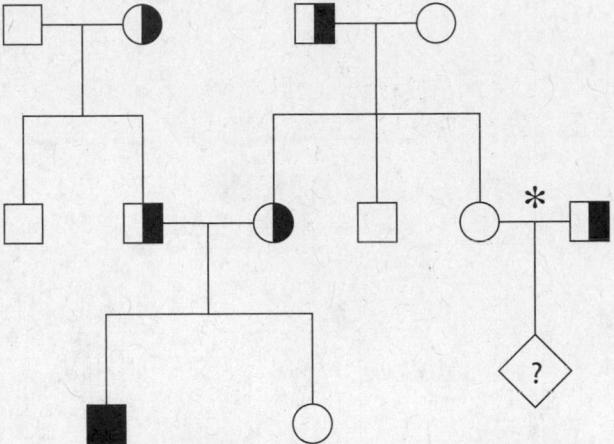

1. How can the person represented by the solid square at the bottom of the pedigree chart best be described?

   A. a healthy female
   B. a male with cystic fibrosis
   C. a male who is a carrier for cystic fibrosis
   D. a female with an unknown allele combination

2. Place an X on the pedigree chart to indicate each person who has the genotype CC.

3. The asterisk (*) in the pedigree chart indicates a couple who are planning to start a family. They want to know their chances of having a child with cystic fibrosis. What is their probability of having a child with the disease? (It might help to draw a Punnett square.)

   A. 0 percent
   B. 25 percent
   C. 50 percent
   D. 100 percent

Answers are on pages 657–658.

CHAPTER 4

Evolution

Evolutionary Relationships

Lions, tigers, and cheetahs are different species of large cats. Although they live in different parts of the world, scientists believe that these, and all large cats, are related through a now-extinct ancestor species. **Common ancestry** is the theory that related organisms evolved from a shared ancestor. The following table summarizes the evidence scientists use to explain the evolution of organisms from ancestral species.

Evidence of Common Ancestry

Evidence	Example
Fossil record Organizing fossils by age shows gradual change in organisms.	Fossils show how gradual change over time has produced the modern horse. Eohippus Mesohippus Merychippus Modern horse
Homologies Different organisms have similarities in body structures, DNA sequences, and development.	Different animals have similar bones in their forearms. Human Cat Whale Bat
Biogeography Similar but unique organisms exist in similar environments around the world.	Finches on differents islands in the Galapagos appear similar but have developed unique beak shapes. Large ground finch Medium ground finch Small tree finch Warbler finch

Cladograms

A **cladogram** is a diagram that uses shared characteristics to show how organisms are related. Organisms are arranged on branches based on the characteristics each has. Look at the following cladogram. The lancelet is the first branch because it has none of the characteristics being compared. The lamprey is second because it has one of the characteristics, a vertebral column (spine). The wolf has all of the characteristics.

Cladogram

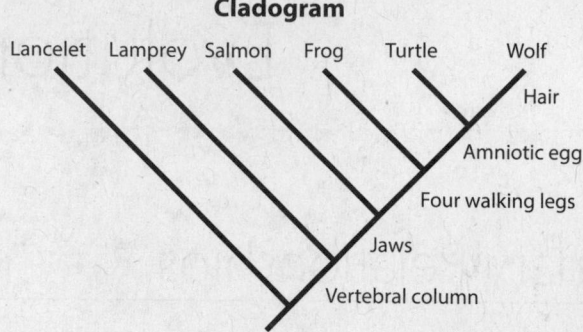

The more characteristics two organisms share, the more closely they are assumed to be related. Based on this cladogram, the turtle is more closely related to the wolf than the salmon is, because the turtle and wolf share all characteristics but one.

EXERCISE 1

Evolutionary Relationships

Directions: Choose the best answer for each of the following items.

Questions 1 and 2 are based on the following cladogram.

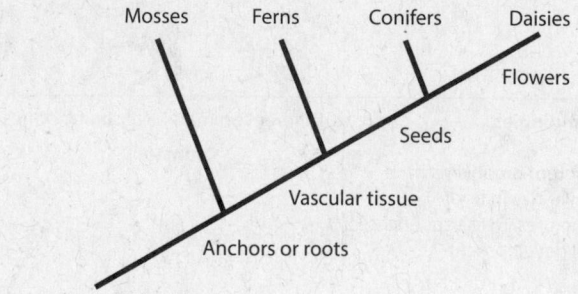

1. According to the information in the cladogram, which two plant species are most closely related?

   A. ferns and daisies
   B. conifers and ferns
   C. daisies and mosses
   D. mosses and conifers

2. The cladogram was created using which type of evidence for common ancestry?

   A. fossil records
   B. biogeography
   C. molecular homologies
   D. homologous structures

Answers are on page 658.

Evolution by Natural Selection

Consider the long neck of a giraffe. Ancestral giraffes had necks of varying lengths and ate grass. During periods when grass was scarce, giraffes with longer necks were able to eat the leaves off of trees. Since these giraffes were better able to find food, they were more likely to survive and reproduce than the giraffes with shorter necks. Gradually over time, the proportion of long-necked giraffes increased until no short-necked giraffes were left. This process of some members of a species being better able to survive and reproduce than others is called **natural selection**.

Farmers and animal breeders use a similar process called **artificial selection**. Natural selection works on traits that affect organisms' ability to survive in their environment. In artificial selection, humans specifically choose two organisms to breed based on desired traits. Farmers, for example, might specifically breed two tomato plants that are the most resistant to disease. A dog breeder might choose to breed two dogs that have the most desirable temperament.

You can tell that selection is occurring when a specific version of a trait becomes more or less common in a species. Look at the following peppered moth example. During England's industrial revolution, smog from factories caused the tree trunks that the moths lived on to darken. The graph shows that during this time period, dark-winged moths increased and light-winged moths decreased. This means that the dark-winged moths had an advantage. It was harder for predators to see them, so more of them survived and reproduced. Natural selection was occurring.

Peppered Moth Wing Coloration over Time

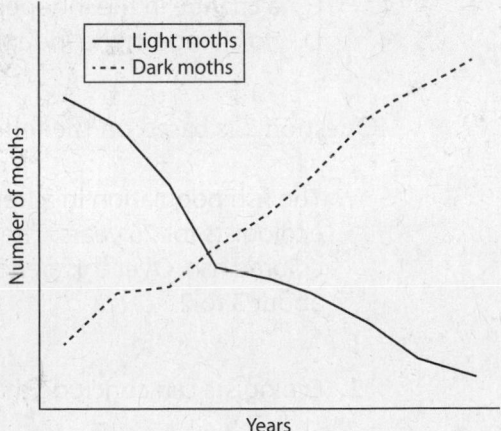

Requirements for Selection

Natural selection causes species to evolve. For natural selection to act on a species, though, two conditions must be met. First, the species must show **variation in traits**. In peppered moths, for example, the wing-color trait has two versions (dark and light). When the moths' environment changed, natural selection favored the dark-winged moths. If all of the moths had the same color wings to begin with, natural selection wouldn't have had anything to favor.

A species must also show **differential survivability**. This means that one version of the trait must provide a greater chance of survival. The dark-winged moths were better able to survive and reproduce than the light-winged moths, so their numbers increased. If light-winged moths were able to survive just as well as dark-winged moths, natural selection would not occur.

EXERCISE 2

Evolution by Natural Selection

Directions: Choose the best answer for each of the following items.

Question 1 is based on the following passage.

> In a scientific study, a change in the independent variable results in a change in the dependent variable. For example, a change in tree trunk color resulted in a change in wing-color frequencies in England's peppered moth population.

1. When studying natural selection, which of the following observations would provide the clearest proof that selection is happening?

   A. a change in the dependent variable
   B. no change in the dependent variable
   C. a change in the independent variable
   D. no change in the independent variable

Question 2 is based on the following passage.

> The fish population in a freshwater lake has been monitored by local ecologists for 26 years. The population includes both dark- and light-colored fish. Over this period, the ratio of dark to light fish has remained about 3 to 2.

2. Ecologists can conclude that natural selection is NOT occurring because

   A. the fish do not have enough variation in body color.
   B. the fish have enough food and do not need to change.
   C. neither body color has a greater effect on fish survival.
   D. humans are causing artificial selection to occur instead.

Answers are on page 658.

Chapter 4 ~ Evolution | 551

Evolutionary Change

An **adaptation** is a trait shared by all members of a species that helps them survive or reproduce in their unique environment. Natural selection leads to adaptations. Think back to natural selection in giraffes. Long necks were more beneficial than short necks. Long necks became more common over time, and now only long-necked giraffes exist. A long neck has become an adaptation of the giraffe species. A few more examples of adaptations are listed in the following table.

Organism	Adaptation	Benefit
Cactus	Sharp spines	Improves survival by providing protection against being eaten by animals
Cheetah	Fast running ability	Improves survival by improving chances of getting food when hunting
Many bird species	Elaborate and colorful feathers in males	Improves reproductive chances by helping males attract mates

Species develop adaptations because the environment exerts something called **selection pressure**. Selection pressure is anything in the environment that affects a species' survival. The following table describes different types of selection pressure.

Selection Pressure	May Include	Example
Limited resources	Food sources Clean water Living space Suitable mates	In an environment where food is scarce during the winter, a species may develop the adaptation of hibernating until spring.
Environmental threats	Predators Human activity Disease	In an environment where predators hunt by sight, a species may develop the adaptation of blending in, or camouflage.

Speciation

When a new species evolves from an existing species, the process is called **speciation**. In general, speciation happens when some members of a species develop adaptations that are different from the rest of the species. This often happens if a group becomes geographically separated from the original population. The selection pressures in the new environment may cause the separated group to develop new adaptations. Many new adaptations over time eventually cause the group to become a separate species.

The Galapagos finches are a well-studied example of speciation. Small groups of a finch species originally living on the mainland settled on a variety of islands in the Galapagos off the coast of South America. Over time, each group developed a unique beak shape as an adaptation to the food available on their island. Now, each island has its own unique finch species.

EXERCISE 3

Evolutionary Change

Directions: Choose the best answer for each of the following items.

1. Complete the table with terms from the section.

Adaptation	Selection Pressure
a) male frogs sing to attract females	_____
b) snakes get moisture only from food	_____
c) some birds, such as swallows, build nests on walls	_____

2. Complete the statement with a term from the section.

If two populations of a species develop different adaptations,

_____ might happen.

Answers are on page 658.

CHAPTER 5

Ecosystems

Energy in Ecosystems

Energy is constantly cycling through ecosystems. In most ecosystems, there are four important feeding levels that determine the direction of energy flow. Energy is moved from one level to another as organisms are consumed.

- **Producers** are organisms (usually plants) that convert some of the sun's energy into stored chemical energy.

- **Primary consumers** are herbivores. They obtain energy by consuming producers.

- **Secondary consumers** are carnivores that consume primary consumers for energy.

- **Decomposers** are organisms that obtain energy by breaking down dead organisms from the three other levels.

Flow of Energy

Models, such as the following **energy pyramid**, allow us to visualize the feeding relationship between organisms at different levels. They show the energy gained and lost over time. Producers form the base of the pyramid. The size of each block is proportional to the amount of available energy.

Energy Pyramid

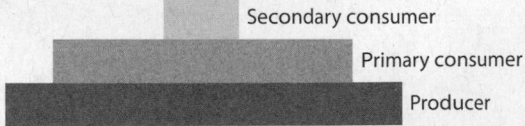

Secondary consumer

Primary consumer

Producer

Conservation of Energy

Only a small percentage of a feeding level's energy is passed up to the next level. Examine the following leaf diagram.

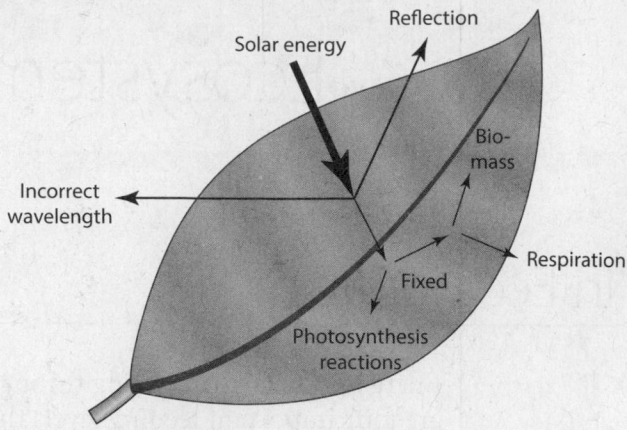

In a plant, not all of the available solar (light) energy actually makes it into the leaf. The energy that does make it into the leaf is made usable by **photosynthesis**. That energy may then be used during respiration. The energy that remains can be lost in several ways, one of which is heat. Finally, whatever energy is left in the leaf becomes available to the next feeding level when the plant is eaten.

EXERCISE 1

Energy in Ecosystems

Directions: Choose the best answer for each of the following items.

Questions 1 and 2 refer to the following drawing and information.

Arrows indicate the direction of energy flowing in and out of the cow.

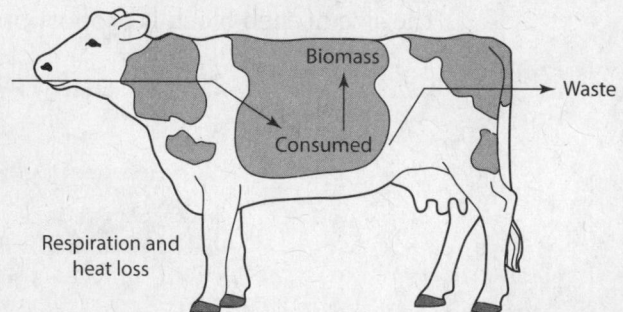

1. The arrow between "consumed" and "respiration and heat loss" is missing. Mark an arrow on the diagram to indicate the direction of energy flow.

2. The cow would best fit which of the following roles?

   A. producer
   B. decomposer
   C. primary consumer
   D. secondary consumer

Answers are on page 659.

Matter in Ecosystems

Food Chains

One way to represent feeding relationships is with a **food chain**. This model uses arrows to show the direction in which matter and energy are transferred between organisms.

A Food Chain

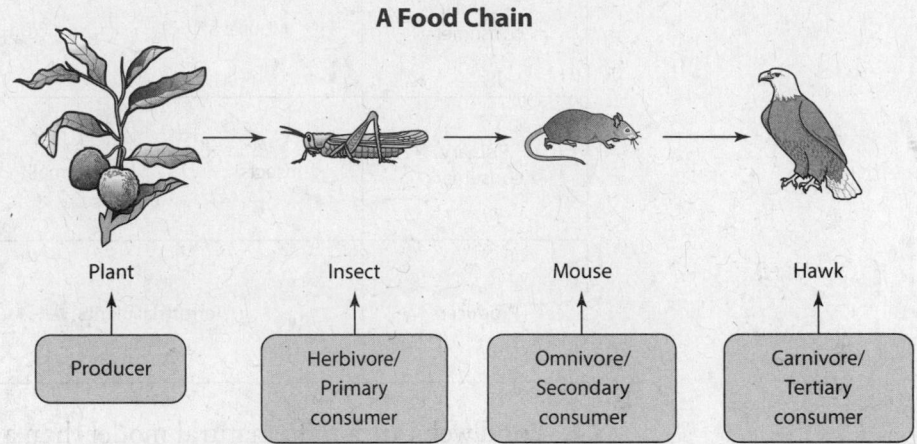

Plant	Insect	Mouse	Hawk
Producer	Herbivore/ Primary consumer	Omnivore/ Secondary consumer	Carnivore/ Tertiary consumer

As you can see, each organism in the food chain represents a feeding (trophic) level in the passage of materials and energy. A food chain typically has no more than five links, because the amount of energy left by the fifth link is only a tiny portion of what was available at the first link.

Food Webs

Most ecosystems are complicated. They cannot be modeled by a single, unbranched food chain, because most organisms depend on more than one other species for food. The best way to model these feeding relationships is with elaborate **food webs**.

A Food Web

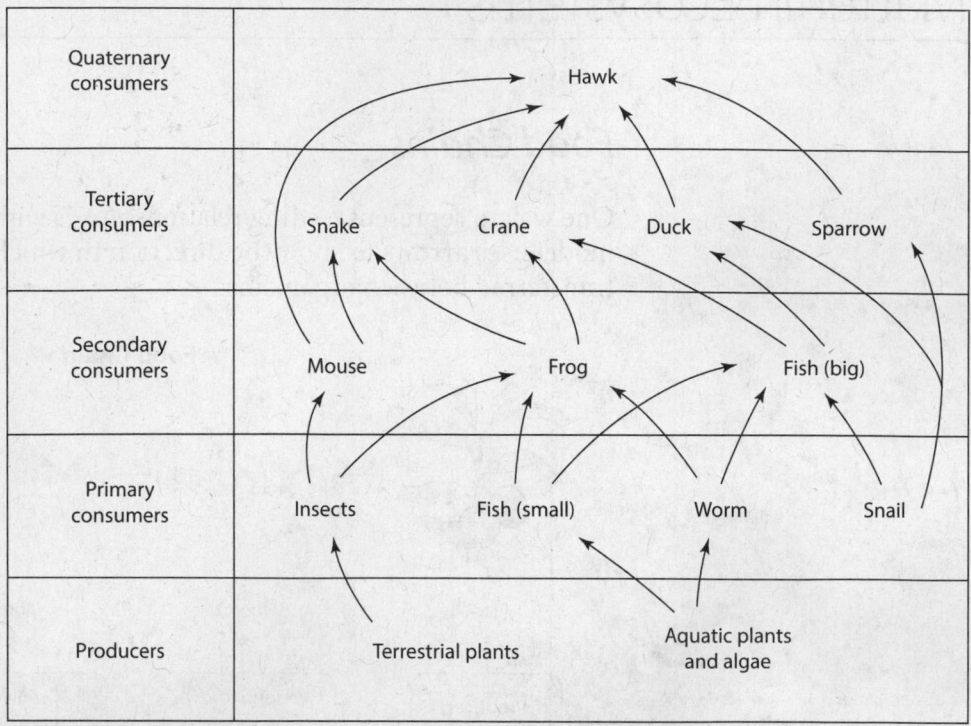

Food webs are a more natural model than a food chain because they show all possible feeding relationships at each feeding level. Some consumers feed at several different levels. The duck in this food web may eat snails (primary consumers) and big fish (higher-level consumers). Omnivores, including humans, eat producers as well as consumers from different levels.

Food webs also help identify limitations in communities. Consider what might happen to the frog population if pollution led to the destruction of aquatic plants. The organisms in the next feeding level would lose an important food source. The entire food web would be negatively impacted.

EXERCISE 2

Matter in Ecosystems

Directions: Choose the best answer for each of the following items.

1. Complete the statement with a term from the section.

    The arrow in a food chain shows the direction in which _____ and _____ are moving through the food chain.

2. The best model of organisms' complex feeding relationships is a(n)

    A. food web.   C. energy link.
    B. food chain.   D. energy pyramid.

Capacity for Change

A population is a group of organisms of the same species living in an area. The **carrying capacity** of a population is the maximum number of organisms that a particular environment can support over time. For example, when populations are less than the carrying capacity of a particular environment, births will exceed deaths until the carrying capacity is reached.

The following graph illustrates a population with a constant, but limited, food supply. During the lag phase the population size grows very slowly, and organisms mature and adapt to their environment. When food is plentiful, the population grows quickly (exponential growth phase). When the population size outgrows the amount of available food, growth begins to plateau (stationary phase, in which the carrying capacity of the population is reached).

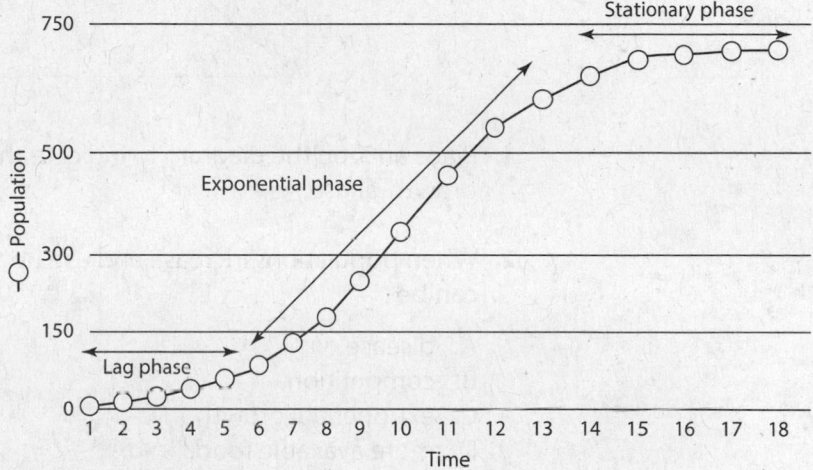

Population Growth over Time

Limiting Factors

The following diagram shows six factors that can limit population size. For example, if competition between members of a species, or individuals of different species, for food or space increases, the population size will decrease. Other **limiting factors** can include the effects of a disease, changes in the amount of available space or light, and other environmental effects.

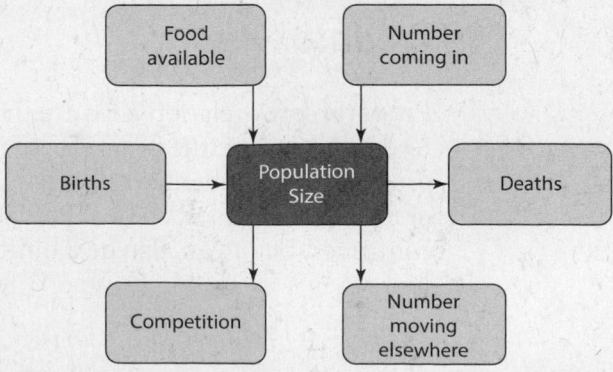

Factors Limiting Population Size

EXERCISE 3

Capacity for Change

Directions: Choose the best answer for each of the following items.

Question 1 is based on the following diagram.

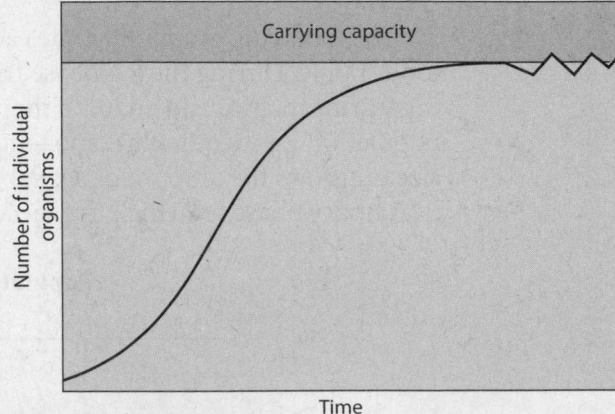

1.⸱ Place an X on the diagram to indicate the correct location of the slow growth phase.

2. When populations increase and use up the available resources, the result can be

   A. disease.
   B. competition.
   C. exponential growth.
   D. more available food.

Answers are on page 659.

Relationships in Ecosystems

Predator-Prey

Predator-prey relationships are those in which one organism (the predator) feeds on another (the prey). These relationships help ecosystems function properly. Remember that energy is moved through an ecosystem by way of food webs or food chains. Predation ensures that the flow of energy continues, but it can also be a limiting factor on population size.

In the following graph, the prey population declines sharply several times. Each decline is followed by a crash in the predator population because of the reduced source of food. As a result of the reduced predator population, the prey population is able to rebound. This is followed by a rise in the predator numbers. Predator-prey relationships are important for the health of natural populations. Usually it is the young, old, or injured members of a population that are caught by predators. Predation restricts the size of the prey population within the limits of the resources that are available.

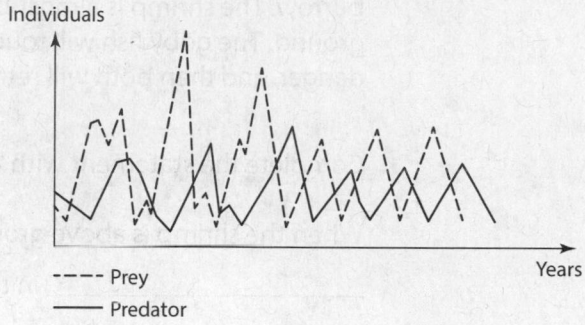

A Predator-Prey Relationship

Symbiosis

Another type of relationship that impacts many species' survival is **symbiosis**. This relationship occurs when there is a close and long-term association between members of different species. There are several different types of symbiosis. Examine the following chart to compare and contrast the different types of symbiotic relationships.

Symbiotic Relationships

Relationship	Definition	Examples
Parasitism	Relationship in which one organism (the parasite) benefits while the other (the host) is harmed	Tapeworms living in the intestines of a cat Tick living on a dog
Mutualism	Relationship in which both species benefit	Ants living in and protecting an acacia tree Clownfish living amongst sea anemones
Commensalism	A relationship in which one species benefits and the other species is neither harmed nor benefited	Hermit crabs using gastropod shells for shelter Spiders building webs on plants

Relationships in Ecosystems

Directions: Choose the best answer for each of the following items.

Questions 1 and 2 are based on the following passage.

A goby fish sometimes lives together with a shrimp. The shrimp digs and cleans up a burrow in the sand, and both the fish and shrimp live in the burrow. The shrimp is almost blind and at risk of being eaten when above ground. The goby fish will touch the shrimp with its tail to warn it of danger, and then both will retreat into the burrow.

1. Complete the statement with a term from the section.

   When the shrimp is above ground, it takes on the role of

   _____ in the predator-prey relationship.

2. What type of relationship exists between the goby fish and the shrimp?

   A. parasitism
   B. mutualism
   C. predator-prey
   D. commensalism

Answers are on page 659.

Disruption of Ecosystems

Conditions in ecosystems are always changing. Sometimes they change quickly and dramatically, due to floods or fire. Sometimes they change slowly as new species are introduced and begin to take over an area. Available food, water, and fluctuating temperatures also play a role in the balance, or equilibrium, of an ecosystem.

In the following chart, four common disturbances in ecosystems are identified and described.

Type of Disturbance	Description
Flooding	Occurs when an overflow of water covers land not normally covered by water. Ecosystems of water-based habitats are also impacted by runoff containing sediments and pollutants.
Habitat destruction	A process in which a natural habitat is displaced or destroyed and is not able to support the species present. Human activity such as urban sprawl, mining, drilling, logging, and clearing of forests for farmland are the principal causes.
Desertification	Occurs when relatively dry land regions become increasingly arid. Bodies of water begin to dry up, causing loss of plant and animal life. It is primarily caused by climate change and human activities such as deforestation.
Invasive species	Occurs when nonnative species that adversely affect the habitats and ecology of an area are introduced to the area. Species, such as plants or animals, may disrupt the ecosystem by outcompeting the native species for limited resources such as food and space.

These disturbances lead to changes. Take, for example, a forest fire in a national park. Thousands of acres of trees, shrubs, and grasses are destroyed. However, over time, plants begin to grow in the scorched soil. The following diagram illustrates the **succession** that follows the disruption of a forest ecosystem.

Succession Stages After a Fire

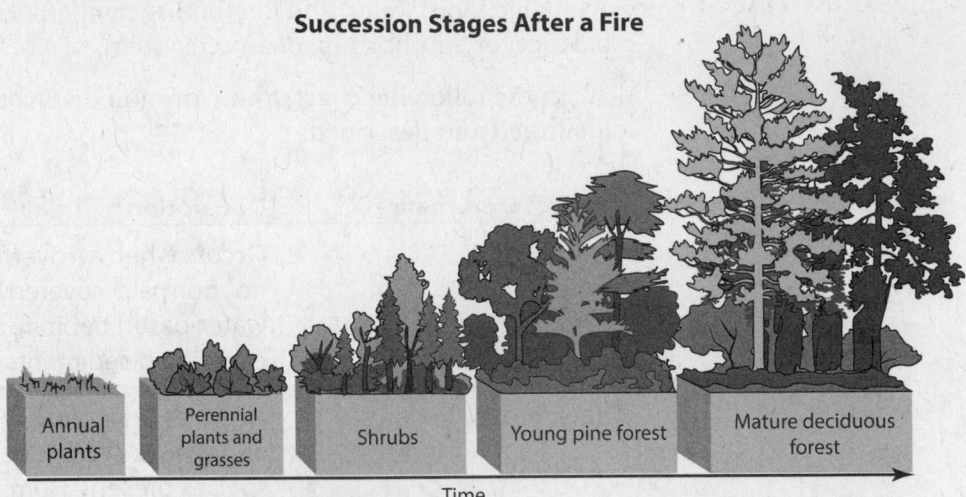

Annual plants | Perennial plants and grasses | Shrubs | Young pine forest | Mature deciduous forest

Time

Extinction

Sometimes an ecosystem is so completely changed that it can no longer support certain species. **Extinction** is the disappearance of a species when the last of its members dies. Although extinction can happen as a result of natural processes, human activities including hunting, urbanization, and the destruction of forests to create farmland are primarily responsible for the habitat destruction that eventually leads to extinctions.

EXERCISE 5

Disruption of Ecosystems

Directions: Choose the best answer for each of the following items.

1. Indicate your answer choice by connecting the events to the correct examples.

   The kudzu vine, introduced to help prevent   Flooding
   soil erosion, climbs over trees, blocking sunlight.

   Runoff containing sediment and fertilizers   Desertification
   pollutes a freshwater ecosystem.

   Overgrazing of plants in semiarid areas   Invasive species
   destroys fragile plant cover.

2. Complete the sentence with a term from the section.

   Human activities have increased the rate of habitat destruction and

   caused the _____ of many species of wildlife.

Answers are on page 660.

CHAPTER 6

The Human Body and Health

Body Systems

The human body is composed of **organ systems** that work interactively to carry out the functions of life. The following table identifies the 11 major organ systems and the functions involved with the different body systems.

Organ System	Functions	Organs
Integumentary	Barrier to invading organisms and chemicals Temperature control	Skin Hair Subcutaneous tissues
Skeletal	Supports body Protects internal organs Mineral storage Blood formation	Bones Cartilage Ligaments Bone marrow
Muscular	Locomotion Heat production	Muscles Tendons
Nervous	Coordinates activities of other organ systems Responds to sensations	Brain Spinal cord Nerves Eyes Ears
Endocrine	Regulates body functions by chemicals (hormones)	Pituitary gland Parathyroid gland Thyroid gland Adrenal gland Thymus Pancreas Gonads

(continued)

Organ System	Functions	Organs
Circulatory	Transports oxygen and nutrients to tissues Removes waste products	Heart Blood Blood vessels
Lymphatic	Returns tissue fluids to blood Defense against foreign organisms	Spleen Lymph nodes Thymus Lymphatic vessels
Respiratory	Oxygen/carbon dioxide exchange	Lungs Trachea Larynx Nasal cavities Pharynx
Digestive	Processes foods Absorption of nutrients into body	Stomach Intestinal tract Liver Pancreas Esophagus Salivary glands
Urinary	Elimination of wastes Regulates pH and volume of blood	Kidneys Urinary bladder Urethra
Reproductive	Produces egg cell (female) and sperm cells (male) Environment for growth of fetus (female)	*Female:* ovaries, uterus, mammary glands, external genitalia *Male:* testes, prostate gland, external genitalia

Interaction Between Body Systems

Most tasks in the body need the support of two or more organ systems working together. In your body, organ systems work together to complete the tasks needed to keep you alive.

The circulatory, digestive, and respiratory systems work together to carry out the process of cellular respiration. The respiratory system brings oxygen into the lungs, and the digestive system breaks food down into nutrients such as glucose. The circulatory system transports glucose from the digestive system to the cells. It also moves oxygen from the lungs to the cells and returns carbon dioxide waste to the lungs.

Another example is the organ system teamwork needed to walk, run, or lift an object. The muscular, skeletal, and nervous systems must all cooperate to produce even the most simple movements that propel our bodies. The following diagram highlights some specific ways that these systems work together

How Body Systems Work Together

```
                          ┌──────────────────────┐
                          │    Skeletal System    │
                          └──────────────────────┘

┌──────────────────┐                                    ┌──────────────────┐
│ Skull protects the│      ┌────────────────────┐       │ Skeletal muscles move│
│ brain, and vertebrae│    │ Provides skeletal muscle│   │ bone, and tendons │
│ protect spinal cord.│    │ something to pull against│  │ connect muscle    │
└──────────────────┘       │ so that skeletal muscle│    │ to bone.          │
                           │ can move.          │        └──────────────────┘
┌──────────────────┐       └────────────────────┘
│ Spinal cord travels down│
│ vertebral column and│
│ delivers the messages│
│ from the brain to the│
│ rest of the body.   │
└──────────────────┘

┌──────────────────┐                                    ┌──────────────────┐
│  Nervous System  │                                    │  Muscular System │
└──────────────────┘                                    └──────────────────┘

                  ┌──────────────────────┐
                  │ Cerebrum of brain     │
                  │ controls movement,    │
                  │ while cerebellum      │
                  │ controls voluntary    │
                  │ movement.             │
                  └──────────────────────┘
```

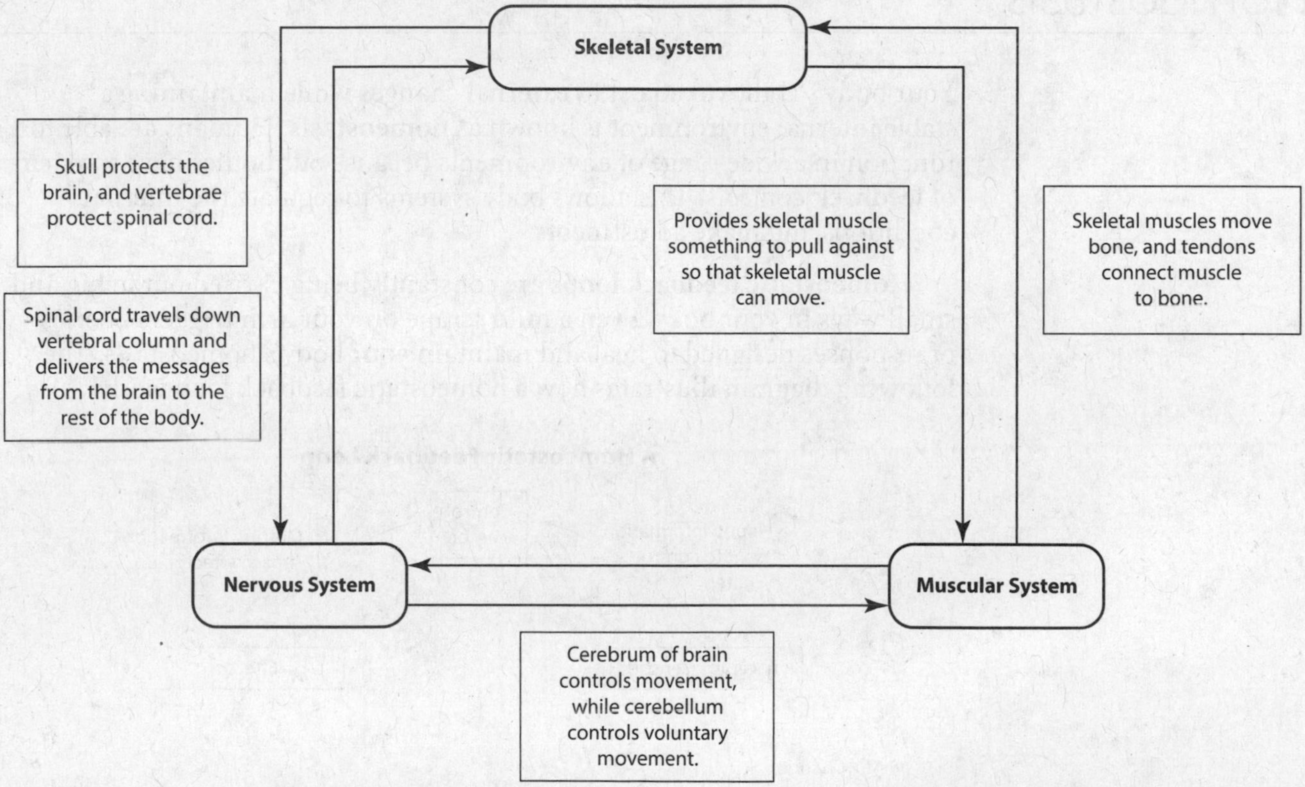

EXERCISE 1

Body Systems

Directions: Choose the best answer for each of the following items.

1. Which organ system regulates both the volume and pH of blood?

   A. circulatory
   B. respiratory
   C. lymphatic
   D. urinary

2. Complete the statement with terms from the section.

The three organ systems primarily responsible for the running

motion of an athlete in a relay race are _____,

_____, and _____.

Answers are on page 660.

Homeostasis

Your body's ability to adjust to external changes while maintaining a stable internal environment is known as **homeostasis**. Humans are able to function in a wide range of environments because our bodies have a system of feedback controls. This allows body systems to regulate the internal conditions and make adjustments.

Homeostatic feedback loops are constantly being carried out in big and small ways in your body. Even a mild scrape on your arm triggers a series of responses designed to heal and maintain your body's homeostasis. The following diagram illustrates how a homeostatic feedback loop works.

A Homeostatic Feedback Loop

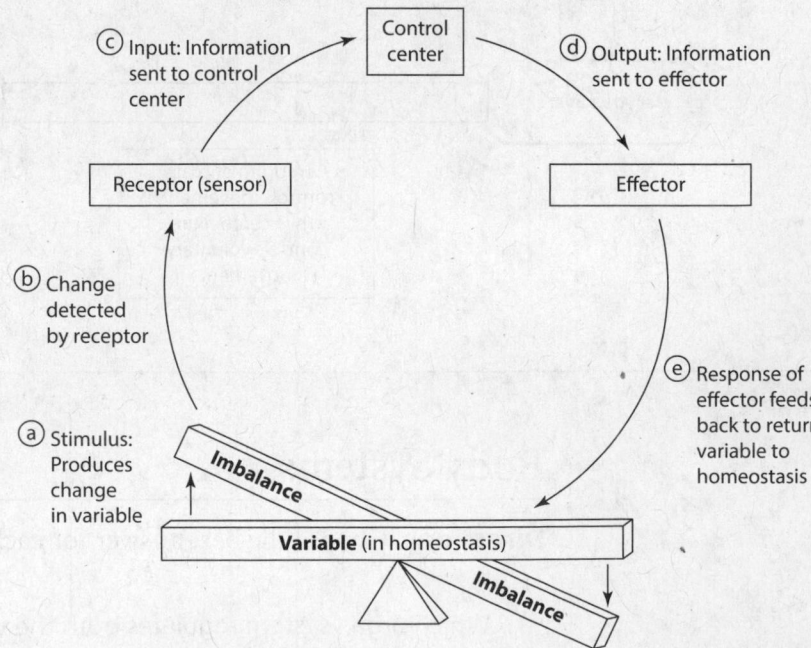

There are two main types of feedback loops. **Negative feedback** is a process that happens when body systems need to slow down or completely stop a process that is occurring. Your digestive system uses a negative feedback loop to regulate the use of your stomach. You don't need your stomach churning if you are not eating!

Positive feedback encourages a physiological process. It amplifies your body's response to a stimulus until negative feedback can take over. Take, for example, the process of digestion. Your body makes an enzyme called pepsin that helps to digest food. Before that takes place, your body usually secretes an inactive enzyme called pepsinogen in your stomach. As pepsinogen is converted to a different enzyme, pepsin, it triggers a process that helps convert other pepsinogen molecules. This cascade effect quickly supplies your stomach with enough pepsin molecules needed to digest proteins.

Effects of External Environments

Homeostatic feedback also occurs in response to changes in the external environment. It can be clearly seen when your body regulates temperature. For example, think about how you feel when you are standing in the hot sun and becoming overheated. In this situation, the response to overheating is stimulation of the sweat glands. Receptors in your skin monitor and sense the rising body temperature. The receptors respond by sending a message to your brain, which then alerts the sweat glands in the skin. The sweat glands act as effectors when they respond to your brain's message to make a change. Sweating cools you and reduces body temperature, thus restoring homeostasis.

Now, suppose that it is very cold and you go outside without a coat. Your body wants to maintain its normal 98.6°F temperature, so it automatically adjusts. To stay warm, hair follicles on your arms tighten and stand up higher to retain heat. Your muscles will also shiver to generate heat through movement. If your body failed to respond, you would be at risk of hypothermia, a life-threateningly cold body temperature.

Homeostasis

Directions: Choose the best answer for each of the following items.

1. Indicate your answer choice by connecting the terms to correct places in the homeostatic feedback loop. (**Note:** On the real GED® test, you will click on the words you choose and "drag" each one into position in the diagram.)

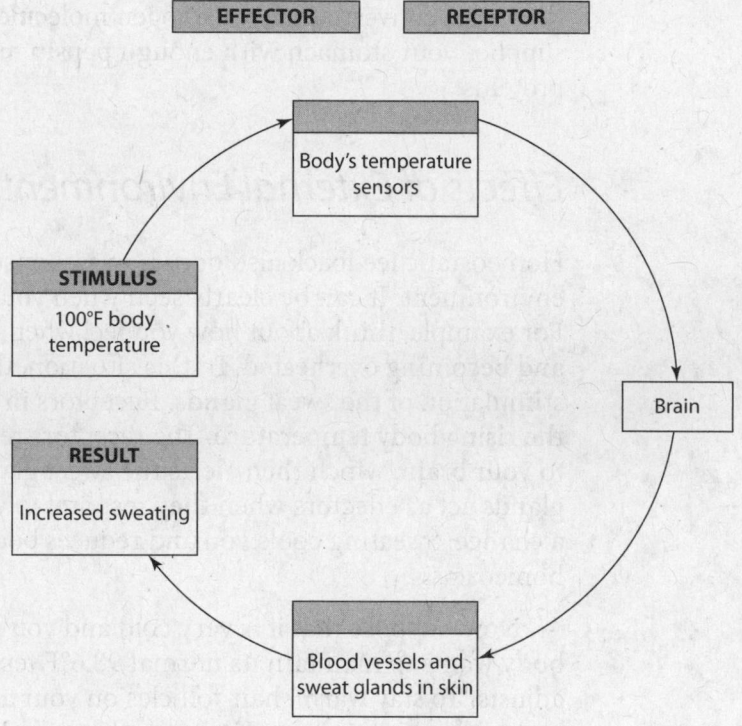

2. Prolonged exposure to the sun at the beach would most likely disrupt homeostasis in the

   A. skin because of the potential for a sunburn.
   B. liver because of increased liquid consumption.
   C. muscles because of exhaustion from swimming.
   D. lungs because of secondhand smoke and exhaust fumes.

Answers are on page 660.

Nutrition

Your body's ability to carry out all the chemical reactions needed to maintain homeostasis depends on six types of **nutrients**. The following table identifies the essential nutrients, the roles they play in helping your body to function properly, and some foods in which the nutrients are found.

Nutrient	Role in Body Functions	Found in . . .
Protein	Building and repairing cells	Beans, meat, fish, and dairy products
Fats	Energy and for cell membranes	Dairy products, vegetable and animal oils
Water	Fills up cells and dissolves chemicals	Water, consumed as a beverage or found in foods
Carbohydrates	Used for energy	Grains, bread, sweets, vegetables, pasta, rice, fruit
Minerals	Calcium for healthy bones Iron for blood	A variety of foods such as meat, dairy, fruits, etc.
Vitamins	Used in small amounts to help enzymes	Small amounts in fresh fruit, vegetables, cereal, etc.

Another source of nutrients is bacteria. Many types of helpful bacteria live inside your digestive system. These **symbiotic bacteria** assist in breaking down food and make the essential vitamins B and K. In return, the bacteria benefit from a stable environment inside your intestines.

Nutrition Concepts

A well-balanced diet is an important component of your overall health. Deficiencies in certain types of nutrients can even lead to disease. For example, a lack of vitamin D can result in bones not hardening properly. Too little of the mineral iron can lead to anemia, a disorder affecting red blood cells.

The energy your body needs is measured in **calories**. The number of calories in a food tells how much energy that food provides. The following chart shows the amount of energy, in calories, found in 1 gram of fat, protein, and carbohydrate.

Fat	1 gram = 9 calories
Protein	1 gram = 4 calories
Carbohydrates	1 gram = 4 calories

Eating the proper amount of each type of nutrient is one key to staying healthy. Just as deficiencies in nutrients can cause problems, so also can too much of a certain type of nutrient. Excessive amounts of protein in a diet can lead to a buildup of toxins that can harm your kidneys. Excessive amounts of fat can eventually lead to obesity.

Information about the types and amounts of nutrients in packaged food can be found on the nutritional labels. The following illustration points out important details found on labels, such as the number of calories and the amount of proteins, carbohydrates, vitamins, and minerals per serving size.

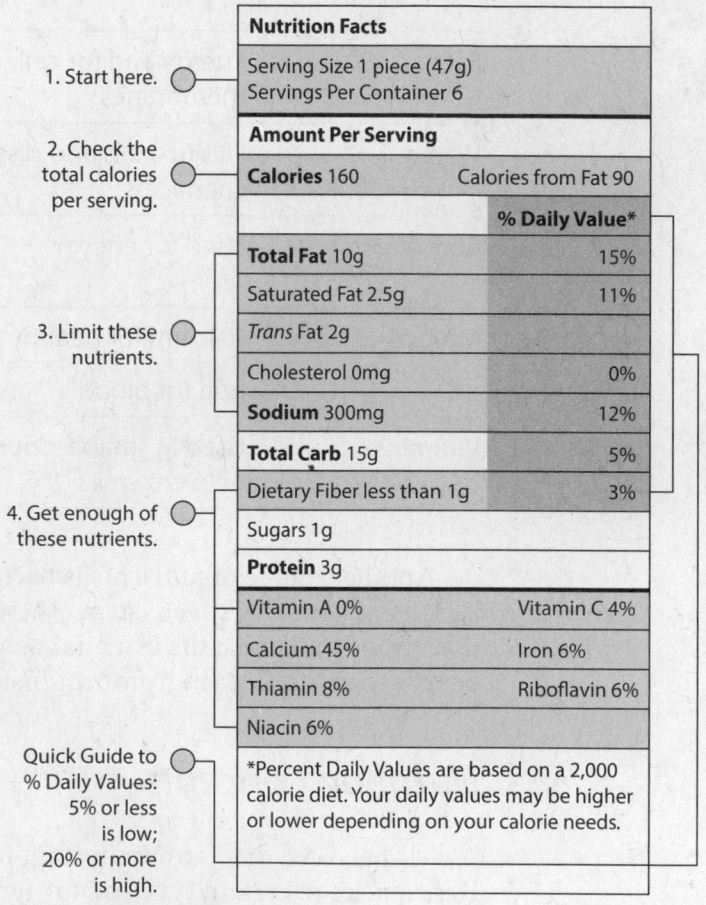

1. Start here.

2. Check the total calories per serving.

3. Limit these nutrients.

4. Get enough of these nutrients.

Quick Guide to
% Daily Values:
5% or less
is low;
20% or more
is high.

Nutrition Facts

Serving Size 1 piece (47g)
Servings Per Container 6

Amount Per Serving

Calories 160	Calories from Fat 90
	% Daily Value*
Total Fat 10g	15%
Saturated Fat 2.5g	11%
Trans Fat 2g	
Cholesterol 0mg	0%
Sodium 300mg	12%
Total Carb 15g	5%
Dietary Fiber less than 1g	3%
Sugars 1g	
Protein 3g	
Vitamin A 0%	Vitamin C 4%
Calcium 45%	Iron 6%
Thiamin 8%	Riboflavin 6%
Niacin 6%	

*Percent Daily Values are based on a 2,000 calorie diet. Your daily values may be higher or lower depending on your calorie needs.

Nutrition

Directions: Choose the best answer for each of the following items.

1. How many calories are in 9 grams of fat?

   A. 9
   B. 10
   C. 18
   D. 81

2. Which of the following nutrients is important for bone health?

   A. vitamins
   B. minerals
   C. proteins
   D. carbohydrates

3. A person taking antibiotics for a long time might be at risk for which of the following?

   A. anemia
   B. reduced energy
   C. vitamin K deficiency
   D. toxicity of the kidneys

Answers are on page 660.

Disease and Pathogens

Another way that your body's homeostasis can be disrupted is through disease and pathogens. **Pathogens** are microorganisms or viruses that cause disease. The following table identifies five of the most common ways in which pathogens can be transmitted, or spread.

Method of Transmission	Explanation	Example
Droplet infection (through the nose or mouth)	When you cough, sneeze, or talk, tiny droplets fly out of your mouth and nose. If you have an infection, those droplets will contain microorganisms. Other people breathe in the droplets, along with the viruses or bacteria they contain.	Flu Tuberculosis Common cold
Direct contact (skin)	Some diseases are spread by direct contact of the skin.	Athlete's foot Genital herpes
Contaminated food and water (through the mouth)	Eating raw or undercooked food or drinking water contaminated by sewage means you take large numbers of microorganisms straight into your digestive tract.	*Water:* cholera and amoebic dysentery *Food:* Salmonella
By body fluids (through breaks in the skin)	Pathogens can enter the body through body fluids (blood), cuts and scratches, or needle punctures.	HIV/AIDS Hepatitis
Vectors (usually through the skin or through the mouth)	A vector is an animal that spreads disease-causing organisms from one host to another without suffering any harm itself. Vectors include mosquitoes and houseflies.	Malaria Dysentery West Nile virus

Prevention of Disease

Many diseases can be prevented by simple **sanitation** methods. Adopting healthy behaviors such as washing your hands often and covering your mouth and nose when you cough or sneeze can reduce and prevent illness. Being aware of what you eat and drink and how carefully you prepare the food is also important for good health.

Immunizations are another way to prevent infections. Many infectious diseases, such as measles, polio, tetanus, and diphtheria, can be controlled with vaccines. A **vaccine** introduced into your body enables you to develop immunity without suffering from the actual disease that the vaccine prevents.

Effects of Disease on Populations

Prior to vaccinations, many infectious diseases had devastating results. Millions of lives were lost in widespread viral epidemics. Between the 15th and 18th centuries, the arrival of European colonists to the Americas introduced several deadly viruses. Some Native American populations were reduced by 80 percent from diseases such as smallpox, measles, and influenza. The damage done by these viruses helped the colonists to conquer the native populations and changed the course of history. Widespread outbreaks of diseases still have the power to change demographics and even lead to extinction.

EXERCISE 4

Disease and Pathogens

Directions: Choose the best answer for each of the following items.

1. The best way to prevent *Salmonella* poisoning is by

    A. boiling your water.
    B. using mosquito repellant.
    C. covering your mouth when you sneeze.
    D. not consuming raw foods such as eggs.

2. Complete the statement with a term from the section.

    Up to _____ percent of the members of Native

    American populations were affected by diseases such as smallpox.

Answers are on pages 660–661.

Life Science

Directions: Choose the best answer for each of the following items.

1. A heterotroph is an organism that must consume other organisms to obtain nutrients and energy. Which process can heterotrophs not perform?

   A. mitosis
   B. respiration
   C. fermentation
   D. photosynthesis

2. The following flowchart describes the evolutionary process that scientists believe occurred when a small group of finches from Ecuador migrated to a nearby island in the Galapagos. Connect each evolutionary term on the right to the correct step in the flowchart.

The island has a limited supply of the seeds that the finches are used to eating but has an abundant supply of insects.	**speciation**
↓	
Finches with slightly narrower beaks are better able to catch insects. Narrow-beaked finches begin to have a survival advantage over broad-beaked finches.	**adaptation**
↓	
In each new generation, the proportion of narrow-beaked finches increases. Eventually, the island's entire finch population has narrow beaks.	**natural selection**
↓	
As the island finch population acquires unique adaptations, it eventually becomes a new species distinct from the finches in Ecuador.	**selection pressure**

Question 3 is based on the following table.

Guinea Pig Inheritance

Gene	Dominant Allele	Recessive Allele
Fur color	Dark (F)	Light (f)
Eye color	Black (E)	Red (e)

3. How many different combinations of alleles would produce a guinea pig with dark fur and red eyes?

   A. 1
   B. 2
   C. 3
   D. 4

Questions 4, 5, and 6 are based on the following passage.

Some bacteria and viruses are pathogens that cause disease in humans. A bacterium is composed of a single cell with no nucleus. A virus is composed of DNA encased in a protective protein coat. Both contain enzymes. A bacterium and a virus are shown in the following diagram.

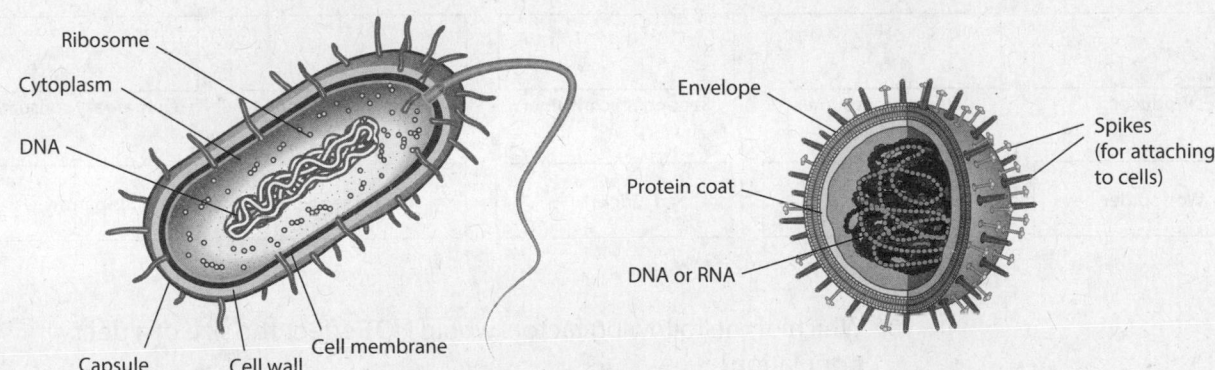

4. Which characteristic best explains why most scientists do not consider viruses to be living things?

   A. Viruses lack cells.
   B. Viruses have no nucleus.
   C. Viruses contain no DNA.
   D. Viruses can contain enzymes.

5. Bacteria, like all cells, use the instructions in DNA to make proteins.

   Place a circle on the diagram to indicate the cell structure that is responsible for building proteins.

6. Which of the following are the two best methods to reduce the spread of diseases caused by pathogens?

    A. sanitation and immunization
    B. immunization and isolation
    C. isolation and antibiotics
    D. antibiotics and sanitation

7. Anemia is primarily a nutrient deficiency. Which nutrient is deficient in a person with anemia, and what body system is most affected?

    A. protein, nervous system
    B. water, lymphatic system
    C. vitamins, digestive system
    D. minerals, circulatory system

8. Which of the following is an example of a mutualistic relationship?

    A. tapeworms living in the intestines of a cat
    B. intestinal bacteria that make vitamins B and K
    C. hermit crabs using gastropod shells for shelter
    D. a wisteria vine growing up and over an oak tree

9. Connect each organism with its correct role in the food chain. (**Note**: On the real GED® test, you will click on the words you choose and "drag" each one into position in the diagram.)

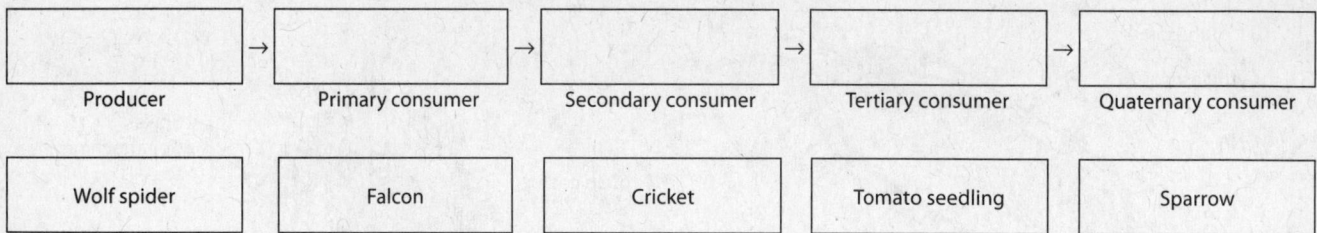

10. Which of the following factors would NOT affect the size of a deer population?

    A. the number of fawns born in the spring
    B. the number of new deer joining the herd
    C. the number of male deer hunted and killed
    D. the number of juvenile female deer in the herd

Answers are on page 661.

PART 2

Physical Science

CHAPTER 7

Chemical Interactions

Structures of Matter

Atomic Particles

All **atoms** are made up of the same three basic particles: protons, electrons, and neutrons. The atoms of different substances have a different number of particles in each atom.

Protons have a positive charge, and **electrons** have a negative charge. **Neutrons** do not have a charge. Another difference between the particles is their mass. Protons and neutrons each weigh about 2000 times as much as an electron.

Following is a model of a helium atom. Notice that the atom is nearly empty and is not a solid object at all. The middle part of the atom is called the **nucleus**. This is where you always find the protons and neutrons. The nucleus contains most of the mass of an atom and has a positive charge, since all the protons are located here. The electrons orbit around the nucleus.

Helium Atom

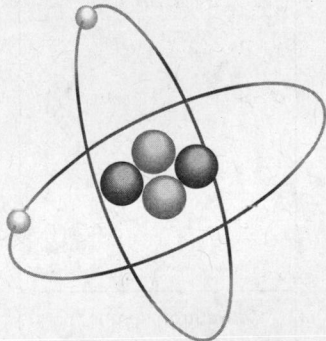

To describe atoms and their nuclei, we use letters and numbers. The letters are a key to the name of the atom. The helium atom is represented by the letters He. The mass number (top number) tells how many protons and neutrons are in the nucleus. The atomic number (bottom number) tells how many protons are in the nucleus. You can see that helium has 2 protons and a mass of 4.

$$_{2}^{4}\text{He}$$

The number of electrons is the same as the number of protons. Because the positively charged protons balance the negatively charged electrons, overall the atom has a neutral charge.

Ions and Isotopes

Sometimes the number of particles in an atom can change. The following table illustrates the results of changes to the numbers of electrons, protons, or neutrons in atoms. If the number of electrons in an atom is changed, protons and electrons are no longer in balance, and the atom becomes a charged particle. Charged particles are called **ions**. If the number of protons in an atom is changed, the atom becomes a completely different element. Atoms with fewer or more neutrons than protons are called **isotopes**.

Change	Result
Electron number	
Proton number	
Neutron number	

Molecules, Elements, and Compounds

Many times, individual atoms are bonded together with other atoms. A **molecule** is a particle made of two or more atoms bonded together. If the atoms are the same type, then the molecule is classified as an **element**.

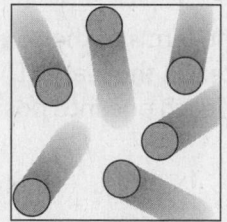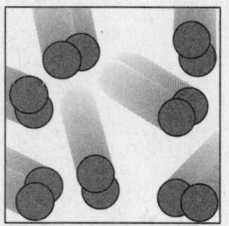

(1) Atoms of a single element   (2) Molecules of a single element

Molecules can also be made of two or more different types of atoms. In this case, the molecule is called a compound. A **compound** is made of two or more elements that have been chemically bonded.

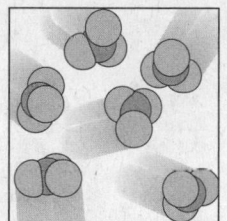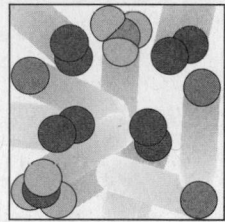

(3) Molecules of a compound   (4) Mix of elements and a compound

EXERCISE 1

Structures of Matter

Directions: Choose the best answer for each of the following items.

1. Connect the terms to the correct place on the chart. One term will not be used. (**Note**: On the real GED® test, you will click on the words you choose and "drag" each one into position in the chart.)

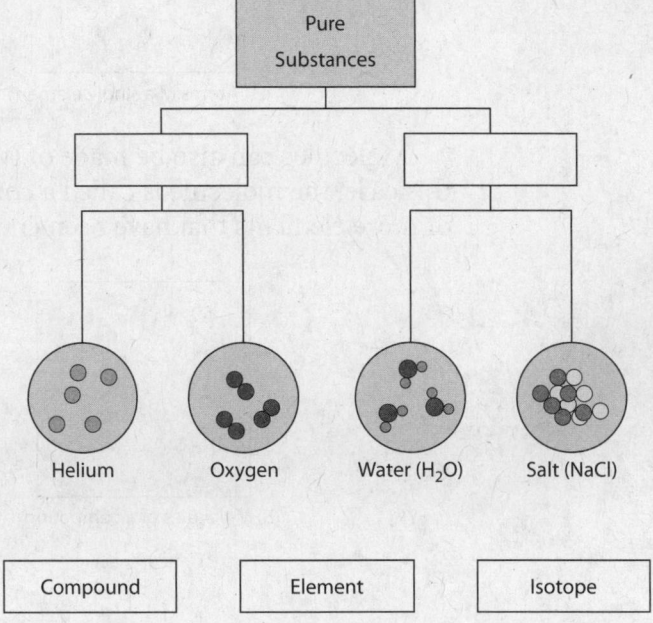

Question 2 is based on the following illustration.

$$^{12}_{6}C$$

2. How many protons does the carbon atom have in its nucleus?

   A. 1
   B. 6
   C. 12
   D. 18

Answers are on page 662.

Physical and Chemical Properties

There are over 100 different elements, each with a unique arrangement of protons, neutrons, and electrons. Scientists use a chart called the **periodic table** to arrange the elements by their atomic number. Each square of the periodic table supplies four important facts, as shown in the following illustration.

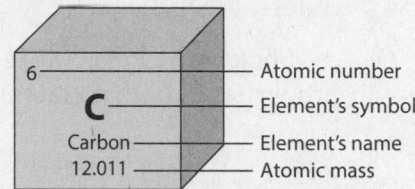

6 —— Atomic number
C —— Element's symbol
Carbon —— Element's name
12.011 —— Atomic mass

In the periodic table, the elements are organized according to their physical and chemical properties. Metals with similar properties are grouped together on the left side of the table. Nonmetals are grouped on the right side of the table.

Periodic Table of the Elements

1 H Hydrogen 1.008																	2 He Helium 4.0026
3 Li Lithium 6.94	4 Be Beryllium 9.0122											5 B Boron 10.81	6 C Carbon 12.011	7 N Nitrogen 14.007	8 O Oxygen 15.999	9 F Fluorine 18.988	10 Ne Neon 201.80
11 Na Sodium 22.990	12 Mg Magnesium 24.305											13 Al Aluminum 26.982	14 Si Silicon 28.085	15 P Phosphorus 30.974	16 S Sulfur 32.06	17 Cl Chlorine 35.45	18 Ar Argon 39.948
19 K Potassium 39.098	20 Ca Calcium 40.078	21 Sc Scandium 44.956	22 Ti Titanium 47.867	23 V Vanadium 50.942	24 Cr Chromium 51.996	25 Mn Manganese 54.938	26 Fe Iron 55.845	27 Co Cobalt 58.933	28 Ni Nickel 58.693	29 Cu Copper 63.546	30 Zn Zinc 65.38	31 Ga Gallium 69.723	32 Ge Germanium 72.630	33 As Arsenic 74.922	34 Se Selenium 78.97	35 Br Bromine 79.904	36 Kr Krypton 83.798
37 Rb Rubidium 85.468	38 Sr Strontium 87.62	39 Y Yttrium 88.900	40 Zr Zirconium 91.224	41 Nb Niobium 92.906	42 Mo Molybdenum 95.95	43 Tc Technetium (98)	44 Ru Ruthenium 101.07	45 Rh Rhodium 102.91	46 Pd Palladium 106.42	47 Ag Silver 107.87	48 Cd Cadmium 112.41	49 In Indium 114.723	50 Sn Tin 118.71	51 Sb Antimony 121.76	52 Te Tellurium 127.60	53 I Iodine 126.90	54 Xe Xenon 131.29
55 Cs Cesium 132.91	56 Ba Barium 137.33	57–71	72 Hf Hafnium 178.49	73 Ta Tantalum 180.95	74 W Tungsten 183.84	75 Re Rhenium 186.21	76 Os Osmium 190.23	77 Ir Iridium 192.22	78 Pt Platinum 195.08	79 Au Gold 196.97	80 Hg Mercury 200.59	81 Tl Thallium 204.38	82 Pb Lead 207.2	83 Bi Bismuth 208.98	84 Po Polonium (209)	85 At Astatine (210)	86 Rn Radon (222)
87 Fr Francium (223)	88 Ra Radium (226)	89–103	104 Rf Rutherfordium (265)	105 Db Dubnium (268)	106 Sg Seaborgium (271)	107 Bh Bohrium (270)	108 Hs Hassium (277)	109 Mt Meitnerium (276)	110 DS Darmstadtium (281)	111 Rg Roentgenium (280)	112 Cn Copernicium (285)	113 Uut Ununtrium (284)	114 Fl Flerovium (289)	115 Uup Ununpentium (288)	116 Lv Livermorium (293)	117 Uus Ununseptium (294)	118 Uuo Ununoctium (294)

57 La Lanthanum 138.91	58 Ce Cerium 140.12	59 Pr Praseodymium 140.91	60 Nd Neodymium 144.24	61 Pm Promethium (145)	62 Sm Samarium 150.36	63 Eu Europium 151.96	64 Gd Gadolinium 157.25	65 Tb Terbium 158.93	66 Dy Dysprosium 162.50	67 Ho Holmium 164.93	68 Er Erbium 167.26	69 Tm Thulium 168.93	70 Yb Ytterbium 173.05	71 Lu Lutetium 174.97
89 Ac Actinium (227)	90 Th Thorium 232.04	91 Pa Protactinium 231.04	92 U Uranium 238.03	93 Np Neptunium (237)	94 Pu Plutonium (244)	95 Am Americium (243)	96 Cm Curium (247)	97 Bk Berkelium (247)	98 Cf Californium (251)	99 Es Einsteinium (252)	100 Fm Fermium (257)	101 Md Mendelevium (258)	102 No Nobelium (259)	103 Lr Lawrencium (262)

Chemical properties include flammability, combustibility, and reactivity with other chemicals. These properties are observed when one substance interacts with another substance. A **physical property** can be noted without observing how the substance interacts with others. Color, melting point, and density are a few examples of physical properties.

Density, in particular, is a characteristic physical property of a substance. It is the relationship between the substance's mass and its volume. Remember that volume is how much space a substance takes up.

$$\text{Density} = \frac{\text{Mass}}{\text{Volume}}$$

The density of a substance is determined by the mass, size, and arrangement of its atoms. Objects with the same volume but different mass will have different densities.

Look at the following table. It identifies different chemical and physical properties of both metals and nonmetals.

Metals	Nonmetals	Physical Property	Chemical Property
Strong	Soft and/or brittle	X	
Malleable and ductile	Brittle	X	
High melting and boiling points	Low melting and boiling points	X	
Reacts with oxygen to form basic oxides	Reacts with oxygen to form acidic oxides		X
Good conductors of electricity and heat	Poor conductors of electricity and heat	X	
Shiny	Dull	X	
High density	Low density	X	
When they form ions, the ions are positive.	When they form ions, the ions are negative (hydrogen is the exception).		X
Solids at room temperature (except mercury)	Solids, liquids, and gases at room temperature	X	

States of Matter

States of matter are considered physical properties. **Solids** have particles packed in a regular pattern and are dense. There is very little space between the particles. Most metals, such as gold and silver, are in a solid state at room temperature. When a solid is heated, its particles gain energy and expand. When the particles reach the melting point, they break away from their positions and enter a liquid state.

Solid

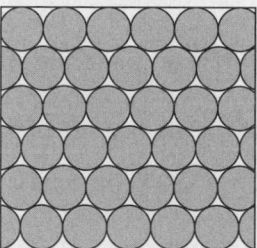

Liquids take the shape of the container in which they are placed, meaning that the particles are not in a fixed position. Liquids are dense because there is a small amount of space between the particles. Mercury (a metal) and bromine (a nonmetal) are in a liquid state at room temperature. When a liquid is heated to the boiling point, the particles gain energy and expand, changing state into a gas. When the particles contain even more energy, evaporation can take place. When liquids are cooled, they can solidify and enter a solid state.

Liquid

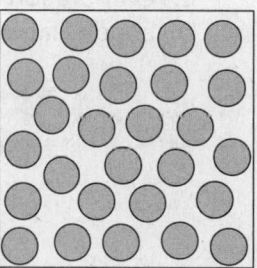

Gases have very low densities because there are huge amounts of space between the particles. Gases are easily compressed and have no shape, filling up whatever space is available as the particles move around. Many nonmetals, including helium, oxygen, and hydrogen, are in a gas state at room temperature. When a gas is cooled, the particles lose energy, causing them to move more slowly and closer together until the gas becomes a liquid. This change of state is called condensation.

Gas

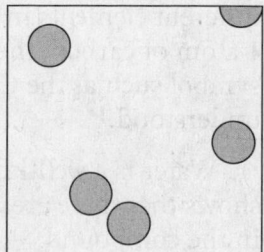

Physical and Chemical Properties

Directions: Choose the best answer for each of the following items.

1. Complete the statement with the appropriate number answer.

   The density of a metal with a volume of 30 milliliters and a mass of
   120 kilograms is _____.

2. Which of the following elements is NOT a solid at room temperature?

   A. gold
   B. silver
   C. mercury
   D. hydrogen

3. Which change of state occurs when a liquid is cooled and the particles lose energy and stop moving?

   A. liquefaction
   B. solidification
   C. evaporation
   D. condensation

Answers are on page 662.

Chemical Formulas and Equations

The periodic table of elements uses one- or two-letter symbols to represent each element. But how do you represent a compound? The answer is a chemical formula. A **chemical formula** is a combination of symbols that represents the elements in a compound. For example, the formula for carbon dioxide is CO_2.

The subscript numbers in a formula show the ratio of the atoms of different elements in that compound. In the case of carbon dioxide, for every 1 atom of carbon, there are 2 atoms of oxygen in the compound. If a letter symbol such as the C for carbon does not have a subscript, the number 1 is understood.

Water is a well-known compound with the formula H_2O. The subscript 2 shows that there are 2 atoms of hydrogen (H) for every 1 atom of oxygen (O) in the compound.

Using symbols instead of words allows you to write chemical equations. **Chemical equations** summarize what happens in chemical reactions. They tell you what substances you begin with (the reactants) and what substances you end with (the products). The number of reactants and products can vary, depending on the reaction.

For example, iron reacts with sulfur to produce iron sulfide. This equation would be written as follows:

$$Fe \quad + \quad S \quad \rightarrow \quad FeS$$

Iron	Sulfur	Iron sulfide
(reactant)	(reactant)	(product)

Conservation of Mass

Even though the arrangement of atoms is different at the end of a reaction from what it was at the start, all the atoms present at the start are still present at the end. In the case of iron and sulfur, there is one atom of iron on the reactant side and one atom of iron on the product side of the equation. The same is true for sulfur.

This principle is known as the **conservation of mass**. During a chemical reaction, matter is neither created nor destroyed. In other words, during a chemical reaction, the amount of matter involved does not change. The total mass of the reactants will always equal the total mass of the products.

Balancing Chemical Equations

Because mass is conserved during chemical reactions, chemical equations must be balanced. To **balance an equation**, first look at the formulas. Try writing the equation with words first. Then, use the symbols to write the equation.

Take the reaction resulting in water as an example. Hydrogen gas reacts with oxygen gas to form water when a spark is added to the mixture.

$$H_2 + O_2 \rightarrow H_2O$$

Now, check to make sure that you have the same number of atoms on one side of the reaction as you do on the other side. This is known as balancing the equation.

In this case, there are 2 oxygen atoms on the left but only 1 on the right. To correctly represent the reaction and balance the equation, you use a coefficient. A coefficient is a number placed in front of a chemical formula that tells you how many atoms or molecules of each reactant and product participate in the reaction. If the coefficient is 1, it is understood and not written.

In this case, you need to multiply the H_2O on the right by the coefficient 2.

$$H_2 + O_2 \rightarrow 2H_2O$$

This gives you 2 oxygen atoms on both sides, but now you have 2 hydrogen atoms on the left and 4 hydrogen atoms on the right. So you also need to multiply the H_2 by the coefficient 2 to have a balanced chemical equation.

$$2H_2 + O_2 \rightarrow 2H_2O$$

Limiting Reactants

In chemistry, there is usually too much of one reactant and not enough of another. The reactant that is used up first and prevents more product from being made is referred to as the **limiting reactant**. The substance that does not get used up as a reactant is called the excess reactant.

Suppose you start with 4 hydrogen gas molecules and 1 oxygen gas molecule. Can you make 4 water molecules?

$$4H_2 + O_2 \rightarrow 4H_2O$$

No, you cannot because you have only 1 oxygen gas molecule. In your reaction, you will run out of O_2 before you run out of H_2. Oxygen gas is the limiting reactant.

Types of Chemical Reactions

So far, all of the reactions in this section have been examples of **synthesis reactions**. A synthesis reaction is one in which two or more substances combine to make a more complex substance. Another example is the reaction between magnesium and oxygen to form magnesium oxide.

$$2Mg + O_2 \rightarrow 2MgO$$

There are several other types of chemical reactions. A **decomposition reaction** happens when compounds are broken down into simpler products. An example is the decomposition of hydrogen peroxide into water and oxygen gas.

$$2H_2O_2 \rightarrow 2H_2O + O_2$$

A **replacement reaction** occurs when one element replaces another in a compound, or when two elements in different compounds trade places. An example of a replacement reaction can be seen when rock that contains copper oxide is heated in the presence of charcoal, which is pure carbon, to obtain copper. The carbon found in the charcoal replaces copper in the copper oxide to form carbon dioxide and copper metal.

$$2CuO + C \rightarrow 2Cu + CO_2$$

EXERCISE 3

Chemical Formulas and Equations

Directions: Choose the best answer for each of the following items.

Questions 1 through 3 are based on the following information.

Iron oxide reacts with carbon monoxide to produce iron and carbon dioxide.

1. Which of the following word equations is correct?

A. iron + iron oxide → carbon monoxide + carbon dioxide
B. iron oxide → carbon monoxide + iron + carbon dioxide
C. carbon monoxide + iron oxide + iron → carbon dioxide
D. iron oxide + carbon monoxide → iron + carbon dioxide

2. Which of the following equations is correctly balanced?

A. $Fe_2O_3 + CO → 2Fe + 3CO_2$
B. $Fe_2O_3 + 3CO → 2Fe + 3CO_2$
C. $Fe_2O_3 + 2CO → 2Fe + CO_2$
D. $Fe_2O_3 + CO → 2Fe + 2CO_2$

3. Which type of equation is described?

A. limiting
B. synthesis
C. replacement
D. decomposition

Answers are on page 662.

Solutions and Solubility

When you think about the word *solution*, what comes to mind? Many people think about something liquid, like a saline solution, a mixture made of salt and water. In chemistry, a **solution** is a homogenous (same throughout) mixture of two or more substances in which the particles are very small (from 0 to 100 nanometers). The substances can be solids, liquids, or gases. Air is a solution that includes dissolved water vapor in a mixture made up of oxygen, carbon dioxide, nitrogen, and various other gases. Metal alloys such as sterling silver are also solutions.

There are two parts to any solution. The substance that is dissolved is called the **solute**. The solute is usually present in a smaller amount than the substance in which it is dissolved. The **solvent** is the substance that does the dissolving and is usually present in a greater amount.

The most common solvent is water. In solutions where water is the solvent, the mixture formed is called an **aqueous solution**. In the following image, sugar is the solute and water is the solvent. The sugar-water mixture is the solution.

Dissolving of Sugar in Water

Water

Sugar solution

Sugar

Solubility

For now, we will focus on aqueous solutions. The **concentration** of a solution refers to how much of the solute is dissolved in the liquid. **Solubility** is the maximum amount of solute that will dissolve in a certain amount of water at a given temperature. Take a look at the following solubilities graph. You can see that as temperature increases, most solids increase in solubility. However, gases decrease in solubility as temperature rises.

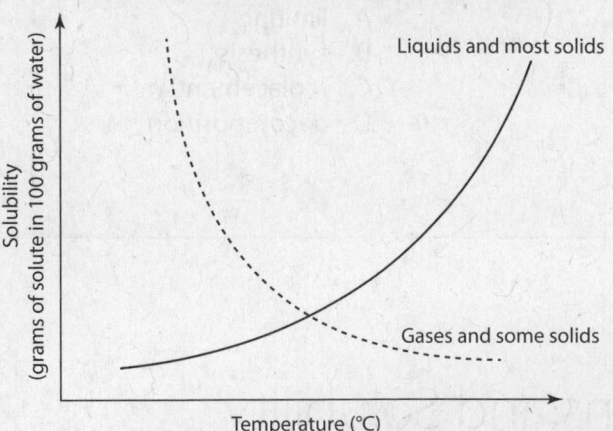

Saturation

A true solution appears clear. If it has color, you can still see through it. If there are undissolved particles, the solution will be cloudy. So, what happens when water can no longer dissolve a certain substance? This is referred to as **saturation**. It is the point at which a solution can dissolve no more of that substance, and any additional amounts of it will appear as undissolved particles. There are three degrees of saturation, as shown in the following table.

Concentration	What It Means	Example
Unsaturated	If you add more solute to the liquid, it would keep dissolving.	One teaspoon of salt placed into a bucket of water creates an unsaturated solution. If you added another teaspoon of salt, it would dissolve too.
Saturated	The liquid has dissolved the maximum amount of solute that is possible at that temperature.	Adding spoon after spoon after spoon of sugar to a single cup of iced tea. At some point, there is too much solute (sugar). The solution is saturated and the rest of the sugar falls to the bottom of the cup.
Supersaturated	The liquid contains more solute than it can theoretically dissolve at a given temperature.	This occurs if you have a very hot saturated solution and slowly cool it down. The solubility of the solute decreases as the solution cools. Hot solutions can dissolve more than cold solutions. These solutions are not stable and crystallize easily.

Weak and Strong Solutions

Solutions can be described as dilute (weak) or concentrated (strong). **Dilute** means that a small amount of solute is dissolved in the solvent. **Concentrated** means that there is a lot of solute dissolved in the solvent.

The acidity, alkalinity, or neutrality of a solution is also described in terms of strength. In a strong acid, nearly all of the acid molecules will form ions, whereas in a weak acid only some of the molecules will form ions. The strength of the solution is shown using a scale of numbers called the **pH scale**. The pH numbers range from 0 to 14.

- Solutions with pH numbers less than 7 are **acidic**. Examples include citrus juices. The lower the pH number, the stronger is the acid.

- Solutions with pH numbers greater than 7 are **alkaline**. An example is milk. The higher the pH number, the stronger is the alkali.

- A solution with a pH of exactly 7 is considered **neutral**. Water is neutral.

EXERCISE 4

Solutions and Solubility

Directions: Choose the best answer for each of the following items.

1. Which of the following Is NOT an example of a solution?

   A. water
   B. gasoline
   C. salt water
   D. 14-karat gold

2. A dilute solution of lemon juice, with a pH of 1.5, would be classified as a

   A. neutral.
   B. weak acid.
   C. strong acid.
   D. weak alkali.

3. Connect the terms to the correct image and description. (**Note**: On the real GED® test, you will click on the words you choose and "drag" each one into position in the diagram.)

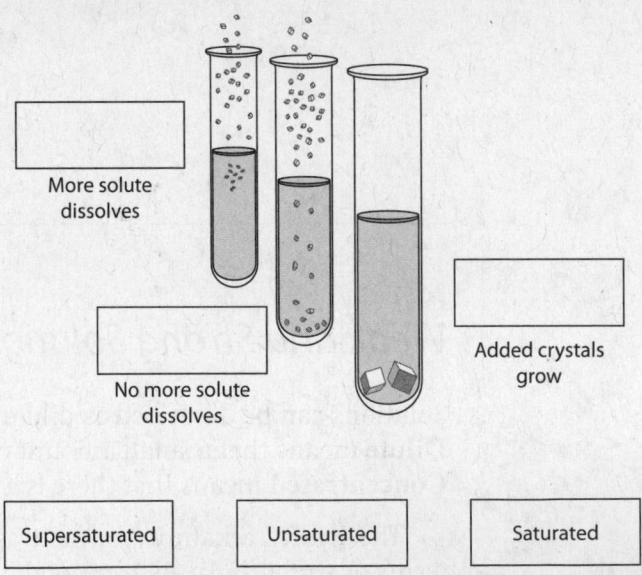

More solute
dissolves

No more solute
dissolves

Added crystals
grow

| Supersaturated | Unsaturated | Saturated |

Answers are on page 662.

CHAPTER 8

Energy

Types of Energy

Turning a lightbulb on and running a mile both require energy, but not the same kind. **Energy** is simply described as the ability to do work. Energy exists in many forms, including:

- **Chemical energy** stored in a substance's chemical bonds
- **Electrical energy** carried in electrical charges
- **Radiant energy** carried in electromagnetic waves, like light
- **Mechanical energy** related to an object's motion and position
- **Nuclear energy** stored in the nuclei of a substance's atoms
- **Thermal energy** related to a substance's temperature

Notice that mechanical energy depends on two characteristics of an object. The energy that an object has because of its position is called **potential energy**. Potential energy is often described as stored energy. The energy that an object has because of its motion is called **kinetic energy**. An object's total mechanical energy can be determined by adding its potential and kinetic energy. We will take a closer look at some of the other forms of energy later in the section.

Energy Transformations

Energy cannot be created or destroyed. It can, however, be converted (or transformed) from one form to another. During photosynthesis, for example, plants convert sunlight (radiant energy) to food (chemical energy). When you walk, run, or perform any kind of motion, the chemical energy from the food you ate is converted to kinetic energy. Some of the chemical energy from your food is also converted to thermal energy as you release body heat.

Types of Energy

Directions: Choose the best answer for each of the following items.

Question 1 is based on the following information.

> To determine the best location in a greenhouse to grow seedlings, a gardener places seedlings in various locations. She puts 2 seedlings by a north-facing window, 2 seedlings by an east-facing window, and 2 in the center of the greenhouse. The gardener measures the height of each plant every 3 days. After 2 weeks, the gardener compares the growth of the plants in each location.

1. Complete the gardener's hypothesis with a type of energy from the section.

   The rate of a seedling's growth is affected by the amount of

   _____ energy it is exposed to.

2. For each energy transformation, indicate the forms of energy involved. (**Note:** On the real GED® test, you will click on the words and "drag" them into position on the diagram.)

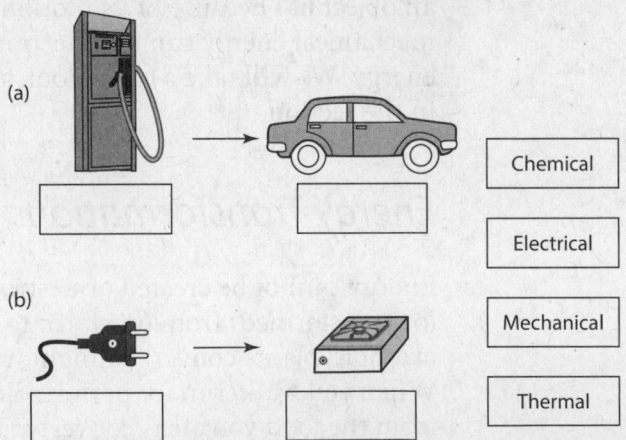

(a)

(b)

Chemical

Electrical

Mechanical

Thermal

Answers are on page 663.

Waves

Energy can be transported by oscillations (repetitive movements) called **waves**. Waves can travel through substances or empty space. The following diagram shows the two types of wave motion.

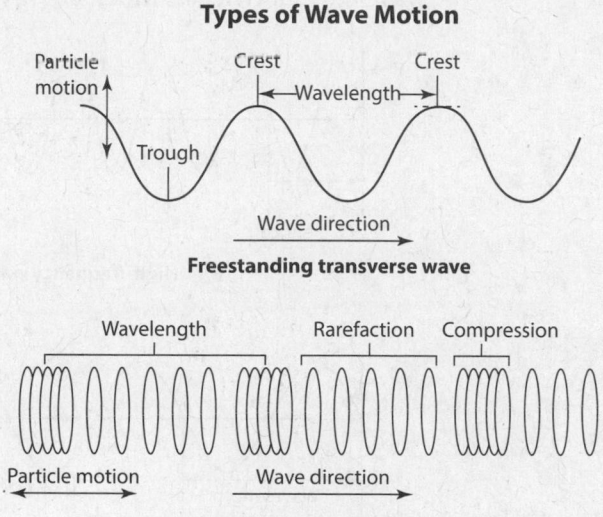

Types of Wave Motion

Freestanding transverse wave

Freestanding longitudinal wave

Notice that both waves in the diagram are traveling from left to right. The type of wave produced depends on how the substance's particles move. If the particles move up and down, a **transverse wave** is produced. The direction of a transverse wave is always perpendicular to the movement of the particles. Think about a jump rope. If one person whips one end of the jump rope up and down while another person holds the other end steady, a transverse wave will ripple through the jump rope. Light energy is transferred by transverse waves.

If the particles move backward and forward, a **longitudinal wave** is produced. The direction of a longitudinal wave is always parallel to the movement of particles. Think about a toy spring. If one person quickly compresses one end of the spring while another person holds the other end steady, a longitudinal wave will ripple through the spring. Sound energy is transferred by longitudinal waves.

Parts of Waves

The two most important characteristics of a wave are wavelength and frequency. **Wavelength** is the distance between corresponding parts of a wave. Notice on the transverse wave in the previous diagram that wavelength is measured from one crest to the next crest. The wavelength of a transverse wave can also be measured from trough to trough, or between any two corresponding points on the wave. Look back at the longitudinal wave in the previous diagram. Notice that the wavelength is measured from compression to compression.

Frequency is the total number of wavelengths that pass a specific point per second. In general, the higher a wave's frequency, the more energy it carries. Look at the following diagram. Each graph shows a total time of 1 second. The top graph shows a wave that produces 6 wavelengths per second. The bottom graph shows a wave that produces 3 wavelengths per second. Since the top wave's frequency is twice the bottom wave's frequency, the top wave carries twice as much energy.

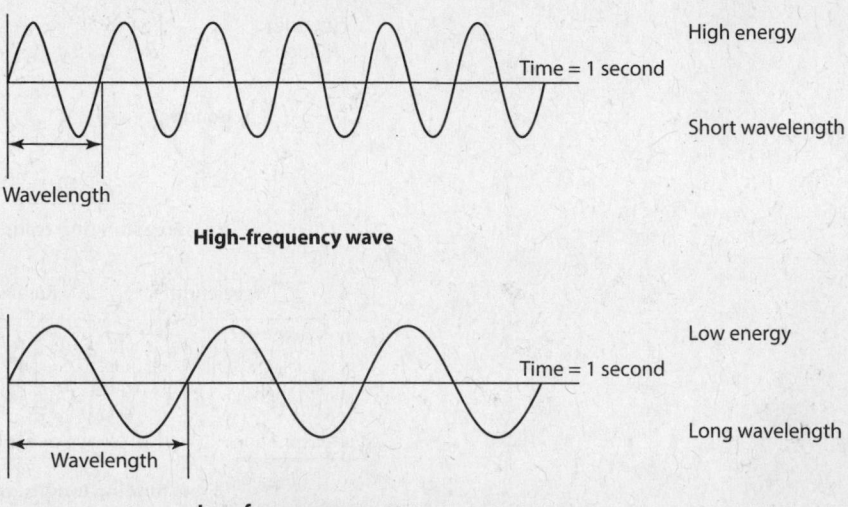

Also notice the difference in wavelength between the two waves in the diagram. The shorter a wave's wavelength, the higher its frequency, and vice versa. This means that waves with a shorter wavelength tend to carry more energy.

Types of Electromagnetic Radiation

Energy that is produced by the movement of electrically charged particles is called **electromagnetic radiation**. Visible light and other forms of electromagnetic radiation are transferred by the seven types of waves shown in the following diagram. Notice that electromagnetic waves are organized according to their wavelength. Radio waves have the longest wavelengths, and gamma rays have the shortest. This also means that radio waves have the lowest frequency and energy, while gamma rays have the highest frequency and energy.

Types of Electromagnetic Radiation

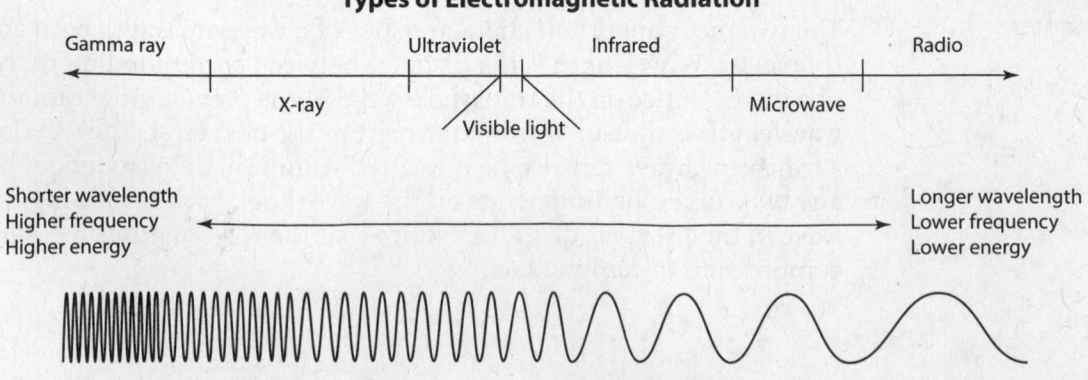

Uses and Dangers of Electromagnetic Radiation

Each type of electromagnetic radiation has a unique set of uses based on wavelength. Some of the common uses of each type of radiation are listed in the following table.

Type of Radiation	Common Uses
Radio	Radio stations
	Wireless communication
Microwave	Weather radar
	Microwave ovens
	GPS
Infrared	Remote controls
	Thermal imaging
Visible light	Can be seen by the human eye
Ultraviolet	Vitamin D production in human body
	Sterilizing medical equipment
X-ray	Medical x-rays
	Airport security
Gamma ray	Cancer treatments
	Medical imaging
	Food pasteurization

There are also dangers associated with exposure to electromagnetic radiation. In general, the shorter the wavelength, the more dangerous the radiation. Radio waves and microwaves are believed to be relatively safe. High doses of infrared, visible light, and ultraviolet radiation can cause burns. X-rays and gamma rays are known to cause DNA mutation, cell destruction, and cancer. When these types of radiation are used, precautions are taken to minimize exposure. Prolonged exposure to any type of electromagnetic radiation can be damaging to your health.

Waves

Directions: Choose the best answer for each of the following items.

Questions 1 and 2 are based on the following diagram.

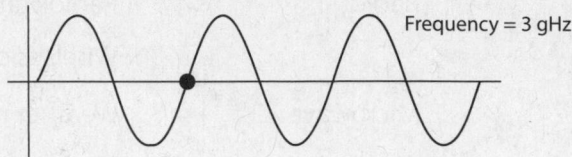

1. Using the dot as the starting point, place an X on the wave to indicate one wavelength.

2. Visible light has an approximate frequency of 300,000 gHz or higher. Based on its frequency, the wave in the diagram represents which type of wave?

   A. radio waves
   B. x-rays
   C. ultraviolet rays
   D. gamma rays

3. Which type of radiation would be most appropriate to use to boil water?

   A. visible light
   B. ultraviolet
   C. gamma rays
   D. microwaves

Answers are on page 663.

Heat

The particles that make up any substance are constantly moving. **Temperature** is the measure of the average speed of the particles in a substance. In general, particles move slowest in a solid, faster in a liquid, and fastest in a gas. This is the reason, for example, that ice (solid state) has a lower temperature than liquid water, and liquid water has a lower temperature than water vapor (gas state).

Heat is the transfer of energy between substances based on the difference in the substances' temperatures. Energy is always transferred from a substance with a higher temperature to a substance with a lower temperature. When an ice cube melts, energy from the warmer air flows into the cold ice cube. This causes the ice cube's particles to move faster, raising its temperature and causing it to change from solid to liquid.

Remember that energy is the ability to do work. When heat is transferred to a substance, its particles move faster because work is done on the substance.

Heat Transfer

The following diagram shows the three ways that heat can be transferred.

Convection

Conduction

Radiation

Conduction transfers heat between two substances that are directly touching. When you touch a hot pot handle, the heat transfers directly from the handle to your hand. In conduction, energy will continue to be transferred until the temperatures of the two substances are equal.

Convection transfers heat by the movement of a liquid or gas. Look at the water in the diagram. As the water in the bottom of the pot gets warmer, it also gets less dense. The less dense warm water moves toward the top of the pot, and the denser cool water moves to the bottom. This movement creates currents that circulate the heat throughout the water.

Radiation transfers heat by electromagnetic waves rather than through contact or movement of substances. As shown in the diagram, heat radiating from a fire can be felt without actually touching the fire itself. Heating food in the microwave and the sun heating Earth are also examples of heat radiation.

EXERCISE 3

Heat

Directions: Choose the best answer for each of the following items.

Questions 1 and 2 are based on the following information.

> When a coffee mug is taken out of the cabinet, it is cool to the touch. A few seconds after hot coffee is poured into the mug, the mug begins to feel warm to the touch.

1. Which type of heat transfer is occurring between the coffee and the mug?

   A. radiation
   B. convection
   C. conduction
   D. none of these

2. Which statement best explains why the mug feels hot?

   A. The air transfers energy to the mug.
   B. The air transfers energy to the coffee.
   C. The mug transfers energy to the coffee.
   D. The coffee transfers energy to the mug.

Answers are on page 663.

Energy in Reactions

Endothermic Reactions

When chemicals react, the amount of energy before and after the reaction is different. When the products contain more total energy than the original reactants, the reaction is **endothermic**. The following diagram shows the change in energy for an endothermic reaction.

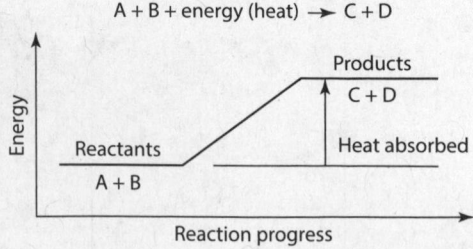

Endothermic Reaction

A + B + energy (heat) ⟶ C + D

An endothermic reaction must absorb energy (heat) from the environment. For this reason, the reaction makes the container in which it occurs feel cold. Instant cold packs, for example, contain two chemicals that undergo an endothermic reaction when the barrier between them is broken.

Exothermic Reactions

Reactions that release energy into the environment are **exothermic**. In an exothermic reaction, the products contain less total energy than the original reactants. The following diagram shows the change in energy for an exothermic reaction.

Exothermic Reaction

$A + B \rightarrow C + D + energy$ (heat)

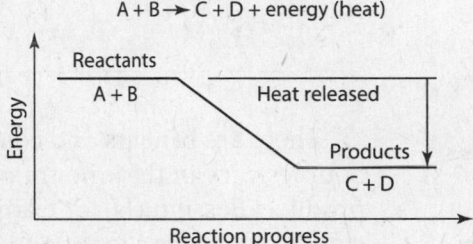

Exothermic reactions make the surroundings feel warm because they release energy (heat) into the environment. You can feel the heat coming from a fire because the burning (oxidation) of fuels, such as wood, is an exothermic reaction.

EXERCISE 4

Energy in Reactions

Directions: Choose the best answer for each of the following items.

1. Complete the statement with a term from the section.

   Photosynthesis is an endothermic reaction because plants must absorb

   _____ from the sun in order for the reaction to occur.

2. Complete the statement with a term from the section.

   Respiration is an _____ reaction because it releases

   energy for cells to use.

Answers are on page 663.

Sources of Energy

Energy is involved in almost every aspect of daily life. Using kitchen appliances, heating and cooling homes, and commuting to work or school are just a few of the ways people use energy every day. The energy we use comes from a variety of sources. The following table lists some common energy sources.

Common Energy Sources	Description
Fossil fuels (petroleum, natural gas, coal)	Drilled or mined from deposits within the earth
Solar	Energy absorbed from sunlight
Nuclear	Energy released from radioactive atoms

There are benefits and costs associated with using any energy source. Sources vary in the amount of energy they provide and the pollution they produce. Fossil fuels, for example, can provide a lot of energy, but they can also produce a lot of pollution. Burning fossil fuels releases smog and greenhouse gases like carbon dioxide. Oil spills can also cause major damage to ecosystems. Nuclear power plants can provide a lot of energy, but they produce radioactive waste. Solar energy produces little, if any, pollution, but it produces a relatively small amount of energy.

EXERCISE 5

Sources of Energy

Directions: Choose the best answer for each of the following items.

Questions 1 and 2 are based on the following graph.

U.S. Energy Use (2010)

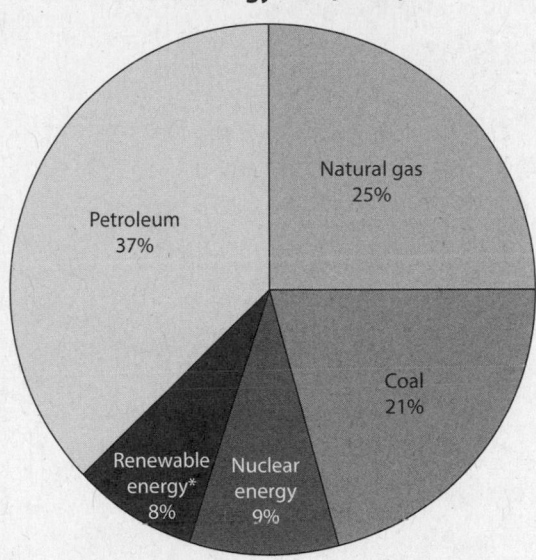

*Renewable energy includes wind, solar, biomass, geothermal, and hydroelectric.

1. Complete the statement with a term from the section.

    In 2010, approximately 83 percent of the energy used in the United States came from _____.

2. Which energy source would be least likely to increase pollution with increased usage?

    A. coal
    B. nuclear
    C. renewable
    D. petroleum

Answers are on page 663.

CHAPTER 9

Motion and Force

Motion

You probably know that speed describes how fast something is moving. An object's **speed** can be calculated by dividing the distance it traveled by the amount of time it was traveling. The speed equation is as follows.

speed = distance ÷ time

$v = d \div t$

Note that speed is represented by a lowercase v in the equation. This is because the equation can be used to calculate both speed and velocity. **Velocity** is speed in a specific direction. Think about a car traveling at a speed of 40 miles per hour (mph). Now look at the following example. Whether the car is traveling toward Location B or back toward Location A, its speed remains 40 mph. The car's velocity, however, changes when the car's direction changes. The car has a velocity of positive 40 mph when traveling toward Location B, but negative 40 mph when traveling back to Location A.

Location A	40 mph → ← 40 mph	Location B		Location A	+40 mph → ← −40 mph	Location B
	Speed				**Velocity**	

You probably recognize that when an object speeds up, it is accelerating. **Acceleration** actually describes any change in an object's velocity. If an object speeds up, slows down, or changes direction, it is accelerating.

An object's acceleration can be calculated by subtracting its original (old) speed from its final (new) speed, and dividing by the time it took to change between speeds. The acceleration equation is as follows.

acceleration = (final velocity − original velocity) ÷ time

$a = (v_2 - v_1) \div t$

Momentum and Collisions

When an object is moving, the product of its mass and velocity is called its **momentum**. The larger an object is and the faster it moves, the greater its momentum. The momentum equation is as follows. Note that momentum is represented by a lowercase p.

momentum = mass × velocity

$p = m \times v$

When objects collide, they transfer momentum to one another. Look at the following example. When the cars collide, their masses do not change. Their velocities, however, do change. The cars' velocities change because they have transferred momentum.

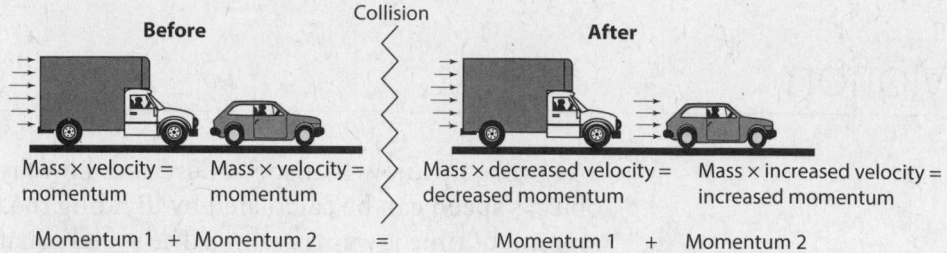

Notice that the total combined momentum of the two cars, however, does not change. The total momentum is always the same before and after a collision. Like energy, momentum cannot be created or destroyed, only transferred between objects.

Another important characteristic of objects in collisions is inertia. **Inertia** is the tendency of an object to resist change in its motion. Objects that are at rest tend to stay at rest. Objects in motion tend to stay in motion.

Think about what happens when a car stops abruptly. When the car was moving, the people inside it were also moving. When the car stops, the peoples' inertia causes them to continue moving forward until something forces them to stop. Safety features like seat belts and airbags are designed to reduce injuries during a collision by stopping peoples' inertia.

EXERCISE 1

Motion

Directions: Choose the best answer for each of the following items.

Questions 1 and 2 are based on the following graph.

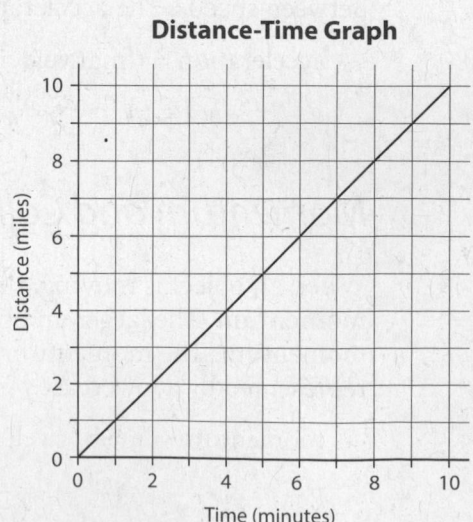

1. Complete the statement with a number.

   The object represented in the graph was moving with a speed of

   _____ miles per minute.

2. What type of acceleration is demonstrated by the object in the graph?

   A. speeding up
   B. slowing down
   C. no acceleration
   D. changing direction

3. Which object has the greatest momentum: a 60-gram tennis ball traveling at 20 meters per second or a 600-gram basketball traveling at 2 meters per second?

   A. the basketball
   B. the tennis ball
   C. neither ball has momentum
   D. their momentum is the same

Answers are on page 664.

Force

When you push or pull on something, you exert a **force**. All objects exert forces on each other. In fact, most objects have multiple forces acting on them at the same time.

Forces may be balanced or unbalanced. Balanced forces do not affect an object's motion. Unbalanced forces cause an object to accelerate (speed up, slow down, or change direction). Think about two dogs pulling on opposite ends of a rope toy. If each dog pulls with the same amount of force, the forces are balanced and the rope does not move in either direction. If one dog pulls with more force, the forces are unbalanced and the rope accelerates toward the stronger dog.

Newton's Laws

In the late 1600s, the English physicist Sir Isaac Newton developed three laws that explain how forces cause objects to move. Scientists use these three laws as the basis for understanding the movement of all objects on Earth and in the universe. The following table describes how Newton's laws can be used to understand the motion of a skateboard.

Newton's Laws of Motion

Law	Explanation	Example
1st Law of Motion: Law of Inertia	An object at rest will stay at rest, and an object in motion will continue moving with the same velocity in a straight line, unless acted on by an unbalanced force.	A skateboard resting on the sidewalk does not move until someone pushes it. When you push with a forward force greater than the force of friction (backward force), the skateboard will accelerate forward.
2nd Law of Motion: $F = ma$	An object's acceleration depends on its mass and the net force applied to it. This relationship is represented by the equation: force = mass × acceleration ($F = m \times a$).	The more force you use to push a skateboard, the more the skateboard will accelerate. It takes more force to accelerate a skateboard with a larger mass.
3rd Law of Motion: Action-Reaction	If one object exerts a force on a second object, the second object exerts an equal force back on the first object.	When your foot pushes down on the ground, the ground pushes back on your foot, pushing you and your skateboard forward.

Gravity

Sir Isaac Newton also identified the **law of universal gravitation**. This law says that every object attracts every other object with a force determined by the objects' masses and the distance between them. The name for this force is **gravity**. The relationship between gravity, mass, and distance is shown in the following diagram.

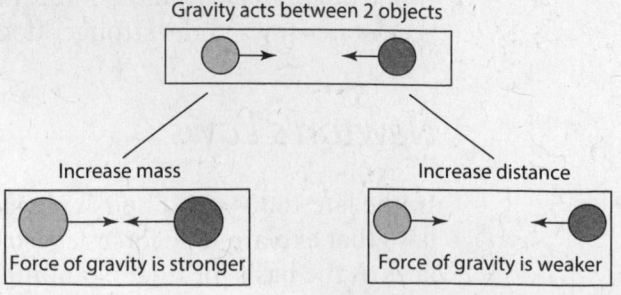

Gravity acts between 2 objects

Increase mass — Force of gravity is stronger

Increase distance — Force of gravity is weaker

The law of universal gravitation explains why the moon orbits Earth and Earth orbits the sun. The force of gravity keeps the smaller object orbiting around the larger object. This law also explains why, on Earth, things fall. Because Earth has such a large mass and we are so close to it, the gravity between Earth and the objects on it is very strong.

When gravity is the only force acting on an object, the object is in **free fall**. An object in free fall accelerates, or continually speeds up, as it falls toward the ground at a constant rate of approximately 10 m/s^2. True free fall cannot actually happen inside Earth's atmosphere, because the force of air resistance is always working against gravity.

Mass and Weight

Mass is the amount of matter in an object. **Weight** measures the force of gravity on an object. On Earth, your mass and weight are the same. In space, however, weight depends on location. If your weight on Earth is 170 pounds, for example, your weight on the moon would be about 28 pounds. The moon is smaller than Earth, so it would exert a smaller gravitational force on you than Earth does. Your mass on the moon would still be the same, though, because the amount of matter you contain does not change.

EXERCISE 2

Force

Directions: Choose the best answer for each of the following items.

Questions 1 and 2 are based on the following diagram.

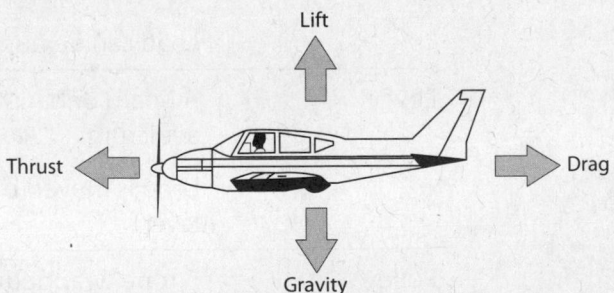

1. Place a circle on the diagram to indicate the two forces that must be balanced in order for the airplane to maintain a constant altitude (height).

2. Which law can be used to determine the amount of thrust required to cause the airplane to accelerate at a certain rate?

   A. first law of motion
   B. third law of motion
   C. second law of motion
   D. law of universal gravitation

Answers are on page 664.

Work and Machines

Consider two boxes, one empty and one full of books. You push the empty box across the floor easily. You push and push on the box full of books, but you can't get it to move. Scientists consider only one of these tasks to be work.

In science, **work** happens when a force causes an object to move a distance. You exerted force on both boxes, but only the empty one moved a distance. You did work only on the empty box. Even though you might have exerted more force trying to move the full box, no work was done, because the full box didn't move.

The amount of work done on an object is calculated by multiplying the force applied by the distance the object moves. The work equation is as follows.

work = force × distance

$w = F \times d$

Simple Machines

Simple machines make work easier, usually by reducing the applied force necessary at the expense of the distance over which that force is applied. The six types of simple machines are listed in the following table.

Simple Machine	Function	Example
Inclined plane	A flat surface placed at an angle Load can be pushed or rolled up or down.	Ramp
Lever	A board or bar that pivots on a support called a fulcrum Load is moved by applying force to part of the lever.	Seesaw
Pulley	A rope wrapped around one or more wheels Load can be attached to rope or wheel and lifted.	Crane
Screw	An inclined plane wrapped around a lever Turning a screw causes it to move up or down.	Screw
Wedge	An inclined plane that moves A wedge is used to split objects.	Ax
Wheel and axle	A wheel with a rod through it Load can be attached to the axle and moved.	Doorknob

Mechanical Advantage and Power

When you use a simple machine, the amount of work you do stays the same, but the force you exert changes. Simple machines can change the direction of your force. Look at the examples shown in the following figure. A screw moves downward as you turn it clockwise. It is easier to turn a screw into a piece of wood than to push the screw straight into the wood. As you push downward, a wedge pushes outward to split an object. Even though you are still doing the same amount of work, splitting wood by swinging an ax downward is much easier than pulling the wood apart with your hands.

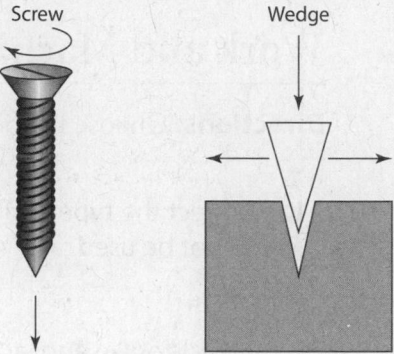

Simple machines can also change the amount of the force you need to apply. If the amount of force that comes out of a machine (output force) is greater than the amount of force you apply to the machine (input force), then the machine is said to amplify force. A machine's **mechanical advantage** tells you how much the machine amplifies force.

Think about the work equation, $w = F \times d$. Remember that simple machines cannot change the total amount of work done. If you want to reduce the amount of (input) force, there must be a trade-off. To do the same amount of work using less force, the distance traveled must increase. Look at the ramp example shown. Lifting the box directly up would require less distance, but more force. Using a ramp increases the total distance you move the box, but it lets you use less force.

Shorter distance
requires more force

Longer distance
requires less force

Power is the amount of work a machine can do in a certain amount of time. The faster a machine performs work, the greater its power. A machine's power can be calculated by dividing the amount of work it does by the amount of time in which it performs the work. The power equation is as follows.

power = work ÷ time

$P = w \div t$

Work and Machines

Directions: Choose the best answer for each of the following items.

1. Connect the type of simple machine with the correct item. Some names will not be used.

   a) slide   inclined plane

   b) twist-top lid and jar   lever

   c) hammer   pulley

   d) paint roller   screw

                                   wedge

                                   wheel and axle

2. Complete the statement using an amount based on the information in the section.

   A simple machine that requires half the input force requires you to travel

   _____ the distance.

Answers are on page 664.

Physical Science

Directions: Choose the best answer for each of the following items.

Questions 1 and 2 are based on the following passage.

Thermite is a mixture of a metal powder (aluminum) and metal oxide (iron oxide). When ignited, the metals in the mixture react to produce a burst of extremely high temperature. Thermite is used to cut or weld steel, as when repairing train tracks.

1. The chemical equation for a thermite reaction is shown. Balance the equation by adding coefficients.

$$\underline{\hspace{2cm}} Al + Fe_2O_3 \rightarrow Al_2O_3 + \underline{\hspace{2cm}} Fe$$

2. The thermite reaction is an example of which type of reaction?

   A. synthesis
   B. exothermic
   C. endothermic
   D. decomposition

3. Which of the following is a property of most metals?

   A. soft and brittle
   B. form negative ions
   C. solid at room temperature
   D. high melting and low boiling point

Questions 4 through 6 are based on the following passage.

A student wants to observe the properties of solutions with various amounts of saturation. She uses a common photograph developing chemical, sodium hyposulfite, as the solute and water as the solvent.

EXPERIMENT 1

A test tube is filled with 2 milliliters of water, and 1 gram of hyposulfite crystals is added to the test tube. The test tube is shaken to dissolve the crystals. The crystals dissolve rapidly, and the solution in the test tube becomes clear.

EXPERIMENT 2

Two grams of hyposulfite crystals are added to 2 milliliters of water in a test tube. After several minutes of shaking the test tube, the crystals dissolve. The solution is cloudy.

EXPERIMENT 3

Three grams of hyposulfite crystals are added to 4 milliliters of water in a test tube. The test tube is shaken and the crystals dissolve. The solution in the test tube becomes clear.

EXPERIMENT 4

Thirty grams of hyposulfite crystals are added to 2 milliliters of water. The mixture is heated to a gentle boil. Then the test tube is placed in a container of cold water until it returns to room temperature. Small crystalline particles are observed in the solution.

4. Which of the following is a possible source of error in the experimental design?

   A. using 2 milliliters of water in experiment 1
   B. using 30 grams of crystals in experiment 4
   C. using 4 milliliters of water in experiment 3
   D. using 2 grams of hyposulfite in experiment 2

5. Which of the experiments produced a supersaturated solution?

   A. Experiment 1
   B. Experiment 2
   C. Experiment 3
   D. Experiment 4

6. Which type of heat transfer is demonstrated by the boiling mixture in Experiment 4?

   A. radiation
   B. convection
   C. conduction
   D. combustion

7. Gamma rays are the most dangerous type of electromagnetic radiation because they

   A. transfer the most energy.
   B. have the lowest frequency.
   C. have the highest wavelength.
   D. are not visible to the human eye.

8. A truck is traveling down the highway at a speed of 65 miles per hour. Which other piece of information is needed to determine the truck's momentum?

   A. truck's mass
   B. distance traveled
   C. truck's acceleration
   D. amount of travel time

9. A student wants to test how different types of flooring affect the motion of a toy car. Which of the following experimental designs should the student use?

   A. Choose 3 cars with equal masses. Push cars down a ramp onto 3 different types of flooring. Observe the car that traveled the farthest on each type of flooring.
   B. Choose 3 cars with different masses. Allow cars to roll down a ramp onto 3 different types of flooring. Observe the car that traveled the farthest on each type of flooring.
   C. Choose 3 cars with equal masses. Allow cars to roll down a ramp onto 3 different types of flooring. Observe the distance traveled by each car on each type of flooring.
   D. Choose 3 cars with different masses. Push cars down a ramp onto 3 different types of flooring. Observe the distance traveled by each car on each type of flooring.

10. Which of the following tasks is NOT considered work?

   A. trying to turn on a stuck water faucet
   B. pushing a wheelbarrow over a flat lawn
   C. rolling a trash can down a steep driveway
   D. dragging a bag of raked leaves behind you

Answers are on pages 664–665.

PART 3

Earth and Space Science

CHAPTER 10

Space Systems

The Age of Earth

It is estimated that Earth formed about 4.6 billion years ago. Scientists use three major types of evidence when determining the age of Earth and of objects on Earth: landforms, fossils, and radiometric dating.

The processes that build up and wear down landforms today are the same processes that have been at work throughout Earth's history. Understanding these processes allows scientists to learn about Earth's history just by looking at the structure and composition of landforms.

One process scientists study is the formation of sedimentary rock. Over time, as sediment (weathered material) settles, it becomes compacted into layers of sedimentary rock. Look at the following diagram. Since new sediment is added to the top of sedimentary rock, the youngest layers are at the top and the oldest layers are at the bottom. This allows scientists to determine the relative age of the layers in a landform.

Layers of Sedimentary Rock

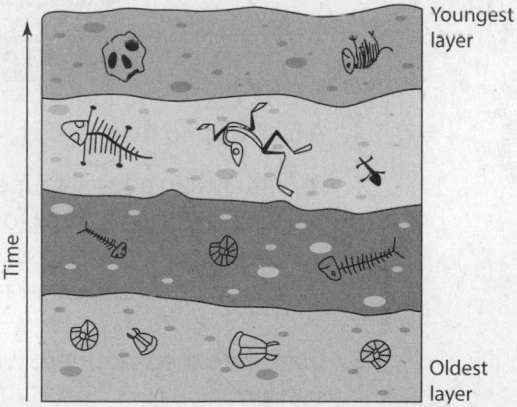

Fossils are remains (shells or bones) or evidence (imprints) left behind by dead organisms. Fossils are most often found in sedimentary rock. As shown in the diagram, the age of a fossil can be determined by looking at the layer it is found in. The opposite is also true. Finding a fossil whose age is already known can provide information about the layer it is found in.

Comparing rock layers and fossils provides information about the relative age of objects on Earth. **Radiometric** (or radioactive) **dating** provides the exact, or absolute, age of objects on Earth. Remember that an element has a specific number of protons in its nucleus. Some elements have radioactive isotopes, or versions that turn into another element by losing a proton. Carbon-14 and uranium-235 are radioactive isotopes used by scientists in radiometric dating.

The amount of time it takes half of an isotope's atoms to change into another element is called the half-life. For example, uranium-235 (U) has a half-life of 1 billion years. After 1 billion years, half of the U-235 atoms in a rock will have turned into lead (Pb) atoms. After 2 billion years, half of the remaining U-235 atoms in the rock will have turned into lead atoms, so only one-quarter of the original total will remain. The process will continue at the same pace. By looking at the number of U-235 atoms that remain, scientists can determine the age of the rock.

EXERCISE 1

The Age of Earth

Directions: Choose the best answer for each of the following items.

Question 1 is based on the following diagram.

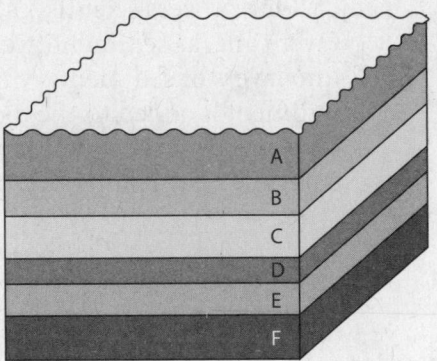

1. A fossil found in layer C is

   A. older than a fossil found in layer E.
   B. younger than a fossil found in layer A.
   C. the same age as a fossil found in layer D.
   D. the same age as other fossils found in layer C.

2. Complete the statement with a number based on the information in the section.

   The half-life of carbon-14 is about 5,730 years. After 5,730 years an object

   originally containing 100 carbon-14 atoms can be expected to have about

   _____ carbon-14 atoms left.

Answers are on page 665.

The Solar System

Solar means sun. Our **solar system** is made up of the sun and all objects that orbit the sun. The **sun** is a star located at the center of our solar system. We'll discuss stars in more detail later.

Remember that all objects exert gravitational force on each other. Since the sun is the largest object in the solar system, its gravity keeps all other objects orbiting around it. After the sun, the largest objects in the solar system are the round-shaped **planets**. The following diagram shows the relative locations of the eight planets in the solar system.

The Solar System

The planets are sometimes broken into two groups. The four smaller planets located closest to the sun all have rocky surfaces and are called the **terrestrial planets**. The four larger planets farther from the sun all have gaseous surfaces and are called the **gas giants**. Recently, a new category of planet was created called dwarf planets or minor planets. One example of these objects is Pluto.

Any natural object in space that orbits a planet is called a **moon**. You know that Earth has one moon. A planet may have no moons, like Mercury, or several moons, like Jupiter. We'll look more closely at Earth's moon later.

Asteroids are another type of object in the solar system. An asteroid is a large, irregularly shaped chunk of rock. Although asteroids exist throughout the solar system, most are found in a band called the asteroid belt. The asteroid belt separates the gas giants from the terrestrial planets.

Comets are made up of frozen gases and dust particles and are usually smaller than asteroids. Some comets orbit the sun continuously. Others orbit the sun once and then travel off into space. Halley's Comet is a famous comet that continuously orbits the sun. Its orbit passes by Earth every 76 years.

Interactions Between Earth and the Solar System

Earth orbits, or revolves, around the sun. Earth completes one **revolution** around the sun every 365¼ days. We call one revolution of Earth a year.

Earth also spins, or rotates, on an axis. Earth completes one **rotation** every 24 hours. We call one rotation of Earth a day. Earth's rotation and revolution are shown on the following diagram.

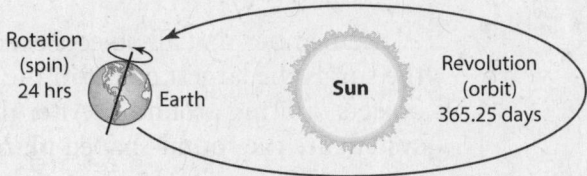

Earth's Rotation and Revolution

Interactions between Earth, the moon, and the sun cause Earth to experience eclipses and tides. An **eclipse** is caused by the positions of the sun and moon in relation to Earth. An eclipse happens when one object in space blocks light from reaching another object. The following diagram shows the two types of eclipses that can occur. During a solar eclipse, the moon blocks sunlight from reaching Earth. In a lunar eclipse, Earth blocks sunlight from reaching the moon.

Solar and Lunar Eclipses

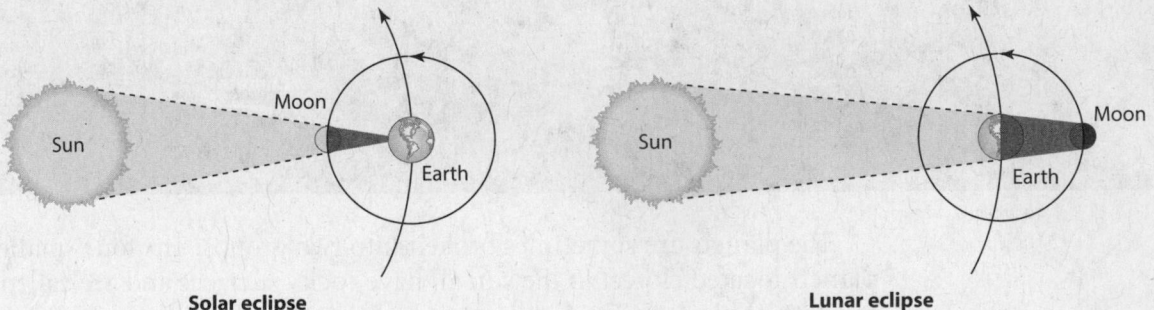

The daily rises and falls of ocean levels are called **tides**. A high tide occurs when the ocean reaches its highest point on the shore. A low tide occurs when the ocean reaches its lowest point on the shore. Shorelines experience two high tides and two low tides every day.

Tides are caused by the pull of the moon's gravity as Earth rotates on its axis. Look at the following tides diagram. As the moon orbits Earth, its gravity pulls on the water in the ocean. This causes the ocean to bulge on the sides closest to and opposite of the moon. Shores within the bulge areas experience high tide. Shores not located in the bulge areas experience low tide. As Earth rotates, the bulges stay in line with the moon, causing different locations to experience high tide at different times throughout a day.

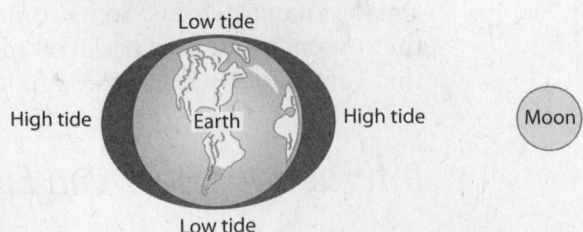

The sun's gravitational force also affects tides. Look at the following diagram. When the sun is in line with the moon, they both pull the ocean in the same direction. This causes extra high and extra low tides called the **spring tides**. When the sun and moon are perpendicular to each other, they pull the ocean in different directions. This causes only minor differences in high and low tides, a condition referred to as the **neap tides**.

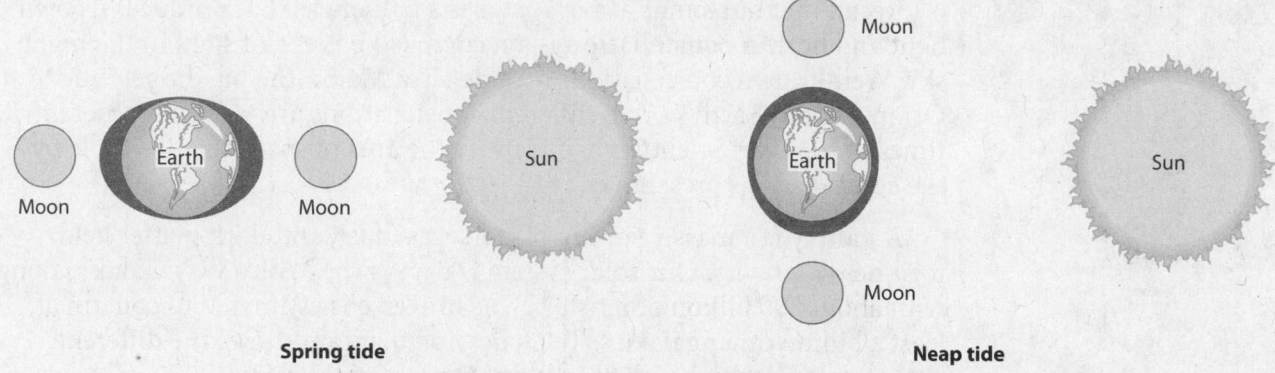

Spring tide   **Neap tide**

EXERCISE 2

The Solar System

Directions: Choose the best answer for each of the following items.

1. Complete the following statement with terms from the section.

    Earth is classified as a _____ planet because it has a

    _____ surface.

2. The daily cycle of night and day is caused by

    A. Earth's rotation.
    B. the sun's gravity.
    C. Earth's revolution.
    D. the moon's revolution.

Answers are on page 665.

The Universe

The total of all matter and energy that exists is called the **universe**. The different objects that exist in our solar system are found throughout the universe. The universe contains many other solar systems, as well as other types of objects.

Recall that our sun is a star. A **star** is a ball of gas that produces its own light and heat. A **constellation** is a recognized pattern of stars in the night sky. Well-known constellations include Ursa Major (the big dipper) and Orion. Due to Earth's orbit, different constellations are visible at different times of the year. Scientists can identify the area of space that is visible by the constellations present.

A **galaxy** is a massive group of stars, gas, dust, and dark matter held together by gravity. Our solar system is part of the Milky Way Galaxy, along with about 200 billion other stars. The universe is estimated to contain at least a billion other galaxies. The following diagram shows the different shapes galaxies can have. The Milky Way is a spiral galaxy.

Types of Galaxies

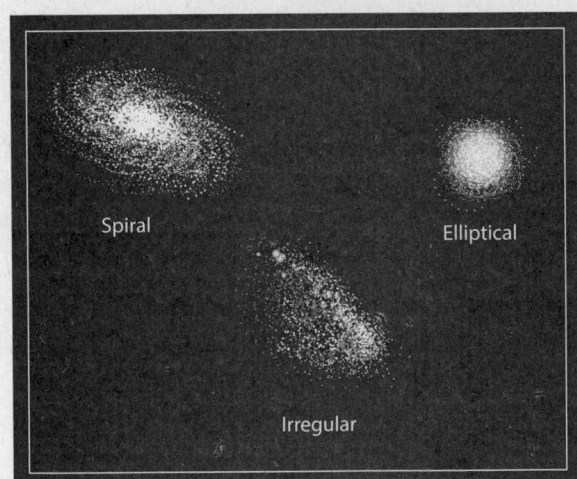

Age and Development of the Universe

Scientists believe that the universe formed 10 to 20 billion years ago. The most widely accepted model of how the universe began is called the **Big Bang theory**. According to this theory, all of the matter and energy in the universe was once contained in an area the size of an atom. An enormous explosion (Big Bang) caused the matter and energy to rapidly expand outward, creating the universe. Scientists believe the universe has been expanding ever since.

Age and Development of Stars

Stars vary in composition, size, and age. All stars, however, follow the same basic life cycle. A star forms in a cloud of gas and dust called a **nebula**. Gravity causes some gas and dust to pull inward, forming a **protostar**. A protostar then turns into a **main sequence** star. A star spends most of its life as a main sequence star.

The fusion of hydrogen (H) atoms into helium (He) atoms causes main sequence stars to release heat and light. A star dies when it runs out of hydrogen. A main sequence star that has run out of fuel will eventually stop glowing and become a black dwarf. **White dwarfs** are stars that are close to dying out.

Sometimes a protostar is too massive to become a main sequence star. These **supergiant** stars die in a sudden explosion called a **supernova**. The death of a supergiant can result in a **black hole**.

EXERCISE 3

The Universe

Directions: Choose the best answer for each of the following items.

1. The Big Bang theory provides the leading model for the formation of the

    A. Earth.
    B. universe.
    C. solar system.
    D. Milky Way galaxy.

2. The death of a supergiant star can result in a

    A. nebula
    B. main sequence star
    C. white dwarf
    D. black hole

Answers are on page 665.

CHAPTER 11

Earth Systems

The Structure of Earth

There are three main layers that make up Earth's interior. Each layer has its own materials, properties, and conditions as shown in the following table.

Properties of Earth's Interior Layers

Property	Crust	Mantle	Core
Fraction of Earth	< 1% of mass	About 70%	About 30%
State	Broken rock	Plastic	Semiliquid
Depth (kilometers)	0–30	30–3030	3030–6370
Density (grams/cubic centimeter)	2.7	3.5–5.5	10–12
Representative chemical composition	SiO_2	$(Fe, Mg) SiO_4$	Fe, Ni
Temperature (Kelvin)	300–500	500–3000	3000–5300
Pressure (atmospheres)	1–1000	$10^3–10^6$	$10^6–10^7$

The outermost layer is called the **crust**. This is a thin outer layer of rock that includes both the dry land and the ocean floor that cover Earth's surface. The crust beneath the ocean is referred to as **oceanic crust** and consists mostly of dense, dark, finely textured rock called basalt. **Continental crust** forms the continents. It consists mainly of granite, a lighter, less dense rock with larger crystals than those found in basalt.

Underneath the crust there is a boundary of hot rock. This is the **mantle**. It is composed mainly of silicate rocks that contain lots of iron, nickel, and magnesium. The uppermost part of the mantle and the crust are similar. Together, they form a rigid layer called the **lithosphere**. Below the lithosphere, temperature and pressure increase with depth. This added heat and pressure results in less rigid rock that is somewhat bendable and plastic-like. The **asthenosphere** is a soft layer of the mantle where material can flow freely.

Earth's Interior Layers

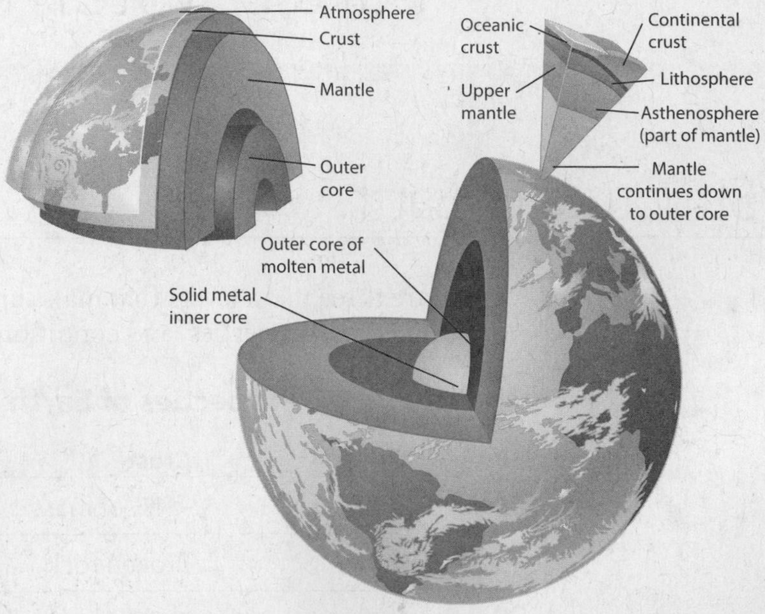

Earth's **core** also consists of two parts: a molten, liquid **outer core** and a solid, dense **inner core**. Both parts are made up of metals like iron and nickel. Together, the inner and outer cores are just slightly smaller than the moon.

Tectonic Plates

The following image may look more like a puzzle to you than a map. It illustrates how oceanic crust and continental crust come together in sections to make up seven primary **tectonic plates** and many other smaller plates. All of the tectonic plates have names that usually refer to their proximity to certain landmasses, oceans, or regions of the globe. These plates slowly move, or float, on the mantle by means of convection currents. **Convection currents** are hot currents of molten rock that cause the plates above them to move 1 or 2 centimeters each year.

Earth's Tectonic Plates

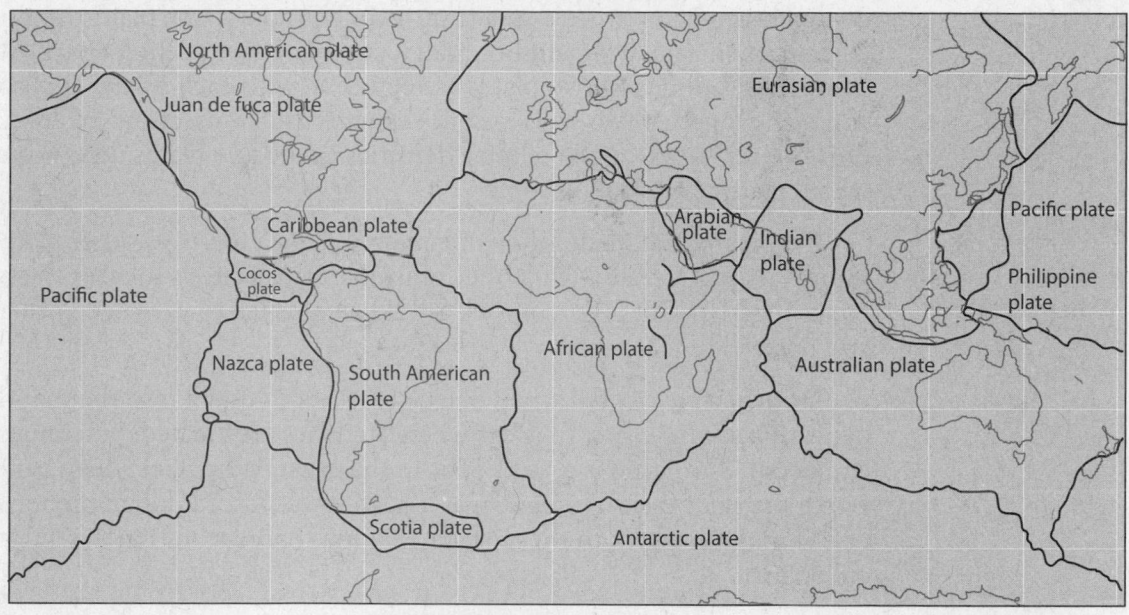

The motion of the tectonic plates provides an explanation for the formation of ocean basins, mountains, and continental shelves. **Continental shelves** are gently sloping, shallow sections of the ocean floor that extend outward from the edge of a continent. **Ocean basins** are vast geologic regions below sea level that cover nearly 75 percent of Earth's surface. Ocean basins contain features such as deep-sea trenches and mountain-like ocean ridges. Tectonic plates are the key to the formation of these features.

Features of the Ocean Basin

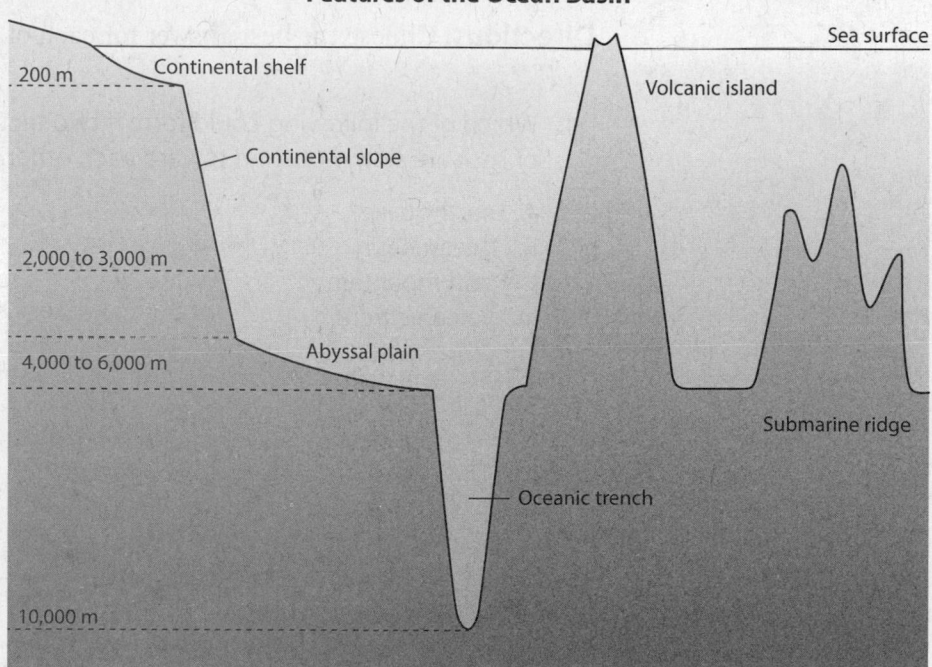

There are different types of plate boundaries including transform, divergent, and convergent. At a transform boundary, one plate is sliding past another. At a divergent boundary, two plates are pulling apart. At a convergent boundary, two plates are colliding with each other. This collision can bring together two sections of oceanic crust, two sections of continental crust, or one of each. The relative densities of the two plates determine which plate comes out on top.

Mountains are made when one plate slides on top of another plate. **Fold mountains** are created when the collision of two plates squeezes the two plates together. The layers of rock are slowly pushed toward each other and rise upward in folds.

Trenches are created when one plate is forced down into the mantle beneath a second plate. In areas where trenches are created, **volcanoes** can occur. A volcano is a weak spot in the crust. When heat deep beneath Earth's surface melts the plate material that was forced down, molten rock called **magma** is sent to the surface. Magma that reaches Earth's surface is called **lava**.

The movement of two tectonic plates sliding past each other can create earthquakes. **Earthquakes** are formed by the shifting and breaking of the surface rocks. The break in the crust where earthquakes can occur is called a fault. Faults usually occur along plate boundaries.

EXERCISE 1

The Structure of Earth

Directions: Choose the best answer for each of the following items.

1. Which of the following could form if two tectonic plates collide and layers of rock are slowly pushed toward each other?

   A. earthquake
   B. ocean basin
   C. fold mountains
   D. volcanic trench

2. Connect the correct terms to each diagram label. (**Note**: On the real GED®
test, you will click on the words you choose and "drag" each one into
position on the diagram.)

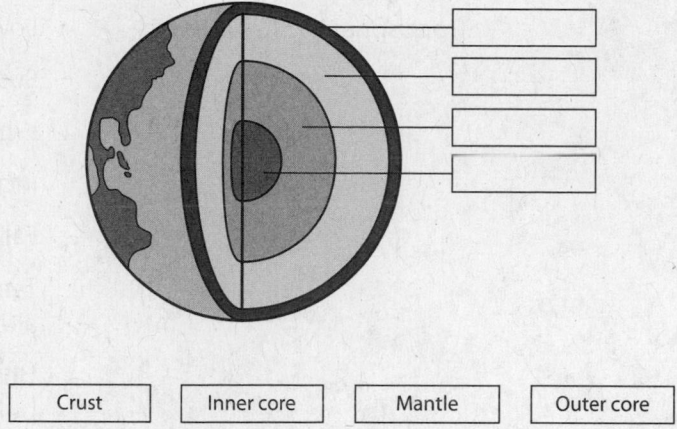

| Crust | Inner core | Mantle | Outer core |

Answers are on page 666.

Earth's Atmosphere

Scientists estimate that Earth formed around 4.6 billion years ago. After
a certain passage of time, it is thought that gases from Earth's core were
expelled from volcanoes. The envelope of gases that now surrounds the
planet is called Earth's **atmosphere**. These gases are most dense at sea level
and become increasingly thinner higher in the atmosphere.

The atmosphere exists as a series of layers, each having its own
characteristics. The following table lists the characteristic features of each
layer as well as its location relative to sea level.

Layers of Earth's Atmosphere

Atmospheric Region	Location (km)	Features
Troposphere	0–10 km	Lowest region of the atmosphere
		Sustains life
		Where all weather occurs
		Increased wind speeds with height
		Fall in pressure with height
		Temperature decreases with increasing altitude (6.4 degrees per 1000 m)
		Unstable layer due to presence of clouds, pollution, water vapor, and dust
Stratosphere	10–30 km	Temperatures increase with height.
		Ozone, a form of oxygen, is concentrated here.
		Ozone absorbs ultraviolet (UV) radiation from the sun and warms this layer.
		Winds increase with height but pressure falls.
		Some jet aircraft fly here.
Mesosphere	30–50 km	Rapid fall in temperature with height caused by lack of water vapor, clouds, or dust
		Temperatures very low (as low as −130 degrees Celsius) and winds high
		Space shuttle orbits within this layer.
Thermosphere	50–400 km	Rapid increase in temperature with height due to steady influx of solar energy
		Temperatures in excess of 1000 degrees Celsius
Ionosphere	Extending 50–600 km above sea level	Electrified region that contains large concentrations of ions and free electrons
		Important for radio wave propagation
Exosphere	Extending 480 km above sea level	Merges into the regions of Earth's magnetic field, radiation belt, and outer space

Atmospheric Gases

The air around us, part of the tropospheric layer, is a mixture of gases. It contains 78 percent nitrogen, 20 percent oxygen, and trace amounts of several other gases, including hydrogen and carbon dioxide.

Gases in Earth's atmosphere hold in heat from the sun and help to support life in the troposphere. The process by which gases in the atmosphere trap solar energy is called the **greenhouse effect**. Greenhouse gases include water vapor, carbon dioxide, and methane.

Effects of Gases on Earth

Human activities can add greenhouse gases to the atmosphere. This may be contributing to steadily increasing temperatures over the last century. Global warming is a gradual increase in the temperature of Earth's atmosphere that can lead to **climate change**.

Another global change in the atmosphere involves the ozone layer. Ozone (O_3) is a molecule made up of three oxygen atoms. Ozone works as a protective blanket in the stratosphere, filtering harmful ultraviolet (UV) rays from the sun before they reach Earth.

Scientists have identified areas where the ozone layer has become increasingly thin. They believe that a group of chlorine compounds known as chlorofluorocarbons, or CFCs, are the main culprit. CFCs were widely used in refrigerators, air conditioners, and spray cans until the late 1980s. Unlike most chemical compounds released into the air, CFCs do not break down easily or quickly. Instead, they last for decades, rising into the stratosphere where ultraviolet radiation breaks down the CFC molecules into chlorine. The chlorine atoms then break ozone down into oxygen atoms, destroying the protective ozone layer.

The following image and table identify various sources of pollution that impact the integrity of the ozone layer, the quality of the air you breathe, and your overall health.

Sources of Air Pollution

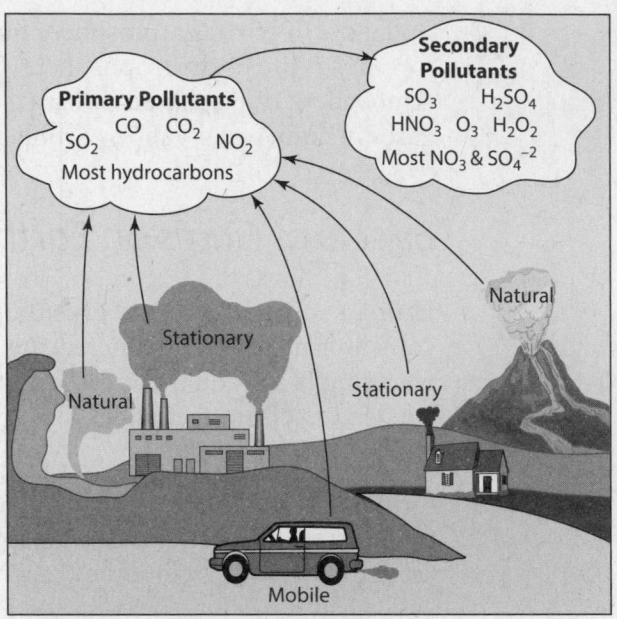

Main Air Pollutants

Pollutant	Source	Effects on Human Health
Particles—measured by Air Particle Index (API)	Internal combustion engines (e.g., cars and trucks) Industry (e.g., factories) Burning wood Cigarette smoke	Long-term exposure is linked to: • Lung cancer • Heart disease • Lung disease • Asthma attacks
Nitrogen dioxide (NO_2)	Motor vehicles are the biggest contributors. Other combustion processes	• Exposure to high levels of NO_2 may lead to lung damage or respiratory disease. • It has also been linked to asthma and respiratory problems.

Pollutant	Source	Effects on Human Health
Carbon monoxide (CO)	Motor vehicle exhaust and burning of materials such as coal, oil, and wood. It is also released from industrial processes and waste incineration.	When inhaled, carbon monoxide enters the bloodstream and disrupts the supply of oxygen to the body's tissues.
Lead (Pb)	Is largely derived from the combustion of lead additives in motor fuels as well as lead smelting.	Retards learning in children and the development of their nervous system.
Hydrocarbons (HC)—chemical compounds composed of hydrogen and carbon atoms	Most fuel combustion processes result in the release of hydrocarbons to the environment. The largest fuel sources are natural gas and petrol. They are also a component of the smoke from wood fires.	Exposure can cause headaches or nausea, while some compounds may cause cancer. Some may also damage plants.

EXERCISE 2

Earth's Atmosphere

Directions: Choose the best answer for each of the following items.

1. What chemicals are the major cause of the depletion of ozone?

   A. hydrocarbons
   B. carbon dioxide
   C. nitrogen dioxide
   D. chlorine compounds

2. Connect the correct term to each layer of the atmosphere. One term will not be used. (**Note:** On the real GED® test, you will click on the words you choose and "drag" each one into position in the diagram.)

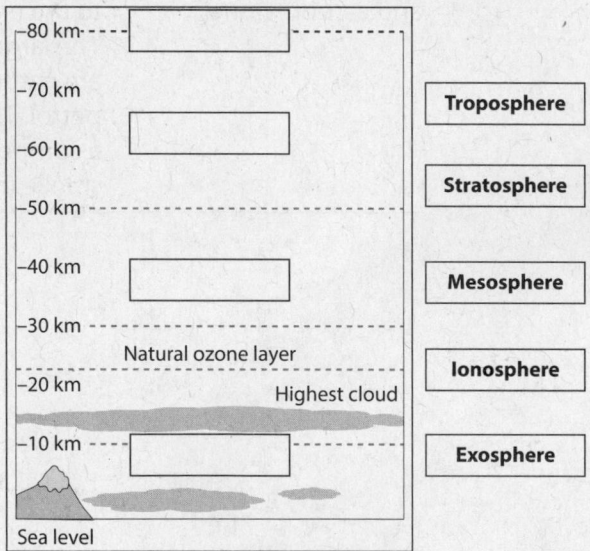

Answers are on page 666.

Weathering and Erosion

Two of the primary agents of change on Earth are wind and water. Wind and water interact powerfully to constantly change Earth's surface through weathering and erosion.

Weathering is the process of breaking down or dissolving minerals and rocks on Earth's surface. Water, ice, temperature changes, acids, salt, plants, and animals can all be agents of weathering. Once rock is broken down, wind, water, and gravity can transport the bits of rocks and minerals away.

This process is called **erosion**. No rock on Earth's surface is hard enough to resist weathering.

Weathering can be a mechanical or a chemical process, and often the two types work together. Chemical weathering occurs when the materials that make up rocks and soil are changed by chemical means. Sometimes carbon dioxide from the soil or air combines with water to produce carbonic acid. This is a weak acid that can dissolve rock, and it is particularly effective on limestone. Rust, through the process of oxidation, is also an agent of chemical weathering.

Mechanical (or physical) weathering causes rocks to crumble. One way water weathers rocks is the freeze-thaw process. Water enters cracks in the rock. When the temperatures drop and the water freezes, it expands. This places pressure on the rocks around it, causing rocks to crack and split over time.

Wind

Wind can also be an agent of weathering. The wind carries dust, sand, and other small grit particles that repeatedly strike the surface of rocks, resulting in a gradual wearing away of the rock. This process is called wind abrasion and can be compared to sandblasting.

What exactly is wind, and how is it caused? **Wind** is the movement and flow of gases on Earth's surface. It is caused by the uneven heating of the surface by the sun. Winds are generated by differences in atmospheric pressure. For example, at the equator, the sun warms the water and land more than on the rest of the planet. This warm equatorial air rises higher into the atmosphere and then flows toward the poles. This is a called a low pressure system. At the same time, a high pressure system composed of dense, cooler air flows toward the equator to replace the heated air.

How Winds Are Generated

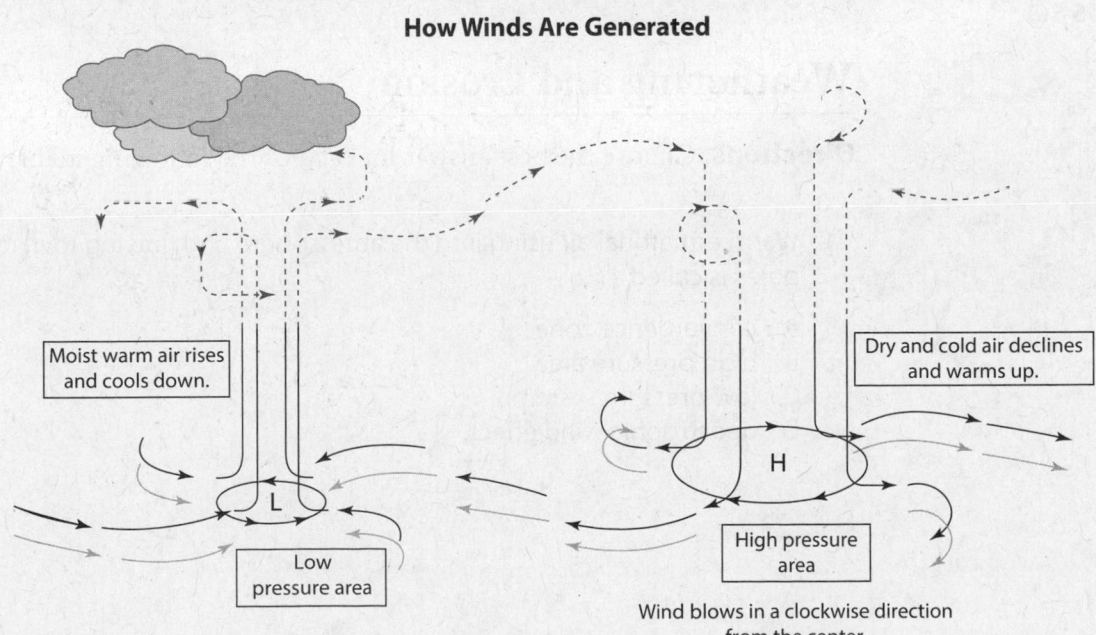

Moist warm air rises and cools down.

Dry and cold air declines and warms up.

Low pressure area

High pressure area

Wind blows in a clockwise direction from the center.

Generally, winds blow from high pressure areas to low pressure areas. The boundary between a high pressure area and a low pressure area is called a **front**. The complex relationships between fronts result in different types of weather and wind patterns.

Winds that regularly blow from a single direction over a specific area of Earth are called prevailing winds. Areas where prevailing winds meet are referred to as convergence zones. These winds usually blow east-west rather than north-south because of what is called the **Coriolis effect**.

The Coriolis Effect

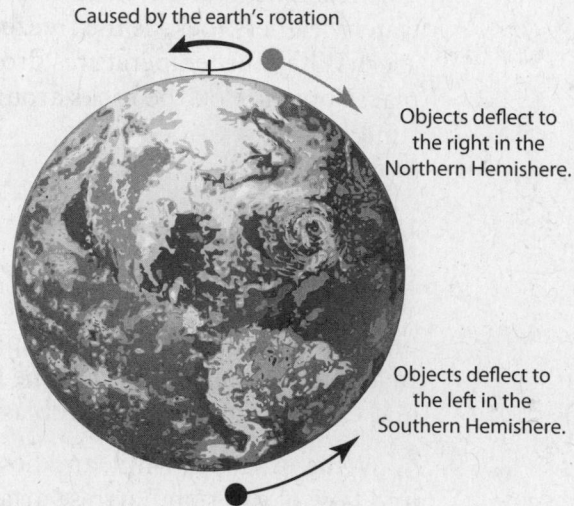

Caused by the earth's rotation

Objects deflect to the right in the Northern Hemishere.

Objects deflect to the left in the Southern Hemishere.

Earth's rotation generates a circulation pattern that makes wind systems twist counterclockwise in the Northern Hemisphere and clockwise in the Southern Hemisphere. The Coriolis effect causes some winds to travel along the edges of the high and low pressure systems.

EXERCISE 3

Weathering and Erosion

Directions: Choose the best answer for each of the following items.

1. Warm equatorial air rising into the atmosphere and flowing toward the poles is called a

   A. convergence zone.
   B. high pressure area.
   C. low pressure system.
   D. geostrophic wind effect.

2. Which of the following is an example of chemical weathering?

A. frost action
B. oxidation
C. abrasion
D. erosion

Answers are on page 666.

The Oceans

Over 70 percent of Earth's surface is covered by water. The ocean is what makes Earth appear blue when viewed from space and what makes all life on Earth possible.

Ocean water is a mixture of water and salts. It has an average **salinity** of about 3.5 percent. This means that for every 1000 grams of seawater, there are approximately 35 grams of dissolved salts. The molecules that compose those salts are predominantly chlorine and sodium ions. Other ions found in seawater are sulfates, magnesium, calcium, and potassium. Seawater also contains dissolved gases such as nitrogen, oxygen, and carbon dioxide. Seawater is also denser than both pure water and fresh water because the dissolved salts add mass without contributing much to the overall volume of the water.

Ocean Currents

Currents are streams of water running through a larger body of water that are set in motion by a variety of factors. Ocean currents can be either warm or cold. The temperature of a current affects the temperature of the coastal areas toward which it flows.

Currents flowing near the surface of the oceans transport warm water from the equator to the poles and cool water back toward the equator. You have already learned about the Coriolis effect in which winds are influenced by Earth's rotation. The paths of ocean currents are also influenced by this effect.

Cold, deep currents transport oxygen and nutrients to organisms living in the ocean's depths. Ocean food chains are constantly recycled because of the upwelling of ocean currents. The following diagram illustrates how upwelling occurs.

Upwelling of Ocean Water

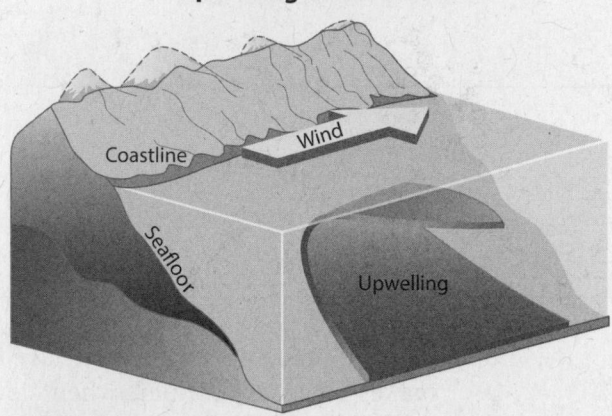

When winds push surface water away from the shore, deep currents of cold water rise to take its place. Nutrients from various depths become available to nourish new plankton growth, which provides food for fish.

Some ocean currents are very large and powerful. One you may be familiar with is the Gulf Stream. This is a warm surface current that originates in the tropical Caribbean Sea and influences weather patterns all over the globe. Warm-water currents sometimes displace the cold Humboldt Current along the west coast of South America. This phenomenon, called El Niño, can affect weather patterns over large areas of the globe.

The ocean has several layers that receive varying amounts of sunlight. The surface zone is the smallest and warmest, reaching down about 200 meters and making up only 5 percent of the ocean's depth. Beneath it is the twilight zone, making up about 20 percent of the ocean depths. This zone reaches from 200 meters to 1000 meters in depth. It is cold and dimly lit to dark. Below the twilight zone is the deep ocean zone, making up 75 percent of the ocean. In this zone, there is constant cold and no sunlight.

Coral Reefs

Coral reefs can be found in the sunny and shallow surface zones of the ocean. Coral reefs are created by colonies of tiny coral animals that produce a hard structure around their soft bodies. Microscopic, symbiotic algae called zooxanthellae live in the bodies of coral animals and provide them with food produced by photosynthesis. Coral reefs provide diverse habitats for many organisms.

One-quarter of all ocean species depend on coral reefs for food and shelter. This is a remarkable statistic when you consider that coral reefs take up less than 1 percent of Earth's surface. Coral reef ecosystems also have tremendous impact on humans, providing food, shoreline protection from storms, ingredients for medicines, and jobs based on tourism. Sadly, humans are also the greatest threat to coral reefs. Pollution, destructive fishing, acidification of ocean water, and invasive species have all taken a negative toll.

EXERCISE 4

The Oceans

Directions: Choose the best answer for each of the following items.

1. The average salinity of ocean water is

   A. 3.5 percent.
   B. 5 percent.
   C. 20 percent.
   D. 75 percent.

2. Complete the statement with terms from the section.

   Currents flowing near the ocean's surface transport heat from the

   _____ to the _____ and then

   move cool water back to equatorial regions.

Answers are on page 666.

CHAPTER 12

Interactions Between Earth's Systems and Living Things

Cycles in Nature

Every living thing depends upon oxygen, nitrogen, and carbon dioxide in the atmosphere. Water is also key to life on Earth. Will these life-sustaining substances ever get used up and disappear? Fortunately, the answer is no. Look at the following four diagrams. Each illustrates an important cycle of matter found in nature.

Nitrogen Cycle

In the **nitrogen cycle**, nitrogen moves from the air to the soil, into living things, and back into the air. Nitrogen enters the food chain when nitrogen compounds called nitrates are absorbed from the soil by plants. Plants convert nitrates into usable nitrogen compounds. These compounds are transferred between organisms through feeding (trophic) levels starting when primary consumers feed on the plants. Decaying plants and animals also return nitrogen to the soil with the help of nitrogen-fixing bacteria. These bacteria produce nitrates from the nitrogen compounds found in decaying matter. Denitrifying bacteria play a role when they return nitrogen to the atmosphere by converting nitrates to nitrogen gas.

The Nitrogen Cycle

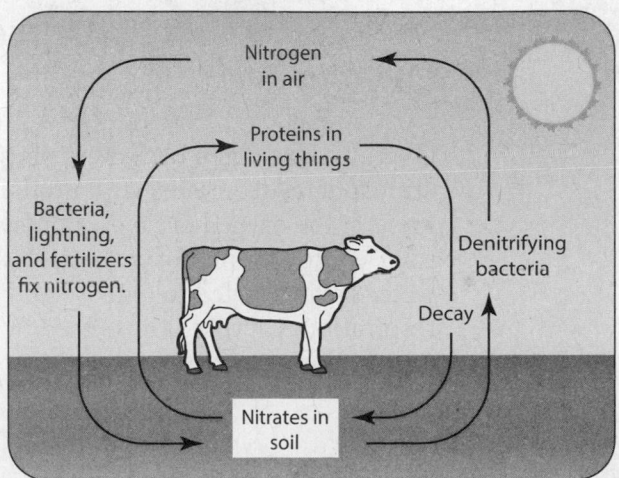

Carbon Cycle

The **carbon cycle** is a system involving living things and the nonliving matter in Earth's crust, oceans, and atmosphere. In this cycle, carbon is transferred from one part of the environment to another. The energy that drives the cycle is provided by the sun and Earth's core. Organic compounds, such as carbohydrates, proteins, and lipids, are formed in producers when carbon is made usable (fixed) from carbon dioxide by the process of photosynthesis. The fixed carbon is moved through the feeding levels from primary consumers to secondary consumers and beyond. Carbon continues to be recycled through the processes of respiration, decay by decomposers, and the combustion of fossil fuels.

The Carbon Cycle

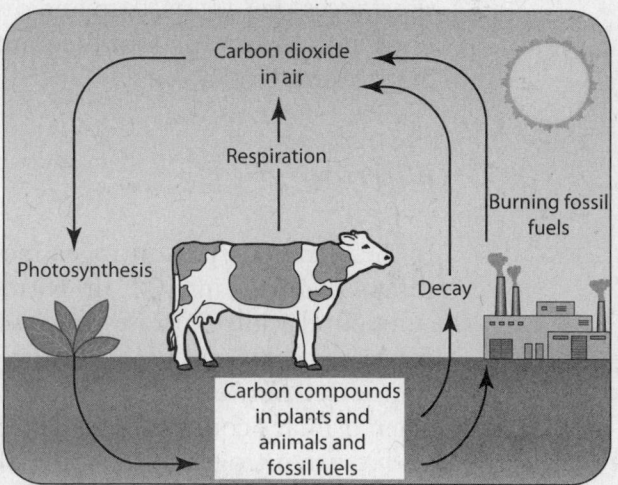

Remember that fossil fuels (petroleum, natural gas, or coal) are drilled or mined from underground deposits. We burn fossil fuels to extract energy. The burning releases gases, including carbon dioxide, into the atmosphere. Excess carbon dioxide contributes to the greenhouse effect.

Oxygen Cycle

Overall, the **oxygen cycle** describes the movement of oxygen within the atmosphere, organisms, and nonliving matter on Earth's crust. The driving force in the oxygen cycle is photosynthesis. Remember that producers use solar energy for photosynthesis. Using that energy, carbon dioxide and water are converted to glucose and oxygen. Plants use some glucose to fuel respiration. Glucose is also used in the making of fats and proteins.

The Oxygen Cycle

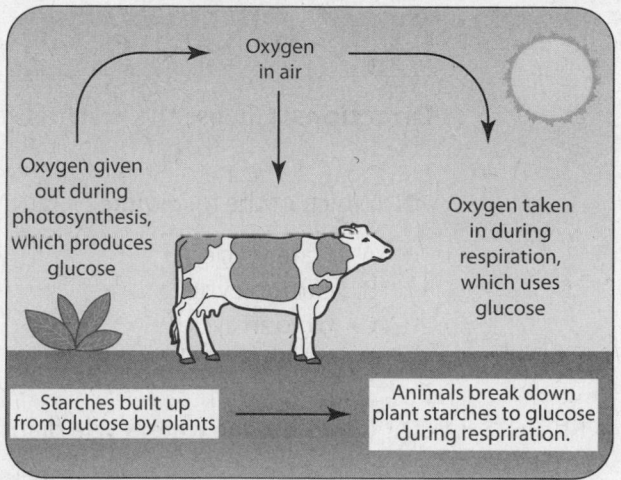

Water Cycle

The **water cycle** describes the continuous process of transporting water from the oceans to the atmosphere, then to the land, and then returning it to the oceans. The processes of evaporation, condensation, and precipitation make up the water cycle.

The Water Cycle

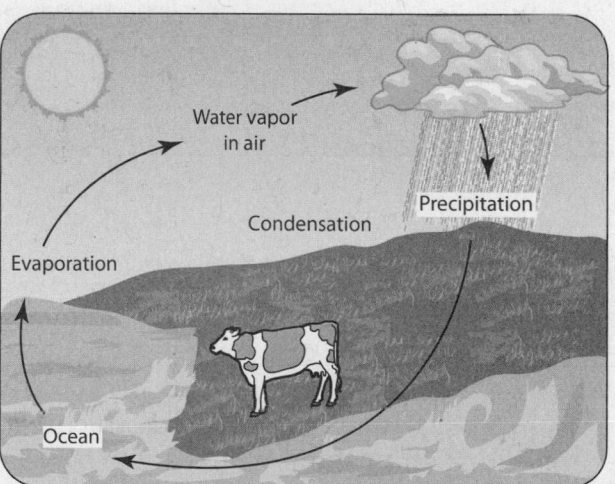

Cycles in Nature

Directions: Choose the best answer for each of the following items.

1. Which of the following cycles is dependent upon bacteria?

   A. water cycle
   B. carbon cycle
   C. oxygen cycle
   D. nitrogen cycle

2. Complete the water cycle diagram using terms from the section.

Water Cycle

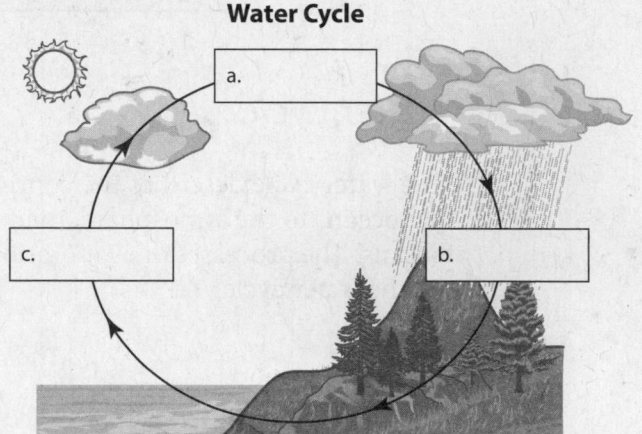

Answers are on page 667.

Natural Hazards

Nature can also be a destructive force. A **natural hazard** is the threat of a natural event that can have a negative effect on organisms and the environment. There is a wide range of events that can be classified as natural hazards, from droughts to volcanic explosions. In order for a physical event to be defined as hazardous, there must be the potential for the loss of life.

Certain areas are more vulnerable to natural hazards. For example, cities built on or near tectonic plate boundaries are far more likely to be negatively impacted by earthquakes. Coastal cities are much more vulnerable to hurricanes. Additionally, the impact of hazards can be increased by human activity. For instance, flooding and landslides are more likely to result from heavy rainfall if poor farming practices have removed vegetation from hill slopes.

The following table identifies four types of natural hazards and indicates the probability that each will occur in any given calendar year. Notice that the frequency, or likelihood, of each natural hazard occurring is calculated according to the potential severity of the event. For example, there is an 86 percent probability of a flood occurring that will lead to at least 10 fatalities and 0.4 percent (four-tenths of a percent) probability of a flood occurring that will lead to 1000 or more fatalities.

Natural Hazard	Frequency	Severity**
Earthquakes	0.11*	10 fatalities
	0.001	1,000 fatalities
Hurricanes	0.39	10 fatalities
	0.06	1,000 fatalities
Floods	0.86	10 fatalities
	0.004	1,000 fatalities
Tornados	0.96	10 fatalities
	0.006	1,000 fatalities

 * 0.11 = 11% probability
** Minimum fatality estimate

Effects of Natural Hazards

The short- and long-term effects that a natural hazard has on an area depend on a number of factors. In general, the less economically developed a country is, the more damage it is likely to sustain, both economically and in terms of loss of life. The more people there are and the more vulnerable they are to a disaster, the greater the impact of a natural hazard. The following table identifies six reasons for the discrepancy in effects between less and more developed countries.

	Less Economically Developed	More Economically Developed
Population	Denser populations	Populations are more spread out.
Finance	Lack the financial authority to demand strict building legislation codes	Well-financed governments require strict building codes.
Education	Increased vulnerability because people are often not taught where to go during an emergency	Educated about what to do in the event of a hazard
Insurance	Homes are rarely insured.	Homes can be insured against damage from hazards, which offsets the cost of rebuilding.
Economy	Dependent on a cash crop; if a hazard wipes out the entire crop, then the whole economy suffers	Economy has more stability.
Infrastructure	Power, communication, water and sewage systems sustain long-term damage	Highly organized emergency services and communications ensures the population in need of help receives assistance as quickly as possible; this reduces the spread of disease and death.

Clearly, the short- and long-term effects from a natural hazard can be markedly different, depending on the area of the world in which the hazard occurs. Short-term effects in a more developed area will include loss of power and communication, damage to water and sewage systems, infrastructure damage, financial loss, injuries, sickness, and death. In a less developed area, many of those short-term effects become long-term effects, and disasters may eventually lead to failed economies and outbreaks of disease. More developed areas typically have few, if any, long-term effects.

Hazard Mitigation

There are some steps that can be taken to mitigate the impact of natural hazards. **Mitigation** is an effort to reduce the loss of property and life by lessening the impact of the disaster. Structural mitigation techniques involve building dams, dikes, levees, and containment ponds to hold water or slow its flow. Other structures, like storm shelters, are designed for the specific purpose of saving lives. These are common in tornado-prone areas.

Building practices such a land use regulations, building codes, and zoning ordinances are effective nonstructural mitigation techniques. Building codes specify what types of materials can be used to build homes and businesses based on criteria such as strength, durability, flammability, and resistance to water and wind. As you can imagine, in a city built near a fault line, such as San Francisco, the building codes might require building practices that are different from those in cities that are not built near fault lines.

EXERCISE 2

Natural Hazards

Directions: Choose the best answer for each of the following items.

1. Which of the following statements best explains why less-developed countries experience more long-term effects from natural hazards?

   A. Poverty and population density increase the impacts of natural hazards.
   B. Highly organized emergency services reduce the spread of disease and death.
   C. Education about action during a hazard reduces the vulnerability of the population.
   D. Building standards do not specify what types of materials can be used to build homes.

Question 2 is based on the following table.

Natural Hazard	Frequency	Severity**
Earthquakes	0.11*	10 fatalities
	0.001	1000 fatalities

 * 0.11 = 11% probability
** Minimum fatality estimate

2. The probability of an earthquake that results in loss of life for more than 1000 people in any given calendar year is

   A. 0 percent.
   B. 0.1 percent.
   C. 1 percent.
   D. 11 percent.

Answers are on page 667.

Natural Resources

The wind, water, and rock that can be sources of natural hazards also supply us with a wide range of **natural resources** that are essential for our daily lives. The following illustration shows nine different resources that humans rely on. Notice that each resource is classified as renewable or nonrenewable.

Renewable Resource		Nonrenewable Resource	
Biomass (heating, electricity, transportation)	3.9%	Oil (transportation, manufacturing)	37.4%
Hydropower (electricity)	2.5%	Natural Gas (heating, manufacturing, electricity)	24%
Geothermal (heating, electricity)	0.4%	Coal (manufacturing, electricity)	22.6%
Wind (electricity)	0.5%	Uranium (electricity)	8.5%
Solar (light, heating, electricity)	0.1%		

Renewable resources are those that will never run out, either naturally or through proper management. Resources that are naturally occurring and renewable include the wind, waves, air, and sunlight. Resources that require proper management to remain **sustainable** (able to be maintained over time at an acceptable level) include forests, soil, water, fish, and wildlife.

Nonrenewable resources are those that will eventually run out; they have a finite supply. Minerals such as diamonds and iron ore (used to make steel) are classified as nonrenewable resources. Though they are naturally occurring, their formation took millions of years. Nuclear energy relies on minerals such as uranium and plutonium. Minerals are extracted from rocks through the process of mining.

Fossil fuels are another category of nonrenewable resources. These substances are primarily used as energy sources. Fossil fuels include oil, coal, and natural gas. Oil and natural gas are thought to have formed slowly, over millions of years, from the decomposition of plants and animals. Over time, the dead organisms were compressed between layers of sediment that added pressure. Eventually, rock was formed, and, in areas that lacked oxygen, heat and pressure turned the remains of the organisms into oil and natural gas.

Some of those rocks, such as limestone or sandstone, have networks of small holes called pores. Oil (a liquid) seeps into the holes in the rocks. Natural gas also diffuses into porous rocks. Oil and natural gas are extracted using techniques such as drilling and hydraulic fracturing.

Sustainability of Resources

Untapped deposits of coal and oil are becoming increasingly difficult to locate. Additionally, there are serious concerns about how much is left and how long the reserves will last. Some estimates suggest that oil reserves could run out in approximately 50 years, and coal reserves in approximately 300 years. These estimates spotlight a need for greater fuel efficiency and a decreased reliance on nonrenewable resources for energy. As dependence on renewable energy sources grows, people must also accept the responsibility to properly manage and sustain those sources.

EXERCISE 3

Natural Resources

Directions: Choose the best answer for each of the following items.

1. Which of the following could be classified as a sustainable renewable resource, with proper management?

   A. sunlight
   B. wind
   C. forests
   D. minerals

2. Why are natural resources such as coal and oil not considered renewable?

   A. Oil is difficult to locate and extract.
   B. Coal reserves will last 300 years or more.
   C. Fossil fuels contribute to the greenhouse effect.
   D. The formation of coal and oil takes millions of years.

Answers are on page 667.

Earth and Space Science

Directions: Choose the best answer for each of the following items.

Question 1 is based on the following diagram.

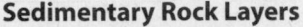

Sedimentary Rock Layers

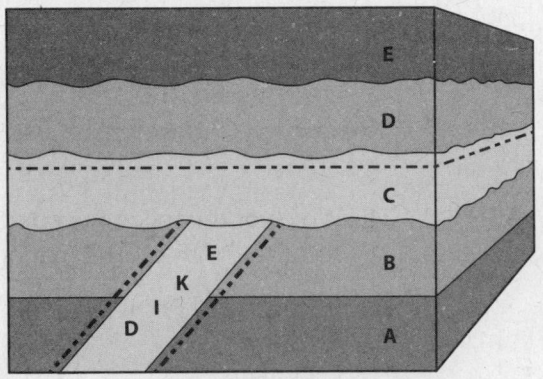

1. A dike is a sheet of rock that forms in a crack within an existing rock layer. Scientists have used radiometric dating to determine that the dike in the diagram formed 85 million years ago, and rock layer D formed 80 million years ago.

    Place an X on the diagram to indicate the rock layer that must be between 80 and 85 million years old.

2. Scientists observe a previously unidentified object in the solar system. What information would best help scientists identify whether the object is an asteroid or comet?

    A. the size of the object
    B. the object's composition
    C. the location of the object
    D. the number of times the object has orbited the sun

3. Which type of star is the sun?

    A. protostar
    B. supergiant
    C. black dwarf
    D. main sequence

4. In which of the following atmospheric layers does temperature increase with height?

   A. thermosphere only
   B. ionosphere and stratosphere
   C. troposphere and mesosphere
   D. stratosphere and thermosphere

5. Areas where prevailing winds meet are referred to as

   A. convergence zones.
   B. upwelling zones.
   C. twilight zones.
   D. surface zones.

6. Why are zooxanthellae algae important to coral reef systems? Because they

   A. act as a producer in the coral reef food web.
   B. provide diverse habitats for many organisms.
   C. produce the unique color for which corals are known.
   D. make a hard protective structure around the soft coral bodies.

7. Which of the following natural resources would be the best choice for an environmentally conscious company looking for a sustainable energy source?

   A. coal
   B. wind
   C. nuclear energy
   D. natural gas

8. A nonprofit group wants to help a less economically developed country prepare for disasters. The group plans to host free seminars to educate community leaders about proper building codes and emergency preparedness techniques.

   Discuss the strengths and weaknesses of this plan. Include multiple pieces of evidence from the text to support your answer.

   Indicate your response on a separate sheet of paper. This task may take approximately 10 minutes.

Answers are on pages 667–668.

Science

PART 1 LIFE SCIENCE

Chapter 1 Structures and Functions of Life

Exercise 1: Cells, Tissues, and Organs

1. **Correct answer: B.** According to the cell theory, cells are the smallest unit of life. That means that anything that is made of cells (even a single cell) is a living thing.

2. **Correct answer: specialized.** Each different cell type is specialized to carry out specific functions in the body.

Exercise 2: Cell Functions and Components

1. **Correct answer: B.** All cells need to extract energy from food, but they do not all produce food. Only the cells of producers (like plants) produce food. All other organisms extract energy from the food they consume.

2. **Correct answer: energy.** Without mitochondria, the cell would not be able to convert food into energy. This lack of energy would prevent the cell from carrying out necessary processes.

Exercise 3: Cell Division

1. **Correct answer is shown in the following diagram.** In mitosis, chromosomes line up during metaphase and split apart during anaphase. In this particular cell, the chromosomes appear to have lined up and may be starting to separate. This indicates that the cell is transitioning from metaphase to anaphase.

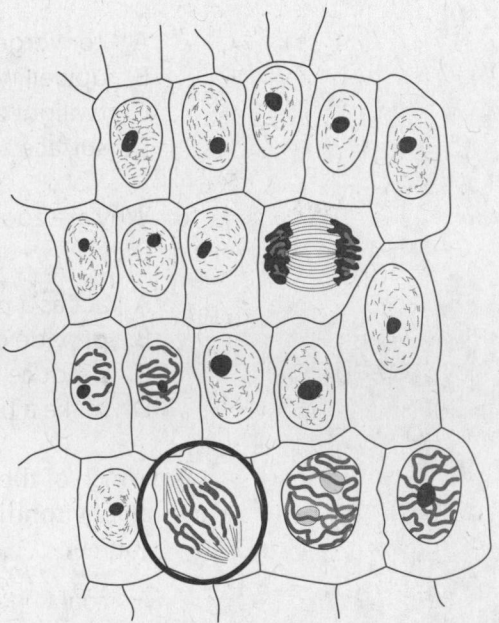

2. **Correct answers: a) mitosis and meiosis, b) mitosis, c) meiosis, d) mitosis and meiosis,** and **e) meiosis.** Body cells reproduce themselves by separating into two identical cells during mitosis. Meiosis produces four reproductive cells, each with half the DNA of a normal body cell. Crossing over occurs during Prophase I of meiosis. Both mitosis and meiosis begin with the copying of the cell's DNA. Because mitosis produces new body cells and meiosis produces reproductive cells, both processes are required in humans.

Chapter 2 Life Functions and Energy Intake

Exercise 1: Energy for Life Functions

1. **Correct answer: D.** Leaves release oxygen into the environment as a product of the photosynthesis reaction. Because the bubbles are coming from the leaves, they are most likely oxygen gas being released.

2. **Correct answers: a) Respiration, b) Respiration, c) Fermentation, d) Fermentation.** Respiration converts a lot of energy, but it can only do so when oxygen is available. Fermentation converts a little energy when oxygen is not available. Human cells use respiration most of the time, but will use fermentation temporarily when the oxygen supply is low.

Chapter 3 Heredity

Exercise 1: DNA and Chromosomes

1. **Correct answers: RNA** and **protein.** The central dogma of gene expression states that the instructions in DNA are converted to RNA, which is then used by a ribosome to build a protein. This process occurs in the same way in all cells.

2. **Correct answer: C.** Egg and sperm are reproductive cells that each contain half the normal number of chromosomes (23 in humans). When these reproductive cells unite, their chromosomes combine to produce a new cell with a complete set of chromosomes (46 in humans).

3. **Correct answer: B.** The two chromatids that make up a chromosome are exact copies of each other. Every gene present on one chromatid is also present on the other.

Exercise 2: Alleles and Traits

1. **Correct answer: C.** The addition of an extra base results in a mutation in a gene. A mutation produces a new allele of the gene.

2. **Correct answer: D.** Before crossing over, the two chromatids of the same chromosome are identical. During crossing over, the inside chromatids of the chromosomes trade segments. The inside chromatid is no longer identical to its partner.

3. **Correct answer: C.** All lizards lack the genes necessary for the ability to produce body heat. In this case, the environment is not turning any genes on or off.

Exercise 3: Simple Inheritance

1. **Correct answer: B.** In a pedigree chart, a square represents a male and a solid shape represents a person with the disease being studied.

2. **Correct answer: the 6 empty circles and squares.** A person with the genotype CC is healthy because cystic fibrosis is caused only by the recessive genotype cc. In a pedigree chart, an empty shape represents a person who is healthy, or does not have the disease being studied, and is not a carrier of the disease.

3. **Correct answer: A.** The pedigree chart shows that the woman has the genotype CC and the man has the genotype Cc. Based on the following Punnett square, the couple has no

chance of having a child with cystic fibrosis (genotype cc).

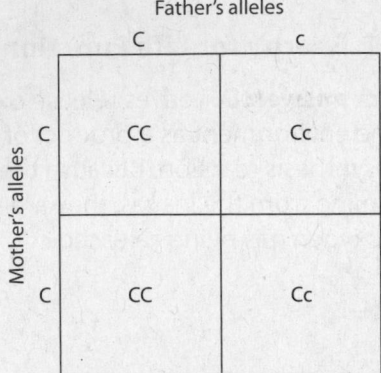

Chapter 4 Evolution

Exercise 1: Evolutionary Relationships

1. **Correct answer: B.** The closer two organisms are on a cladogram, the more closely they can be assumed to be related. Ferns and conifers are listed directly next to each other on the cladogram. They share two of the characteristics being studied.

2. **Correct answer: D.** The cladogram compares structural characteristics of the different plant types. Similar, or homologous, structures in different organisms is evidence that the organisms share a common ancestor.

Exercise 2: Evolution by Natural Selection

1. **Correct answer: A.** A change in the dependent variable shows that natural selection is occurring. In the peppered moths example, the dependent variable is the proportion of dark- and light-winged moths observed. Because these proportions changed over time, natural selection was occurring.

2. **Correct answer: C.** If one version of a trait provides no advantage over the other, no

change in the proportions will be observed. Because the proportion of dark to light fish remained about the same over time, the ecologists can assume that no selection occurred because there is no differential survivability.

Exercise 3: Evolutionary Change

1. **Correct answers: a) suitable mates, b) clean water, c) living space** or **human activity.** Frogs compete for suitable mates by singing to impress females. If clean water is limited, snakes can get all the moisture they need from their food instead of drinking water. When living space is limited, especially when humans destroy natural habitats, swallows can build nests on natural and man-made walls instead of in trees.

2. **Correct answer: speciation.** Speciation describes the evolutionary process of creating a new species. Accumulating different adaptations will eventually lead different groups of a species to become separate species altogether.

Chapter 5 Ecosystems

Exercise 1: Energy in Ecosystems

1. **Correct answer depicts an arrow pointing toward "Respiration and heat loss."** This indicates that energy consumed is lost through respiration and heat.

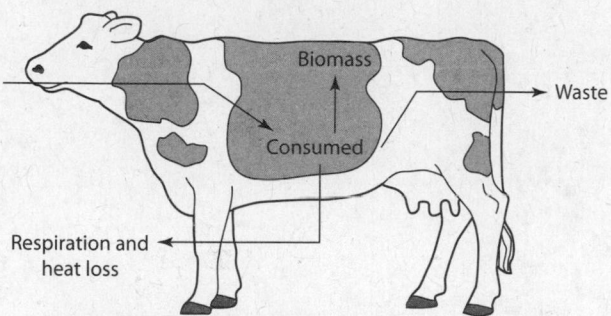

2. **Correct answer: C.** The cow best fits the role of a primary consumer because it is a herbivore that feeds on plants. The cow obtains energy by consuming producers such as grass.

Exercise 2: Matter in Ecosystems

1. **Correct answers: matter** and **energy.** A food chain uses arrows to show the direction in which matter and energy are transferred from producer to primary consumer to secondary consumer, and so on.

2. **Correct answer: A.** Food webs are a more natural model than a food chain because they show all the possible feeding relationships at each trophic level in a community.

Exercise 3: Capacity for Change

1. **Correct answer: at the bottom of the S.**

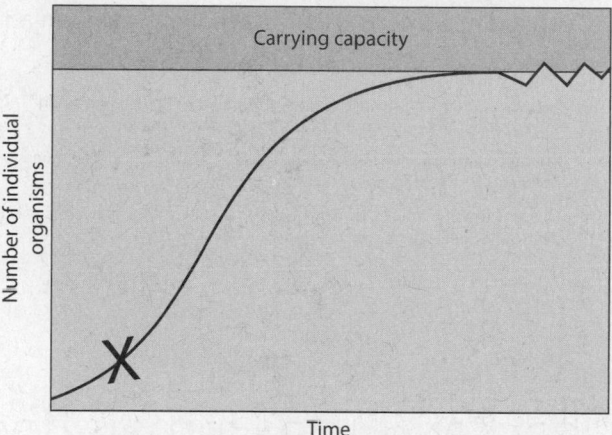

The slow growth phase of the graph is also referred to as the lag phase, denoted on the graph showing Population Growth Over Time.

2. **Correct answer: B.** When resources are limited, a growing population will have to compete to acquire those resources.

Exercise 4: Relationships in Ecosystems

1. **Correct answer: prey.** The shrimp is in danger of being eaten by a competing organism. In this relationship, the shrimp takes on the role of prey and the competitor is the predator.

2. **Correct answer: B.** Both the goby fish and the shrimp benefit from their relationship. The goby fish gains shelter, and the shrimp receives protection from predation.

ANSWERS AND EXPLANATIONS

Exercise 5: Disruption of Ecosystems

1. **Correct answer is shown in the table.**
   The kudzu vine is an example of an invasive species. It is an introduced species that outcompetes a native species for resources. Polluted runoff impacting an environment is an example of flooding, and overgrazing in an arid area is an example of desertification.

The kudzu vine, introduced to help prevent soil erosion, climbs over trees, blocking sunlight.	Flooding
Runoff containing sediment and fertilizers pollutes a freshwater ecosystem.	Desertification
Overgrazing of plants in semiarid areas destroys fragile plant cover.	Invasive species

2. **Correct answer: extinction.** Human activities, including hunting, urbanization, and the destruction of forests to create farmland are primarily responsible for the habitat destruction that eventually leads to extinction.

Chapter 6 The Human Body and Health

Exercise 1: Body Systems

1. **Correct answer: D.** The organs of the urinary system are responsible for elimination of wastes and regulating both the pH and volume of blood.

2. **Correct answer: skeletal, muscular,** and **nervous systems.** The skeletal and muscular systems cooperate as muscles move bone and tendons connect muscle to bone, while the brain and nerves control movement and deliver messages to the specific parts of the body.

Exercise 2: Homeostasis

1. The **receptor** is the body's temperature sensors and the **effector** is the response seen in the blood vessels and sweat glands in the skin. A sensory receptor is a structure that recognizes a stimulus, and an effector is the part of the body capable of responding to a stimulus.

2. **Correct answer: A.** Prolonged exposure to the sun increases the likelihood of a first- or second-degree sunburn that would injure the outer layer of skin cells.

Exercise 3: Nutrition

1. **Correct answer: D.** 1 gram of fat equals 9 calories; therefore 9 grams of fat would be equivalent to 81 calories (9×9).

2. **Correct answer: B.** Minerals, such as calcium, are essential for bone building.

3. **Correct answer: C.** Antibiotics can kill the symbiotic bacteria living in the intestinal tract. These bacteria produce vitamins K and B.

Exercise 4: Disease and Pathogens

1. **Correct answer: D.** Salmonella can be found in raw foods such as chicken or eggs. Thoroughly cooking these foods can prevent the transmission of this pathogen.

2. **Correct answer: 80.** Some Native American populations were reduced by 80 percent from diseases such as smallpox, measles, and influenza.

Practice: Life Science

1. **Correct answer: D.** Photosynthesis is the process of using the energy in sunlight to make food. A heterotroph must consume other organisms for food because it cannot perform photosynthesis to make food.

2. **Correct answers: selection pressure, natural selection, adaptation,** and **speciation.** The environment exerts selection pressure on the finches by providing a limited food supply. Natural selection favors the finches with the best beaks for obtaining food (insects). Narrow beaks become an adaptation of the island finches when no more broad-beaked finches exist. Speciation occurs when the island finches become their own species.

3. **Correct answer: B.** Dark fur can be produced by the allele combinations FF or Ff. Red eyes can only be produced by the allele combination ee. This means that a guinea pig with dark fur and red eyes can only be produced in two ways: FF with ee, or Ff with ee.

4. **Correct answer: A.** According to the cell theory, all living things are composed of cells. Viruses do not have cells, so most scientists consider them to be nonliving.

5. **Correct answer: ribosome.** The ribosomes are the sites where proteins are made within a cell.

6. **Correct answer: A.** Many diseases can be prevented with simple sanitation methods such as handwashing. Immunizations provide resistance to many other types of pathogenic diseases.

7. **Correct answer: D.** An anemic person is deficient in iron, a type of mineral. Anemia is a disorder that affects red blood cells, part of the circulatory system.

8. **Correct answer: B.** Intestinal bacteria that live in human digestive systems are an example of a type of symbiotic relationship called mutualism. The bacteria receive a habitat and food source while humans benefit from the synthesis of essential nutrients.

9. **Correct answer:** The tomato seedling is the producer and should be listed first. The correct order for the food chain is as follows: **Tomato seedling** (Producer) → **Cricket** (Primary consumer) → **Wolf spider** (Secondary consumer) → **Sparrow** (Tertiary consumer) → **Falcon** (Quaternary consumer)

10. **Correct answer: D.** The number of juvenile female deer in the herd would not affect the size of the deer population because they are already accounted for. Additionally, juvenile, or immature, deer are not breeding and reproducing, and thus adding to the population size.

PART 2 PHYSICAL SCIENCE
Chapter 7 Chemical Interactions

Exercise 1: Structures of Matter

1. **Correct answer:** The box on the left should be labeled **Element**. The box on the right should be labeled **Compound**. Elements can be both single atoms or molecules of the same atom. Compounds are molecules made up of two or more elements that have been chemically bonded.

2. **Correct answer: B.** The atomic number, shown in the bottom left corner, represents the number of protons in an atom's nucleus. The carbon atom has 6 protons.

Exercise 2: Physical and Chemical Properties

1. **Correct answer: 4 kg/mL.** Density is calculated by dividing the mass by the volume. Thus 120 is divided by 30, yielding 4.

2. **Correct answer: C.** Mercury, a metal, is in a liquid state at room temperature.

3. **Correct answer: B.** When a liquid cools and enters a solid state, the particles become fixed and packed into dense patterns, resulting in a change of state called solidification.

Exercise 3: Chemical Formulas and Equations

1. **Correct answer: D.** The interaction between the reactants iron oxide and carbon monoxide is shown with a plus sign. The arrow indicates that the reaction has taken place and the products, iron and carbon dioxide, are written on the right side.

2. **Correct answer: B.** The iron atoms are balanced by writing a coefficient of 2 in front of iron. A coefficient of 3 for carbon dioxide and for oxygen balances the carbon and oxygen atoms.

3. **Correct answer: C.** The equation is a replacement reaction because the iron in iron oxide is displaced.

Exercise 4: Solutions and Solubility

1. **Correct answer: A.** Water is a single substance rather than a homogenous mixture of substances. It is commonly the solvent in solutions.

2. **Correct answer: C.** The smaller the number on the pH scale, the stronger the acid. Therefore, lemon juice with a pH of 1.5 is a strong acid.

3. **Correct answer: (counterclockwise starting from the left) Unsaturated, Saturated, Supersaturated.** The unsaturated solution indicates that more solute can be dissolved, while the saturated illustration shows that nothing else can be dissolved. The supersaturated solution demonstrates crystallization.

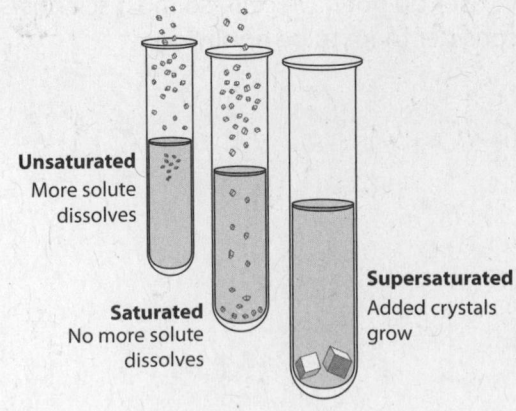

Unsaturated
More solute dissolves

Saturated
No more solute dissolves

Supersaturated
Added crystals grow

Chapter 8 Energy

Exercise 1: Types of Energy

1. **Correct answer: radiant.** Placing the seedlings in different locations within the greenhouse affects the amount of direct sunlight the plants receive. Sunlight is a form of radiant energy.

2. **Correct answers: a) Chemical to Mechanical and b) Electrical to Thermal.** The chemical energy stored in gasoline is converted to mechanical energy when the car moves. The electrical energy traveling through a power cord is converted to thermal energy when the stove is used to cook food.

Exercise 2: Waves

1. **Correct answer is shown in the following diagram.** Wavelength is measured between two corresponding parts of a wave. Because the dot is placed on the *x*-axis where the wave is sloping upward, the X should be placed in the next location where the wave crosses the *x*-axis as it slopes upward. The distance between the dot and the X indicates one wavelength.

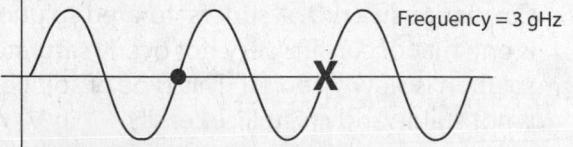

Frequency = 3 gHz

2. **Correct answer: A.** The frequency of the wave shown is 3 gHz, much less than the frequency of visible light. Radio waves have a lower frequency than visible light waves.

3. **Correct answer: D.** Water can be boiled in a microwave oven, which uses microwaves. Microwaves are effective at heating water and food and are relatively safe with reasonable exposure.

Exercise 3: Heat

1. **Correct answer: C.** Heat is transferred as the result of direct contact between the coffee and the mug. This is an example of conduction.

2. **Correct answer: D.** Energy is transferred from the high temperature substance (coffee) to the low temperature substance (mug). Energy is transferred in the form of heat. As more energy transfers from coffee to mug, the mug's temperature increases.

Exercise 4: Energy in Reactions

1. **Correct answer: energy.** Endothermic reactions, like photosynthesis, must absorb energy from the environment. Because energy is absorbed, the products of an endothermic reaction contain more energy than the original reactants.

2. **Correct answer: exothermic.** Exothermic reactions, like respiration, release energy into the environment. In the case of respiration, the environment is the cell where the reaction takes place.

Exercise 5: Sources of Energy

1. **Correct answer: fossil fuels.** According to the graph, petroleum, natural gas, and coal make up a combined 83 percent of the United States' sources of energy in 2010. These energy sources are all considered fossil fuels.

2. **Correct answer: C.** Renewable energy includes energy sources like solar energy, which produces very little pollution. Increasing the use of renewable energy sources like solar energy is least likely to increase pollution.

Chapter 9 Motion and Force

Exercise 1: Motion

1. **Correct answer: 1.** The distance traveled is 10 miles in 10 minutes. Using the speed equation $v = d/t$, 10 miles divided by 10 minutes is 1 mile per minute.

2. **Correct answer: C.** The straight line on the graph shows that the object was moving at the same speed for the entire 10 minutes. This means that the object had no acceleration.

3. **Correct answer: D.** For the tennis ball, 60 g × 20 m/s = 1200 g m/s. For the basketball, 600 g × 2 m/s = 1200 g m/s. The tennis ball has a small mass but travels quickly, while the basketball has a large mass and travels slowly.

Exercise 2: Force

1. **Correct answers: Lift** and **Gravity.** If the forces of lift and gravity are balanced, the plane will not accelerate up or downward.

2. **Correct answer: C.** Newton's second law of motion, or $F = m \times a$, can be used to determine how much thrust is required to achieve a certain acceleration. Multiplying the plane's mass by the desired acceleration will give the required force (thrust).

Exercise 3: Work and Machines

1. **Correct answers: a) inclined plane, b) screw, c) lever,** and **d) wheel and axle.** A slide is a ramp and a lid screws onto a jar. Applying force to one end of a hammer applies an output force at the hammer's other end. On a paint roller, the roller itself is a wheel and the handle provides the axle.

2. **Correct answer: double.** A simple machine does not change the amount of work done. If a simple machine decreases the amount of input force, it must also increase the distance used proportionally.

Practice: Physical Science

1. **Correct answer: $2Al + Fe_2O_3 \rightarrow Al_2O_3 + 2Fe$.** To balance the two atoms of aluminum on the product side, a coefficient of 2 must be added to aluminum on the reactant side. The same process occurs for iron, adding a coefficient of 2 on the product to balance the 2 iron atoms on the reactant side of the equation.

2. **Correct answer: B.** The thermite reaction is exothermic because it releases energy into the environment. The burst of high temperature produced by the reaction releases energy in the form of heat.

3. **Correct answer: C.** Most metals, with the exception of mercury, are in a solid state at room temperature. Metals are also generally strong and malleable, have high melting and boiling points, and form positive ions.

4. **Correct answer: C.** The amount of water used is a control in the experiment. Changing the amount from 2 mL to 4 mL indicates a source of error in the experimental design by introducing another variable that will introduce inconclusive data.

5. **Correct answer: D.** A supersaturated solution is one that occurs if a very hot overly saturated solution is slowly cooled. This type of solution is not stable and crystallizes easily.

6. **Correct answer: B.** A boiling liquid is an example of convection. Heat is transferred throughout the mixture as the warm, less dense liquid at the bottom rises toward the top and the cold, more dense liquid sinks to the bottom.

7. **Correct answer: A.** Gamma rays have the highest frequency of all electromagnetic radiation, allowing them to transfer the most energy. The more energy a wave transports, the more harmful exposure to the wave can be.

8. **Correct answer: A.** An object's momentum is the product of its mass and velocity. The velocity of the truck is given. To calculate the truck's momentum, its mass must also be known.

9. **Correct answer: C.** To test the effect of flooring type on car motion, all other variables that could affect the toy cars' motion should be kept constant. This means that the cars should have equal mass and should be allowed to roll down the ramp. The distance traveled by all cars should be recorded.

10. **Correct answer: A.** Work is done when applying a force to an object results in the object moving a distance. Although a force is applied to the faucet, the handle is stuck and does not move. This means that no work is done on the faucet.

PART 3 EARTH AND SPACE SCIENCE

Chapter 10 Space Systems

Exercise 1: The Age of Earth

1. **Correct answer: D.** Fossils found within the same sedimentary rock layer are considered to have the same relative age. When the sediment becomes compressed into rock, the fossil remains of organisms that died around the same time are preserved within the rock.

2. **Correct answer: 50.** After one half-life, half of the original carbon-14 atoms, or 50 total, would still exist. The other half would have changed into another element.

Exercise 2: The Solar System

1. **Correct answers: terrestrial** and **rocky.** Earth is one of the four inner planets that are closest to the sun. Earth's location in the solar system and solid, rocky surface identify it as one of the terrestrial planets.

2. **Correct answer: A.** Earth takes 24 hours to complete one rotation on its axis. At any given time, half of Earth is in darkness (night) and half is in sunlight (day). The part of Earth that is in day or night changes as Earth rotates.

Exercise 3: The Universe

1. **Correct answer: B.** Scientists believe that the universe formed as the result of a giant explosion termed the Big Bang.

2. **Correct answer: D.** A supergiant star can die in a giant explosion called a supernova. The explosion can result in the creation of a black hole.

Chapter 11 Earth Systems

Exercise 1: The Structure of Earth

1. **Correct answer: C.** Fold mountains happen when the collision of two plates squeezes the two plates together. The layers of rock are slowly pushed toward each other.

2. The correct answers, from top to bottom, are **Crust, Mantle, Outer core, Inner core**. The crust is the surface of the Earth, and the mantle is located just below. The inner core is the center of the Earth's interior and is ringed by the outer core.

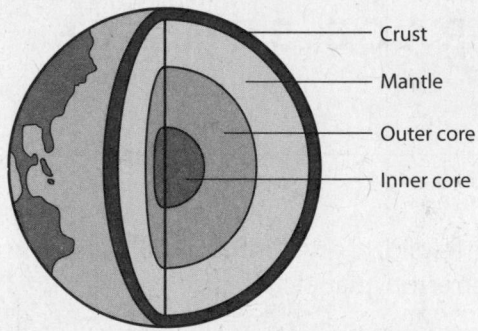

Crust
Mantle
Outer core
Inner core

Exercise 2: Earth's Atmosphere

1. **Correct answer: D.** Chlorofluorocarbons, or CFCs, are a type of chlorine compound that degrades the ozone layer by breaking ozone down into oxygen atoms.

2. The correct answers from top to bottom are **Ionosphere, Mesosphere, Stratosphere,**

Troposphere. The ionosphere extends from 50 to 600 km; thus it would cover the section at 80 km. Below that, the atmospheric layers in descending order are mesosphere, stratosphere, and troposphere.

Exercise 3: Weathering and Erosion

1. **Correct answer: C.** A low pressure system is caused when warm air from equatorial regions rises higher into the atmosphere and then extends toward the north and south poles.

2. **Correct answer: B.** Oxidation occurs when rock is chemically altered by the interaction between iron and oxygen. It is more commonly referred to as rusting.

Exercise 4: The Oceans

1. **Correct answer: A.** For every 1000 grams of seawater, there are approximately 35 grams of dissolved salts, resulting in a salinity of 3.5 percent.

2. **Correct answers: equator** and **poles.** Currents near the surface move heat from the equator to the north and south poles, and back toward the equator.

Chapter 12 Interactions Between Earth's Systems and Living Things

Exercise 1: Cycles in Nature

1. **Correct answer: D.** Nitrogen-fixing bacteria produce nitrates from organic nitrogen compounds, and denitrifying bacteria return nitrogen to the atmosphere by converting nitrates to nitrogen gas.

2. **Correct answers: a) Condensation, b) Precipitation, c) Evaporation.** Water vapor condensation in clouds leads to precipitation, and water is returned to the land or sea. The sun's heat provides the energy for evaporation, and the water from Earth's surface is returned to the atmosphere.

Exercise 2: Natural Hazards

1. **Correct answer: A.** In general, in less-developed countries, the poverty level is higher than in more highly developed countries. Also, population density, meaning the number of people in a given area, increases vulnerability to disaster.

2. **Correct answer: B.** The chance that an earthquake might occur that has the severity to cause the deaths of over 1000 people is 0.001, or 0.1 percent.

Exercise 3: Natural Resources

1. **Correct answer: C.** Forests are considered a sustainable resource because they require proper management to be sustained and stay viable.

2. **Correct answer: D.** Though they are naturally occurring, coal and oil took millions of years to form, making them a finite resource.

Practice: Earth and Space Science

1. **Correct answer: layer C.** In the diagram, layer C is below layer D, but above the dike. This means that the age of layer C must be between that of layer D (80 million years) and that of the dike (85 million years).

2. **Correct answer: B.** Asteroids are composed of rock, and comets are composed of frozen gas and dust. Identifying the composition of the object will tell scientists what type of object it is.

3. **Correct answer: D.** The sun produces light and heat. This means it is actively converting hydrogen to helium, which is a characteristic of main sequence stars.

4. **Correct answer: D.** The stratosphere is characterized by temperatures that increase with height because ozone in this layer absorbs UV radiation. In the thermosphere, temperature increases with height because of a steady influx of solar energy.

5. **Correct answer: A.** Winds that blow from a single direction over a specific area of Earth are called prevailing winds. Areas where prevailing winds meet are referred to as convergence zones.

6. **Correct answer: A.** Microscopic, symbiotic algae called zooxanthellae live in the bodies of coral animals and provide them with food produced by photosynthesis.

7. **Correct answer: B.** A company concerned about the environment would select a renewable and sustainable energy source such as wind power.

8. **The correct response contains:**
   - A clear and well-developed explanation of the strengths in a plan to educate about building codes and emergency preparedness
   - A clear and well-developed explanation of the weaknesses in a plan to educate about building codes and emergency preparedness
   - Complete support from the passage

SAMPLE PAPER

The effects of natural hazards tend to be more severe and long lasting in less economically developed areas. While the need for education on emergency preparedness and building codes is great, the realities of an impoverished population may not allow people to attend the seminars. Even though the seminar is free, people may not be free to attend. Economies dependent on cash crops often require long workdays with no time off. Additionally, a plan to educate people about how to build a home that can structurally survive a natural hazard is unlikely to be successful. In less economically developed countries, government authorities may lack the means to implement and enforce strict building codes. However, if community leaders are able to attend the seminars, the program could see some success if the leaders share what they learned with the rest of the community.

Social Studies

The Social Studies Test

The Social Studies section of the GED® test measures your knowledge of key social studies topics and how well you are able to analyze and interpret documents and other social studies information. There are 45 questions on the Social Studies test, and you will have 90 minutes to complete the entire test, including 25 minutes for writing an extended response (essay). Half of the questions focus on U.S. government and civics. The rest cover U.S. history, world history, economics, and geography.

Questions on the Social Studies test may ask about the information in a short passage, a map, a graph, a table, or some other graphic presentation of social studies data. Sometimes two or three questions will refer to the same passage, graph, or table.

Most Social Studies questions are multiple choice with four answer choices. Others use interactive formats such as drag and drop, fill-in-the-blank, and drop-down. See "Introducing the GED® Test" at the beginning of this book for an explanation and samples of these formats.

The Social Studies Review

The following section of this book presents a comprehensive review of the knowledge that is tested on the Social Studies test. Each main topic is followed by a short exercise to measure how well you have mastered that subject. The exercise questions include examples of the kinds of short passages, charts, tables, and other graphics that you will encounter on test day. These exercises will help you become familiar with the Social Studies question types. If you have already taken the Social Studies Pretest at the start of this book, make sure to study those sections of the Social Studies review that correspond to the questions you missed or found difficult.

This Social Studies review section is organized as follows:

Social Studies

Answers and explanations for all of the practice questions in this section are located at the end of the section.

CHAPTER 1

Civics and Government

Types of Historical and Modern Governments

Governments are institutions that make, interpret, and implement laws for the people in a community. These processes maintain order in society and provide security for citizens.

There have been many different kinds of governments throughout history, and many different kinds exist today. In the United States, the citizens play an important role in government. Through elections, Americans choose their leaders. United States citizens benefit from a government that was created to protect their rights and freedoms.

Most governments throughout history can be classified into four basic types: oligarchy, monarchy, dictatorship, and democracy.

An **oligarchy** is a political system in which power is held by a small group of people. These people are usually members of an upper class such as nobles or military officers. They are not elected by the citizens. In an oligarchy, the rulers typically exercise power in their particular interests rather than on behalf of society at large.

In a **monarchy,** power is held by a king, queen, emperor, or empress. This leader generally rules until the end of his or her life. Then leadership is passed on to his or her heirs. In a traditional monarchy, the leader has absolute power. In a **constitutional monarchy** such as Great Britain or the Netherlands, the ruler's powers are limited by laws that may be written or unwritten. In modern constitutional monarchies, the ruler has little power and functions mainly as a ceremonial head of state.

A **dictatorship** is a type of government in which a single leader exercises absolute power over nearly every aspect of life in a country, including political, social, and economic issues. The leader, or dictator, is not bound by any rules and can enact or change laws at will. Elections, if they are permitted, are usually meaningless because no transfer of power is allowed.

In a **democracy**, citizens exercise power on their own behalf. The earliest democracy was established in the small city-state of Athens in ancient Greece in 510 BCE. This was a **direct democracy** in which all citizens participated directly in making laws and in the government. Today's democracies, in much larger nations, are **representative democracies** in which citizens elect representatives to carry out the functions of government. In a democracy, every citizen has a voice, either directly or through elected representatives, in how the country is governed. When the head of state is a person elected by voters (rather than a hereditary constitutional monarch), this form of government is called a **republic**.

A democracy may be either parliamentary or presidential. A **parliamentary democracy**, such as those in Australia, Great Britain, and Canada, is a type of government in which government leaders are chosen by the political party that holds a majority of seats in the legislature, or parliament, based on elections. If no party holds a majority, several parties may work together to form a coalition government. Executive power is exercised by a prime minister, premier, or chancellor, assisted by cabinet members. The prime minister is the head of the government and is the leader of the political party that has the most seats in parliament. The government remains in office as long as the parliament supports its policies.

A **presidential democracy,** such as those in the United States and France, functions somewhat differently. This kind of democracy is headed by a powerful chief executive, called the president, who is elected by the voters, generally for a set number of years. The president is separate from the legislature and exercises a considerable amount of independent power, but his or her actions are limited by the constitution and other laws.

EXERCISE 1

Types of Historical and Modern Governments

Directions: Choose the best answer to each of the following questions.

1. In which of the following governments does a leader have the most control over citizens' lives?

   A. oligarchy
   B. monarchy
   C. dictatorship
   D. democracy

2. Read each characteristic of a democracy. In the space, indicate whether each characteristic is found in a direct or representative democracy. Use **D** for direct democracy and **R** for representative democracy.

   _____ Every citizen can place proposals on the ballot, and a proposal becomes law if the majority vote for it.

   _____ Citizens elect a legislature to rule the country.

   _____ Delegates represent the wishes of the voting citizens.

   _____ Power to veto laws rests with the citizens themselves.

Answers are on page 829.

Basic Principles of American Constitutional Democracy

The founders of the American political system based their ideas on a number of principles developed by earlier thinkers in Great Britain and elsewhere in Europe. One of these principles, the philosophy of **natural rights**, was included in the Declaration of Independence.

According to this idea, individuals have certain rights just by the fact that they are human beings. These rights are derived from nature; they are not allowed by a ruler or permitted by a law. Also, they are absolute and not revocable. The idea of natural rights dates back to the European Enlightenment of the 17th and 18th centuries. The Scottish philosopher John Locke (1632–1704) stated that the duty of government is to protect people's rights to life, liberty, and property. The Declaration of Independence states that people are "endowed by their Creator with certain unalienable Rights," and states that these include the rights to life, liberty, and the pursuit of happiness.

A second principle that contributes to American democracy is **popular sovereignty**. According to this principle, the government derives its power from the **consent of the governed**. Furthermore, people who are subject to the government's decisions have the right to a voice in deciding how those decisions are reached. This was a fundamental belief of the 18th-century American colonists who demanded a say in how the colonies were governed. Following the Revolutionary War, the idea of popular sovereignty was one of the bases on which the government of the United States was founded. The people, through their elected representatives, have a voice in how governmental decisions are made.

Constitutionalism is a way of thinking that combines the ideas of a limited government and the rule of law. These ideas are found throughout the Constitution of the United States. The government is entitled to exercise certain powers, but its powers are also limited in order to protect the rights of the citizens. **Limited government** means that government's powers are spelled out and also limited by the laws and the Constitution. **The rule of law** means that neither the citizens nor the government officials are permitted to break the laws or to violate the Constitution.

The idea of constitutionalism was written into the Preamble of the U.S. Constitution. The Preamble states that the government is given the powers needed to protect the people, but that its powers are limited and cannot be used unjustly against the citizens.

Because the U.S. government is based on the consent of the governed, **majority rule** is an important basic concept. Simply put, decisions are made by a vote of more than half of the people who participate, whether it is an election or an act of the legislature.

The founders were also aware that a majority might abuse its power and might not respect the rights of a minority. In a democracy, majority rule needs to be limited so that **minority rights** are guaranteed. Those with unpopular views, whether they are individuals or minority groups, must be protected from oppression by the majority. One way this protection is granted in the United States is by the Bill of Rights, which protects the basic rights of individual citizens.

Another important principle, called **federalism**, provides for the separation of powers and functions between the federal government and the governments of the states. The **federal government** exercises supreme power throughout the country and has exclusive control over issues such as:

- Declaring war

- Making treaties with other countries

- National defense

- Regulating trade

The **state governments** control:

- Functions that are not assigned to the federal government

- Local issues covered by state and local laws

The Tenth Amendment to the U.S. Constitution grants powers to the states that the Constitution has not assigned specifically to the federal government.

EXERCISE 2

Basic Principles of American Constitutional Democracy

Directions: Read the following statements, and then choose the principle that is addressed.

1. "All . . . will bear in mind this sacred principle, that though the will of the majority is in all cases to prevail, that will to be rightful must be reasonable; that the minority possess their equal rights, which equal law must protect and to violate would be oppression." —Thomas Jefferson

   A. limited government
   B. minority rights
   C. popular sovereignty
   D. natural rights philosophy

2. Everyone deserves to enjoy certain freedoms and to have the opportunity to obtain a reasonable quality of life.

   A. limited government
   B. minority rights
   C. popular sovereignty
   D. natural rights philosophy

3. Citizens are able to voice their opinions on the rules and laws by which they are expected to live.

   A. limited government
   B. minority rights
   C. popular sovereignty
   D. natural rights philosophy

4. The Scottish philosopher John Locke declared that the duty of government is to protect people's rights to life, liberty, and property.

   A. limited government
   B. minority rights
   C. popular sovereignty
   D. natural rights philosophy

5. At the time the U.S. Constitution was written, the federal government was not permitted to raise money for itself and had to depend on the states to provide the funds needed to operate the country.

   A. limited government
   B. minority rights
   C. popular sovereignty
   D. natural rights philosophy

Answers are on page 829.

Structure and Design of the U.S. Federal Government

The structure of the U.S. federal government is based on a principle called the **separation of powers**. The Constitution divides the federal government into three branches: the executive branch (the President), the legislative branch (Congress), and the judicial branch (the court system). In this way, power is divided. The division prevents any one branch of the government from having too much power. It also means that if one branch abuses its power, the other two are available to restrain it. Thus each branch checks the power of the other two. This is known as a system of **checks and balances**. This division of government into three branches was first proposed by the French political philosopher Montesquieu in the 18th century. He believed that this division of power promoted liberty. The idea of separation of powers is one of the main components of modern constitutional government.

Checks and Balances

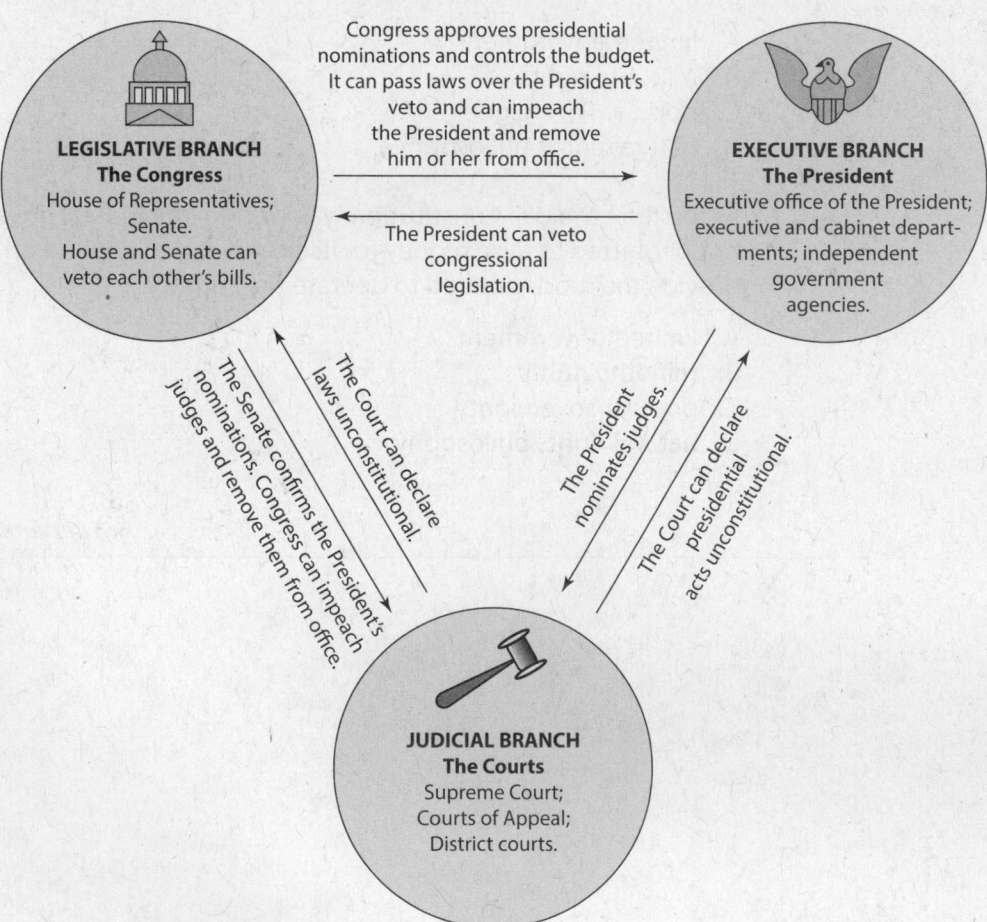

Each of the three branches of government serves a distinct purpose. The **legislative** branch, which is Congress, makes the laws. The **executive** branch is the President and the members of his or her administration. The President is elected separately from the members of Congress. The executive branch is responsible for enforcing the laws. It also has the power to veto acts of Congress, thus limiting the power of the legislative branch. The **judicial** branch, which is the court system, is responsible for interpreting the laws.

EXERCISE 3

Structure and Design of the U.S. Federal Government

Directions: Follow the instructions to answer the question.

1. Read each of the following statements. For each one, decide which branch of government is being checked by the action described. Then indicate the column in the table where each statement belongs. (**Note**: On the real GED® test, you will click on each statement and "drag" it into position in the diagram.)

How Each Government Branch Is Controlled by Checks and Balances

Action That Checks the Legislative Branch	Action That Checks the Executive Branch	Action That Checks the Judicial Branch

The President nominates judges to the Supreme Court.	Congress has the power to remove the President from office.
The Supreme Court decides if laws enacted by Congress follow the guidelines of the Constitution.	The Senate must confirm persons nominated for the Supreme Court.
The Supreme Court determines whether the actions of the President are permitted by the Constitution.	The President has the power to veto laws enacted by Congress.

Answers are on page 829.

The Legislative Branch

The legislative branch of government, the U.S. Congress, is composed of two houses. These are the **House of Representatives**, or the lower house, and the **Senate**, or the upper house. These two houses are equal in power. They differ in how they are elected and in the number of members in each house. Members of the House are elected from districts that each include a roughly equal number of voters. The districts are redrawn ("reapportioned") every 10 years based on the results of a census. States with larger populations contain more electoral districts and therefore elect more members to the House. Members of the House serve two-year terms. In the Senate, by contrast, each state is represented by two senators, regardless of the state's population. Thus states with small populations have the same number of votes in the Senate as states with large populations. Senators are elected by all the voters in a state. They serve six-year terms, with one-third up for election every two years. The **Speaker of the House** is the presiding officer of the House and is elected by the members. He or she is typically the leader of the majority party.

The powers of Congress are listed in Article I of the U.S. Constitution. These listed powers are called **enumerated powers**, although the **elastic clause** allows Congress to stretch its powers to fit specific situations as needed. Some of the enumerated powers held by Congress include the power to tax, to regulate commerce and the currency, to introduce bills, to declare war, to maintain the army and navy, to admit new states into the Union, to approve treaties, and to impeach the President. Most of these powers are shared by both houses; however, some are assigned to either the Senate or the House only.

EXERCISE 4

The Legislative Branch

Directions: Use the map to answer the following questions.

**Apportionment of the U.S. House of Representatives
Based on the 2010 Census**

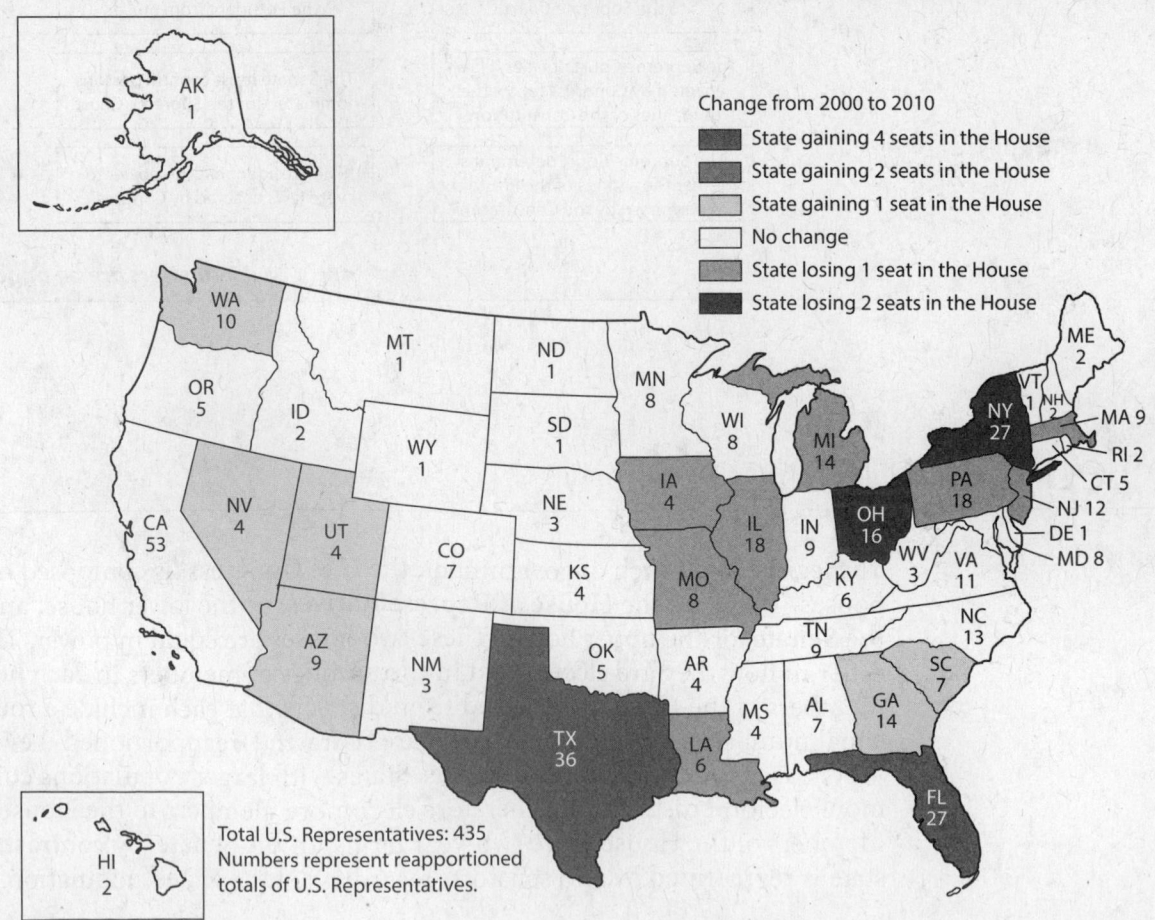

Change from 2000 to 2010
- State gaining 4 seats in the House
- State gaining 2 seats in the House
- State gaining 1 seat in the House
- No change
- State losing 1 seat in the House
- State losing 2 seats in the House

Total U.S. Representatives: 435
Numbers represent reapportioned totals of U.S. Representatives.

1. During the 113th Congress, which began on January 3, 2013, California had 53 representatives. What does that indicate?

   A. California had a greater population than any other state at the time the Constitution was ratified.
   B. At the time of this session of Congress, the population of California was greater than that of any other state.
   C. More voters in California participated in the 2012 presidential election than in any other state.
   D. California has the greatest land area, in square miles, of any state in the country.

2. What can you infer based on the map?

   A. Texas has always had 36 representatives because it is the largest state by area.
   B. Certain states will always have the greatest number of representatives.
   C. The number of representatives for each state can change every 10 years based on census results.
   D. Western states such as California and Oregon have a greater number of representatives than states in the east.

3. Which state gained the most representatives in 2010?

   A. California
   B. Florida
   C. Georgia
   D. New York

Answers are on page 829.

The Executive Branch

The executive branch of the government includes the **President**, the **Vice President**, and the agencies that enforce the laws of the United States. The President, who is the head of the government of the United States, is elected by the people for a four-year term, and may serve no more than two terms. Article II of the Constitution outlines the responsibilities of the President, which include serving as commander-in-chief of the armed forces, appointing judges to the Supreme Court, nominating major executive officers, executing and enforcing laws enacted by Congress, and vetoing bills sent by Congress as he sees fit. Congress can override the President's veto of a law with a two-thirds vote of both houses.

The U.S. Constitution gives the President the power to negotiate and sign treaties with other countries. These treaties must be ratified by a two-thirds vote of the Senate. The Constitution also requires the President to give Congress information regarding the **State of the Union**, which is traditionally an address to a joint session of Congress each year in January. The Constitution also established three qualifications for being elected President: a candidate must be at least 35 years old, must be a natural-born citizen of the United States, and must have lived in the country for a minimum of 14 years.

The Vice President assumes the presidency if the President is unable to complete a term, for example, if he or she becomes disabled or dies. Thus the Vice President's major responsibility is to be prepared to take on the responsibilities of the President at a moment's notice. The Vice President also serves as president of the Senate, where his or her vote may be needed to break a tie. Other vice presidential duties are assigned at the President's discretion. The Speaker of the House is third in line to succeed the President, following the Vice President.

EXERCISE 5

The Executive Branch

Directions: Choose the best answer to each of the following questions.

1. The Constitution specifies the wording of the oath of office of the President of the United States. Read the following excerpts from the Constitution.

   > Before he enter on the Execution of his Office, he shall take the following Oath or Affirmation: "I do solemnly swear (or affirm) that I will faithfully execute the Office of President of the United States, and will to the best of my Ability, preserve, protect and defend the Constitution of the United States."

   What is the central idea of the oath of office? The President will

   A. protect the people of the United States.
   B. support the U.S. Constitution.
   C. work to preserve the land of the United States.
   D. amend the U.S. Constitution as he or she finds it necessary.

2. What inference can be made about why the framers of the Constitution included the oath of office?

   A. They wanted to ensure that every presidential inauguration included the same words.
   B. They believed that every President would need to be protected and defended while in office.
   C. They wanted to ensure that all future Presidents would follow the guidelines established in the Constitution.
   D. They believed that the Constitution should be mentioned every four years so no one would forget about it.

3. Read the following:

> [The President] shall have power, by and with the advice and consent of the Senate, to make treaties, provided two thirds of the Senators present concur; and he shall nominate, and by and with the advice and consent of the Senate, shall appoint ambassadors, other public ministers and consuls, judges of the Supreme Court, and all other officers of the United States, whose appointments are not herein otherwise provided for, and which shall be established by law: but the Congress may by law vest the appointment of such inferior officers, as they think proper, in the President alone, in the courts of law, or in the heads of departments.

—Excerpt from the U.S. Constitution

Which statement best reflects the point of view of the framers of the Constitution?

A. No single person should have too much power in the government.
B. The Senate should have the power to appoint people to certain public offices.
C. Congress is better able to make decisions about treaties than the President.
D. The President should not make any decisions without the consent of Congress.

Question 4 is based on the following graph.

Party Affiliations of the First 44 Presidents

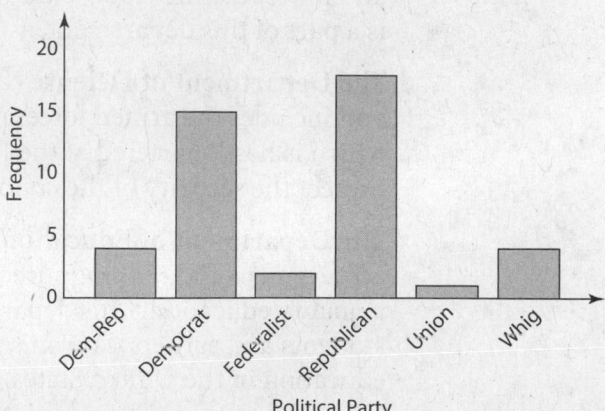

4. Based on the graph, which statement is true?

A. Most Presidents have had more than one party affiliation.
B. There have been more Republican than Democratic Presidents.
C. The last four Presidents have been affiliated with the Whig party.
D. The next President is more likely to be a Democrat than Republican.

Answers are on page 829.

The President's Cabinet

Within the three branches of government are many people who play important roles in the running of the country. The **cabinet** is a group whose role is to advise the President on subjects related to each member's office. This group includes not only the Vice President of the United States but also the heads of executive departments, including the Attorney General and the secretaries of Agriculture, Commerce, Defense, Education, Energy, Health and Human Services, Homeland Security, Housing and Urban Development, Interior, Labor, State, Transportation, Treasury, and Veteran's Affairs. Each of these officials is appointed by the President and then confirmed by the Senate and is responsible for running a major federal agency and for carrying out the day-to-day operations of the federal government. Each cabinet member takes the title of "Secretary" of his or her department, with the exception of the head of the justice department, who is known as the Attorney General. Following the Vice President, the Speaker of the House, and the Senate President pro tempore, the cabinet members are included in the line of succession to the presidency in the order in which their departments were created.

Each of the departments and agencies over which the cabinet members preside takes responsibility for a different set of government functions.

- The **Department of Agriculture** is responsible for ensuring the safety of food and regulating farming.

- The **Department of Commerce** is responsible for improving the living standards of the citizens of the country through economic development, and for regulating trade, banking, and the economy. The Census Bureau is a part of this department, as is the Patent and Trademark Office.

- The **Department of Defense** (DOD) is the largest government agency and includes the armed forces of the United States. This department, which is headquartered at the Pentagon in Washington, D.C., helps protect the security of the country.

- The **Department of Education** is responsible for promoting student achievement and making sure that all students have equal access to a quality education. This department administers financial aid for students and gathers data on schools in order to guide improvements for education in the United States.

- The **Department of Energy** regulates utilities and is responsible for ensuring the security of the country's power supplies. It also promotes new technology to conserve energy resources. The department provides funds for scientific research in this area.

- The **Department of Health and Human Services** includes the Food and Drug Administration (FDA), the Centers for Disease Control (CDC), and the National Institutes of Health and Administration on Aging. This department works to ensure the health of U.S. citizens and administers Medicare and Medicaid, which provide health insurance to approximately 25 percent of Americans.

- The **Department of Homeland Security** was established following the terrorist attacks of 2001 and is responsible for security within the United States, and for patrolling the borders. This department was created by combining 22 executive branch agencies. It includes the Immigration and Naturalization Service, the U.S. Secret Service, the U.S. Coast Guard, and the Transportation Security Administration.

- The **Department of Housing and Urban Development** (HUD) promotes affordable home ownership for U.S. citizens and makes sure that there is no discrimination against those trying to purchase a home. It provides mortgage and loan insurance, administers public housing, and offers assistance to the homeless.

- The **Department of the Interior** works to protect, conserve, and nurture national resources, including national parks and wildlife. This department manages about 20 percent of the land in the United States and protects endangered species. Agencies such as the Fish and Wildlife Service and the Bureau of Indian Affairs fall under the responsibility of this department.

- The **Department of Justice** is the largest law office in the world. It is responsible for enforcing the laws and for protecting the interests of U.S. citizens. It works to ensure public safety, control crime, and seek justice for individuals who are guilty of committing crimes. It includes a total of 40 organizations, including the Federal Bureau of Investigation (FBI), the Federal Bureau of Prisons, and the Drug Enforcement Administration (DEA).

- The **Department of Labor** enforces labor laws in the United States and protects the safety and rights of workers. The programs of this department deal with job training, minimum wage levels, unemployment insurance, and discrimination in hiring. The Occupational Safety and Health Administration (OSHA) and the Bureau of Labor Statistics are part of this department.

- The **Department of State** is responsible for diplomatic relations with other countries and works to develop and implement the foreign policies of the President. This agency and its representatives reflect the United States as part of the worldwide community. The Secretary of State, who leads this department, is the President's top advisor on foreign policy.

- The **Department of Transportation** is responsible for maintaining and ensuring the safety of the nation's transportation network. It was responsible for establishing the Interstate Highway System, and it includes the Federal Highway Administration, the Federal Aviation Administration, and the National Highway Traffic Safety Administration.

- The **Department of the Treasury** collects taxes, manages federal finances, produces coins and currency, and oversees the financial and economic stability of the United States. It works with other agencies, with the governments of foreign countries, and with international financial institutions to raise the standard of living and encourage economic growth worldwide.

- The **Department of Veterans' Affairs** offers medical care for veterans who are wounded or ill and administers benefits to those who have served in the armed forces and to their families.

EXERCISE 6

The President's Cabinet

Directions: Choose the best answer to each of the following questions.

1. There are currently about 25 million living American veterans. Of these, approximately 75 percent served the country either during a time of war or during an official time of hostility. This means that about one-fourth of the population of the United States, about 70 million people, could be eligible for veterans' benefits as a result of either being a veteran or being a family member or survivor of a veteran.
   Based on this information, which conclusion can be drawn?

   A. The Secretary of Veteran's Affairs oversees a very large budget.
   B. Benefits for veterans and their families will run out within the next decade.
   C. The Department of Veteran's Affairs will have to decrease the amount of benefits awarded.
   D. Family members of veterans should not receive benefits because they did not serve our country.

2. Which department was created most recently?

   A. Department of the Treasury
   B. Department of Defense
   C. Department of Education
   D. Department of Homeland Security

Answers are on page 829.

The Judicial Branch

The judicial branch of the federal government includes the **Supreme Court**, the most powerful court in the country, whose responsibility is to determine whether or not laws are constitutional. This process is called **judicial review**. The judicial branch is also responsible for determining the meaning of laws and whether or not laws have been followed.

The Supreme Court is composed of nine justices who are appointed by the President and confirmed by the U.S. Senate. The justices serve for life. The **Chief Justice** is the head of this elite group; the others are known as associate justices. The exact number of justices is determined by Congress. Although there have been nine members since 1869, this number had formerly been as low as six. A decision is reached when a majority of these justices agree. One responsibility of the Chief Justice is to administer the oath of office at presidential inaugurations. Another is to preside over impeachment hearings.

According to Article III of the Constitution, the Supreme Court is empowered to rule on cases that involve a state and citizens from a different state, controversies between states, and patent and copyright issues. Because the Supreme Court's responsibility is to interpret what a law means, it generally does not hold trials. The justices may, however, accept legal briefs, hear arguments, or ask questions of the parties in the case.

In addition to the Supreme Court, the judicial branch also includes the United States district courts and United States courts of appeal. The district courts try most federal cases. The courts of appeal are responsible for reviewing appealed district court cases. These courts must abide by the decisions and interpretations of the Supreme Court. Once the Supreme Court makes a ruling or interprets a law, the inferior courts must apply this interpretation to other cases.

The Judicial Branch

Directions: Questions 1 and 2 are based on the following table. Use the information in the table to fill in the blanks.

Chief Justices of the United States

Chief Justice	Appointed by President	Judicial Oath Taken	Date Service Terminated
Jay, John	Washington	October 19, 1789	June 29, 1795
Rutledge, John	Washington	August 12, 1795	December 15, 1795
Ellsworth, Oliver	Washington	March 8, 1796	December 15, 1800
Marshall, John	Adams, John	February 4, 1801	July 6, 1835
Taney, Roger Brooke	Jackson	March 28, 1836	October 12, 1864
Chase, Salmon Portland	Lincoln	December 15, 1864	May 7, 1873
Waite, Morrison Remick	Grant	March 4, 1874	March 23, 1888
Fuller, Melville Weston	Cleveland	October 8, 1888	July 4, 1910
White, Edward Douglass	Taft	December 19, 1910	May 19, 1921
Taft, William Howard	Harding	July 11, 1921	February 3, 1930
Hughes, Charles Evans	Hoover	February 24, 1930	June 30, 1941
Stone, Harlan Fiske	Roosevelt, F.	July 3, 1941	April 22, 1946
Vinson, Fred Moore	Truman	June 24, 1946	September 8, 1953
Warren, Earl	Eisenhower	October 5, 1953	June 23, 1969
Burger, Warren Earl	Nixon	June 23, 1969	September 26, 1986
Rehnquist, William H.	Reagan	September 26, 1986	September 3, 2005
Roberts, John G., Jr.	Bush, G. W.	September 29, 2005	

1. The Chief Justice who has held this office for the longest period of time is

   _____.

2. The longest serving Chief Justice held this position for approximately

   _____ years.

Answers are on page 830.

Amending the Constitution

According to Article IV of the U.S. Constitution, the Constitution can be modified. Only 27 changes have been made despite the fact that thousands have been proposed. These changes or additions to the Constitution are called **amendments**. The fact that the Constitution can be modified allows the government to adapt to changes that take place in the country.

The amendment process, which is spelled out in Article IV of the Constitution, begins one of two ways. Either Congress or a group of state legislatures can propose a change. The President plays no role in the process. The proposed amendment is presented to the states in the form of a joint resolution. Each state governor then submits the amendment to his or her state legislature. After an amendment has been proposed, three-fourths of the state legislatures must ratify, or approve, the change before it becomes law. The only amendment to have been ratified by all 50 states was the Twentieth Amendment. This amendment set the beginning and ending dates for presidential and congressional terms.

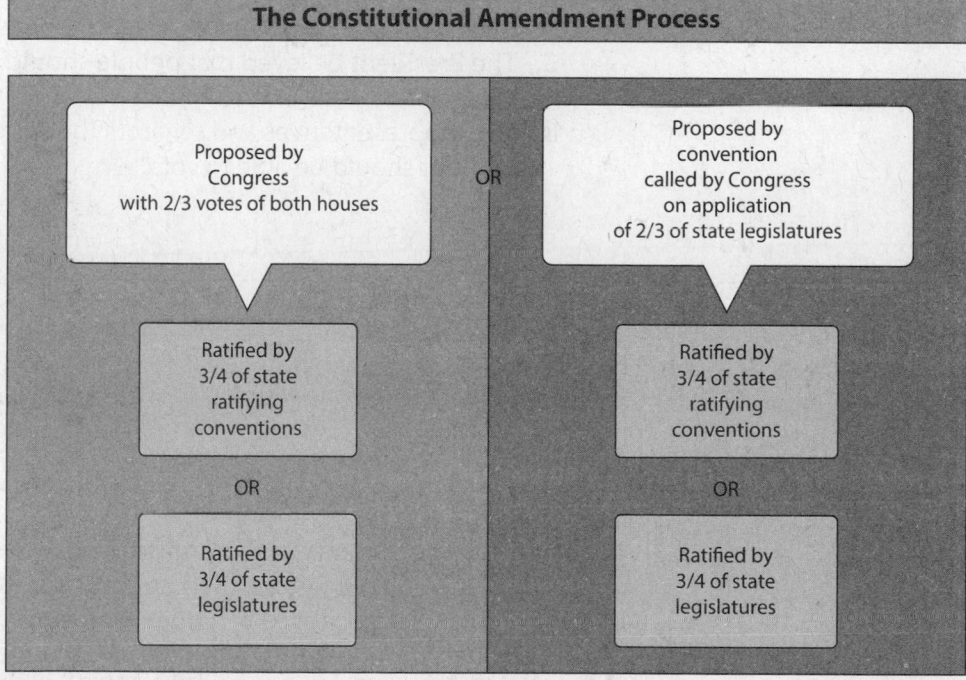

The Constitutional Amendment Process

Proposed by Congress with 2/3 votes of both houses

OR

Proposed by convention called by Congress on application of 2/3 of state legislatures

Ratified by 3/4 of state ratifying conventions

OR

Ratified by 3/4 of state legislatures

Ratified by 3/4 of state ratifying conventions

OR

Ratified by 3/4 of state legislatures

Amending the Constitution

Directions: Choose the best answer to each of the following questions.

1. What can be inferred from the ratification of the Twentieth Amendment?

   A. Most states do not believe amendments are necessary.
   B. States do not believe that the start and end dates for political terms are important.
   C. All 50 states will never agree on proposed amendments in the future.
   D. Just one amendment was ratified by all 50 states.

2. Congress once debated a proposed amendment that would have lowered the voting age from 18 to 16, but the proposal was defeated. What point of view does this defeat reflect?

   A. A minority of representatives and senators favored raising the minimum voting age.
   B. Most legislators believed that high school students are ready to vote.
   C. The President believed that people should not be allowed to vote at 16 years of age.
   D. Most representatives and senators thought that only people aged 18 or older should be able to vote.

Answers are on page 830.

The Bill of Rights

The first 10 amendments to the Constitution, which were proposed and ratified by the First Congress, are known as the **Bill of Rights**. These amendments were proposed by James Madison in 1789 because several states wanted the Constitution to provide stronger protection for individual liberties. The amendments in the Bill of Rights place specific restrictions on the government's power and guarantee certain rights and **civil liberties** to the citizens. These civil liberties include freedom of religion, freedom of speech, freedom of the press and assembly, and freedom from unreasonable searches and seizures.

Bill of Rights

Amendment I	Freedom of religion, speech, the press, assembly, and petition
Amendment II	Right to keep and bear arms in order to maintain a well-regulated militia
Amendment III	No quartering of soldiers in private homes without the owner's consent
Amendment IV	Freedom from unreasonable searches and seizures
Amendment V	Right to due process of law; freedom from self-incrimination and double jeopardy
Amendment VI	Rights of accused persons, such as the right to a speedy and public trial by jury
Amendment VII	Right of trial by jury in civil cases
Amendment VIII	Freedom from excessive bail and from cruel and unusual punishments
Amendment IX	Rights in addition to those stated in the Constitution
Amendment X	Powers reserved to the states

EXERCISE 9

The Bill of Rights

Directions: Choose the best answer to each of the following questions.

1. Read each statement. Determine which amendment in the Bill of Rights applies to each situation. Write the number of the amendment on the line.

_____ A newspaper prints an editorial criticizing the actions of a political candidate.

_____ A person is selected to be a member of a jury during the trial of someone accused of criminal activity.

_____ During a routine traffic stop, authorities demand to search for stolen goods in the driver's vehicle.

_____ A person is tried for a crime and found not guilty; however, many in the community believe that the verdict is wrong and the accused should be tried again.

_____ A homeowner purchases a personal firearm after robberies are committed in the neighborhood.

2. Several amendments in the Bill of Rights, including Amendments IV, V, and VI (4, 5, and 6), provide protection for people who are accused of a crime. Indicate which of the following rights are covered by these amendments by placing an X on the line.

_____ Protection against being tried twice for the same crime

_____ The right to freely practice religion

_____ The right to a speedy trial

_____ The right to freedom of the press

_____ Protection from being forced to house soldiers

_____ The right to bear arms

_____ The right to avoid self-incrimination

3. Read the following passage, and then answer the question.

> The happy Union of these States is a wonder; their Constitution a miracle; their example the hope of Liberty throughout the world.

> —*President James Madison (1829)*

What did Madison mean by the phrase "the hope of Liberty throughout the world"?

A. People in other countries look at the United States and hope that someday Americans will be free.

B. Everyone around the world will someday enjoy the same rights as citizens of the United States.

C. People in the United States do not believe that people in other countries will also gain liberty.

D. People in other countries will see that it is possible for a government to protect the freedom of its people.

Answers are on page 830.

Citizens' Rights and Civic Responsibilities

The Bill of Rights guarantees certain civil rights of American citizens. Other rights protected by the federal government but not included in the Bill of Rights are economic rights. These include the right to own property or a business. The government also protects people from discrimination by enacting laws that ensure equal treatment of people regardless of race, religion, age, or gender.

American citizens have responsibilities to their country and community as well. **Civic responsibilities** are key to making a democratic system of government work. Civic responsibilities of the citizens in the United States include paying taxes, registering for military service, performing jury service, and obeying federal, state, and local laws. Paying taxes provides the government with the funds needed to provide public goods and services, such as schools, law enforcement, roads, and parks. Serving on juries enables those accused of crimes to have a trial before a jury of their peers, as guaranteed by the Bill of Rights. Registering for military service helps to protect the country.

Civic responsibilities also include voting. Because the United States is a democracy, it is important for people to voice their opinions by voting. Citizens who have reached the age of 18 can register to vote and thus help select government officials and influence government policy.

Of the 27 amendments to the Constitution, four address who is able to vote. These amendments stipulate that citizens must be 18 years old or older, and may be men or women of any race. The amendments also guarantee that citizens are not required to pay a special tax in order to vote.

Citizens' Rights and Civic Responsibilities

Directions: Use the following Official Ballot to answer Questions 1 and 2.

OFFICIAL BALLOT
PRESIDENTIAL GENERAL ELECTION
NOVEMBER 6, 2012

PAGE 1

STATE OF MARYLAND, BALTIMORE CITY

INSTRUCTIONS

To vote, completely fill in the oval ⬤ to the left of your choice(s). Mark only with a #2 pencil. DO NOT ERASE. If you make a mistake you may request a new ballot. If your vote for a candidate or question is marked in such a manner that your intent is not clearly demonstrated, your vote for that office may not be counted. To protect the secrecy of your vote, do not put your name, initials, or any identifying mark on your official ballot.

To vote for a candidate whose name is not printed on the ballot, write in the name of the candidate on the designated write-in line under that office title and completely fill in the oval ⬤ to the left of the write-in candidate's name.

PRESIDENT AND VICE PRESIDENT
OF THE UNITED STATES
Vote for One

◯ **Barack Obama** — Democratic
Illinois
And
Joe Biden
Delaware

◯ **Mitt Romney** — Republican
Massachusetts
And
Paul Ryan
Wisconsin

◯ **Gary Johnson** — Libertarian
New Mexico
And
James P. Gray
California

◯ **Jill Stein** — Green
Massachusetts
And
Cheri Honkala
Pennsylvania

◯
_____
Write-in

U.S. SENATOR
Vote for One

◯ **Ben Cardin** — Democratic
◯ **Daniel John Bongino** — Republican
◯ **Dean Ahmad** — Libertarian
◯ **S. Rob Sobhani** — Unaffiliated
◯
_____
Write-in

JUDGE, COURT OF APPEALS
APPELLATE CIRCUIT 6
Robert M. Bell
Vote Yes or No
For Continuance in Office

◯ YES
◯ NO

JUDGE, COURT OF SPECIAL APPEALS
AT LARGE
Stuart R. Berger
Vote Yes or No
For Continuance in Office

◯ YES
◯ NO

JUDGE, COURT OF SPECIAL APPEALS
APPELLATE CIRCUIT 6
Shirley M. Watts
Vote Yes or No
For Continuance in Office

◯ YES
◯ NO

QUESTION 1
Constitutional Amendment
(Ch. 394 of the 2011 Legislative Session)
Qualifications for Prince George's County
Orphans' Court Judges

(Amending Article IV, Section 40 of the Maryland Constitution)

Requires judges of the Orphans' Court for Prince George's County to be admitted to practice law in this State and to be a member in good standing of the Maryland Bar.

◯ **For the Constitutional Amendment**
◯ **Against the Constitutional Amendment**

1. Fill in the blank with the name of the candidate who is running for judge of Court of Special Appeals Appellate Circuit 6. _____

2. James P. Gray is running for which office?

   A. President
   B. U.S. senator
   C. Vice President
   D. Court of Appeals judge

3. Suppose a voter wants to vote for a candidate who is not listed as running for the U.S. Senate. Using the information on the ballot, what can the voter do?

   A. Contact the Senate
   B. Notify a poll worker
   C. Create a new ballot that includes the unlisted candidate
   D. Write in the name of the unlisted candidate on the ballot

Answers are on page 830.

Political Parties

Political parties are organizations that seek power and influence within the government. The members of a party share similar opinions and ideas about many issues. The members of a party choose a candidate to run for a government office and work to gain public support and votes for their chosen candidate.

In the early years of the United States, there were political parties that were different from the ones we see today. The issues they faced were different from the ones that are the focus of politics today. The first political parties were established by people who had differing visions for the future of America. Thomas Jefferson wanted the federal government to play a less active role. He wanted the powers of the President to be limited, and he wanted the United States to have a close relationship with France. Alexander Hamilton, on the other hand, believed that the United States should have a strong federal government. He also wanted the country's President to be strong. He believed that the country should have a strong relationship with Great Britain.

Today in the United States, the two main political parties are the **Democrats** and the **Republicans**. There are also a number of minor parties, but the nature of the political system makes it difficult for minor-party ("third party") candidates to win elections.

Each of the two main parties includes people with a range of different viewpoints. However, each one also has a central core of defining beliefs. In general, Democrats are more liberal, or left wing, and support a broad, more active role for the federal government. Democrats also support laws favoring workers and strong, government-run social programs. Republicans, on the other hand, are more conservative, or right wing, and generally favor the rights of the states rather than the federal government. They support policies that favor business owners and managers and private solutions to social problems.

Political Parties in the United States

Time Period	Major Parties	Important Issues	Minor Parties
1787–1792	Federalist, Anti-federalist	Power of the federal government vs. state and local governments, Bill of Rights	None
1792–1824	Federalist, Democrat-Republican	Federalists supported Hamilton's financial plans, protective tariffs, Great Britain against France, greater power for the national government. Democrat-Republicans opposed Hamilton's plans, supported France in its war against Great Britain.	None
1824–1854	Whig, Democrat	Democrats (led by Andrew Jackson) favored expelling Native Americans from the western territories and opening them to settlement; opposed tariffs. Whigs supported modernizing the economy with high protective tariffs; opposed the expansion of slavery into the western territories.	Anti-Masonic, Liberty, Free Soil, Know-Nothing
1854–1896	Republican, Democrat	Republicans favored high protective tariffs and opposed the expansion of slavery into the western territories. After the Civil War, they sought to impose harsh terms on Southern secessionists. Democrats supported low tariffs but were split on permitting the expansion of slavery into the western territories.	Whig-American, Southern Democrat, Constitutional Union, Prohibition
1896–1932	Republican, Democrat	Republicans opposed the Spanish-American War and other overseas expansionist policies; after World War I they returned to a pro-business position and opposed federal controls. Democrats supported regulation of industry, particularly railroads, and Progressive issues, including child labor laws, women's rights, and the income tax.	Populist, Progressive, Prohibition
1933–Today	Democrat, Republican	Democrats support an activist government that addresses economic and social problems, that regulates industry and finance, and that guarantees civil rights and minority rights. Republicans support low taxes, a limited role for government, and policies that favor business owners and managers; they oppose government regulation of industry and finance, government spending on social programs, and policies favoring labor unions.	Union, States Rights, American Independent, Independent, Reform, Green

EXERCISE 11

Political Parties

Directions: Choose the best answer to each of the following questions.

1. According to the preceding table, in what period were today's political parties established?

   A. late 1700s
   B. early 1800s
   C. mid- to late 1800s
   D. early 1900s

2. Which statement is true?

   A. All U.S. citizens are represented politically by one or the other of the two main political parties.
   B. Members of different political parties in the United States rarely share any viewpoints on political issues.
   C. A range of political beliefs exists among the citizens of the United States.
   D. The number of major political parties in the United States has varied widely over time.

3. The political party that has a majority in the House of Representatives or the Senate is called the "majority party." The other party is called the "minority party." If a Republican is the majority party leader in the Senate, what does this indicate?

   A. There are more Republicans than Democrats in the Senate.
   B. There are more Republicans than Democrats in the House of Representatives.
   C. More Republicans than Democrats were elected to office in the last election.
   D. A Republican was most recently elected as President of the United States.

Answers are on page 830.

Political Campaigns, Elections, and the Electoral Process

In the United States, presidential **elections** are held every four years on the first Tuesday of November. Elections for senators and representatives are held at the same time. Senators and representatives are also elected in "off-year" elections, which take place midway through the four-year presidential term. In advance of the main "general" elections, political parties hold a series of **primary elections**. In these elections, candidates from the same party for the same office run against one another to determine which one will be the party's nominee in the general election.

Candidates spend many months running their **political campaigns** in order to gain the support of the most voters. During this organized effort to persuade people to support them, candidates share their ideas about necessary policy changes and spread their message about why they deserve to be elected. Messages are spread through personal appearances, phone calls, websites, mailings, and television and radio advertisements. Research is conducted to determine who should be included in the candidate's target audience and what issues are important to these people. Candidates ask supporters to join the campaign by helping to spread the message and making financial contributions.

Despite the fact that millions of citizens vote for their favored candidates in these elections, the President is not elected directly by the people. Rather, the citizens elect members of the **Electoral College**, which is the formal body that actually elects the President. The number of electors for each state is equal to the number of senators and representatives from that state in Congress. These electors cast votes for the presidential candidates. In order to win the presidency, a candidate must receive at least half of the electoral votes. Generally, the candidate who receives the majority of the citizens' votes within a state receives all of the electoral votes for that state. Because of the way the Electoral College works, a candidate who receives a majority of citizens' votes nationwide may still fail to gain a majority of electoral votes and thus lose the presidency.

The following map shows which candidate in the 2012 presidential election won the electoral votes for each state. Although the number of states won by each candidate is similar, the number of electoral votes each received was quite different.

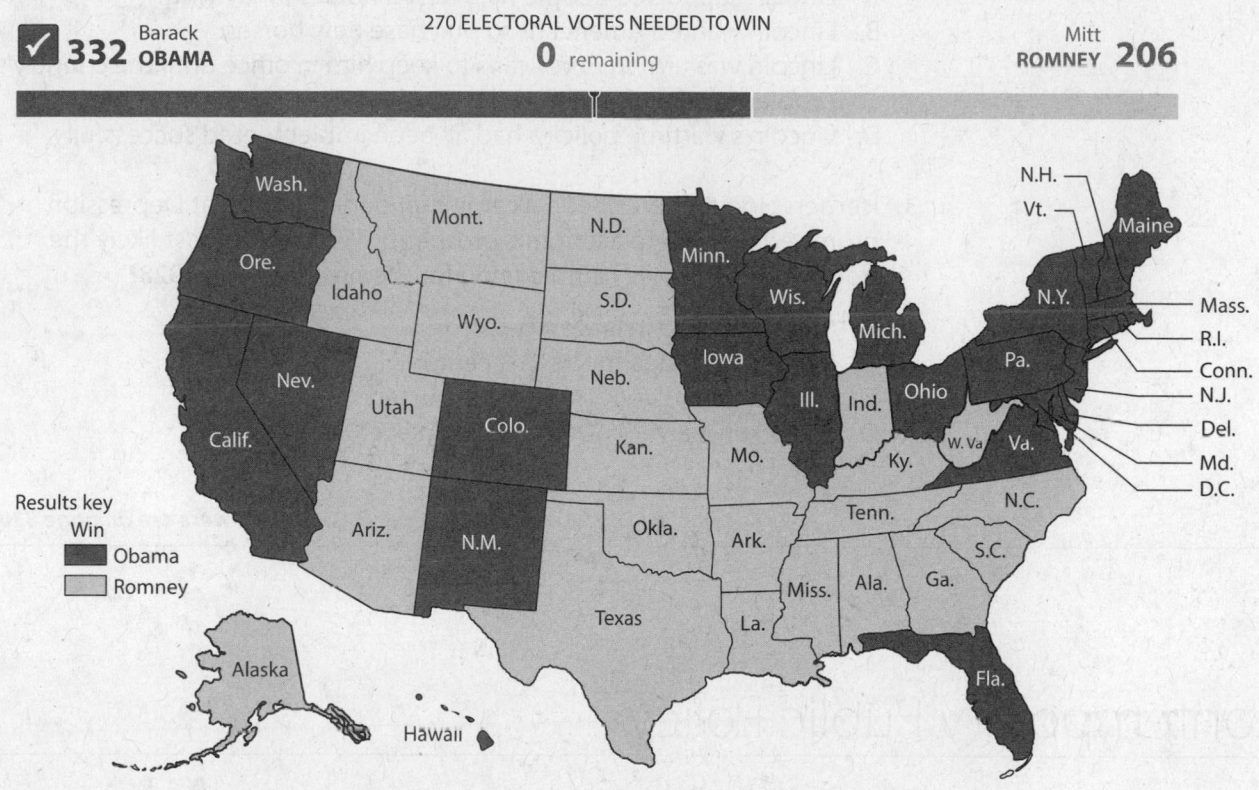

Results of 2012 Presidential Election

270 ELECTORAL VOTES NEEDED TO WIN

☑ **332** Barack OBAMA

0 remaining

Mitt ROMNEY **206**

Results key
Win
■ Obama
■ Romney

EXERCISE 12

Political Campaigns, Elections, and the Electoral Process

Directions: Choose the best answer to each of the following questions.

1. Which claim is supported by the information in this section?

    A. The states that are largest in area have the greatest number of electoral votes.

    B. The President is elected by receiving the majority of votes from voters on Election Day.

    C. A presidential candidate who receives the majority of votes from voters nationwide may still lose the election.

    D. In order to win a majority of electoral votes, a candidate must win the election in a majority of states.

2. During elections, candidates often use slogans to help voters remember a key point about them or their campaign on Election Day. During his 1864 reelection campaign in the midst of the Civil War, President Abraham Lincoln's slogan was "Don't swap horses in the middle of the stream." What point was he trying to make?

   A. Lincoln supported people who raised horses for a living.
   B. Lincoln wanted Americans to purchase new horses.
   C. Lincoln was urging Americans to keep him in office until the country's problems were resolved.
   D. Lincoln's wartime policies had all been implemented successfully.

3. Herbert Hoover's presidential campaign during the Great Depression promised a return to economic prosperity. Which was most likely the slogan he used while campaigning for the presidency in 1928?

   A. Sunflowers die in November
   B. Building a bridge to the 21st century
   C. Hoover we trusted—now we're busted
   D. A chicken in every pot (and a car in every backyard)

Answers are on page 830.

Contemporary Public Policy

Public policy is whatever course of action a government adopts regarding a given issue. The actions taken may include passing laws, enforcing rules or regulations, and providing funding or other resources. Most of the public policies of the United States are implemented through the executive branch of the government. When deciding upon a public policy, it must be determined who will benefit from the policy and who will be responsible for the costs. Some major categories of public policy include criminal justice, culture and society, economic affairs, education, the environment, government operations, health, social welfare, and foreign affairs and national security.

Interest groups are groups of people who share a common interest or a common concern, and who come together to influence the government to adopt a certain policy or to make decisions that support their cause. The goal of these groups may benefit the members of the group, a part of society, or the public in general. Interest groups try to influence public policy by providing information and education on an issue, by advocating for the issue in public speeches or the media, or by organizing campaigns to influence lawmakers to support their cause. Because a democracy is government by the people, interest groups have an important influence on the shaping of public policy.

EXERCISE 13

Contemporary Public Policy

Directions: Use the following graph to answer Questions 1 and 2.

In a recent year, a controversial proposal was on the ballot in a certain state. Contributions by interest groups supporting or opposed to the proposition are shown in the graph.

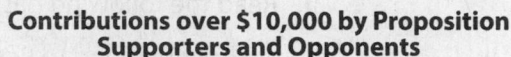

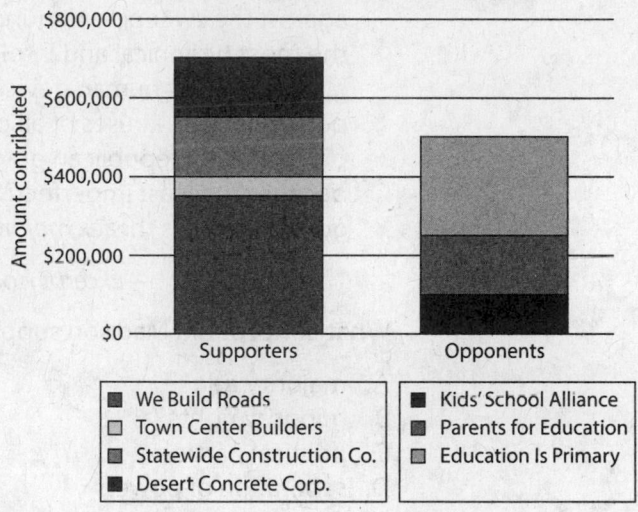

1. _____ donated the largest amount of money to oppose the proposition.

2. Which interest group donated approximately $350,000 to support the proposition?

   A. We Build Roads
   B. Kids' School Alliance
   C. Statewide Construction Company
   D. Parents for Education

Answers are on page 830.

Civics and Government

Directions: Choose the best answer to each of the following questions.

1. Read the following passage, and then answer the question.

   > [E]very friend to Republican government ought to raise his voice
   > against the sweeping denunciation of majority governments as
   > the most tyrannical and intolerable of all governments. . . . [N]o
   > government of human device and human administration can be
   > perfect; . . . the abuses of all other governments have led to the
   > preference of republican government as the best of all governments,
   > because the least imperfect; [and] the vital principle of republican
   > governments is the *lex majoris partis*, the will of the majority.

   —*Excerpt from a letter by President James Madison (1833)*

   What concept did Madison support in this letter?

   A. majority rule
   B. minority rights
   C. political parties
   D. separation of powers

2. Which of the following means that people have the right to request the
   government to adopt or change a particular policy?

   A. Freedom of speech
   B. Freedom of assembly
   C. Freedom of the press
   D. Freedom of petition

3. Read the following passage, and then answer the question.

   > The Senate of the United States shall be composed of two Senators
   > from each State, elected by the people thereof, for six years; and each
   > Senator shall have one vote.

   —*Excerpt from Seventeenth Amendment to the U.S. Constitution*

   Before this amendment was adopted, senators were elected by the various
   state legislatures. This amendment gave voters themselves the right to
   elect senators. What was the effect of this change?

   A. Senators became directly responsible to the voters who elected them.
   B. More people registered to vote so that they could participate in
      electing senators.
   C. States with greater numbers of voters would have greater
      representation in the Senate.
   D. The number of senators increased dramatically.

PRACTICE

Question 4 is based on the following timeline.

Early Supreme Court Justices

Members in the Timeline

	G. Washington	J. Adams	T. Jefferson	J. Madison	J. Monroe	J. Q. Adams	
	1790	1800	1810	1820		1830	
	John Rutledge	Alfred Moore	Brockholst Livingston			Robert Trimble	
	John Blair	Oliver Ellsworth	Thomas Todd				Henry Baldwin
	John Jay	Samuel Chase			Smith Thompson		
	William Paterson		Gabriel Duvall				
	Thomas Johnson	William Johnson					
	James Iredell	John Marshall					
	William Cushing		Joseph Story				
	James Wilson	Bushrod Washington					
							John McLean
	1790	1800	1810	1820		1830	

4. According to the timeline, which President appointed Justice Robert Trimble to the Supreme Court?

A. George Washington
B. John Q. Adams
C. Thomas Jefferson
D. James Madison

5. In New England, town meetings are held. All of the citizens who are of voting age gather to discuss political issues. The citizens then vote, and decisions are made by majority rule. This is an example of which concept?

A. Monarchy
B. Aristocracy
C. Direct democracy
D. Representative democracy

6. Read the following passage, and then answer the question.

So we can gut education to pay for more tax breaks for the wealthy, or we can decide that in the United States of America, no child should have her dreams deferred because of an overcrowded classroom. No family should have to set aside a college acceptance letter because they don't have the money. No business should have to look for workers in China because they can't find ones with the right skills here in the United States. So, Ohio, I am asking you to help me recruit 100,000 new math and science teachers. Help me improve early childhood education. Help me give two million workers the chance to learn the skills they need at community colleges that will lead directly to a new job. Help us work with colleges and universities to cut the cost of tuition. Help us meet those goals. Help us choose that future for America.

—Excerpt from a speech by President Barack Obama
during the 2012 election campaign

Which is a public policy that Obama is proposing?

A. retraining U.S. workers to give them new job skills
B. building more affordable public housing
C. recruiting foreign workers for U.S. businesses
D. reducing taxes for middle-class families

Question 7 is based on the following graph.

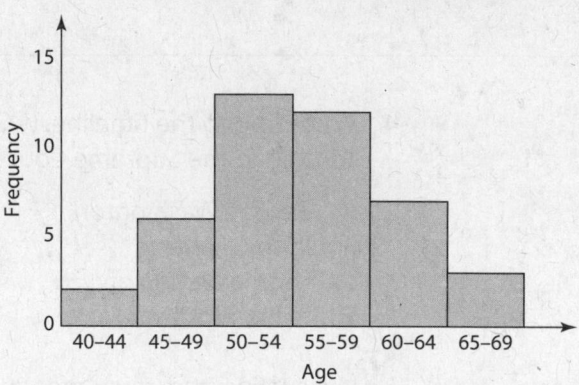

Presidents' Ages at Inauguration

7. According to the graph, which statement accurately interprets the data?

A. Most Presidents were inaugurated while in their 50s.
B. Most Presidents were inaugurated while in their 60s.
C. A few Presidents were inaugurated while younger than 40 years old.
D. Fewer Presidents were inaugurated while in their 60s than in their 40s.

8. Which quotation from the U.S. Constitution best indicates that the nation is a democracy?

A. "We the people of the United States . . ."
B. ". . . in order to form a more perfect Union"
C. "All legislative powers herein granted shall be vested in a Congress . . ."
D. ". . . executive power shall be vested in a President."

9. Which is an example of the checks and balances in the U.S. government?

    A. Under the U.S. Constitution, power is divided between the federal government and the state governments.
    B. The legislative branch of government is Congress, which is divided into the Senate and the House of Representatives.
    C. The executive branch of government can propose laws and is responsible for carrying out laws enacted by Congress.
    D. By a two-thirds vote of the Senate and House, Congress can pass a law despite a veto by the President.

10. Read the following quotation, and then answer the question.

    The local interests of a state ought, in every case, to give way to the interests of the Union.

    > —*Alexander Hamilton, in a speech to the New York Convention of 1788 assembled for the purpose of ratifying the Constitution*

    Which statement reflects Hamilton's point of view?

    A. The federal government should hold more power than the state governments.
    B. Powers should not be divided between the federal and state governments.
    C. It is important for the federal government to be granted additional power.
    D. The Constitution should have given more powers to individual states.

Answers are on page 830.

CHAPTER 2

United States History

European Exploration of the Americas

The first Europeans to reach North America were Vikings from what is now Norway, under a leader named Leif Ericson. In about the year 1000 they established a settlement in what is now Newfoundland, but the settlement was soon abandoned.

In 1492 the Italian explorer **Christopher Columbus**, sailing on behalf of the king and queen of Spain, sailed west from Spain in search of a route to Asia that would be faster than the traditional route around Africa. Trade with Asia was very attractive to Europeans, so there was great interest in finding a better route, Columbus was unaware, however, that the continents of North America and South America blocked his path to Asia. When Columbus and his crew made landfall in what is now the Bahamas, they thought they had reached islands near India off the coast of Asia. For this reason, they called the people living there Indians. After Columbus returned home from the New World, he later made three more voyages to Central and South America.

Soon, other explorers came to explore the New World. In the 1500s, Spanish explorers came to North America in search of gold. Juan Ponce de Leon was the first European to reach what is now the United States when he and his crew landed in Florida. Within a few years, Hernando de Soto was sent to settle this area. He traveled through much of what is now the southeastern states and was the first European to reach the Mississippi River. Francisco Vasquez de Coronado explored what is now the American Southwest. Amerigo Vespucci, for whom the Americas are named, was the first European to sight the mouth of the Amazon River.

Other European explorers continued Columbus's quest to find a sea route to Asia. John Cabot, whose voyage was financed by England, landed in Canada. Cabot returned to England to report finding rich fishing areas. The Italian Giovanni da Verrazano, in the service of the French King Francis I, explored the Atlantic coast of North America. He was the first European to enter New York Bay. In 1608, Samuel de Champlain established the first permanent French settlement in Canada when he founded a fur-trading post named Quebec. The Dutch, also in search of a way to reach Asia, sent English ship captain Henry Hudson on this quest in 1609. He sailed up what is now called the Hudson River in New York, claiming land on which the Dutch started a colony called New Netherland the next year.

Wherever the Europeans claimed land in the New World, they established settlements and spread their culture. Their influence, including language, customs, and foods, is visible today.

European Exploration of the Americas

Directions: Read the following passage, and then answer the questions.

19 September. Continued on, and sailed, day and night, twenty-five leagues, experiencing a calm. Wrote down twenty-two. This day at ten o'clock a pelican came on board, and in the evening another; these birds are not accustomed to go twenty leagues from land. It drizzled without wind, which is a sure sign of land. The Admiral was unwilling to remain here, beating about in search of land, but he held it for certain that there were islands to the north and south, which in fact was the case and he was sailing in the midst of them. His wish was to proceed on to the Indies, having such fair weather, for if it please God, as the Admiral says, we shall examine these parts upon our return. Here the pilots found their places upon the chart: the reckoning of the Nina made her four hundred and forty leagues distant from the Canaries, that of the Pinta four hundred and twenty, that of the Admiral four hundred.

—*Excerpt from Christopher Columbus's diary of his voyage in 1492*

1. Indicate an X next to the statements that helped Columbus know that he and his crew were nearing land.

   _____ They sailed day and night.

   _____ Two pelicans landed on the boat.

   _____ The admiral wanted to keep sailing.

   _____ There was a light rain with no wind.

2. What is the meaning of the word *league* as it is used in this passage?

   A. an organization
   B. a unit of distance
   C. the captain of a ship
   D. the depth of a body of water

Answers are on page 831.

The English Colony in Virginia

The English also wanted to establish colonies in North America. In 1585 a group of English colonists made a settlement on Roanoke Island, off the coast of what is now North Carolina. However, the colonists later disappeared without a trace. Approximately 20 years later, a group of

English merchants were granted permission from the king of England to start a new settlement in North America. About 100 people sailed to the area now known as **Virginia**, where they established a town called Jamestown. This was the first permanent English colony in what is now the United States. Since the majority of these colonists did not know how to farm, most of them soon died. But soon one of the survivors, John Rolfe, learned from the Native Americans in the area that tobacco was a successful local crop. Knowing that tobacco was popular in England but grew poorly there, the people of Jamestown began growing and selling this crop, for which people in England were willing to pay a high price. This income allowed the settlers to purchase the food and supplies they needed from their home country, and thus the colony was able to survive. In 1619 the colonists in Virginia created an elected legislature called the House of Burgesses. Most of these elected representatives were members of the Church of England (also called the Anglican Church), and soon this became the official church of the colony, forcing members of other religions to move away from the area.

George Washington was elected to the House of Burgesses in 1758 and served in this position for 15 years. Patrick Henry and Thomas Jefferson were also members of this legislature. At the time Washington was elected as a burgess, each county sent two representatives, who by law had to be male landowners and at least 21 years old.

EXERCISE 2

The English Colony in Virginia

Directions: Choose the best answer to each of the following questions.

1. Which of the following contributed to the successful establishment of the colony at Jamestown?

   A. Receiving the king's permission to found a settlement
   B. Growing tobacco for sale to England
   C. Instituting an official church
   D. Creating the House of Burgesses

2. What claim about the House of Burgesses can be supported by the text?

   A. Some important American leaders began their political careers in the House of Burgesses.
   B. All of the members of the House of Burgesses later became presidents of the United States.
   C. The House of Burgesses was modeled on the example of the United States Congress.
   D. Most people in Virginia were qualified to be elected to the House of Burgesses because they owned land.

Answers are on page 831.

English Colonies in New England and Maryland

During the early 1600s, other English settlements were established on the Atlantic coast of North America. A small group of Separatists, so called because they sought religious freedom from the Church of England, set sail on the *Mayflower* to establish a religious settlement in Virginia. These people called themselves Pilgrims. Like many before them, they landed in an area different from the one they had intended, and they found themselves in what is now **Massachusetts**. In order to set up a government for their colony, which they called Plymouth, the Pilgrims drafted the **Mayflower Compact**, which established a set of basic laws.

Another English religious group, the Puritans, also seeking freedom from the Church of England, set sail for North America in order to establish a colony based on their own religious beliefs. These settlers landed in an area north of Plymouth and built their colony near what is now Boston. The Puritans called their settlement the Massachusetts Bay Colony. This colony proved to be very successful, and many other Puritans came from England to join it. By the 1640s, approximately 20,000 Puritans lived in this region, and as a result, the area became known as New England.

Religion played a significant role in the government of the Massachusetts Bay Colony, and only male colonists who were members of the church and who owned land were able to vote. Despite these regulations, the people of this colony still enjoyed more self-government than those in many other colonies. However, there were some who felt that the Puritan leaders should not have so much control over the colonists' lives. One prominent colonist named Roger Williams believed that the government should not establish laws dealing with religion. As a result, he was banished by the Puritan leaders. Williams went on to found a new colony, **Rhode Island**, in 1636. In Rhode Island, government and religion were kept separate, and people could worship as they chose.

Thomas Hooker, a minister, also disagreed with some of the laws established by the Puritan leaders. He led a small group of colonists to an area in **Connecticut** to establish a community in which all men could vote, regardless of whether or not they were members of the church. The colony of **New Hampshire** was established when colonists from the Massachusetts Bay Colony moved farther north to settle.

Around this same time, in 1632, King Charles I of England gave North American land to Cecilius Calvert, an English noble also known as Lord Baltimore. Calvert, a Catholic, founded the colony of **Maryland** so that members of his religion could escape the religious persecution they often faced in England.

EXERCISE 3

English Colonies in New England and Maryland

Directions: Choose the best answer to each of the following questions.

Use the following timeline to answer Question 1.

Timeline of the Pilgrims' Voyage

1619	September 1620	October 1620	November 9, 1620	November 11, 1620
The Pilgrims are given a land patent from the London Virginia Company, with plans to establish an American colony where they can enjoy religious freedom.	Aboard the *Mayflower*, the Pilgrims leave England, headed for Virginia.	Storms throw the *Mayflower* off course.	The *Mayflower* makes landfall at Cape Cod, Massachusetts.	The Pilgrims draft the Mayflower Compact to establish their own government because they did not arrive at their intended destination in another colony. John Carver becomes the first governor.

1. Which is a true statement inferred from the timeline?

   A. It was unusual for weather to impact the course of a ship.
   B. It was John Carver's idea to create the Mayflower Compact.
   C. The Pilgrims were disappointed that they did not land in Virginia.
   D. The Pilgrims recognized the importance of establishing a government.

2. Read the following passage, and then answer the question.

   > In the name of God, Amen. We whose names are underwritten, the loyal subjects of our dread sovereign lord King James, by the grace of God, of Great Britain, France, and Ireland King, Defender of the Faith, etc.
   >
   >   Having undertaken, for the glory of God, and advancement of the Christian faith, and honor of our king and country, a voyage to plant the first colony in the northern parts of Virginia, do by these presents solemnly and mutually in the presence of God and one of another, covenant, and combine ourselves together into a civil body politic, for our better ordering and preservation, and furtherance of the ends aforesaid; and by virtue hereof to enact, constitute, and frame such just and equal laws, ordinances, acts, constitutions, offices from time to time, as shall be thought most meet and convenient for the general good of the colony: unto which we promise all due submission and obedience. In witness whereof we have hereunder subscribed our names; Cape Cod, the 11th of November, in the year of the reign of our

sovereign lord King James, of England, France and Ireland eighteenth and of Scotland fifty-fourth, Anno Domini 1620.

—Excerpt from the Mayflower Compact

Which of the following true statements is the *central idea* of the document?

A. The Pilgrims agreed to spread the ideas of their Christian faith.
B. The colony would always be submissive to God and to King James.
C. The laws included in the compact must be obeyed by all of the Pilgrims.
D. The Pilgrims agreed to follow any laws that were later set for the colony.

3. Determine which religious group was the basis for the formation of each settlement listed. Indicate Catholic, Puritan, or Pilgrim beside the name of each colony.

Settlement	Religious Group
Maryland	_____
Massachusetts Bay Colony	_____
Plymouth	_____

4. Three colonies were established when people left the Massachusetts Bay Colony. These three colonies were _____, _____, and _____.

Answers are on page 831.

The Thirteen Colonies Take Shape

In 1663 the new king of England, Charles II, wanted to start another colony in North America. Several European countries, including England, all claimed the land located south of the colony of Virginia. Charles hoped that by establishing a colony in this area, he would keep France and Spain out of the region. The colony that King Charles founded was called Carolina. Colonists began to settle this area because of its quality farmland. In 1729 the colony was separated into **North Carolina** and **South Carolina**.

In 1664 the Dutch colony of New Netherland was taken over by English forces. The King of England gave the colony to his brother James, the Duke of York, who kept part of the territory and renamed it **New York**. James gave the rest of the territory to two of his friends, John Berkeley and George Carteret, who divided it into two colonies, which later joined to become **New Jersey** in 1702. James and his friends who owned New Jersey all lived in England, and they found it difficult to control their land from such a great distance. These men chose governors to rule the colonies, and each governor selected a small group of leaders to advise him. The colonists were also given the opportunity to elect representatives to an assembly to work with the governor to enact laws.

During this time, William Penn, an Englishman who belonged to a religious group known as Quakers, hoped to start a colony in which people could peacefully coexist despite religious differences. Quakers believed that everyone should have the freedom to worship as he or she wished. However, they were often punished for such beliefs in England because everyone was expected to belong to the Church of England. In 1681, Penn was given a large piece of land in North America as repayment for money owed to his family by King Charles II. This new land was called **Pennsylvania**, and colonists there enjoyed freedom of worship as well as the opportunity to elect representatives to the colony's assembly. Penn was later given more land by the Duke of York. This land was part of Pennsylvania for a time, but later it became a new colony, **Delaware**.

In 1732, King George II of England started another colony in an attempt to keep the French and Spanish out of the area to the south of South Carolina. This land was given to James Oglethorpe, who named the colony **Georgia** in honor of the king. As an English lawmaker, Oglethorpe established strict rules for this new colony. Colonists were not allowed to consume alcohol, own slaves, or make their own laws. Oglethorpe did, however, envision a colony for debtors and the poor, who would have the opportunity to begin new lives and avoid imprisonment for their debts in England. He brought a group of these people to the colony, free of charge, and gave them small pieces of land to farm.

By the mid-1700s, there were 13 English colonies along the Atlantic coast: New Hampshire, Massachusetts, Rhode Island, Connecticut, New York, New Jersey, Pennsylvania, Maryland, Delaware, Virginia, North Carolina, South Carolina, and Georgia. These colonies, while distinct in many ways, were all based on some of the traditions of England's government. The populations of the colonies grew steadily, as many were enticed by the economic and political conditions offered, as well as by the opportunity to own land.

The 13 American Colonies

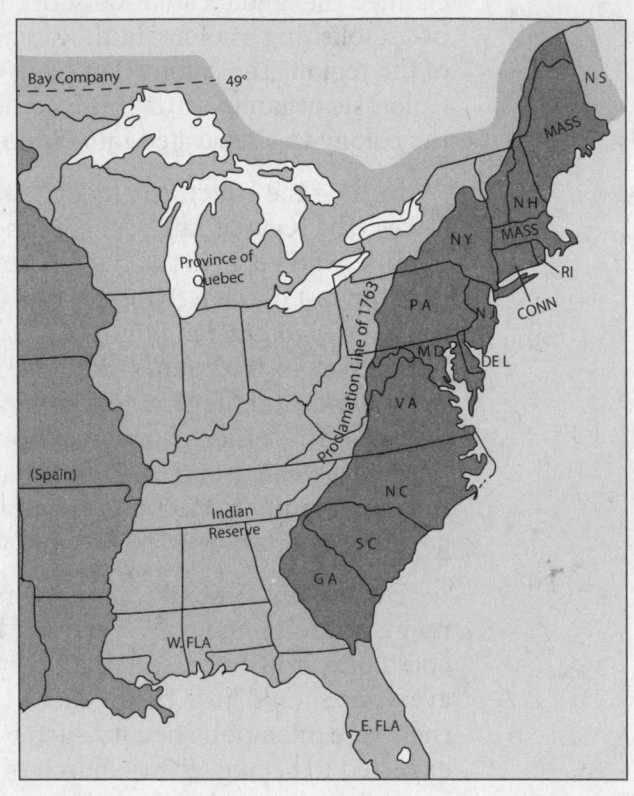

EXERCISE 4

The Thirteen Colonies Take Shape

Directions: Choose the best answer to each of the following questions.

1. Read each of the following phrases. Indicate an X before each phrase that describes a reason the English colonists came to America.

   _____ Political freedom

   _____ Gold

   _____ Economic opportunity

   _____ Escape persecution

   _____ Search for the Fountain of Youth

   _____ Establishment of trade

Questions 1 and 2 are based on the following graph.

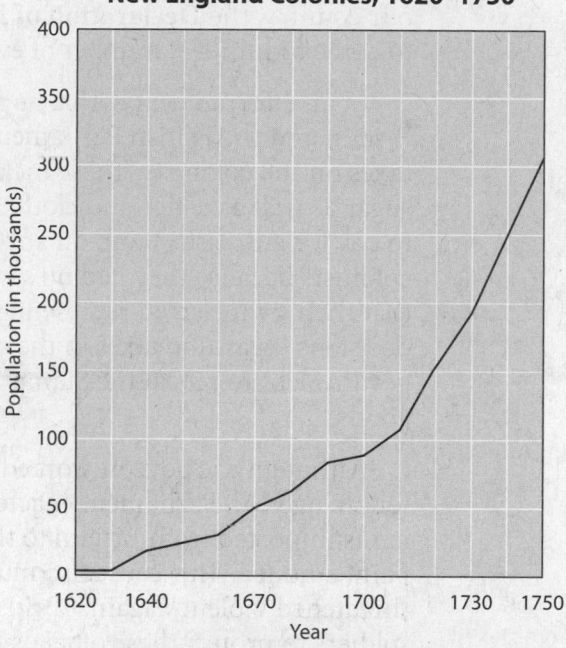

**Colonist Population of the
New England Colonies, 1620–1750**

2. Which conclusion can be drawn based on the data in the graph?

  A. Colonists became increasingly dissatisfied with their decision to come to New England.
  B. Colonists became increasingly satisfied with their decision to come to New England.
  C. Colonists came to the New England colonies in decreasing numbers over time.
  D. Colonists came to the New England colonies in increasing numbers over time.

3. Which statement accurately reflects the data in the graph?

  A. The fewest colonists arrived in the New England colonies after 1750.
  B. The greatest number of colonists arrived in the New England colonies before 1620.
  C. More than 300,000 colonists had arrived in the New England colonies by 1750.
  D. More than 100,000 colonists had arrived in the New England colonies by 1640.

Answers are on page 831.

Tensions Rise Between the Colonies and Great Britain

When considering the historical documents that have shaped the history of our country, the **Declaration of Independence** is likely to be one of the first to come to mind. A number of events led to the drafting of this document.

In an effort to deal with a huge war debt, King George III of Great Britain and the British Parliament enacted a number of laws that imposed taxes on the colonists. These included the **Sugar Act of 1764**, which taxed sugar as well as coffee and cloth. The **Stamp Act of 1765** required colonists to pay for a British stamp on any official document. These acts angered the colonists because they had no say in the passing of the laws. They believed that their own elected representatives, rather than Parliament, should make decisions regarding taxes in the colonies. In order to convince the British government to repeal the Stamp Act, many colonists boycotted British goods.

Although the boycott worked and the Stamp Act was repealed the following year, Parliament enacted new taxes. The **Townshend Acts** taxed items imported from Britain to the colonies, such as lead, glass, paper, paint, and tea. This caused so much anger among the colonists that they threatened violence against British tax officials. As a result, Britain sent soldiers to protect these officials from the colonists, an act that frustrated the colonists even further. Again, the taxed items were boycotted and the colonists substituted American-made goods for British imports. Britain eventually repealed many of the taxes but retained the tax on tea as a way of asserting Britain's right to tax the colonists.

In 1770 in Boston, an argument between a group of colonists and a British soldier grew to include several soldiers. Shots were fired, killing five colonists in what was called the **Boston Massacre**. This event greatly increased the colonists' distrust and resentment of the British government.

In 1773 the **Tea Act** gave a British company the right to sell low-priced tea to the colonists. The price of the tea included a tax to which the colonists had not consented. Again, the colonists were angered by what they called "taxation without representation." A group of colonists dumped the tea into Boston Harbor, an event now known as the **Boston Tea Party**. In response, the British Parliament passed the **Intolerable Acts**. These laws were intended to punish the colonists by closing the port of Boston and bringing the government of Massachusetts under tighter British control.

EXERCISE 5

Tensions Rise Between the Colonies and Great Britain

Directions: Choose the best answer to each of the following questions.

Questions 1 and 2 are based on the following graph.

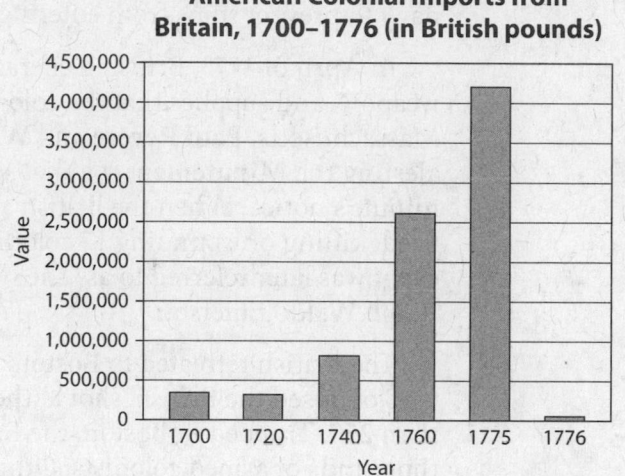

American Colonial Imports from Britain, 1700–1776 (in British pounds)

1. According to the graph, in which year were the most goods imported from Britain into the colonies?

   A. 1700
   B. 1775
   C. 1776
   D. 1740

2. Between which years did the value of colonial imports from Britain increase the most?

   A. 1720–1740
   B. 1740–1760
   C. 1760–1775
   D. 1775–1776

Answers are on page 831.

The First Continental Congress and the Beginning of the American Revolution

In September 1774 the delegates from the colonies held the **First Continental Congress** in Philadelphia, Pennsylvania, to demand that the Intolerable Acts be repealed. They asked to have the same rights as other English citizens, and not to be taxed without their consent. Britain responded by sending 3,000 soldiers to occupy Boston, and by sending the navy to prevent ships from entering or leaving Boston Harbor.

In April of 1775, British General Thomas Gage set out to destroy weapons and supplies that the colonists were storing in **Concord**, Massachusetts. **Paul Revere** and **William Dawes** raced ahead of them, alerting the **Minutemen**, colonial soldiers who would be ready to fight at a minute's notice. When the British arrived at nearby **Lexington**, shots were fired, killing or wounding 17 colonists and wounding a British soldier. This event was later referred to as "the shot heard 'round the world" by the poet Ralph Waldo Emerson.

The British retreated to Boston. On their way the **Patriots**, colonists who opposed the British, shot at the soldiers and killed or wounded more than 250. Trapped in Boston, the British found themselves surrounded by thousands of armed colonists. Other Patriots built a fort on Breed's Hill, located across the Charles River from Boston. From there they fired cannons at the British until they ran out of gunpowder. The British then captured the fort. Nevertheless, in this fierce battle, the Patriots killed or wounded more than half of the British soldiers and proved their ability as fighters.

EXERCISE 6

The First Continental Congress and the Beginning of the American Revolution

Directions: Read the following passage, and then answer the questions.

I have made a rule, whenever in my power, to avoid becoming the draughtsman of papers to be reviewed by a public body. I took my lesson from an incident which I will relate to you. When I was a journeyman printer, one of my companions, an apprentice hatter, having served out his time, was about to open shop for himself. His first concern was to have a handsome signboard, with a proper inscription. He composed it in these words, "John Thompson, Hatter, makes and sells hats for ready money," with a figure of a hat subjoined. But thought he would submit it to his friends for their amendments. The first he showed it to thought the word "Hatter" tautologous, because followed by the words "makes hats," which showed he was a hatter. It was struck out. The next observed that the word "makes" might as well be omitted, because his customers would not care who made the hats. If good and to their mind, they would buy them, by whomsoever made. He struck it out. A third said he thought the words "for ready money" were useless, as it was not the custom of the place to sell on credit. Everyone who purchased expected to pay. They were parted with, and the inscription now stood, "John Thompson sells hats." "Sells hats!" says the next friend. "Why, nobody will expect you to give them away. What then is the use of that word?" It was stricken out, and "hats" followed it, the rather as there was one painted on the board. So the inscription was reduced ultimately to "John Thompson," with the figure of a hat subjoined.

—Excerpt from a statement by Benjamin Franklin to the First Continental Congress, explaining why he did not want to participate in writing the documents of the Congress

1. What was the message Franklin wanted to convey by telling this story?

    A. He wanted to be a hatter, not a writer.
    B. He recognized the fact that he was not a skilled writer.
    C. He believed that his apprentice should write the document.
    D. He believed that no matter what he wrote in the document, someone would change it.

2. What did the poet Emerson mean by the phrase "the shot heard 'round the world"?

    A. The guns used by the soldiers were extremely loud.
    B. People in many nations would become aware of what the colonists had done.
    C. The colonists wanted to invade other countries.
    D. The soldiers used guns that had come from other countries.

Answers are on page 831.

The Second Continental Congress and the Declaration of Independence

The **Second Continental Congress** began in May of 1775 in Philadelphia in the building now known as Independence Hall. The members determined that a new army, the **Continental Army**, should be created, and that these soldiers would be well trained in order to be prepared for the war that was anticipated against Britain. **George Washington** was chosen as the commander. Over the next several months, the Continental Army trained. Meanwhile, the British soldiers retreated from Boston in March 1776.

In early 1776, **Thomas Paine** wrote a popular pamphlet called "**Common Sense**," which presented strong arguments for separating the colonies from Britain. The pamphlet was very widely read in the colonies and greatly increased support for independence. The colonists were also inspired by the **Magna Carta**, a document signed by the English King John in 1215. This document established certain key rights for people in Britain, such as the right to a representative government with powers over taxation, the right to trial by jury, and the right to due process in legal matters. The colonists believed that they had been deprived of these rights and were determined to recover them, by establishing their own government if necessary.

The delegates to the Second Continental Congress decided that the 13 colonies should be self-governing. They asked one of the delegates, **Thomas Jefferson** from Virginia, to explain in writing their reasons for the break with the government of Great Britain. He composed the **Declaration of Independence**. The document was approved by the Second Continental Congress on July 4, 1776, a date that has since been recognized as the birth of the United States.

EXERCISE 7

The Second Continental Congress and the Declaration of Independence

Directions: Choose the best answer to each of the following questions.

Question 1 is based on the following passage.

> We hold these truths to be self-evident, that all men are created equal, that they are endowed by their Creator with certain unalienable Rights, that among these are Life, Liberty and the pursuit of Happiness.— That to secure these rights, Governments are instituted among Men, deriving their just powers from the consent of the governed, —That whenever any Form of Government becomes destructive of these ends, it is the Right of the People to alter or to abolish it, and to institute new Government, laying its foundation on such principles and organizing its powers in such form, as to them shall seem most likely to effect their Safety and Happiness.

> —*Excerpt from the Declaration of Independence (1776)*

1. The Declaration of Independence lists rights that should not be taken away. Indicate these rights with an X on the line before each one.

    _____ Liberty

    _____ Life

    _____ Power

    _____ Pursuit of happiness

    _____ Safety

    _____ Truthfulness

2. The Second Continental Congress chose which of the following to be the Commander of the Continental Army?

A. George Washington
B. Thomas Jefferson
C. Thomas Paine
D. Benjamin Franklin

Answers are on page 831.

The Revolutionary War

Even after the Declaration of Independence was signed, about 20 percent of Americans still favored British rule of the colonies. These people were known as **Loyalists** because they were loyal to King George III. The beginning of the **Revolutionary War** forced the colonists to decide which side they would support.

Battles continued for several years, first in New York and Pennsylvania and later in the southern colonies. George Washington and his army were outnumbered by the British, but the Americans had the advantage of fighting on familiar ground. Eventually, Britain proved unable to sustain and supply a large military force over a long period in distant North America. In addition, in 1778 France joined the war on the American side, providing the colonists with money, arms, and naval support.

In October 1781, the British surrendered at Yorktown in the last large battle of the war. In September 1783, the war ended with the signing of the **Treaty of Paris**, which granted independence to the United States. It also gave the new country more land.

EXERCISE 8

The Revolutionary War

Directions: Choose the best answer to each of the following questions.

Questions 1 through 3 are based on the following table.

Major Battles of the American Revolution

Date	Battle	American Commander(s)
April 19, 1775	Lexington-Concord	Capt. John Parker
June 17, 1775	Bunker (Breed's) Hill	Gen. Israel Putnam, Col. William Prescott
Dec. 31, 1775	Quebec	Gen. Richard Montgomery
Aug. 27, 1776	Long Island	Gen. George Washington
Oct. 26, 1776	White Plains	Gen. George Washington
Dec. 26, 1776	Trenton	Gen. George Washington
Sept. 11, 1777	Brandywine	Gen. George Washington
Sept. 19, 1777	Saratoga (Freeman's Farm)	Gen. Horatio Gates
Oct. 4, 1777	Germantown	Gen. George Washington
Oct. 7, 1777	Saratoga	Gen. Horatio Gates
Dec. 5, 1777	White Marsh	Gen. George Washington
June 8, 1778	Monmouth Courthouse	Gen. George Washington
Sept. 16, 1779	Siege of Savannah	Gen. Benjamin Lincoln
Mar. 29, 1780	Siege of Charleston	Gen. Benjamin Lincoln
Sept. 28, 1781	Siege of Yorktown	Gen. George Washington, Gen. Rochambeau

1. The battles of the American Revolution lasted for approximately
   _____ years.

2. During which year did the greatest number of major battles of the Revolution occur?

   A. 1775
   B. 1776
   C. 1777
   D. 1788

3. During the Battle of Trenton, the American forces were led by which commander?

A. Israel Putnam
B. Richard Montgomery
C. George Washington
D. Horatio Gates

Answers are on page 831.

From the Articles of Confederation to the U.S. Constitution

The first government of the new country operated under a document called the **Articles of Confederation**. Each of the 13 colonies, now the 13 states, wanted to have its own authority, which limited the power of the central government. This posed a problem when facing major issues such as regulating trade and national defense.

In 1787 delegates from the states met to amend the Articles of Confederation in order to correct these problems. Instead, those delegates created the **Constitution of the United States**, which continues in force today. The U.S. Constitution is actually the oldest such document currently in effect in the world today. The Constitution created a federal system with a central government and state governments. The central government is divided into three branches: executive, legislative, and judicial. It has power over functions involving the entire nation, such as defense and the regulation of trade. The state governments maintain authority over all functions not specifically assigned to the central government.

The following chart compares the Articles of Confederation and the U.S. Constitution.

Articles of Confederation	Constitution of the United States
No State shall be represented in Congress by less than two, nor by more than seven Members; and no person shall be capable of being delegate for more than three years, in any term of six years; nor shall any person, being a delegate, be capable of holding any office under the united states, for which he, or another for his benefit receives any salary, fees or emolument of any kind.	All legislative Powers herein granted shall be vested in a Congress of the United States, which shall consist of a Senate and House of Representatives.
Each State shall maintain its own delegates in a meeting of the states, and while they act as members of the committee of the states.	Representatives and direct Taxes shall be apportioned among the several States which may be included within this Union, according to their respective Numbers.
In determining questions in the united states, in Congress assembled, each state shall have one vote.	The Senate of the United States shall be composed of two Senators from each State, chosen by the Legislature thereof for six Years; and each Senator shall have one Vote.

During the drafting of the Constitution two distinct political groups emerged: the **Federalists** and the **Anti-Federalists**. The Federalists were mostly those who wanted the central government to have control over the states. The Anti-Federalists, on the other hand, thought that the states would not have enough freedom if the central government was too strong. The following list shows the reasons why the Anti-Federalists objected to the Constitution.

Anti-Federalists' Reasons for Objecting to the Constitution

Opposed the strong central government outlined in the Constitution

Believed that a strong central government threatened the power of the states and the rights of individuals

Thought that a Bill of Rights should be included

Feared that the Constitution favored the wealthy

Compromises were made to ensure that the concerns of both groups were addressed. The **Bill of Rights**, comprising the first 10 amendments to the Constitution, was later added to guarantee individual rights.

EXERCISE 9

From the Articles of Confederation to the U.S. Constitution

Directions: Choose the best answer to each of the following questions.

1. The Preamble to the U.S. Constitution begins with the words "We the people...." Which of the following is indicated by these words?

   A. Rights are guaranteed to certain people.
   B. The people who wrote the document are powerful.
   C. The power of the government comes from the people.
   D. Some people deserve to be given more rights than others.

2. Which group wanted a Bill of Rights to be included in the Constitution?

   A. Federalists
   B. Anti-Federalists
   C. Senators
   D. Representatives

Answers are on page 832.

The War of 1812

Over the next several years, the boundaries of the United States expanded. In 1803, while Thomas Jefferson was President, the Louisiana Purchase added a large area of land to the country. This purchase from France doubled the size of the United States.

The following map shows the territorial expansion of the United States during the presidency of Thomas Jefferson.

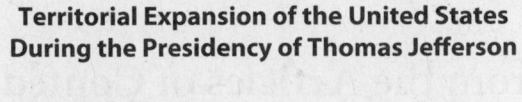

**Territorial Expansion of the United States
During the Presidency of Thomas Jefferson**

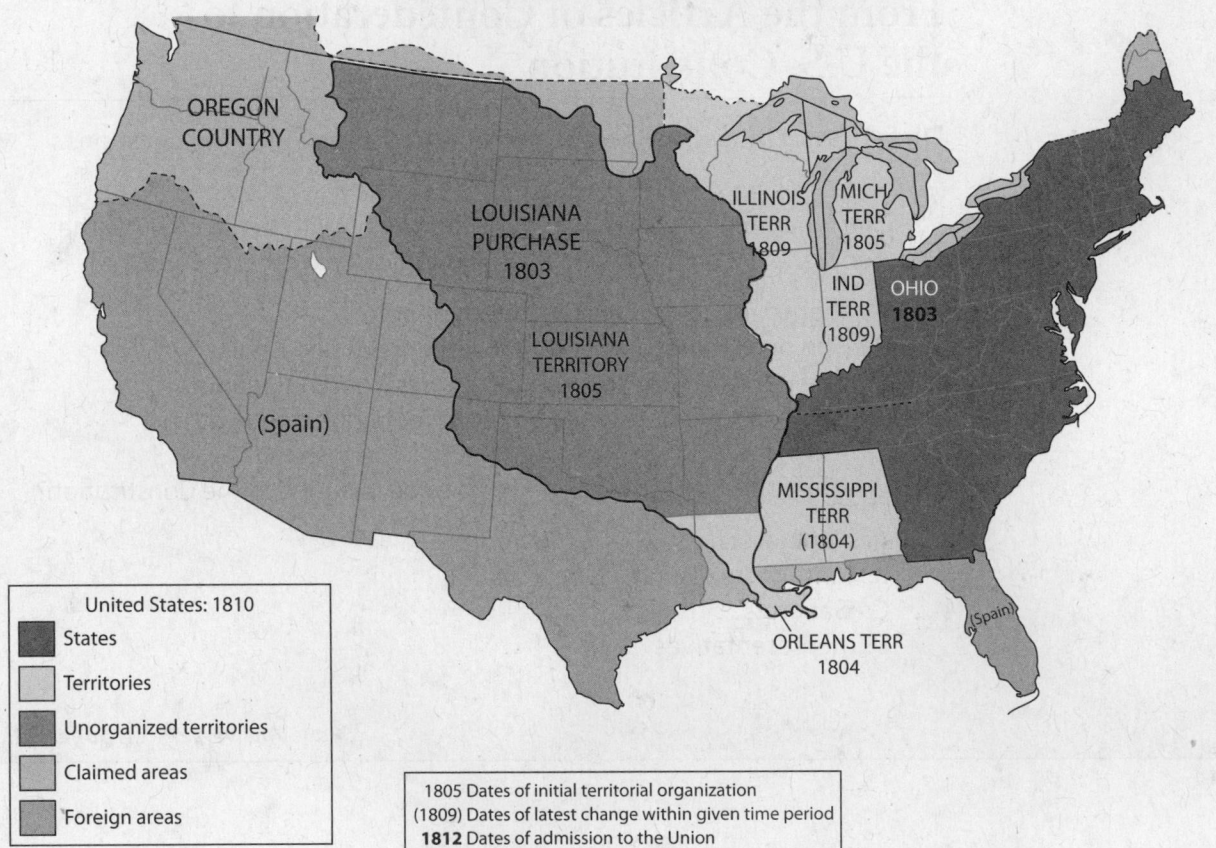

OREGON
COUNTRY

LOUISIANA
PURCHASE
1803

ILLINOIS
TERR
1809

MICH
TERR
1805

IND
TERR
(1809)

OHIO
1803

LOUISIANA
TERRITORY
1805

(Spain)

MISSISSIPPI
TERR
(1804)

(Spain)

ORLEANS TERR
1804

United States: 1810
- States
- Territories
- Unorganized territories
- Claimed areas
- Foreign areas

1805 Dates of initial territorial organization
(1809) Dates of latest change within given time period
1812 Dates of admission to the Union

During this period, Great Britain and France were at war with each other in Europe. As President, Thomas Jefferson tried to keep the United States neutral in this conflict. When James Madison became President in 1808, he too wanted the United States to remain neutral, and he wanted trade to continue with both Britain and France. However, when British naval vessels stopped American merchant ships at sea and forced captured American sailors to serve in the British navy, Americans were outraged. Americans also believed the British were supplying weapons to the Native Americans who were fighting with settlers in the West. For these reasons, Congress declared war on Britain in June 1812. The British navy then began blocking U.S. ships bound for France as a way to stop trade and harm the American economy.

In August 1814, Washington, D.C., was attacked by the British. The British burned buildings in the city, including the White House. Although the Americans did win some battles, neither country was winning the war, and the **Treaty of Ghent** was signed to end the conflict. The treaty did not award territory to either country; each country ended with the same territory it had prior to the start of the war.

The British blockades that had blocked overseas trade during the war caused shortages of many products. As a result, Americans began to manufacture many goods for themselves. The war thus produced not only a strong sense of nationalism, but also a time of prosperity for Americans.

EXERCISE 10

The War of 1812

Directions: Choose the best answer to each of the following questions.

1. Which event led the United States to enjoy a period of prosperity in the early 1800s?

   A. fighting a war and winning some battles
   B. signing the Treaty of Ghent
   C. manufacturing goods to substitute for products formerly obtained by trade
   D. being invaded by a British army that attacked the capital

2. Which event led to the United States becoming involved in the war between Britain and France?

   A. Washington, D.C., was attacked by a British army.
   B. France sold a vast North American territory to the United States.
   C. British naval vessels stopped American ships and captured U.S. sailors.
   D. The British navy blocked U.S. ships in order to interfere with French trade.

Answers are on page 832.

The Monroe Doctrine

When James Monroe was elected President of the United States two years after the end of the War of 1812, he was concerned that European armies might again invade the United States or other countries in the Americas. In 1823, Monroe announced a new foreign policy called the **Monroe Doctrine.** Under this policy, the United States proclaimed that it would resist, by force if necessary, any effort by European countries to establish new colonies in North or South America or to attack any countries in the Americas. The United States also promised to remain neutral in any European conflicts as long as the European countries did not interfere in the Americas. The Monroe Doctrine was significant in that it introduced the United States as a player in worldwide politics.

The Monroe Doctrine

Directions: Choose the best answer to each of the following questions.

1. Read the following passage, and then answer the question.

   > In the discussions to which this interest has given rise and in the arrangements by which they may terminate the occasion has been judged proper for asserting, as a principle in which the rights and interests of the United States are involved, that the American continents, by the free and independent condition which they have assumed and maintain, are henceforth not to be considered as subjects for future colonization by any European powers.

   > —*Excerpt from President James Monroe's State of the Union Address, 1823*

   What is the central idea of this excerpt?

   A. No other countries can establish colonies in the Americas.
   B. The United States plans to begin more colonies in the future.
   C. Each of the states in the United States is free and independent.
   D. The continents of the Americas can be ruled by European powers.

2. Read the following passage, and then answer the question.

   > Our policy in regard to Europe, which was adopted at an early stage of the wars which have so long agitated that quarter of the globe, nevertheless remains the same, which is, not to interfere in the internal concerns of any of its powers; to consider the government de facto as the legitimate government for us; to cultivate friendly relations with it, and to preserve those relations by a frank, firm, and manly policy, meeting in all instances the just claims of every power, submitting to injuries from none.

   > —*Excerpt from President James Monroe's State of the Union Address, 1823*

   What is the central idea of this excerpt?

   A. The United States believes that wars in Europe have lasted for too long.
   B. The United States will not interfere with events in European countries.
   C. The United States will submit to the governments of the European countries.
   D. The United States plans to model its government after the governments in Europe.

Answers are on page 832.

U.S. Policy Toward Native Americans

Following the end of the War of 1812, U.S. military officer **Andrew Jackson** and his army defeated a group of Creek Native Americans in what is now Alabama. The Creeks were forced to cede about 22 million acres of land in Georgia and Alabama to the United States. Jackson then invaded Spanish Florida to fight the Seminoles, acquiring more land in this area. Between 1814 and 1824, Jackson negotiated many additional treaties with Native American peoples. Under these treaties, the Native Americans gave up land in what is now the southeastern United States for land in the West.

The Cherokee, who lived mainly in Georgia and nearby areas, appealed to the U.S. Supreme Court to protect their land from settlers. In 1831, after several failed attempts, the tribe won their suit. The Court ruled that the tribe had the right to their own government and that the laws of Georgia did not apply to them. The state, however, refused to follow this ruling, and Jackson, who was now President of the United States, refused to enforce it.

Shortly after Jackson took office, Congress passed the **Indian Removal Act**. This act authorized the forcible removal of Native Americans east of the Mississippi River to a new "Indian territory" in the West.

In Florida, the majority of the Seminoles refused to leave their land. As a result, the U.S. army waged three wars against them in the mid-1800s. Eventually, the U.S. government paid the remaining Seminoles to move to land in the West

Among the Cherokee, a small minority faction agreed to a treaty with the United States permitting removal of the tribe to the West. The majority, however, wished to remain on their lands. When the tribe had not moved west by the deadline in the treaty, the U.S. government sent troops to expel 16,000 Cherokee by force. Their journey west was called the **Trail of Tears** because 4,000 Cherokee died along the way of hunger, cold, and disease.

By 1837, a total of 46,000 Native Americans had been expelled from their lands in the East by Jackson and his administration. Jackson's policy added 25 million acres of land for settlers.

U.S. Policy Toward Native Americans

Directions: Choose the best answer to each of the following questions.

1. Read the following passage, and then answer the question.

   The instrument in question is not the act of our Nation; we are not parties to its covenants; it has not received the sanction of our people. The makers of it sustain no office nor appointment in our Nation, under the designation of Chiefs, Head men, or any other title, by which they hold, or could acquire, authority to assume the reins of Government, and to make bargain and sale of our rights, our possessions, and our common country. And we are constrained solemnly to declare, that we cannot but contemplate the enforcement of the stipulations of this instrument on us, against our consent, as an act of injustice and oppression, which, we are well persuaded, can never knowingly be countenanced by the Government and people of the United States; nor can we believe it to be the design of these honorable and high minded individuals, who stand at the head of the Govt., to bind a whole Nation, by the acts of a few unauthorized individuals. And, therefore, we, the parties to be affected by the result, appeal with confidence to the justice, the magnanimity, the compassion, of your honorable bodies, against the enforcement, on us, of the provisions of a compact, in the formation of which we have had no agency.

   —*Excerpt from a letter by Cherokee Chief John Ross to the Senate and House of Representatives in 1836, describing the treaty signed by a minority of the tribe, authorizing removal of the Cherokee to the West*

   Which reflects the opinion of the author?

   A. The Cherokee people have been treated unfairly.
   B. The Cherokee accept the treaty and believe it to be fair.
   C. The Cherokee are eager to move to the West.
   D. The U.S. government will not help the Cherokee.

2. The American lawmakers who enacted the Indian Removal Act most likely believed which of the following?

   A. Native Americans can stay in the Southeastern states.
   B. Native Americans will benefit from moving to a new territory.
   C. The land in the West is better for Native Americans than the land in the Southeast.
   D. The United States has more rights to the land in the Southeast than the Native Americans do.

Answers are on page 832.

Manifest Destiny

In 1845, while James Polk was President, the United States annexed the Texas Republic. This event reignited efforts to further expand the United States. Many people, including many in positions of power, believed that the country had a **"manifest destiny"** to occupy the entire North American continent, from the Atlantic Ocean to the Pacific Ocean. After defeating Mexico in the **Mexican-American War** in 1846–1848, the United States gained huge new territories in the West. During a four-year period, the area of the United States increased by more than 60 percent. Large numbers of people migrated westward, and new territories and states were organized in areas west of the Mississippi River. In 1849, gold was discovered in California, and thousands of Americans headed west to the goldfields. California became a state in 1850.

EXERCISE 13

Manifest Destiny

Directions: Choose the best answer to each of the following questions.

1. People who believed in the idea of *manifest destiny* thought that the United States should eventually include all the land between

    A. Texas and the Mississippi River.
    B. Texas and the Pacific Ocean.
    C. the Atlantic Ocean and the Pacific Ocean.
    D. the Atlantic Ocean and Texas.

2. In the late 1840s the United States gained new territories in western North America by

    A. purchasing Texas from Mexico.
    B. establishing a state government in California.
    C. defeating Mexico in a war.
    D. conquering the Texas Republic.

Question 3 is based on the following graph.

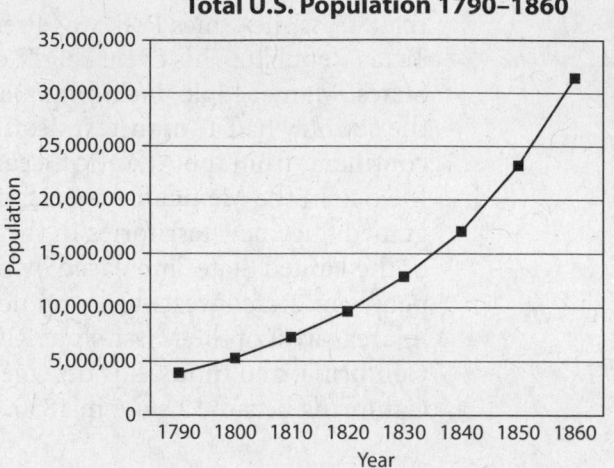

Total U.S. Population 1790–1860

3. How do the data in the graph relate to the idea of manifest destiny?

A. The addition of new territories in the mid-1800s caused the population of the United States to increase.

B. The rapid growth of the U.S. population in the mid-1800s created a demand for more territory.

C. There was not enough population growth in the 1800s to justify the addition of new territories.

D. Enough land was gained in the 1840s to support the increasing population.

Answers are on page 832.

Civil War and Reconstruction

In the early 1800s, there were important economic, cultural, and political differences between the various regions of the country. As a result, the different regions favored different policies and made different demands on the central government. The problems caused by these regional differences were called **sectionalism**.

In the northern states, the economy was increasingly based on industry and trade. Northerners supported policies that favored manufacturing, including high tariffs that protected new industries from foreign competition.

In the southern states, by contrast, the economy was based on agriculture, much of it using slave labor. Southerners favored policies that protected slavery and that supported southern exports of agricultural goods such as cotton. They also opposed high tariffs, which made manufactured goods more expensive.

Over time, the sectional differences between North and South became greater and greater. Sectionalism caused people to become more loyal to their region than to the country as a whole. Political strife between northerners and southerners became more and more intense.

The biggest issue dividing the country was slavery. As each new territory was added to the Union, a decision had to be made about whether it would permit slavery (as a "slave state") or ban it (as a "free state"). Some people, particularly many southerners, believed that the residents of each state or territory should have the right to make this and other important decisions for themselves. This idea was called "states' rights." Many southerners hoped thereby to increase the number of slave states and thus the power of the South in Congress. Other people thought that slavery should be banned in the new territories, but permitted to continue in areas where it was already allowed. Some people, known as **Abolitionists**, thought that slavery was wrong and should not be allowed in any state. Although compromises were attempted, a lasting solution to the issue of slavery was not found.

In 1857 a slave named Dred Scott sued for his freedom when his master took him into a free territory. The Supreme Court ruled that slaves like Scott were property that belonged to the master and had no legal rights. The southern states supported the **Dred Scott decision**, but the northern states did not. The Dred Scott case divided the states even further.

In 1860, Abraham Lincoln, the candidate of the new Republican Party, was elected President. Lincoln promised no restrictions on slavery in the states where it already existed, but he opposed permitting it to expand to new states. The southern states claimed that this was unfair and rejected any further attempts to limit slavery. They voted to form their own government and secede from the United States. The southern states established the **Confederate States of America** and elected Jefferson Davis of Mississippi as President. Lincoln believed the southern states were not obeying the laws and that this act could not be tolerated.

In April 1861 the Confederacy launched the **Civil War** by firing on Fort Sumter, a federal base in the harbor of Charleston, South Carolina. In the war that followed, the North had many advantages over the South. Not only did the North already have an established army, it also had stronger financial institutions, more industry, greater natural resources, and many more miles of railroad. However, most battles were fought in the South, where southerners had the advantage of familiarity with the local terrain. The war lasted four years and cost the lives of more than 600,000 men.

In 1862, Lincoln's **Emancipation Proclamation** decreed that all slaves in the states at war with the Union were henceforth free. Following this, 180,000 former slaves joined the Union army to fight against the South. In April 1865, the war ended when the general of the Confederate army, **Robert E. Lee**, surrendered to the Union commander, **Ulysses S. Grant**.

Following the Civil War, the nation needed to be reunited. Lincoln had a **Reconstruction** plan that would allow the southern states to rejoin the Union. However, he was assassinated by a southern sympathizer shortly after the war ended. Andrew Johnson, from Tennessee, became the President. In December 1865 the **Thirteenth Amendment to the U.S. Constitution** was passed, abolishing slavery in the United States. President Johnson's Reconstruction policy angered many radical Republicans in Congress, who considered it to be too lenient toward the South. The radical Republicans wanted the South to be punished as an enemy that had been at war with the Union. When the southern legislatures enacted **Black Codes** (laws restricting the rights of African Americans), the radicals claimed they were trying to avoid compliance with the Thirteenth Amendment. The radicals supported the **Freedman's Bureau,** which helped the freed slaves.

When the radicals in Congress passed laws protecting the freedoms of the former slaves, President Johnson vetoed some of them. However, the radicals still managed to pass the **Fourteenth Amendment,** which granted citizenship to the former slaves, and the **Fifteeenth Amendment,** which outlawed restrictions on voting based on race.

EXERCISE 14

Civil War and Reconstruction

Directions: Choose the best answer to each of the following questions.

1. Place an X before each phrase that names an issue that led to the Civil War.

   _____ Lack of farmland for a growing population

   _____ The expansion of slavery into new territories

   _____ War with Mexico

   _____ Differences between North and South on economic issues

   _____ The election of President Abraham Lincoln

   _____ New amendments to the U.S. Constitution

Question 2 is based on the following timeline.

Civil War Events of 1865

January 15	February 3	February 19	March 3	March 25– April 2	April 3–4	April 9	April 14
1,841 killed in battles for Fort Fisher, NC	Lincoln and the Confederate Peace Commission meet in Virginia	Confederates leave Charleston, SC	Freedman's Bureau is created by the Union Congress	17,000 killed In the Battle of Petersburg in Virginia	Lincoln arrives in Richmond	General Lee surrenders at Appomattox Courthouse, Virginia	Lincoln is assassinated

2. Which statement is true, based on the information in the timeline?

   A. January was the most deadly month of fighting in 1865.

   B. More Civil War battles were fought in 1865 than in any other year.

   C. President Lincoln was assassinated less than a week after the end of the Civil War.

   D. Much of the military action in the last few months of the war took place in North Carolina.

Answers are on page 832.

The United States Becomes a Major Industrial Nation

The United States underwent two Industrial Revolutions. The first began in 1793, with the invention of the **cotton gin**. This machine could process as much cotton in one day as 1000 slaves; southern planters found that it multiplied their profits tenfold. The invention of the steamboat, which could sail upstream against the current, made it possible to move huge boatloads of cotton north; this made possible a thriving New England textile industry.

The first wave of the U.S. national transportation system included canals, paved roads, and the **transcontinental railroad**, completed in 1869. The purpose of a national system of transportation was to link the agricultural and industrial regions so that both would benefit as sellers expanded into new territories and found new markets for their goods. For example, the railway boom made possible the cattle boom of the 1870s. Railroads took the cattle north to the slaughterhouses of Chicago. As profits grew, so did the sizes of towns and the movement of settlers.

There were no safety or wage regulations to protect factory workers until after the Civil War. Owners set wages as low as they could, demanded a 60- to 85-hour workweek, and shrugged off unsafe working conditions because the constant flood of new immigrants meant that dissatisfied or injured workers could easily be replaced. Factories exposed workers to high levels of industrial pollution. Machinery was dangerous to operate at the best of times—more so when workers were always exhausted from the long hours. **Labor unions** and federal regulations to protect the workers finally arrived with the Second Industrial Revolution.

The Second Industrial Revolution took place during the post–Civil War era. Instant long-distance communication (telegraph, telephone), a machine that could produce a perfectly printed letter (typewriter), and cheap, steady lamplight with the flick of a switch (the electric lightbulb) made great changes in the way people lived and worked. Before electricity, most people rose and went to bed with the sun; when electricity was perfected, people could work or enjoy themselves in brightly lit rooms all through the night if they wanted to.

The **Bessemer process**, which made possible the easy and cheap conversion of iron ore into steel, led to a rise in steel production and became the most important factor in the success of the Second Industrial Revolution. Men at the head of heavy industries and large-scale construction companies made fortunes, and American cities became forests of skyscrapers, suspension bridges, and elevated train lines. With the rise of the reform-minded **Progressive Party** and the creation of labor unions, workers were also in a position to enjoy some of the profits of their labor.

EXERCISE 15

The United States Becomes a Major Industrial Nation

Directions: Chose the best answer to each of the following questions.

Questions 1 and 2 refer to the following political cartoon from 1896.

"I am confident the workingmen are with us."

Cartoon by Homer Davenport

1. The cartoon shows a man with his foot resting on money bags. This image most likely represents

   A. a striking coal miner.
   B. a wealthy industrialist.
   C. a foreign diplomat.
   D. President Ulysses S. Grant.

2. The man in the cartoon holds a whip draped across a skull marked "Labor." The cartoonist most likely means that the man in the chair

   A. supports the Progressive Party.
   B. wants to restrict immigration.
   C. does not support labor unions.
   D. favors attacking foreign countries.

Answers are on page 832.

The United States Becomes a World Power

At the start of the 20th century, the United States was a wealthy and strong nation, but not a world power. Occupied with internal issues such as the Civil War, Reconstruction, industrialization, and westward expansion, the United States had taken very little active interest in world affairs. In 1900, Western Europe dominated world politics and the world economy. Great Britain, France, Austria-Hungary, Russia, and the recently unified Germany were the **great powers** of the world.

The United States had several motives for acquiring colonies. The first was to gain trade partners on favorable terms—partners that could supply natural resources the United States could not, such as sugar, rubber, and coffee. The second was to establish naval bases. The third was simply to prove to the world that the United States was a great power—a force other nations would have to reckon with. Between 1898 and 1903, the United States annexed Hawaii, Guam, Puerto Rico, and the Philippines, made Cuba a **protectorate**, and took control of the construction of the Panama Canal. The United States would retain control of this important trade route for most of the 20th century.

The United States Becomes a World Power

Directions: Choose the best answer to the following question.

Question 1 is based on the following political cartoon from the era of the Spanish-American War (1898).

1. In the cartoon, a "goddess of liberty" heralds freedom for Cuba, Puerto Rico, and the Philippines. The man in the background represents

    A. Europe.
    B. the United States.
    C. Abraham Lincoln.
    D. the King of Spain.

The answer is on page 832.

World War I

World War I—called at the time the "Great War"—marked the United States' first major entry into world affairs. The war began in 1914 as a territorial conflict among European nations, with the Central Powers (Austria and Germany) on one side and the Entente or Allied Powers (Britain, Russia, and France) on the other. By 1916, the United States was supplying money and arms to the Allied Powers; U.S. troops joined the fight in late 1917, and the Central Powers surrendered in November 1918.

Despite its late entry into the war, the United States was treated as an equal partner at the **peace conference**, marking the first time in history that a non-European nation had played a major role in the peace settlements of a European war. The United States had played a small but crucial role on the battlefield, and it ended the war in a much stronger military and economic position than the European nations, which had suffered much greater losses. Ironically, President Woodrow Wilson's dream of the **League of Nations**—an international organization to settle differences over a conference table, taking up arms only as a last resort—was realized without American participation.

EXERCISE 17

World War I

Directions: Choose the best answer to each of the following questions.

Questions 1 and 2 are based on the following political cartoon from 1919 commenting on the formation of the League of Nations. The sign reads "This League of Nations Bridge was designed by the President of the U.S.A."

The Gap in the Bridge
Cartoon by Leonard Raven-Hill.
Appeared in *Punch* magazine, December 10, 1919.

1. In the cartoon, the reclining figure, representing the United States, can best be described as

   A. indifferent.
   B. eager.
   C. angry.
   D. ashamed.

2. The artist of this cartoon is suggesting that the League of Nations

   A. has too many members and does not need the United States.
   B. will be headquartered in England and Italy rather than in Belgium and France.
   C. will not be successful without the United States as a member.
   D. needs to build a bridge from France to England.

Answers are on page 832.

The Great Depression

The Great Depression began with the **crash** of the **stock market** in October 1929. Although the United States had weathered several financial panics since the 1790s, this one was nicknamed "great" because it was the worst, longest-lasting economic crisis in U.S. history.

The simple cause of the stock market crash was the practice of **margin buying**, which had become common during the 1920s. Speculators would borrow money and buy stock, then keep an eye on its value and sell it as soon as its price went up. The large number of speculators meant that share prices were constantly fluctuating, usually upward. This meant a booming market built on an insubstantial foundation of unpaid debt. When buyers lost confidence in the market and began selling their shares, prices dropped and debts fell due. Banks failed because people could not repay their loans. When a bank failed, everyone who had an account with that bank lost all of his or her money; there was no mechanism in place to protect account holders from loss. Across the nation, businesses closed and workers were laid off. Landlords evicted tenants who could not pay rent. Millions could not make their mortgage payments and so lost their houses. All social and economic classes were affected.

The failure of businesses and banks coincided with many months of **drought** in the Great Plains, turning the 50-million-acre Breadbasket into the **Dust Bowl**. The topsoil in this region was a thin layer over hard, dry dirt. With no rain to keep it moist and anchored in place, the thin topsoil blew away during **dust storms**, and the crops failed. Thousands of small farmers lost everything they had. These "**Okies**" (nicknamed for the state of Oklahoma, although they were from several neighboring states as well) migrated westward, hoping for a fresh start in the favorable climate of California. All they found there was hostility, prejudice, and starvation wages.

Many Americans blamed the Depression on President Herbert Hoover, who had failed to predict it and seemed not only unable but unwilling to resolve it. People who had lost their homes built shantytowns called "**Hoovervilles**" in ironic tribute to the President. In the 1932 presidential election, Hoover lost in a landslide to Franklin Delano Roosevelt.

Roosevelt immediately took action to address the financial crisis. His **New Deal** programs created millions of jobs and restored the nation's banks to a sound financial footing. During Roosevelt's first term, unemployment dropped by about 8 percent. Unsurprisingly, he was reelected in 1936 in the greatest landslide in 100 years.

EXERCISE 18

The Great Depression

Directions: Choose the best answer to each of the following questions.

1. Which statement is supported by the preceding text?

    A. The Great Plains was the region least affected by the Great Depression.
    B. Proper farming techniques are essential to maintaining healthy soil.
    C. Immigrants from New York and California settled in the Dust Bowl area in the 1930s.
    D. In the Great Plains in the 1930s, crops failed because of drought and dust storms.

Question 2 is based on the following graph.

U.S. Unemployment Percentage, 1910–1960

2. According to the graph, the unemployment percentage in the United States reached a peak of 21 percent in

    A. 1924.
    B. 1934.
    C. 1941.
    D. 1949.

Answers are on page 832.

World War II

It took World War II to bring the United States out of the Depression and back to prosperity. The military draft and the change to a war production economy combined to put millions of Americans back to work. The United States officially entered the war in December 1941, after Japan attacked the American naval base at Pearl Harbor, Hawaii. America was faced with a two-front war; it joined Britain's battle against Nazi Germany in Western Europe, and it sent troops to the Pacific to fight the Japanese. The United States was a formidable ally against Germany because of its almost unlimited manpower and its ability to produce an endless flow of military supplies and weapons.

The war in Europe ended in the spring of 1945; Japan held out until the United States dropped atomic bombs on Hiroshima and Nagasaki at the end of August 1945. At the peace conference at Potsdam, Germany, it was clear that the United States and the Soviet Union were the only great powers left in the world. The munitions industry had completely reinvigorated the American economy, American casualties had been minor compared to European losses, and the United States itself was far from the combat zones and physically undamaged. Britain, France, and the other European nations recovered, but they would never again be more than second-rate powers.

At the time of the Japanese attack on Pearl Harbor, more than 110,000 Americans of Japanese descent were living on the West Coast of the United States. The U.S. government feared espionage and sabotage in this part of the country and moved these Japanese-Americans to internment camps in the middle of the country and California for the duration of the war. This detainment was later recognized by the United States as a violation of these citizens' human and civil rights.

EXERCISE 19

World War II

Directions: Read the following passage, and then answer the question.

Armed defense of democratic existence is now being gallantly waged in four continents. If that defense fails, all the population and all the resources of Europe and Asia, and Africa and Austral-Asia will be dominated by conquerors. And let us remember that the total of those populations in those four continents, the total of those populations and their resources greatly exceed the sum total of the population and the resources of the whole of the Western Hemisphere—yes, many times over.

In times like these it is immature—and, incidentally, untrue—for anybody to brag that an unprepared America, single-handed and with one hand tied behind its back, can hold off the whole world.

—Excerpt from a speech to Congress by President
Franklin Roosevelt, January 6, 1941

1. What message is President Roosevelt giving to Congress and the American people?

   A. The United States can easily beat any enemy in the world.
   B. Other countries will defend democracy, so Americans need not worry.
   C. The defense of democracy is already a lost cause.
   D. Americans need to begin preparing seriously for possible war.

The answer is on page 832.

Postwar America

Following World War II, Americans enjoyed an era of prosperity and plenty after the hard times of the Great Depression. In 1944, the **GI Bill**, also known as the Servicemen's Readjustment Act, was passed in Congress. This bill provided benefits to veterans to help them transition back into civilian life after serving their country. Under this act, assistance was provided immediately to servicemen and women. Although some changes occurred over time, the original bill provided three main benefits:

• Subsidized education or career training

• Guaranteed low-interest loans for homes, businesses, or agriculture

• One year of unemployment benefits if the veteran was unable to obtain work

The GI Bill gave veterans the chance to get a college education, buy a house or a farm, attend training school for a particular profession, or start a business. This enabled many to marry, start families, and move to the newly built **suburbs**. People began buying cars, television sets, and other consumer goods.

Also after the war, Americans moved to rebuild the European countries that were devastated by the years of fighting. Secretary of State George Marshall proposed a plan to help rebuild Europe in order to provide political stability and help the world economy. Congress then passed the Economic Cooperation Act of 1948, also known as the **Marshall Plan**, which helped to restore productivity in the areas of agriculture and industry, prevented famine, and helped the nations of Europe avoid political chaos.

Postwar America

Directions: Choose the best answer to each of the following questions.

Questions 1 and 2 are based on the following passage.

> The modern system of the division of labor upon which the exchange of products is based is in danger of breaking down.... Aside from the demoralizing effect on the world at large and the possibilities of disturbances arising as a result of the desperation of the people concerned, the consequences to the economy of the United States should be apparent to all. It is logical that the United States should do whatever it is able to do to assist in the return of normal economic health to the world, without which there can be no political stability and no assured peace. Our policy is not directed against any country, but against hunger, poverty, desperation, and chaos. Any government that is willing to assist in recovery will find full cooperation on the part of the USA. Its purpose should be the revival of a working economy in the world so as to permit the emergence of political and social conditions in which free institutions can exist.
>
> —*Excerpt from a speech on the Marshall Plan by Secretary of State George C. Marshall, June 5, 1947*

1. Based on the passage, you can infer that Marshall

   A. wanted defeated Germany and Japan to pay for global economic recovery after World War II.
   B. thought that the United States should play a leading role in global economic recovery after World War II.
   C. favored letting European allies solve their own economic problems.
   D. believed that only allies of the United States deserved to receive American economic aid.

2. Secretary of State Marshall would most likely agree with which of the following statements?

   A. The United States should take no further part in international affairs.
   B. The biggest threat to stability in Europe is political parties that promote democracy.
   C. Prosperity is possible only under conditions of political and social stability.
   D. Efforts to aid postwar economic recovery should focus only on U.S. allies.

Answers are on page 832.

The Cold War

In foreign affairs, the late 1940s ushered in a new era of "**Cold War**" between the two **superpowers**: the United States and the Soviet Union. With their opposing political systems and economic policies, these World War II allies quickly became enemies; throughout the Cold War, each tried to contain the other's sphere of influence. The war was called "cold" because the two enemies did not actually fire on one another.

To counter the Soviet threat, the United States and its European allies created a military alliance called the **North Atlantic Treaty Organization** (NATO). In 1947, President Harry Truman called for immediate economic and military support for Greece and Turkey to protect those countries from a possible Soviet-backed Communist takeover. Under the **Truman Doctrine**, the United States promised similar help to all countries threatened by Communism.

Germany was another Cold War flashpoint. At the end of World War II, Germany had been divided into West Germany and East Germany. East Germany was a Communist country dominated by the Soviet Union. West Germany was a non-Communist ally of the United States, Great Britain, and France. The city of Berlin was also divided. In 1948 the Soviet Union attempted to force the United States and its allies to leave West Berlin by blocking access to the city. The allies responded by delivering supplies to Berlin by airplane in what was called the **Berlin Airlift**. In 1961 the East Germans built the Berlin Wall to separate their part of the city from the part controlled by the allies. In the meantime, the Soviet Union joined with East Germany, Hungary, Poland, Romania, Bulgaria, and Czechoslovakia to form the military alliance called the **Warsaw Pact**.

When civil wars erupted in Korea and Vietnam, the Soviets backed one side and the United States the other. The Korean War ended in a stalemate and the Vietnam War in a Communist victory.

The Cold War started to break down during the 1980s when **Mikhail Gorbachev** became leader of the Soviet Union. Gorbachev relaxed controls over Soviet society and over the Warsaw Pact countries. In 1989 those countries overthrew their Communist governments and broke free of Soviet control, and East Germany and West Germany were soon reunited. In 1991 the Soviet Union itself collapsed as Communism proved to be economically unsustainable. The Soviet government was replaced by a non-Communist Russia and other independent republics. The Cold War was over.

The Cold War

Directions: Choose the best answer to the following question.

1. All of the following statements about the Cold War are true except:

   A. The Truman Doctrine, first applied to Greece and Turkey, was later also applied to other countries threatened by Communist takeover.
   B. Although World War II was over, Americans remained willing to play an active role in global affairs.
   C. The end of the Cold War resulted in part from changes in policy by the Soviet government.
   D. Attempts by the Soviet Union to expel the United States and its allies from West Berlin were eventually successful.

The answer is on page 832.

The Civil Rights Movement and the Women's Movement

In postwar America, racial discrimination remained a major problem. In many states, particularly in the South, so-called "Jim Crow laws" dating from the late 19th and early 20th centuries enforced a system of legal **segregation**, or separation of the races. Laws providing for "separate but equal" accommodations for different races had been upheld by the Supreme Court in a case called *Plessy v. Ferguson* (1896).

After World War II, a **Civil Rights movement** took root. Americans eager to claim the leadership of the "free world" against Communist foes began to realize that the legal segregation of African Americans seriously undermined that claim. Furthermore, African Americans who had fought for freedom overseas were no longer willing to accept legal restrictions when they returned home. President Harry S. Truman ordered the integration of the U.S. military.

In 1954, a milestone decision was made in the Supreme Court case *Brown v. Board of Education*. The court, led by **Chief Justice Earl Warren**, ruled it unconstitutional to separate children in public schools based on race. Through the decade that followed, African Americans used nonviolent protests and civil disobedience to protest against racial discrimination. Black students across the South staged a series of **sit-ins** that ended segregation in many public places. Martin Luther King Jr., a clergyman from Georgia, organized and led many of these protests, which were often met with violence.

In response to growing public sympathy for the protesters, Congress passed the **Civil Rights Act of 1964**, which outlawed discrimination in schools, colleges, places of employment, and public accommodations such as restaurants and public transportation. This was followed by the **Voting Rights Act of 1965**, which outlawed restrictions that had been used to prevent African Americans from voting.

In postwar society, women also began protesting against discrimination. Women had won the right to vote in 1919 through the passage of the **Nineteenth Amendment** to the U.S. Constitution, but they were still kept out of many jobs and positions of influence in society. During World War II, many women had gone to work in traditionally male jobs (including military service) and proved very capable. After the war, women were no longer content with the old assumption that they should have no ambitions beyond marriage and children. By the 1960s, more and more women were getting college educations and competing for skilled professional jobs. A proposed Equal Rights Amendment to the Constitution failed to pass, but American women made great strides toward social and legal equality during the last decades of the 20th century.

EXERCISE 22

The Civil Rights Movement and the Women's Movement

Directions: Choose the best answer to each of the following questions.

Question 1 is based on the following passage.

> Our Constitution is color-blind, and neither knows nor tolerates classes among citizens.
>
> —*Excerpt from a statement by Justice John Marshall Harlan, the only Supreme Court justice to dissent from the ruling in the case of* Plessy v. Ferguson

1. In which way did Justice Harlan's opinion differ from that of the other justices? He believed that

A. all races and classes are guaranteed the same rights.
B. the Constitution supports the idea of "separate but equal."
C. civil rights should be based on class, but not on race.
D. citizens should be given equal opportunities, even if laws keep them separate.

Question 2 is based on the following passage.

> So I say to you, my friends, that even though we must face the difficulties of today and tomorrow, I still have a dream. It is a dream deeply rooted in the American dream that one day this nation will rise up and live out the true meaning of its creed—we hold these truths to be self-evident, that all men are created equal. . . . And when we allow freedom to ring, when we let it ring from every village and hamlet, from every state and city, we will be able to speed up that day when all of God's children—black men and white men, Jews and Gentiles, Catholics and Protestants—will be able to join hands and to sing in the words of the old Negro spiritual, "Free at last, free at last, thank God Almighty, we are free at last."

—Excerpt from a speech by Dr. Martin Luther King Jr.
at the March on Washington, 1963

2. Which statement reflects King's opinion?

A. People should be separate based on religious beliefs, but not based on race.
B. It is time for people in the United States to be guaranteed religious freedom.
C. Each state should have the freedom to determine which rights are offered based on race.
D. The Declaration of Independence intended all to receive equal treatment regardless of race.

Answers are on page 832.

The Great Society, the Vietnam War, and Watergate

When **Lyndon B. Johnson** became President in 1963 following the assassination of President John F. Kennedy, he sought to complete some of the programs begun by the late President. Johnson persuaded Congress to pass not only the Civil Rights Act of 1964 (see the previous section) but also the **Economic Opportunity Act of 1964** and other measures intended to alleviate poverty and boost employment. Johnson declared his intention to create a **Great Society** in which poverty would be eliminated.

However, starting in 1965, Johnson's administration became increasingly embroiled in the **Vietnam War**, an effort to prevent a Communist takeover of a country in Southeast Asia. Eventually more than 600,000 U.S. troops were sent to Vietnam, but victory over Vietnamese guerrilla fighters proved elusive. As the war dragged on, protests against it mounted in the United

States. Finally, in 1968, peace talks were begun and Johnson retired from public life.

His successor as President, Richard M. Nixon, continued the peace talks but also pursued the war for another four years. U.S. troops were not finally withdrawn from Vietnam until 1973. During the 1972 presidential campaign, burglars were arrested in the Democratic National Committee's office in the Watergate building in Washington, D.C. Eventually it was revealed that the burglars had ties to the Nixon administration and that White House officials were attempting to cover up their involvement. Faced with the threat of impeachment over this **Watergate Scandal**, Nixon resigned the presidency in 1974.

EXERCISE 23

The Great Society, the Vietnam War, and Watergate

Directions: Choose the best answer to each of the following questions.

1. Which of the following is an opinion, not a fact?
   A. Despite the start of peace talks in 1968, United States forces remained in Vietnam until 1973.
   B. As President, Lyndon Johnson continued to pursue policies begun by President John Kennedy.
   C. The protests against the Vietnam War were harmful to the nation and disrespectful of the soldiers who served.
   D. President Nixon's resignation in 1974 resulted directly from the involvement of his administration in the Watergate Scandal.

Question 2 is based on the following passage.

> Although the economic well-being and prosperity of the United States have progressed to a level surpassing any achieved in world history, and although these benefits are widely shared throughout the Nation, poverty continues to be the lot of a substantial number of our people. The United States can achieve its full economic and social potential as a nation only if every individual has the opportunity to contribute to the full extent of his capabilities and to participate in the working of our society. It is, therefore, the policy of the United States to eliminate the paradox of poverty in the midst of plenty in this Nation by opening to everyone the opportunity for education and training, the opportunity to work and the opportunity to live in decency and dignity. It is the purpose of this Act to strengthen, supplement, and coordinate efforts in furtherance of that policy.

> —*Excerpt from the Statement of Purpose of the Economic Opportunity Act, 1964*

2. Which of the following is the central idea of the passage?

    A. No one should have to live in poverty in such a prosperous country.

    B. If everyone had a quality education, the nation would be more prosperous.

    C. Many people in our society are wealthy; however, a few are forced to live in poverty.

    D. Because everyone contributes to his or her full potential, our country has progressed farther than any other.

Answers are on page 833.

Presidencies in the Late 20th Century

Former Hollywood actor and California Republican governor **Ronald Reagan** served two terms as President in 1980–1988. His administration implemented highly conservative policies, both political and economic, that would have long-lasting effects. Tax rates were lowered and regulations on industry were loosened in an effort to stimulate economic growth. A massive military buildup was also undertaken. In foreign affairs, Reagan's government followed an aggressive anti-Communist policy and provided support to antigovernment rebels in Central America. Eventually, however, administration officials became mired in the so-called Iran-Contra scandal, which involved secret funding of the rebels with the proceeds from arms sales to Iran.

Politics in the 1990s were dominated by the Democrat Bill Clinton, who served as President from 1992 to 2000. Clinton's achievements were primarily domestic. In a time of great financial prosperity, with record-low poverty and unemployment rates, the Clinton administration introduced social policies such as the Family and Medical Leave Act (FMLA) and welfare reform. Customs barriers between the United States, Canada, and Mexico were dramatically lowered by the North American Free Trade Agreement (NAFTA), stimulating imports and exports among the three countries of North America.

EXERCISE 24

Presidencies in the Late 20th Century

Directions: Choose the best answer to the following question.

Question 1 is based on the following graph.

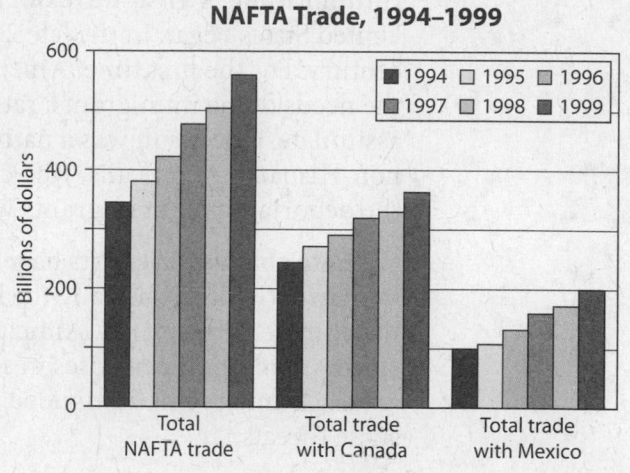

NAFTA Trade, 1994–1999

1. According to the graph, in what year did total NAFTA trade first exceed $500 billion dollars?

A. 1996
B. 1997
C. 1998
D. 1999

The answer is on page 833.

Issues Facing the United States at the Start of the 21st Century

The first decade of the 21st century was a time of crisis and dramatic changes. In the presidencies of George W. Bush (2000–2008) and Barack Obama (2008–2016), the United States faced several major challenges.

- **Economic issues.** Following a crisis in the financial markets and the collapse of several major financial institutions in 2008, the United States and other industrial countries entered a prolonged period of slow economic growth and high unemployment. This worsened a long-term trend toward increasing economic inequality, which saw a growing share of the country's wealth and profits flow to those in the highest income brackets.

- **Technology.** At the turn of the 21st century, a technological revolution swiftly changed the way Americans communicate. The advent of e-mail, cell phones, personal computers, online social networks, and portable **Internet** access made sweeping changes to society, both at home and on the job. Financial security and personal privacy became major social and legal concerns due to a rise in **hacking,** the practice of illegally breaking into electronic data systems.

- **Immigration.** A great wave of Latin American immigration to the United States began in the late 20th century and continued into the 21st century. For the first time, American culture began changing to meet the needs of the immigrants, rather than expecting the immigrants to assimilate. One result was a nativist backlash among some groups of non-Hispanic Americans, who called for increased border security and the deportation of immigrants who lacked proper documentation.

- **Climate change.** Scientists have become increasingly concerned that human activities, especially the burning of fossil fuels, are changing the climate of the planet. Anticipated changes include droughts, severe storms, and significant rises in sea level that will likely flood coastal areas. Opinion remains divided regarding the most effective response to these threats.

- **Overseas military operations.** After Arab terrorists attacked the United States on **September 11, 2001,** destroying the World Trade Center in New York and damaging the Pentagon in Washington, D.C., there was a violent breach in U.S.-Arab relations. U.S. troops attacked the fundamentalist Islamic group Al Qaeda and its local allies in Afghanistan, and in 2003, U.S. forces invaded Iraq and toppled its government. After an occupation marked by violence, the United States withdrew from Iraq in 2011. Fighting by U.S. forces continued against Al Qaeda forces in Afghanistan and in other Arab countries.

United States History

Directions: Choose the best answer to each of the following questions.

1. Which U.S. Constitutional amendment gave women the right to vote?

   A. Nineteenth
   B. Twentieth
   C. Twenty-first
   D. Twenty-second

Question 2 is based on the following timeline.

1808	1809	1810	1812	1814	1816	1817	1818
U.S. abolishes slave trade.	James Madison becomes President; Abraham Lincoln born.	Population of the U.S. is 7,239,881.	Louisiana becomes the 18th state; U.S. declares war on Britain.	British forces burn Washington, D.C.; Francis Scott Key writes the poem "The Star Spangled Banner," which becomes the national anthem.	Indiana becomes the 19th state.	Mississippi becomes the 20th state; James Monroe becomes the 5th President.	Congress adopts a U.S. flag with 13 red and white stripes and a white star for each state; Illinois becomes the 21st state.

2. Place an X beside each conclusion that can be drawn by the timeline.

   _____ James Madison was against the slave trade.

   _____ James Monroe was the fifth President of the United States.

   _____ The United States declared war on Great Britain in 1812.

   _____ Abraham Lincoln encouraged Illinois to join the United States as a free state.

   _____ Lyrics to the national anthem were written by Frances Scott Key.

PRACTICE

Question 3 is based on the following table.

Estimated Population of the Middle Colonies, 1630–1780 (in thousands)

Year	Delaware	New Jersey	New York	Pennsylvania	Total
1630			0.4		0.4
1640			1.9		1.9
1650	0.2		4.1		4.4
1660	0.5		4.9		5.5
1670	0.7	1.0	5.8		7.4
1680	1.0	3.4	9.8	0.7	14.9
1690	1.5	8.0	13.9	11.4	34.8
1700	2.5	14.0	19.1	18.0	53.5
1710	3.6	19.9	21.6	24.4	69.6
1720	5.4	28.8	36.9	31.0	103.1
1730	9.2	37.5	48.6	51.7	147.0
1740	19.9	51.4	63.7	85.6	220.5
1750	28.7	71.4	76.7	119.7	296.5
1760	33.2	93.8	117.1	183.7	427.9
1770	35.5	117.4	162.9	240.1	555.9
1780	45.4	139.6	210.5	327.3	722.9

3. Which colony had the largest population in 1720?

A. New Jersey
B. New York
C. Pennsylvania
D. Delaware

Question 4 is based on the following passage.

Perhaps the sentiments contained in the following pages, are not yet sufficiently fashionable to procure them general favor; a long habit of not thinking a thing wrong, gives it a superficial appearance of being right, and raises at first a formidable outcry in defence of custom. But the tumult soon subsides. Time makes more converts than reason.

—*Excerpt from "Common Sense" by Thomas Paine (1776)*

4. Which statement best reflects the ideas Paine included in this introduction? He believed that people

   A. would never read or understand his statements and reasoning.
   B. would always think that the ideas shared in the text were wrong.
   C. who are sufficiently fashionable have a habit of correct thinking.
   D. may not have been ready to hear the information he would share in the text.

5. Place an X next to countries that were Axis Powers in World War II.

   _____ United States

   _____ Japan

   _____ Germany

   _____ Great Britain

Question 6 is based on the following map.

The Columbian Exchange

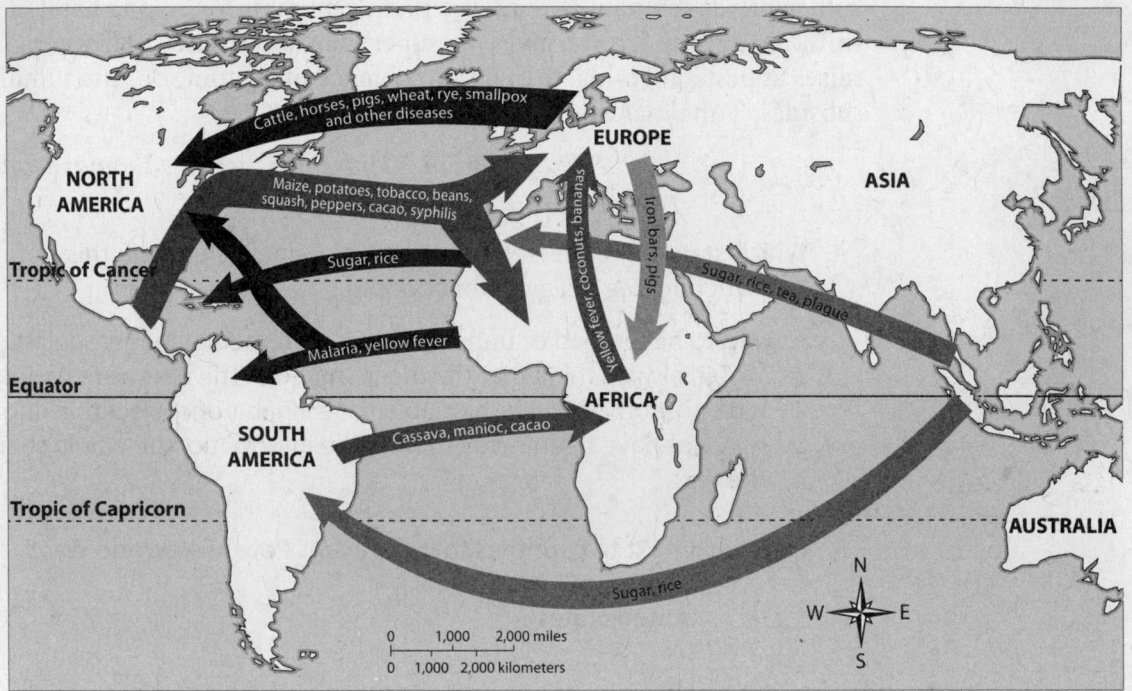

6. The "Columbian Exchange" refers to a time beginning with Columbus's voyage in 1492 and extending through the years of discovery. During this time, plants, animals, diseases, and technology were exchanged between the Old and New Worlds, changing the ways of life for both Europeans and Native Americans. Based on the map, which statement is true?

A. Pigs were transported to Europe from Africa.
B. Smallpox was carried from Europe to North America.
C. Tobacco was shipped from Africa to North America.
D. Plague was carried from North America to Asia.

PRACTICE

Question 7 is based on the following map.

Events in the War of 1812

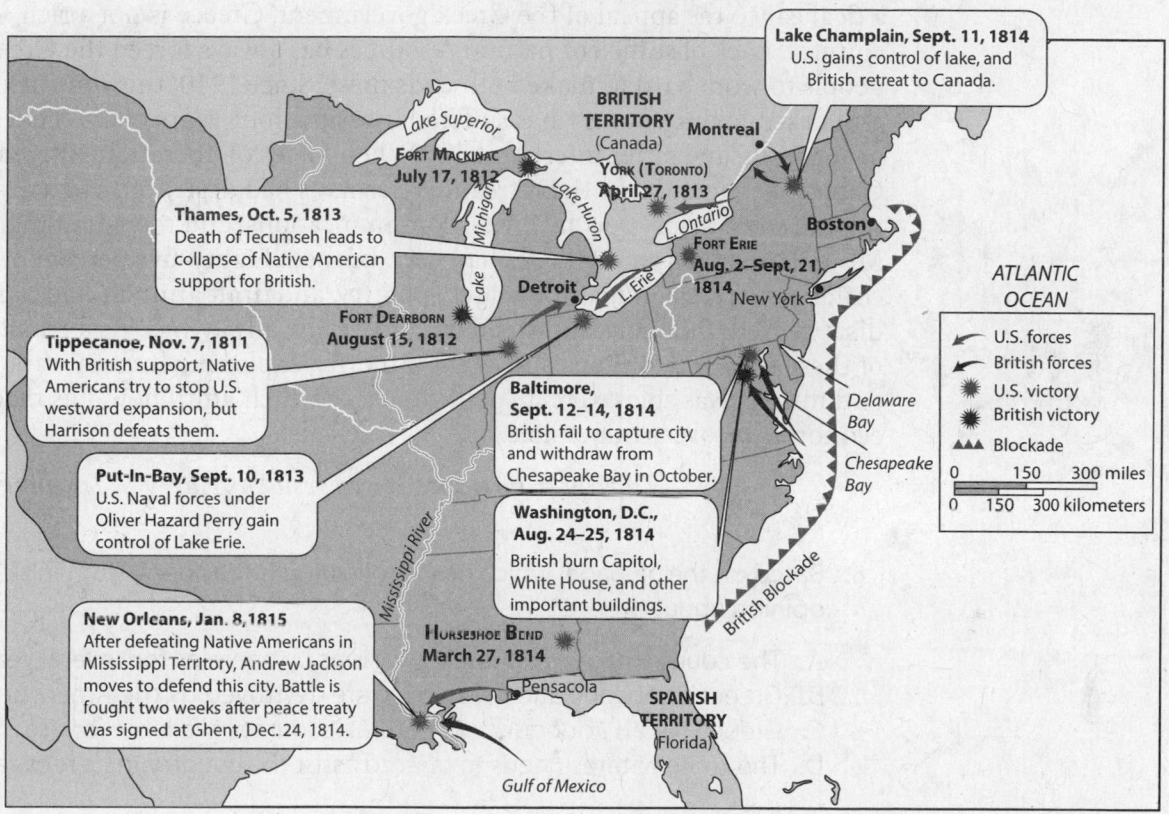

7. The map shows some events that occurred during the War of 1812. According to the map, which battle was won by Andrew Jackson?

A. The Battle of Tippecanoe
B. The Battle of Fort Dearborn
C. The Battle of New Orleans
D. The Battle of Fort Erie

Question 8 is based on the following passage.

I do not believe that the American people and the Congress wish to turn a deaf ear to the appeal of the Greek government. Greece is not a rich country. Lack of sufficient natural resources has always forced the Greek people to work hard to make both ends meet. Since 1940, this industrious and peace-loving country has suffered invasion, four years of cruel enemy occupation, and bitter internal strife. When forces of liberation entered Greece they found that the retreating Germans had destroyed virtually all the railways, roads, port facilities, communications, and merchant marine. More than a thousand villages had been burned. Eighty-five percent of the children were tubercular. Livestock, poultry, and draft animals had almost disappeared. Inflation had wiped out practically all savings. As a result of these tragic conditions, a militant minority, exploiting human want and misery, was able to create political chaos which, until now, has made economic recovery impossible.

—*Excerpt from a speech by President Harry S. Truman (1947)*

8. Based on the passage, which of the following is President Truman's opinion about Greece?

   A. The country has not suffered invasions by enemies for several years.
   B. Greece's transportation systems were destroyed by the Americans.
   C. Greece has an abundance of natural resources available for use.
   D. The United States needs to offer to assist the country in its recovery.

9. Which President of the United States is best known for programs to eliminate poverty?

   A. George W. Bush
   B. Ronald Reagan
   C. Richard M. Nixon
   D. Lyndon B. Johnson

10. Before the Civil War, which section of the United States was the most industrialized?

   A. Northeast
   B. Southwest
   C. Midwest
   D. Southeast

Answers are on page 833.

CHAPTER 3

World History

The Earliest Civilizations

A **civilization** is more than a group of people; it represents the next step toward social organization. In a civilization, people organize governments and social classes, establish writing systems, build cities, create works of art, study science and mathematics, and invent new ways of doing things.

To sustain human life, two things are required: a **temperate** climate and ready sources of food and fresh water. Under the right conditions, this leads to a surplus of food and thus an increase in health, life span, and income. With extra resources and more spare time, people turn to pursuits beyond the hunting and gathering of food—they create civilizations. All the early human civilizations have left us written records, scientific discoveries, beautiful art objects, and works of architecture that go well beyond simple shelters from the weather.

Human beings began to organize themselves into civilizations around 3500 BCE (Before the Common Era). The **Fertile Crescent** (present-day Iraq, Syria, and Egypt) was home to the early civilizations. This period of human civilization is called the **Bronze Age** for the copper-tin alloy people discovered around 3000 BCE. Bronze produced stronger and sturdier tools and weapons than copper alone.

Mesopotamia (present-day Iraq) gave the world its first written language, its first organized religion, the basics of modern mathematics, the wheel (used first for making pottery, then for transportation), and the first literary epic (*The Descent of Inana*). The first city-states were created in southern Mesopotamia by a people called the Sumerians. Archaeologists have unearthed many luxury objects at Sumerian sites, including musical instruments, game boards, and jewelry. These artifacts allow us to conclude the existence of a wealthy class of Sumerians: only the wealthy can purchase luxury items. The objects' fine quality shows that the Sumerians were skilled artisans. The use of metal in a region where no metal exists proves that the Sumerians traded with other civilizations (probably in the Indus Valley in present-day Pakistan).

The Babylonian Empire came into being around 2000 BCE. Babylonians could plot the fixed stars, follow the course of the sun, and predict lunar eclipses. Their mathematicians were the first to use the number 60 as a base for measuring circles, spheres, and time; we use that system today. Babylonian law codes, such as the Code of Hammurabi, show that in ancient times, people valued the concept of abstract justice and believed in punishing criminals. Another great civilization arose at the same time in the Nile River valley in Egypt. The Great Pyramids of Egypt prove that the Egyptians were able not only to design monumental buildings, but also to plan and carry out their construction—a remarkable engineering feat in an era with no technology beyond the wheel and the lever. Less is known about the Indus Valley Civilization in present-day Pakistan because historians have not yet been able to decipher its written records. However, this civilization did leave behind planned cities with impressive works of architecture and sophisticated drainage systems.

EXERCISE 1

The Earliest Civilizations

Directions: Choose the best answer to each of the following questions.

1. Based on the information above, which of the following statements is NOT true?

   A. The earliest known civilizations arose in what is now the Middle East.
   B. The written records of the ancient Indus Valley people remain a mystery to this day.
   C. Babylonian mathematicians established systems and conventions that we still use today.
   D. Early civilizations discovered that using copper for tools was better than using bronze.

2. Based on the information above, which of the following statements is an opinion, not a fact?

   A. Some Sumerians must have been wealthy, considering the luxurious items found by archaeologists.
   B. Archaeologists have found clear evidence that Sumerians traded with other ancient civilizations.
   C. The Sumerians had a clear understanding of basic mathematics.
   D. A Sumerian writer created the first known work of literary fiction, *The Descent of Inana*.

Answers are on page 833.

Early China

China has existed as a culturally unified entity since at least 1000 BCE; aspects of Chinese culture that may date back even further include the domestication of silkworms, the production of ceramic and jade objects, and the use of chopsticks. The classical Chinese written language, originating well before 1000 BCE, served as an important unifying force in ancient Chinese kingdoms; although different dialects were spoken in different regions, written Chinese was the same everywhere.

The early Chinese settlements were located along the rivers—the highways of the ancient world. China was isolated from the Fertile Crescent not only by distance, but by obstacles such as deserts and mountain ranges. There is no evidence that ancient China and the ancient Near East had any knowledge of one another.

K'ung-fu-tzu, known in the West as Confucius, became as influential in Chinese thought and culture as Jesus would later become in the West. Born in the sixth century BCE into the minor nobility, Confucius became a teacher and a scholar. Confucius supported the established order of society, in which everyone had a place. If each person knew and kept his place, did his duty, and respected tradition, society would function smoothly. By the same token, personal integrity would guarantee a wise and just use of authority.

Under the Han dynasty (206 BCE–AD 220) China achieved a free-market economy, the invention of paper, a universal law code, and a merit-based bureaucracy. This period also saw the establishment of the **Silk Road**, a major overland trade route from Luoyang in the east all the way to Constantinople and Alexandria in the west. Horses from Iran, luxury objects from Rome, silks from China, spices and cotton from India, and stories and ideas from all cultures were traded along the Silk Road.

EXERCISE 2

Early China

Directions: Choose the best answer to each of the following questions.

1. Before the establishment of the Silk Road, the peoples of the Fertile Crescent and China

    A. shared a common language and religion.
    B. were unable to domesticate horses.
    C. were unaware of each other's existence.
    D. made war on each other repeatedly.

2. Based on the information above, which of the following existed in China as early as 1000 BCE?

    A. wine
    B. diamond jewelry
    C. steel
    D. chopsticks

Answers are on page 833.

Early India

Geography played a major role in the isolation of ancient India. The Himalayas, which include some of the world's tallest mountains, blocked access from the north; the other two sides of the triangular peninsula border on the Indian Ocean. This unique geographical location ensured that India could be invaded only from the northwest, through present-day Pakistan.

The Aryans, Eastern Europeans who invaded and settled in Persia and the Indus Valley around 1500 BCE, had a lasting influence on Indian culture. Historians believe that **Hinduism** is a mix of Indian and Aryan ideas and beliefs. Hinduism links a religious belief in sacrifice with a caste system based on duty to others; it continues to hold sway over present-day India.

Siddhartha Gautama, born into the nobility in 563 BCE, is known to history as the Buddha (the title means "Enlightened One"). The Buddha taught that since all suffering and conflict in the world came from frustrated ambition, passion, or egotism, the elimination of these emotions would lead to contentment and spiritual peace. **Buddhism** also opposed the caste system. Today, Buddhism has its greatest influence in China, not India.

EXERCISE 3

Early India

Directions: Choose the best answer to the following question.

1. Based on the information above, it can be assumed that

   A. Himalayan mountain passes made easy routes for invaders.
   B. the caste system, which still influences Indian society, has existed for centuries.
   C. the Buddha fought the caste system by becoming a powerful and wealthy emperor.
   D. the Aryans entered India from the east by traveling from Mongolia through Nepal.

The answer is on page 833.

Classical Greece

The beginning of an identifiable Greek culture goes back to 2000 BCE and the arrival of the Achaeans from the present-day Balkan region of southeastern Europe. The peninsular and island culture of Greece meant a close relationship with the sea; trading was done by boat, and the navies of the Greek states became the strongest and best of the era.

The Greek idea of abstract **philosophy**—that people could use their reasoning powers to understand the workings of the universe—is Greece's most important contribution to the development of Western culture. During the Greek Classical Age (roughly 750–400 BCE), the Greeks created the basis of Western art, architecture, literature, science, philosophy, and government.

At a time when the world was ruled by the principle of the divine right of emperors, some of the Greek city-states featured a new form of government called **democracy**. This was not democracy as we understand it today; neither slaves nor free women had many legal rights or freedoms, and only men in positions of power (about 10 percent of the total population) could vote. Still, the government did give some of its citizens some say in the laws they had to live by. This principle of government by the consent of the governed would eventually hold sway throughout the Western world.

The northern Greek kingdom of Macedonia took over the Greek civilization under Philip II and his son and successor Alexander the Great. During the 4th century BCE, Alexander's wars of conquest spread Greek culture, language, and customs all the way from the Danube River in Europe to the Indus River in India.

EXERCISE 4

Classical Greece

Directions: Choose the best answer to each of the following questions.

1. Based on the information above, you can assume that

   A. the Roman emperors modeled their laws on those of Greek emperors.
   B. Greek navies were superior to all others in the ancient world.
   C. Alexander the Great tried to conquer China but failed to do so.
   D. democracy ended in Greece because of slave revolts.

2. What claim about philosophy is supported by the information above?

   A. The philosophers of ancient Greece continue to be read and studied.
   B. The word *philosophy* comes from *philo*, meaning love, and *sophia*, meaning wisdom.
   C. Alexander the Great was an avid student of philosophers such as Socrates.
   D. The ancient Greek language used in philosophical texts is no longer understood.

Answers are on page 833.

Rome

The Roman Empire (500 BCE–AD 476) was the largest and most impressive political achievement of the ancient world. With the aid of its bureaucracy and army, Rome brought all the Western civilizations together into a unified whole that allowed each individual culture to flourish. The phrase "Western Civilization" refers to the Greco-Roman heritage—the history, culture, and understanding of the world common to all Western nations that were part of the Roman Empire or influenced by it.

The key to the Roman Empire's success and longevity was tolerance. Roman rulers allowed diversity to flourish, requiring only three things: obedience to the Roman law code, payment of taxes, and loyalty to the Roman state. Worship of the Roman gods was mandatory, but the people might also worship any other gods they pleased.

Romans adopted elements of mythology, religion, and culture from the Greeks and the Etruscans (an earlier Italian people). Rome's most important original achievements were in law, government, and engineering. Latin, the Roman language, would be the common language of all educated Westerners for well over 1000 years after the Empire fell. Rome began as a monarchy, but in 509 BCE a republic was established. Both **patricians** (aristocrats) and **plebeians** (commoners) were represented in the Senate, and the plebeians' representatives had veto power over those of the patricians. By 100 BCE the republic had become a dictatorship, but the institution of the Senate endured.

Christianity came into existence under the Roman Empire as a new sect of **Judaism**, the ancient religion of the Hebrews. Judaism was revolutionary for two things: its followers worshipped only one god instead of many, and its moral code (the Ten Commandments) applied to all people, from monarchs to slaves. This defied the common ancient belief that monarchs were divine and not to be questioned.

Christians and Jews worship the same god, but Christians believe that Jesus of Nazareth was the son of God, the Messiah or Christ (both words mean "anointed one") whose appearance on earth was foretold in the Hebrew Bible. After Jesus' execution, his most influential follower, Paul, preached his message of universal love and eternal salvation through the eastern half of the Roman Empire. To make Christianity appeal to his culturally Greek audience, Paul blended Hebrew beliefs with elements of Hellenistic culture and religion, such as the abstract philosophy of the Trinity. Christianity spread rapidly across the Roman Empire, and would hold sway throughout Western Europe for centuries to come.

By the 4th century AD, the Roman Empire had become too large to govern effectively from one city; it split into two halves, with the eastern half eventually breaking away altogether as the Byzantine Empire, governed from Constantinople (founded AD 330). Disagreements over dogma split the Christian religion; Rome became the seat of Roman Catholicism, while Constantinople became the seat of Eastern Orthodoxy. Rome was culturally Latin while Constantinople was culturally Greek—another reason for the division. Finally, the Roman Empire was mired in economic troubles and faced serious threats of invasion from the north.

EXERCISE 5

Rome

Directions: Choose the best answer to each of the following questions.

Questions 1 and 2 are based on the following map.

The Roman Empire: Expansion to 133 BCE

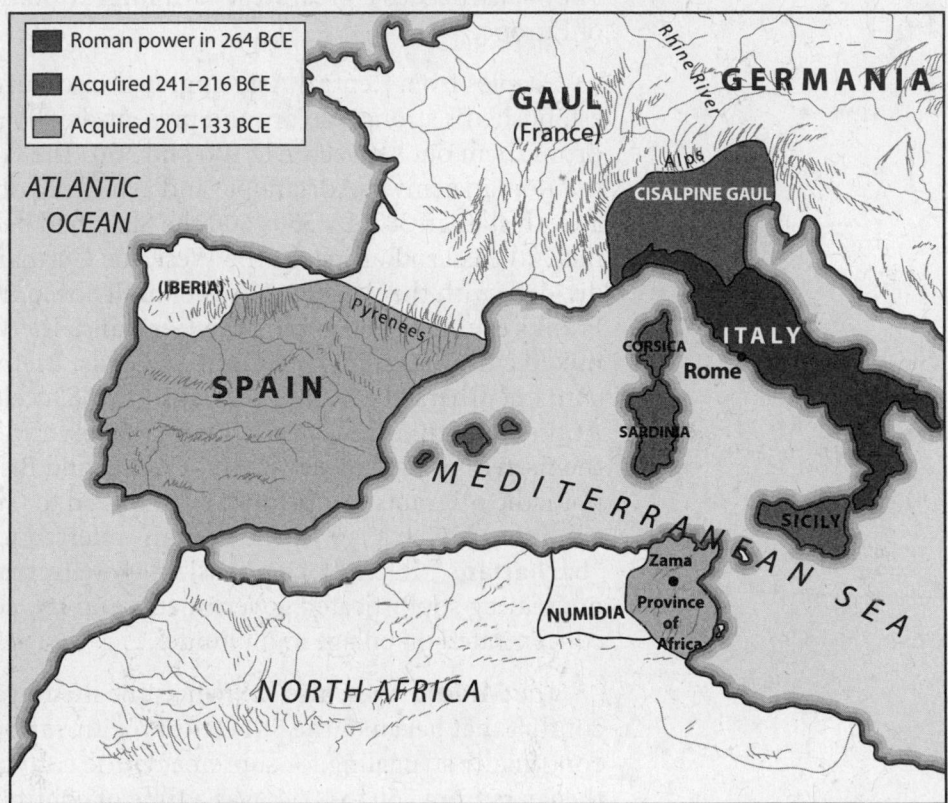

1. During which time period did the Roman Empire expand to include Spain?

   A. before 264 BCE
   B. 241–218 BCE
   C. 201–133 BCE
   D. after 133 BCE

2. Which statement is true?

   A. By 133 BCE the Roman Empire included regions on two continents.
   B. The Roman Empire reached to the Atlantic Ocean by 264 BCE.
   C. Britain was acquired by the Roman Empire in 133 BCE.
   D. Gaul was acquired by the Roman Empire before 264 BCE.

Answers are on page 833.

The Great Migration and the Middle Ages

From the 6th millennium BCE, people had inhabited the **steppes** of Central Asia—bleak grasslands bordered by the Ural Mountains and the Gobi desert. Small tribes of people roamed the harsh terrain, following the herds on which they depended for milk and meat. By mastering horses and learning to work with iron—they were the first people to make wheels with spokes—the Central Asian tribes became formidable bands of warriors. They spearheaded a great westward **migration** that ended in the settlement of Europe.

Peoples from Central Asia migrated into Europe in waves. The Goths established a stronghold around present-day Poland and Hungary; the Huns drove them out between AD 100 and 300. The Goths moved south, defeating the Roman army at Adrianople and achieving official Roman recognition of a Goth state in 382. By 550–600 the Slavs had become the dominant culture in southeastern Europe. In the West, the Germanic tribe of the Franks divided, with the West Franks eventually becoming the French and the East Franks eventually becoming the Germans. The West Franks dominated a mixed culture that included Roman Gauls, Bretons, Belges, Vikings, and a mix of others; the East Franks absorbed Slav elements into their culture. At the same time, the Sueves, Burgundians, and Anglo-Saxons established themselves in present-day Spain, France, and Britain. The culture of these nomadic migrants was primitive compared to Greco-Roman Classical civilization, which is why the Romans referred to all the Northern peoples as "**barbarians**." Instead of emphasizing intellectual and artistic achievement or creating sophisticated governments and law codes, the Northern tribes concentrated on pillage and plunder.

The **Middle Ages**, also known as the **medieval** period, was an era of conflict that began in the 5th century with various migrating peoples continually struggling for supremacy. The early medieval period, especially the years from 750 to 1054, was a time of continual raids on France, Britain, and Eastern Europe by Viking tribes from Scandinavia. In the same period, Vikings traveling through what is now Russia founded the cities of Kiev and Novgorod; the local Muscovy princes would later absorb these states into the expanding Russian empire. After the Christian conversion of Vladimir I in 988, Kiev became culturally more Slavic and Byzantine. To meet the threat of the Viking invaders, the local Slavs began reorganizing themselves along Viking-style political lines; this led to greater social organization and thence to true civilization rather than tribal culture.

EXERCISE 6

The Great Migration and the Middle Ages

Directions: Choose the best answer to each of the following questions.

1. Which of the following tribes of nomadic migrants became part of West Frank culture?

   A. Sueves
   B. Burgundians
   C. Bretons
   D. Slavs

2. Viking tribes traveled through many parts of Europe, including areas in which of the following modern-day countries?

   A. Spain
   B. Portugal
   C. Greece
   D. Russia

Answers are on page 833.

Feudalism

The feudal system developed during this early **medieval** era—not only in Europe, but also in India, China, and Japan. The social contract between classes was based on an oath of loyalty, which people of this era considered legally binding. The monarch provided warriors with vast land grants and noble titles in exchange for their loyal military service. The warrior thus became the **lord** of a large estate—the ruler of his own small feudal realm, in which he protected and housed his **vassals** in exchange for their military service, loyalty, and obedience. The "lord" of the estate might even be a lady; very few medieval women were warriors (there were rare exceptions even to this rule, such as Joan of Arc), but some women achieved positions of great power through marriage or widowhood.

The monarch and the lords worked out an uneasy balance of power. The monarch wanted to control the realm and command the obedience of all his subjects, but the lords held so much independent power on their estates that they might easily defy the monarch, even though they agreed that the monarch ruled by divine right. The **Magna Carta** is an example of what could happen when the lords united against the monarch. King

John of England had such a disgraceful record of bad administration and unwise rule that in 1215, the lords forced him to sign the Magna Carta, which specifically stated that even the monarch was not above the law, and laid the foundations for the parliamentary system that England would eventually adopt.

EXERCISE 7

Feudalism

Directions: Choose the best answer to each of the following questions.

1. Feudal vassals were given housing and farmland by lords in exchange for

   A. military service and obedience.
   B. a promise of marriage.
   C. giving up one child for slavery.
   D. taxes on sales at the local market.

2. King John of England signed the Magna Carta following disputes with

   A. the king of France.
   B. English lords.
   C. English commoners.
   D. French knights.

Answers are on page 834.

The Middle East and Africa

Islam, the religion that would eventually unify the entire Near East, was founded in the early 7th century in Arabia. Muslims worship the same god as Jews and Christians; Allah is simply the Arabic name for him. Muslims regard Jesus as a great prophet, but secondary to Islam's founder, Muhammad. Islam is based on the Five Pillars: faith, prayer, alms, fasting, and pilgrimage to Mecca.

By the end of the 10th century, Islam had taken firm hold on a sizeable region of the world. Muhammad was not only the founder of a major world religion; he was also an extraordinary political leader who unified all the Arab tribes under one central government for the first time in their history. Muslim armies conquered an empire that was highly diverse, embracing Turkish, Persian, and North African cultural and artistic traditions. The Muslims even penetrated Europe as far as northern Spain; they would remain in power on the Iberian Peninsula for the better part of 800 years.

Starting in the 15th century, much of the Middle East was controlled by Ottoman Turkish rulers based in Constantinople. Under the Ottomans, the Islamic world reached a zenith of cultural, literary, and artistic achievement—but soon lagged behind the West, partly due to its inability or refusal to embrace new scientific methods. While Europeans devised their first printing press in 1455, the Arab peoples did not acquire this technology until 1727. At a time when a pendulum clock was an ordinary household object in Europe, it was a curiosity and a rare luxury in India. Beginning around the mid-1700s, the Ottoman Empire steadily lost power and influence; the Islamic world would not play a significant power role in international politics again until the 1970s.

The major African civilizations of the first millennium included Nubia, located on the Nile River in what is now Sudan and southern Egypt, and Axum, located in what is now northern Ethiopia. The kingdom of Ghana, on the coast of West Africa, prospered from about 830 to 1235. It traded extensively by camel caravan with the countries north of the Sahara desert, providing them with gold, ivory, and salt. Foreign invasion, religious conversion, and international trade are the major themes of these civilizations.

The Middle East and Africa

Directions: Choose the best answer to each of the following questions.

1. Which statement is supported by the information above?

   A. The Muslim empire required its Persian, Turkish, and North African subjects to abandon their native cultures.
   B. The African kingdom of Ghana had little contact with the outside world.
   C. The kingdom of Nubia was located in what is now northern Ethiopia.
   D. The Ottoman Empire lasted from the 15th century into the 20th century.

2. According to the text, which of the following statements is an opinion, not a fact?

   A. Muslim rulers governed Spain for hundreds of years.
   B. The Ottoman Empire grew steadily weaker after the mid-1700s.
   C. The kingdom of Nubia was the greatest of the ancient African civilizations.
   D. Muslim armies conquered Persia, Turkey, and much of North Africa.

Answers are on page 834.

Civilizations in the Americas

Native Americans created numerous civilizations throughout the Americas. In North America, hundreds of different peoples developed ways of life that were well adapted to the continent's different environments. Their settlements were often linked by long-distance trade networks. In the eastern forests, people lived in villages and lived by hunting, fishing, and farming based on growing maize (corn). In the Great Plains, people followed a nomadic lifestyle and survived by hunting bison and other animals. In the desert southwest, Native Americans built towns and practiced agriculture, often by irrigation.

To the south, Native American people created advanced civilizations and established empires. The Maya dominated Central America and built stone cities with large temples before AD 900. They developed a complex writing system and an accurate calendar. Later the Aztecs conquered a large empire in what is now Mexico and built their capital city where Mexico City is located today.

Farther south, in the Andes Mountains of South America, the Inca created an empire that lasted until the early 1500s. The Inca built large cities and developed an efficient administration system to make their empire run smoothly. The Aztec and the Inca civilizations flourished until their conquest by the Spanish in the early 16th century.

EXERCISE 9

Civilizations in the Americas

Directions: Choose the best answer to the following question.

1. Based on the information above, you can infer that
   A. the Maya kept careful track of days and years.
   B. Native American tribes in North America had little contact with each other.
   C. no Native Americans ever lived in large cities.
   D. native peoples in Central America failed to develop a writing system.

The answer is on page 834.

Renaissance and Reformation in Europe

Two important factors made the **Renaissance**, a cultural movement that began in Italy around 1350, a great turning point in Western history. One was a resurgence of interest in Classical philosophy, literature, and art. The second was a sharp rise in literacy—the effect of the development of moveable type and the printing press.

The Koreans invented movable type; it was modified in Germany and ended up having a much greater effect in the West than in Korea and China. With books readily available, people could read on their own instead of simply trusting what the learned authorities told them.

The religious movement called the **Reformation** began in 1517 with the founding of the Lutheran Church. By 1600, thousands of Europeans—particularly Northern Europeans—were worshipping in Lutheran, Calvinist, and Anglican churches. The success of **Protestantism** (it gets its name because its believers *protested* against Catholic doctrine) had multiple causes: a growing realization that the Catholic Church was neither all-powerful nor morally above reproach, a rise in secular political power, and the perfection of the printing process. People could now read the Bible (and all other books) for themselves; they no longer had to accept the Church's interpretation of Scripture.

EXERCISE 10

Renaissance and Reformation in Europe

Directions: Choose the best answer to each of the following questions.

1. Based on the text, which of the following statements is true?

   A. Protestantism was the result of protests against the Lutheran Church.
   B. The concept of movable type, or the printing press, was not invented in Europe.
   C. The Renaissance began in Korea and China before spreading to Western Europe.
   D. Calvinists thought that only church officials should be permitted to read.

2. Based on the information above, it can be inferred that

   A. Lutherans, Calvinists, and Anglicans do not agree on Christian dogma.
   B. the Catholic Church was opposed to Classical literature and art.
   C. the sharp rise in literacy in Europe had a profound effect on history.
   D. people in southern Europe were predominantly Muslim.

Answers are on page 834.

The Scientific Revolution, the Enlightenment, and the Industrial Revolution

The **Scientific Revolution** was a time of great progress in human understanding of the laws of the universe. This era changed not only *what* people thought but, more important, *how* they thought. The discoveries of the Scientific Revolution (such as the moons of Jupiter and the paths of the planets around the sun) were the product of practical experimentation rather than abstract philosophy.

The *philosophes* (French for *philosophers*) of the 18th-century **Enlightenment** applied this scientific process of critical thinking to social and political problems. They argued that all people were born free and equal and that individuals should be able to make their way in the world as reasonable beings as to how they wished to live. Their works encouraged people to believe that they did not have to accept existing conditions and that they could create new institutions to their own liking. In the end, Enlightenment teachings led directly to major revolutions in British North America and in France.

Later on in the 18th and 19th centuries, the **Industrial Revolution** demonstrated a third way of using the process of observation and experimentation: by applying it to the mechanical challenges of manufacturing and agriculture. New machines appeared with bewildering rapidity, permanently altering the pace of human life and shifting the Western economy from a basis in agriculture to a basis in mass production.

EXERCISE 11

The Scientific Revolution, the Enlightenment, and the Industrial Revolution

Directions: Choose the best answer to each of the following questions.

1. The *philosophes* of the Enlightenment applied what process to social and political problems?

   A. resource management, like that used in agriculture
   B. mass production, like that used in manufacturing
   C. critical thinking, like that used in science
   D. cataloguing, like that used in libraries

2. The progress and discoveries of the Scientific Revolution were based on

   A. the opinions of French aristocrats.
   B. the machines of the Industrial Revolution.
   C. practical experimentation rather than abstract philosophy.
   D. the migration of workers form rural areas to big cities.

Answers are on page 834.

The Age of Exploration

At the end of the 1400s, European monarchs began sponsoring voyages of exploration beyond the world they knew. Their purposes were fourfold: trade, conquest and expansion, religious conversion, and curiosity.

- **Trade.** The **natural resources** of the colonized regions—Asia, Africa, and the Americas—included such non-European items as rice, coffee, sugar, rubber, silk, cotton, gold, diamonds, and spices. West Africa was also the source of slave labor throughout the 18th century. Colonization meant that Europeans could set their own prices for what they bought from the colonies and what they sold to them.

- **Conquest, expansion, and profit.** A larger population meant more revenue for the crown in taxes, more income for the churches in tithes, and more soldiers in the army. Therefore three of the most powerful branches of society—the court, the clergy, and the military—were united in the desire to explore the seas and lands beyond Europe in the hope of establishing colonies that would make them richer and stronger than their neighbors.

- **Religious conversion.** The third motive, religious conversion, was a product of the universal Christian belief that it was a Christian's duty to convert non-Christians and thus save their souls.

- **Curiosity.** The last motive, and a very powerful one, was the universal human sense of adventure and curiosity—the drive to find out things that has characterized human beings since the beginning of civilization.

EXERCISE 12

The Age of Exploration

Directions: Choose the best answer to each of the following questions.

1. Which of the following was NOT a motive of explorers in the Age of Exploration?

    A. conquest
    B. religious conversion
    C. curiosity
    D. hostility

2. True or False? Religious conversion was a key objective in the Age of Exploration because Christian explorers thought it was their duty to convert non-Christians to Christianity.

Answers are on page 834.

Building Empires

Nations become empires in two ways—either by swallowing up adjoining land and thus expanding their borders or by seizing colonies some distance away. Rome, China, India, Russia, and the United States are examples of the first type of empire (the United States would acquire a few offshore colonies at the turn of the 20th century). Spain, France, Prussia (later Germany), and Britain are examples of the second.

The European powers colonized the entire continent of Africa (except Ethiopia and Liberia), and all the Southeast Asian kingdoms except Siam (present-day Thailand). These colonies could not match the military might of the invaders, so they had to accept foreign rule.

Spain colonized all of Mexico, Central America, most of South America except for Brazil, and the Philippines in Asia. It also conquered nearly one-third of the present-day United States. Portugal colonized Brazil as well as Angola, Mozambique, and Guinea-Bissau in Africa and Macau in Asia.

France colonized Vietnam, much of North and West Africa, Canada, the Great Lakes region, and the Louisiana Territory, which it later sold to the United States. French Canada was conquered by Britain. France and Britain fought over control of India; in 1850 Britain won the fight and would govern India until after World War II. Britain also held colonies in Africa and Asia and sent settlers to colonize Australia and New Zealand.

The European countries profited from the colonies by extracting natural resources such as gold, oil, metals, and timber. The colonies also served as protected markets for the goods manufactured in Europe. The age of colonization ended with World War II for two reasons; the European powers could no longer afford to maintain colonies, and the people who lived in the colonized countries began to rebel against foreign rule.

EXERCISE 13

Building Empires

Directions: Choose the best answer to the following question.

1. For each country or region in the following list, indicate which country colonized it by writing the name in the proper column in the table. Then indicate the column in the table where each statement belongs. (**Note**: On the real GED® test, you will click on the country name and "drag" it into position in the diagram.)

Spain	Portugal	Britain	France

Central America	Macau	India
The Philippines	Mexico	Australia
Brazil	South America (except Brazil)	Mozambique
New Zealand	Vietnam	Louisiana Territory
Angola	Great Lakes Region	Guinea-Bissau

The answers are on page 834.

Revolutions in Britain and France

Between 1689 and 1789, the West saw three major political revolutions—one in England, one in America, and one in France.

In Great Britain, 50 years of violent conflict between Parliament and the absolutist monarchy led to the **Glorious Revolution**. In 1649, following defeat in battle, Charles I was captured by Parliamentary forces and executed for treason; after a brief military dictatorship under Oliver Cromwell, Charles's son Charles II was crowned in 1660. When Charles II died and his unpopular Catholic brother became king as James II, Parliament rebelled, inviting James's Protestant daughter Mary and her husband William of Orange (in Holland) to rule jointly. James II fled to France, and the Glorious Revolution was won without a shot being fired. The English Bill of Rights, passed by Parliament in 1689, ushered in a new era of individual rights and **constitutional monarchy**.

In the **French Revolution** of 1789, commoners rebelled against an absolute monarch and an overprivileged **aristocracy**. Unable to devise a viable republican government to replace the monarchy, France became a military **dictatorship** under Napoleon Bonaparte. His attempt to conquer all of Europe united all the other nations against France and ended in his defeat and exile. The French monarchy was restored, but with constitutional limits on the monarch's power.

EXERCISE 14

Revolutions in Britain and France

Directions: Choose the best answer to each of the following questions.

1. According to the information above, which of the following statements is true?

   A. William and Mary were childless and assumed that the monarchy would end with them.
   B. No actual battles were fought during the Glorious Revolution of 1688.
   C. The French Revolution was an uprising against the military dictatorship of Napoleon Bonaparte.
   D. James II of England fled to France in 1649 following the execution of his father Charles I.

2. The English and French revolutions both eventually led to what change in the powers of the monarch?

   A. Constitutional limits were placed on the monarch's powers.
   B. The monarch became a military dictator.
   C. All restrictions on the monarch's powers were removed.
   D. All of the monarch's powers were transferred to Parliament.

Answers are on page 834.

New Political Ideas in the 19th Century

Many new political forces came into being in the 19th century—**liberalism**, **socialism**, **nationalism**, **conservatism**, and **Marxism**. This table explains what each term means.

Political Philosophy	Definition/Description
Conservatism—the philosophy of those who looked back toward the era of absolute monarchy	Hereditary monarchy is the best form of government.
	Those of aristocratic birth should hold government office because they know best how to run the country.
	A hereditary monarch and well-born ministers of state will keep their end of the social contract—they will act in the best interests of their people.
	The social and political arrangements created by history are the best ones; tampering with them is perilous.
	A free press is dangerous; the government is the best judge of what should be published.
Liberalism—the philosophy of those who looked ahead toward an age of constitutional government, legal rights, and free enterprise	A limited monarchy with a freely elected legislative assembly and a written constitution is the best form of government.
	Voting rights should be limited to property owners because they are generally better educated and have a greater stake in the government.
	Educated, qualified people of merit, regardless of their birth, should hold government office.
	Citizens should have individual rights such as private property and freedom of speech.
Socialism—the belief that government control of the economy can reduce or eradicate social injustice	The good of the whole people is more important than the rights of the individual.
	What benefits one citizen benefits all citizens; therefore all citizens should cooperate with and help one another.
	The government should control business and industry and regulate wages and prices in order to promote economic and social justice and equality.
Marxism—the philosophy developed by Karl Marx and Friedrich Engels; states that the working class should take power through an international revolution	Social classes are inherently enemies, opposed to one another's interests.
	The worker is a far more valuable member of society than the owner because the worker produces goods while the owner produces nothing.
	Workers, not owners or managers, should enjoy the greatest share of the profits of their labor.
	Workers should themselves run the industries in which they work.

Political Philosophy	Definition/Description
Nationalism—pride in one's ethnic, cultural, and linguistic heritage and support for the interests of the nation in world affairs	A nation should be composed of people who share the same linguistic, ethnic, and cultural heritage. People who do not share that heritage may not be considered part of the nation. Generally a unifying force in a culturally homogenous nation such as France. Generally a divisive, explosive force in a multiethnic empire such as Austria-Hungary.

EXERCISE 15

New Political Ideas in the 19th Century

Directions: Choose the best answer to each of the following questions.

1. Which political philosophy holds that government should control business and regulate wages and prices?

   A. liberalism
   B. socialism
   C. nationalism
   D. conservatism

2. Nineteenth-century conservatives and liberals both supported monarchy, but they differed in regard to

   A. the right to strike.
   B. freedom of the press.
   C. pride in their country.
   D. government control of business.

Answers are on page 834.

Political Developments in 19th-Century Europe

Examples of constitutional governments in Great Britain, France, and the United States led to loud calls for written constitutions in many European nations. One wave of European revolutions took place in 1830 and another in 1848. In those revolutions, the forces of liberalism, which supported representative government, scored some victories—although conservative governments were still in power in several countries at the end of the century.

One of the most conservative was the Austro-Hungarian Empire, which included a diverse mix of Germans, Czechs, Hungarians, Croats, and Italians. **Nationalism**—pride in one's culture and language—made all these groups chafe at living in an empire instead of being independent. The growing strength of nationalism was a major factor in the unification of Italy in 1861 and of Germany in 1871. Nationalism in Ireland made the Irish restive under British rule and led to some reforms in Britain's Irish policy.

Nationalism also contributed to the decline and fall of the Ottoman Empire. Throughout the 10th century the Ottomans steadily lost territory and influence, until the Empire was eliminated altogether after World War I. In 1923 the Empire was transformed into Turkey, a secular Islamic republic.

In Russia, a rebellion in 1905 did not succeed in overthrowing the tsar, but it did lay the groundwork for the Revolution of 1917.

EXERCISE 16

Political Developments in 19th-Century Europe

Directions: Choose the best answer to each of the following questions.

1. Which statement is supported by the text?

   A. Ireland gained independence from Great Britain in 1871.
   B. The unification of Italy resulted from the revolutions of 1830.
   C. Nationalism divided Austria-Hungary, but it united the states that joined to form Italy and Germany.
   D. The Czechs and Croats were the most liberal groups in Austria-Hungary.

2. Which conclusion can be drawn about the Ottoman Empire?

   A. In the later 19th century, the Ottomans became close allies of the French.
   B. The armies of Europe were no match for the forces of the Ottoman Empire.
   C. The people of Turkey still refer to themselves as Ottomans.
   D. Throughout the 19th century the Ottoman Empire steadily lost territory and influence.

Answers are on page 834.

World War I and the Russian Revolution

World War I (called the **Great War** at the time, since no one anticipated World War II) happened primarily for two reasons. The first was nationalism: nationalist agitation among Serbs and other Slavs in Austria's Balkan provinces threatened the power of the Austro-Hungarian Empire, and German nationalism had led to a major buildup of the German military during the 1910s. The second reason for going to war was maintaining the European **balance of power**. The unification of Germany had created a large, strong, powerful nation-state whose ambitions caused grave concern to Britain, Russia, and especially France. Those three countries formed a defensive alliance. Germany allied itself with Austria-Hungary. When a Serb nationalist assassinated an Austrian archduke at Sarajevo in 1914, Austria declared war on Serbia, Russia mobilized to defend the Serbs, and the alliances went into action. Soon Britain, France, and Russia (the "Allies") were at war with Germany, Austria, and the Ottoman Empire (the "Central Powers").

The war wrecked the European economy; Russian farmers and workers were especially hard hit. Tsar Nicholas II was unable to take control and improve matters. Resentment against the tsar led to a popular uprising in 1917, and as a result Nicholas abdicated. After a chaotic power struggle, control of the government passed to the leftist Bolshevik Party led by V. I. Lenin. Lenin signed a peace treaty with Germany, withdrew Russian troops from the war, and began to convert the newly renamed Soviet Union into a Communist dictatorship. Britain and France, dismayed by the abrupt withdrawal of a powerful ally, were heartened when the United States joined the war. The tide turned in the Allies' favor and Germany agreed to an armistice on November 11, 1918.

At the peace conference, the Allied leaders did three things to restore the balance of power in Europe. First, they partially redrew the map of Europe along nationalist lines, creating new states, expanding others, and breaking up the Austro-Hungarian Empire. Second, after making Germany accept responsibility for the war, they reduced Germany's strength by ordering the Germans to maintain the German Rhineland as a demilitarized zone, to pay enormous **reparations**, and to reduce the size of the German army and navy. Third, the Allied leaders created the **League of Nations** as an international forum for resolving conflicts and maintaining peace.

World War I and the Russian Revolution

Directions: Choose the best answer to each of the following questions.

1. Which event upset the European balance of power and led to World War I?

   A. the unification of Germany as a powerful, ambitious nation state
   B. revolution in Russia and its transformation into a Communist dictatorship
   C. the breakup of Austria-Hungary into separate nations
   D. the weakness of the Allies compared to the Central Powers

2. After the war, the Allies redrew the map of Europe in response to the wishes of

   A. the Central Powers.
   B. Russian Communists.
   C. European nationalists.
   D. the League of Nations.

3. At the peace conference, the Allies imposed harsh measures on Germany. You can infer that these measures were intended to

   A. stop Germany from joining the Soviet Union.
   B. prevent Germany from starting another war.
   C. encourage a revival of the German economy.
   D. keep the League of Nations from interfering in German affairs.

Answers are on page 834.

The Rise of Fascism

During the 1920s and 1930s, **fascist** governments arose in Italy, Germany, Spain, and Eastern Europe; by 1937, Japan was also under strict military rule, and Communist forces were on the rise in China.

Fascism was a political doctrine that promoted extreme nationalism as a way of achieving national unity and eliminating domestic social and economic strife. In this it differed from Communism, which in theory offered a new social order run by the working class, and fascists and Communists despised each other. In day-to-day practice, however, fascism and Communism often amounted to the same thing—absolute dictatorship of a police state, with only one political party that tolerated no opposition.

In Germany, the fascists, who were called National Socialists ("Nazis"), also implemented policies of racial persecution, particularly of Jews, whom they blamed for the country's economic and other ills. Social and political developments of the period gave rise to these dictatorships. The first was the rise of mass political parties. The second was dissension among liberals in government and parliaments and their helplessness to respond effectively when a massive economic depression struck in the 1930s. The third was the large class of World War I veterans who made an enthusiastic audience for nationalist rhetoric.

EXERCISE 18

The Rise of Fascism

Directions: Choose the best answer to each of the following questions.

1. According to the text, the rise of fascism in Germany was aided by

   A. the rejection of nationalism by all political parties.
   B. the growing strength of Communist parties in Asia.
   C. the government's failure to effectively combat economic depression.
   D. interference in German politics by outsiders.

2. German fascists used which of the following to attract supporters?

   A. alliance with the Communists
   B. strikes for higher wages
   C. promises to veterans that there would be no more wars
   D. extreme nationalism

Answers are on page 834.

World War II

World War II was a war of German aggression—a war fought partly to change the defeat of World War I into a victory and partly to take over Europe as Napoleon had temporarily succeeded in doing at the beginning of the 19th century.

World War II began in 1939 when Germany, after taking over Austria and Czechoslovakia, invaded Poland. France and Great Britain declared war, but Germany soon conquered the Netherlands, Belgium, and France and launched air attacks on Britain. After failing to conquer Britain, Germany began an invasion of the Soviet Union. Germany and its ally Italy (the "Axis" powers) maintained control of the war until late 1942. Their well-planned invasions succeeded more or less by surprise. The German troops were extremely effective, and Germany and Italy eventually controlled almost all of Europe and a sizable chunk of North Africa.

In the Pacific, Japan had invaded the Manchurian region of China and was seeking further conquests. It joined Germany and Italy in the Axis alliance, and when Japan attacked the United States at Pearl Harbor in Hawaii in 1941, Germany also declared war on the United States. Great Britain, the United States, and the Soviet Union then joined in a great alliance to defeat Germany, and their numerical and economic strength eventually turned the tide. Additionally, the distant American factories were well out of danger of being bombed or captured, so the Allied source of tanks and munitions never dried up.

During the time when Germany ruled most of Europe, the fascist Nazis implemented extreme racial persecution measures within the occupied countries. Approximately six million European Jews were forced into concentration camps and murdered—an event known as the **Holocaust**. Millions of other Europeans were also killed by the Nazis.

The war is accurately called a world war because of the extent of the fighting outside of Europe. After more than three years of fighting in the Pacific, Japan finally conceded defeat after it was attacked with nuclear weapons in 1945.

EXERCISE 19

World War II

Directions: Choose the best answer to each of the following questions.

1. Great Britain and France declared war on Germany in 1939 after Germany invaded

    A. Poland.
    B. Austria.
    C. France.
    D. the Netherlands.

Question 2 is based on the following passage.

> Yesterday, December 7, 1941—a date which will live in infamy—the United States of America was suddenly and deliberately attacked by naval and air forces of the Empire of Japan. The United States was at peace with that nation, and, at the solicitation of Japan, was still in conversation with its government and its emperor looking toward the maintenance of peace in the Pacific.
>
> —*Excerpt from the speech to Congress by President Franklin Roosevelt, requesting a declaration of war, December 8, 1941*

2. According to the speech, December 7, 1941, will "live in infamy" because

    A. the attack on Pearl Harbor had no effect on the United States.
    B. the United States was already at war with Germany in Europe.
    C. Japan had never before attacked another country.
    D. the attack on the United States was unprovoked, with no declaration of war.

Answers are on page 834.

The End of European Dominance and the Formation of the European Union

At the start of the 20th century, Europe was the world's most powerful region, controlling many parts of Asia and most of Africa. After 1945, the former European powers had no resources to spare for their colonial empires; all their energies and resources were concentrated on rebuilding. The postwar era therefore saw a wave of independence throughout all of Africa. It was not gained easily, peacefully, or overnight, and in some African nations it led to an era of harsh military rule, corruption, and violent social and political unrest.

India also finally broke free from British rule and was divided into two separate states: a Hindu India and an Islamic Pakistan. Millions of Indian Muslims immediately crossed the border into Pakistan, while Pakistani Hindus fled to India.

During the late 1950s, Western European nations began to profit from the experience of their wartime alliance; they realized they were stronger united than they were on their own, and that peaceful cooperation was better than wars of conquest. A European Economic Community was created, and this led to the formation of the **European Union (EU)** in 1991. EU nations are entirely independent and self-governing, but they share common foreign and security policies and they cooperate on matters of domestic policy and affairs of international justice. They have had a common currency, the euro, since 1999.

EXERCISE 20

The End of European Dominance and the Formation of the European Union

Directions: Choose the best answer to the following question.

Question 1 is based on the following timeline.

Countries Joining the European Union

1957	1973	1981	1986	1995	2004	2007	2013
Belgium	Denmark	Greece	Portugal	Austria	Cyprus	Bulgaria	Croatia
France	Ireland		Spain	Finland	Czech Republic	Romania	
Germany	United Kingdom (Great Britain)			Sweden	Estonia		
Italy					Hungary		
Luxembourg					Latvia		
Netherlands					Lithuania		
					Malta		
					Poland		
					Slovakia		
					Slovenia		

1. According to the timeline, how many countries joined the European Union in 2004?

   A. 3
   B. 6
   C. 8
   D. 10

The answer is on page 834.

The End of the Soviet Union

By 1945, the Soviet Union held total political sway over all of Eastern Europe. Puppet Communist governments under the control of Moscow existed in all these small Slavic nations except Yugoslavia, ruled by the fiercely independent Marshall Tito. Germany was divided into two nations, democratic West Germany and Communist East Germany. A political border nicknamed the **Iron Curtain** would exist between Western and Eastern Europe from the late 1940s until 1989. In the divided city of Berlin, the Iron Curtain became an actual concrete wall in 1961; the **Berlin Wall** would be the most powerful symbol of the Cold War. The Soviet Union did not hesitate to use brute force in suppressing popular uprisings and attempts at reform such as the **Prague Spring** of 1968.

Soviet Communism proved economically unfeasible, despite major Soviet victories in the "**space race**" with the United States. Each superpower tried to outdo the other in exploring the universe beyond Earth. After the death of dictator Joseph Stalin and a lengthy period of economic stagnation, a gradual thaw in Soviet policy eventually led to the end of the Cold War, successful political uprisings, and the coming of democratic government to Eastern Europe. The Berlin Wall was demolished in 1989, and the Soviet Union broke up into independent republics in 1991.

EXERCISE 21

The End of the Soviet Union

Directions: Choose the best answer to the following question.

1. Which of the following contributed to the collapse of the Soviet Union?

    A. the suppression of the "Prague Spring"
    B. the division of Germany into two nations
    C. a lengthy period of economic stagnation
    D. the building of the Berlin Wall

The answer is on page 835.

China Today

Communist one-party rule was established in China in 1949 after a civil war. After several decades of isolation, a certain amount of market free enterprise was reintroduced, and Communist China began rising to world prominence and power. The early 21st century has been a time of great prosperity for some groups and regions in China.

However, the country continues to suffer grave social problems. Chinese citizens do not have unrestricted access to outside information sources, the press is censored, and political dissidence is not tolerated.

Tens of thousands of workers earn extremely low wages turning out electronic devices; cheap, low-quality clothing and household items; and other export items, which the United States and other nations continue to import because the prices are so low.

EXERCISE 22

China Today

Directions: Choose the best answer to the following question.

Question 1 is based on the following graph.

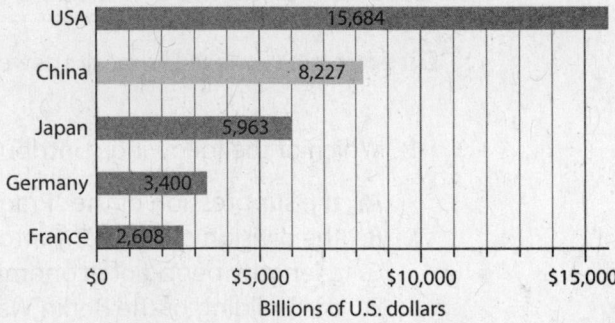

Gross Domestic Products, 2011–2012

	Billions of U.S. dollars
USA	15,684
China	8,227
Japan	5,963
Germany	3,400
France	2,608

1. According to the graph, China's gross domestic product (GDP) in 2011–2012 was approximately

   A. $2.6 trillion.
   B. $3.4 trillion.
   C. $8.2 trillion.
   D. $15.7 trillion.

The answer is on page 835.

The Arab World

A massive demand for oil in the post–World War II era led to an enormous economic change in the Middle East. As the source of most of the world's oil, the region leapt into a position of international consequence and great prosperity almost overnight. In 1960, five of the Arab nations created a cartel called the Organization of Petroleum Exporting Countries (**OPEC**) with the purpose of regulating oil prices and controlling the supply of oil to the rest of the world. Today, OPEC has 12 member nations including 4 in Africa and 2 in South America.

Most Middle Eastern nations are either military dictatorships or monarchies; the press is heavily censored in these countries. In many of these countries, Islamic leaders constantly pressure their governments to enforce Islamic values and practices.

The creation of the state of Israel in the late 1940s caused great turmoil in the region, and the situation was worsened when Israel began a long-term occupation of territories with Arab populations during the "Six-Day War" in 1967. In 2011 a series of popular uprisings in Arab countries (dubbed the **Arab Spring**) raised hopes for the creation of democratic governments, but they also opened new conflicts between pro-Western liberals and Islamists.

EXERCISE 23

The Arab World

Directions: Choose the best answer to the following question.

1. What claim about the modern Middle East is supported by the text?

   A. In many Middle Eastern countries, politics and religion are frequently intertwined.
   B. The state of Israel was created after the "Six-Day War" in 1967.
   C. OPEC allows only Middle Eastern countries as members.
   D. The "Arab Spring" put an end to monarchies in the Middle East.

The answer is on page 835.

World History

Directions: Fill in the blank with the word or phrase that makes the sentence true.

1. The earliest human civilizations occurred in a region we call the

   _____ because its climate was ideal for good harvests.

   A. Silk Road
   B. Rift Valley
   C. Spice Islands
   D. Fertile Crescent

2. The Romans referred to Northern tribes like the Goths and Huns as

   _____ because Northern tribal culture was based on plunder and pillage, not on building cities, writing law codes, and creating works of art.

   A. patricians
   B. plebeians
   C. barbarians
   D. Gauls

3. The medieval kingdom of Ghana, located in _____, was known for its long-distance trade network of precious metals and spices.

   A. West Africa
   B. Persia
   C. Arabia
   D. the Indus Valley

4. _____, defined as pride in one's country's ethnic and cultural heritage, was a major force driving political change in 19th-century Europe.

   A. Communism
   B. Liberalism
   C. Socialism
   D. Nationalism

5. _____ was a medieval system that bound together people of different social classes with oaths of loyalty and mutual responsibilities and duties.

   A. Slavery
   B. Feudalism
   C. Colonialism
   D. Monarchy

Choose the best answer to each of the following questions.

6. The thinkers of the 18th-century Enlightenment taught that people do not have to accept existing conditions and can create new institutions to their own liking. Which of the following is true in regard to this idea?

   A. Few people thought it was important.
   B. Europeans used it to justify their empires.
   C. It was popular with European kings.
   D. It inspired the American and French Revolutions.

Question 7 is based on the following passage.

We have before us an ordeal of the most grievous kind. We have before us many, many long months of struggle and of suffering. You ask, what is our policy? I can say: It is to wage war, by sea, land and air, with all our might and with all the strength that God can give us; to wage war against a monstrous tyranny, never surpassed in the dark, lamentable catalogue of human crime. That is our policy. You ask, what is our aim? I can answer in one word: It is victory, victory at all costs, victory in spite of all terror, victory, however long and hard the road may be; for without victory, there is no survival.

—*Excerpt from a speech by Prime Minister Winston Churchill to the British Parliament early in World War II*

7. Which of the following can be inferred from the speech?

   A. Churchill wanted the British to know that they faced a long and difficult war.
   B. Churchill wanted Parliament to realize that Britain faced defeat.
   C. Many people in Britain did not think the war was worth fighting.
   D. Churchill thought that the war would soon be over.

8. The colonial power that ruled India until 1947 was

   A. Spain.
   B. France.
   C. Great Britain.
   D. Portugal.

9. Which of the following is true in regard to the European Union (EU)?

   A. EU nations have never shared a common currency.
   B. EU nations cooperate on matters of domestic policy.
   C. EU nations all obey a single central government.
   D. EU nations joined together in order to conquer other countries.

Question 10 is based on the following graph.

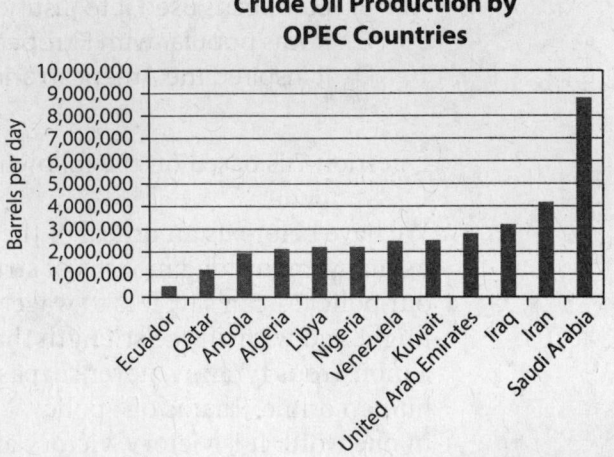

Crude Oil Production by OPEC Countries

10. According to the graph, every OPEC country produces at least 2 million barrels of oil per day except

    A. Algeria and Angola.
    B. Nigeria and Liberia.
    C. Iran and Saudi Arabia.
    D. Qatar, Ecuador, and Angola.

Answers are on page 835.

CHAPTER 4
Economics

Fundamental Economic Concepts

The term **economics** refers to the continuous exchange of goods, services, and resources that is necessary in any human society.

The most basic principle of economics is that you cannot get something for nothing; everything has a **cost**. You have to give something up in order to get something. Cost may not be a matter of money, or not money alone. It may be computed in money, time, effort, or a combination of those things. Also, the things you want may not be material things. They may be intangibles like academic success or excellence in a particular sport. **Individual choice** also plays an important role in economics. Individuals make choices about what to do and not do, or what to buy or not to buy. Every economic issue involves individual choice. People must also make choices about what to give up in order to make a particular purchase. **Opportunity cost** refers to gains that are passed over in the choice of doing one thing instead of another.

To make the best economic choices, you can conduct a **cost-benefit analysis**. This means weighing the cost (what you have to give up) against the benefits (what you will gain). For example, if you want to produce a product, you need to add up all the costs involved in producing that product (and the opportunity costs involved in producing that product instead of doing something else) and compare those costs to the income you are likely to earn from selling the product. You will want to know whether the likely income exceeds the costs.

Goods and services in an economy are produced by labor and capital working in conjunction. **Labor** refers to workers and the work they do— mental work as well as physical work. **Capital** is the wealth used to finance a business. Capital can include money, buildings, or the equipment used in manufacturing. **Wages** refers to the money workers earn from their labor.

Profit is the excess capital earned when a good is sold for more than it cost to produce. A business has a **comparative advantage** in producing a particular good if it can produce that good at a lower cost than any other business can. A business with a comparative advantage can make a greater profit.

Productivity refers to the output per unit of labor, or the rate at which goods or services are produced.

Entrepreneurship is the quality of being an entrepreneur, or someone who owns and manages a business and therefore shoulders the risk and effort involved in running that business.

Specialization means focusing on a limited area of economic activity. Companies or individuals that specialize usually do so because the chosen activity is one they do well, or one that earns them the most profit.

An economic **incentive** motivates or encourages people to do something. Positive economic incentives reward people financially for making certain choices and behaving a certain way. For example, a tax deduction for gifts to charity is an incentive for people to donate to charities.

A **balanced budget** is one in which income is equal to or greater than expenses. If you spend more than your income and borrow to make up the shortfall, you will end up in **debt**. Some people find that their debts grow so large they cannot repay them. In extreme cases of debt, individuals can declare **bankruptcy,** a legal procedure in which the individual's property is used to repay a portion of the debt.

EXERCISE 1

Fundamental Economic Concepts

Directions: Choose the best answer to each of the following questions.

1. A business decides that it will reduce expenses if it purchases an updated computer system. This business has made a(n) _____.

   A. incentive
   B. balanced budget
   C. cost-benefit analysis
   D. comparative advantage

2. The money and equipment that a business uses to create a product are called its _____.

   A. comparative advantage
   B. capital
   C. competition
   D. specialization

Answers are on page 835.

Microeconomics and Macroeconomics

Microeconomics

A **market** is any place where the seller of a particular good or service can meet with buyers. **Microeconomics** is the study of individual markets.

Markets operate according to the **law of supply and demand**. **Supply**, simply stated, is the amount of a good that is available. **Demand** is the amount of an item that consumers wish to purchase.

When an item is scarce, demand can be greater than the available supply, and the **price** of the item will rise. By contrast, if the item is so abundant that the supply is greater than the demand, the price of the item will fall.

When the price of an item rises, producers tend to supply more of it in an effort to increase their profits. This trend is shown in the following supply curve.

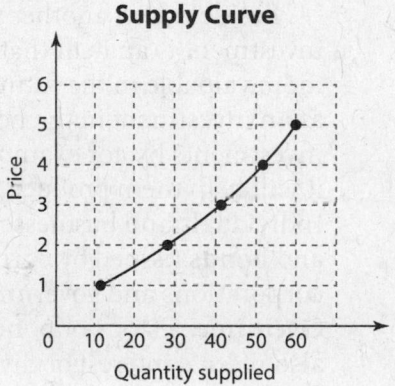

By contrast, when the price of an item falls, consumers tend to demand more of it because they consider it to be a better buy. This trend is shown in the following demand curve.

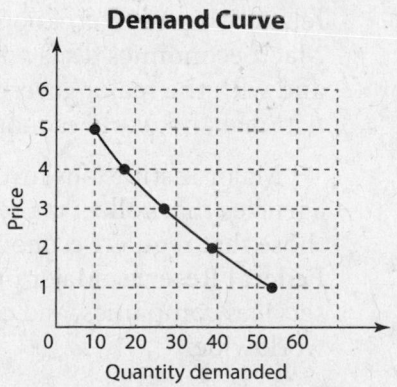

Equilibrium is the price at which the supply and demand for an item are balanced. At the equilibrium price, producers can sell all that they produce, and consumers can purchase all that they demand.

Small businesses and larger companies and corporations form the major part of a market-based economy. Companies earn money by selling goods or services. They spend money to pay wages and to purchase supplies and equipment or goods for resale. The purpose of these operations is to earn profits; that is, to take in more money than the company spends. The company can save profits, distribute them to owners and/or workers, or invest them in ways that expand or improve the business. A company may spend more than it earns. The excess spending is called a loss or a **deficit**. If a company fails to earn a profit, it can wind up in bankruptcy, and it may go out of business.

Competition occurs when more than one seller provides the same good or service. Sellers compete to attract buyers for their product. They set prices that attract consumers, or they improve their product in order to offer consumers better value.

A **monopoly**, by contrast, occurs when a seller is the only one to offer a certain good or service. When a seller has a monopoly, he or she can charge a higher price than would be possible in a competitive market because that particular good or service is not available from anyone else.

Besides sales, another way to earn money is through **investments**. An investment is an item that is purchased in the hope that it will become more valuable in the future. For example, an individual may buy a house as an investment in the hope that it will increase in value. Businesses make investments by, for example, purchasing new equipment in the hope that it will help them produce more and better products and earn more money. Individuals and businesses also purchase **stock** (issued by corporations) and **bonds** (issued by corporations or governments) as investments. The corporations and governments sell the stocks and bonds to raise money. Over time, a stock or bond may increase in value, and the purchaser may also receive interest or dividends.

Macroeconomics

The study of the overall workings of a national economy, and of its relationship to international markets, is called **macroeconomics**. Macroeconomics deals with what nations as a whole produce and trade, and with the major government and private institutions that operate in the national and world economy.

Major institutions involved in macroeconomics include government agencies that collect tax revenue, such as the **Internal Revenue Service**, and those that regulate economic activity on a national scale, such as the **U.S. Federal Reserve**. Major private institutions include leading banks, financial services companies, and corporations doing business nationwide and worldwide.

Fiscal policy refers to the way in which government collects and spends tax revenues. Each year, the President presents a budget to Congress regarding fiscal policy. Congress then considers which programs to fund.

Monetary policy relates to the supply of money, which is controlled by factors such as interest rates and reserve requirements for banks. Monetary policies include manipulating the money supply or interest rates in order to promote economic growth or to combat inflation. **Tariffs** are taxes or duties paid on specified classes of imports or exports. A tariff adds to the cost of an imported good and is one of several trade policies a country can enact.

Economists define **inflation** as a general, ongoing rise in the prices of goods and services. The inflation rate is generally reported as an annual percentage. In other words, if the inflation rate is 5 percent, prices in general have risen by 5 percent in a year, and consumers' dollars will now buy less than they did formerly. **Deflation**, on the other hand, refers to a general reduction of prices in an economy.

Gross domestic product, or GDP, is one of the primary indicators used to measure the strength of a country's economy. It represents the total dollar value of all the goods and services produced by a country over a specific time period. The gross domestic product is the main measure of production in the United States.

Another gauge of a country's economic health is the **unemployment** rate. A person actively searching for employment who is unable to find work is considered unemployed. Every month, the U.S. Bureau of Labor Statistics reports the percentage of Americans who are unemployed. During the Great Depression of the 1930s, unemployment rates in the United States reached 25 percent of all workers. The rate in the mid-2010s was between 7 and 8 percent. While policymakers strive for low unemployment rates, what exactly is acceptable has changed over time.

EXERCISE 2

Microeconomics and Macroeconomics

Directions: Choose the best answer to each of the following questions.

1. True or False? Microeconomics concerns itself with national and governmental economic policies.

2. The point at which supply and demand are balanced is called

   _____.

Answers are on page 835.

Banking and Credit

Banks provide services such as **checking** and **savings** accounts, and they offer loans and credit cards at a cost. Checking accounts allow customers to deposit their money into the account and then use the money to pay for goods and services by writing checks. Many banks charge a fee for maintaining a checking account. Savings accounts allow customers to deposit money into the account and earn interest on the account balance. The amount of interest paid is a percentage of the balance in the account. Deposits in checking and savings accounts up to $250,000 are insured by the Federal Deposit Insurance Corporation (FDIC), an independent agency created by the U.S. Congress.

Banks earn money by making loans to individuals and businesses. You can borrow money to make a purchase, but you must pay back the sum you borrowed plus additional money called **interest**. Interest represents the cost of borrowing. For a very expensive purchase such as a house, you can arrange a **mortgage** with a bank. The bank pays the seller in full at the time of purchase, and you repay the bank an agreed amount per month, most often over a period of 30 years. The monthly mortgage payments include interest charges based on the total number of years of the loan. Early repayment means you pay less overall, because you save the interest charges. The mathematical equation for calculating interest is $R \times P \times T = I$ (Rate × Principle × Time = Interest). Other expensive purchases for which people routinely take out loans include cars and college educations.

Many banks also offer credit cards. **Credit** is an arrangement that allows consumers to finance a purchase without having to pay the total cost at the time the purchase is made. When a credit cardholder makes a purchase, the bank pays the seller on the cardholder's behalf. The cardholder then repays the bank, with interest if repayment is not made immediately. The bank also collects a fee from the seller for processing the transaction. There are many **consumer and credit laws** in place to protect the rights of people and businesses that interact with credit card companies and to establish rules for the credit industry.

EXERCISE 3

Banking and Credit

Directions: Choose the best answer to each of the following questions.

1. What might a bank offer to a customer?

   A. loans
   B. savings accounts
   C. credit cards
   D. all of the above

2. True or False? The FDIC is the National Bank of the United States.

Answers are on page 835.

The Role of Government in the National Economy

In a capitalist economy, business and industry are in private hands, and a free, competitive market sets wages and prices. In a socialist economy, the government owns all business and industry and fixes prices artificially. A mixed economy is a combination of these two systems. The United States has developed as a largely capitalist economy. Most other Western nations have mixed economies.

In the United States, the federal, state, and local governments have income (called **revenue**) and expenses. Revenue comes mainly from two sources: payment of taxes and the sale of bonds. **Income tax** is a percentage of individual or business income paid to the government. **Sales tax** is a small percentage added to the price of an item or a service. A **government bond** is, in effect, a loan. Investors pay the government the price of the bond. They can cash in the bond at any time, but the longer they hold it, the more it is worth, because the government pays them interest based on the length of time they hold the bond.

Governments use these sources of revenue to meet their expenses. For the federal government, expenses include financing the armed forces and paying the salaries of all government workers all the way up to the President. The federal government also funds education at all levels; runs programs such as Medicare, Medicaid, and Social Security; regulates commerce and enforces safety standards; provides funding for the arts and scientific research; maintains national parks and nature preserves; and helps to fund and maintain a national transportation system.

State taxes pay for things like the state police force and bridge and highway maintenance. Local city taxes pay for things like public schools, garbage collection, the library system, and municipal parks. State governments also depend on taxes for their revenue. Each state determines what taxes it will assess. For example, Pennsylvania charges a state income tax but does not charge sales tax on clothing.

The federal government helps to manage the national economy by setting tax rates and interest rates and by regulating businesses and industries. It sets and enforces rules governing minimum wages, workplace standards, and fair business practices. For example, it can penalize large financial institutions that have been found to have defrauded customers in numerous states. States regulate certain industries by requiring them to follow specified rules when doing business within the state.

EXERCISE 4

The Role of Government in the National Economy

Directions: Follow the instructions below.

1. For each of the following items, decide whether it is a function of the federal government or of the state or local government. Then indicate in which column of the chart each item belongs. (**Note:** On the real GED® test, you will click on the items and "drag" them into position on the chart.)

Federal Government Function	State/Local Government Function

Equip the armed forces	Maintain the national parks
Support the highway patrol	Pay the President's salary
Regulate interstate commerce	Enforce national safety standards
Maintain bridges and highways	Finance public schools
Provide funding for scientific research	Manage Social Security
Fund garbage collection	

Answers are on page 835.

International Trade

A **trade** is an exchange—something you do not need for something you want. In international trade, people and businesses **export** (sell to foreigners) the goods they do not need, and **import** (buy from foreigners) the goods they want.

Geography is closely connected to international trade. A nation's geographic location determines its climate and its **natural resources**. Nations must trade to obtain the natural resources or manufactured products they cannot provide for themselves. Often a nation will have **surplus** of products it can trade away. For example, Argentina's climate is perfect for raising cattle—but all wrong for growing coffee. The cattle can supply all the meat the Argentines need with plenty left over to trade away for the coffee they cannot produce.

Nations also export natural resources or manufactured goods in order to earn income. The income is used to create or buy more goods and services, which strengthens the nation's economy. A nation that is well suited to manufacture a certain product can often undersell competitors and earn substantial profits from foreign trade.

It is easy to see the connection between international trade and foreign policy. Economics can drive foreign policy, and foreign policy can dictate economic choices. **Colonization** is one example of how economics can drive foreign policy. When a country acquires a colony, it controls the trade relationship. This fact helped to shape a foreign policy of aggressive European colonization from about 1500 to 1945, when colonies in Asia, Africa, and the Americas provided a number of commodities and resources Europeans could not produce for themselves—coffee, tea, sugar, cotton, spices, potatoes, copper, tin, and many more.

Trading with other independent nations is different from trading with a colony because the bargaining power between the two is more equal. If a nation is your enemy, it may refuse to trade with you—or it may demand unreasonably high prices for its goods. If an enemy nation is rich in a commodity you want to import, you are under economic pressure to improve your political relations with that nation. If nations can become allies, they are much more likely to come to a trade agreement that will please both sides. But sometimes, a nation may decide that the best way to obtain natural resources from a neighboring country is through a war of conquest.

A nation that has a political dispute with another country may sometimes employ a tactic called an **embargo** in order to apply pressure against its opponent. When you establish an embargo against a country, you do not export to that country and you do not import its goods. This means finding alternatives to whatever goods that country produces. An example of this occurred during the U.S. Civil War, when, for political reasons, Britain decided to break off trade relations with the Confederacy. Instead of importing American cotton, Britain imported cotton from India until after the war ended and the Confederacy rejoined the Union.

International Trade

Directions: Choose the best answer to each of the following questions.

Questions 1 and 2 are based on the following graphs and information.

The graphs show current U.S. imports and exports for the following:

- Agricultural products: soybeans, fruit, corn, etc.
- Industrial supplies: chemicals, crude oil, etc.
- Capital goods: computers, telecommunications equipment, motor vehicle parts, office machines, etc.
- Consumer goods: automobiles, clothing, toys, furniture, medicines, etc.

1. According to the first graph, nearly half of all U.S. exports are

   A. agricultural products.
   B. industrial supplies.
   C. capital goods.
   D. consumer goods.

2. According to the graphs, the United States imports

   _____ as many consumer goods as it exports.

   A. half
   B. twice
   C. three times
   D. exactly

Answers are on page 835.

Key Economic Events in U.S. History

The economy of the United States has been shaped by many events during its history. The causes of these financial events have included actions by individuals, natural and social processes, and the influence of ideas.

In early American history, the federal government had little involvement in economic affairs. One economic issue that stirred controversy was the proposal to create a national bank. At the urging of Alexander Hamilton, Congress established the Bank of the United States in 1791. Many, including Thomas Jefferson, opposed this action. The bank had a 20-year charter, which expired in 1811.

There were also doubts about the government's right to interfere in economic matters. However, in 1824, in the case of *Gibbons v. Ogden*, the Supreme Court ruled that Congress had the right to regulate interstate commerce, under Article I of the Constitution. The court said that the only limits on Congress's power in this area were those specifically stated in the Constitution. The court also said that the states could not interfere with the use of harbors and rivers.

Beginning in the early 1800s, the country's westward expansion was a key economic event. Settlers established farms in the Midwest and the Great Plains, motivated by a sharp rise in agricultural commodity prices and new methods of shipping farm products to world markets. The discovery of gold in California in 1849 speeded up the pace of western migration and brought new wealth to many. The second half of the 19th century was the great age of railroad building and the rapid growth of industries based on steel and coal.

After the end of the 19th century, government began taking a more active role in economic affairs. It did so in response to demands from farmers, businesspeople, and labor movements that the government intercede on their behalf. The **Interstate Commerce Act** (1887) strengthened the role of Congress in regulating trade across state lines and increased its power to regulate railroads. The **Sherman Antitrust Act** (1890) gave Congress the power to limit the establishment of business monopolies.

The **Federal Reserve Act** (1913) created the modern banking system. This act established the Federal Reserve System, under which the country is divided into 12 Federal Reserve Districts. The system includes the Federal Reserve Board as the primary governing body of all U.S. banks, as well as 12 regional Federal Reserve Banks, one in each District. The Federal Reserve banks jointly implement the monetary policies decided on by the federal government. Each bank also regulates the commercial banks in its district.

In the 1930s, in response to the Great Depression, President Franklin Roosevelt and Congress enacted a set of far-reaching economic measures called the **New Deal**. These measures were needed to address the dire economic conditions and to help those who were suffering. The New Deal greatly expanded the role of the federal government in domestic affairs. Some of its programs provided food, shelter, and financial security to those in economic need. Others provided funds for building dams, roads, bridges, and other large structures. These building projects provided employment for thousands of people. Another major New Deal program, Social Security, still provides a guaranteed income to millions of Americans.

World War II brought an end to the Depression. The demand for weapons, ships, and airplanes created jobs and paychecks for millions of workers. When the war was over, people spent money freely on everything that had been postponed during the war years: starting families, buying houses, and purchasing all kinds of consumer goods developed by new industries. The result was an unprecedented economic boom that lasted for 25 years. During this period, the United States consolidated its position as the greatest economic power in the world.

EXERCISE 6

Key Economic Events in U.S. History

Directions: Choose the best answer to each of the following questions.

1. President Roosevelt's response to the Great Depression was the New Deal policy, which

   A. discouraged economic growth in the United States.
   B. discouraged unemployed people from finding work.
   C. funded the building of roads, dams, and other infrastructure projects.
   D. encouraged people to buy stock on margin.

2. At the end of World War II there was strong economic growth due to

   A. a housing boom.
   B. increased consumer demand.
   C. development of new industries.
   D. all of the above.

Answers are on page 836.

Economics

1. The Great Depression lasted into the late 1930s. How did economic conditions change when the United States entered World War II?

   A. More people were employed.
   B. Investment in new factories declined.
   C. Fewer people owned homes.
   D. The funds people had in savings decreased.

2. A sharp rise in the prices of agricultural commodities was just one factor that drove the westward expansion that began in the United States in 1807. Another was the search for

   A. spices.
   B. gold.
   C. religious freedom.
   D. trade routes.

3. Which of the following established the modern banking system in the United States?

   A. Sherman Antitrust Act
   B. Interstate Commerce Act
   C. Federal Reserve Act
   D. The New Deal

4. Which is the definition of profit?

   A. money received over a period of time
   B. purchase of an item in the hope that it will increase in value
   C. the point at which the supply of an item equals the demand for it
   D. excess income after expenses are paid

5. Place an X beside the people or groups responsible for determining the federal government's fiscal policy.

   _____ Congress

   _____ President

   _____ Supreme Court

   _____ Secretary of Defense

Question 6 is based on the following table.

Stockholders' Profit, 2005

Industry	Percentage
Toiletries and cosmetics	41.4
Beverages (alcoholic)	32.6
Tobacco	32.1
Beverages (soft drinks)	26.2
Building materials	22.9
Food processing	21.2
Pharmaceutical	18.3
Petroleum (producing)	16.9
Petroleum (integrated)	15.5
Computer software	13.8
Medical services	13.0
Computers and peripherals	12.7
Publishing	12.3
Chemicals (specialty)	12.3
Apparel	12.0
Value line market	11.6
Auto parts	11.4
Automobiles and trucks	10.0
Furniture and home furnishings	9.9
Machinery	9.3
Metal fabricating	9.2
Trucking	9.0
Aerospace and defense	8.9
Metals and mining	8.5
Chemicals (basic)	8.2
Forest products	2.5
Tire and rubber products	2.0
Precision instruments	−0.2
Electronics	−1.3

6. According to the table, in which of the following industries did stockholders earn the greatest percentage of profits?

   A. electronics
   B. computer software
   C. building materials
   D. aerospace and defense

Question 7 is based on the following map.

Federal Reserve Banks and Districts

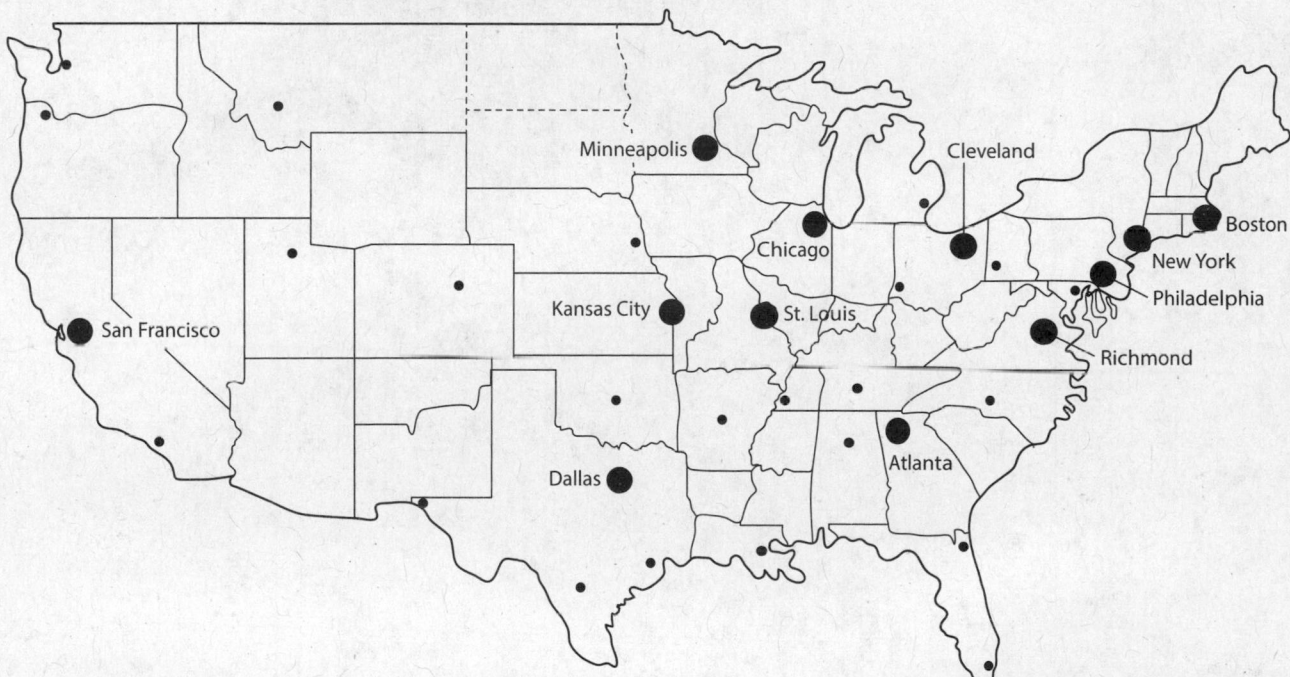

7. What does the location of these banks most likely indicate?

   A. There are more people in Boston than in San Francisco.
   B. The northeastern United States is the main center of banking activity in the country.
   C. Banking activity is concentrated in the western portion of the United States.
   D. Banking practices in the Midwest are radically different from those in the South.

8. Short response:

The price of any product depends largely on the law of supply and demand. How do supply and demand affect price?

```
✂ Cut   📋 Copy 📋 Paste  ↶ Undo ↷ Redo
```

Answers are on page 836.

CHAPTER 5

Geography

Ecosystems

Over millions of years, physical processes have shaped and reshaped Earth's surface. The continents we know today did not always exist in their current form. Over time, landmasses break away from one another or collide with one another, forming new landmasses. Forces inside Earth cause mountain ranges to rise up, but over time, wind and water wear the rocks away. As a result, Earth has a highly varied landscape. Different locations have different landforms and different climates, and they are inhabited by different groups of plants and animals.

The **climate** of a region encompasses many things: the prevailing winds, temperatures, and the amount and type of **precipitation**, averaged over time. Climate is affected by geographical factors such as the proximity of mountains or large bodies of fresh or salt water. Climate can change when any of these factors changes.

The term **ecosystem** refers to the ongoing interaction between the land, the climate, and living organisms in a particular location. All the factors work together in a certain way to create a natural system that sustains the organisms that live there. For example, in a forest in a temperate region of North America, trees produce nuts and fruits as part of their reproductive cycle. Small animals and birds survive by eating the nuts and fruits. Wolves and hawks survive by preying on the smaller animals and birds. Other animals survive by eating the insects that live in the soil and on the trees. The remains of dead plants and animals supply nutrients to the soil that nourish plants and trees. The whole system works together to sustain one generation of living things after another.

Earth is divided into many different ecosystems. For example, the **tropical** ecosystem of the South America rain forests is completely different in terms of climate, precipitation, and living organisms from the **desert** ecosystem in the southwestern United States. Much of the United States and Western Europe is located in an area of moderate climate called the **temperate** zone.

Ecosystems

Directions: Choose the best answer to each of the following questions.

1. Which of the following is not a global ecosystem?

   A. Temperate
   B. Desert
   C. Tropical
   D. Deciduous

Question 2 is based on the following passage.

> Storms from the Pacific Ocean usually drop their moisture when they reach the western slopes of the mountains in California, Oregon, and Washington. The area east of the mountains, where little rain falls, is said to be in a *rain shadow*.

2. What kind of ecosystem would you expect to find in a rain shadow?

   A. Temperate
   B. Desert
   C. Tropical
   D. Arctic

Answers are on page 836.

Geography and the Development of Human Societies

Geography largely determines how and where people live. The climate and the physical features, or **topography**, of the land are very important. Areas with very cold climates, like northern Canada, are sparsely populated. Areas with very dry climates also generally have few inhabitants. Mountainous areas with harsh climates are usually less populated than plains, where farming is easier. Throughout history, people have tended to settle in places where the soil is fertile, where fresh water is abundant, and where travel is relatively easy. That is why, for example, river valleys in the temperate zones, such as the Nile valley in Egypt or the Yangtze valley in China, were the sites of the earliest civilizations. Today population tends to be greatest in coastal areas, often near harbors where shipping makes it easy to transport people and goods. These areas attract people because they provide comparatively more economic opportunities.

Geography and climate affect the choices people make. The climate determines the clothing people wear, the crops they grow, the animals they raise for food, and the kinds of transportation they use. For example, the Italian peninsula is mountainous, with dry, rocky soil. Together with the mild temperatures of the Mediterranean region, this makes the perfect environment for growing grapes. These geographical factors have made Italy a major producer and exporter of wine since the days of ancient Rome.

Geography also affects conflicts between human societies. Countries must always consider how easily they can defend their borders. Countries with natural border defenses such as wide oceans or high mountain ranges are easier to defend than countries located in the middle of broad plains and surrounded by hostile neighbors.

Geographical factors can also dictate success or failure in war. Distance is one important factor—this was especially true before the invention of airplanes. The farther an army marches from its sources of supply, the greater the risk of defeat. Invading armies can also encounter harsh, unfamiliar weather conditions or mountainous terrain that makes transportation difficult. Geography has been a major factor in wars throughout human history.

EXERCISE 2

Geography and the Development of Human Societies

Directions: Choose the best answer to each of the following questions.

1. Which of the following is NOT a reason why many cities are built beside rivers?

    A. The surrounding area is fertile and suitable for agriculture.
    B. Fresh water for people and livestock is readily available.
    C. Ports make travel and trade quick and convenient.
    D. River banks are easy to defend against invaders.

2. _____ are natural borders that countries have used as defenses against invaders and conquerors.

    A. Broad plains
    B. Wide river valleys
    C. High mountains
    D. Dry, rocky soils

Answers are on page 836.

Human Changes to the Environment

Human beings have significantly altered every natural environment in which they have settled.

They turn over the soil and sow crops. They may fell whole forests in order to clear land for farming or building. They create systems for irrigation and waste disposal. They build walls and fences to mark property borders. Large human civilizations go beyond these steps. They build bridges, roads, and cities. Since the beginning of the industrial age, people have been building factories, mines, and railroads. All these human activities alter an environment.

Large human societies need to manage resources. A **natural resource** is something of value that is supplied by the environment that is needed by or useful to living beings. This includes water, forests, minerals, air, animals, fossil fuels, plants, and rocks. Since the start of the Industrial Revolution in the early 19th century, people have been consuming natural resources at an ever-increasing rate. Some natural resources, such as coal, oil, and natural gas, are limited or finite. With continual use, they will one day run out. **Sustainability** refers to a way of using natural resources without depleting or destroying them.

Industrialization has produced pollution of air, land, and water on a massive scale. The problem has only grown worse over time; as the 21st century begins, it has resulted in **global warming**. Average temperatures have risen all over Earth, melting glaciers and causing sea levels to rise. Societies have responded to environmental problems in a variety of ways, creating a "**green movement**." People recycle used products in order to reduce the amount of waste. They plant gardens in cities, on vacant land, and on rooftops. Farmers have changed their farming methods to make better use of the soil. Some farmers forgo the use of manufactured pesticides to raise **organic** crops However, not all nations participate in these protective measures; some fear damage to their economies if they have to convert factories to cleaner, more environmentally responsible methods of production and waste disposal.

EXERCISE 3

Human Changes to the Environment

Directions: Choose the best answer to the following question.

Question 1 is based on the following graph.

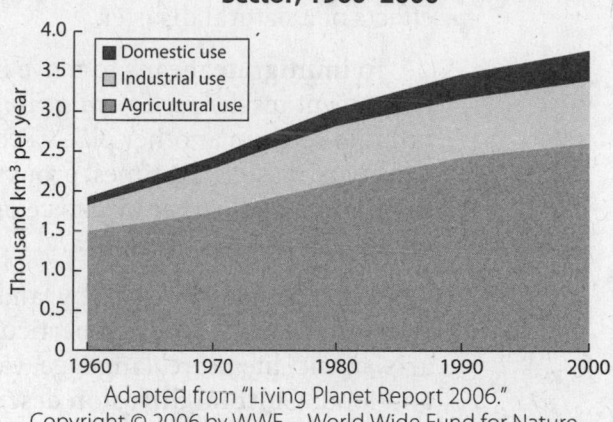

Global Water Withdrawals by Sector, 1960–2000

Adapted from "Living Planet Report 2006."
Copyright © 2006 by WWF—World Wide Fund for Nature.

1. According to the graph, in which decade did total water use begin to exceed 3,000 km³ per year?

   A. 1970s
   B. 1980s
   C. 1990s
   D. 2000s

2. According to the graph, the amount of water used for agriculture

   increased from 1,500 km³ per year in 1960 to _____ in 2000.

   A. 2,000 km³ per year
   B. 2,500 km³ per year
   C. 3,000 km³ per year
   D. 3,500 km³ per year

Answers are on page 836.

Human Migration

Migration is the movement of large numbers of people from one country, place, or region to another. Human migrations have occurred throughout history prompted by population trends and issues. There is a connection between human migration and geography and environment. In many cases, people migrate to regions where farmland is available or where crops can be grown more successfully. People also migrate in order to find a better climate, to obtain jobs or natural resources, or to avoid poverty, wars, or the effects of a natural disaster.

To **immigrate** means to move into a country, usually to establish permanent residence. To **emigrate**, on the other hand, means to leave in order to settle in another place. People may immigrate or emigrate for a variety of reasons. At times, groups of people have been dispersed outside of their homelands either by choice or involuntarily. This scattering of groups of people is called a **diaspora**.

When people move to new lands, they experience new culture. **Culture** refers to the way of life of a particular group of people. This includes their arts, music, literature, language, values, religion, shared beliefs, clothing, and food. **Cultural diffusion** describes the spread of cultural ideas to new groups of people. This can take place when people with different cultures live in close proximity to one another. Over time, contact between the cultures leads to a mix. Cultural diffusion can also occur when one country conquers another and the defeated people are forced to accept the culture of the victors. Today, technology such as the media and the Internet plays a part in the widespread sharing of cultural ideas and beliefs. When people from different ethnic backgrounds integrate into the main culture of a society, they are said to **assimilate**. People in this situation do not necessarily abandon their traditional culture, but they accept many of the cultural ideas and practices of the dominant main culture.

EXERCISE 4

Human Migration

Directions: Choose the best answer to each of the following questions.

1. Tex-Mex, a combination of traditional Mexican cuisine and foods popular with American settlers in Texas, is an example of

   _____.

   A. assimilation
   B. migration
   C. cultural diffusion
   D. sustainability

2. Read the passage, and then answer the question.

> The great famine of 1845–1852 in Ireland was a catastrophe for the Irish. As many as 80 percent of Irish people left home and settled in countries as far away as the United States, Canada, Argentina, Australia, and New Zealand. This mass emigration was one of history's great diasporas.

Which of the following would NOT be termed a diaspora?

A. the expulsion of Jewish people from Europe prior to and during World War II

B. the enslavement of West African people and their forcible transportation to the New World

C. the migration of Chinese people throughout Southeast Asia in search of better economic opportunities

D. The conquest of Native American peoples in South America by the Spanish

Answers are on page 836.

Population Trends and Issues

In early history, nearly all people lived in rural societies centered on agriculture. By contrast, much of today's world is an urban society in which most people live in towns and cities. Today more than 50 percent of the world's population lives in urban areas. This is the first time in history that this has been true. The growth of urban populations is expected to continue. There are numerous reasons for this trend. Cities offer many more opportunities for employment, education, and health care than rural areas with lower populations.

However, moving from a rural area to an urban area does not guarantee a higher quality of life. Particularly in developing countries in Asia, Africa, or Latin America, many people who move to cities with little or no resources of their own soon find themselves living in poverty. In those countries, the cities do not provide enough economic opportunities to support the rapidly increasing population. Poverty levels are usually highest in areas where population growth is fastest.

In 2013 the estimated total world population was 7.2 billion. This is expected to increase to 10.9 billion by the beginning of the next century. Most of this population growth is expected to occur in developing countries. In the more developed countries—the European and North American countries and Japan—population growth is much slower, mainly because family size is typically significantly smaller.

Population Trends and Issues

Directions: Choose the best answer to the following questions.

Questions 1 and 2 are based on the following graph.

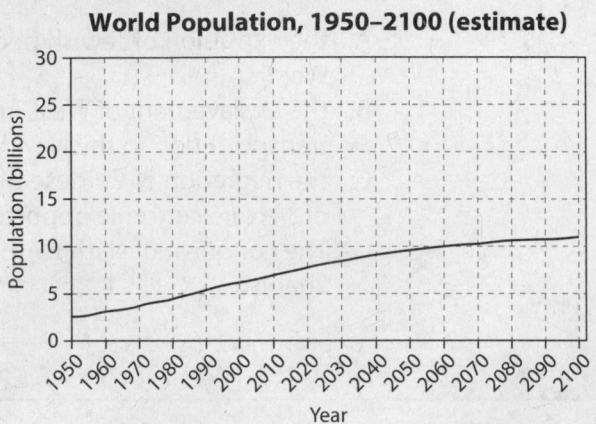

World Population, 1950–2100 (estimate)

1. Based on the graph, which inference can be made?

   A. Experts can predict the world's exact population in the year 2100.
   B. Experts agree that the world's population will decrease by 2100.
   C. The world's population is expected to continue to increase over the next 75 years.
   D. The world's population is expected to triple in the second half of the 21st century.

2. True or False? By 2070, the world's population is expected to be three times as great as it was in 1970.

Answers are on page 836.

Geography Tools and Skills

We use the term **place** or **region** to refer to a location on Earth. A place is an individual location—a single country, town, or city. A region is a group of locations—the collective identity of several adjoining countries, states, or provinces.

Various tools are used to show the spatial organization of people, places, and environments on Earth's surface. A **globe** is the most accurate representation because it is the same spherical shape as Earth. However, even the largest globe is scaled down so far in size from the actual Earth that it cannot show much detail. Flat **maps** distort the actual curvature of the land, but a close-up map of a small area can show much more detail than a globe.

Different types of **maps** can show many physical and human characteristics of places and regions. Take for instance an ordinary map of the United States. It shows how Americans decided to divide their country into specific states for political purposes. You might take the same map and shade it to show the different regions: Northeast, Midwest, Southeast, Southwest, and Northwest. You might shade the map in different colors to show where different major crops are grown—such as wheat, corn, potatoes, and oranges. You might shade the map to show average temperature, rainfall, or elevation above sea level.

Maps come in many varieties. A **political map** shows the names and borders of countries, provinces or states, cities, and towns. A **topographical map** shows comparative elevation above sea level. A **climate map** can show which areas receive the most and least annual rainfall and which have the coldest and hottest temperatures.

You can locate any place on Earth by plotting its **latitude** and **longitude**. When you look at a globe, you will see a crisscross grid of latitude and longitude lines. A location's latitude gives its distance north or south of the **equator**. A location's longitude is an angular measure giving its distance east or west of the **prime meridian**, a north-south line running through a location near London in Great Britain. Latitude and longitude are measured in **degrees** (°) and **minutes** ('). The equator is considered to be 0° latitude. The north and south pole are located at 90° north and 90° south latitude, respectively. The prime meridian is considered to be 0° longitude.

Latitude and Longitude

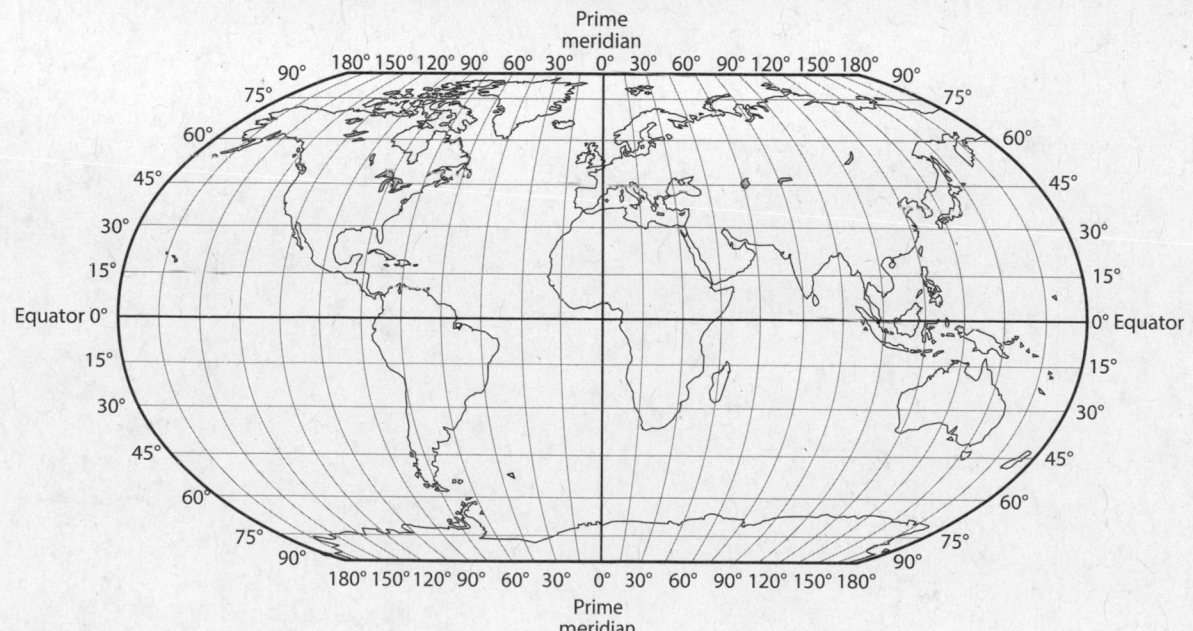

EXERCISE 6

Geography Tools and Skills

Directions: Choose the best answer to each of the following questions.

1. If you want to plan a route for a hiking trip in a mountainous area, which kind of map would you be likely to consult?

   A. climate
   B. political
   C. highway
   D. topographical

2. The equator crosses which continents?

   A. South America, Africa, and Asia
   B. North America, Europe, and Asia
   C. South America, Europe, and Australia
   D. North America, Africa, and Asia

Answers are on page 836.

Geography

Directions: Choose the best answer to each of the following questions.

1. Which statement is true regarding how geography affects the development of societies?

   A. Groups of people often establish their first settlements in mountainous regions.
   B. People usually locate their settlements away from large bodies of water.
   C. The availability of natural resources influences where people settle.
   D. Societies develop in areas where health care is easily available.

Question 2 is based on the following graph.

Greenhouse Gases in the Atmosphere

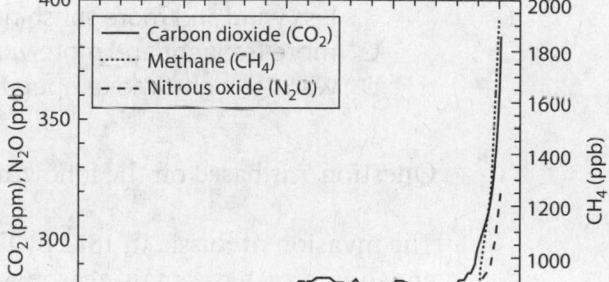

Source: United States Environmental Protection Agency

2. Which of the following can be inferred from this graph?

   A. Greenhouse gases in the atmosphere have increased rapidly since the start of industrialization in the 18th century.
   B. Greenhouse gases in the atmosphere have decreased as world population has increased.
   C. There was less carbon dioxide than methane in the atmosphere before Europeans colonized the New World.
   D. There was more carbon dioxide in the atmosphere before the European colonization of the New World than there is today.

3. True or false? Humans have often migrated in search of land available for farming.

4. The Prime Meridian

   A. measures distance from east to west.
   B. is located near the equator
   C. is located at 0 degrees longitude.
   D. measures distance from north to south.

5. At which location is the climate most likely to be temperate?

   A. 5 degrees north latitude
   B. 40 degrees north latitude
   C. 25 degrees south latitude
   D. 75 degrees south latitude

6. By comparison to a tropical ecosystem, a temperate ecosystem has

   A. cooler temperatures and less rainfall.
   B. less wind and more sunshine.
   C. more frequent and more violent storms.
   D. warmer nighttime temperatures.

Question 7 is based on the following passage.

The invasion of Russia in 1812 by French troops commanded by Napoleon ended in disaster. A main reason was that the French were unprepared for the Russian winter. They had expected fighting to end before winter began, and therefore did not have proper clothing or supplies. The French soldiers were still wearing summer uniforms when snow began falling. In the icy conditions, many died from hypothermia or starvation. As a result, the French were forced to retreat, and the campaign ended in failure.

7. Which of the following statements is supported by the passage?

   A. The French retreated because they were outnumbered by the Russians.
   B. Napoleon's army was overwhelmed by the Russian climate.
   C. The French invasion failed because the Russians had better generals.
   D. The Russians considered the winter of 1812–1813 to be comparatively mild.

Answers are on page 836.

Social Studies Essay Writing

The GED Social Studies test includes an extended-response task. Test-takers have 25 minutes to examine one or more source texts and to write a response based on a question prompt, using evidence from the texts. Primary and secondary source documents will be used. Sometimes a source will be presented alone; in other cases sources will be presented in pairs for comparison.

Scoring

The scoring rubric used for Social Studies extended-response questions focuses on three writing fundamentals:

1. Argument analysis and use of evidence

2. Idea development and organizational structure

3. Clarity and command of the English language

These fundamentals are the three categories (called traits) that are used to develop a raw score for the extended-response answer. Using a four-point scale, Trait 1 is worth up to 2 points. Traits 2 and 3 are worth 1 point each. The final raw score is double-weighted to produce a possible 8-point raw score that is included in the overall score for the Social Studies section.

How to Approach the Social Studies Extended-Response Question

To do your best on the Social Studies extended-response question, you need to understand what the scorers are looking for in your response. Then you need to develop a time-management strategy to make sure you have enough time to formulate your response and execute it effectively.

The following sections describe each of the three traits that the scorers look for in your essay.

Trait 1: Argument Analysis and Use of Evidence

In the context of an essay test, the word *argument* does not mean a dispute or fight between people. It means the ideas, assertions, and explanations that a writer uses to take a stand on an issue. Your essay will be scored based on how well you establish and support your point of view (or argument), using the sources provided. Here is a simplified version of the rubric used to determine your score for this trait.

Trait 1: Creation of Arguments and Use of Evidence

Score	Description
2	Creates an argument based on the source text(s). Shows a clear understanding of the relationships among the ideas, events, and persons mentioned in the source text(s) and their historical context.
	Supports the argument with evidence from primary and secondary sources.
	Connects the argument clearly to both the prompt and the source texts.
1	Shows some understanding of the relationships among the ideas, events, and persons mentioned in the source text(s).
	Supports the argument with some evidence from primary and secondary sources.
	Connects the argument to both the prompt and the source text(s).
0	Shows little or no understanding of the relationships among the ideas, events, and persons mentioned in the source text(s) or their historical context.
	May or may not create an argument; presents little or no evidence to support the argument.
	Does not connect an argument to either the prompt or the source text(s).

An essay that receives 2 points for this trait will respond directly to the question raised in the prompt and will demonstrate that the test-taker has a firm grasp of the issues and concepts presented in the source text(s).

In your essay, you should avoid a response that merely summarizes the source texts. Incorporating your own ideas about the topic—along with evidence from the sources—is allowed and encouraged, but avoid delving too deep into your personal experiences and opinions. The ideas you present can be your own, but do not let them distract or deviate from the question at hand.

For example, if the source texts discuss the Cuban Missile Crisis of 1961, you might mention U.S.-Cuban relations throughout the Cold War and even the continuation of the Cuban trade embargo to this day, if they are relevant to the point you wish to make. But you should not discuss at length whether you agree with today's embargo or describe how your grandmother left Cuba in 1960.

Trait 2: Idea Development and Organizational Structure

Idea development is the way in which you construct your argument using evidence from the source text(s). How you organize your points will determine how well you score. To do well, you need to do more than simply break your essay into paragraphs. You need to show a logical progression from one point to the next so that each point you make reinforces your main idea. Here is a simplified version of the rubric used to determine your score for this trait:

Trait 2: Development of Ideas and Organizational Structure

Score	Description
1	Organizes ideas in a sensible sequence and clearly shows links between main ideas and details.
	Develops ideas in a generally logical manner; elaborates on several ideas.
	Shows awareness of the audience and the purpose of the writing task.
0	Organization of ideas is unclear or lacking.
	Develops ideas poorly or illogically; elaborates on just a single idea.
	Shows no awareness of the purpose of the writing task.

For example, once you have stated the main idea of your argument ("Kennedy's calm, careful behavior throughout the Cuban Missile Crisis was the main reason why the world escaped nuclear war"), present your evidence in a clear, logical order. Your explanation might not be clear if, say, you began by describing the Cuban leader Fidel Castro, then gave examples of how Kennedy was calm and careful, and ended with a discussion of why Cuba and Russia were allies during the Cold War. Also, you should not spend time on lengthy presentations of background information. Stay focused on your argument. Build your thesis step by step and point by point. Don't just list ideas in random order.

Trait 3: Clarity and Command of the English Language

This last trait deals explicitly with your knowledge of the English language and the principles of good writing. There are specific language standards that you should understand before test day and use correctly in your response. Here is a simplified version of the rubric used to determine your score for this trait:

Trait 3: Clarity and Command of Standard English Conventions

Score	Description
1	Uses largely correct sentence structure in regard to the following: • Frequently confused words and homonyms • Subject-verb agreement • Pronoun usage, including agreement with antecedent, unclear references, and pronoun case • Placement of modifiers and correct word order for logic and clarity • Capitalization • Use of apostrophes with possessive nouns • Punctuation
	Uses largely correct sentence structure and varies structure from sentence to sentence; is generally fluent and clear with regard to the following: • Correct subordination, coordination, and parallelism • Avoidance of wordiness and awkwardness • Use of transitional words, conjunctive adverbs, and other words that aid organizational clarity • Avoidance of run-on sentences or sentence fragments • Standard usage at a level appropriate to on-demand, draft writing
	May make some errors in usage and mechanics, but these do not interfere with understanding.

Score	Description
0	Has minimal control of basic conventions regarding frequently confused words, subject-verb agreement, pronoun usage, word order, and capitalization.
	Sentence structure is consistently flawed with little or no variation; has minimal control over conventions regarding correct and fluent sentence structure and standard usage at a level appropriate to on-demand, draft writing.
	Makes severe and frequent errors in usage and mechanics that interfere with meaning. OR Response is insufficient to demonstrate level of mastery over usage and mechanics.

Time-Management Strategies

You only have 25 minutes to review the source text(s), formulate your thesis, organize your response, write it, and then proofread it for errors. That means you need to approach the extended-response question with an action plan that you can implement effectively on test day.

A successful, high-scoring answer cannot be written off the cuff. You need to spend some time preparing what you are going to say before you begin typing.

First, read the prompt and make sure you understand what it is asking. The prompt's wording will help you focus on what the test graders are looking for in your response: What is the key issue, and why was that source text chosen to illustrate that issue?

Next, spend about 5 minutes organizing your response. What is your thesis? What evidence will you use to back up your claim? If you work out these details before you begin, your argument will be strong and well supported, and you are more likely to score 2 points for Trait 1.

In what order will you present your evidence? Will you use direct quotes from the source text? Which ones? If you draft an outline of your response, you will have a better chance of scoring a point for Trait 2. Remember to write a sentence or two presenting your thesis at the beginning of your essay and summarizing your conclusions at the end.

Now you have 15 to 20 minutes to write your response. Write a thoughtful response using the conventions of Standard English. Start new ideas with a new paragraph. Proper paragraphing not only indicates to your reader that you have moved on to the next thought or idea, it is also crucial to readability. A long block of text makes it difficult for the reader to process your prose.

After completing your response, take 3 to 5 minutes to proofread what you have written. Make sure you have followed your outline. Are your points in a logical order? Look for errors in grammar, syntax, and spelling. Is your sentence structure varied? These last few minutes may not seem like much, but they can make a big difference to your score, especially for Trait 3.

Sample Extended-Response Prompts and Essays

Now let's look at some sample Social Studies extended-response prompts and some sample high-scoring essays.

Directions: Read the following source texts:

Four score and seven years ago our fathers brought forth on this continent a new nation, conceived in liberty, and dedicated to the proposition that all men are created equal. . . . It is rather for us to be here dedicated to the great task remaining before us—that from these honored dead we take increased devotion to that cause for which they gave the last full measure of devotion—that we here highly resolve that these dead shall not have died in vain—that this nation, under God, shall have a new birth of freedom—and that government of the people, by the people, for the people, shall not perish from the earth.

—*Excerpt from President Abraham Lincoln's Gettysburg Address, November 19, 1863*

I have a dream that one day this nation will rise up and live out the true meaning of its creed—we hold these truths to be self-evident that all men are created equal.

I have a dream that one day on the red hills of Georgia the sons of former slaves and the sons of former slave-owners will be able to sit down together at a table of brotherhood.

I have a dream that one day even the state of Mississippi, a desert state, sweltering with the heat of injustice and oppression, will be transformed into an oasis of freedom and justice.

I have a dream that my four little children will one day live in a nation where they will not be judged by the color of their skin but by the content of their character.

I have a dream today!

—*Excerpt from Dr. Martin Luther King's "I Have a Dream" speech, August 28, 1963*

Explain how the excerpt from Dr. Martin Luther King's speech reflects the enduring issue expressed in the excerpt from the Gettysburg Address. In your essay, incorporate relevant and specific evidence from the two excerpts and your own knowledge of the enduring issue, as well as the circumstances surrounding the writing of the Gettysburg Address and the civil rights movement.

Here is a sample high-scoring essay response to this prompt:

While the nation was still in the grip of the bitter Civil War, President Abraham Lincoln delivered what is now called the Gettysburg Address, today one of the most widely known and revered speeches in American history. Although the speech took only minutes to deliver, President Lincoln was able to clearly and eloquently express, to a nation weary of war and loss, the reason why the Union needed to endure and be victorious—to preserve forever the cause of freedom and justice on earth. In Dr. Martin Luther King's famous speech, delivered purposely on the steps of the Lincoln Memorial in Washington, D.C., he gave the same reason, also to a weary people. He spoke to the nation, but specifically to the "soldiers" of the civil rights movement as they continued the fight, begun 100 years earlier, for equality.

Lincoln begins his speech by drawing a link between the ideals of the America Revolution and the reasons why the Civil War is being fought. He echoes the exact words of the preamble of the Declaration of Independence, stating that the United States was founded on "the proposition that all men are created equal." King makes the same allusion, expressing his hope that the United States will "rise up and live out the true meaning of its creed."

Because the President is speaking at the dedication of a memorial at the site of an important battle, he mentions the soldiers who fought and died, and the cause for which they gave their lives. He emphasizes that the people they left behind should maintain their determination to see the fight to the end, so that "these dead shall not have died in vain." King too uses his speech as a rallying cry, describing his dream for America in moving detail—a vision of brotherhood and "oasis of freedom"—a dream that can only come true if the people remain steadfast in the struggle for equal rights. This idea echoes Lincoln's vision of a "new birth of freedom" for the United States.

Clearly, these two brilliant orators were able to move the nation and fortify its resolve at crisis points in United States history by focusing on the promise of freedom on which the nation was founded.

The scorers might rate this response as follows:

- **Trait 1.** The writer's argument illustrates clearly that she understands that the "enduring issue" in the excerpt from the Gettysburg Address— continuing the fight for freedom and justice—is reflected in King's famous "I Have a Dream" speech. In many cases, the writer quotes specific examples from both speeches to defend her argument of how the two texts relate to each other. In addition, the writer illustrates her own background knowledge of both the events of the Civil War as well as those of the civil rights movement.

- **Trait 2.** The writer structures her argument and organizes her thoughts effectively. In order to connect the two texts, she presents her examples in a logical order and elaborates on why each specific reference supports her thesis.

- **Trait 3.** Not only is the response free of obvious grammatical or spelling errors, the language used is also fluent, clear, and varied. Conventions of Standard English (such as capitalization) are properly used. Some repetition (of words such as "freedom" and "fight") is understandable and permissible, and the punctuation error in paragraph 3, where the period is outside of the quotation mark, does not detract from meaning.

Here is another set of sample Social Studies extended-response prompts.

Directions: Read the following source texts:

Three millions of people, armed in the holy cause of liberty, and in such a country as that which we possess, are invincible by any force which our enemy can send against us. . . . The battle, sir, is not to the strong alone; it is to the vigilant, the active, the brave. Besides, sir, we have no election. If we were base enough to desire it, it is now too late to retire from the contest. . . . Is life so dear, or peace so sweet, as to be purchased at the price of chains and slavery? Forbid it, Almighty God!—I know not what course others may take; but as for me, give me liberty or give me death!

—*Excerpt from Patrick Henry's speech before the*
Virginia House of Burgesses, March 23, 1775

I had great regard for British diplomacy which has enabled them to hold the Empire so long. Now it stinks in my nostrils, and others have studied that diplomacy and are putting it into practice. They may succeed in getting, through these methods, world opinion on their side for a time; but India will speak against that world opinion. She will raise her voice against all the organized propaganda. I will speak against it. Even if all the United Nations opposed me, even if the whole of India forsakes me, I will say, "You are wrong. India will wrench with non-violence her liberty from unwilling hands." I will go ahead not for India's sake alone, but for the sake of the world. Even if my eyes close before there is freedom, non-violence will not end.

—*Excerpt from "I Will Go Ahead" speech by Mahatma Gandhi, delivered in Bombay on August 8, 1942*

Explain how Gandhi's "I Will Go Ahead" speech reflects the enduring issue expressed in the excerpt from the Patrick Henry's speech. Incorporate relevant and specific evidence from both excerpts and your own knowledge of the enduring issue, as well as the circumstances surrounding the American Revolution and India's independence from British colonial rule.

Here is a sample high-scoring essay response to this prompt:

The British Empire was one of the largest and greatest empires in human history; it stretched to every corner of the globe. Although it is just a small island in the North Sea, Great Britain grew in power and strength over the course of many centuries. By the time Patrick Henry and his fellow colonists took up the cause of American independence, Great Britain had amassed the greatest navy in the world, and its colonies supplied the government with unbounded wealth. Just over 150 years later, another colony began the fight to freedom from British rule. Although Mahatma Gandhi chose a path of civil disobedience, his foe was no less formidable. In both these speeches, Henry and Gandhi address how their fellow citizens have the strength to fight the power of Great Britain, and they are explicit about the price that must be paid for that freedom.

Henry believes he and his revolutionary allies are "invincible," but it is not because they can match the force of the British Empire. He does not deny that his enemy is a fearsome foe, and that it will use every weapon in its arsenal to defeat them. Instead, Henry emphasizes that the fight "is not to the strong alone." Instead, the revolutionaries are "the vigilant, the active, the brave"—and that is why they have a chance at success. Gandhi also alludes to greatness of British Empire, the power it has and the way it may use both its military power and its diplomatic influence to sway other nations to agree with it. Yet Gandhi insists that India will not falter; its strength is not in force, but in perseverance and the justice of its cause, speaking out "against that world opinion" and "against all the organized propaganda."

Henry and Gandhi also make personal connections to the cause. They reiterate their resolve to stay in the fight, regardless of the actions of others, and regardless of whether it takes their lives. Henry ends his speech with some of the most well-known words in American history: "I know not what course others may take; but as for me, give me liberty or give me death!" Gandhi also uses the first person to personalize his point, and says that his actions are not dictated by those of others. He asserts, "I will say, 'You are wrong.

India will wrench with non-violence her liberty from unwilling hands.' I will go ahead. . . . Even if my eyes close before there is freedom, non-violence will not end." He emphasizes the importance of non-violence in India's struggle for independence, even if he should die before freedom is achieved.

The remarkable parallel between the experiences of these two revolutionaries, wrestling with the same colonial power, is evident in their similar views—Great Britain can be defeated, and that is a cause for which they are ready to pay the ultimate price.

The scorers might rate this response as follows:

- **Trait 1.** The writer begins by showing substantial background knowledge of the history of the British Empire and providing context to both the American Revolution and India's fight for independence. In her analysis, she elaborates on specific phrases from both speeches, at times using direct quotes to support her argument.

- **Trait 2.** The writer uses evidence in a logical progression to support her thesis. She shows the connection between two distinct ideas that appear in both excerpts (first, that while Britain is powerful, it is not invincible; and second, that the speakers make personal connections to the cause), and she organizes her ideas and evidence effectively.

- **Trait 3.** The sentence structure is correct and varied. Vocabulary is fluent and interesting. The writer shows understanding of English language conventions, and the response does not contain any errors in grammar, spelling, or usage.

Social Studies

Chapter 1 Civics and Government

Exercise 1: Types of Historical and Modern Governments

1. **Correct answer: C**

2. __D__ Every citizen can place proposals on the ballot, and a proposal becomes law if the majority vote for it.

   __R__ Citizens elect a legislature to rule the country.

   __R__ Delegates represent the wishes of the voting citizens.

   __D__ Power to veto laws rests with the citizens themselves.

Exercise 2: Basic Principles of American Constitutional Democracy

1. **Correct answer: B**

2. **Correct answer: D**

3. **Correct answer: C**

4. **Correct answer: D**

5. **Correct answer: A**

Exercise 3: Structure and Design of the U.S. Federal Government

1.

How Each Government Branch Is Controlled by Checks and Balances

Action That Checks the Legislative Branch	Action That Checks the Executive Branch	Action That Checks the Judicial Branch
The Supreme Court decides if laws enacted by Congress follow the guidelines of the Constitution.	Congress has the power to remove the President from office.	The President nominates judges to the Supreme Court.
The President has the power to veto laws enacted by Congress.	The Supreme Court determines whether the actions of the President are permitted by the Constitution.	The Senate must confirm persons nominated for the Supreme Court.

Exercise 4: The Legislative Branch

1. **Correct answer: B**

2. **Correct answer: C**

3. **Correct answer: B**

Exercise 5: The Executive Branch

1. **Correct answer: B**

2. **Correct answer: C**

3. **Correct answer: A**

4. **Correct answer: B**

Exercise 6: The President's Cabinet

1. **Correct answer: A**

2. **Correct answer: D**

ANSWERS AND EXPLANATIONS

Exercise 7: The Judicial Branch

1. **Correct answer: John Marshall**
2. **Correct answer: 34**

Exercise 8: Amending the Constitution

1. **Correct answer: D**
2. **Correct answer: D**

Exercise 9: The Bill of Rights

1. __1(I)__ A newspaper prints an editorial criticizing the actions of a political candidate.

   __6(VI)__ A person is selected to be a member of a jury during the trial of someone accused of criminal activity.

   __4(IV)__ During a routine traffic stop, authorities demand to search for stolen goods in the driver's vehicle.

   __5(V)__ A person is tried for a crime and found not guilty; however, many in the community believe that the verdict is wrong and the accused should be tried again.

   __2(II)__ A homeowner purchases a personal firearm after robberies are committed in the neighborhood.

2. __X__ Protection against being tried twice for the same crime

   _____ The right to freely practice religion

   __X__ The right to a speedy trial

   _____ The right to freedom of the press

   _____ Protection from being forced to house soldiers

   _____ The right to bear arms

   __X__ The right to avoid self-incrimination

3. **Correct answer: D**

Exercise 10: Citizens' Rights and Civic Responsibilities

1. **Correct answer: Shirley M. Watts**
2. **Correct answer: C**
3. **Correct answer: D**

Exercise 11: Political Parties

1. **Correct answer: C**
2. **Correct answer: C**
3. **Correct answer: A**

Exercise 12: Political Campaigns, Elections, and the Electoral Process

1. **Correct answer: C**
2. **Correct answer: C**
3. **Correct answer: D**

Exercise 13: Contemporary Public Policy

1. **Correct answer: Education Is Primary**
2. **Correct answer: A**

Practice: Civics and Government

1. **Correct answer: A**
2. **Correct answer: D**
3. **Correct answer: A**
4. **Correct answer: B**
5. **Correct answer: C**
6. **Correct answer: A**
7. **Correct answer: A**
8. **Correct answer: A**
9. **Correct answer: D**
10. **Correct answer: A**

Chapter 2 United States History

Exercise 1: European Exploration of the Americas

1. _____ They sailed day and night.

   ___X___ Two pelicans landed on the boat.

   _____ The admiral wanted to keep sailing.

   ___X___ There was a light rain with no wind.

2. **Correct answer: B**

Exercise 2: The English Colony in Virginia

1. **Correct answer: B**

2. **Correct answer: A**

Exercise 3: English Colonies in New England and Maryland

1. **Correct answer: D**

2. **Correct answer: D**

3. | Settlement | Religion |
   | --- | --- |
   | Maryland | Catholic |
   | Massachusetts Bay Colony | Puritan |
   | Plymouth | Pilgrim |

4. **Correct answer: Connecticut, New Hampshire, Rhode Island**

Exercise 4: The Thirteen Colonies Take Shape

1. ___X___ Political freedom

   _____ Gold

   ___X___ Economic opportunity

   ___X___ Escape persecution

   _____ Search for the Fountain of Youth

   ___X___ Establishment of trade

2. **Correct answer: D**

3. **Correct answer: C**

Exercise 5: Tensions Rise Between the Colonies and Great Britain

1. **Correct answer: B**

2. **Correct answer: B**

Exercise 6: The First Continental Congress and the Beginning of the American Revolution

1. **Correct answer: D**

2. **Correct answer: B**

Exercise 7: The Second Continental Congress and the Declaration of Independence

1. ___X___ Liberty

   ___X___ Life

   _____ Power

   ___X___ Pursuit of happiness

   _____ Safety

   _____ Truthfulness

2. **Correct answer: A**

Exercise 8: The Revolutionary War

1. **Correct answer: 6**

2. **Correct answer: C**

3. **Correct answer: C**

ANSWERS AND EXPLANATIONS

Exercise 9: From the Articles of Confederation to the U.S. Constitution

1. Correct answer: C
2. Correct answer: B

Exercise 10: The War of 1812

1. Correct answer: C
2. Correct answer: C

Exercise 11: The Monroe Doctrine

1. Correct answer: A
2. Correct answer: B

Exercise 12: U.S. Policy Toward Native Americans

1. Correct answer: A
2. Correct answer: D

Exercise 13: Manifest Destiny

1. Correct answer: C
2. Correct answer: C
3. Correct answer: B

Exercise 14: Civil War and Reconstruction

1. _____ Lack of farmland for a growing population

   ___X___ The expansion of slavery into new territories

   _____ War with Mexico

   ___X___ Differences between North and South on economic issues

   ___X___ The election of President Abraham Lincoln

   _____ New amendments to the U.S. Constitution

2. Correct answer: C

Exercise 15: The United States Becomes a Major Industrial Nation

1. Correct answer: B
2. Correct answer: C

Exercise 16: The United States Becomes a World Power

1. Correct answer: B

Exercise 17: World War I

1. Correct answer: A
2. Correct answer: C

Exercise 18: The Great Depression

1. Correct answer: D
2. Correct answer: B

Exercise 19: World War II

1. Correct answer: D

Exercise 20: Postwar America

1. Correct answer: B
2. Correct answer: C

Exercise 21: The Cold War

1. Correct answer: D

Exercise 22: The Civil Rights Movement and the Women's Movement

1. Correct answer: A
2. Correct answer: D

ANSWERS AND EXPLANATIONS

Exercise 23: The Great Society, the Vietnam War, and Watergate

1. **Correct answer: C**
2. **Correct answer: A**

Exercise 24: Presidencies in the Late 20th Century

1. **Correct answer: C**

Practice: United States History

1. **Correct answer: A**
2. _____ James Madison was against the slave trade.

   __X__ James Monroe was the fifth President of the United States.

   __X__ The United States declared war on the British in 1812.

_____ Abraham Lincoln encouraged Illinois to join the United States as a free state.

__X__ Lyrics to the national anthem were written by Frances Scott Key.

3. **Correct answer: B**
4. **Correct answer: D**
5. _____ United States

   __X__ Japan

   __X__ Germany

   _____ Great Britain

6. **Correct answer: B**
7. **Correct answer: C**
8. **Correct answer: D**
9. **Correct answer: D**
10. **Correct answer: A**

Chapter 3 World History

Exercise 1: The Earliest Civilizations

1. **Correct answer: D**
2. **Correct answer: A**

Exercise 2: Early China

1. **Correct answer: C**
2. **Correct answer: D**

Exercise 3: Early India

1. **Correct answer: B**

Exercise 4: Classical Greece

1. **Correct answer: B**
2. **Correct answer: A**

Exercise 5: Rome

1. **Correct answer: C**
2. **Correct answer: A**

Exercise 6: The Great Migration and the Middle Ages

1. **Correct answer: C**
2. **Correct answer: D**

ANSWERS AND EXPLANATIONS

Exercise 7: Feudalism

1. Correct answer: A
2. Correct answer: B

Exercise 8: The Middle East and Africa

1. Correct answer: D
2. Correct answer: C

Exercise 9: Civilizations in the Americas

1. Correct answer: A

Exercise 10: Renaissance and Reformation in Europe

1. Correct answer: B
2. Correct answer: C

Exercise 11: The Scientific Revolution, the Enlightenment, and the Industrial Revolution

1. Correct answer: C
2. Correct answer: C

Exercise 12: The Age of Exploration

1. Correct answer: D
2. Correct answer: True

Exercise 13: Building Empires

1.

Spain	Portugal	Britain	France
Central America	Brazil	India	Great Lakes Region
Mexico	Angola	Australia	Louisiana Territory
The Philippines	Guinea-Bissau	New Zealand	Vietnam
South America (except Brazil)	Mozambique		
	Macau		

Exercise 14: Revolutions in Britain and France

1. Correct answer: B
2. Correct answer: A

Exercise 15: New Political Ideas in the 19th Century

1. Correct answer: B
2. Correct answer: B

Exercise 16: Political Developments in 19th-Century Europe

1. Correct answer: C
2. Correct answer: D

Exercise 17: World War I and the Russian Revolution

1. Correct answer: A
2. Correct answer: C
3. Correct answer: B

Exercise 18: The Rise of Fascism

1. Correct answer: C
2. Correct answer: D

Exercise 19: World War II

1. Correct answer: A
2. Correct answer: D

Exercise 20: The End of European Dominance and the Formation of the European Union

1. Correct answer: D

Exercise 21: The End of the Soviet Union

1. **Correct answer: C**

Exercise 22: China Today

1. **Correct answer: C**

Exercise 23: The Arab World

1. **Correct answer: A**

Practice: World History

1. **Correct answer: D**
2. **Correct answer: C**
3. **Correct answer: A**
4. **Correct answer: D**
5. **Correct answer: B**
6. **Correct answer: D**
7. **Correct answer: A**
8. **Correct answer: C**
9. **Correct answer: B**
10. **Correct answer: D**

Chapter 4 Economics

Exercise 1: Fundamental Economic Concepts

1. **Correct answer: C**
2. **Correct answer: B**

Exercise 2: Microeconomics and Macroeconomics

1. **Correct answer: False**
2. **Correct answer: equilibrium**

Exercise 3: Banking and Credit

1. **Correct answer: D**
2. **Correct answer: False**

Exercise 4: The Role of Government in the National Economy

1.

Federal Government Function	State/Local Government Function
Equip the armed forces	Support the highway patrol
Maintain the national parks	Maintain bridges and highways
Pay the President's salary	Finance public schools
Regulate interstate commerce	Fund garbage collection
Enforce national safety standards	
Provide funding for scientific research	
Manage Social Security	

Exercise 5: International Trade

1. **Correct answer: C**
2. **Correct answer: B**

Exercise 6: Key Economic Events in U.S. History

1. **Correct answer: C**
2. **Correct answer: D**

Practice: Economics

1. **Correct answer: A**
2. **Correct answer: B**
3. **Correct answer: C**
4. **Correct answer: D**

5. __X__ Congress
   __X__ President
   _____ Supreme Court
   _____ Secretary of Defense
6. **Correct answer: C**
7. **Correct answer: B**
8. **Sample answer:** If the demand for a product is greater than the supply, the price of that product will rise. If the supply is greater than the demand, the price of the product will fall. At the equilibrium price, supply and demand are balanced. At that price, producers can sell all they produce, and consumers can buy all of the product that they want.

Chapter 5 Geography

Exercise 1: Ecosystems

1. **Correct answer: D**
2. **Correct answer: B**

Exercise 2: Geography and the Development of Human Societies

1. **Correct answer: D**
2. **Correct answer: C**

Exercise 3: Human Changes to the Environment

1. **Correct answer: B**
2. **Correct answer: B**

Exercise 4: Human Migration

1. **Correct answer: C**
2. **Correct answer: D**

Exercise 5: Population Trends and Issues

1. **Correct answer: C**
2. **Correct answer: False**

Exercise 6: Geography Tools and Skills

1. **Correct answer: D**
2. **Correct answer: A**

Practice: Geography

1. **Correct answer: C**
2. **Correct answer: A**
3. **Correct answer: True**
4. **Correct answer: C**
5. **Correct answer: B**
6. **Correct answer: A**
7. **Correct answer: B**

Posttests

How to Use the Posttests

Now that you have finished studying the lessons and exercises in this book, it is time to measure your readiness to take the real GED® test. There are four posttests in this section, one in each GED® test subject area: Reasoning Through Language Arts (RLA), Mathematical Reasoning, Science, and Social Studies. Each one is designed to match the real exam as closely as possible in format and degree of difficulty. When you take these posttests, your results will help you to determine whether you are ready to take the real GED® test and, if not, which topics you still need to review.

To make the best use of these posttests, follow these four steps:

1. **Take the posttests one at a time.** Do not try to work through all four posttests in one session.

2. **Take each posttest under test conditions.** Find a quiet place where you will not be disturbed. Take the posttest as if it were the actual GED® test. Work though the posttest from beginning to end in one sitting. Mark your answers directly on the test pages. Observe the time limit given at the start of the test. If you have not finished the posttest when time runs out, mark the last question you answered, and then note how much longer it takes you to complete the test. This information will tell you if you need to speed up your pace and, if so, by how much.

3. **Answer every question.** On the real GED® test, there is no penalty for wrong answers, so it makes sense to answer every question, even if you have to guess. If you don't know an answer, see if you can eliminate one or more of the answer choices. The more choices you can eliminate, the better your chance of guessing correctly!

4. **Check your answers in the Answers and Explanations section at the end of each posttest.** Pay particular attention to the explanations for questions you missed.

5. **Fill out the Evaluation Charts.** These charts are located at the end of each Answers and Explanations section. Mark the numbers of the questions you missed, and the chart will show you if you still need to review certain topics.

The number of questions and time limit for each posttest are shown in the following chart.

Posttest	Number of Questions	Time Limit
Reasoning Through Language Arts		
Part 1: Multiple choice	64	95 minutes
(break)		(10-minute break)
Part 2: Essay	1 essay question	45 minutes
Mathematical Reasoning	50	90 minutes
Science	40	90 minutes
Social Studies	45	90 minutes

Reasoning Through Language Arts (RLA)

This Reasoning Through Language Arts (RLA) Posttest is designed to help you determine how well you have mastered this GED® test subject area and whether you are ready to take the real GED RLA test.

This test has the same number of questions as the real GED RLA test: 64 items in multiple-choice or other formats and one essay question. The question formats are the same as the ones on the real exam and are designed to measure the same skills. Most of the questions are based on reading passages that are selections from either fiction selections or nonfiction sources. Most of the questions are in multiple-choice format, but you will also see questions in other formats, such as fill-in-the-blank items and simulated click-and-drag and drop-down items. On the real GED® test, you will indicate your answers by clicking on the computer screen. For this paper-and-pencil practice test, mark your answers directly on the page. Write your essay on a separate sheet of paper.

To get a good idea of how you will do on the real exam, take this test under actual exam conditions. Complete the test in one session and follow the given time limit. If you do not complete the test in the time allowed, you will know that you need to work on improving your pacing.

Try to answer as many questions as you can. There is no penalty for wrong answers, so guess if you have to. In multiple-choice questions, if you can eliminate one or more answer choices, you can increase your chances of guessing correctly.

After you have finished the test, check your answers in the Answers and Explanations section that follows the posttest. Then use the Evaluation Chart at the end of the Answers and Explanations section to determine the skills and content areas in which you need more practice.

Now turn the page and begin the Reasoning Through Language Arts (RLA) Posttest.

Reasoning Through Language Arts (RLA)

Part 1: Multiple Choice

64 questions | **95 minutes**

Use the excerpt for Items 1 through 5:

Excerpt Adapted from *A Village Singer*

by Mary Wilkins Freeman

1   The trees were in full leaf, a heavy south wind was blowing, and there was a loud murmur among the new leaves. The people noticed it, for it was the first time that year that the trees had so murmured in the wind. The spring had come with a rush during the last few days.

2   The murmur of the trees sounded loud in the village church, where the people sat waiting for the service to begin. The windows were open; it was a very warm Sunday for May.

3   The church was already filled with this soft sylvan music—the tender harmony of the leaves and the south wind, and the sweet, desultory whistles of birds—when the choir arose and began to sing.

4   In the center of the row of women singers stood Alma Way. All the people stared at her, and turned their ears critically. She was the new leading soprano. Candace Whitcomb, the old one, who had sung in the choir for forty years, had lately been given her dismissal. The audience considered that her voice had grown too cracked and uncertain on the upper notes. There had been much complaint, and after long deliberation the church officers had made known their decision as mildly as possible to the old singer. She had sung for the last time the Sunday before, and Alma Way had been engaged to take her place. With the exception of the organist, the leading soprano was the only paid musician in the large choir. The salary was very modest; still, the village people considered it large for a young woman. Alma was from the adjoining village of East Derby; she had quite a local reputation as a singer.

5   Now she fixed her large solemn blue eyes; her long, delicate face, which had been pretty, turned paler; the blue flowers on her bonnet trembled; her little thin gloved hands, clutching the singing book, shook perceptibly; but she sang out bravely. The most formidable mountain height of the world,

self-distrust and timidity, arose before her, but her nerves were braced for its ascent. In the midst of the hymn she had a solo; her voice rang out piercingly sweet; the people nodded admiringly at one another; but suddenly there was a stir; all the faces turned toward the windows on the south side of the church. Above the din of the wind and the birds, above Alma Way's sweetly straining tones, arose another female voice, singing another hymn to another tune.

6   "It's her," the women whispered to each other; they were half aghast, half smiling.

7   Candace Whitcomb's cottage stood close to the south side of the church. She was playing on her parlor organ, and singing, to drown out the voice of her rival.

8   Alma caught her breath; she almost stopped; the hymn book waved like a fan; then she went on. But the long husky drone of the parlor organ and the shrill clamor of the other voice seemed louder than anything else.

9   When the hymn was finished, Alma sat down. She felt faint; the woman next to her slipped a peppermint into her hand. "It ain't worth minding," she whispered, vigorously. Alma tried to smile; down in the audience a young man was watching her with a kind of fierce pity.

10   In the last hymn Alma had another solo. Again the parlor organ droned above the carefully delicate accompaniment of the church organ, and again Candace Whitcomb's voice clamored forth in another tune.

11   After the benediction, the other singers pressed around Alma. She did not say much in return for their expressions of indignation and sympathy. She wiped her eyes furtively once or twice, and tried to smile. William Emmons, the choir leader, elderly, stout, and smooth-faced, stood over her and raised his voice. He was the old musical dignitary of the village, the leader of the choral club and the singing schools. "A most outrageous proceeding," he said. People had coupled his name with Candace Whitcomb's. The old bachelor tenor and old maiden soprano had been wont to walk together to her home next door after the Saturday-night rehearsals, and they had sung duets to the parlor organ. People had watched sharply her old face, on which the blushes of youth sat pitifully, when William Emmons entered the singing seats. They wondered if he would ever ask her to marry him.

12   And now he said further to Alma Way that Candace Whitcomb's voice had failed utterly of late, that she sang shockingly, and ought to have had sense enough to know it.

13   When Alma went down into the audience room, in the midst of the chattering singers, who seemed to have descended, like birds, from song flights to chirps, the minister approached her. He had been waiting to speak to her. He was a steady-faced, fleshy old man, who had preached from that

POSTTEST: Reasoning Through Language Arts (RLA)

one pulpit over forty years. He told Alma, in his slow way, how much he regretted the annoyance to which she had been subjected, and intimated that he would endeavor to prevent a recurrence of it. "Miss Whitcomb—must be—reasoned with," said he; he had a slight hesitation of speech, not an impediment. It was as if his thoughts did not slide readily into his words, although both were present. He walked down the aisle with Alma, and bade her good morning when he saw Wilson Ford waiting for her in the doorway.

1. What does Candace Whitcomb do to upset Alma Way?

    A. She sings over her.
    B. She interrupts the service.
    C. She comes into the church.
    D. She watches her sing.

2. Which quotation from the passage supports the idea that Alma Way is nervous?

    A. "The murmur of the trees sounded loud in the village church, where the people sat waiting for the service to begin."
    B. "Now she fixed her large solemn blue eyes; her long, delicate face, which had been pretty, turned paler; the blue flowers on her bonnet trembled; her little thin gloved hands, clutching the singing book, shook perceptibly; but she sang out bravely."
    C. "In the midst of the hymn she had a solo; her voice rang out piercingly sweet; the people nodded admiringly at one another; but suddenly there was a stir; all the faces turned toward the windows on the south side of the church."
    D. "Again the parlor organ droned above the carefully delicate accompaniment of the church organ, and again Candace Whitcomb's voice clamored forth in another tune."

3. What can be inferred about Candace Whitcomb?

    A. She is angry that she had been replaced.
    B. She wants to show that her voice is as good as ever.
    C. She is happy that she has more free time for herself.
    D. She thinks that her organ is better than the church organ.

4. Why does the woman give Alma Way a peppermint?

    A. to show support
    B. to help her voice
    C. to give her energy
    D. to share her candy

5. Why is it surprising that William Emmons spoke critically of Candace Whitcomb to Alma Way?

    A. He was the leader of the choir.
    B. He was against having Alma Way perform.
    C. He was with Candace Whitcomb when she sang.
    D. He was linked romantically to Candace Whitcomb.

6. The following memo contains several numbered blanks, each marked "Select. . . ." Beneath each one is a set of choices. Indicate the choice from each set that is correct and belongs in the blank. (**Note:** On the real GED® test, the choices will appear as a "drop-down" menu. When you click on a choice, it will appear in the blank.)

From: Rosemarie Kelder

To: All Employees:

Subject: Company Fundraiser

We are organizing a company fundraiser to benefit Habitat for Humanity. We will be having a silent auction at the Oceanic Resort on June 1, and we will need volunteers to help organize and run the event as well as individuals to seek donations for our silent auction.

The benefit is a terrific opportunity for many of you to give back to the community. As you know, Select 1... ▼ that become homes to people who never thought they would be able to afford one.

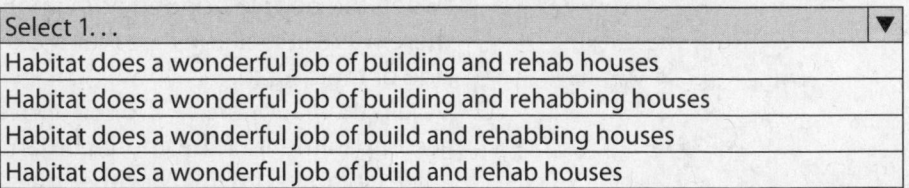

Select 1... ▼
Habitat does a wonderful job of building and rehab houses
Habitat does a wonderful job of building and rehabbing houses
Habitat does a wonderful job of build and rehabbing houses
Habitat does a wonderful job of build and rehab houses

Select 2... ▼ They include coupons from restaurants, beauty salons, and retail shops as well as from artists and craftspeople. If any of you has a connection with a possible donor, please do your best to convince your connection that this is a worthy cause.

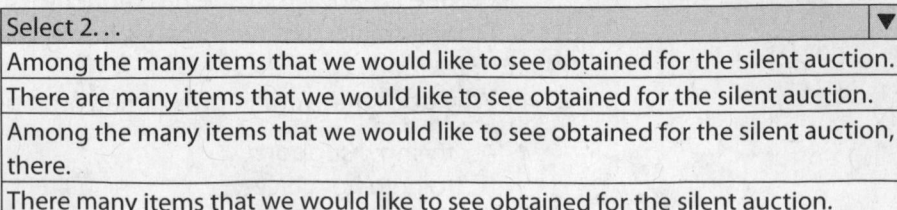

Select 2... ▼
Among the many items that we would like to see obtained for the silent auction.
There are many items that we would like to see obtained for the silent auction.
Among the many items that we would like to see obtained for the silent auction, there.
There many items that we would like to see obtained for the silent auction.

Perhaps you have something that you could donate Select 3... ▼

Select 3... ▼
itself.
theirselves.
yourselves.
themselves.

I, for instance, am donating a week's stay at my condo in Puerto Rico. Some of you may be willing to buy tickets to theater productions and donate them. If you come up with any idea, please do participate.

Select 4... ▼ We will need people to set up and then oversee the auction and, of course, break everything down at the end of the evening.

Select 4... ▼
During the auction itself there is a sign-up sheet in the lunch room for those of you who would like to give up your time.
There is during the auction itself a sign-up sheet in the lunchroom for those of you who would like to give up your time.
There is a sign-up sheet in the lunchroom during the auction itself for those of you who would like to give up your time.
There is a sign-up sheet in the lunchroom for those of you who would like to give up your time during the auction itself.

Food and drink will be provided by our company, so attendees will have an enjoyable time.

Select 5... ▼ because there will be so many items that you will want to bid on as well.

Select 5... ▼
Do plan on attending, even if you cannot volunteer time, and please brought your wallets, credit cards, or checkbooks
Do plan on attending, even if you cannot volunteer time, and please is brining your wallets, credit cards, or checkbooks
Do plan on attending, even if you cannot volunteer time, and please bring your wallets, credit cards, or checkbooks
Do plan on attending, even if you cannot volunteer time, and please brings your wallets, credit cards, or checkbooks

Use the following two excerpts for Items 7 through 16:

The Emancipation Proclamation

by President Abraham Lincoln (1863)

1   Whereas, on the twenty-second day of September, in the year of our Lord one thousand eight hundred and sixty-two, a proclamation was issued by the President of the United States, containing, among other things, the following, to wit:

2   "That on the first day of January, in the year of our Lord one thousand eight hundred and sixty-three, all persons held as slaves within any State or designated part of a State, the people whereof shall then be in rebellion against the United States, shall be then, thenceforward, and forever free; and the Executive Government of the United States, including the military and naval authority thereof, will recognize and maintain the freedom of such persons, and will do no act or acts to repress such persons, or any of them, in any efforts they may make for their actual freedom.

3   "That the Executive will, on the first day of January aforesaid, by proclamation, designate the States and parts of States, if any, in which the people thereof, respectively, shall then be in rebellion against the United States; and the fact that any State, or the people thereof, shall on that day be, in good faith, represented in the Congress of the United States by members chosen thereto at elections wherein a majority of the qualified voters of such State shall have participated, shall, in the absence of strong countervailing testimony, be deemed conclusive evidence that such State, and the people thereof, are not then in rebellion against the United States."

4   Now, therefore I, Abraham Lincoln, President of the United States, by virtue of the power in me vested as Commander-in-Chief, of the Army and Navy of the United States in time of actual armed rebellion against the authority and government of the United States, and as a fit and necessary war measure for suppressing said rebellion, do, on this first day of January, in the year of our Lord one thousand eight hundred and sixty-three, and in accordance with my purpose so to do publicly proclaimed for the full period of one hundred days, from the day first above mentioned, order and designate as the States and parts of States wherein the people thereof respectively, are this day in rebellion against the United States, the following, to wit:

5   Arkansas, Texas, Louisiana, (except the Parishes of St. Bernard, Plaquemines, Jefferson, St. John, St. Charles, St. James Ascension, Assumption, Terrebonne, Lafourche, St. Mary, St. Martin, and Orleans, including the City of New Orleans) Mississippi, Alabama, Florida, Georgia, South Carolina, North Carolina, and Virginia, (except the forty-eight

counties designated as West Virginia, and also the counties of Berkley, Accomac, Northampton, Elizabeth City, York, Princess Ann, and Norfolk, including the cities of Norfolk and Portsmouth[)], and which excepted parts, are for the present, left precisely as if this proclamation were not issued.

6   And by virtue of the power, and for the purpose aforesaid, I do order and declare that all persons held as slaves within said designated States, and parts of States, are, and henceforward shall be free; and that the Executive government of the United States, including the military and naval authorities thereof, will recognize and maintain the freedom of said persons.

7   And I hereby enjoin upon the people so declared to be free to abstain from all violence, unless in necessary self-defence; and I recommend to them that, in all cases when allowed, they labor faithfully for reasonable wages.

8   And I further declare and make known, that such persons of suitable condition, will be received into the armed service of the United States to garrison forts, positions, stations, and other places, and to man vessels of all sorts in said service.

9   And upon this act, sincerely believed to be an act of justice, warranted by the Constitution, upon military necessity, I invoke the considerate judgment of mankind, and the gracious favor of Almighty God.

10   In witness whereof, I have hereunto set my hand and caused the seal of the United States to be affixed.

11   Done at the City of Washington, this first day of January, in the year of our Lord one thousand eight hundred and sixty three, and of the Independence of the United States of America the eighty-seventh.

12   By the President: ABRAHAM LINCOLN

13   WILLIAM H. SEWARD, Secretary of State.

President Barack Obama's Proclamation on the 150th Anniversary of the Emancipation Proclamation

1   On December 31, 1862, our Nation marked the end of another year of civil war. At Shiloh and Seven Pines, Harpers Ferry and Antietam, brother had fought against brother. Sister had fought against sister. Blood and bitterness had deepened the divide that separated North from South, eroding the bonds of affection that once united 34 States under a single flag. Slavery still suspended the possibility of an America where life and liberty were the birthright of all, not the province of some.

2   Yet, even in those dark days, light persisted. Hope endured. As the weariness of an old year gave way to the promise of a new one, President Abraham Lincoln issued the Emancipation Proclamation—courageously declaring that on January 1, 1863, "all persons held as slaves" in rebellious areas "shall be then, thenceforward, and forever free." He opened the Union Army and Navy to African Americans, giving new strength to liberty's cause. And with that document, President Lincoln lent new moral force to the war by making it a fight not just to preserve, but also to empower. He sought to reunite our people not only in government, but also in freedom that knew no bounds of color or creed. Every battle became a battle for liberty itself. Every struggle became a struggle for equality.

3   Our 16th President also understood that while each of us is entitled to our individual rights and responsibilities, there are certain things we cannot accomplish on our own. Only a Union could serve the hopes of every citizen, knocking down the barriers to opportunity and giving each of us the chance to pursue our highest aspirations. He knew that in these United States, no dream could ever be beyond our reach when we affirm that individual liberty is served, not negated, by seeking the common good.

4   It is that spirit that made emancipation possible and codified it in our Constitution. It is that belief in what we can do together that moved millions to march for justice in the years that followed. And today, it is a legacy we choose not only to remember, but also to make our own. Let us begin this new year by renewing our bonds to one another and reinvesting in the work that lies ahead, confident that we can keep driving freedom's progress in our time.

5   Now therefore, I, Barack Obama, President of the United States of America, by virtue of the authority vested in me by the Constitution and the laws of the United States, do hereby proclaim January 1, 2013, as the 150th Anniversary of the Emancipation Proclamation. I call upon all Americans to observe this day with appropriate programs, ceremonies, and activities that celebrate the Emancipation Proclamation and reaffirm the timeless principles it upheld.

6   In witness whereof, I have hereunto set my hand this thirty-first day of December, in the year of our Lord two thousand twelve, and of the Independence of the United States of America the two hundred and thirty-seventh.

7. What was the purpose of the Emancipation Proclamation?

    A. to allow formerly enslaved people to own property
    B. to free enslaved people in areas that were then in rebellion
    C. to fine the states that continued to permit slavery
    D. to free enslaved people everywhere in the United States

8. Which description expresses the main idea of the Emancipation Proclamation?

   A. The United States will expel from the country all the states and parts of states where slavery still exists.

   B. The United States will allow formerly enslaved people to join the military only if they are from states that allow slavery to exist.

   C. The United States will institute lawsuits against the areas where slavery is still practiced in order to have it declared illegal.

   D. The United States declares that in the areas then in rebellion, all people who have been enslaved are henceforth free.

9. What is President Obama's viewpoint on the Emancipation Proclamation?

   A. The Emancipation Proclamation was not actually written by President Lincoln.

   B. The United States is a better country because of the Emancipation Proclamation.

   C. The Emancipation Proclamation is actually less important than was once thought.

   D. The Emancipation Proclamation should not have been issued during wartime.

10. Why does President Obama mention that the Emancipation Proclamation allowed African Americans to serve in the Union army and navy?

    A. to contrast the differences between the Union army and navy

    B. to suggest that the Union army and navy were short of volunteers

    C. to show that the Proclamation applied to both soldiers and civilians

    D. to point out that the freed slaves aided the Union war effort

Use this excerpt for Item 11:

"It is that belief in what we can do together that moved millions to march for justice in the years that followed."

11. Why does President Obama include this sentence in his proclamation?

    A. to criticize modern Americans for their failure to live up to the spirit of the Emancipation Proclamation

    B. to make young Americans more aware of their individual rights and responsibilities

    C. to point out that the Emancipation Proclamation has been an important inspiration for later generations of Americans

    D. to support his view that the Emancipation Proclamation was overly idealistic

12. Which sentence from President Obama's proclamation is evidence that he thinks there is more to do to achieve the goal of freedom?

A. "At Shiloh and Seven Pines, Harpers Ferry and Antietam, brother had fought against brother."

B. "Yet, even in those dark days, light persisted."

C. "Let us begin this new year by renewing our bonds to one another and reinvesting in the work that lies ahead, confident that we can keep driving freedom's progress in our time."

D. "I call upon all Americans to observe this day with appropriate programs, ceremonies, and activities that celebrate the Emancipation Proclamation and reaffirm the timeless principles it upheld."

13. Indicate where each sentence belongs in the chart. (**Note:** On the real GED® test, you will click on each sentence and "drag" it into position in the chart.)

Emancipation Proclamation	President Barack Obama's Proclamation

Certain states and parts of states are currently in rebellion against the United States.

People who join together can maintain and expand freedom.

The Emancipation Proclamation turned the Civil War into a war for liberty and equality.

The slaves in the rebellious areas must be freed and be paid for their work.

14. How does the tone of President Obama's proclamation differ from that of the Emancipation Proclamation? President Obama's proclamation is

    A. angrier in tone than the Emancipation Proclamation.
    B. less emotional in tone than the Emancipation Proclamation.
    C. more inspirational in tone than the Emancipation Proclamation.
    D. more formal in tone than the Emancipation Proclamation.

15. Which of the following is an important difference between the Emancipation Proclamation and President Obama's proclamation?

    A. The Emancipation Proclamation is an official government document, but President Obama's proclamation is only a private letter.
    B. The Emancipation Proclamation contains threats of war, but President Obama's proclamation is a call for peace.
    C. The Emancipation Proclamation applied only to members of the military, but President Obama's proclamation applies to everyone.
    D. The Emancipation Proclamation is an official order, but President Obama's proclamation is merely an appeal.

16. Both President Lincoln and President Obama are concerned with the fight for freedom. How do their perspectives differ?

    A. President Lincoln says that the fight is just beginning; President Obama believes that the fight is won.
    B. President Lincoln is focused on immediate measures; President Obama is focused on the longer term.
    C. President Lincoln believes that the Emancipation Proclamation will abolish slavery; President Obama thinks that it was a failure.
    D. President Lincoln wants all citizens to have equal civil rights; President Obama thinks that economic equality is more important.

17. The following memo contains several numbered blanks, each marked "Select. . . ." Beneath each one is a set of choices. Indicate the choice from each set that is correct and belongs in the blank. (**Note:** On the real GED® test, the choices will appear as a "drop-down" menu. When you click on a choice, it will appear in the blank.)

To: All Employees

From: Charles Houston, Chief Security Officer

Subject: Security Changes

While it has been our practice to issue ID swipe cards that could be used on a 24-hour, 7-day-a-week basis, this policy will no longer be in effect. Select 1... ▼

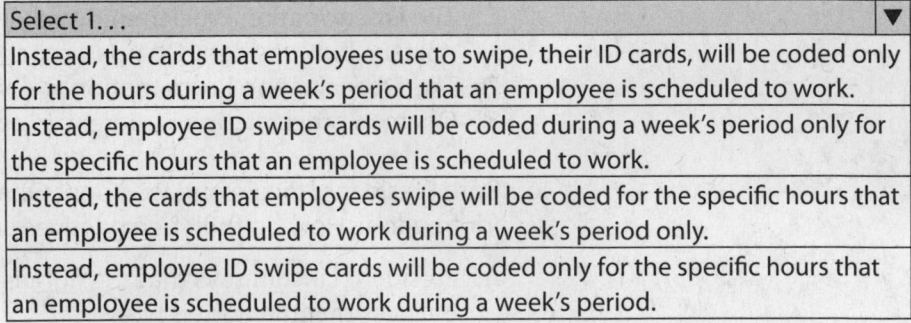

Select 1... ▼
Instead, the cards that employees use to swipe, their ID cards, will be coded only for the hours during a week's period that an employee is scheduled to work.
Instead, employee ID swipe cards will be coded during a week's period only for the specific hours that an employee is scheduled to work.
Instead, the cards that employees swipe will be coded for the specific hours that an employee is scheduled to work during a week's period only.
Instead, employee ID swipe cards will be coded only for the specific hours that an employee is scheduled to work during a week's period.

We have made the change because it has come to our attention that some swipe cards are being used inappropriately, and this will ensure that does not happen in the future.

While we have had a lax attitude about having employees wear their ID swipe cards, this is to be changed as well. We are now asking employees to wear their ID swipe cards at all times for easier verification of employment.

Select 2... ▼ changes are being made to the way visitors are admitted into the building.

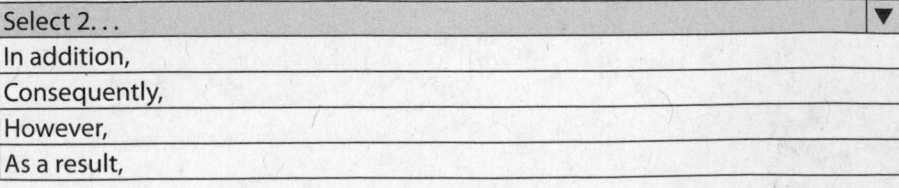

Select 2... ▼
In addition,
Consequently,
However,
As a result,

Starting immediately, all visitors to our facility will be required to sign in at the reception area prior to meeting up with the appropriate party. While on-site, guests must wear [Select 3... ▼] visitor cards at all times.

Select 3... ▼
there
their
theyre
they're

Visitor cards will only work during business hours. Visitors must return their visitor cards before leaving the building. If they should forget, they will face a fine.

While it might seem clear enough from a security perspective, we remind all employees that they should not let anyone into the building who does not have an ID swipe card on his or her person. Instead, employees should ask the person who they are here to see and offer to call that person for them. [Select 4... ▼]

Select 4... ▼
Anyone who senses that there is something out of the ordinary should call security. We will handle the problem.
Anyone who senses that there is something out of the ordinary should call security, we will handle the problem.
Anyone who senses that there is something out of the ordinary should call security: We will handle the problem.
Anyone who senses that there is something out of the ordinary should call security we will handle the problem.

We are sure that these new security measures will make for a safer work area.

Use the excerpt for Items 18 through 22:

Adapted Excerpt from "Gift of the Magi"

by O. Henry

1   One dollar and eighty-seven cents. That was all and sixty cents of it was in pennies. Three times Della counted it: one dollar and eighty-seven cents, and the next day would be Christmas.

2   Della stood by the window and looked out. Tomorrow would be Christmas Day, and she had only $1.87 with which to buy Jim a present. She had been saving every penny she could for months, with this result.

3   Now, there were two possessions of the James Dillingham Youngs in which they both took a mighty pride. One was Jim's gold watch that had been his father's and his grandfather's. The other was Della's hair. Had the queen of Sheba lived in the flat across the airshaft, Della would have let her hair hang out the window someday to dry just to depreciate Her Majesty's jewels and gifts. Had King Solomon been the janitor, with all his treasures piled up in the basement, Jim would have pulled out his watch every time he passed, just to see him pluck at his beard from envy.

4   So now Della's beautiful hair fell about her rippling and shining like a cascade of brown waters. It reached below her knee. And then she did it up again nervously and quickly. Once she faltered for a minute and stood still while a tear or two splashed on the worn red carpet.

5   On went her old brown jacket; on went her old brown hat. She fluttered out the door and down the stairs to the street. Where she stopped the sign read: "Mne. Sofronie. Hair Goods of All Kinds." One flight up Della ran, and collected herself, panting.

6   "Will you buy my hair?" asked Della.

7   "I buy hair," said Madame. "Take yer hat off and let's have a sight at the looks of it."

8   Down rippled the brown cascade.

9   "Twenty dollars," said Madame, lifting the mass with a practiced hand.

10   "Give it to me quick," said Della.

11   Oh, and the next two hours she spent ransacking the stores for Jim's present.

12   She found it at last. It surely had been made for Jim and no one else. It was a platinum fob chain simple and chaste in design. It was even worthy of The Watch. As soon as she saw it she knew that it must be Jim's. Grand as the watch was, he sometimes looked at it on the sly on account of the old leather strap that he used in place of a chain.

13   When Della reached home she got out her curling irons and lighted the gas and went to work repairing the ravages made by generosity added to love.

14   Within forty minutes her head was covered with tiny, close-lying curls that made her look wonderfully like a truant schoolboy.

15   At 7 o'clock the coffee was made and the frying-pan was on the back of the stove hot and ready to cook the chops.

16   Jim was never late. She heard his step on the stair away down on the first flight, and she turned white for just a moment. She whispered: "Please God, make him think I am still pretty."

17   The door opened and Jim stepped in and closed it. He looked thin and very serious. Poor fellow, he was only twenty-two—and to be burdened with a family!

18   Jim stopped inside the door, as immovable as a setter at the scent of quail. His eyes were fixed upon Della, and there was an expression in them that she could not read, and it terrified her. It was not anger, nor surprise, nor disapproval, nor horror, nor any of the sentiments that she had been prepared for.

19   "Jim, darling," she cried, "don't look at me that way. I had my hair cut off and sold because I couldn't have lived through Christmas without giving you a present. It'll grow out again—you won't mind, will you? My hair grows awfully fast. Say 'Merry Christmas!' Jim, and let's be happy. You don't know what a nice—what a beautiful, nice gift I've got for you."

20   "You've cut off your hair?" asked Jim, laboriously, as if he had not arrived at that patent fact yet even after the hardest mental labor.

21   "Cut it off and sold it," said Della. "Don't you like me just as well, anyhow?" Out of his trance Jim seemed quickly to wake. He enfolded his Della.

22   Jim drew a package from his overcoat pocket and threw it upon the table.

23   "Don't make any mistake, Dell," he said, "about me. I don't think there's anything in the way of a haircut that could make me like my girl any less. But if you'll unwrap that package you may see why you had me going a while at first."

24   White fingers and nimble tore at the string and paper. And then an ecstatic scream of joy; and then, alas! a quick change to tears and wails. For there lay The Combs—the set of combs, side and back, that Della had worshipped long in a Broadway window. They were expensive combs, she knew, and her heart had simply craved and yearned over them without the least hope of possession. And now, they were hers, but the tresses that should have adorned the coveted adornments were gone. And then Della leaped up like a little singed cat and cried, "Oh, oh!"

25   Jim had not yet seen his beautiful present. She held it out to him eagerly upon her open palm. "Isn't it a dandy, Jim? I hunted all over town to find it. Give me your watch. I want to see how it looks on it."

26   Instead of obeying, Jim tumbled down on the couch and put his hands under the back of his head and smiled. "Dell," said he, "let's put our Christmas presents away and keep 'em a while. They're too nice to use just at present. I sold the watch to get the money to buy your combs. And now suppose you put the chops on."

18. Which event develops the theme of "Gift of the Magi"?

    A. Della selling her hair.
    B. Della curling her hair.
    C. Della counting her money.
    D. Della putting on her jacket.

19. Which quotation from the passage supports the idea that Della had mixed feelings about selling her hair?

    A. "She had been saving every penny she could for months, with this result."
    B. "Once she faltered for a minute and stood still while a tear or two splashed on the worn red carpet."
    C. "Oh, and the next two hours she spent ransacking the stores for Jim's present."
    D. "Within forty minutes her head was covered with tiny, close-lying curls that made her look wonderfully like a truant schoolboy."

20. What effect does the phrase *rippling and shining like a cascade of brown waters* in paragraph 4 have?

    A. It shows that Della had brown hair.
    B. It tells the reader that Della's hair was long.
    C. It suggests that Della may have dyed her hair.
    D. It helps the reader realize how beautiful Della's hair is.

21. Indicate where each sentence belongs in the chart. (**Note:** On the real GED® test, you will click on each sentence and "drag" it into position in the chart.)

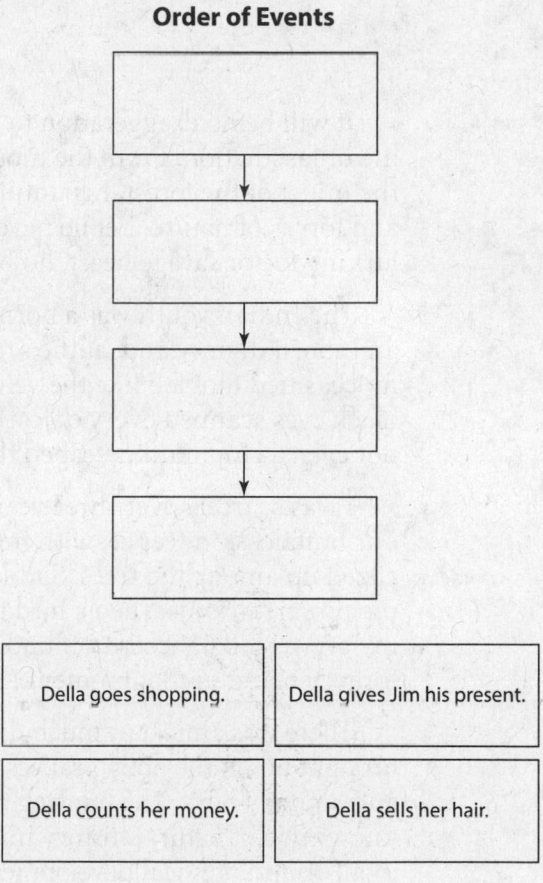

Order of Events

| Della goes shopping. | Della gives Jim his present. |
| Della counts her money. | Della sells her hair. |

22. What is the purpose of Jim saying to "put the chops on" in paragraph 26?

    A. It shows he wants to get on with life.
    B. It shows that he has eaten very little.
    C. It shows he is displeased with his wife.
    D. It shows he does not know how to cook.

Use the excerpt for Items 23 through 32:

Adapted Excerpt from *Indian Boyhood*

by Charles A. Eastman

1   It will be no exaggeration to say that the life of the Indian hunter was a life of fascination. From the moment that he lost sight of his rude home in the midst of the forest, his untutored mind lost itself in the myriad beauties and forces of nature. Yet he never forgot his personal danger from some lurking foe or savage beast, however absorbing was his passion for the chase.

2   The Indian youth was a born hunter. Every motion, every step expressed an inborn dignity and, at the same time, a depth of native caution. His moccasined foot fell like the velvet paw of a cat—noiselessly; his glittering black eyes scanned every object that appeared within their view. Not a bird, not even a chipmunk, escaped their piercing glance.

3   I was scarcely over three years old when I stood one morning just outside our buffalo-skin teepee, with my little bow and arrows in my hand, and gazed up among the trees. Suddenly the instinct to chase and kill seized me powerfully. Just then a bird flew over my head and then another caught my eye, as it balanced itself upon a swaying bough. Everything else was forgotten and in that moment I had taken my first step as a hunter.

4   There was almost as much difference between the Indian boys who were brought up on the open prairies and those of the woods, as between city and country boys. The hunting of the prairie boys was limited and their knowledge of natural history imperfect. They were, as a rule, good riders, but in all-round physical development much inferior to the red men of the forest.

5   Our hunting varied with the season of the year, and the nature of the country which was for the time our home. Our chief weapon was the bow and arrows, and perhaps, if we were lucky, a knife was possessed by someone in the crowd. In the olden times, knives and hatchets were made from bone and sharp stones. . . .

6   We hunted in company a great deal, though it was a common thing for a boy to set out for the woods quite alone, and he usually enjoyed himself fully as much. Our game consisted mainly of small birds, rabbits, squirrels and grouse. Fishing, too, occupied much of our time. We hardly ever passed a creek or a pond without searching for some signs of fish. When fish were present, we always managed to get some. Fish-lines were made of wild hemp, sinew or horse-hair. We either caught fish with lines, snared or speared them, or shot them with bow and arrows. In the fall we charmed them up to the surface by gently tickling them with a stick and quickly threw them out. We have sometimes dammed the brooks and driven the larger fish into a willow basket made for that purpose.

7   It was part of our hunting to find new and strange things in the woods. We examined the slightest sign of life; and if a bird had scratched the leaves off the ground, or a bear dragged up a root for his morning meal, we stopped to speculate on the time it was done. If we saw a large old tree with some scratches on its bark, we concluded that a bear or some raccoons must be living there. In that case we did not go any nearer than was necessary, but later reported the incident at home. An old deer-track would at once bring on a warm discussion as to whether it was the track of a buck or a doe. Generally, at noon, we met and compared our game, noting at the same time the peculiar characteristics of everything we had killed. It was not merely a hunt, for we combined with it the study of animal life. We also kept strict account of our game, and thus learned who were the best shots among the boys.

8   I am sorry to say that we were merciless toward the birds. We often took their eggs and their young ones. My brother Chatanna and I once had a disagreeable adventure while bird-hunting. We were accustomed to catch in our hands young ducks and geese during the summer, and while doing this we happened to find a crane's nest. Of course, we were delighted with our good luck. But, as it was already midsummer, the young cranes—two in number—were rather large and they were a little way from the nest; we also observed that the two old cranes were in a swampy place nearby; but, as it was moulting-time, we did not suppose that they would venture on dry land. So we proceeded to chase the young birds; but they were fleet runners and it took us some time to come up with them.

9   Meanwhile, the parent birds had heard the cries of their little ones and come to their rescue. They were chasing us, while we followed the birds. It was really a perilous encounter! Our strong bows finally gained the victory in a hand-to-hand struggle with the angry cranes; but after that we hardly ever hunted a crane's nest. Almost all birds make some resistance when their eggs or young are taken, but they will seldom attack man fearlessly.

23. Why does the narrator describe the Indian boy's foot as *the velvet paw of a cat* in paragraph 2?

    A. to explain what a moccasin is like
    B. to show that Indian boys liked cats
    C. to tell why an Indian boy wears moccasins
    D. to suggest how quiet an Indian boy's step is

24. Fill in the blank.

    One type of bird that will attack a man if it thinks its young are at risk is

    the _____.

25. In what way does the information about the narrator when he was three support the main idea? It shows that

    A. Indian boys are poor marksmen.
    B. Indian boys are not interested in wildlife.
    C. many Indian boys are not interested in hunting.
    D. the hunting instinct is natural to an Indian boy.

26. Which quotation from the passage supports the idea that the Indian boys studied animal life?

    A. "Just then a bird flew over my head and then another caught my eye, as it balanced itself upon a swaying bough."
    B. "We have sometimes dammed the brooks and driven the larger fish into a willow basket made for that purpose."
    C. "An old deer-track would at once bring on a warm discussion as to whether it was the track of a buck or a doe."
    D. "Meanwhile, the parent birds had heard the cries of their little ones and come to their rescue."

27. What was the main weapon that Indian boys used?

    A. sticks
    B. knives
    C. hatchet
    D. bow and arrow

28. Why does the narrator include details about the way in which Indian boys caught fish? The narrator wants readers to

    A. learn how catch fish themselves.
    B. know how inventive the Indian boys were.
    C. recognize how strong the Indian boys were.
    D. understand that fish were a staple for the Indians.

29. Indicate each word that DESCRIBES the narrator. (**Note:** On the real GED® test, you will click on the words you choose and "drag" each one into position in one of the blank ovals.)

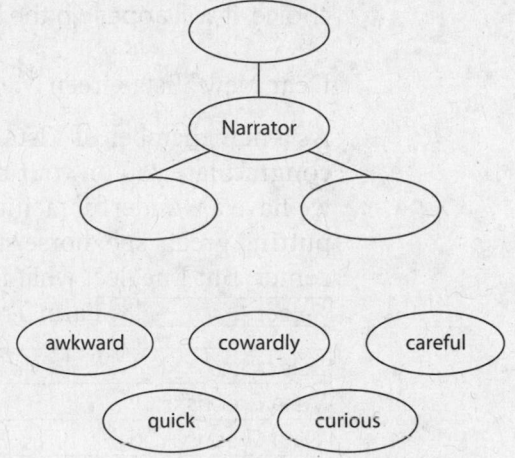

30. At what time of day would the Indian boys get together and discuss their game?

    A. at noon
    B. at sundown
    C. in the evening
    D. early in the morning

31. Why did the narrator and his brother stay away from baby cranes for the most part?

    A. They were not tasty to eat.
    B. They were impossible to catch.
    C. The adult cranes would attack them.
    D. They were considered sacred by the tribe.

32. What were the knives and hatchets that the Indian boys had made from?

    A. clay
    B. wood
    C. bear claws
    D. bone and stones

33. The following letter contains several numbered blanks, each marked "Select. . . ." Beneath each one is a set of choices. Indicate the choice from each set that is correct and belongs in the blank. (**Note:** On the real GED® test, the choices will appear as a "drop-down" menu. When you click on a choice, it will appear in the blank.)

Dear New Vista Green Member:

As a new member of Vista Green Resort Club, we welcome you and congratulate you on your extraordinarily excellent taste. As you know we have a wonderful facility here, complete with tennis courts, pools, putting green, spa, horse stables, premier golf course, and business center. But I neglect what is most likely your favorite spot to relax— Select 1... ▼ Palm Tree Beach, which is just steps from your unit.

Select 1... ▼
Vista Greens'
Vista Greens
Vista Greenes
Vista Green's

We hope you will be staying with us on a regular basis. By joining the club, you are guaranteed the best price for units as long as you commit for at least one Select 2... ▼ per year.

Select 2... ▼
weak
weake
week
weeke

Of course you have the option of staying here much more frequently than that. Just call our reservation desk and book your space. We'll find you an excellent facility at the best available price.

Because you have recently joined our club, we want to reward you with a $50 gift certificate to our lovely Italian Restaurant, Addesso. Select 3... ▼

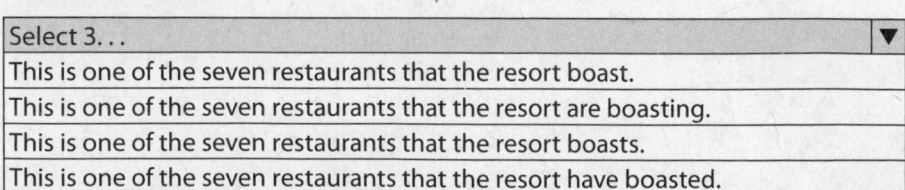

Select 3... ▼
This is one of the seven restaurants that the resort boast.
This is one of the seven restaurants that the resort are boasting.
This is one of the seven restaurants that the resort boasts.
This is one of the seven restaurants that the resort have boasted.

This fine eatery offers exquisite Northern Italian cuisine, so we know you will be pleased to dine there. It is on the top floor of the main building and offers spectacular views as well as delicious food.

Select 4... ▼ You could choose to tour the observatory in town or our neighboring city of Humacao or take the tour of old San Juan, with its wonderful shops and restaurants. In addition, fishing expeditions as well as scuba diving outings can be arranged.

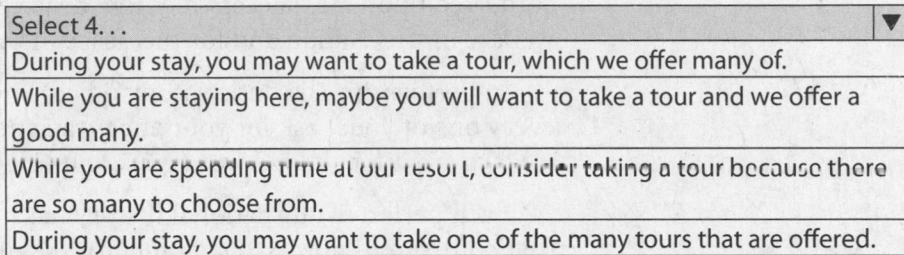

Select 4... ▼
During your stay, you may want to take a tour, which we offer many of.
While you are staying here, maybe you will want to take a tour and we offer a good many.
While you are spending time at our resort, consider taking a tour because there are so many to choose from.
During your stay, you may want to take one of the many tours that are offered.

If you should require anything out of the ordinary during your stay here, please contact me personally and I will ensure that any of your needs are met. Select 5... ▼

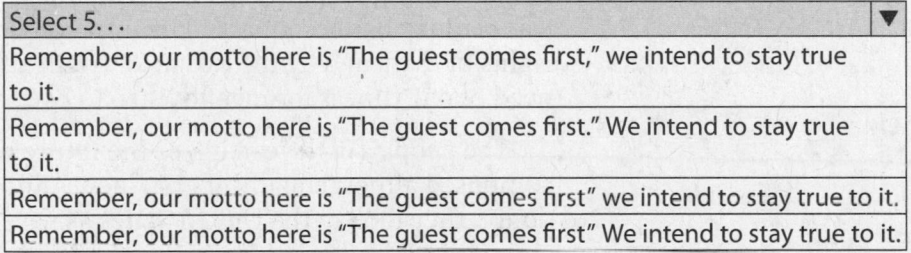

Select 5... ▼
Remember, our motto here is "The guest comes first," we intend to stay true to it.
Remember, our motto here is "The guest comes first." We intend to stay true to it.
Remember, our motto here is "The guest comes first" we intend to stay true to it.
Remember, our motto here is "The guest comes first" We intend to stay true to it.

Again, please drop by my office and say hello. I enjoy meeting all our guests.

Sincerely,

Carlos Julio

Manager
Vista Green Resort Club

Use the following two excerpts for Items 34 through 41:

Excerpt from the Inaugural Address of President Harry S. Truman

1   I accept with humility the honor which the American people have conferred upon me. I accept it with a deep resolve to do all that I can for the welfare of this Nation and for the peace of the world.

2   In performing the duties of my office, I need the help and prayers of every one of you. I ask for your encouragement and your support. The tasks we face are difficult, and we can accomplish them only if we work together.

3   Each period of our national history has had its special challenges. Those that confront us now are as momentous as any in the past. Today marks the beginning not only of a new administration, but of a period that will be eventful, perhaps decisive, for us and for the world.

4   It may be our lot to experience, and in large measure to bring about, a major turning point in the long history of the human race. The first half of this century has been marked by unprecedented and brutal attacks on the rights of man, and by the two most frightful wars in history. The supreme need of our time is for men to learn to live together in peace and harmony.

5   The peoples of the earth face the future with grave uncertainty, composed almost equally of great hopes and great fears. In this time of doubt, they look to the United States as never before for goodwill, strength, and wise leadership.

6   It is fitting, therefore, that we take this occasion to proclaim to the world the essential principles of the faith by which we live, and to declare our aims to all peoples.

7   The American people stand firm in the faith which has inspired this Nation from the beginning. We believe that all men have a right to equal justice under law and equal opportunity to share in the common good. We believe that all men have the right to freedom of thought and expression. We believe that all men are created equal because they are created in the image of God.

8   From this faith we will not be moved.

9   The American people desire, and are determined to work for, a world in which all nations and all peoples are free to govern themselves as they see fit, and to achieve a decent and satisfying life. Above all else, our people desire, and are determined to work for, peace on earth—a just and lasting peace—based on genuine agreement freely arrived at by equals.

10   In the pursuit of these aims, the United States and other like-minded nations find themselves directly opposed by a regime with contrary aims and a totally different concept of life.

11   That regime adheres to a false philosophy which purports to offer freedom, security, and greater opportunity to mankind. Misled by this philosophy, many peoples have sacrificed their liberties only to learn to their sorrow that deceit and mockery, poverty and tyranny, are their reward.

12   That false philosophy is communism.

13   Communism is based on the belief that man is so weak and inadequate that he is unable to govern himself, and therefore requires the rule of strong masters.

14   Democracy is based on the conviction that man has the moral and intellectual capacity, as well as the inalienable right, to govern himself with reason and justice.

15   Communism subjects the individual to arrest without lawful cause, punishment without trial, and forced labor as the chattel of the state. It decrees what information he shall receive, what art he shall produce, what leaders he shall follow, and what thoughts he shall think.

16   Democracy maintains that government is established for the benefit of the individual, and is charged with the responsibility of protecting the rights of the individual and his freedom in the exercise of his abilities.

17   Communism maintains that social wrongs can be corrected only by violence.

18   Democracy has proved that social justice can be achieved through peaceful change.

Excerpt Adapted from the Inaugural Address of President Theodore Roosevelt

1   We have become a great nation, forced by the fact of its greatness into relations with the other nations of the earth, and we must behave as beseems a people with such responsibilities. Toward all other nations, large and small, our attitude must be one of cordial and sincere friendship. We must show not only in our words, but in our deeds, that we are earnestly desirous of securing their goodwill by acting toward them in a spirit of just and generous recognition of all their rights. While ever careful to refrain from wrongdoing others, we must be no less insistent that we are not wronged ourselves. We wish peace, but we wish the peace of justice, the peace of righteousness. We wish it because we think it is right and not because we

are afraid. No weak nation that acts manfully and justly should ever have cause to fear us, and no strong power should ever be able to single us out as a subject for insolent aggression.

2   Our relations with the other powers of the world are important; but still more important are our relations among ourselves. Such growth in wealth, in population, and in power as this nation has seen during the century and a quarter of its national life is inevitably accompanied by a like growth in the problems which are ever before every nation that rises to greatness. Power invariably means both responsibility and danger. Our forefathers faced certain perils which we have outgrown. We now face other perils, the very existence of which it was impossible that they should foresee. Modern life is both complex and intense, and the tremendous changes wrought by the extraordinary industrial development of the last half century are felt in every fiber of our social and political being. Never before have men tried so vast and formidable an experiment as that of administering the affairs of a continent under the forms of a Democratic republic. The conditions which have told for our marvelous material well-being, which have developed to a very high degree our energy, self-reliance, and individual initiative, have also brought the care and anxiety inseparable from the accumulation of great wealth in industrial centers. Upon the success of our experiment much depends, not only as regards our own welfare, but as regards the welfare of mankind. If we fail, the cause of free self-government throughout the world will rock to its foundations, and therefore our responsibility is heavy, to ourselves, to the world as it is to-day, and to the generations yet unborn. There is no good reason why we should fear the future, but there is every reason why we should face it seriously, neither hiding from ourselves the gravity of the problems before us nor fearing to approach these problems with the unbending, unflinching purpose to solve them aright.

3   Yet, after all, though the problems are new, though the tasks set before us differ from the tasks set before our fathers who founded and preserved this Republic, the spirit in which these tasks must be undertaken and these problems faced, if our duty is to be well done, remains essentially unchanged. We know that self-government is difficult. We know that no people needs such high traits of character as that people which seeks to govern its affairs aright through the freely expressed will of the freemen who compose it. But we have faith that we shall not prove false to the memories of the men of the mighty past. They did their work, they left us the splendid heritage we now enjoy. We in our turn have an assured confidence that we shall be able to leave this heritage unwasted and enlarged to our children and our children's children. To do so we must show, not merely in great crises, but in the everyday affairs of life, the qualities of practical intelligence, of courage, of hardihood, and endurance, and above all the power of devotion to a lofty ideal, which made great the men who founded this Republic in the days of Washington, which made great the men who preserved this Republic in the days of Abraham Lincoln.

34. Which quotation from President Truman's excerpt supports the idea that the United States is built on the belief that all people have certain equal rights?

    A. "Each period of our national history has had its special challenges."
    B. "We believe that all men have the right to freedom of thought and expression."
    C. "Above all else, our people desire, and are determined to work for, peace on earth—a just and lasting peace—based on genuine agreement freely arrived at by equals."
    D. "Democracy is based on the conviction that man has the moral and intellectual capacity, as well as the inalienable right, to govern himself with reason and justice."

35. What can be inferred about President Truman's attitude toward communism?

    A. He believes that it might work in some foreign countries.
    B. He thinks it a dangerous philosophy.
    C. He believes that someday all countries will adopt it.
    D. He thinks that it fails to work because people are selfish.

36. What is the meaning of the word *unprecedented* as it is used in paragraph 4 of President Truman's speech?

    A. impossible to foresee
    B. not permitted by law
    C. not like anything previously known
    D. based on no apparent reason

37. At the beginning of his speech, how does President Roosevelt say the United States should act toward other countries?

    A. It should be friendly toward them.
    B. It should ignore them.
    C. It should assist them.
    D. It should be suspicious of them.

38. Which quotation from President Roosevelt's speech supports the idea that he believes the nation is facing a great challenge?

    A. "We have become a great nation, forced by the fact of its greatness into relations with the other nations of the earth, and we must behave as beseems a people with such responsibilities."
    B. "While ever careful to refrain from wrongdoing others, we must be no less insistent that we are not wronged ourselves."
    C. "Our relations with the other powers of the world are important; but still more important are our relations among ourselves."
    D. "If we fail, the cause of free self-government throughout the world will rock to its foundations, and therefore our responsibility is heavy, to ourselves, to the world as it is to-day, and to the generations yet unborn."

39. Based on the information in the speeches, what viewpoint do President Truman and President Roosevelt share?

    A. Communism is a threat to democracy.
    B. America's democratic form of government will last indefinitely.
    C. The problems facing the founding fathers were very different from the ones the country faces today.
    D. The founding fathers foresaw the many political issues that have arisen over the years.

40. How is the tone of President Truman's speech different from the tone of President Roosevelt's speech? President Truman's speech is more

    A. focused on dangers threatening the United States.
    B. optimistic about the future.
    C. unhappy about missed opportunities.
    D. angry about continued opposition to his policies.

41. In what way are the speeches by President Truman and President Roosevelt similar in style?

    A. They both use satire to make a point.
    B. They both use dramatic language to reinforce their ideas.
    C. They both use humor to engage their audience.
    D. They both make heavy use of metaphors and similar literary devices.

42. The following letter contains several numbered blanks, each marked "Select. . . ." Beneath each one is a set of choices. Indicate the choice from each set that is correct and belongs in the blank. (**Note:** On the real GED® test, the choices will appear as a "drop-down" menu. When you click on a choice, it will appear in the blank.)

To: All Students in Class 201

Re: Summer Employment

From: Professor Esposa

You probably will be looking for a summer job, so I thought I would give you some handy tips on how to apply for one. The
$\boxed{\text{Select 1... ▼}}$ a competitive place, so it's a good idea to be prepared in every way.

Select 1... ▼
world's
worlds'
world
worlds

Write an excellent resume. Keep it brief, just one page. Open with a statement about your talents and your goals. List any past experience you have had and explain briefly what each position consisted of. Add information about your education and any volunteer activities that you do. $\boxed{\text{Select 2... ▼}}$

Select 2... ▼
Don't use jargon. Do use language that is similar to what the job description used.
Don't use jargon: Do use language that is similar to what the job description used.
Don't use jargon, do use language that is similar to what the job description used.
Don't use jargon do use language that is similar to what the job description used.

Before you go on an interview, make sure to find out everything you can about the company. What are the company's leaders' goals? What are their needs? How can you be of help to [Select 3... ▼]

Select 3... ▼
him?
them?
themselves?
itself?

When you go for your interview, be confident. Dress comfortably but professionally. [Select 4... ▼] Smile and make eye contact. Be alert and be prepared to tell your interviewer why you would be an asset to this company.

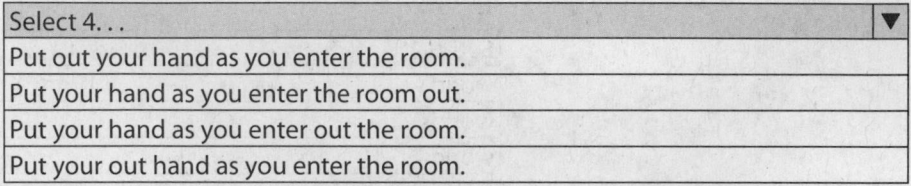

Select 4... ▼
Put out your hand as you enter the room.
Put your hand as you enter the room out.
Put your hand as you enter out the room.
Put your out hand as you enter the room.

One frequent question that interviewers like to ask is for you to name your best and worst trait. Give this some thought before you are interviewed. Try to come up with a positive trait that will impress the interviewer, such as being very thorough. You could also use that for your worst trait—being too thorough, which actually isn't that bad anyway. Just don't tell the interviewer that you hate to work. That would be a mistake.

I feel confident that if you follow these easy suggestions, you will land the job you want. And this will be a great opportunity to test your interviewing skills before you graduate from State, so that you will have experience on how to deal with other potential interviewers.

Use the excerpt for Items 43 through 49:

Excerpt Adapted from Opening Keynote Address at the Annual Biomedical Research Conference for Minority Students

by Dr. Cora Marrett, Deputy Director, National Science Foundation

1   The issue of U.S. global competitiveness continues to be a top priority for the country and across the federal government. The emphasis appears in the directions science funding agencies—the National Institutes of Health, the National Science Foundation, for example—have chosen.

2   Sobering statistics help account for the emphasis on competitiveness. Consider information Staples has compiled. It indicates that the United States ranks 21 out of 30 developed nations on student achievement, as measured by international science assessments. . . . We rank 27th among the developed nations in the percentage of college graduates with degrees in the sciences or engineering.

3   But this is no time for reviewing discouraging statistics, for this conference shows faces of encouragement, of not just a belief in possibilities but experiences with success.

4   Instead, I offer three take-home messages—particularly to the undergraduate and graduate students assembled here. First, the global arena is an inviting one. This message alters somewhat the theme of the meeting. Recall that theme: "Increasing Diversity to Improve Global Scientific Competitiveness." Such a message has been used as a call to action by business leaders, elected representatives and, yes, an organization such as the National Science Foundation.

5   But what might such a message mean to many of you here, who are not yet in the seats of influence you will someday occupy?

6   I suggest that it should encourage you to look beyond the borders of this nation for opportunities and challenges.

7   Yes, your pursuit of the biological and behavioral sciences should indeed improve the competitiveness of the United States. But, if you pursue international research experiences and opportunities, you will contribute substantially to your own development as scientists and that of the nation.

8   Let me elaborate a bit. Global competitiveness requires a science and engineering community that moves easily across borders, taking advantage of developments at the frontier of knowledge, wherever those developments are found. Experiences at the frontier of science are rewarding, both professionally and personally.

9   The second take-home message follows from the first. It is this: Success demands perseverance. How many record books report on those who started but did not complete the race?

10   Third, think of the National Science Foundation as your cheer-leading section, a body that applauds the strides you're making. We cheer you, given our determination, our path-breaking attempts to broaden participation in the science and engineering enterprise of the nation.

11   Let me recount a story of someone on an educational path like yours. Dr. Jagger Harvey began as an NSF Minority Postdoctoral Research Fellow.

12   He took his fellowship to the United Kingdom—Norwich and Cambridge, specifically—where he undertook research on plant viruses. Ultimately, he made significant progress on anti-viral treatments for plants.

13   His interest in plant genetics, international development, and Africa led him to the International Livestock Research Institute in Nairobi, Kenya, where he is a Research Scientist.

14   He recently served on one of the review panels for NSF's BREAD program, or, "Basic Research to Enable Agricultural Development." He is building his career as a biologist both in the United States and in Africa. He's making a difference through his dedication to science in service to human health and well-being.

15   Examples abound that illustrate the importance of perseverance, of persistence.

16   Let me mention the work of two students who participated in the East Asia and Pacific Summer Institutes program that NSF sponsors. Timothy Downing, a UC Berkeley student, went to Japan to study stem cells, out of his interest in the regeneration of the spinal cord.

17   Tim is an outstanding scientist, and it was his involvement in college football that inspired his research on peripheral nerve damage and the disabilities that result. He engineered nerve conduits in rats by seeding neural crest stem cells to repair sciatic nerves. The process accelerated regeneration and shows potential for the engineering of tissue for medical application.

18   Let me turn next to Sook-Lei Liew. She traveled to China for an opportunity to conduct research examining the role of experience on neural networks. She used functional magnetic resonance imaging to explore how experience changes neural activity patterns when people view familiar or unfamiliar socially relevant actions.

19   One of the questions she explored was: What happens when we try to understand *why* someone is doing something?

20   She scanned brain activity of participants as they observed videos of either racially familiar or unfamiliar actors performing familiar or unfamiliar gestures. Her surprising finding: Different regions of the brain were involved in trying to understand unfamiliar in contrast to familiar actions.

21   The processes she observed about how sense-making took place have widespread implications. They give clues, for example, about how a person in an unfamiliar environment may seek to interpret an unknown, culture-specific gesture.

22   Through her journey to a different setting and her perseverance, Lei Liew is now a published author.

23   Let me turn now to my third message: Your success matters greatly to the National Science Foundation.

24   The Foundation has embraced fully the aspirational statement by President Obama to the National Academy of Sciences in 2009. His statement: "Science is more essential for our prosperity, our security, our health, our environment, and our quality of life than it has ever been before. We . . . need to work with our friends around the world."

25   The National Science Foundation recognizes that wasting talent is not an option—not if we are to meet the economic and other needs of the country, in competition and alliance with others across the globe.

43. Which quotation supports the idea that the National Science Foundation supports helping minority students succeed in science?

    A. "The issue of U.S. global competitiveness continues to be a top priority for the country and across the federal government."

    B. "I suggest that it should encourage you to look beyond the borders of this nation for opportunities and challenges."

    C. "Let me mention the work of two students who participated in the East Asia and Pacific Summer Institutes program that NSF sponsors."

    D. "They give clues, for example, about how a person in an unfamiliar environment may seek to interpret an unknown, culture-specific gesture."

44. What do the statistics show about people graduating with degrees in science?

    A. Science is a popular field for American students.

    B. Foreign schools are more appealing to American students.

    C. The United States ranks poorly in the number of science students.

    D. Science students are studying abroad rather than in the United States.

45. Which word is closest in meaning to the word *peripheral* in paragraph 17?

    A. central
    B. habitual
    C. secondary
    D. rational

46. What is the purpose of Dr. Marrett's speech?

    A. to stress that the NSF cannot take sides politically because of its mission statement
    B. to express her feelings about the rankings of the United States for students of science
    C. to show that the NSF is introducing new programs to help minority students study science
    D. to encourage her audience to continue to study science in a way that will benefit them and the world

47. In what way does the information about what the students researched support the main idea?

    A. It supports the idea that scientists must study everything that they find of interest in the world.
    B. It supports the idea that people who study science can make a difference in the world.
    C. It supports the idea that many programs exist for minority students who want to study science.
    D. It supports the idea that more emphasis on science at the early grades would be productive.

48. Based on the speech, what generalization could be made about the NSF's attitude toward the United States?

    A. The country is failing to encourage talented students to study science.
    B. The country is trying hard to improve its education programs to encourage science study.
    C. Most people are unaware of the country's standing in science majors compared to other countries.
    D. It is likely that the country will never train as many people in science as other countries will.

49. Why does Dr. Marrett include the quotation from President Obama?

    A. to show that the President helps support the NSF
    B. to explain why President Obama was returned to office
    C. to explain why the NSF supports the Obama administration
    D. to show that the President is aware of how important science is

Use the excerpt for Items 50 through 55:

Excerpt Adapted from *Main Street*

by Sinclair Lewis

1   The last faculty reception before commencement. In five days they would be in the cyclone of final examinations.

2   The house of the president had been massed with palms suggestive of polite undertaking parlors, and in the library, a ten-foot room with a globe and the portraits of Whittier and Martha Washington, the student orchestra was playing "Carmen" and "Madame Butterfly." Carol was dizzy with music and the emotions of parting. She saw the palms as a jungle, the pink-shaded electric globes as an opaline haze, and the eye-glassed faculty as Olympians. She was melancholy at the sight of the mousey girls with whom she had "always intended to get acquainted," and the half dozen young men who were ready to fall in love with her.

3   But it was Stewart Snyder whom she encouraged. He was so much manlier than the others; he was an even warm brown, like his new ready-made suit with its padded shoulders. She sat with him, and with two cups of coffee and a chicken patty, upon a pile of presidential overshoes in the coat-closet under the stairs, and as the thin music seeped in, Stewart whispered:

4   "I can't stand it, this breaking up after four years! The happiest years of life."

5   She believed it. "Oh, I know! To think that in just a few days we'll be parting, and we'll never see some of the bunch again!"

6   "Carol, you got to listen to me! You always duck when I try to talk seriously to you, but you got to listen to me. I'm going to be a big lawyer, maybe a judge, and I need you, and I'd protect you—"

7   His arm slid behind her shoulders. The insinuating music drained her independence. She said mournfully, "Would you take care of me?" She touched his hand. It was warm, solid.

8   "You bet I would! We'd have, Lord, we'd have bully times in Yankton, where I'm going to settle—"

9   "But I want to do something with life."

10   "What's better than making a comfy home and bringing up some cute kids and knowing nice homey people?"

11   It was the immemorial male reply to the restless woman. Thus to the young Sappho spake the melon-venders; thus the captains to Zenobia; and in the damp cave over gnawed bones the hairy suitor thus protested to the

woman advocate of matriarchy. In the dialect of Blodgett College but with the voice of Sappho was Carol's answer:

12   "Of course. I know. I suppose that's so. Honestly, I do love children. But there's lots of women that can do housework, but I—well, if you HAVE got a college education, you ought to use it for the world."

13   "I know, but you can use it just as well in the home. And gee, Carol, just think of a bunch of us going out on an auto picnic, some nice spring evening."

14   "Yes."

15   "And sleigh-riding in winter, and going fishing—"

16   Blarrrrrr! The orchestra had crashed into the "Soldiers' Chorus"; and she was protesting, "No! No! You're a dear, but I want to do things. I don't understand myself but I want—everything in the world! Maybe I can't sing or write, but I know I can be an influence in library work. Just suppose I encouraged some boy and he became a great artist! I will! I will do it! Stewart dear, I can't settle down to nothing but dish-washing!"

17   Two minutes later—two hectic minutes—they were disturbed by an embarrassed couple also seeking the idyllic seclusion of the overshoe-closet.

18   After graduation she never saw Stewart Snyder again. She wrote to him once a week—for one month.

19   A year Carol spent in Chicago. Her study of library-cataloguing, recording, books of reference, was easy and not too somniferous. She reveled in the Art Institute, in symphonies and violin recitals and chamber music, in the theater and classic dancing. She almost gave up library work to become one of the young women who dance in cheese-cloth in the moonlight. She was taken to a certified Studio Party, with beer, cigarettes, bobbed hair, and a Russian Jewess who sang the Internationale. It cannot be reported that Carol had anything significant to say to the Bohemians. She was awkward with them, and felt ignorant, and she was shocked by the free manners which she had for years desired. But she heard and remembered discussions of Freud, Romain Rolland, syndicalism, the Confederation Generale du Travail, feminism vs. haremism, Chinese lyrics, nationalization of mines, Christian Science, and fishing in Ontario.

20   She went home, and that was the beginning and end of her Bohemian life.

21   The second cousin of Carol's sister's husband lived in Winnetka, and once invited her out to Sunday dinner. She walked back through Wilmette and Evanston, discovered new forms of suburban architecture, and remembered her desire to recreate villages. She decided that she would give up library work and, by a miracle whose nature was not very clearly revealed to her, turn a prairie town into Georgian houses and Japanese bungalows.

22   The next day in library class she had to read a theme on the use of the Cumulative Index, and she was taken so seriously in the discussion that she put off her career of town-planning—and in the autumn she was in the public library of St. Paul.

50. What can be inferred about Carol?

    A. She wants to experience life.
    B. She wants to live a traditional life.
    C. She has little control over her emotions.
    D. She has a stubborn streak that can be annoying.

51. Which quotation supports the story's theme?

    A. "But it was Stewart Snyder whom she encouraged."
    B. " 'Stewart dear, I can't settle down to nothing but dish-washing!' "
    C. "After graduation she never saw Stewart Snyder again."
    D. "She went home, and that was the beginning and end of her Bohemian life."

52. What does Stewart think about Carol?

    A. He knows that she is sensitive.
    B. He feels she needs more challenges.
    C. He understands her need to succeed.
    D. He thinks she would be a good housewife.

53. Indicate each word that DESCRIBES Carol and belongs in the character web. (**Note:** On the real GED® test, you will click on the words you choose and "drag" each one into position in the character web.)

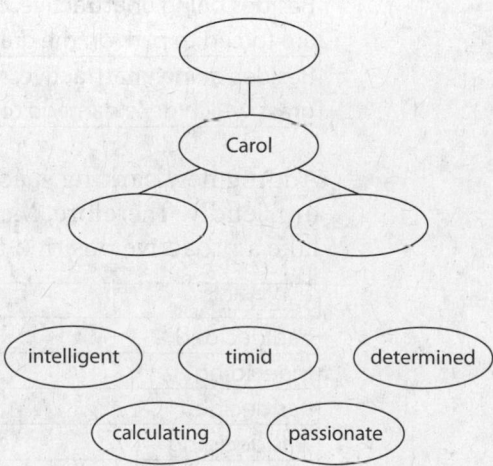

54. What does the author's use of the words *insinuating music* in paragraph 7 suggest?

    A. It suggests that the music was enjoyable to hear.
    B. It suggests that Carol was a lover of classical music.
    C. It suggests that the music had an odd rhythm.
    D. It suggests that the music was making Carol lose her concentration.

55. Why does Carol go to the Bohemian party?

    A. She thinks she might fit in with them.
    B. She wants to show them their errors.
    C. She hopes to teach them about books.
    D. She was doing research for a library course.

56. The following memo contains several numbered blanks, each marked "Select. . . ." Beneath each one is a set of choices. Indicate the choice from each set that is correct and belongs in the blank. (**Note:** On the real GED® test, the choices will appear as a "drop-down" menu. When you click on a choice, it will appear in the blank.)

Memo: To All Employees

Our company has been going through a growth spurt. And because of this, it has become clear that there is not enough parking for everyone.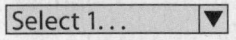

Select 1... ▼
Many times employees are forced to park on the grass, besides being unattractive, which does damage to the ground.
Many times employees are forced to park on the grass, which, besides being unattractive, does damage to the ground.
Besides being unattractive, does damage to the ground, many times employees are forced to park on the grass.
Besides being unattractive, many times employees are forced to park on the grass which does damage to the ground.

Adding new parking spaces is expensive and environmentally unfriendly. Therefore, Management here at Solsuns 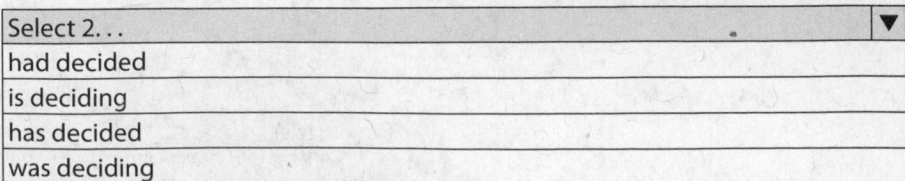 to take a proactive position regarding carpooling.

Select 2... ▼
had decided
is deciding
has decided
was deciding

There are many advantages to carpooling. It helps the environment; you will use less gas and cause fewer emissions. You will save money; by ride sharing, you will end up purchasing less gasoline. It will resolve the company's parking problem. And carpooling will enhance the image of Solsuns with our customers and with our community. Let's set an example and make the concept of driving alone a thing of the past!

Select 3... ▼ Employees who carpool will be given preferred parking spaces. Those who ride the bus will be given rebates toward the cost of the ticket. Bike racks will be installed in the front. We will start construction next week on locker room and shower facilities, and they should be completed in two weeks.

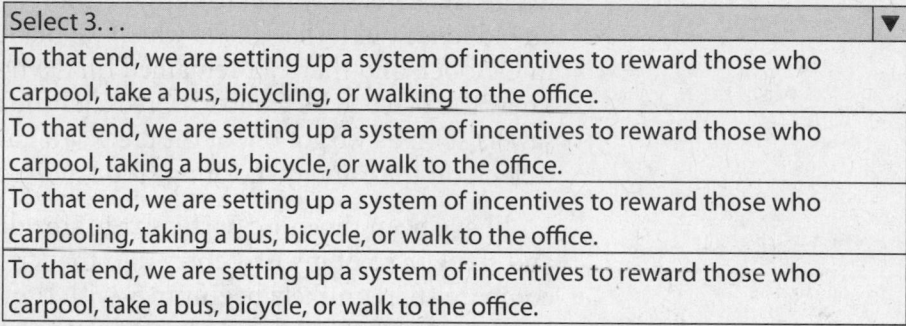

Select 3... ▼
To that end, we are setting up a system of incentives to reward those who carpool, take a bus, bicycling, or walking to the office.
To that end, we are setting up a system of incentives to reward those who carpool, taking a bus, bicycle, or walk to the office.
To that end, we are setting up a system of incentives to reward those who carpooling, taking a bus, bicycle, or walk to the office.
To that end, we are setting up a system of incentives to reward those who carpool, take a bus, bicycle, or walk to the office.

In addition, all employees who participate and use alternative means to driving alone to commute to and from the office will receive a reward equal to 1 percent of their net biweekly income on each paycheck for as long as they continue to participate.

Sign-up sheets are now available. A database will be set up so you can easily find those who live near you, and routes will be mapped. Select 4... ▼

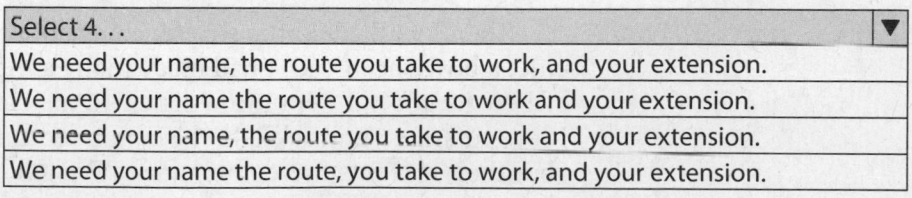

Select 4... ▼
We need your name, the route you take to work, and your extension.
We need your name the route you take to work and your extension.
We need your name, the route you take to work and your extension.
We need your name the route, you take to work, and your extension.

We are very excited here at Solsuns about our new carpooling program.

Use the excerpt for Items 57 through 64:

Excerpt Adapted from *The Autobiography of Benjamin Franklin*

1   However, walking in the evening by the side of the river, a boat came by, which I found was going towards Philadelphia, with several people in her. They took me in, and, as there was no wind, we row'd all the way; and about midnight, not having yet seen the city, some of the company were confident we must have passed it, and would row no farther; the others knew not where we were; so we put toward the shore, got into a creek, landed near an old fence, with the rails of which we made a fire, the night being cold, in October, and there we remained till daylight. Then one of the company knew the place to be Cooper's Creek, a little above Philadelphia, which we saw as soon as we got out of the creek, and arriv'd there about eight or nine o'clock on the Sunday morning, and landed at the Market-street wharf.

2   I have been the more particular in this description of my journey, and shall be so of my first entry into that city, that you may in your mind compare such unlikely beginnings with the figure I have since made there. I was in my working dress, my best cloths being to come round by sea. I was dirty from my journey; my pockets were stuff'd out with shirts and stockings, and I knew no soul nor where to look for lodging. I was fatigued with travelling, rowing, and want of rest, I was very hungry; and my whole stock of cash consisted of a Dutch dollar, and about a shilling in copper. The latter I gave the people of the boat for my passage, who at first refus'd it, on account of my rowing; but I insisted on their taking it. A man being sometimes more generous when he has but a little money than when he has plenty, perhaps thro' fear of being thought to have but little.

3   Then I walked up the street, gazing about till near the market-house I met a boy with bread. I had made many a meal on bread, and, inquiring where he got it, I went immediately to the baker's he directed me to, in Second-street, and ask'd for biscuit, intending such as we had in Boston; but they, it seems, were not made in Philadelphia. So not considering or knowing the difference of money, and the greater cheapness nor the names of his bread, I made him give me three-penny worth of any sort. He gave me, accordingly, three great puffy rolls. I was surpriz'd at the quantity, but took it, and, having no room in my pockets, walk'd off with a roll under each arm, and eating the other. Thus I went up Market-street as far as Fourth-street, passing by the door of Mr. Read, my future wife's father; when she, standing at the door, saw me, and thought I made, as I certainly did, a most awkward, ridiculous appearance. Then I turned and went down Chestnut-street and part of Walnut-street, eating my roll all the way.

4   Thus refreshed, I walked again up the street, which by this time had many clean-dressed people in it, who were all walking the same way. I joined them, and thereby was led into the great meeting-house of the Quakers near the market. I sat down among them, and, after looking round awhile and hearing nothing said, being very drowsy thro' labor and want of rest the preceding night, I fell fast asleep, and continued so till the meeting broke up, when one was kind enough to rouse me. This was, therefore, the first house I was in, or slept in, in Philadelphia.

5   Walking down again toward the river, and, looking in the faces of people, I met a young Quaker man, whose countenance I lik'd, and, accosting him, requested he would tell me where a stranger could get lodging. He brought me to the Crooked Billet in Water-street. Here I got a dinner; and, while I was eating it, several sly questions were asked me, as it seemed to be suspected from my youth and appearance, that I might be some runaway.

6   After dinner, my sleepiness return'd, and being shown to a bed, I lay down without undressing, and slept till six in the evening, was call'd to supper, went to bed again very early, and slept soundly till next morning. Then I made myself as tidy as I could, and went to Andrew Bradford the printer's. I found in the shop the old man his father, whom I had seen at New York, and who, travelling on horseback, had got to Philadelphia before me. He introduc'd me to his son, who receiv'd me civilly, gave me a breakfast, but told me he did not at present want a hand, being lately suppli'd with one; but there was another printer in town, lately set up, one Keimer, who, perhaps, might employ me; if not, I should be welcome to lodge at his house, and he would give me a little work to do now and then till fuller business should offer.

57. Which quotation supports the idea that Benjamin Franklin had a well-developed system of values?

    A. "However, walking in the evening by the side of the river, a boat came by, which I found was going towards Philadelphia, with several people in her."

    B. "The latter I gave the people of the boat for my passage, who at first refus'd it, on account of my rowing; but I insisted on their taking it."

    C. "I was surpriz'd at the quantity, but took it, and, having no room in my pockets, walk'd off with a roll under each arm, and eating the other."

    D. "After dinner, my sleepiness return'd, and being shown to a bed, I lay down without undressing, and slept till six in the evening, was call'd to supper, went to bed again very early, and slept soundly till next morning."

58. What effect does Franklin hope to achieve by using the word *sly* in paragraph 5? It shows that

    A. he was aware of the intent of the questions.
    B. the people asking the questions were impolite.
    C. he was being very careful about what he told anyone.
    D. the people who asked the questions were not all that interested.

59. Fill in the blank.

    Another way to say *countenance* as it is used in paragraph 5 is

    _____.

60. Why does the author include information about seeing his future wife?

    A. to explain how he met his wife
    B. to tell a funny story about himself
    C. to suggest that his wife was self-absorbed
    D. to show that he fell in love with her right away

61. Why was helping to row the ship important to the story? It shows

    A. that Franklin could row well.
    B. what kind of person Franklin was.
    C. how hard it was to travel in the old days.
    D. that the ship could keep going without wind.

62. How does the information about Franklin falling asleep in the Quaker meeting hall support the main idea? It shows that

    A. Franklin was a person who did whatever it took to reach his goal.
    B. Quakers were a friendly group of people who cared about Franklin.
    C. Franklin found it hard to make friends in a city where he knew no one.
    D. Quakers traveling at the time had few places where they could stay.

63. Fill in the blank.

    The Market Street harbor where Franklin arrived was in the city of

    _____.

64. What main idea can be inferred from the passage?

    A. Franklin was narrow-minded.
    B. Franklin was seeking a new life.
    C. Franklin wanted to get married.
    D. Franklin was interested in religion.

Part 2: Essay

1 question | **45 minutes**

Use the following two excerpts for Item 65:

Excerpt Adapted from a Speech by Senator Richard Durbin

1 First, the Electoral College is undemocratic and unfair. It distorts the election process, with some votes by design having more weight than others. Imagine for a moment if you were told as follows: We want you to vote for President. We are going to give you one vote in selection of the President, but a neighbor of yours is going to have three votes in selecting the President.

2 You would say that is not American, that is fundamentally unfair. We live in a nation that is one person—one citizen, one vote.

3 But that is exactly what the Electoral College does. When you look at the states, Wyoming has a population of roughly 480,000 people. In the State of Wyoming, they have three electoral votes. So that means that roughly they have 1 vote for President for every 160,000 people who live in the state of Wyoming—1 vote for President, 160,000 people. My home State of Illinois: 12 million people and specifically 22 electoral votes. That means it takes 550,000 voters in Illinois to vote and cast 1 electoral vote for President. Comparing the voters in Wyoming to the voters in Illinois, there are three times as many people voting in Illinois to have 1 vote for President as in the State of Wyoming.

4 On the other hand, the philosophical underpinning of a direct popular election system is so clear and compelling it hardly needs mentioning. We use direct elections to choose senators, governors, congressmen, and mayors, but we do not use it to elect a President. One-person, one-vote, and majority rule are supposedly basic tenets of a democracy.

5 Second, while it appears smaller and more rural states have an advantage in the Electoral College, the reality of modern presidential campaigns is that these states are generally ignored.

6 One of my colleagues on the floor said: I will fight you, Durbin, on this idea of abolishing the Electoral College. I come from a little state, and if you go to a popular vote to elect a President, presidential candidates will pay no attention to my little state.

7 I have news for my colleagues. You did not see Governor Bush or Vice President Gore spending much time campaigning in Rhode Island or Idaho.

In fact, 14 states were never visited by either candidate during the campaign, while 38 states received 10 or fewer visits. The more populous contested states with their large electoral prizes, such as Florida, Pennsylvania, Ohio, and Wisconsin, really have the true advantage whether we have a direct election or whether we have it by the Electoral College.

8   Third, the Electoral College system totally discounts the votes of those supporting the losing candidate in their state. In the 2000 presidential race, 36 states were never really in doubt. The average percentage difference of the popular vote between the candidates in those states was more than 20 percent. The current system not only discounts losing votes; it essentially adds the full weight and value of those votes to the candidate those voters oppose.

9   Fourth, the winner-take-all rules greatly increase the risk that minor third party candidates will determine who is elected President. In the Electoral College system, the importance of a small number of votes in a few key states is greatly magnified. In a number of U.S. presidential elections, third-party candidates have affected a few key state races and determined the overall winner.

Excerpt from Speech by
U.S. Representative Ron Paul

1   Today's presidential election is likely to be relatively close, at least in terms of popular vote totals. Should either candidate win the election but lose the overall popular vote, we will be bombarded with calls to abolish the Electoral College, just as we were after the contested 2000 presidential election. After all, the pundits will argue, it would be "undemocratic" to deny the presidency to the man who received the most votes.

2   This argument is hostile to the Constitution, however, which expressly established the United States as a constitutionally limited republic and not a direct democracy. The Founding Fathers sought to protect certain fundamental freedoms, such as freedom of speech, against the changing whims of popular opinion. Similarly, they created the Electoral College to guard against majority tyranny in federal elections. The president was to be elected by the 50 states rather than the American people directly, to ensure that less populated states had a voice in national elections. This is why they blended Electoral College votes between U.S. House seats, which are based on population, and U.S. Senate seats, which are accorded equally to each state. The goal was to balance the inherent tension between majority will and majority tyranny. Those who wish to abolish the Electoral College because it's not purely democratic should also argue that less populated states like Rhode Island or Wyoming don't deserve two senators.

3   A presidential campaign in a purely democratic system would look very strange indeed, as any rational candidate would focus only on a few big population centers. A candidate receiving a large percentage of the popular vote in California, Texas, Florida, and New York, for example, could win the presidency with very little support in dozens of other states. Moreover, a popular vote system would only intensify political pandering, as national candidates would face even greater pressure than today to take empty, middle-of-the-road, poll-tested, mainstream positions. Direct democracy in national politics would further dilute regional differences of opinion on issues, further narrow voter choices, and further emasculate political courage.

4   Those who call for the abolition of the Electoral College are hostile to liberty. Not surprisingly, most advocates of abolition are statist elites concentrated largely on the east and west coasts. These political, economic, academic, media, and legal elites overwhelmingly favor a strong centralized federal government, and express contempt for the federalist concept of states' rights. They believe in omnipotent federal power, with states acting as mere glorified federal counties carrying out commands from Washington.

5   The Electoral College threatens the imperial aims of these elites because it allows the individual states to elect the President, and in many states the majority of voters still believe in limited government and the Constitution. Voters in southern, midwestern, and western states—derided as "flyover" country—tend to value family, religion, individual liberty, property rights, and gun rights. Washington elites abhor these values, and they hate that middle and rural America hold any political power whatsoever. Their efforts to discredit the Electoral College system are an open attack on the voting power of the pro-liberty states.

6   Sadly, we have forgotten that states created the federal government, not the other way around. The Electoral College system represents an attempt, however effective, to limit federal power and preserve states' rights. It is an essential part of our federalist balance. It also represents a reminder that pure democracy, mob rule, is incompatible with liberty.

65. Extended response

While Senator Richard Durbin argues that the Electoral College system used in the election of presidents should be changed, U.S. Representative Ron Paul argues that it should continue to be the law of the land.

In your response, analyze both speeches to determine which position is best supported. Use relevant and specific evidence from both sources to support your response.

Write your response in the box on the following page. This task may require approximately 45 minutes to complete.

POSTTEST

Cut   Copy   Paste   Undo   Redo

THIS IS THE END OF THE REASONING THROUGH LANGUAGE ARTS (RLA) POSTTEST.

Reasoning Through Language Arts (RLA)

Answers and Explanations

1. **Correct answer: A.** She sings over her. Alma is clearly upset when she hears Candace Whitcomb singing at the same time she is singing; she can hardly continue because she is so upset.

2. **Correct answer: B.** "Now she fixed her large solemn blue eyes; her long, delicate face, which had been pretty, turned paler; the blue flowers on her bonnet trembled; her little thin gloved hands, clutching the singing book, shook perceptibly; but she sang out bravely." This quotation supports the idea that Alma Way is nervous. The others do not.

3. **Correct answer: A.** She is angry that she had been replaced. The reader can infer from how she behaves that Candace is upset because she has been replaced.

4. **Correct answer: A.** To show support. The woman tells Alma Way that "It ain't worth minding." She is showing her support by giving Alma a candy.

5. **Correct answer: D.** He was linked romantically to Candace Whitcomb. The narrator tells us that people thought William might marry Candace, so this is the reason that it was surprising for him to speak up against her.

6. Drop-down Select . . . 1–5.

   Select 1 correct answer: Habitat does a wonderful job of building and rehabbing houses. In this choice, the verbs *building* and *rehabbing* are parallel; they are in the same form. That is not the case in the other choices.

   Select 2 correct answer: There are many items that we would like to see obtained for the silent auction. The insertion of *There*

are creates a complete sentence. The other choices are fragments; they do not have a subject and verb.

   Select 3 correct answer: yourselves. This is a reflexive pronoun that agrees with the antecedent, *you*. It is a second person plural form, which is required to correctly edit the sentence.

   Select 4 correct answer: There is a sign-up sheet in the lunchroom for those of you who would like to give up your time during the auction itself. The order of the sentence is clear and effective as well as logical.

   Select 5 correct answer: Do plan on attending, even if you cannot volunteer time, and please bring your wallets, credit cards, or checkbooks. The verb *bring* agrees with the subject, *you*, which is understood and requires a plural verb form in the present tense.

7. **Correct answer: B.** To free enslaved people in areas that were then in rebellion. This is the reason that President Abraham Lincoln drafted the Emancipation Proclamation; the answer is in the text itself.

8. **Correct answer: D.** The United States declares that in the areas then in rebellion, all people who have been enslaved are henceforth free. This sums up the main idea of the Emancipation Proclamation; the other choices do not.

9. **Correct answer: B.** The United States is a better country because of the Emancipation Proclamation. President Obama clearly thinks that Lincoln's proclamation was a step forward

in securing the rights of all people in the United States.

10. **Correct answer: D. T**o point out that the freed slaves aided the Union war effort. President Obama says that when Lincoln permitted the freed slaves to enlist in the Union army and navy, they give "new strength to liberty's cause." That is, they aided the Union war effort, and President Obama wants to make sure that their contribution is remembered.

11. **Correct answer: C.** To point out that the Emancipation Proclamation has been an important inspiration for later generations of Americans. By including this sentence, President Obama is saying that the beliefs underlying the Emancipation Proclamation have inspired Americans of all kinds to demand and fight for civil rights and other causes from that time until our own day.

12. **Correct answer: C.** "Let us begin this new year by renewing our bonds to one another and reinvesting in the work that lies ahead, confident that we can keep driving freedom's progress in our time." This sentence shows that President Obama believes that there is more work to be done to ensure that people have the rights the Constitution gives them.

13. **Emancipation Proclamation:**

Certain states and parts of states are currently in rebellion against the United States.

The slaves in the rebellious areas must be freed and be paid for their work.

President Barack Obama's Proclamation:

The Emancipation Proclamation turned the Civil War into a war for liberty and equality.

People who join together can maintain and expand freedom.

14. **Correct answer: C.** President Obama's proclamation is more inspirational in tone than the Emancipation Proclamation.

The Emancipation Proclamation is an official document setting forth an act of government in basic legal terms. President Obama's proclamation, while also an official document, merely asks Americans to observe the anniversary of the Emancipation Proclamation. It uses inspirational language to remind Americans why the Emancipation Proclamation deserves to be commemorated.

15. **Correct answer: D.** The Emancipation Proclamation was an official order, but President Obama's proclamation was merely an appeal. Both are government documents, but the Emancipation Proclamation was an executive order with the force of law and tremendous real-world consequences. President Obama's proclamation, by contrast, is merely an appeal that calls upon Americans to observe an anniversary. There is no expectation that it will be enforced in any way.

16. **Correct answer: B.** President Lincoln is focused on immediate measures; President Obama is focused on the longer term. In regard to the fight for freedom, President Lincoln's Emancipation Proclamation is focused on one single step to be taken immediately: freeing the slaves in the areas then in rebellion "as a fit and necessary war measure." President Obama, on the other hand, takes a longer view, speaking of the spirit that "moved millions to march for justice in the years that followed."

17. Drop down Select . . . 1–4.

Select 1 correct answer: Instead, employee ID swipe cards will be coded only for the specific hours that an employee is scheduled to work during a week's period. This editing creates the most straightforward and clear sentence; the other choices do not.

Select 2 correct answer: In addition,. The preceding sentences described a change in the rules regarding use of the employee ID swipe cards. The introductory phrase "In addition" signals to the reader that the next sentence will describe another new change to the security rules.

Select 3 correct answer: their. This is the way the possessive pronoun is spelled. It makes sense in the sentence.

Select 4 correct answer: Anyone who senses that there is something out of the ordinary should call security. We will handle the problem. The placement of a period between the two complete thoughts, creating two complete sentences, is the edit that is needed to resolve the issue of the run-on sentence.

18. **Correct answer: A.** Della selling her hair. This event develops the theme of the story, a theme of sacrificing something for love. The other events do not advance the theme.

19. **Correct answer: B.** "Once she faltered for a minute and stood still while a tear or two splashed on the worn red carpet." This quotation expresses how mixed Della's feelings were about selling her hair. The others do not.

20. **Correct answer: D.** It helps the reader realize how beautiful Della's hair is. This is the meaning of these figurative words. Her hair seemed like water running down a cascade.

21. **Correct order:**

   Della counts her money.

   Della sells her hair.

   Della goes shopping.

   Della gives Jim his present.

22. **Correct answer: A.** It shows he wants to get on with life. By saying this, Jim shows that he has accepted what happened and wants to move on. He also suggests that in time they will be able to make use of their gifts.

23. **Correct answer: D.** To suggest how quiet an Indian boy's step is. This is the meaning of the simile.

24. Blank should be filled in with: **crane**.

25. **Correct answer: D.** It shows that the hunting instinct is natural to an Indian boy. This choice supports the idea that Indian boys are excellent hunters in spite of their age.

26. **Correct answer: C.** "An old deer-track would at once bring on a warm discussion as to whether it was the track of a buck or a doe." This quotation tells about how the Indian boys studied animal life; it shows how they learned from the tracks of a deer.

27. **Correct answer: D.** Bow and arrow. This information is found in the passage. A close reading will reveal the answer.

28. **Correct answer: B.** The narrator wants readers to know how inventive the Indian boys were. The narrator shows that the Indian boys found various ways to catch the fish; they were inventive.

29. Words that describe the narrator:

   Correct answer: careful. From the way the narrator describes himself and the other Indian boys they are careful when it comes to dangerous animals, such as bears.

   Correct answer: quick. The narrator is clearly quick when he hunts or he wouldn't get his prey.

   Correct answer: curious. The narrator is curious about the animals that he hunts, as are the other Indian boys.

30. **Correct answer: A.** At noon. The narrator tells the reader this in paragraph 7. A close reading will give the answer.

31. **Correct answer: C.** The adult cranes would attack them. This was the point of the story that the narrator tells about the boys' dealings with cranes.

32. **Correct answer: D.** Bone and stones. The answer is stated in the text.

33. Drop down Select . . . 1–5.

   Select 1 correct answer: Vista Green's. This is the correct form for a possessive noun.

   Select 2 correct answer: week. This is the correct spelling for a period of seven days.

   Select 3 correct answer: This is one of the seven restaurants that the resort boasts. The verb *boasts* agrees in number with the subject and is in the present tense because the action takes place in the present.

   Select 4 correct answer: During your stay, you may want to take one of the many tours that are offered. This is the simplest and most straightforward way of communicating the information in this sentence. The other choices are illogical and/or ungrammatical.

   Select 5 correct answer: Remember, our motto here is "The guest comes first." We intend to stay true to it. This choice has a period between the two complete thoughts, so it is not a run-on sentence.

34. **Correct answer: B.** "We believe that all men have the right to freedom of thought and expression." This quotation refers to the fact that the Constitution states that all men are created equal, and that they enjoy certain equal rights.

35. **Correct answer: B.** He thinks it a dangerous philosophy. Judging from the language that President Truman uses to describe Communism, such as calling it "false" and saying it "misleads," it would appear he thinks it is dangerous.

36. **Correct answer: C.** Not like anything previously known. Something that is *unprecedented* has not happened in the past; nothing like it has ever before occurred. This expression fits into the context of the sentence.

37. **Correct answer: A.** It should be friendly toward them. The answer is stated in the text.

President Roosevelt says that America's "our attitude must be one of cordial and sincere friendship."

38. **Correct answer: D.** "If we fail, the cause of free self-government throughout the world will rock to its foundations, and therefore our responsibility is heavy, to ourselves, to the world as it is to-day, and to the generations yet unborn." This quotation supports the idea that President Roosevelt believed the nation was facing a great challenge. The other choices do not.

39. **Correct answer: C.** The problems facing the founding fathers were very different from the ones the country faces today. Both presidents make this point; they note that the founding fathers could not have had any idea of the kind of problems that they are dealing with.

40. **Correct answer: A.** Focused on dangers threatening the United States President Truman's speech is largely about the threat of Communism; there is no support for any of the other choices.

41. **Correct answer: B.** They both use dramatic language to reinforce their ideas. Both Presidents use dramatic words and phrases to get their points across to the audience.

42. Drop down Select . . . 1–4.

   Select 1 correct answer: world's. *World's* is a contraction for *world is*. This is the correct spelling.

   Select 2 correct answer: Don't use jargon. Do use language that is similar to what the job description used. Of the other choices, one uses a colon incorrectly and the other two are run-on sentences that need a period placed between the two complete ideas.

   Select 3 correct answer: them?. This is the correct pronoun because it is in the objective case and agrees with the plural antecedent *leaders*.

Select 4 correct answer: Put out your hand as you enter the room. This is where the word *out* should go in the sentence. The other choices are incorrect.

43. **Correct answer: C.** "Let me mention the work of two students who participated in the East Asia and Pacific Summer Institutes program that NSF sponsors." This information directly supports the idea that NSF supports helping minority students succeed in science.

44. **Correct answer: C.** The United States ranks poorly in the number of science students. The information on the ranking of the United States is stated in the text.

45. **Correct answer: C.** Secondary. This word fits with the context of the sentence and the sentences that follow.

46. **Correct answer: D.** To encourage her audience to continue to study science in a way that will benefit them and the world. Dr. Marrett is interested in increasing the number of American students who go into the field of science; that is why she presents examples of students who have succeeded in the field.

47. **Correct answer: B.** It supports the idea that people who study science can make a difference in the world. This helps Dr. Marrett make the point that science is an important field and one where people can make important discoveries.

48. **Correct answer: A.** That the country is failing to encourage talented students to study science. This is why Dr. Marrett is concerned with the future of the United States and its worldwide standing in terms of the number of science majors.

49. **Correct answer: D.** To show that the President is aware of how important science is. The quotation shows that the NSF is not the only agency that realizes that in order for the nation to become more competitive, more students need to study science.

50. **Correct answer: A.** She wants to experience life. Carol knows she does not want to be a traditional housewife; she tries out what it would be like to be a Bohemian. She is curious about life.

51. **Correct answer: B.** "'Stewart dear, I can't settle down to nothing but dish-washing!'" This quotation supports the theme that one must find one's own way in life.

52. **Correct answer: D.** He thinks she would be a good housewife. We learn this from his conversation with her in the closet.

53. Words that describe Carol:

    Correct answer: intelligent. Carol graduates from college and goes on to study to be a librarian and seems to be doing well at it. She seems intelligent.

    Correct answer: determined. Clearly Carol is determined to make a difference in life.

    Correct answer: passionate. Carol seems to have deep feelings about her life and about experiencing new things. She is passionate about her life.

54. **Correct answer: D.** It suggests that the music was making Carol lose her concentration. The music was making Carol less focused and more romantic. The sentence goes on to say that the music "drained her of independence," so context helps to answer this question.

55. **Correct answer: A.** She thinks she might fit in with them. Carol fancied herself something of a Bohemian, but she finds that she does not fit in at all with real Bohemians.

56. Drop down Select . . . 1–4.

    Select 1 correct answer: Many times employees are forced to park on the grass, which, besides being unattractive, does damage to the ground. The order of the words is logical and the meaning is clear in this choice; the others are not.

Select 2 correct answer: has decided. The verb *has decided* is in the simple past tense, which is called for in this sentence.

Select 3 correct answer: To that end, we are setting up a system of incentives to reward those who carpool, take a bus, bicycle, or walk to the office. The verbs *carpool*, *take*, *bicycle*, and *walk* are parallel.

Select 4 correct answer: We need your name, the route you take to work, and your extension. The correct punctuation is to place commas after every item in a series, including the item before the word *and*.

57. **Correct answer: B.** "The latter I gave the people of the boat for my passage, who at first refus'd it, on account of my rowing; but I insisted on their taking it." This quotation directly supports the idea that Franklin's value system was well developed; even though he rowed, he wanted to pay his passage fee. Fairness was important to him.

58. **Correct answer: A.** He was aware of the intent of the questions. The questions were sly because the people did not want to offend Franklin, but he realized why they were asking them.

59. Blank should be filled in with: **face; the way the person looks**.

60. **Correct answer: B.** To tell a funny story about himself. Franklin put in many details about how silly he looked and the fact that his future wife thought he looked ridiculous in order to tell a funny story about the time they first saw each other.

61. **Correct answer: B.** It shows what kind of person Franklin was. The incident showed that Franklin did not put himself above others; he pitched in when it was needed. That was his character.

62. **Correct answer: A.** It shows that Franklin was a person who did whatever it took to reach his goal. This explanation supports the idea that Franklin was an inventive person who did what he needed to do to reach his goal—in this case to get some sleep.

63. Blank should be filled in with: **Philadelphia**.

64. **Correct answer: B.** Franklin was seeking a new life. The fact that he arrived in Philadelphia with little money and visited a printer to find work suggests that he was seeking a new life.

65. **Extended response.** Decide which of the two arguments you think is stronger. Then support your choice with evidence from the excerpts. In essay questions like this, there is no "right" or "wrong" side.

   The two speeches differ in the fact that Paul uses more emotional arguments than Durbin does, including his main point that majority rule is basically mob rule.

   Paul argues that abolition of the electoral system would be, in effect, unconstitutional because the country was founded not as a direct democracy but rather as a republic. He points out that the states made the federal government and not the other way around and the Electoral College protects the smaller, less powerful states, often considered "flyover states." He takes aim at the elites mainly found on the east and west coasts, saying they want a strong federal government and do not believe in states' rights. He goes so far as to say that pure democracy is incompatible with liberty.

   Durbin's approach is not without emotional statements, but tends to be more down to earth than Paul's. For instance, Paul says that changing the electoral system would make smaller states less important, but Durbin responds by saying that these smaller states are ignored today in campaigns for the most part anyway. Durbin points out that senators and House representatives are voted directly into office, so why not presidents? He calls the electoral system undemocratic and unfair because a vote in a less populated state carries more weight than one in a populous state such as Illinois. Another point that Durbin makes is that because of the Electoral College system, third-party candidates can have more effect than they could with a direct vote election.

If possible, ask an instructor to evaluate your essay. Your instructor's opinions and comments will help you determine what skills you need to practice in order to improve your essay writing.

You may also want to evaluate your essay yourself using the checklist that follows. Be fair in your evaluation. The more items you can check, the more confident you can be about your writing skills. Items that are not checked will show you the essay-writing skills that you need to work on.

My essay:

☐ Creates a sound, logical argument based on the passage(s).

☐ Cites evidence from the passage(s) to support the argument.

☐ Analyzes the issue and/or evaluates the validity of the arguments in the passage(s)

☐ Organizes ideas in a sensible sequence.

☐ Shows clear connections between main points and details.

☐ Uses largely correct sentence structure.

☐ Follows Standard English conventions in regard to grammar, spelling, and punctuation.

Evaluation Chart

Check the Answers and Explanations section of the RLA Posttest to see which answers you got correct and which ones you missed. For each multiple-choice question that you missed, find the item number in the chart below. Check the column on the left to see the test content area for that item. If you missed questions in a particular content area, you need to pay particular attention to that area as you study for the GED® test. The pages of this book that cover that content area are listed in the column on the right.

Content Area	Item Number	Pages to Review
1. Testing Basic English Usage Editing mechanics	6, 17, 33, 42, 56	164–186
2. Testing Reading Comprehension Basic critical reading skills	2, 3, 5, 6, 7, 16, 24, 27, 30, 32, 35, 39, 47, 48, 50, 62, 63, 64	193–203
3. Structure and Author's Choices Sequence of events Structural relationships Author's language	8, 14, 20, 22, 23, 36, 40, 41, 45, 54, 58, 59	209–218
4. Literary Texts (Fiction) Using textual evidence to analyze elements of fiction	1, 2, 3, 4, 5, 18, 19, 21, 28, 29, 31, 50, 51, 52, 53, 55	225–243
5. Informational Texts (Nonfiction) Inferring relationships between ideas Author's viewpoint and purpose Analyzing arguments Rhetorical techniques Author's response to conflicting viewpoints and bias Comparing texts	6, 9, 10, 11, 12, 13, 14, 15, 16, 25, 26, 34, 37, 38, 39, 40, 41, 43, 44, 46, 47, 48, 49, 57, 60, 61, 62	251–270

Mathematical Reasoning

Now that you have reviewed the topics tested on the GED Mathematical Reasoning test, this Mathematical Reasoning Posttest is designed to give you a good idea of your readiness to take the actual exam.

This test has the same number of questions as the real GED Mathematical Reasoning test: 50 items. The questions are in the same formats as the ones on the real exam and are designed to measure the same skills. Some of the questions simply ask you to make calculations. Others describe real-life situations that you must decide how to solve using mathematics. Many of the questions on this test are based on graphs or diagrams. Most of the questions are in multiple-choice format, but you will also see questions that ask you to indicate a point on a graph, write your answer in a box, select an answer from a drop-down menu, or "drag" an answer into the correct position in a math expression or equation. On the real GED® test, you will indicate your answers by clicking on the computer screen. For this paper-and-pencil practice test, mark your answers directly on the page.

To get a good idea of how you will do on the real exam, take this test under actual exam conditions. Complete the test in one session and follow the given time limit. If you do not complete the test in the time allowed, you will know that you need to work on improving your pacing.

Try to answer as many questions as you can. There is no penalty for wrong answers, so guess if you have to. In multiple-choice questions, if you can eliminate one or more answer choices, you can increase your chances of guessing correctly.

After you have finished the test, check your answers in the Answers and Explanations section that follows the posttest. Then use the Evaluation Chart at the end of the Answers and Explanations section to see if there are still content areas in which you need more review and practice.

Now turn the page and begin the Mathematical Reasoning Posttest.

Mathematics Formula Sheet

Area

parallelogram $\quad A = bh$

trapezoid $\quad A = (\frac{1}{2})h(b_1 + b_2)$

Surface Area and Volume

rectangular/right prism $\quad SA = ph + 2B \qquad V = Bh$

cylinder $\quad SA = 2\pi rh + 2\pi r^2 \qquad V = \pi r^2 h$

pyramid $\quad SA = (\frac{1}{2})ps + B \qquad V = (\frac{1}{3})Bh$

cone $\quad SA = \pi rs + \pi r^2 \qquad V = (\frac{1}{3})\pi r^2 h$

sphere $\quad SA = 4\pi r^2 \qquad V = (\frac{4}{3})\pi r^3$

(p = perimeter of base B; $\pi \approx 3.14$)

Algebra

slope of a line $\quad m = \dfrac{(y_2 - y_1)}{(x_2 - x_1)}$

slope-intercept form of the equation of a line $\quad y = mx + b$

point-slope form of the equation of a line $\quad y - y_1 = m(x - x_1)$

standard form of a quadratic equation $\quad ax^2 + bx + c = y$

quadratic formula $\quad x = \dfrac{-b \pm \sqrt{b^2 - 4ac}}{2a}$

Pythagorean theorem $\quad a^2 + b^2 = c^2$

simple interest $\quad I = prt$
(I = interest, p = principal, r = rate, t = time)

Mathematical Reasoning

50 questions | **90 minutes**

1. What is the largest possible value for which $2x^2 + 7x - 30 = 0$?

   A. $\dfrac{5}{6}$

   B. $\dfrac{5}{2}$

   C. 5

   D. 6

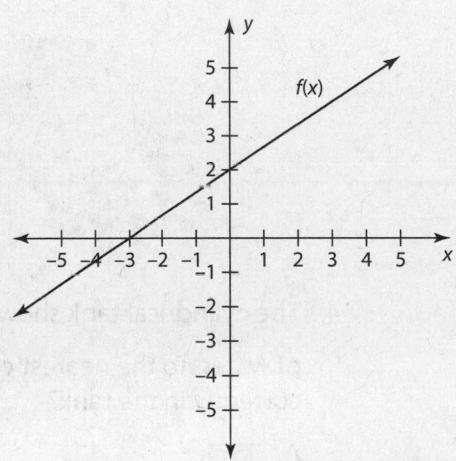

2. The figure above shows the graph of a linear function $f(x)$. If $g(x) = \dfrac{1}{2}x + 8$, then which of the following statements is true when both functions are graphed?

   A. The slope of both lines is the same and positive.
   B. The slope of both lines is the same and negative.
   C. The slope of the line for $f(x)$ is greater than the slope of the line for $g(x)$.
   D. The slope of the line for $f(x)$ is smaller than the slope of the line for $g(x)$.

3. If the slope of line *m* is −2, then what is the slope of a line perpendicular to line *m*?

   A. −2

   B. $-\dfrac{1}{2}$

   C. $\dfrac{1}{2}$

   D. 2

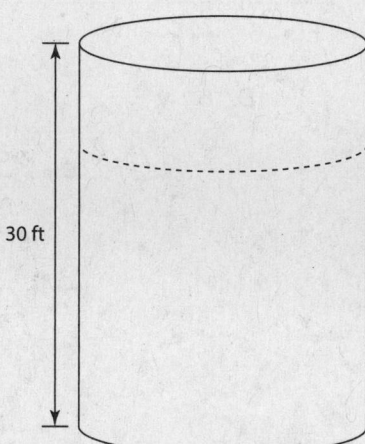

30 ft

4. The cylindrical tank shown above has a radius of 5 feet and is $\dfrac{2}{3}$ full of water. To the nearest cubic foot, how many cubic feet of water are currently in the tank?

   A. 1571
   B. 2356
   C. 6283
   D. 9425

5. Terry can run 5 miles in about 43 minutes. If he runs at the same pace, in how many minutes can Terry run 20 kilometers? State your answer to the nearest minute. (1 mile = 1.6 km)

    A. 63
    B. 69
    C. 108
    D. 172

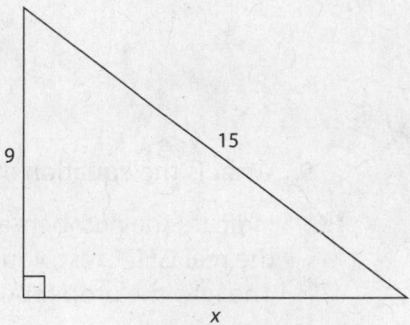

6. What is the value of x in the figure shown above?

    A. 3
    B. 8
    C. 12
    D. 17

7. Line m in a coordinate plane passes through the points (−1, 4) and (0, 9). What is the slope of a line that is parallel to line m? Indicate your answer in the box.

8. A certain piggy bank contains only pennies and quarters. It contains four times as many pennies as quarters. If the bank contains 440 coins, how many are quarters? Indicate your answer in the box.

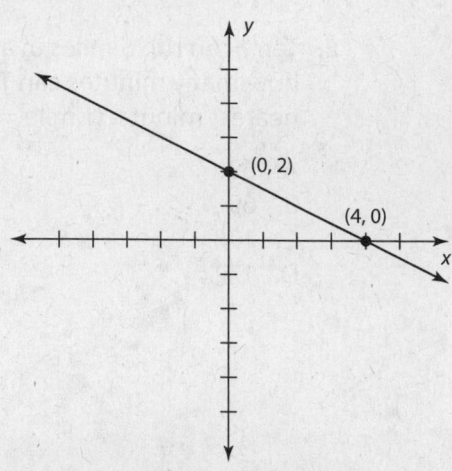

9. What is the equation of the line in the figure shown above?

   Indicate the numbers and variables that complete the equation. (**Note:** On the real GED® test, you will click on the items you choose and "drag" each one into the proper box.)

   $$y = \boxed{} + \boxed{}$$

   | $-2x$ | $-\dfrac{1}{2}x$ | $4x$ | 2 | $\dfrac{1}{2}$ |

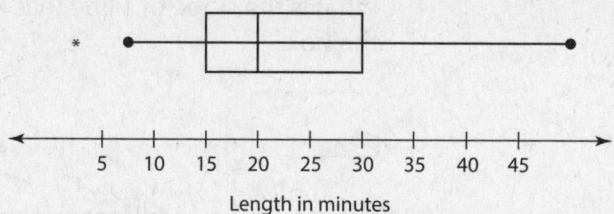

Length in minutes

10. The box plot above represents the length of calls made by a sample of college students over one weekend. Based on this figure, which of the following statements is true?

    A. More than half of the phone calls made were longer than 20 minutes.
    B. The shortest phone call lasted about 8 minutes.
    C. 50% of the phone calls lasted between about 15 and 30 minutes.
    D. 25% of the phone calls were shorter than 30 minutes.

11. The ages of students in a community science club are 13, 11, 14, 12, 8, and 10. What is the range of ages in this club?

    A. 4
    B. 6
    C. 10
    D. 14

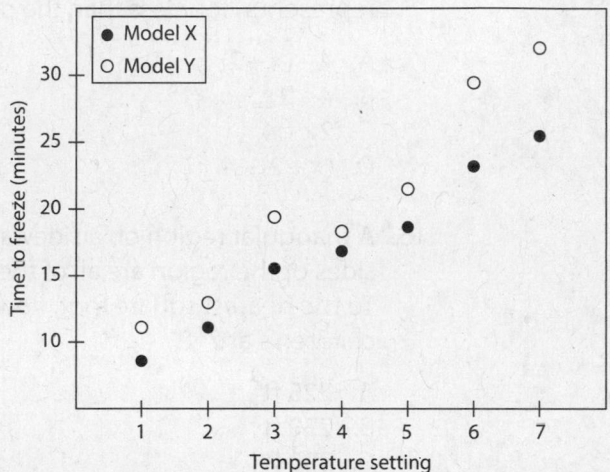

12. The scatter plot shown above represents data collected during the testing of two models of laboratory freezers. In the experiment, it was determined how long it took a 1-cup sample of water to freeze completely solid at seven different temperature settings in each freezer model. Based on the scatter plot, which of the following statements is true?

    A. For model X, the time to freeze was more than 10 minutes for all temperature settings.
    B. For model X, the time to freeze was never longer than 30 minutes at any setting.
    C. For model Y, the time to freeze always increased as the temperature setting increased.
    D. For model Y, the time to freeze was less than for model X for at least one setting.

13. In a class of 31 students, 30 took an exam, and the mean score was 76.5. The remaining student took the exam later. If his score was 98, which of the following is true regarding the mean for all 31 students?

    A. It will be lower than 76.5.
    B. It will remain 76.5.
    C. It will be higher than 76.5.
    D. It is not possible to make a statement about the mean without knowing individual scores.

14. If $k(x) = 4x^2 - 7$, then $k\left(\dfrac{1}{2}\right) =$
    A. −6.
    B. −5.
    C. −4.
    D. −3.

15. If a certain number is represented by x, which of the following expressions represents "four less than the product of the number and two"?
    A. $4 - (x + 2)$
    B. $4 - 2x$
    C. $2x - 4$
    D. $(x + 2) - 4$

16. A triangular region on a sidewalk is reserved for children's chalk art. The sides of the region are all of the same length and the perimeter is 90 feet. To the nearest square foot, how large is the area that is reserved for the children's art?
    A. 225 ft²
    B. 250 ft²
    C. 390 ft²
    D. 450 ft²

17. A single box of product samples contains 45 samples, while a crate holds 18 boxes. How many product samples are there in 20 crates? Indicate your answer in the box.

18. What is the value of the expression $-3x + 5y$ when $x = -1$ and $y = -2$?
    A. −11
    B. −7
    C. −2
    D. 1

19. Of a doctor's patients, the number who are older than 50 is at least 10 more than the number who are under 20. If the doctor has 18 patients who are older than 50, what is the maximum number of patients she could have who are under 20?
    A. 4
    B. 8
    C. 10
    D. 28

20. Suppose that the weight of a single marble is represented by the expression $\dfrac{x+1}{x-8}$ where x is a nonzero whole number. If a bag contains $\dfrac{2x-16}{x-1}$ marbles, which expression represents the weight of all the marbles in the bag?

   A. $\dfrac{2x+2}{x-1}$

   B. $\dfrac{2x^2-2}{x^2+1}$

   C. $\dfrac{x-8}{x-1}$

   D. $\dfrac{2x^2-16}{x^2+8}$

21. Last week, the price of a particular leather jacket was $159. This week, the jacket is on sale for $130. To the nearest tenth of a percent, what is the percent decrease in the price of the jacket?

   A. 11.9%
   B. 14.6%
   C. 18.2%
   D. 22.3%

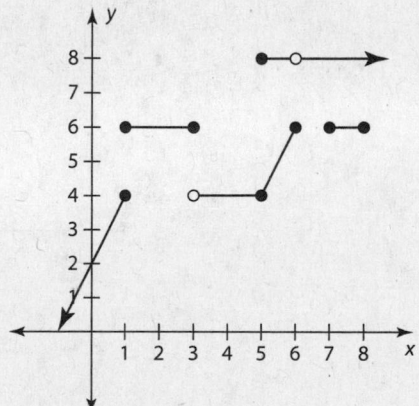

22. In the figure shown above, for which of the following ranges of values is y a function of x?

   A. $0 < x \le 2$
   B. $2 < x \le 4$
   C. $4 < x \le 6$
   D. $6 < x \le 8$

23. $1 - 5(2 - 4^2) =$

    A. −89
    B. −62
    C. 56
    D. 71

24. Two numbers are represented by m and n. Create an equation that represents "5 less than double the product of the two numbers is equal to 2."

    Choose expressions and/or numbers that belong in the boxes to create your answer. (**Note:** On the real GED® test, you will click on the items you choose and "drag" each one into the proper box.)

    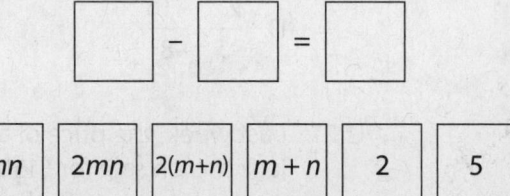

25. Indicate two points on the grid that lie on the line represented by $-3x + y = 5$. (**Note:** On the real GED® test, you will click on the grid to indicate the points.)

    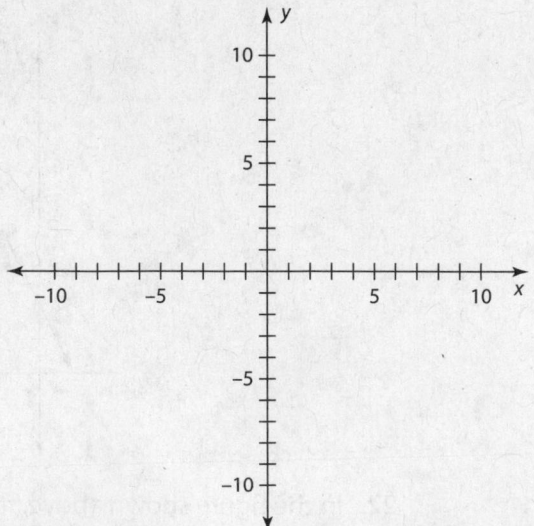

26. If x = −4, what is the value of $\frac{x^2-4}{x}$?

    A. −5
    B. −3
    C. 0
    D. 2

July Expenses

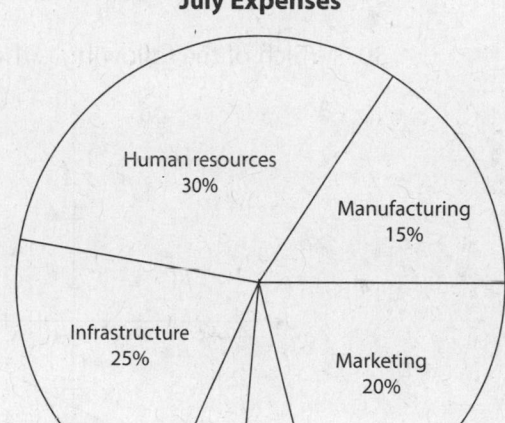

27. The graph above shows the breakdown of July expenses for a recently started business. If the total expenses in July were $40,120, how much of this total was spent on manufacturing?

    A. $2,006
    B. $6,018
    C. $8,024
    D. $12,036

28. In order to calculate the value of a measurement Y, the difference between an initial measurement X and 5 must be divided by the square of X. Which of the following provides a formula for calculating the value of Y based on the initial measurement X?

    A. $X - \dfrac{5}{X^2}$

    B. $\dfrac{1}{5X} - X^2$

    C. $\dfrac{X-5}{X^2}$

    D. $X - \dfrac{\sqrt{X}}{5}$

29. Over a period of five business days, the balance in a checking account at the end of the day was $143.20, $210.50, $187.50, $800.65, and $777.65. What was the mean balance in the account over this period of time?

    A. $187.50
    B. $210.50
    C. $423.90
    D. $657.45

30. Which of the following is the graph of the equation $2x - 4y = 10$?

    A.

    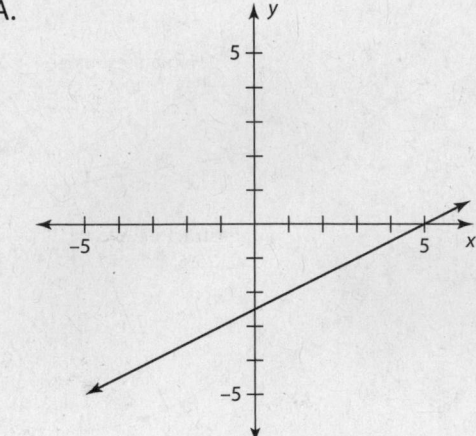

    B.

    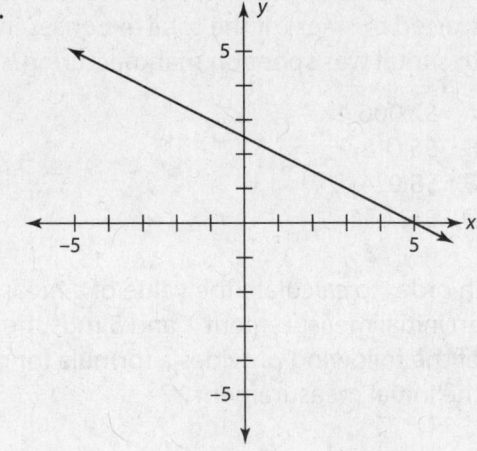

C.

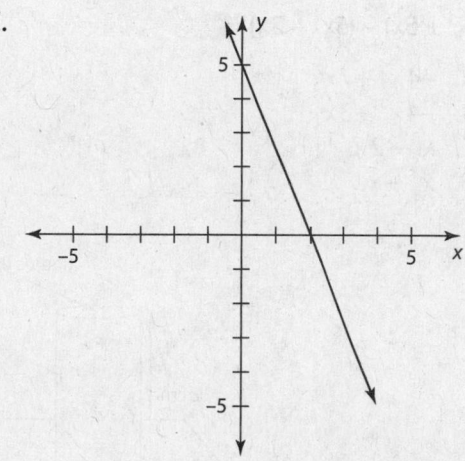

D.

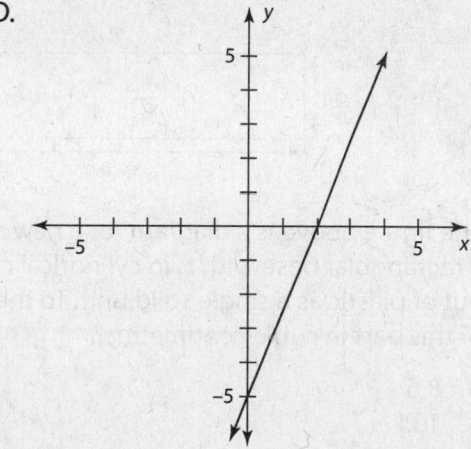

31. Which of the following expressions is the completely factored form of $2x^3 - 10x^2 - 2x$?

   A. $2x(x-5)(x-2)$

   B. $2(x^3 - 5x^2 - x)$

   C. $x(2x^2 - 10x - 2)$

   D. $2x(x^2 - 5x - 1)$

32. What is the solution set of the inequality $-4x + 2 > 3x + 9$?

   A. $x < -1$
   B. $x < 2$
   C. $x > 7$
   D. $x > 11$

33. $(x^3 + 5x) - (5x^3 - 2x) =$

   A. $-4x^3 + 7x$
   B. $-4x^3 + 3x$
   C. $x^3 - 2x$
   D. $x^3 + x$

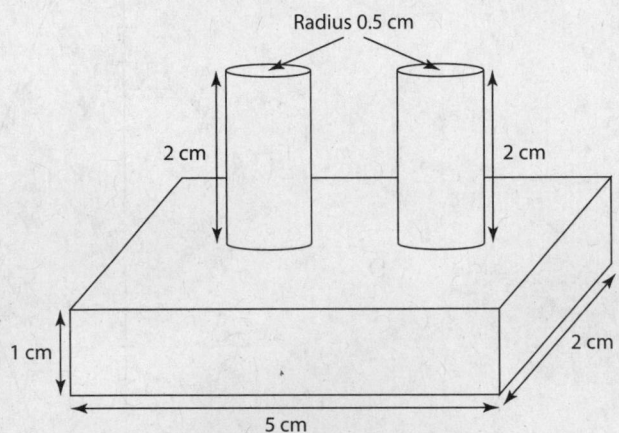

34. The figure above is a diagram for a new machine part. The part consists of a rectangular base with two cylindrical connectors. It will be manufactured out of plastic as a single solid unit. To the nearest tenth, what is the volume of this part in cubic centimeters?

   A. 8.6
   B. 10.1
   C. 11.6
   D. 13.1

35. A Little League team is holding a raffle. Any person may enter the raffle up to three times, but only one winner will be chosen. If a total of 45 people enter the raffle and all 45 enter it three times, what is the probability that any given person will win the raffle?

Item 36 contains a blank marked "Select. . . ." Beneath the blank are four choices. Indicate the choice that is correct and belongs in the blank. (**Note:** On the real GED® test, the choices will appear as a "drop-down" menu. When you click on a choice, it will appear in the blank.)

36. Consider this list of rational numbers: $0.73, \frac{2}{3}, \frac{1}{4}, 2$.

    Rewritten in order from least to greatest, the list would read:

    | Select. . . ▼ |

Select. . . ▼
$0.73, \frac{2}{3}, \frac{1}{4}, 2$
$\frac{1}{4}, 0.73, \frac{2}{3}, 2$
$\frac{1}{4}, \frac{2}{3}, 0.73, 2$
$0.73, \frac{1}{4}, \frac{2}{3}, 2$

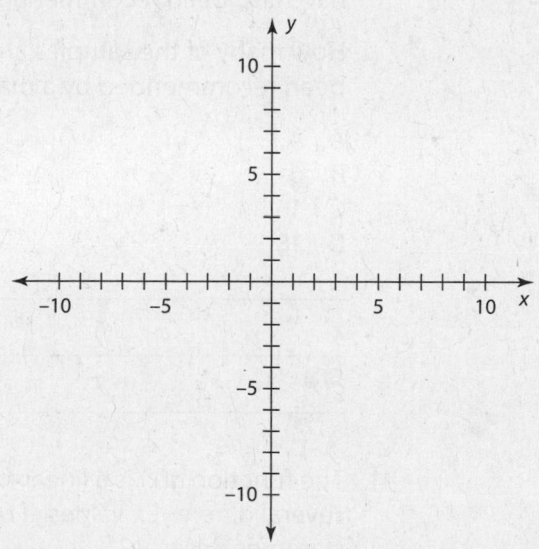

37. On the coordinate plane above, indicate the point (−6, 0). (**Note:** On the real GED® test, you will click on the grid to indicate the point.)

38. Which of the following is equivalent to $\left(4^{\frac{1}{3}}\right)^{\frac{1}{2}}$?

    A. $\dfrac{1}{4^{\frac{1}{2}}}$

    B. $4^{\frac{1}{5}}$

    C. $4^{\frac{1}{6}}$

    D. $\dfrac{1}{4^{\frac{1}{3}}}$

39. At a local grocery store, a 13-ounce box of pasta that usually sells for $2.50 is on sale for $1.38. In terms of price per ounce, how much of a discount does this represent, rounded to the nearest tenth of a cent?

    A. 8.6 cents
    B. 10.6 cents
    C. 19.2 cents
    D. 29.8 cents

40. At a retail cosmetics store, 18 items are offered as free samples. Of these items, 12 are produced by large companies and 10 have been recommended by a magazine. Six are produced by large companies and have also been recommended by a magazine.

    How many of the samples are not produced by large companies but have been recommended by a magazine?

    A. 4
    B. 6
    C. 16
    D. 18

x	−1	0	2
$g(x)$	7	9	13

41. The function $g(x)$ is a linear function. The table above gives its value for several different x values. If $f(x) = -3x + 5$, then which of the following statements is true?

    A. The value of $f(x)$ is larger than the value of $g(x)$ when $x = 0$.
    B. The value of $f(x)$ is smaller than the value of $g(x)$ when $x = 0$.
    C. The value of $f(x)$ is equal to the value of $g(x)$ when $x = 0$.
    D. It is not possible to compare values of $f(x)$ and $g(x)$ when $x = 0$ without more information.

42. If $\frac{1}{2}(x-5)=x$, then $x=$

   A. −10.

   B.   5.

   C. $-\frac{1}{2}$.

   D. $-\frac{5}{2}$.

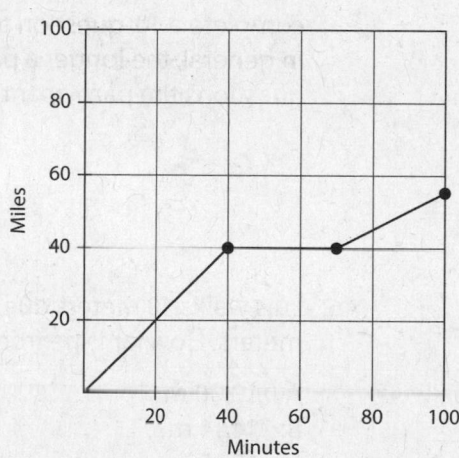

43. The figure above represents the first 100 minutes of the Johnson family's summer road trip. Based on this graph, which of the following statements best describes this portion of the trip?

   A. The family began driving at a steady rate for about 40 minutes and then stopped for the day.
   B. The family began driving at a steady rate for about 40 minutes and then took a 30-minute break before continuing at the same rate as before.
   C. The family began driving at a steady rate for about 40 minutes and then took a 30-minute break before continuing at a slower rate than before.
   D. The family began driving at a steady rate for about 40 minutes and then took a 30-minute break before continuing at a faster rate than before.

44. If $x-9<-5$, which of the following statements about x must be true?

   A. $x>-14$
   B. $x>4$
   C. $x<-14$
   D. $x<4$

Item 45 contains a blank marked "Select. . . ." Beneath the blank are two choices. Indicate the choice that is correct and belongs in the blank. (**Note:** On the real GED® test, the choices will appear as a "drop-down" menu. When you click on a choice, it will appear in the blank.)

Length of time given (minutes)	10	5	2	1	15	8	4	6	1
Number of questions completed	8	4	2	3	9	7	3	4	2

45. In an experiment, participants were given varying amounts of time to complete a 10-question test. Based on the table above, you can say that, in general, the longer a participant was given, the [Select... ▼] questions the participant was able to answer.

Select... ▼
fewer
more

46. Luis walks 10 meters due south, then turns due east and walks another 10 meters. How far is he from his starting point?

A. 10.00 m
B. 14.14 m
C. 15.15 m
D. 20.00 m

47. Line *k* in the coordinate plane passes through the points (2, 6) and (4, 3). What is the slope of a line that is perpendicular to line *k*?

A. $-\dfrac{3}{2}$

B. $-\dfrac{2}{3}$

C. $\dfrac{2}{3}$

D. $\dfrac{3}{2}$

48. A bag of licorice laces contains only red and black laces. The bag contains three times as many red laces as black ones. If the bag contains 240 laces total, then how many red laces are there in the bag?

    A. 60
    B. 120
    C. 150
    D. 180

49. Line k in the coordinate plane passes through the points $(-3, -4)$ and $(1, 2)$. Which is the correct equation of line k?

    A. $3x - 2y + 1 = 0$
    B. $3x + 2y + 1 = 0$
    C. $2x - 3y + 1 = 0$
    D. $2x + 3y + 1 = 0$

50. If $f(x) = 6x^2 + 13x + 5$, then $f(-4) =$

    A. -143.
    B. 49.
    C. 81.
    D. 153.

THIS IS THE END OF THE MATHEMATICAL REASONING POSTTEST.

Answers and Explanations

1. **Correct answer: B.** The left side of the equation can be factored into the terms $(2x-5)(x+6)$. By the zero product rule, the solutions are then $\frac{5}{2}$ and -6.

2. **Correct answer: C.** The function $g(x)$ is written in slope intercept form, so its slope is the coefficient of the x term or $\frac{1}{2}$. The graph of $f(x)$ shows that the line passes through the point $(-3, 0)$ and $(0, 2)$, so using the slope formula, its slope is $m = \frac{2-0}{0-(-3)} = \frac{2}{3}$ which is larger than $\frac{1}{2}$.

3. **Correct answer: C.** The slope of a line perpendicular to m will have a slope that is the negative reciprocal of -2.

4. **Correct answer: A.** The volume of the entire tank is $V = \pi(5)^2(30) = 2356.19$ cubic feet. Two-thirds of this is $\frac{2}{3}(2356.19) \approx 1571$.

5. **Correct answer: C.** Given his pace, Terry can run 1 mile (or 1.6 km) in $\frac{43}{5} = 8.6$ minutes. Therefore, he can run 20 km in $\frac{8.6 \text{ min}}{1.6 \text{ km}}(20 \text{ km}) = 107.5$ min.

6. **Correct answer: C.** Using the Pythagorean theorem, $15^2 = 9^2 + x^2$ and $x^2 = 15^2 - 9^2 = 144 \Rightarrow x = \sqrt{144} = 12$.

7. **Correct answer: 5.** A line that is parallel to m will have the same slope, which is $\frac{9-4}{0-(-1)} = \frac{5}{1} = 5$.

8. **Correct answer: 88.** If P represents the number of pennies and Q the number of quarters, then the information given can

be written as P + Q = 440 and P = 4Q. Using substitution, 4Q + Q = 440 or 5Q = 440. Thus there are $\frac{440}{5} = 88$ quarters in the piggy bank.

9. **Correct answer:** $y = -\frac{1}{2}x + 2$. The slope of the given line is $\frac{0-2}{4-0} = -\frac{1}{2}$, and it crosses the y-axis at the point $(0, 2)$. Using the point-slope form of a line, the equation is $y = -\frac{1}{2}x + 2$.

10. **Correct answer: C.** The box itself on a box plot represents the middle 50% of the data, which is the percentage between the first and third quartiles. Looking on the plot, the box starts at 15, which is the first quartile, and ends at 30, the third quartile.

11. **Correct answer: B.** The range is the difference between the largest and the smallest data value. In this case that is $14 - 8 = 6$.

12. **Correct answer: B.** For model X, the longest time to freeze was about 25 minutes.

13. **Correct answer: C.** Although it may or may not be an outlier, the larger value will essentially "pull" the mean higher.

14. **Correct answer: A.**
$$k\left(\frac{1}{2}\right) = 4\left(\frac{1}{2}\right)^2 - 7 = 4\left(\frac{1}{4}\right) - 7 = 1 - 7 = -6$$

15. **Correct answer: C.** "Four less than" implies subtraction from something. Since product implies multiplication, the statement should show 4 subtracted from 2 times x or $2x - 4$.

16. **Correct answer: C.** If the perimeter is 90 feet, then each side has a length of 30 feet. The height of the triangle will then be a leg of a right triangle with a length of 15 feet and a hypotenuse with a length of 30 feet. Using the Pythagorean theorem, the height is

$\sqrt{30^2 - 15^2} \approx 26$. Thus, the area of the region is approximately $\frac{1}{2}(30)(26) = 390$ square feet.

17. **Correct answer: 16,200.** Each crate will have $45 \times 18 = 810$ samples; therefore, the 20 crates will have $20 \times 810 = 16,200$ samples.

18. **Correct answer: B.** $-3(-1) + 5(-2) = 3 - 10 = -7$

19. **Correct answer: B.** If F represents the number older than 50 and T the number under 20, then $F \geq 10 + T$. Since $F = 18$, this means that $18 \geq 10 + T$ and $8 \geq T$.

20. **Correct answer: A.** The total weight would be the product of the number of marbles times the weight of each marble. In this case that product is
$$\left(\frac{x+1}{x-8}\right)\left(\frac{2x-16}{x-1}\right) = \left(\frac{x+1}{x-8}\right)\left(\frac{2(x-8)}{x-1}\right) = \frac{2(x+1)}{x-1} = \frac{2x+2}{x-1}.$$

21. **Correct answer: C.** The percent decrease is
$$100\% \times \left(\frac{159 - 130}{159}\right) = 18.2\%.$$

22. **Correct answer: B.** The graph shows y as a function of x only when there is one y value for each x value. This can be checked by seeing if a vertical line passes through the graph only once for the entire region being checked. Of the given ranges, this can be done only when x is between 2 and 4.

23. **Correct answer: D.**
$1 - 5(2 - 4^2) = 1 - 5(2 - 16) = 1 - 5(-14) = 1 + 70 = 71$

24. **Correct answer: $2mn - 5 = 2$.** Double the product is represented by 2 times the product of m and n. Five less than this represents subtracting 5 from that value.

25. **Correct answer: Any two points along the line shown below.**

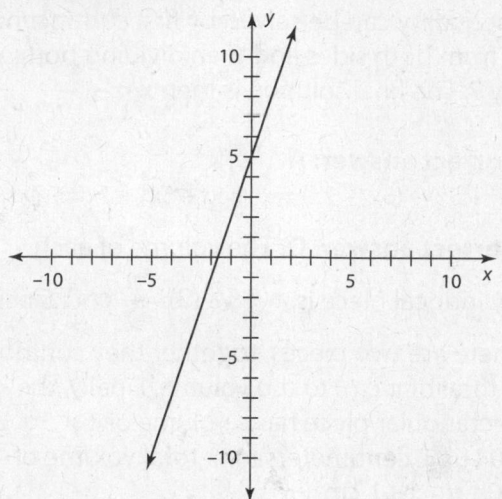

26. **Correct answer: B.** $\dfrac{(-4)^2 - 4}{-4} = \dfrac{16 - 4}{-4} = \dfrac{12}{-4} = -3$

27. **Correct answer: B.** From the chart, 15% of the $40,120 was spent on manufacturing and $0.15 \times 40,120 = 6018$.

28. **Correct answer: C.** The difference between X and 5 is represented by $X - 5$ while the square of X is represented by X^2. Dividing the first by the second: $\dfrac{X - 5}{X^2}$.

29. **Correct answer: C.**
$$\frac{143.20 + 210.50 + 187.50 + 800.65 + 777.65}{5} = 423.90$$

30. **Correct answer: A.** The x intercept of the line is the solution to $2x - 4(0) = 10$ or $x = 5$, while the y intercept of the line is the solution to $2(0) - 4y = 10$ or $y = -\dfrac{5}{2}$. Only the line in answer choice A has these intercepts.

31. **Correct answer: D.** Each term shares a factor of $2x$. Factoring this term out results in the expression $2x(x^2 - 5x - 1)$ where $x^2 - 5x - 1$ is a nonfactorable trinomial.

32. Correct answer: A. Adding $4x$ to both sides of the inequality results in $2 > 7x + 9$. This inequality can be solved by first subtracting 9 from both sides and then dividing both sides by 7. The final solution is then $x < -1$.

33. Correct answer: A.
$(x^3 + 5x) - (5x^3 - 2x) = x^3 + 5x - 5x^3 + 2x = -4x^3 + 7x$

34. Correct answer: D. The volume of each cylindrical piece is $\pi(0.5)^2(2) = \dfrac{\pi}{2}$ cm³. Since there are two pieces, together they contribute a total of π cm³ to the volume. Finally, the rectangular piece has a volume of $1 \times 5 \times 2 = 10$ cubic centimeters for a total volume of $10 + \pi \approx 13.1$ cm³.

35. Correct answer: $\dfrac{1}{45}$. The total number of entries is 3×45, while the total number of entries for any one particular person is 3. Therefore the probability that any one person wins is $\dfrac{3}{3(45)} = \dfrac{1}{45}$.

36. Correct answer: $\dfrac{1}{4}, \dfrac{2}{3}, 0.73, 2$.

37. Correct answer:

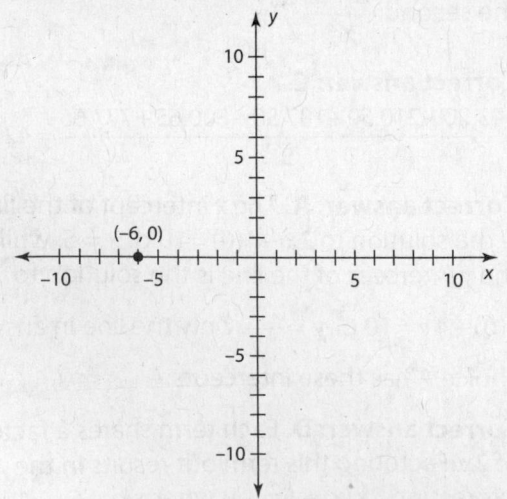

The x coordinate is -6 and the y coordinate is 0, indicating that the point lies at -6 on the x-axis.

38. Correct answer: C. By the rules of exponents, the exponents are multiplied:
$$\left(4^{\frac{1}{3}}\right)^{\frac{1}{2}} = 4^{\frac{1}{3} \times \frac{1}{2}} = 4^{\frac{1}{6}}$$

39. Correct answer: A. Without the discount, the price per ounce was $\dfrac{\$2.50}{13} = \$0.192$ while with the discount, the price per ounce is $\dfrac{\$1.38}{13} = \$0.106$. This represents a difference of $19.2 - 10.6 = 8.6$ cents.

40. Correct answer: A. The 6 that are produced by large companies that have also been recommended by a magazine are counted in the 10 total that have been recommended by a magazine. Therefore there must be $10 - 6 = 4$ that have been recommended by a magazine that aren't produced by a large company. A Venn diagram may be useful here.

41. Correct answer: B. When $x = 0$, the table shows that $g(x)$ has a value of 9, while the value of $f(x)$ at $f(0) = -3(0) + 5 = 5$.

42. Correct answer: B. Distributing the one-half over $x - 5$, this equation is equivalent to $\dfrac{1}{2}x - \dfrac{5}{2} = x$. Solving this equation:
$$\frac{1}{2}x - \frac{5}{2} = x$$
$$-\frac{5}{2} = \frac{1}{2}x$$
$$-5 = x$$

43. Correct answer: C. The flat space in the middle of the graph indicates that time is passing but no new miles are being added. This would be the family's break in the road trip. After this, the new line shows a steady rate, but it has less of a slope than the line before the break. This indicates that the family is now traveling slower than before.

44. **Correct answer: D.** Adding 9 to both sides, $x < 4$. The direction of the inequality will change only if both sides are multiplied or divided by a negative number.

45. **Correct answer: more.** "Based on the table above, you can say that in general the longer a participant was given, the **more** questions the participant was able to answer."

    Although there is some variability, the shorter times generally had fewer questions answered than the longer times. This could also be seen in a scatterplot.

46. **Correct answer: B.** Using the Pythagorean theorem, $10^2 + 10^2 = x^2$ and $x^2 = 100 + 100 = 200 \Rightarrow x = \sqrt{200} = 14.14$.

47. **Correct answer: C.** Line k has a slope of $m = \dfrac{(y_2 - y_1)}{(x_2 - x_1)} = \dfrac{(3-6)}{(4-2)} = -\dfrac{3}{2}$. A line that is perpendicular to k will have the negative reciprocal of that slope, which is $\dfrac{2}{3}$.

48. **Correct answer: D.** If R represents the number of red laces and B the number of black laces, then the information given can be written as $R + B = 240$ and $R = 3B$. Using substitution, $3B + B = 240$ or $4B = 240$. Thus, there are $\dfrac{240}{4} = 60$ black laces in the bag. So, $R = 3B = 3(60) = 180$. Therefore, there are 180 red laces in the bag.

49. **Correct answer: A.** The slope of the line k is:

$$m = \frac{(y_2 - y_1)}{(x_2 - x_1)} = \frac{(2-(-4))}{(1-(-3))} = \frac{6}{4} = \frac{3}{2}$$

Using the point-slope form of a line, the equation is:

$$(y - y_1) = m(x - x_1) \text{ or } (y - y_1) = m(x - x_1)$$

$$y - 2 = \frac{3}{2}(x - 1) \qquad y - (-4) = \frac{3}{2}(x - (-3))$$

$$2y - 4 = 3x - 3 \qquad\qquad y + 4 = \frac{3}{2}(x + 3)$$

$$2y = 3x + 1$$

$$0 = 3x - 2y + 1 \qquad 2y + 8 = 3x + 9$$

$$3x - 2y + 1 = 0 \qquad 2y = 3x + 1$$

$$0 = 3x - 2y + 1$$

$$3x - 2y + 1 = 0$$

50. **Correct answer: B.**

$$f(x) = 6x^2 + 13x + 5$$

$$f(-4) = 6(-4)^2 + 13(-4) + 5$$

$$f(-4) = 6(16) - 52 + 5$$

$$f(-4) = 96 - 52 + 5 = 49$$

Evaluation Chart

Check the Answers and Explanations section of the Mathematical Reasoning Posttest to see which answers you got correct and which ones you missed. For each question that you missed, find the item number in the chart below. Check the column on the left to see the test content area for that item. If you missed questions in a particular content area, you need to pay particular attention to that area as you study for the GED® test. The pages of this book that cover that content area are listed in the column on the right.

Content Area	Item Number	Pages to Review
1. Whole Numbers and Operations	17, 36, 39, 40	307–315
2. Exponents, Roots, and Number Properties	23, 38	317–328
3. Decimal Numbers and Operations	36	329–339
4. Fractions and Operations	36	341–358
5. Ratios, Rates, and Proportions	5	359–364
6. Percents and Applications	21, 27	365–372
7. The Number Line and Negative Numbers	14, 18	373–377
8. Probabililty and Counting	35	379–385
9. Statistics and Data Analysis	10, 11, 12, 13, 29, 45	387–404
10. Algebraic Expressions	20, 24, 26, 28, 48	405–428
11. Solving Equations and Inequalities	1, 8, 15, 18, 19, 31, 32, 33, 42, 44	429–451
12. Graphing Equations	3, 7, 9, 25, 30, 37, 43, 47, 49	453–470
13. Functions	2, 14, 22, 41, 50	471–485
14. Geometry	4, 6, 16, 34, 46	487–500

Science

This Science Posttest is designed to help you determine how well you have mastered this GED® test subject area and whether you are ready to take the real GED Science test.

This test has the same number of questions as the real GED Science test: 40 items. The questions are in the same formats as the ones on the real exam and are designed to measure the same skills. Many of the questions are based on short reading passages on science topics. Some are based on scientific illustrations, diagrams, or other graphics. Most of the questions are in multiple-choice format, but you will also see questions that ask you to draw a line or indicate a point on a diagram, fill in a blank, or write a short answer. On the real GED® test, you will indicate your answers by clicking on the computer screen. For this paper-and-pencil practice test, mark your answers directly on the page. Write your short-answer responses on a separate sheet of paper.

To get a good idea of how you will do on the real exam, take this test under actual exam conditions. Complete the test in one session and follow the given time limit. If you do not complete the test in the time allowed, you will know that you need to work on improving your pacing.

Try to answer as many questions as you can. There is no penalty for wrong answers, so guess if you have to. In multiple-choice questions, if you can eliminate one or more answer choices, you can increase your chances of guessing correctly.

After you have finished the test, check your answers in the Answers and Explanations section that follows the posttest. Then use the Evaluation Chart at the end of the Answers and Explanations section to determine the skills and content areas in which you need more practice.

Now turn the page and begin the Science Posttest.

Science

40 questions | **90 minutes**

Use the following passage for Items 1 through 3:

Respiratory homeostasis involves regulating the amount of oxygen and carbon dioxide in the blood. The exchange of gases takes place between the alveolar sacs in the lungs and the capillaries.

Blood leaving the lungs in the capillaries will have partial pressures of oxygen and carbon dioxide in amounts that are similar to the average values found in the alveoli. If the amount of carbon dioxide in the blood is different from the amount in the alveoli, chemical receptors detect the change and alert the respiratory system to respond.

1. Which of these responses best indicates high levels of carbon dioxide in blood?

   A. fever
   B. coughing
   C. rapid breathing
   D. excessive urination

Use the following diagram for Item 2:

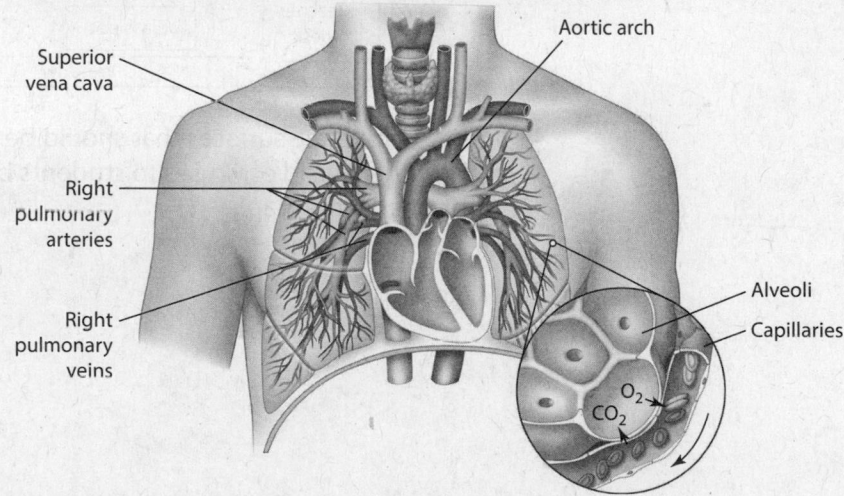

2. Using the information in the passage, identify and mark an **X** on the location of the exchange of gases.

3. Based on the information in the passage, the respiratory, cardiovascular, and nervous systems work together to regulate

    A. capillary action.
    B. ventilation pathways.
    C. blood gas composition.
    D. chemical receptor functions.

Use the following passage and diagram for Item 4:

During flu season, proper hand hygiene is the best way to reduce the spread of infection. Some viruses can live up to eight hours on surfaces made of plastic and metal. Viruses can be transmitted when students rub eyes and noses and then touch a surface. Examine the elementary-classroom map in the following diagram.

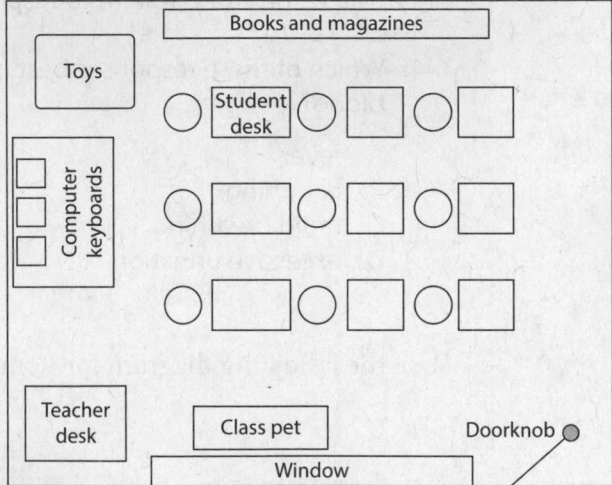

4. Identify the three surfaces that should be cleaned most frequently to reduce the spread of viruses to students by marking an **X** on three labeled locations on the map.

POSTTEST

Use the following passage and diagram for Items 5 through 7:

Energy and nutrients pass through the trophic levels of an ecosystem when organisms feed on one another. The following image shows a terrestrial food chain common in a variety of ecosystems. The arrows show the flow of energy from one organism to the next.

Not pictured in the image are detritivores, often called decomposers. Detritivores are important components of every ecosystem. These organisms derive energy from organic wastes, such as fallen leaves and the remains of dead organisms from other feeding levels. The organic material that composes living things is eventually recycled and returned to the nonliving environment in forms that can be used by plants.

5. The flower in the terrestrial food chain obtains energy for life functions from the process of

   A. acidification.
   B. fermentation.
   C. photosynthesis.
   D. chemosynthesis.

6. On the following diagram, draw lines to match each organism with its correct role in the food chain.

Roles of Organisms in a Terrestrial Food Chain

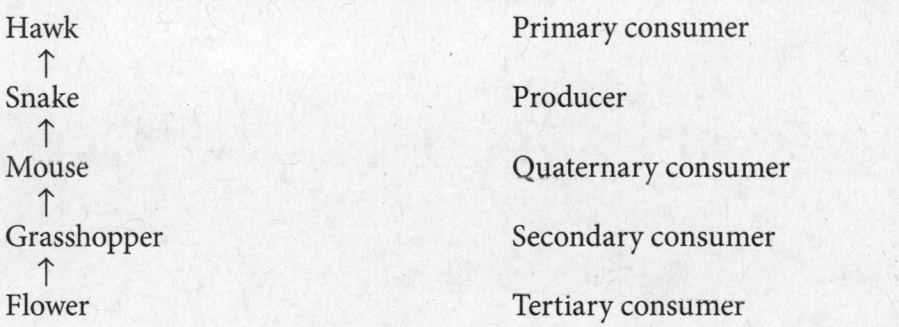

POSTTEST

7. **Short answer**

Consider the role of detritivores in the ecosystem. What effect would a decline in the detritivore community have on this particular terrestrial food chain? Include multiple pieces of evidence from the text to support your answer.

Write your response in the space provided. This task may take approximately 10 minutes to complete.

Use the following passage for Items 8 through 10:

Jane wants to feed her family healthy, nutritious, and organic food without spending a lot of money. She decides to plant her own garden to accomplish these goals. Next to her garden, she builds a cistern to collect rainwater for the plants. For plant health, Jane opts to use beneficial lady beetles, more commonly called ladybugs, to control pests in the garden.

Jane learns that ladybugs are the natural enemies of garden pests such as aphids, mealy bugs, and leafhoppers. Ladybugs benefit plants in a number of ways. While they prefer to feed on aphids, they also eat other foods such as pollen and nectar, acting as pollinators. Jane also stays alert for signs of ant colonies. Ants that feed on the products of aphids can attack and drive off ladybugs, leaving a garden undefended.

8. Which of the following could directly lead to an increase in the ladybug population?

    A. stabilized ant colony
    B. growing aphid population
    C. increased honeybee activity
    D. declining leafhopper population

9. What type of symbiotic relationship is seen when ladybugs fill the role of plant pollinators?

    A. parasitism
    B. mutualism
    C. amensalism
    D. commensalism

10. Jane's garden acts as a small ecosystem composed of both living and nonliving factors. Which of the following incidents could cause a severe imbalance in this environment?

    A. extended drought
    B. pesticides in rain runoff
    C. addition of composted soil
    D. genetically modified seeds

Use the following passage for Items 11 through 13:

Metabolism is the process of converting the calories in food and beverages into energy. The number of calories a body needs to carry out the basic functions of life is called the basal metabolic rate, and it accounts for 60 to 75 percent of the calories burned every day. Several factors determine an individual's basal metabolic rate.

- **Body size and composition:** The bodies of people who are larger or who have more muscle burn more calories, even at rest.

- **Gender:** Men usually have less body fat and more muscle than women of the same age and weight, burning more calories.

- **Age:** As people age, the amount of muscle tends to decrease and fat accounts for more of the weight, slowing down calorie burning and lowering the basal metabolic rate.

11. According to the passage, which of the people described below would have the highest basal metabolic rate?

    A. male, age 25, 6.2 feet tall, muscular
    B. female, age 20, 5.4 feet tall, muscular
    C. male, age 45, 6.5 feet tall, overweight
    D. female, age 75, 5 feet tall, overweight

12. Which statement best explains why people with more muscle have a higher metabolism?

    A. Muscle tissues are organized into three types, cardiac, skeletal, and smooth muscles.
    B. Muscle cells contain more mitochondria, the cellular organelles that produce energy.
    C. Muscle tissues can work without conscious thought, such as involuntary heart muscles.
    D. Muscle cells contain protein filaments that slide past one another, causing contractions.

13. When the calories in food are converted to energy for muscle movement, what type of transformation takes place?

    A. chemical to kinetic
    B. kinetic to chemical
    C. kinetic to mechanical
    D. mechanical to chemical

Use the following passage and chart for Item 14:

Hemophilia is a bleeding disorder in which blood does not clot normally.
Queen Victoria of England was a carrier of this rare genetic disorder.
Examine the Queen's pedigree chart.

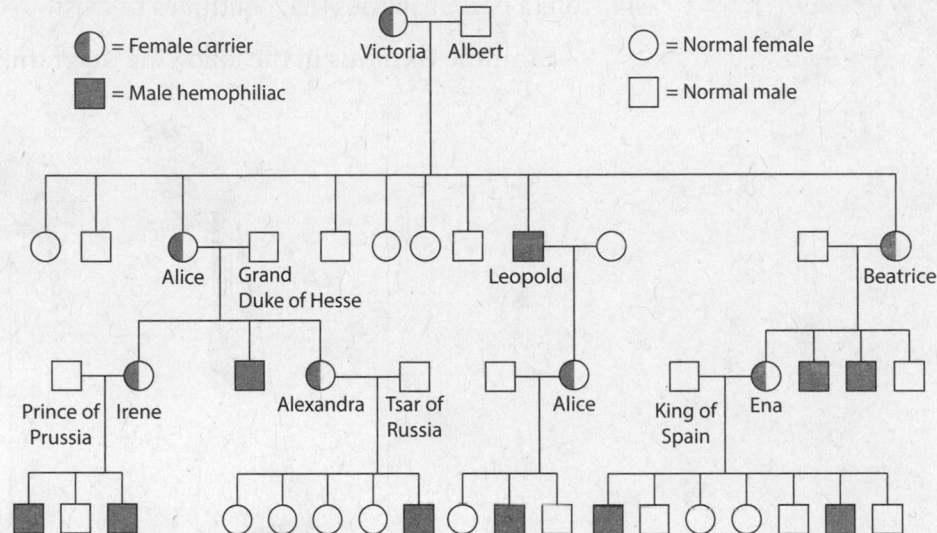

14. Using the information in the chart, write the appropriate number answer
    in the blank.

    Queen Victoria had _____ daughters that were known

    to have carried the gene for hemophilia.

Use the following passage and diagram for Item 15:

There are two patterns of speciation. The first, called anagenesis, takes place when a single population is transformed enough to be called a new species. The second, called cladogenesis, is the budding of one or more new species from a parent species that continues to exist.

Examine the birds in the following diagram.

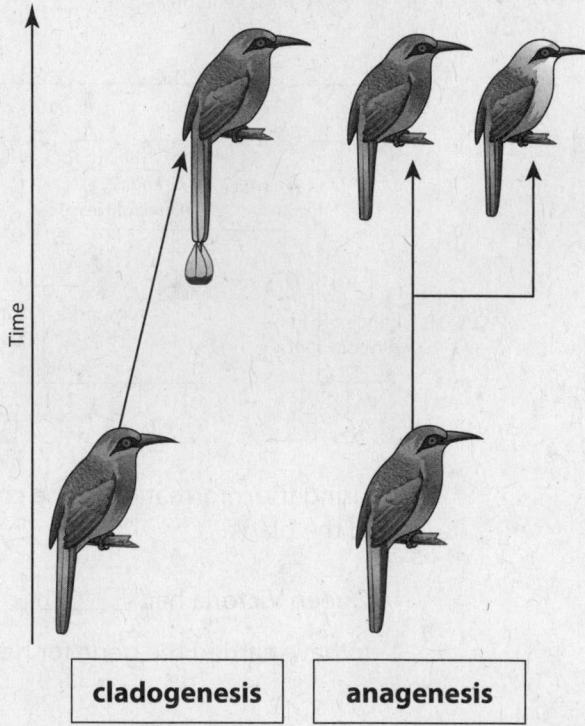

15. Draw a line to connect the correct word with the set of birds that best illustrates the definition.

POSTTEST

Use the following diagram for Item 16:

Types of Heat Transfer

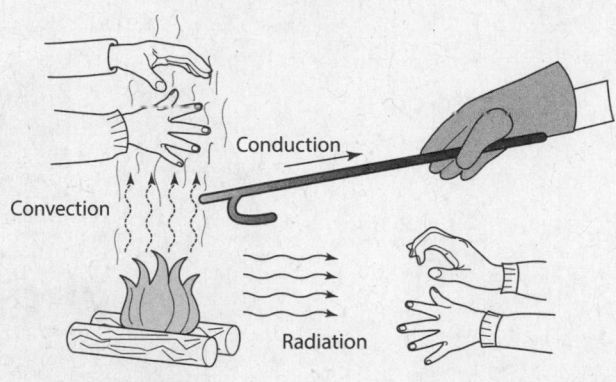

16. Based on the information from the picture, write the appropriate term in the blank.

    In the process of _____, heat is transferred from one particle of matter to another in an object without the movement of the object itself.

Use the following definitions and cartoon for Item 17:

Exothermic reaction: a type of reaction that gives out energy in the form of heat

Endothermic reaction: a type of reaction that takes energy from the surroundings

17. Based on the given information, write the appropriate answer in the blank.

    The reaction shown in the cartoon is a type of _____ reaction.

Use the following pie chart for Item 18:

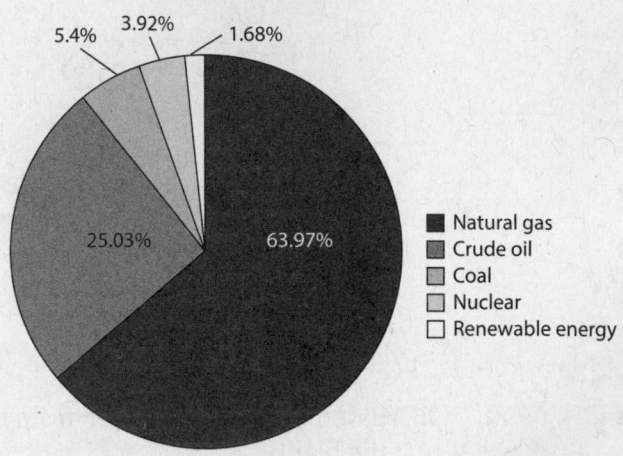

Energy Sources

- Natural gas
- Crude oil
- Coal
- Nuclear
- Renewable energy

18. Approximately what percentage of total energy comes from renewable energy?

A. 2%
B. 4%
C. 5%
D. 25%

Use the following diagram for Item 19:

Electromagnetic Radiation

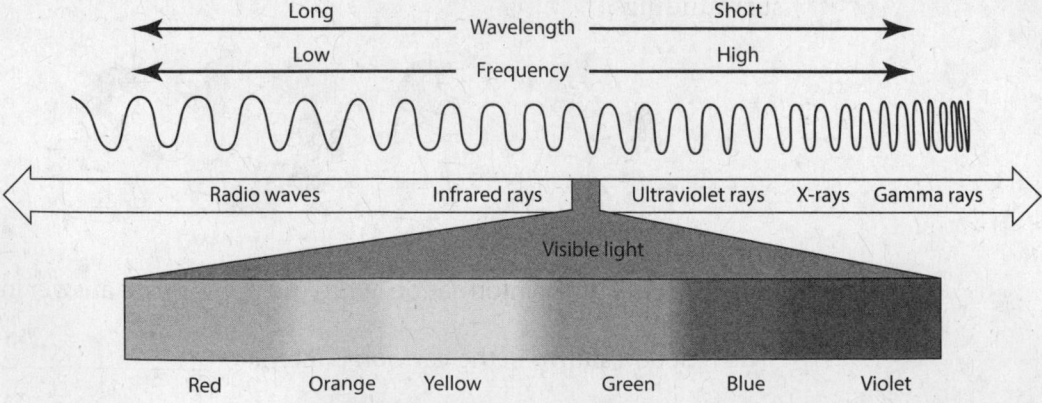

19. Based on the information from the diagram, write the appropriate answer in the blank.

_____ have the shortest wavelengths and the highest frequencies.

Use the following cartoon for Item 20:

20. Which of the following principles of motion is NOT illustrated in this cartoon?

    A. unbalanced force, because there is no seatbelt
    B. constant acceleration, because the velocity may vary
    C. inertia, because the car is at rest and the driver is moving
    D. transfer of momentum, because the driver and car have mass and velocity

Use the following diagram for Item 21:

Third-Class Lever

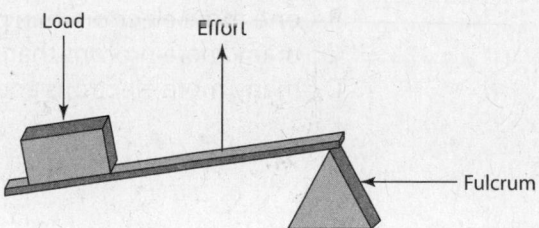

21. Which of these objects would best be classified as a third-class lever?

    A. seesaw
    B. scissors
    C. hammer
    D. wheelbarrow

Use the following graphic for Item 22:

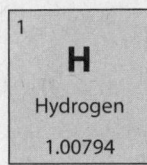

22. How many protons are found in the nucleus of a hydrogen atom?

   A. 1
   B. 1.007
   C. 2.008
   D. 3

Use the following passage for Item 23:

A chlorine atom has seven electrons in its outer shell. It can reach a full outer shell by gaining 1 electron. It will then become the chloride ion, Cl^-.

23. What does it mean when an atom, such as Cl^-, has a negative charge? It contains

   A. one more electron and neutron.
   B. one more electron than protons.
   C. many more protons than electrons.
   D. many more electrons and neutrons.

Use the following chart for Items 24 through 25:

Properties of Metals and Nonmetals

Metals	Nonmetals
Strong	Brittle
Malleable (can be bent or hammered into shapes) and ductile (shaped into wires)	Brittle
React with oxygen to form basic oxides	React with oxygen to form acidic oxides
Sonorous	Dull sound when hit with hammer
High melting and boiling points	Low melting and boiling points
Good conductors of electricity	Poor conductors of electricity
Good conductors of heat	Poor conductors of heat
Mainly solids at room temperature (Exception: mercury is liquid at room temperature.)	Solids, liquids, and gases at room temperature
Shiny when polished	Dull looking
When they form ions, the ions are positive	When they form ions, the ions are negative (except hydrogen that forms a positive ion, H+)
High density	Low density

24. How would a colorless, odorless gas with a very low melting point and a high density at the boiling point best be classified?

    A. as a metal because it has a high density
    B. as a metal because it has a boiling point
    C. as a nonmetal because it is a colorless gas
    D. as a nonmetal because it has a melting point

25. **Short answer**

Consider a copper penny. Using the information in the preceding chart, discuss the properties of the element copper that make it a good choice for jewelry, cookware, and electrical wiring. Include multiple pieces of evidence from the chart to support your answer.

Write your response in the space provided. This task may take approximately 10 minutes to complete.

✂ **Cut** 📋 **Copy** 📋 **Paste** ↺ Undo ↻ Redo

26. Which chemical equation correctly illustrates the following statement?

    Magnesium burns in oxygen to produce magnesium oxide.

    A. $O_2 + MgO \rightarrow 2Mg$
    B. $2Mg + O_2 \rightarrow 2MgO$
    C. $2MgO + O_2 \rightarrow 2Mg$
    D. $2O_2 + 2Mg \rightarrow 4O + 2Mg$

Use the following illustration for Item 27:

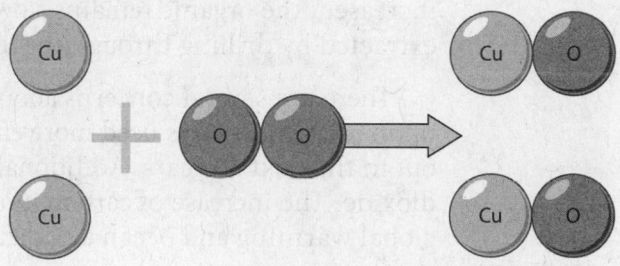

27. Which equation is represented by the symbols shown?

    A. $2Cu + O_2 \rightarrow 2CuO$
    B. $2Cu + 2O \rightarrow CuO_2$
    C. $2Cu + 2O_2 \rightarrow 2CuO_2$
    D. $Cu + 2O \rightarrow Cu2O_2$

Use the following passage for Item 28:

The measure of the concentration of hydrogen ions in a solution is called pH. The lower the pH, the higher the concentration of hydrogen ions in the solution. Measured pH values range from 0 to 14. Strong acids, such as hydrochloric acid, have a pH around 0 to 1. A solution of a strong alkali, such as sodium hydroxide, has a pH of 14.

28. What could be inferred about a substance with a pH of 7?

    A. it is mildly acidic
    B. it is a strong alkali
    C. it is slightly alkaline, not acidic
    D. it is neither acidic nor alkaline

Use the following passage for Items 29 through 31:

Scientists can often tell where crude oil is trapped by looking at the shape and structure of rocks. Oil tends to be located where permeable rocks are in contact with impermeable rocks at a fault line or where impermeable rocks are domed upward.

Crude oil formation began millions of years ago when microscopic ocean plants and animals died. The remains were covered by many layers of sediment that eventually turned to rock. As temperature and pressure increased, the organic remains slowly changed into crude oil. That oil is extracted by drilling through the impermeable rocks.

There are several concerns about the world population's dependence upon oil. Unless oil is used more efficiently, supplies of crude oil could run out in the next 30 years. Additionally, when oil is burned, it gives off carbon dioxide. The increase of carbon dioxide in the atmosphere contributes to global warming and ocean acidification.

29. Based on the passage, which statement best summarizes the locations of crude oil?

    A. Permeable rocks, found underground, trap crude oil inside rocky domes.
    B. Oil is usually located inside impermeable rocks underneath the ocean floor.
    C. Crude oil is found trapped in some of the sedimentary rocks of Earth's crust.
    D. In areas of high temperature, dome-shaped rocks near fault lines house most of the oil.

30. According to the passage, oil supplies may be depleted within the next 30 years. Which statement supports this concern?

    A. Locating oil underground is imprecise.
    B. Formation of oil takes millions of years.
    C. Burning oil contributes to global warming.
    D. Drilling for oil is time consuming and expensive.

31. Based on the information in the passage, in what way does crude oil contribute to climate change?

    A. by increasing acidification of ocean water
    B. by raising air temperature from burning oil
    C. by adding carbon dioxide to the atmosphere
    D. by decreasing the oil reserves in Earth's crust

32. In extreme weather events, strong winds can turn stationary objects into dangerous projectiles. A safe room is a specially designed, hardened, windowless structure inside a home. It is meant to provide protection from flying debris. A home with an underground safe room would best protect a person from which type of natural hazard?

    A. tornado with hail
    B. wildfire with smoke
    C. hurricane with flooding
    D. earthquake with aftershocks

Use the following passage and illustration for Item 33:

Rip currents are narrow, fast-moving belts of water caused by circulation cells. They flow seaward from near the shore. Rip current speeds are typically 1 to 2 feet per second, and they can sweep even the strongest swimmer out to sea.

A Rip Current

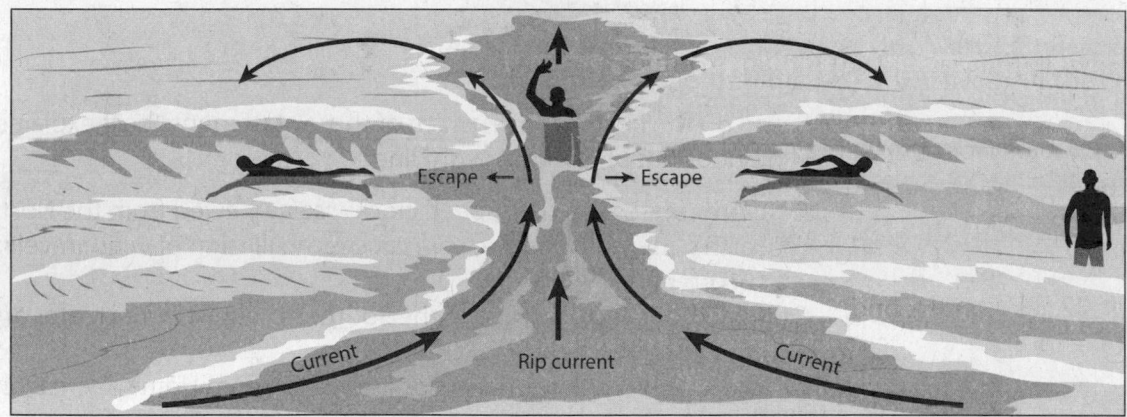

33. A swimmer can best escape a rip current by

    A. standing still in the water.
    B. swimming parallel to the beach.
    C. floating in between the wave breaks.
    D. trying to swim perpendicular to the shoreline.

Use the following passage and illustration for Item 34:

The image illustrates the Coriolis effect. The solid lines on the globe represent the path wind would take if it were not influenced by the Coriolis effect. The dotted lines represent the actual path of wind, as viewed from the equator.

The Coriolis Effect

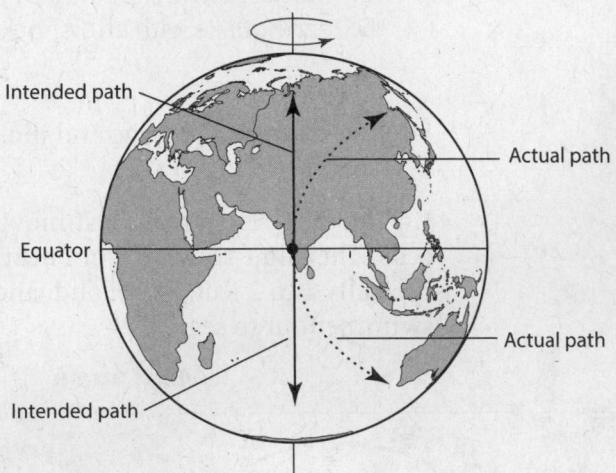

34. Based on the image above, which of these statements best explains why wind does not blow in a straight line?

A. Earth rotates at a high speed clockwise as viewed from the North Pole.
B. Earth's counterclockwise spin causes the illusion of wind traveling in a curved path.
C. Wind traveling over land in the Southern Hemisphere creates areas of high pressure.
D. The spin of Earth causes winds in the Northern Hemisphere to curve to the right.

Use the passage and pictures for Item 35:

The gravitational pull of the sun and the moon influence the tides on Earth. When the moon is in line with the sun, the gravitational pull from the two objects combines. The combined gravitational pull produces extra high and extra low tides twice a month. These types of tides are referred to as spring tides.

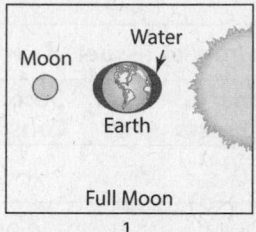
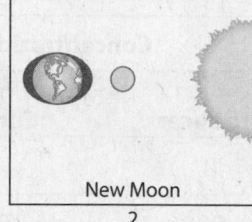
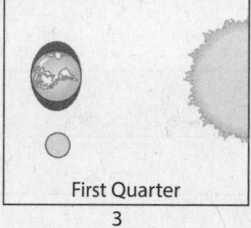
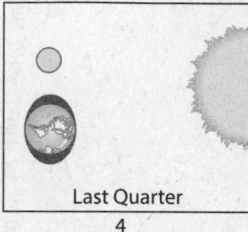

35. Which pictures show the proper conditions to produce a spring tide?

   A. 1 and 2
   B. 2 and 3
   C. 3 and 4
   D. 4 and 1

36. A Punnett square cross yields 50 percent heterozygous traits (Tt) and 50 percent homozygous recessive traits (tt). Which were the MOST likely genotypes of the parents crossed?

   A. TT × tt
   B. Tt × Tt
   C. tt × tt
   D. Tt × tt

37. Which of the following materials would be a good conductor?

   A. a vinyl floor because it does not transfer heat
   B. a plastic spoon because it does not absorb heat
   C. a wool blanket because it slows the transfer of heat from skin
   D. a copper pipe because it accelerates the transfer of heated materials

Use the following passage and table to answer Item 38:

Four substances (A–D) were introduced into a laboratory-based aquatic food chain consisting of producers, primary consumers, and secondary consumers. Samples were taken from each trophic level, and the concentration of each substance was measured in the tissues. The data are shown in the table.

Substance	Concentration (mg/kg tissue)		
	Producer	Primary Consumers	Secondary Consumers
A	0	0	0
B	98	0.0001	0.0001
C	0.005	3.25	28.5
D	0.90	0.92	0.89

38. Which explains the results of substance B?

   A. Each subsequent trophic level accumulated substance B, but could not metabolize it.
   B. Substance B was accumulated by producers, but either excreted or metabolized by consumers.
   C. Substance B could not be absorbed by either producers or consumers.
   D. Substance B was not taken up by producers and therefore not passed up the food chain.

39. Which is MOST specialized with respect to biological organization?

   A. red blood cell
   B. skeletal muscle
   C. circulatory system
   D. lung

POSTTEST

Use the following passage and table to answer Item 40:

Bacterial cells were treated with a hormone that produces specific proteins. The hormone-stimulated cells were then exposed to four different substances (A–D). The effects of each substance on levels of various biologically important molecules are shown in the table.

Substance	DNA Levels	RNA Levels	Protein Levels	ATP Levels
A	0	+	−	0
B	0	−	−	0
C	−	−	−	0
D	0	−	−	−

Key: + increase, 0 no change, − decrease

40. Which process was likely affected by substance A?

   A. DNA replication
   B. transcription
   C. translation
   D. ATP synthesis

THIS IS THE END OF THE SCIENCE POSTTEST.

Answers and Explanations

1. **Correct answer: C.** The values for blood gas composition are established by the amounts of carbon dioxide and oxygen in the alveoli. If blood gas composition, especially carbon dioxide level, moves outside of the homeostatic range, alveolar ventilation will increase. This results in increased respiration, breathing in and out faster, to expel carbon dioxide from the lungs more efficiently.

2. **Correct answer: The X should be at the site where the alveoli and capillaries come into contact with one another.**

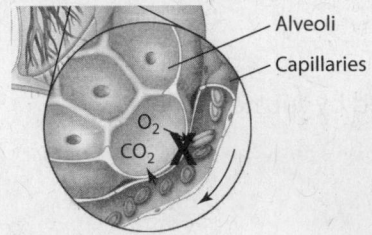

    Oxygen and carbon dioxide are exchanged through the semipermeable membranes of the alveolar sacs and capillaries. Oxygen is inhaled, is transported through the respiratory system, and enters the blood. Carbon dioxide in the blood moves into the respiratory tract and is exhaled.

3. **Correct answer: C.** Chemoreceptors, part of the nervous system, detect changes in blood gas composition, especially of carbon dioxide, that move outside the homeostatic range. These receptors dictate an exchange between the respiratory and cardiovascular systems via the lung-capillary exchange barrier.

4. **Correct answers: The doorknob, computer keyboards, and toys should be marked with an X.**

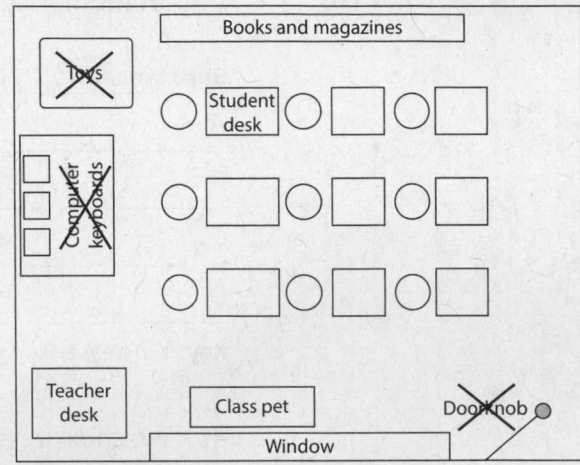

    These surfaces are the most likely to be handled by every member of the class. Doorknobs, computer keyboards, and toys are also composed primarily of plastics and metals, surfaces that harbor viruses for a long time.

5. **Correct answer: C.** The flower in the terrestrial food chain is a primary producer. It is a photosynthetic organism that uses light energy to synthesize sugars and other organic compounds, which are then used as fuel for cellular respiration and growth.

6. **Correct answer: The flower is a producer, the grasshopper is a primary consumer, the mouse is a secondary consumer, the snake is a tertiary consumer, and the hawk is the quaternary consumer.** A producer is always the base of a food chain and is followed by successive levels of consumers.

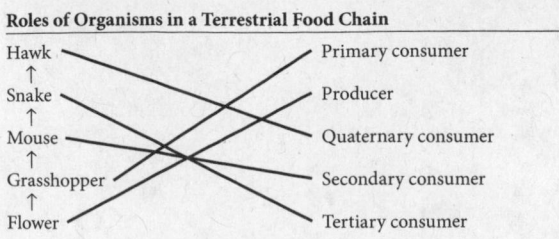

7. Response contains:

3-Point Response
- A clear and well-developed explanation of how a decline in the number of detritivores impacts the terrestrial food chain
- Complete support from the passage

Sample Paper

A decline in the detritivore community could lead to less nutritious soil. Organic waste, such as fallen leaves, contains important nutrients. If the number of decomposers were to drop, this waste might not be decomposed and added back to the earth, resulting in poor soil for the flowers eaten by the grasshoppers. This could lead to a decline in grasshoppers that would impact each additional animal in the terrestrial food chain. The energy left in dead organisms would also not be accessible to the rest of the food chain because it would not be recycled by detritivores and returned to the nonliving community.

2-Point Response
- An adequate or partially articulated explanation of how a decline in the number of detritivores impacts the terrestrial food chain
- Partial support from the passage

Sample Paper

If decomposers began to decline, organic waste would not be broken down. Plants, such as the flowers in the terrestrial food chain, need good soil to grow, and detritivores recycle nutrients into the soil. Other animals in the food chain might decline if the flowers cannot grow in poor soil.

1-Point Response
- A minimal or implied explanation of how a decline in the number of detritivores impacts the terrestrial food chain
- Minimal or implied support from the passage

Sample Paper

Without decomposers, waste would not break down. Flowers could not grow well and the grasshoppers might die.

0-Point Response
- No explanation of how a decline in the number of detritivores impacts the terrestrial food chain
- No support from the passage

8. **Correct answer: B.** Ladybugs require food for themselves and their young in order for their population to thrive. An important way to encourage an increase in ladybug population growth is to have an abundant source of aphids for them to feed on.

9. **Correct answer: B.** The plant and ladybug enjoy a mutualistic relationship. Ladybugs help the plant propagate by pollinating, and the ladybug receives nutrition from the nectar and pollen. The plant also serves as a host home for the ladybug as well as aphids. The ladybug eats the aphids, which are plant parasites, thus benefiting the plant. The plant benefits when the parasitic aphids are removed.

10. **Correct answer: A.** Jane's garden ecosystem would be severely impacted by an extended drought. The rain cistern that she uses to water her plants would dry up without rainfall. Without a steady source of water, the plants would wither, failing to support the insect populations.

11. **Correct answer: A.** Young males, with more muscle and a bigger body size and composition, will burn more calories than young or older females and older males, resulting in a higher basal metabolic rate.

12. **Correct answer: B.** Muscular activity accounts for much of the body's energy consumption. All cells produce adenosine triphosphate (ATP) molecules inside mitochondria. Muscle cells have more mitochondria than any other type of cell, which allows them to respond quickly to the need for doing work.

13. **Correct answer: A.** When calories in food are consumed, the chemical energy held in the sugars is converted in the mitochondria of muscle cells into the kinetic energy of motion.

14. **Correct answer: two.** Of the six daughters born to Queen Victoria, two are denoted on the pedigree chart as being female carriers of the hemophilia gene. Females are denoted with a circle and a carrier female has half of the circle shaded. Alice and Beatrice are designated with half-shaded circles as carrier females.

15. **Correct answer: anagenesis, cladogenesis.** The illustration on the left showing two birds and a single arrow is an example of **anagenesis**. The arrow points to a new species of bird, denoted by the color change and modified tail feathers. The illustration on the right showing a branching of arrows is **cladogenesis**, a type of branching evolution. The originating species still exists, and a new species is also depicted.

16. **Correct answer: conduction.** Conduction is the transfer of thermal energy through direct contact between particles of matter. The picture shows heat from the fire traveling along a metal rod to a person's hand.

17. **Correct answer: exothermic.** Specifically, the reaction shown is a combustion reaction, a type of exothermic reaction, shown by the explosion. The scientist in the cartoon added an oxidizer to a combustible material that reacted to form an oxidized product and release heat.

18. **Correct answer: A.** The graph attributes 1.68 percent, rounded to 2 percent, to renewable energy sources. (Wind power is considered a sustainable energy source and would be classified as renewable on this graph.)

19. **Correct answer: Gamma rays.** Gamma rays are the most penetrating of all the electromagnetic waves and have the greatest amount of energy. These types of waves have the highest frequencies and the shortest wavelengths, and they are used in radiation therapy to kill cancer cells.

20. **Correct answer: B.** Acceleration is the rate of change of velocity. Sometimes an accelerating object will change its velocity by the same amount each second; this is referred to as constant acceleration. A steady change in velocity over time is not clearly illustrated in this image.

21. **Correct answer: C.** A hammer acts as a third-class lever when it is used to drive in a nail. The fulcrum is the wrist at one end of the hammer. The effort is applied through the hand, and the load is the resistance of the surface the nail is piercing at the other end of the hammer.

22. **Correct answer: A.** The atomic number of an element indicates the number of protons in the nucleus of an atom of that particular element. Hydrogen has 1 proton. The periodic table of elements organizes elements by the atomic number, denoted in the upper left corner of the box representing hydrogen.

23. **Correct answer: B.** The designation of Cl^- signifies that the ion contains one more electron than the number of protons. An ion is a charged particle, charged due to an unequal number of electrons and protons.

24. **Correct answer: C.** This element best fits the characteristics of a nonmetal because it is a gas. Metals are usually solids at room temperature, with the exception of mercury, which is a liquid.

25. Response contains:

3-Point Response
- A clear and well-developed explanation of the properties of copper useful for jewelry making, cookware, and electrical wiring
- Complete support from the chart

Sample Paper
Copper is a metal that has a hard and shiny appearance. It is strong and malleable, which are good properties for jewelry. It is strong,

malleable, and a good conductor of heat, which make it a good material for cookware like pots and pans. The ductility of copper and its ability to conduct electricity well make it a good choice for electrical wiring.

2-Point Response
* An adequate or partially articulated explanation of the properties of copper useful for jewelry making, cookware, and electrical wiring
* Partial support from the chart

Sample Paper
A metal like copper is good for jewelry because it is shiny and easy to shape into rings and necklaces. Copper is good for pots and pans because it is a good conductor of heat. It is good for electrical wiring because it can be made into wires.

1-Point Response
* A minimal or implied explanation of the properties of copper useful for jewelry making, cookware, and electrical wiring
* Minimal or implied support from the chart

Sample Paper
Copper is shiny, so it is a good choice for jewelry. It can also be used in pots and pans and wires because it is strong.

0-point response
* No explanation of the properties of copper useful for jewelry making, cookware, and electrical wiring
* No support from the chart

26. **Correct answer: B.** Magnesium oxide is the product, so it is written on the right side of the equation. Oxygen and magnesium are the reactants and are therefore located on the left side of the equation. Because oxygen has 2 atoms, MgO must be multiplied by 2 so that there are 2 oxygen atoms on the product side of the equation. This creates 2 magnesium atoms on the right, so magnesium is multiplied by 2 on the left side to balance the overall equation.

27. **Correct answer: A.** Two atoms of copper react with two atoms of oxygen to form two molecules of copper oxide. This results in two copper atoms and two oxygen atoms shown on each side. $2Cu + O_2 \rightarrow 2CuO$. The numbers In front of the formulas are coefficients, indicating the relative number of molecules or ions of each kind involved in the reaction. Numbers to the lower right of chemical symbols in a formula are subscripts, indicating the specific number of atoms of the element found in the substance. Coefficients and subscripts of 1 are never written; they are understood.

28. **Correct answer: D.** A substance with a pH of 7 falls in the middle of the pH range. It is neither acidic, between 0 and 7, nor alkaline, between 7 and 14. It is a neutral substance, such as distilled water.

29. **Correct answer: C.** Crude oil is found trapped in sedimentary rock layers. Over millions of years, organic matter undergoes high pressures and temperatures and is compressed under layers of permeable and impermeable sediment. The organic matter changes into oil and is trapped between permeable and impermeable layers below Earth's crust.

30. **Correct answer: B.** Crude oil takes millions of years to form and is being depleted more quickly than it is created. Present estimates suggest that world supplies of crude oil will run out in about 30 years unless the oil is used more efficiently.

31. **Correct answer: C.** Photosynthesis by plants and algae uses carbon dioxide from the atmosphere. However, the burning of fossil fuels (coal and oil) is adding carbon dioxide to the atmosphere faster than it can be removed. This means that the level of carbon dioxide in the atmosphere is increasing, contributing to global warming.

32. **Correct answer: A.** A safe room below ground would best protect a person from the flying debris blown about in tornadic force winds. A hardened structure without windows would also protect against any hail. Because the structure is below ground, it could be subjected to flooding, making it not ideal for occupants in flood zones or the path of a storm surge.

33. **Correct answer: B.** In the image, the escape route is marked by arrows parallel to the shoreline. A person is able to move out of the seaward current by swimming alongside the shoreline in a parallel manner, as depicted in the image.

34. **Correct answer: D.** The Coriolis effect describes the turn of the wind to the right in the Northern Hemisphere that is caused by Earth's rotation. It does not impact the wind speed, only the wind direction. In the Northern Hemisphere, the spin of Earth causes winds to curve to the right; the winds curve to the left in the Southern Hemisphere.

35. **Correct answer: A.** Spring tides occur at the full moon and the new moon each month. The sun and moon together produce extra high and extra low tides because they are in line and their gravitational pull is added together. When the sun and moon are at right angles, the sun's pull is subtracted from the moon's and the variation in tides is less, resulting in neap tides.

36. **Correct answer: D.** $Tt \times tt$ will yield 50 percent Tt and 50 percent tt. You can verify this by making a Punnett Square for this cross.

37. **Correct answer: D.** A copper pipe is an excellent conductor of heat and electricity. The materials in the other choices are good insulators.

38. **Correct answer: B.** The appearance of substance B in producers indicates that they could absorb substance B and accumulate it in their tissues. However, the absence of substance B in consumers indicates that they could either excrete or metabolize substance B.

39. **Correct answer: C.** With respect to biological organization: cells < tissue < organ < organ system. So the circulatory system is the most specialized.

40. **Correct answer: C.** In the hormone-stimulated cells, substance A causes no change in DNA or ATP levels, so it does not alter DNA replication or ATP synthesis. However, the increase in RNA and subsequent decrease in protein levels indicate that RNA is being made, but not translated into protein. So, translation is the most likely process affected by substance A.

Evaluation Chart

Check the Answers and Explanations section of the Science Posttest to see which answers you got correct and which ones you missed. For each question that you missed, find the item number in the following chart. Check the column on the left to see the test content area for that item. If you missed questions in a particular content area, you need to pay particular attention to that area as you study for the GED® test. The pages of this book that cover that content area are listed in the column on the right.

Content Area	Item Number	Pages to Review
Part 1 Life Science		
1. Structures and Functions of Life	1, 2, 3, 39	523–531
2. Life Functions and Energy Intake	5, 11, 12, 13	533–535
3. Heredity	14, 36, 40	537–545
4. Evolution	15	547–552
5. Ecosystems	6, 7, 8, 9, 10, 38	553–563
6. The Human Body and Health	4	565–575
Part 2 Physical Science		
7. Chemical Interactions	17, 22, 23, 24, 25, 26, 27, 28	581–594
8. Energy	16, 18, 19, 37	595–605
9. Motion and Force	20, 21	607–614
Part 3 Earth and Space Science		
10. Space Systems	35	621–627
11. Earth Systems	33, 34	629–643
12. Interactions Between Earth's Systems and Living Things	18, 29, 30, 31, 32	645–653

Social Studies

This Social Studies Posttest is designed to help you determine how well you have mastered this GED® test subject area and whether you are ready to take the real GED Social Studies test.

This test has the same number of questions as the real GED Social Studies test: 45 items in various formats including one essay question. The question formats are the same as the ones on the real exam and are designed to measure the same skills. Many of the questions are based on historical documents or on short reading passages on social studies topics. Some are based on graphics such as a map, a diagram, or an illustration. You will also see questions based on paired passages.

Most of the questions are in multiple-choice format, but you will also see questions in other formats, such as fill-in-the-blank items and simulated click-and-drag and drop-down items. On the real GED® test, you will indicate your answers by clicking on the computer screen. For this paper-and-pencil practice test, mark your answers directly on the page. Write your essay on a separate sheet of paper.

To get a good idea of how you will do on the real exam, take this test under actual exam conditions. Complete the test in one session and follow the given time limit. If you do not complete the test in the time allowed, you will know that you need to work on improving your pacing.

Try to answer as many questions as you can. There is no penalty for wrong answers, so guess if you have to. In multiple-choice questions, if you can eliminate one or more answer choices, you can increase your chances of guessing correctly.

After you have finished the test, check your answers in the Answers and Explanations section that follows the posttest. Then use the Evaluation Chart at the end of the Answers and Explanations section to determine the skills and content areas in which you need more practice.

Now turn the page and begin the Social Studies Posttest.

Social Studies

45 questions | **90 minutes**

1. What type of government has a king or queen with powers limited by written or unwritten rules, and a legislature that enacts the laws?

   A. constitutional monarchy
   B. constitutional democracy
   C. democratic republic
   D. federal republic

2. A common type of oligarchy is a junta, a government led by a committee of military leaders. Which of the following is characteristic of an oligarchy?

   A. Power is effectively exercised by all citizens.
   B. One ruler holds supreme power.
   C. A small group of people control the state.
   D. A god or deity is recognized as ruler.

3. Fill in the blank.

   Under the principle of _____, the U.S. government is divided into three different branches, each with its own duties and responsibilities.

   Indicate the choice that is correct and belongs in the blank. (**Note:** On the real GED® test, the choices will appear as a "drop-down" menu. When you click on a choice, it will appear in the blank.)

4. Rights that are independent of laws of government and therefore cannot be taken away by a government act are [Select... ▼]

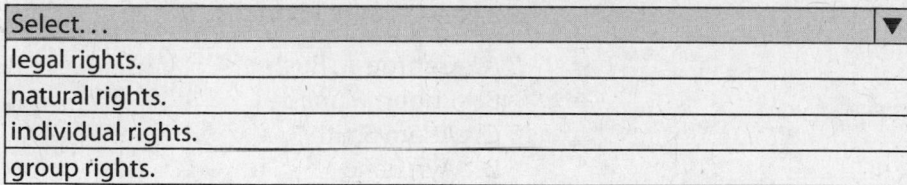

Select... ▼
legal rights.
natural rights.
individual rights.
group rights.

Use the following graph to answer Items 5 through 7:

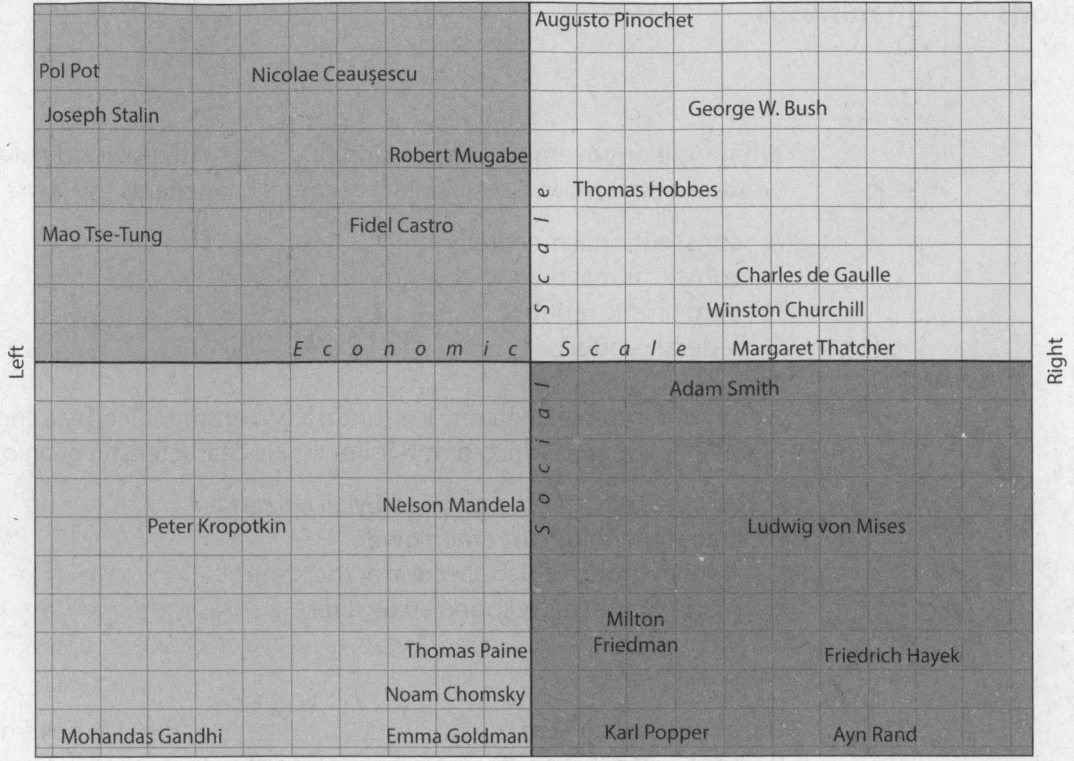

5. What does this graph show?

   A. a comparison of the economic and social beliefs of various public figures
   B. an overview of various kinds of governmental systems
   C. a detailed look at diverse economic systems
   D. an explanation of the difference between leftist and rightist politics

6. According to the graph, which of the following would be best described as a conservative libertarian?

   A. George W. Bush
   B. Robert Mugabe
   C. Adam Smith
   D. Ayn Rand

7. According to the graph, which of the following is most likely to have socialist political views?

   A. Karl Popper
   B. Thomas Hobbes
   C. Mohandas Gandhi
   D. Robert Mugabe

POSTTEST

Use the following chart for Items 8 through 10:

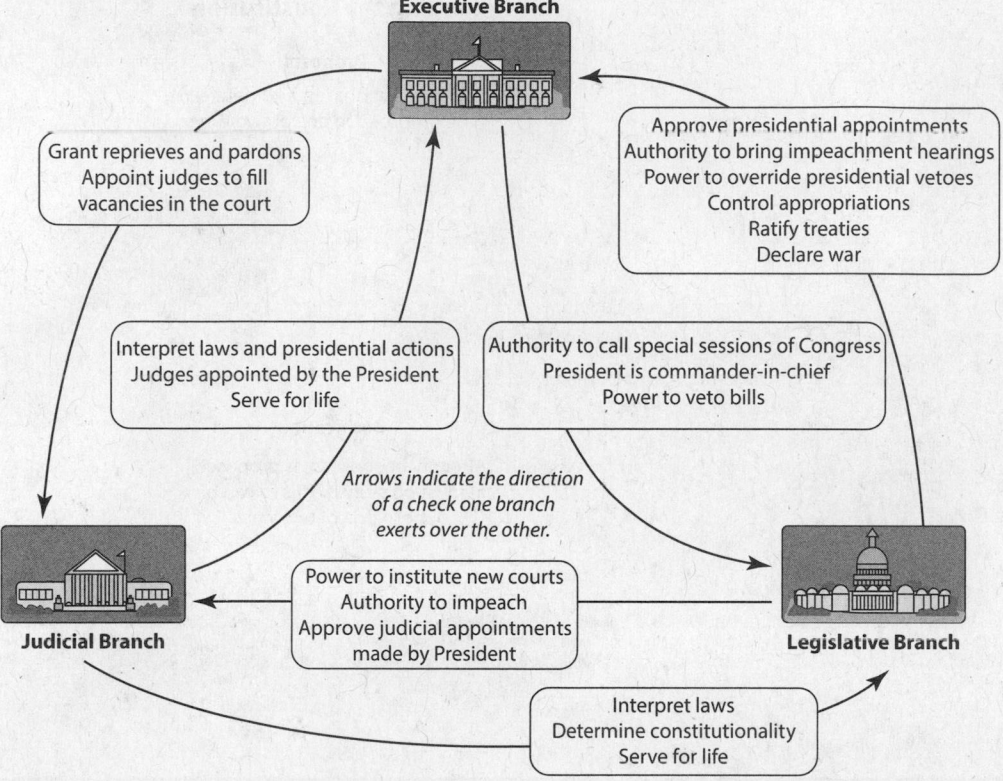

Executive Branch

Grant reprieves and pardons
Appoint judges to fill
vacancies in the court

Approve presidential appointments
Authority to bring impeachment hearings
Power to override presidential vetoes
Control appropriations
Ratify treaties
Declare war

Interpret laws and presidential actions
Judges appointed by the President
Serve for life

Authority to call special sessions of Congress
President is commander-in-chief
Power to veto bills

*Arrows indicate the direction
of a check one branch
exerts over the other.*

Judicial Branch

Power to institute new courts
Authority to impeach
Approve judicial appointments
made by President

Legislative Branch

Interpret laws
Determine constitutionality
Serve for life

8. What does the chart represent?

    A. the functioning of democracy in a typical parliamentary republic
    B. the process by which an act of the U.S. Congress becomes a law
    C. the power of the U.S. President to appoint members of the government
    D. checks and balances of power between branches of the U.S. government

9. Which branch of the U.S. government has the power to impeach the President?

    A. executive
    B. legislative
    C. judicial
    D. All branches have the power to impeach.

10. U.S. presidents may retain influence over the Supreme Court long after they have left office. Which of the following explains this?

    A. Presidents appoint Supreme Court justices, who serve lifetime terms.
    B. Former presidents advise their successors on choosing Supreme Court justices.
    C. Former presidents have the power to impeach Supreme Court justices.
    D. Supreme Court justices consult former presidents before ruling on cases.

POSTTEST

Use the following diagram for Items 11 through 13:

Amending the Constitution

Proposal

A Constitutional amendment can
be proposed in one of two ways:

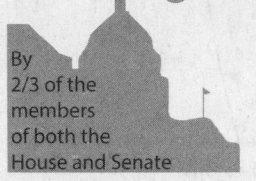

By
2/3 of the
members
of both the
House and Senate

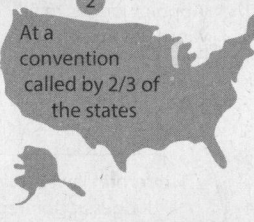

At a
convention
called by 2/3 of
the states

Ratification

After an amendment is proposed,
it must be ratified. This to can be
done in one of two ways:

By
3/4 of the state
legislatures

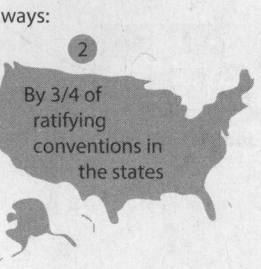

By 3/4 of
ratifying
conventions in
the states

11. What is the first step in amending the U.S. Constitution?

    A. The President sends a proposed amendment to Congress.
    B. An amendment is ratified by three-quarters of the state legislatures.
    C. An amendment is proposed by Congress or by a Constitutional convention.
    D. State legislatures send a proposed amendment to the President.

12. An amendment can be ratified if it is approved by

    A. three-quarters of the House of Representatives.
    B. three-quarters of the Senate.
    C. two-thirds of both the House of Representatives and the Senate.
    D. three-quarters of the state legislatures.

13. An amendment can be proposed if it is approved by

    A. three-quarters of the Senate.
    B. two-thirds of the House of Representatives.
    C. two-thirds of both the House of Representatives and the Senate.
    D. three-quarters of the state legislatures.

Use the following illustration for Items 14 through 16:

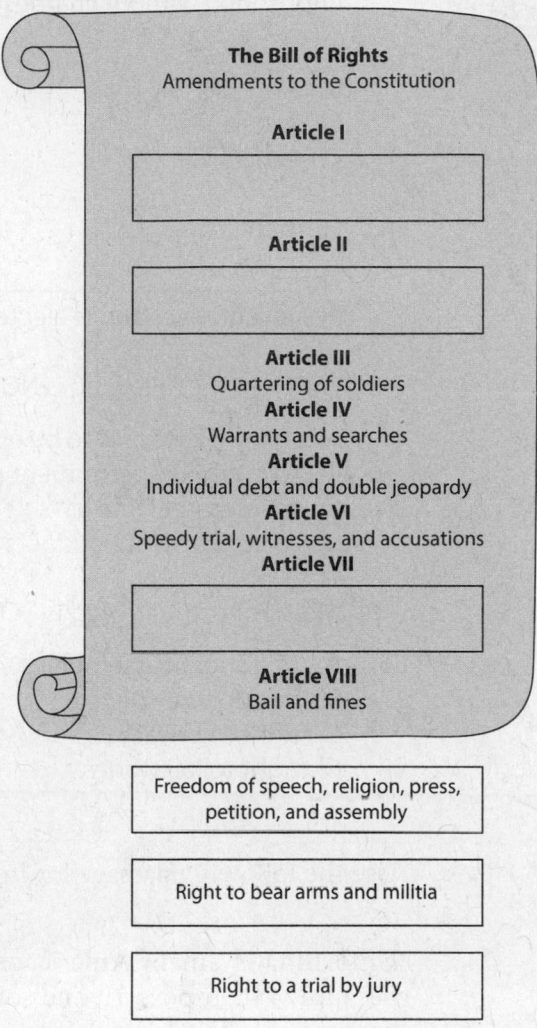

The Bill of Rights
Amendments to the Constitution

Article I

Article II

Article III
Quartering of soldiers
Article IV
Warrants and searches
Article V
Individual debt and double jeopardy
Article VI
Speedy trial, witnesses, and accusations
Article VII

Article VIII
Bail and fines

Freedom of speech, religion, press, petition, and assembly

Right to bear arms and militia

Right to a trial by jury

14. Match each description below the Bill of Rights to its correct Article number. (**Note:** On the real GED® test, you will click on each choice and "drag" it into position in the list.)

15. Which article of the Bill of Rights protects a person from being arrested for writing an article that is highly critical of the President?

   A. Article I
   B. Article III
   C. Article VI
   D. Article VIII

16. Which article of the Bill of Rights guarantees that you cannot be imprisoned without charges for a lengthy period?

    A. Article II
    B. Article V
    C. Article VI
    D. Article VIII

17. Fill in the blank.

    The _____ is the presiding officer of the U.S. House of Representatives and is elected by the majority party.

18. Which of the following is NOT a responsibility of state legislatures?

    A. to introduce bills to be enacted into law
    B. to initiate impeachment procedures against state officials
    C. to interpret state laws
    D. to vote on state budgets

19. Which of the following is NOT considered a civil liberty?

    A. freedom of assembly
    B. freedom of speech
    C. right to privacy
    D. right to fair wages

Use the following passage for Items 20 and 21:

Unfortunately, many Americans live on the outskirts of hope—some because of their poverty, and some because of their color, and all too many because of both. Our task is to help replace their despair with opportunity. This administration today, here and now, declares unconditional war on poverty in America. I urge this Congress and all Americans to join with me in that effort.

It will not be a short or easy struggle, no single weapon or strategy will suffice, but we shall not rest until that war is won. The richest nation on earth can afford to win it. We cannot afford to lose it. One thousand dollars invested in salvaging an unemployable youth today can return $40,000 or more in his lifetime.

Poverty is a national problem, requiring improved national organization and support. But this attack, to be effective, must also be organized at the state and the local level and must be supported and directed by state and local efforts. For the war against poverty will not be won here in

POSTTEST

Washington. It must be won in the field, in every private home, in every public office, from the courthouse to the White House.

The program I shall propose will emphasize this cooperative approach to help that one-fifth of all American families with incomes too small to even meet their basic needs.

Excerpted from President Lyndon Johnson's State of the Union address delivered in 1964

20. Based on this excerpt, who does President Johnson believe should be responsible for ending poverty in the United States?

    A. all citizens
    B. Congress
    C. the Supreme Court
    D. the White House

21. In this excerpt, what is one reason Johnson believes some Americans "live on the outskirts of hope"?

    A. bad government
    B. lack of education
    C. racism
    D. selfishness

22. How many electoral votes does a candidate need in order to win a presidential election?

    A. three-fourths of the votes
    B. two-thirds of the votes
    C. a majority of the votes
    D. all of the votes

Use the following graph for Item 23:

U.S. Public Debt Ceiling Since 1981 (in trillions of dollars)

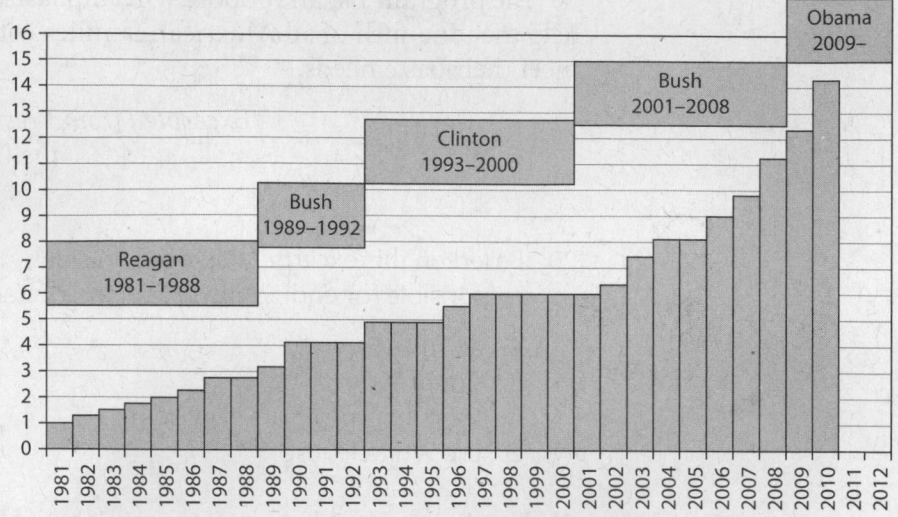

23. For the period covered by the graph, under which President did the U.S. public debt ceiling increase the most?

A. Ronald Reagan
B. Bill Clinton
C. George W. Bush
D. Barack Obama

Use the following passage for Item 24:

When in the Course of human events, it becomes necessary for one people to dissolve the political bands which have connected them with another, and to assume among the powers of the earth, the separate and equal station to which the Laws of Nature and of Nature's God entitle them, a decent respect to the opinions of mankind requires that they should declare the causes which impel them to the separation.

24. This passage is an excerpt from the

A. Declaration of Independence.
B. Bill of Rights.
C. Emancipation Proclamation.
D. Monroe Doctrine.

Use the following map for Item 25:

Westward Expansion of the United States

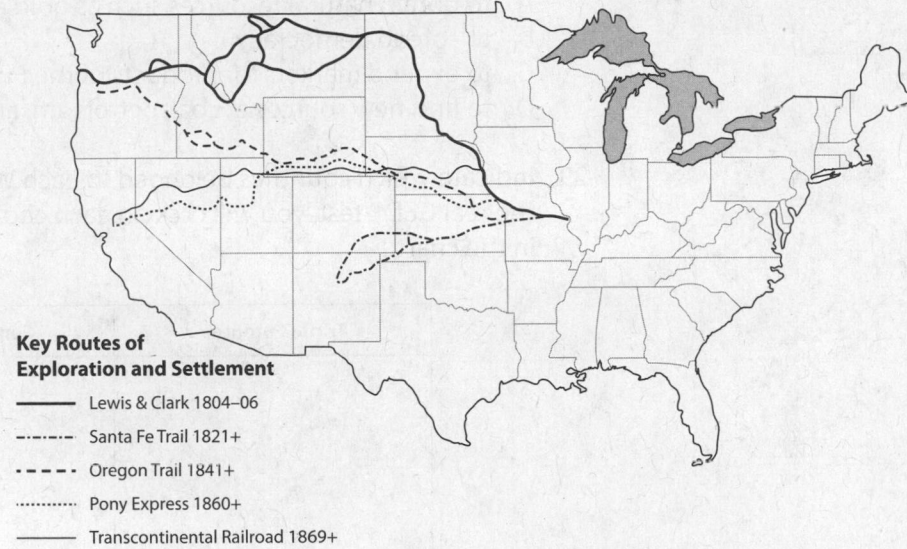

Key Routes of Exploration and Settlement

——— Lewis & Clark 1804–06

–·–·–· Santa Fe Trail 1821+

– – – – Oregon Trail 1841+

············ Pony Express 1860+

——— Transcontinental Railroad 1869+

25. Based on the map, which of the following is true?

    A. Settlers followed the Oregon Trail to the Pacific Northwest.
    B. The Lewis and Clark Expedition discovered a direct route to California.
    C. The Transcontinental Railroad followed the route of the Lewis and Clark Expedition.
    D. The Santa Fe Trail linked the Great Lakes to the Pacific Ocean.

26. Which of the following amendments to the U.S. Constitution was NOT passed as a result of the Civil War?

    A. The Thirteenth Amendment
    B. The Fourteenth Amendment
    C. The Fifteenth Amendment
    D. The Nineteenth Amendment

27. Fill in the blank.

Laws passed between 1876 and 1965 that mandated "separate but equal" segregation in the southern United States were known collectively by the colloquial name _____.

28. Which of the following was a motivator for European colonization of the Americas in the 15th and 16th centuries?

    A. to obtain natural resources such as gold and furs
    B. to spread democracy
    C. to expand markets for products of the European Industrial Revolution
    D. to find new sources of coal, petroleum, and other fossil fuels

29. Indicate which countries belonged to each World War I alliance. (**Note:** On the real GED® test, you will click on each choice and "drag" it into position in the chart.)

Triple Entente	Central Powers

German Empire	France
Ottoman Empire	United Kingdom
Austro-Hungarian Empire	Russian Empire

30. Who was the ruler of Russia who was overthrown by the Russian Revolution that began in 1917?

    A. Joseph Stalin
    B. Vladimir Lenin
    C. Nicholas II
    D. Leon Trotsky

Use the following map for Item 31:

Europe After World War II

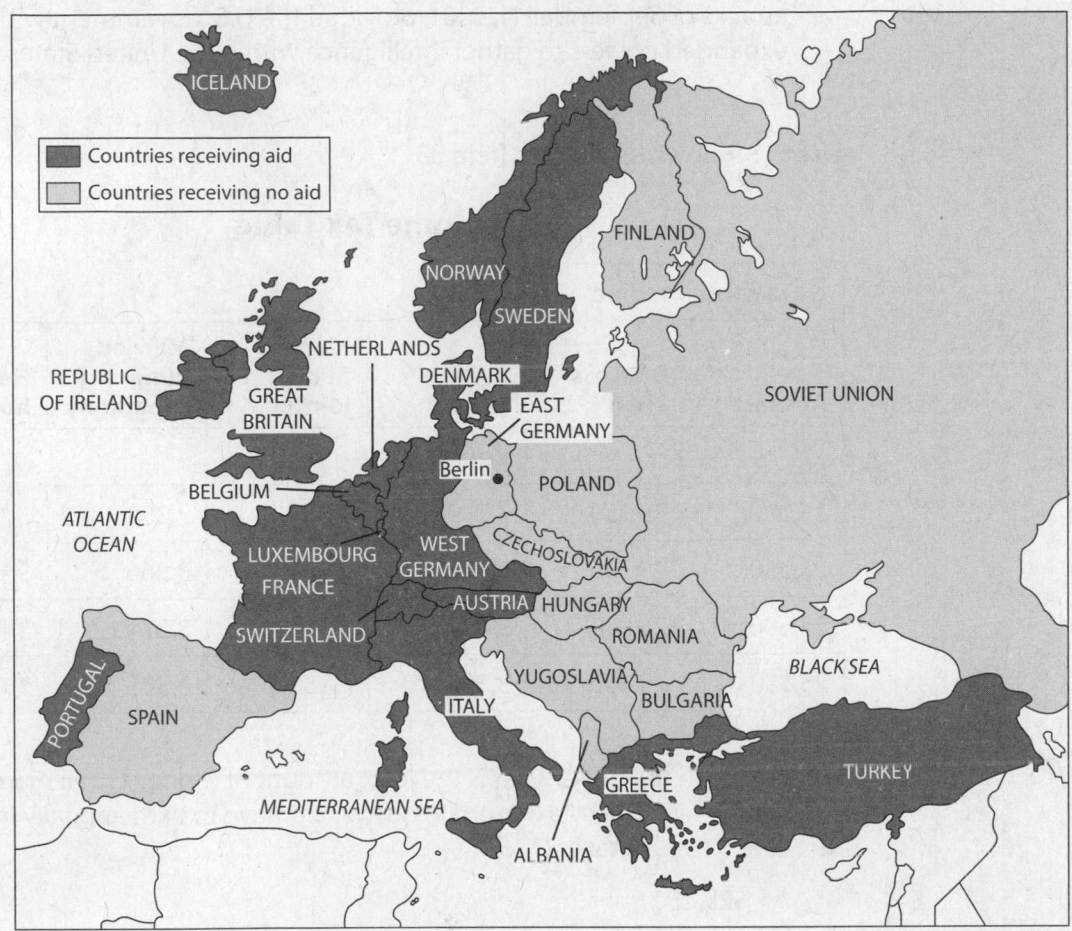

31. Indicate the choice that is correct and belongs in the blank, marked "Select...." (**Note:** On the real GED® test, the choices will appear as a "drop-down" menu. When you click on a choice, it will appear in the blank.)

The map shows the countries that received aid under the

| Select... ▼ |

Select...	▼
Warsaw Pact.	
Truman Doctrine.	
Great Society.	
Marshall Plan.	

32. Fill in the blank.

The _____, a law passed following the terrorist attacks of September 11, 2001, provided the U.S. government with greatly expanded powers to gather intelligence within the United States.

Use the following table for Item 33:

Income Tax Table

Taxable Income					
At Least	But Less Than	Single	Married filing jointly	Married filing separately	Head of a household
		Your tax is—			
25,200	25,250	3,359	2,934	3,359	3,176
25,250	25,300	3,366	2,941	3,366	3,184
25,300	25,350	3,374	2,949	3,374	3,191
25,350	25,400	3,381	2,956	3,381	3,199

33. Based on the table, what is the least amount of money that a married couple filing their tax return jointly would have to earn annually in order to owe $2,949 in taxes?

A. $25,250
B. $25.400
C. $25,300
D. $25,250

34. In what year was the stock market crash that started the Great Depression?

A. 1909
B. 1919
C. 1929
D. 1939

35. During the first quarter of the year, Green Thumb Gardening just broke even. However, during the second quarter of the year, good advertising brought in more customers, and the company was finally able to earn more money than it needed to operate. During the quarter, income from sales exceeded operating costs by $10,000. What is the term in economics for this excess of income over operating costs?

    A. investment
    B. profit
    C. capital
    D. productivity

Use the following illustration for Item 36:

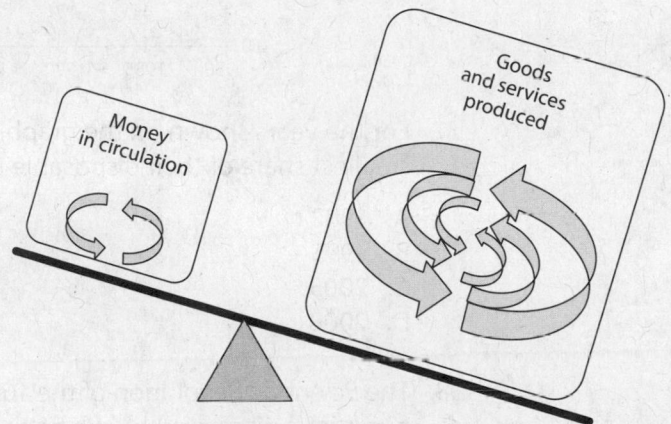

36. What economic phenomenon is represented by the illustration?

    A. recession
    B. inflation
    C. monopoly
    D. deflation

Use the following graph for Item 37:

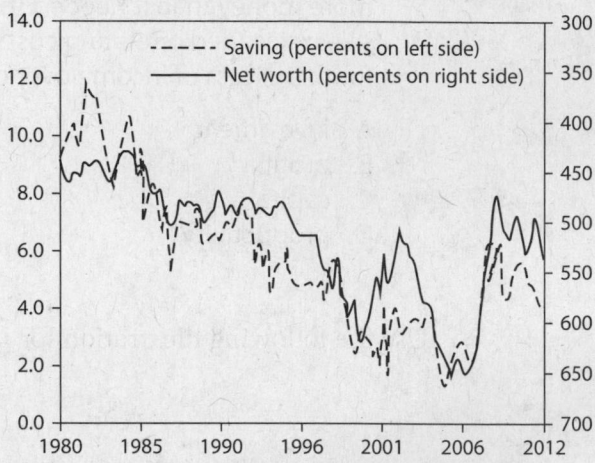

Household Saving Rate and Wealth
(percent of household disposable income)

37. For the years shown on the graph, in which year did households save the smallest share of their disposable income?

  A. 1982
  B. 1995
  C. 2005
  D. 2008

38. The Scientific Revolution of the 16th and 17th centuries was a time of numerous discoveries in the fields of mathematics, medicine, and science. Which of the following was NOT a discovery of the Scientific Revolution?

  A. the fact that the blood circulates continuously from the arteries to the veins
  B. the physical laws governing the motion of objects that have mass and gravity
  C. the heliocentric view of the solar system according to which Earth and the other planets revolve around the sun
  D. the idea that atoms are composed of smaller protons, neutrons, and electrons

39. Which of the following is an essential characteristic of capitalism?

  A. private ownership and operation of industry for profit
  B. state ownership of the banking system
  C. government control of all wages and prices
  D. a society that is not divided into separate social classes

Use the following map for Item 40:

Invasions of the Roman Empire 100–500 CE

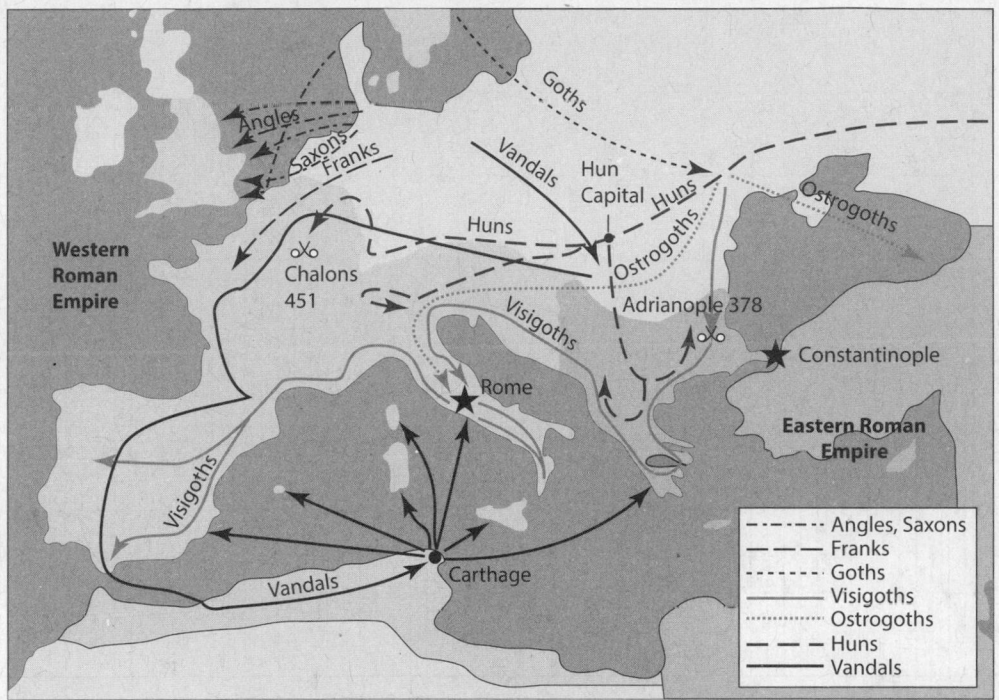

40. Which of the following can you NOT tell from the map?

A. The dates of the invasions of England by the Angles and Saxons
B. The time frame for the various invasions of the Roman Empire
C. The path through Europe taken by the Huns
D. The name of the people who invaded Roman North Africa

41. Philadelphia was the site of the First and Second Continental Congresses and the original capital city of the United States. Which of the following made Philadelphia the logical choice to host the national government?

A. Its central location in the colonies and the original states
B. Its year-round temperate climate
C. Its large, ethnically varied population
D. Its booming local economy

Use the following graph for Item 42:

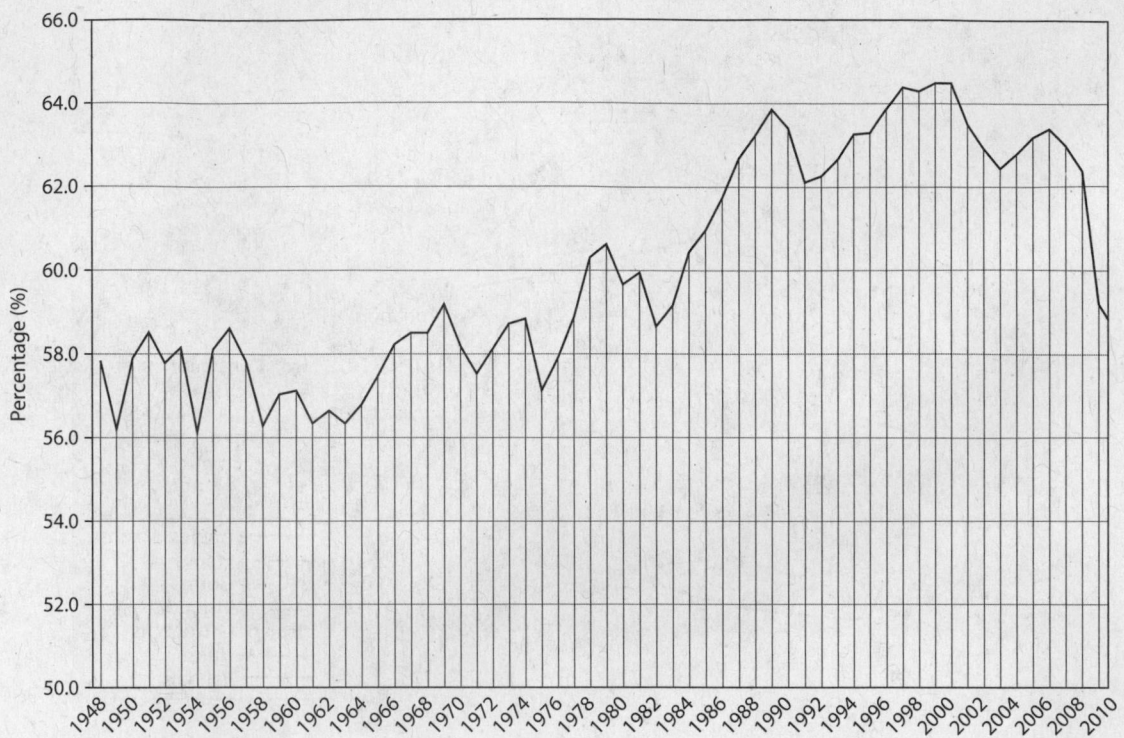

Percentage of U.S. Population Employed

42. According to the graph, in what year was the greatest share of the U.S. population employed?

A. 1950
B. 1970
C. 1990
D. 2000

Use the following passage for Item 43:

In the late 18th century, Samuel Slater, the apprentice of an English cotton spinner, brought his knowledge of English textile manufacturing techniques to Rhode Island in New England and helped to build the first factory in the United States. By the time of the Civil War, there were over 1200 cotton factories in the United States.

43. The American cotton textile industry prospered by using English manufacturing techniques and an ample supply of cotton from

A. Great Britain.
B. India.
C. New England.
D. the American South.

44. Fill in the blank.

   The last state to join the United States was _____.

Use the following excerpt for Item 45:

Remarks from President Barack Obama at Mexico National Museum of Anthropology, Friday May 3, 2013

First, let's do more to expand the trade and commerce that creates good jobs for our people. We already buy more of your exports than any other country. We sell more of our exports to Mexico than we do to Brazil, Russia, India and China—combined. Mexican companies are investing more in the United States, and we're the largest foreign investor in Mexico—because we believe in Mexico, and we want to be a partner in your success.

Guided by the new economic dialogue that President Peña Nieto and I announced yesterday, let's do more to unlock the true potential of our relationship. Let's keep investing in our roads, bridges and border crossings so we can trade faster and cheaper. Let's help our smaller businesses, which employ most of our workers, access new markets—the big markets right across the border. Let's empower our young entrepreneurs as they create the startups that can transform how we live. And let's realize the Trans-Pacific Partnership, this year, so our two nations can compete and win in the fast-growing markets of the Asia Pacific.

Second, let's not just sell more things to each other, let's build more things together. With many of our companies operating in both our countries, parts are now being shipped back and forth across the border as they're assembled. So every day, U.S. and Mexican workers are building things together—cars, aircraft, computers, satellites.

I believe this is only the beginning. Given the skills of our workers, it makes even more sense for companies from around the world to set up shop in our countries. As Mexico reforms, we'll be able to do even more business together. And the more that our companies collaborate, the more competitive they'll be and the more products we'll sell to the world.

Third, as we secure our economic future, let's secure our energy future, including the clean energy we need to combat climate change. Our nations are blessed with boundless natural beauty—from our coastlines and farmlands to your tropical forests. And just as the science of climate change is undeniable, so is the fact that our economies must become greener.

In the United States, we've made historic commitments to clean and renewable energy, and reduced our emissions of harmful carbon pollution. Here in Mexico, you're a leader in cutting carbon emissions and in helping developing countries do the same. Together, let's keep building new clean energy partnerships by harnessing wind and solar and the good jobs that come with them. Let's keep investing in green buildings and smart grid technologies so we're making our planet cleaner and safer for future generations.

Fourth—and this is part of staying competitive, too—let's do more together in education so our young people have the knowledge and skills to succeed. Here in Mexico you've made important progress—with more children staying in school longer, and record numbers of students like you getting a university education.

Just imagine how much the students of our two countries could do together and learn from each other. That's why President Peña Nieto and I announced a new partnership in higher education—to encourage more collaboration between our universities and students. We're going to focus on science, technology, engineering and math. It's part of my broader initiative called 100,000 Strong in the Americas. We want 100,000 students from the United States studying in Latin America, including Mexico. And we want 100,000 Latin American students—including Mexicans like you—to come study in the United States.

Finally, to help energize your careers and spark the industries of the future, let's truly invest in innovation, research and development. Here in Mexico, you're now a global leader in graduating engineers and technicians. One of Mexico's leading scientists, Rafael Navarro-González, is helping analyze data from the rover on Mars.

Together, let's remember that every dollar and every peso that we invest in research and development returns so much more to our economies—more jobs, more opportunity. So let's forge new partnerships in areas like aerospace, IT, nanotechnology, biotechnology, and robotics. Let's answer the hope of a young woman—a student at the National Polytechnic Institute—who spoke for many in your generation, so eager to make your mark. She said, "give us jobs as creators." Give us jobs as creators.

POSTTEST

45. **Extended response**

What was President Obama's purpose in giving this speech? What plans or goals was he seeking to promote?

Write a short essay response to identify and explain the purpose of President Obama's speech. Incorporate relevant and specific examples from the text to support your ideas.

Write your response in the space provided. This task may require 25 minutes to complete.

THIS IS THE END OF THE SOCIAL STUDIES POSTTEST.

Answers and Explanations

1. **Correct answer: A.** Constitutional monarchy. This form of government is headed by a monarch, or king or queen, whose powers are limited by a written or unwritten constitution. A parliament or other legislature enacts the laws.

2. **Correct answer: C.** A small group of people control the state. In an oligarchy, a small group or class of people run the government. Those people gain power in a variety of ways, such as by force or through family ties.

3. **Correct answer: separation of powers**

4. **Correct answer: natural rights.** Natural rights are considered those that all persons have by virtue of being human; they are not granted by the state and cannot be taken away by the state.

5. **Correct answer: A.** A comparison of the economic and social beliefs of various public figures. On the chart, political leaders such as Margaret Thatcher (Prime Minister of the United Kingdom in the 1980s), Joseph Stalin, and George W. Bush are placed according to where their beliefs fall on the economic scale and social scale.

6. **Correct answer: D.** Ayn Rand. Rand is all the way to the right on the economic scale, meaning that her economic beliefs are very conservative (i.e., free-market capitalist). Rand is also at the very Libertarian end of the social scale; she is the most Libertarian of all the persons named on the chart.

7. **Correct answer: C.** Mohandas Gandhi. Socialism is a leftist economic philosophy based on public ownership of the means of production. Gandhi is located at the far left of the economic scale.

8. **Correct answer: D.** Checks and balances of power between branches of the U.S. government. The chart shows the responsibilities of each branch of government and what power each branch has over the other two branches.

9. **Correct answer: B.** Legislative. Under the U.S. Constitution, the legislative branch has the power to impeach.

10. **Correct answer: A.** Presidents appoint Supreme Court justices, who serve lifelong terms. A President can appoint a judge with similar political views, and that judge may make decisions that align with those political views throughout his or her lifelong term.

11. **Correct answer: C.** An amendment is proposed by Congress or by a Constitutional convention. The President does not propose amendments, and ratification occurs after an amendment is proposed.

12. **Correct answer: D.** Three-quarters of the state legislatures. A Constitutional amendment must be ratified by either three-quarters of the state legislatures or three-quarters of ratifying conventions in the states.

13. **Correct answer: C.** Two-thirds of both the House of Representatives and the Senate. A Constitutional amendment can be proposed if it is approved by two-thirds of both houses of Congress or at a convention called by two-thirds of the states.

14. **Correct answers:**

    Article I: Freedom of speech, religion, press, petition, and assembly

    Article II: Right to bear arms and militia

    Article VII: Right to a trial by jury

15. **Correct answer: A.** Article I. The first article guarantees freedom of speech and freedom of the press.

16. **Correct answer: C.** Article VI. Article VI guarantees that persons who are accused of

a crime cannot be held for a lengthy period without charges. Accused persons have the right to know the charges against them and to obtain a speedy trial.

17. **Correct answer: Speaker of the House**

18. **Correct answer: C.** To interpret state laws. Interpreting state laws is a function of the judiciary branch.

19. **Correct answer: D.** Right to fair wages. Civil liberties are rights and freedoms that belong to individuals, such as freedom of speech, freedom of assembly, and the right to privacy. Workers can demand fair wages, but a right to fair wages is not normally considered a civil liberty.

20. **Correct answer: A.** Johnson states that the war on poverty must be a joint effort in both the public and privates spheres of American culture, meaning that all Americans are responsible for ending poverty.

21. **Correct answer: C.** Johnson states near the beginning of this excerpt that some people "live on the outskirts of hope" because of "their color." By this, he means they face racial discrimination.

22. **Correct answer: C.** A majority of the votes. In the U.S. electoral process, a candidate for President must receive a simple majority, or just more than half, of the total electoral votes.

23. **Correct answer: C.** George W. Bush. In the period covered by the chart, during the presidency of George W. Bush the U.S. public debt ceiling increased by more than $5 trillion.

24. **Correct answer: A.** Declaration of Independence. Adopted by the Continental Congress in 1776, the Declaration was an official statement that the 13 American colonies were severing their ties to Great Britain. The passage should be familiar, but if it is not, textual clues such as the words "to dissolve the political bands" should help indicate the correct answer.

25. **Correct answer: A.** Settlers followed the Oregon Trail to the Pacific Northwest. The Oregon Trail started in Missouri and led across the northern Rocky Mountains to the Pacific Northwest. The other choices are contradicted by information from the map.

26. **Correct answer: D.** The Nineteenth Amendment. The Thirteenth, Fourteenth, and Fifteenth Amendments were passed following the Union victory in the Civil War. The Thirteenth Amendment made slavery illegal, the Fourteenth protected the rights of the freed slaves, and the Fifteenth prohibited the government from refusing the right to vote based on race. The Nineteenth Amendment, ratified in 1920, granted women the right to vote.

27. **Correct answer: Jim Crow**

28. **Correct answer: A.** European colonizers went to the Americas in the 15th and 16th centuries in search of wealth from natural resources such as gold and furs. Regarding the other choices, in the 15th and 16th centuries, no European country was a democracy, the Industrial Revolution was still far in the future, and there was yet no great demand for fossil fuels such as coal and petroleum.

29. **Correct answers:**

    Triple Entente: Russian Empire, France, United Kingdom

    Central Powers: German Empire, Austro-Hungarian Empire, Ottoman Empire

30. **Correct answer: C.** Nicholas II. In February 1917, following a revolt in the capital city of St. Petersburg, the tsar, or emperor, Nicholas II abdicated his throne. A temporary government was set up that was later overthrown by Bolshevik revolutionaries.

31. **Correct answer: Marshall Plan.**

32. **Correct answer: Patriot Act**

33. **Correct answer: C.** Based on the table, a couple paying $2,949 in taxes earned between $25,300 and $25,350.

34. **Correct answer: C.** The stock market crashed on Tuesday, October 29, 1929.

35. **Correct answer: B.** Profit. In economics, profit is the positive difference between how much a business spends and its total revenue. If the gardening business earned more money than it spent on materials and operations, it made a profit.

36. **Correct answer: D.** Deflation. Deflation is said to occur when the prices of goods and services decrease throughout the whole economy. The image shows a scale tilting rightward because "Goods and services produced" outweigh "money in circulation." In other words, there are too many goods and services for sale in comparison to the amount of money consumers have available, so prices tend to fall until a new equilibrium is reached.

37. **Correct answer: C.** 2005. In the year 2005, the percentage of household disposable income devoted to savings reached the lowest point shown on the graph, less than 2 percent. Net worth, by contrast, reached a high point of about 650 percent of household disposable income at around the same time (note that the scale for net worth on the right side of the graph gets higher as you move from top to bottom—the reverse of the savings scale on the left side of the graph).

38. **Correct answer: D.** The idea that atoms are composed of smaller protons, neutrons, and electrons. Scientists did not discover the particles that compose the atom until the late 19th and early 20th centuries. The other choices are all discoveries of the earlier Scientific Revolution.

39. **Correct answer: A.** private ownership and operation of industry for profit. A capitalist economic system is characterized by private ownership of the means of production (resources, factories, etc.) and a free-market economy in which goods and services are produced for profit. In a socialist economic system, by contrast, the means of production are owned by the state, which also sets wages and prices. The ostensible goal of such a system is the elimination of unjust economic inequality and the rational, planned allocation of goods and resources.

40. **Correct answer: A.** The dates of the invasions of England by the Angles and Saxons. No dates for those particular invasions are shown on the map, but the overall time frame for all the barbarian invasions—100 to 500 CE—is shown. The routes taken by the different barbarian peoples are marked, and it is clear that it was the Vandals who invaded Roman North Africa.

41. **Correct answer: A.** It made sense to choose a central location as a gathering place for leaders from all the colonies and later all the states. This meant that each person would have to travel the least possible distance in an era when long-distance travel was slow, uncomfortable, and risky.

42. **Correct answer: D.** 2000. The graph shows the percentage of the U.S. population that was employed in each year from 1948 to 2010. The peak was reached in the year 2000, when a little more than 64 percent of the population was employed.

43. **Correct answer: D.** The cotton that fueled the early textile manufacturing industry in New England came mostly from the American South, where it was one of that region's major cash crops.

44. **Correct answer: Hawaii**

45. **Extended response.** In response to this prompt, you should explain that the purpose of President Obama's speech was to encourage closer economic cooperation between the United States and Mexico. You should then cite the many specific proposals in the speech that support this main point.

A high-scoring essay will include some mention of the economic contrasts between the United States and Mexico to provide a context for President Obama's ideas.

If possible, ask an instructor to evaluate your essay. Your instructor's opinions and comments will help you determine what skills you need to practice in order to improve your essay writing.

You may also want to evaluate your essay yourself using the checklist that follows. Be fair in your evaluation. The more items you can check, the more confident you can be about your writing skills. Items that are not checked will show you the essay-writing skills that you need to work on.

My essay:

☐ Creates a sound, logical argument based on the passage.

☐ Cites evidence from the passage to support the argument.

☐ Analyzes the issue and/or evaluates the validity of the arguments in the passage.

☐ Organizes ideas in a sensible sequence.

☐ Shows clear connections between main points and details.

☐ Uses largely correct sentence structure.

☐ Follows Standard English conventions in regard to grammar, spelling, and punctuation.

POSTTEST

Evaluation Chart

Check the Answers and Explanations section of the Social Studies Posttest to see which answers you got correct and which ones you missed. For each question that you missed, find the item number in the following chart. Check the column on the left to see the test content area for that item. If you missed questions in a content area, you need to pay particular attention to that area as you study for the GED® test. The pages of this book that cover that content area are listed in the column on the right.

Content Area	Item Number	Pages to Review
1. Civics and Government	1, 2, 3, 4, 5, 6, 7, 8, 9, 10, 11, 12, 13, 14, 15, 16, 17, 18, 19, 20, 21, 22, 23, 24	671–699
2. United States History	24, 25, 26, 27, 32, 34, 41, 43, 44	705–750
3. World History	28, 29, 30, 31, 38, 39, 40	757–787
4. Economics	23, 33, 34, 35, 36, 37, 39, 42, 45	791–802
5. Geography	40, 41, 43, 44, 45	807–816